The Collected Poems of
Elizabeth Barrett Browning

The Collected Poems of
Elizabeth Barrett Browning

with an Introduction and Notes by
SALLY MINOGUE

Wordsworth Poetry Library

For my husband
ANTHONY JOHN RANSON
with love from your wife, the publisher.
Eternally grateful for your unconditional love.

Readers who are interested in other titles from
Wordsworth Editions are invited to visit our website at
www.wordsworth-editions.com

First published 2015 by Wordsworth Editions Limited
8B East Street, Ware, Hertfordshire SG12 9ET

ISBN 978 1 84022 588 4

Wordsworth Editions
is the company founded in 1987 by
MICHAEL TRAYLER

Typeset in Great Britain by Antony Gray

Printed and bound in Great Britain by Clays Ltd, Elcograf S.p.A.

Contents

INTRODUCTION
page ix

WORKS CITED
page xxxii

FURTHER READING
page xxxiii

from *Poems*
published in 1844

Poems

published in 1850

Sonnets from the Portuguese
(1846) published 1850
page 277

Aurora Leigh
published in 1856

from The Seraphim and Other Poems
published in 1838

from Poems before Congress
published in 1860

from Last Poems
published in 1862

Introduction

The poetic ambition of Elizabeth Barrett Moulton-Barrett (to use her full christened name) was set in place at the age of six, when her father rewarded a poem she had written with a ten-shilling note and the title of Poet Laureate of Hope End. At this point the money, though a hefty sum, would have meant little to her; she was the first-born of wealthy parents, her adored younger brother Edward always beside her, living securely in the grandiloquence of their Gloucestershire estate Hope End. In any case, she later recalled that the title of poet meant much more to her than the ten shillings. Some forty years later her name would be touted for the actual Poet Laureateship. Yet today she is popularly known only through a very small part of her oeuvre, and in spite of a revival in the 1970s and 1980s under the auspices of feminism, her critical reputation remains in decline. In *The New Oxford Book of Victorian Verse*, for example, first published in 1987, but reissued as recently as 2008, Christopher Ricks gives her a grudging five entries, with only one of the *Sonnets from the Portuguese*.[1] Such a decline in reputation has happened to many a poet, but Barrett Browning is a particularly interesting case, since her name is still well known but great portions of her work are not. This is in part the result of a prolific poetic output; nineteenth- and early-twentieth-century editions of her complete *Poetical Works* run to over 600 pages – and that's printing in double columns. She liked writing long poems: her earliest serious poem, *The Battle of Marathon* (1820, finished when she was only fourteen), runs to twenty pages, and with the arrogance of youth is written in a Homeric strain. Also counted among her *Juvenilia*, though written when she was twenty, is *An Essay on Mind* (1826), whose subject matter and heroic couplets give it an eighteenth-century tone. Both the poem and its scholarly Preface and Notes are peppered with the names of Plato and Aristotle, Descartes, Locke and Leibniz, Bacon and Newton. We must respect her learning here, of which more later, but we have chosen not to include either of these early poems, or indeed her long 1838 poem *The Seraphim*, in this collection. While these three poems announce three key areas of her interest, the classical, the philosophical and the religious (all of which are represented in other of her works included here), as poems they are derivative, over-mannered, often

1 By comparison, he awards George Meredith seventeen of the sonnets from his sequence *Modern Love* .

arcane in subject matter, and prolix. Her long poem *Casa Guidi Windows* (1851) is politically and historically esoteric, exploring and supporting the quest for Italian unification, and though it is a considerable work, it lies beyond the scope of this collection.

We have preferred to concentrate on the body of work which fully demonstrates her importance either in her own lifetime or in the present. Her Victorian poetic reputation was made by *Poems 1844* (though we exclude the religious verse play *A Drama of Exile*) and was consolidated by *Poems 1850*, both collections in which we can hear her distinctive voice and characteristic concerns. Her popular audience today is founded on her love poems to Robert Browning, written during their courtship but disguised on their later publication as translations, under the title *Sonnets from the Portuguese* (1846, published 1850). Her strikingly original epic poem *Aurora Leigh* (1856) was the basis for the revival of her modern critical reputation; it is her most fully achieved work. It also reflects her commitment to Italy, as do some of the shorter poems in our selection. Several significant shorter poems, including some from *Last Poems,* published posthumously in 1862, conclude the selection. This edition thus seeks to make a fully representative selection of her best poetry available to a wider public, and in this Introduction I hope to highlight her distinctive qualities, her powerful poetic legacy and some of the reasons she deserves to be more widely read.

I look everywhere for Grandmothers

Though we characteristically know our poet as Elizabeth Barrett Browning, the name she adopted after her marriage, for a large part of her poetic career she published under the name Elizabeth B. Barrett, and she was fiercely protective of her individuality, her singleness even, both as an artist and as a woman.[2] She was aware very early on of the complications visited on the artist by gender, having read Mary Wollstonecraft at the age of twelve, and she recalled to her close correspondent Mary Russell Mitford that at that time: 'I was inconsolable for not being born a man.'[3] However, being born a woman did not immediately visit on her early life the usual disadvantages. Her talent was extraordinarily precocious, and it was

2   The poet used Elizabeth B. Barrett in her early publications, and Elizabeth Barrett Barrett for *Poems 1844*; for publications subsequent to her marriage she used Elizabeth Barrett Browning. I use Barrett for the poet's writings pre-marriage, and Barrett Browning for her post-marriage work, in common with most recent practice.

3   Letter to Mary Russell Mitford, 24 December 1844. All quotations from Barrett Browning's correspondence, unless otherwise stated, are from the Baylor-

encouraged enthusiastically by her father, in this respect (and perhaps only in this respect) not the usual Victorian patriarch. He allowed her to be tutored alongside her brother, so that from the ages of eleven to fourteen she learnt Greek and Latin; and though Edward's departure to Charterhouse meant the loss of the tutor, she continued her studies on her own behalf. Her father guided her reading in his extensive library, and when she wrote *The Battle of Marathon* he had it privately printed.

The confidence bred from this body of learning, and from the early practice with poetic forms, combined with the imprimatur of her father's approval, made her from the first a serious poet who seems not to have suffered any hesitancy, or indeed any lack of publishing success, on account of 'not being born a man'. But she was acutely aware of the lack of female models in the English poetry she so much loved:

> England has had many learned women, not merely readers but writers of the learned languages, in Elizabeth's time and afterwards, – women of deeper acquirements than are common now in the greater diffusion of letters: and yet where were the poetesses? [. . .] I look everywhere for Grandmothers & see none. It is not in the filial spirit I am deficient, I do assure you – witness my reverent love of the grandfathers! – [4]

Thus in 1845 Elizabeth Barrett uncannily prefigured Virginia Woolf's more famous complaint-cum-diagnosis in *A Room of One's Own* some eighty years later. The masculine bias of literary history which was to be laid bare by Woolf's scalpel might itself have been altered by Barrett Browning if she had actually become Poet Laureate. After Wordsworth's death in 1850, *The Athenaeum* proposed her as the best candidate for the post: 'There is no living poet of either sex who can prefer a higher claim'[5] (*The Athenaeum*, April 1850). This was not an empty boast. Barrett had by her late thirties

---

Wellesley website, www.baylor.edu/lib/browningletters. The Armstrong Browning Library at Baylor University and Wellesley College, Wellesley, Massachusetts, have collaborated to make digitally available all the Brownings' correspondence at their disposal.

4 Letter to Henry Fothergill Chorley, 7 January 1845
5 These words were written by the same Henry Chorley to whom Barrett had written about the lack of literary grandmothers, and he was a long-term supporter of her work, but his judgement must have been underwritten editorially by *The Athenaeum*. Although her biographer Margaret Forster (pp. 245–6) suggests that *The Athenaeum* put her forward only as part of an attack on the Laureateship itself, this view is countered by Marjorie Stone (p. 31); she and many other critics consider her suggested candidacy to have been entirely serious.

already produced a substantial and varied body of work, some of her manuscript poems were circulated among contemporary poets including Wordsworth, and her *Poems 1844* had cemented her reputation and crowned it with international critical success, particularly in America. By 1850 she was far better known and more greatly admired as a poet than was her husband. However, it was Alfred Tennyson who actually landed the Laureateship – which might look like a confirmation of the inevitable and grist to Woolf's mill. It has taken another 160 years to have our first female Poet Laureate, Carol Ann Duffy, and Robert Browning's poetry is now more widely discussed and more readily available than his wife's.

Poetry has been as serious a thing to me as life itself

In her Preface to *Poems 1844*, the collection which marked a significant step up in the literary hierarchy, Barrett lays her cards on the table about the importance of being a poet, speaking of

> the mission of the poet, of the self-abnegation implied in it, of the great work involved in it, of the duty and glory [. . .] and of the obvious truth, above all, that if knowledge is power, suffering should be acceptable as a part of knowledge.[6]

To be a poet is to take on a special mantle; and in 'A Vision of Poets' in the 1844 collection (p. 59) Barrett shows a male poet being led through a number of lessons about his relationship to the world which he must then amalgamate in the final vision that the poet's sacrifice is like Christ's suffering, and the poet's duty is finally to God, or at least is God-given. His pilgrimage is rather like Dante's into the Inferno except in reverse, with poets such as Homer and Aeschylus, Chaucer and Milton, Burns and Byron, raised in infinite glory:

> These were poets true,
> Who died for Beauty, as martyrs do
> For Truth –   [p. 69, ll. 289–91]

Beauty and truth come at a price:

> But where the heart of each should beat,
> There seemed a wound instead of it,
> From whence the blood dropped to their feet,
>   [p. 73, ll. 427–9]

6 *The Works of Elizabeth Barrett Browning*, Wordsworth Editions, 1994, pp. 103–4

The poet's task is then a noble, a spiritual one, but it can't be undertaken without spilling some blood. Though Barrett rests the poem on the person of a male poet, she herself enters the poem in the first person in its Conclusion: 'One by one / I traced his footsteps' (p. 87, ll. 825–6). And though there is only one female poet, Sappho, in the poem's pantheon, she is thrillingly depicted and addressed:

> And Sappho, with that gloriole
>
> Of ebon hair on calmèd brows.
> O poet-woman! None forgoes
> The leap, attaining the repose!   [pp. 69–70, ll. 318–21]

The 'gloriole / Of ebon hair' clearly identifies the poet herself with Sappho, and it is evident from her remarks in the Preface that she places herself unhesitatingly in the person of the poet, grandmothers or no. She might have seen her own physical pain as part of the necessary sacrifice, but the business of being a true poet in any case involves pain because of its profound importance:

> Poetry has been as serious a thing to me as life itself; and life has been a very serious thing: there has been no playing at skittles for me in either [. . .] I have done my work, so far, as work – [. . .] and as work I offer it to the public – [7]

This is a defiant statement: poetry is important work, and work is important to a woman just as much as to a man. It is also a challenge to her readership to take that work seriously.

What then of that work? *Poems 1844* comprises a wide variety of forms and subjects. Barrett sometimes seems to be trying out genres and modes of poetry for size, adapting them to her own ends, often subverting them through her female voice, sometimes inhabiting other voices including male ones ('Lady Geraldine's Courtship', parts of 'Rime of the Duchess May') and experimenting with verse form and metre. The ballad forms ('The Romaunt of the Page', 'The Lay of the Brown Rosary', 'Rime of the Duchess May', 'The Lost Bower') to my mind remain problematic for today's reader, with their archaism of form, vocabulary and subject matter. However, Dorothy Mermin points out: 'Through narrative [Barrett] could examine, modify, and criticise conventional ideas about women's place in life and art, and her first major effort to do so occurs in her ballads' (Mermin, p. 89).

---

7   *The Works of Elizabeth Barrett Browning*, op. cit., p. 104

Stone argues even more strongly that the ballad's 'energy, its strong heroines, its elemental passions of love and revenge, its frank physicality and its sinewy narrative conflicts allowed her to circumvent the ideologies of passionless purity and self-sacrifice confining middle-class Victorian women' (Stone, p. 95). As Mermin documents, these were the poems of hers that in their day found most favour and helped to make her reputation. They are also the poems that seem most Victorian to the modern reader, remote in their habits of mind and diction. But if this is part of their difficulty it is surely also part of the appeal of Barrett's writing. If we can sink ourselves back as readers into the swing of the narrative, into the broad gestures of emotion; we can enter a world in which (in 'The Romaunt of the Page', p. 17) a wife could disguise herself as her knight-husband's page and accompany him, unrecognised, to his knightly wars, to be rewarded only by his contempt for any wife who would be 'unwomaned' by such a deed (p. 22, l. 196). The milieu may be ancient but beneath the ballad's surface Barrett explores an inverse inequality between man and woman – the woman is prepared to sacrifice all, even her womanhood, to protect her husband, but that very act of being 'unwomaned' makes her sacrifice pointless to him. As the wife-page bitterly perceives,

> 'Your wisdom may declare
> That womanhood is proved the best
> By golden brooch and glossy vest
> The mincing ladies wear;' [p. 23, ll. 198–201]

Under cover of the drama of 'The Romaunt of the Page', Barrett can reveal the unseeing simple-mindedness of the man, the heroic love of the woman, and the bitter understanding that the woman comes to:

> 'Have I renounced my womanhood,
> For wifehood unto *thee*,
> And is this the last, last look of thine
> That ever I shall see?' [p. 25, ll. 276–9]

The knight's judgement is on any wife who would, as he sees it, compromise her womanhood; he never understands that the page is his actual wife – but that is part of his blindness. For her part the wife-page sees only too clearly that for her the mistake has been to renounce her true womanhood for the reduced position of wife. For this she is rewarded only by the husband's blinkered lack of appreciation of the double sacrifice she has made, first in renouncing her independence to become his wife, and second in sacrificing her own life for his.

Did the Victorian reader catch any of this nuance? The appeal of these poems was largely sensational, the revived ballad form allowing an exotic subject matter, a heightened physical and emotional situation and an archaic poetic language. The poem ends in the blaze of the wife-page's actual bodily sacrifice under the 'Paynim's' scimitar, with the Christian rites of mourning for a convent's dead Abbess leading the reader out of the poem – nothing very radical there. None the less, Barrett certainly uses the genre to explore topics that the traditional ballad had never explored. Certainly her own views on the nature of being a woman accorded with her wife-page's. She despised the standard feminine social graces, the 'golden brooch and glossy vest / The mincing ladies wear'. She was extremely suspicious of marriage, admiring the ideal in the abstract but as she wrote to Robert at the height of their courtship (23 December 1845): 'To see the marriages that are made every day! – worse than solitudes and more desolate!' (Karlin [ed.], p. 175) Nor was she slow to castigate men to him; in the same letter she writes:

> Oh – to see how these things are set about by *men*! To see how a man, carefully holding up on each side the skirts of an embroidered vanity to keep it quite safe from the wet, will contrive to tell you in so many words that he . . . might love you if the sun shone! And women are to be blamed!
> [Karlin, p. 176]

The ballads are never this explicit, but the one which most openly addresses both the gender and the class divide is 'Lady Geraldine's Courtship' (p. 45). This was the culmination of Barrett's ballad writing, and was justly acclaimed, even though it was written at top speed to provide a filler to balance out the two volumes of *Poems 1844*. The speaker in the poem is male, lowly, and a poet; the object of his love, Lady Geraldine, is moneyed and aristocratic, but he is allowed into her circle by virtue of being a poet. There is then already a gender and power reversal. The narrative form is interesting, since the major part of the poem is a retrospective verse letter the poet Bertram writes to his friend, outlining his love, hopeless because of the class and financial divide between himself and Lady Geraldine. This has been confirmed as he thinks by Geraldine herself, whom he has overheard apparently stating her commitment to marry in her own class:

> 'Whom I marry, shall be noble,
> Aye, and wealthy. I shall never blush to think how he was born.'
> [p. 53, ll. 263–4]

However, the separate Conclusion of the poem turns round on this long despairing epistle, bringing us suddenly into the present as 'Bertram finished the last pages' (p. 57, l. 370) – a reversal of what Keats does at the end of 'The Eve of St Agnes', where the present suddenly becomes the past: 'And they are gone: ay, ages long ago / These lovers fled away into the storm' (Keats, p. 255). Barrett instead thrusts us from the narrative past created by Bertram's letter into the current of the present, as Lady Geraldine takes the initiative and declares her love to him, remoulding her earlier words:

> 'Very rich he is in virtues, – very noble – noble, certes;
> And I shall not blush in knowing that men call him lowly born.'
>
> [p. 58, ll. 412–13]

Thus class and gender stereotypes are overturned, and the lovers can go forth from the ballad into their own modern world.

The verse form is key to the power of this poem, with its interweaving alternate lines of sixteen and fifteen syllables. The length of the lines is unusual enough in itself, but Barrett also employs a trochaic metre, with the stress falling on the first syllable of the foot (the metre which most people are familiar with from Henry Wadsworth Longfellow's poem *The Song of Hiawatha*, 1855). Alfred, Lord Tennyson had also used a trochaic rhythm intermittently in *The Lady of Shalott* (1832), but he employed (as Longfellow did later) the standard eight-syllable line (trochaic tetrameter). Barrett's originality lies in her binding two tetrameters together to make the long sixteen-syllable line, then cutting short the second and fourth lines of each stanza to fifteen syllables. In addition, in the main body of the poem, Barrett uses an abab rhyme scheme, so that the final trochee of the first and third lines is usually a double rhyme ('flowing', 'going', p. 48, ll. 93 and 95; 'slackly', 'blackly', p. 49, ll. 125 and 127; 'shadow', 'meadow', p. 51, ll. 189 and 191; 'gazes', 'praises', p. 56, ll. 362 and 364) – what used to be called a feminine ending. The long lines allow a swelling of rhythm matching the high emotion of the narrative, while the repeated double rhymes in the first and third lines of the stanza, with their final weak syllable, create a mesmeric rhythm which carries the reader along. Conversely there is a resolving effect from the final strong syllable in each alternate line. In a knowing display of metrical virtuosity, Barrett demonstrates what a woman poet can do when she chooses to take on the conventions of a traditionally male-authored form, and under cover of that form she slips in radical ideas about male/female partnership in a classic subversion from within.

Barrett's politics were not always disguised. There is a clear strand in all her work of protest against social injustice, evident in *Poems 1844* in 'The Cry of the Children' (p. 128) and 'The Cry of the Human' (p. 153). These poems respond specifically to the social consequences of economic conditions, the former focusing on child labour in an increasingly industrialised England, the latter on the effect of the Corn Laws in driving up the price of bread and leading to what were known as the Hungry Forties, when many of the poorest in society actually starved to death. 'The Cry of the Children' alternates the children's voices themselves with that of the narrating poet, while 'The Cry of the Human' is in a declamatory voice with the repeated refrain 'Be pitiful, O God'. Again, these might be seen as classically Victorian poems, in their use of a language of pathos which can become sentimental; but there are also echoes of Percy Bysshe Shelley's 'The Mask of Anarchy' (1819) and William Blake's 'London' (1794), particularly in their understanding of the institutional nature of the social ills they attack. The titular cry of the children is:

> 'How long,' they say, 'how long, O cruel nation,
>   Will you stand, to move the world, on a child's heart, –
> Stifle down with a mailed heel its palpitation,
>   And tread onward to your throne amid the mart?
> Our blood splashes upward, O gold-heaper,'
>
> [p. 132, ll. 153–7]

The image of the metal-tipped boot stamping down on the innocent is a classic trope of brutal authoritarianism, though stamping on a child's beating heart gives it an extra twist; and here the whole nation is implicated, corrupted by the values of the market place and the lure of gold allied to power. 'Our blood splashes upward' again invokes Christian sacrifice, but this is a world in which even God is ' "speechless as a stone" ' (p. 132, l. 126).

The economic system in which capital is worth more than the human soul is even more vigorously attacked in 'The Cry of the Human':

> Our thoughts grow blank, our words grow strange,
>   We cheer the pale gold-diggers –
> Each soul is worth so much on 'Change,
>   And marked, like sheep, with figures.   [p. 154, ll. 41–4]

These 'Condition of England' poems sit oddly alongside Barrett's ballads, and in the ordering in the 1844 collection they jostle with frankly silly poems such as 'To Flush, my Dog':

> Pleasures wag on in thy tail,
> Hands of gentle motion fail
>   Nevermore, to pat thee!   [p. 144, ll. 94–6]

The weaknesses of dog-lovers extend even to serious poets. However, the very mixedness of *Poems 1844* is perhaps part of its strategy. Again, Barrett can slip powerful attacks on capitalism in alongside poems instinct with Victorian sentimentality. Today's reader might question her discrimination, but her own contemporary audience took in the politics with the pathos. As a collection, it was a resounding success.

How Do I Love Thee?

It was reading *Poems 1844*, and specifically seeing his name mentioned in 'Lady Geraldine's Courtship', that prompted Robert Browning to write to Elizabeth Barrett.[8] He exclaimed at the start of his very first letter to her (10 January 1845), 'I love your verses with all my heart, dear Miss Barrett', going on to praise 'the fresh strange music, the affluent language, the exquisite pathos and true new brave thought' (Karlin, p. 1). This is essentially a fan letter, from a self-styled 'loyal fellow craftsman' who is conscious of being very much the junior partner. Yet it has already a strangely intimate tone, perhaps because their go-between, John Kenyon, who moved freely in literary circles, had hinted at Barrett's likely openness to his approach. In any event, later in the letter he presses on: 'I do, as I say, love these books with all my heart – and I love you too.' A lot of epistolary ink was spilt between this audacious, flirtatious opening gambit in January 1845 (to which Barrett replied in kind) and the final act of secret marriage and making a new life together in Italy in September 1846.

The romantic story of the semi-invalid Elizabeth's elopement with the poet Robert Browning, six years her junior, in defiance not only of her authoritarian father's wishes but of her own self-entombment in her room in Wimpole Street, has interfered with rather than enhanced the modern reader's knowledge of her poetry. The popular 1934 film, *The Barretts of Wimpole Street*, reinforced the romance of that narrative. It remains a compelling one, and it has inevitably brought *Sonnets from the Portuguese* to the foreground, to the exclusion in the popular imagination of her other work. That effect aside, *Sonnets from the Portuguese* are powerful and radical in their own terms, and they can rightly claim our attention.

There was a significant revival of the sonnet during the Victorian period, and Alison Chapman has argued that 'the most significant contribution of the Victorians to the sonnet renaissance was the revival of the sonnet sequence' (Cronin, Chapman and Harrison [eds], p. 105). *Sonnets from the Portuguese* stands alongside George Meredith's *Modern Love* as a sequence

8   See Browning's letter to Barrett, 16 November 1845, in Karlin, p. 155.

which has survived to speak to the twenty-first-century reader. Isobel Armstrong places them in both a formalist and a feminist frame, noting that they 'chart the struggle of the feminine subject to take up a position which is free of dependency', but that they do this often through deliberately breaking away from 'the established regularities of the sonnet form' (p. 356). Rebecca Stott sees them as investigating the 'epistemology of love' and radically recasting an essentially masculine convention, that of courtly love (Avery and Stott, p. 143). Chapman sums up these recent changes of emphasis in critical approaches to the *Sonnets* and adds her own, saying 'there has been a welcome shift ... away from explaining the autobiographical nature of the sequence and its perceived sentimentality, towards accounts of the different ways in which agency and authorship are put into question' (Cronin, Chapman and Harrison, p. 106). This critical eagerness to escape from a reductive autobiographical reading is understandable, but it is counter-intuitive. These forty-four sonnets would not have been written if the love affair between Barrett and Browning had not taken place, any more than the extraordinary sequence of letters they exchanged during this period could have been written without it.

When Barrett asked 'How do I love thee?' (Sonnet 43, p. 300), it was no abstract question. Courtly love sonnets of the Petrarchan era might indeed have imagined an idealised non-bodily love, but part of the radical nature of Barrett's sonnets is that here is a real woman addressing a real man. We see this most notably in the way she plays on the image of her hair in the early stages of the sequence. From the very first sonnet, with its arresting image – 'a mystic Shape did move / Behind me, and drew me backward by the hair' (Sonnet 1, ll. 10–11, p. 279) – hair comes to represent the speaker's bodily self and perhaps her desire. The 'Shape' that draws her backward 'by the hair' is ' "not Death, but Love" ' (Sonnet 1, l. 14); however, the sense of a blinded, disempowered female subject, pulled into submission from behind, and by the hair, is a disquieting one with which to announce a radically female sonnet sequence. But perhaps this is to forget that Barrett is doing something far more radical as the controlling poet, by taking charge both of the sonnet sequence and of the way she represents desire. Certainly she plays with the motif of the dark curls she barters with her lover as a coded (or possibly unconscious) emblem of her virginity: 'I never gave a lock of hair away / To a man, dearest, except this to thee' (Sonnet 18, ll. 1–2, p. 287). In the same poem she plays on the idea of their age difference through reference to her hair, now less vigorous than it once was: 'My hair no longer bounds to my foot's glee, / [. . .] It only may / Now shade on two pale cheeks, the mark of tears' (ll. 6–9). 'Tears' is rhymed with 'funeral-shears' (l. 11).

The image of her locks curling on her cheeks in the shapes of shed tears is contrasted in the following sonnet, Sonnet 19, with her lover's curl received in exchange, 'As purply black [. . .] it is so black!' (ll. 5–9) 'Purple' is used consistently in relation to the lover she casts repeatedly in the sequence's early stages as more vigorous than herself. In Sonnet 9 she avers:

> I will not soil thy purple with my dust,
> Nor breathe my poison on thy Venice-glass,
>
> [ll. 11–12, p. 283]

This is in part classic self-abnegation; but there is a genuine, perhaps a sexual, anxiety here. 'Breathe my poison'; 'Soil thy purple' – these images derive in part from Barrett's consciousness of herself as an invalid, a marred self who perhaps cannot answer to the 'purple' vigour of the new lover:

> Cheeks as pale
> As these you see, and trembling knees that fail
> To bear the burden of a heavy heart, –
> [. . .] O Belovèd, it is plain
> I am not of thy worth nor for thy place!
>
> [Sonnet 11, ll. 2–10, p. 284]

While there was good reason for Barrett to think in this way (the age difference alone might have troubled social convention with the disturbing spectre of a sexually predatory female), this dramatisation of the enfeebled self in the earlier part of the sequence cuts against the idea of the empowered female poet taking charge of her own represented desire. But it is a dramatisation engineered by the poet, perhaps in part for the purposes of the shape of the sequence, which mirrors the progressing openness of their actual love for each other and with it a shifting balance of power.

In Sonnet 22 she suddenly turns on her heel with a galvanising image of equality:

> When our two souls stand up erect and strong,
> Face to face, silent, drawing nigh and nigher,
> Until the lengthening wings break into fire
> At either curvèd point, –
>
> [ll. 1–4, p. 289]

The language is suddenly firmer, brisker, and at the same time more overtly passionate. The first line is worthy of John Donne. In Sonnet 24, she begins with another striking image:

> Let the world's sharpness like a clasping knife

> Shut in upon itself and do no harm
> In this close hand of Love, now soft and warm,
> And let us hear no sound of human strife
> After the click of the shutting.   [ll. 1–5, p. 290]

This brilliantly brings together their personal spiritual love, its physical warmth, the sense of safety it provides as all sharpness is put away not just between themselves but within the world, and the added sense that love between two people can even blot out human strife. This accords with Barrett Browning's belief, expressed at all stages of her poetic development, that love has a special and spiritual force beyond the needs of two people. But it also contains, again a Donne-like, intense shrinking of the world as the love between two people expands to encompass it, making 'one little roome, an every where' ('The Good-morrow', Donne, p. 7).

The *Sonnets* do also clearly express physical desire, coded through images, in Sonnet 29 those of budding and breaking:

> I think of thee! – my thoughts do twine and bud
> About thee, as wild vines, about a tree, [. . .]
> Rustle thy boughs and set thy trunk all bare,
> And let these bands of greenery which insphere thee,
> Drop heavily down,   [ll. 1–11, p. 293]

Against these powerfully intense images of curling hair and twining vines, angel wings bursting into fire and closing clasp knives holding in all the sharpness of the world, the best known Sonnet 43 (p. 300), 'How do I love thee? Let me count the ways', seems predictable and less interesting – it is after all a favourite reading at weddings. It may simply be that we know it too well.

What must be celebrated in *Sonnets from the Portuguese* is a woman poet at the height of her powers taking a major English poetic form, the sonnet, and an ancient and by convention masculine mode, the courtly love-sonnet sequence, and making both her own under the influence of a powerful passion for another human being – as it happens, a man. She thus reverses the standard relationship: she is the inscriber, he the inscribed. That the inscribed is also a poet makes the reversal all the sharper; that she does not show the poems to Browning until after their marriage makes them seem even more a depth-charge waiting to be released, both poetically and personally.

I seek no copy now of life's first half

In Sonnet 42 (p. 299), the one before the penultimate poem of the sequence, 'How do I love thee?', Barrett seems to stand on a pivot between her life in the past and that to come. As decisively as she agreed to marry Browning and escape her father, her self-confinement, and England itself, here she puts away her past and grasps her future:

> While budding, at thy sight, my pilgrim's staff
> Gave out green leaves with morning dews impearled.
> I seek no copy now of life's first half:
> Leave here the pages with long musing curled,
> And write me new my future's epigraph, [ll. 9–13]

As elsewhere in the sequence, the imagery of budding implies both a sensual and a spiritual regeneration, as the pilgrim's staff, once dead wood, breaks into new leaf. But the central metaphor is a writerly one, drawing on the fair copy a writer makes from her manuscript draft. 'I seek no copy now' seems a rejection of her earlier writing self, along with her earlier confined and invalided self: 'Leave here the pages . . . ' And if her husband-poet is to write her future's epigraph, it is only an epigraph. Her new future work lies ahead, and she will be grasping the pen.

The principal fruit of that regeneration would be *Aurora Leigh*, a poem which seemed to spring new-minted from Barrett Browning's creative imagination. But before that she wrote her hymn to Italy, *Casa Guidi Windows* (not included in this collection), in which she explores the quest for Italian unification, which was being enacted on what was now her doorstep. Italy became a deep source of inspiration to Barrett Browning, and increasingly she measured England against it. Forster describes her relationship to Italy as a 'love affair', and explains her 'sudden and extreme' support for its quest for independence in term of her personal situation:

> There was such an exaggerated element of personal identification with Italy that it does not seem too fanciful to suggest that she saw the country as the victim of an oppressor just as she had been the victim of her father's oppression. [Forster, p. 214]

This view may be based on Sandra Gilbert's detailed argument that Italy became the nurturing mother to her, as an artist and as a woman, replacing both her actual father and the patriarchy he represented.[9] There were also

9   Sandra M. Gilbert, 'From Patria to Matria: Elizabeth Barrett Browning's

more prosaic reasons for Barrett Browning's love of Italy: its climate seems to have done her frail health good, it was the place where she found personal fulfilment in what is generally agreed to have been a happy marriage and where she became a mother to her greatly loved son Pen. Such contentment might have bred a lessening in creativity. But as we have seen, poetry was a vocation for her, and she and Browning when planning their marriage had looked forward to its being a period of joint creativity. After the publication of a consolidated *Poems 1850*, some of which I will touch on later (and which included *Sonnets from the Portuguese*), and then *Casa Guidi Windows* in 1851, she went back to the seed of an idea she had had many years earlier for an experimental poem. Michele Martinez notes that she had been writing to both John Kenyon and Mary Russell Mitford in the latter part of 1844 about her idea for a 'novel-poem'. Then in a letter to Mitford on 30 December 1844 she develops her ambition to write 'a poem of a new class' (Martinez, pp. 1–2). The end-of-the-year date suggests her looking ahead to her poetic plans for 1845, a year which in fact was taken up with the cataclysmic meeting and courtship with Browning. Then in one of her earliest letters to Robert, in February 1845, we see that the seed has germinated:

> But my chief *intention* just now is the writing of a sort of novel-poem – a poem as completely modern as 'Geraldine's Courtship', running into the midst of our conventions, & rushing into drawing-rooms & the like 'where angels fear to tread'; & so, meeting face to face & without mask, the Humanity of the age, & speaking the truth as I conceive of it, out plainly. [Karlin, p. 28]

However, it remained no more than a rudimentary seedling, because (as she goes on to say) she did not yet have a story 'and I like to make my own stories, because then I can take liberties with them in the treatment'.

Perhaps these earlier words were in her mind when she did make a start (generally agreed to be early in 1853) and knew she had her story, that of a female poet looking back to her earlier life and her emotional, spiritual and pre-eminently her poetic development. The consonances with Barrett Browning's own life are evident, and there is a rich confidence in her readiness to explore large questions in relation to her own progress as a poet. But, unlike the case with *Sonnets from the Portuguese* (where the notion

---

Risorgimento', in *Victorian Women Poets: Emily Brontë, Elizabeth Barrett Browning, Christina Rossetti* (Bristow [ed.], pp. 132–66)

of translation is tacked on only to disguise their autobiographical genesis), here the poet is at pains to fictionalise this narrative. Aurora Leigh is a character in her own story, much as the first person Jane Eyre is a character in hers. This is how she announces herself:

> Of writing many books there is no end;
> And I who have written much in prose and verse
> For other's uses, will write now for mine, –
> Will write my story for my better self
>
> [*Aurora Leigh*, Book 1, ll. 1–4, p. 303]

This then, it emerges, is the story of a woman poet, told by herself, and for her 'better self' – an entirely female enterprise in inception. Her opening lines invoke other famous epic openings – Virgil's 'Arms and the man I sing', Milton's 'Of man's first disobedience [. . .] Sing, Heavenly Muse' (Virgil, translated by Dryden, p. 1064; Milton, p. 168). The model of epic, male-authored and devoted to a male subject, is thus combined with the voice of a female artist, in a form perhaps peculiar to this one example, 'a sort of novel-poem'. Instead of twelve books we have nine, echoing 'the nine books of the prophetic Cumaean Sibyl and the nine months of a woman's pregnancy'.[10] Barrett Browning's blank verse allows her the spread and freedom she needs. The voice in this poem has leapt forward dramatically from *Poems 1844*. The prosaic line and colloquial tone leads the reader into a story rich in drama but not melodramatically or sentimentally told; indeed the laconic, conversational tone of the narrative could be bathetic. But it is lifted by a long series of metaphors, usually female in conception, punctuated by simple factual statements ('I write', Book 1, l. 29, p. 304; 'There, ended childhood', Book 1, l. 215, p. 309; 'Then, something moved me', Book 1, l. 661, p. 321; 'With that he vanished', Book 2, ll. 556, p. 349). The combination of narrative drive and psychological interest allied to metaphorical power, but told in an ordinary human voice, enmeshes the reader, just as Barrett's ballads had done by different means.

As the self-told story of a poet's life, *Aurora Leigh* has an obvious precedent in Wordsworth's *The Prelude*, but its tone is quite different, deriving from its novelistic aspect. Where Wordsworth's central interest is himself and the growth of his own 'poet's mind' (ineluctably a male one), the use of the narrator Aurora Leigh displaces the first person of the poem from the poet

10 *Elizabeth Barrett Browning: Aurora Leigh and Other Poems*, John R. G. Bolton and Julia Bolton Holloway (eds), Penguin Books, London, 1995, p. 467

who generates it.[11] This allows an intermixing of discourses which for Stone produces a 'teeming, heterogeneous text' (Stone, p. 137) and which Stott characterises as the 'eclectic grafting of diverse genres' (Avery and Stott, p. 117). This text is the opposite of egocentric, trying to represent at various times and in various ways different genders, different classes, different countries and cultures, multifarious views of what it is to be an artist, what it is to be a woman, and what it is to be a woman-artist. It investigates up-to-the-minute socio-economic questions while retaining its unfashionable epic mode, prefiguring Joyce's *Ulysses* by putting an ordinary person at the centre of a heroic form, but being more radical in making that person a woman. It concerns itself with problematic topics such as prostitution, rape and illegitimacy. It questions the supremacy of men and the centrality of marriage, suggesting instead a model of female friendship. But its most revolutionary aspect is its female voice, trumpeting the right of a woman to be a poet; in doing so it employs a central metaphor of breast-milk in a way that might have made many a Victorian gentleman (and perhaps a twenty-first-century one) queasy. Even Barrett Browning's great supporter Chorley found it difficult to swallow – the text, that is; its eclecticism disturbed him. Here is a sample of the breast-milk metaphor, which Barrett Browning wields almost mischievously:

> Never flinch,
> But still, unscrupulously epic, catch
> Upon the burning lava of a song
> The full-veined, heaving, double-breasted Age:
> That, when the next shall come, the men of that
> May touch the impress with reverent hand, and say,
> 'Behold, – behold the paps we all have sucked!
> This bosom seems to beat still, or at least
> It sets ours beating: this is living art,
> Which thus presents, and thus records true life.'
>
> [Book 5, ll. 213–22, p. 441]

It's not surprising that the feminist critics of the 1970s and 1980s seized on *Aurora Leigh* as a key example of a female text which had been suppressed by the power of patriarchy. Here Aurora, in the key midway point of the poem, looks back to her past work, her ballads and her pastoral, and sees

11 The subtitle of *The Prelude* is 'Growth of a Poet's Mind'. See *The Poetical Works of William Wordsworth*, edited by Thomas Hutchinson, OUP, 1950.

them as failing. Her response, however, is to look to something more challenging, nothing less than the regeneration of the epic to represent 'this live, throbbing age, / That brawls, cheats, maddens, calculates, aspires' (Book 5, ll. 203–4, p. 441). And who better to do it than a woman poet? She champions the ability of the epic to reflect the modern age better than the medievalism of the poet who 'trundles back his soul five hundred years, / Past moat and drawbridge, into a castle-court' (Book 5, ll. 191–2, p. 441) – a thinly veiled reference to Tennyson. It is only after this discussion that the imagery of ink as milk emerges.

This passage calls to mind Sonnet 42, in which Barrett looks back at her old poetic life and forward to her new one. But how assured she is now in this new genre, which allows her to speak freely without speaking personally. She has the novelist's wide scope, inhabiting other minds and hearts. Sonnet 42 is recalled in another way, through the image of writing, here replaced by the more confident image of printing. Aurora is able to imagine future male readers touching the 'impress' (the print) reverently, and at the same time seeing the printed ink in the same terms as a mother's milk. 'Behold the paps we all have sucked' reminds both male and female readers that they can draw literary succour from a female poet's imprint. Audaciously here, Barrett Browning puts the words of recognition in male mouths; the men of the next age recognise the female model ('the paps we all have sucked'), an inversion of the usual model of the female poet following the male. Not only is the writer female, and giving milk through her poetry, but the Age itself is 'double-breasted', 'full-veined', 'heaving'. The Age is female, and its bosom sets the male bosoms beating. This is more than a reversal, it is a conquest. Barrett Browning concludes, in the male voice of those who have received the female poet's 'lava':

> 'this is living art,
> Which thus presents and thus records true life.'

The *National Review* responded as one might expect:

> Burning lava and a woman's breast! And concentrated in the latter the fullest ideas of life. It is absolute pain to read it. No man could have written it [. . .][12]

The reviewer carries on to note, accurately, that Barrett Browning's text is

---

12 Quoted in the Introduction to *Elizabeth Barrett Browning: Aurora Leigh and Other Poems*, Cora Kaplan, p. 13. Subsequent references are to Kaplan's Introduction and are embedded in the text under Kaplan.

'never without uneasiness to her readers'. In this she is like Charlotte Brontë, who always caused disturbance.

Part of the way Barrett Browning disturbs in *Aurora Leigh* is through the biting eye she turns on her fellow humans; but she also shares an ironic raised eyebrow with the reader. Through the persona of Aurora she allows herself the tone of amazed amusement at the ways of men (and women too, but especially men) that we glimpsed in her letter to Browning picturing a man lifting up the skirts 'of an embroidered vanity to keep it safe from the wet'. Aurora's cousin Romney Leigh is in the earlier part of the poem the main butt of this irony:

> [. . .] sometimes he should seem to sigh my way;
> It made him easier to be pitiful,
> And sighing was his gift.
>
> [Book 1, ll 530–2, p. 317]

In the long discussion between them in Book 2, Romney dismisses Aurora's ability to be a poet, while breezily admitting that he has not read a page of her book, then counsels that she share with him the path of social duty. Aurora is stung, and delivers a sting in return:

> 'A woman's always younger than a man
> At equal years, because she is disallowed
> Maturing by the outdoor sun and air,
> And kept in long-clothes past the age to walk.
> Ah well, I know you men judge otherwise!
> You think a woman ripens as a peach,
> In the cheeks, chiefly.'
>
> [Book 2, ll. 329–35, p. 343]

But Romney blunders earnestly on to ask her to be his wife. And he doesn't learn his lesson; having been rebuffed by Aurora (' "You want a helpmate, not a mistress, sir" ', Book 2, l. 402, p. 345), he later proposes marriage to Marian Erle out of a theoretical desire to close the difference between them in class, to ' "Compress the red lips of this gaping wound" ' (Book 4, l. 127, p. 405). Both proposals echo that of St John Rivers to Jane Eyre to make a missionary partnership in marriage (one of many echoes of Brontë's novel).

Barrett Browning's wit lies in her acerbic observation, and one of the reasons *Aurora Leigh* has appealed to a twentieth- and twenty-first-century audience is that the modern reader can meet and share her knowing look. But sometimes she sets up her targets too easily. It must be said that Romney is hard done by in the poem: made to carry the can for the faults of his male counterparts, ridiculed by Aurora for his perfectly reasonable concern for his fellow creatures – and then blinded to boot before he is allowed the grace of Aurora's love (another Brontë borrowing). He is, of course, terribly grateful.

There is then a fault-line in the poem, concomitant with its ambitiously effulgent statement of female poetic ambition. Cora Kaplan skewers the problem thus: 'This sisterhood is bought in the narrative at the expense of a representation of the poor as a lumpen motley of thieves, drunkards, rapists and childbeaters' (Kaplan, pp. 11–12). Kaplan is writing out of a particular historical moment, about an earlier historical moment. It's not for her to worry about the unfair representation of men; her concern is with women, but also with class. She is thinking of twentieth-century feminist politics when she says of the poem, 'We have only to look at [. . .] the vicious picture of the rural and urban poor, to see that there are painful contradictions in a liberal feminist position on art or politics' (Kaplan, p. 11). She certainly has a point about Barrett Browning's representation of her female working-class character, Marian Erle. Like Elizabeth Gaskell's Ruth, Marian is made to suffer both for her class and for the ills that have been visited on her through no fault of her own. Ruth dies; poor Marian has to put up first with Romney's do-gooding love, and then with the insufferably patronising friendship of a noble Aurora.

A similar problem arises in one of Barrett Browning's most extraordinary poems, 'The Runaway Slave at Pilgrim's Point' (p. 219). It is remarkable that she takes on the voice of a black woman slave. But can she do that authentically? The obvious point of comparison here is her contemporary Walt Whitman, who likewise inhabits consciousnesses he cannot himself know. But Whitman identifies fully with the individuals he gives voice to, and he has the advantage of being American, with an American voice. The runaway slave, however passionate her appeal, speaks in a middle-class Englishwoman's cadences and vocabulary. However, she does not behave like an Englishwoman, and Barrett Browning imagines herself into the feelings of a woman who is driven to kill her baby because his whiteness reminds her of the white man's rape which engendered him. The poem is an attack not just on America, with its supposed values of liberty and equality, but on God himself:

> O God, [we] cried to Thee
> Though nothing didst Thou say.
> Coldly Thou sat'st behind the sun!

[Verse 13, ll. 87–9, p. 221]

Barrett Browning is herself a passionate believer, as many of her poems attest, but in imagining the consciousness of the black slave (as she likewise imagines the feelings of the poverty-stricken children made to labour in factories) she sees through their eyes that God is missing.

The same sort of imaginative understanding is there at times in the depiction of Marian. Barrett Browning at her best shows that poetic instinct which can lead to the extended metaphor through which Marian explains herself to Aurora, understands herself, and so gives the reader an inward understanding;

> Because that world of yours has dealt with me
> As when the hard sea bites and chews a stone
> And changes the first form of it. I've marked
> A shore of pebbles bitten to one shape
> From all the various life of madrepores;
> And so, that little stone, called Marian Erle,
> Picked up and dropped by you and another friend,
> Was ground and tortured by the incessant sea
> And bruised from what she was, –
>
> [*Aurora Leigh*, Book 6, ll. 803–12, pp. 492–3]

The poet who can think herself into this metaphorical inwardness will always captivate her readers, now as then.

My Elixir

Until the age of fifteen, Elizabeth seems to have been highly active physically as well as intellectually. Then an illness which also afflicted her sisters became fixed, and she became fixed on it. Its onset in puberty, after the departure of Edward to Charterhouse, and the resemblances to anorexia and ME lead us to think of it in our twenty-first-century terms. However, there was clearly an underlying physical illness, possibly tubercular, affecting both the lungs and the spine, sometimes active, sometimes dormant, and resulting in a general debility. What is not in doubt is that it was pathologised beyond its natural extent, with several doctors prescribing many cures, and Barrett being led to nurture her illness rather than resist it. In this her family colluded. The self-incarceration in Wimpole Street may have been in part the result of extreme depression following the death of her beloved brother Edward by drowning in a sailing accident, for which she took responsibility as she had begged for his company when she was convalescing in Torquay. Yet while in August 1843 she professed herself not even strong enough to be taken by chair to Kenyon's house for a change of scene, she was at the same time devoting tremendous energy to her prospective *Poems 1844*, and her physical ailments do not seem to have interfered in any way with her creativity. Indeed Stone (p. 19), and Simon Avery (Avery and Stott, p. 41) both suggest that her illness allowed her the space and time to read and write, freed from the normal female social and domestic demands. In Wimpole Street, between 1841 and 1844, she had a room of her own with a vengeance, scarcely moving outside it, but living a profoundly creative writing life within it.

Intertwined with her illness was the palliative she was prescribed for it from the age of fifteen: laudanum, a solution containing morphine which was an acceptable form of opium. She called it 'my elixir', and took it in combination with ether. In January 1842 she strongly recommended to Mary Russell Mitford that she should get hold of it if she could:

> My elixir has a sort of ubiquitous influence upon all parts of my system –
> quiets my mind, calms my pulse – warms my feet – spirits away the stray
> headache – gives me an appetite – relieves my chest – to say nothing of
> the bestowment of those sudden pleasant feelings belonging by right to
> better health and extreme youth.[13]

Indeed. Browning would have something to contend with. After their marriage, he wanted her to give it up, and she did so temporarily in 1848 (which must have been exceedingly difficult given her long addiction) in order to sustain her one successful pregnancy. But it was embedded in her life, and perhaps especially her writing life. Stone suggests that like a number of the Romantic poets Barrett 'converted opium-enhanced reverie into an additional source of poetic creativity' (Stone, p. 19). Here, as elsewhere, her outward conventionality belied a transgressive interior.

As we have seen, Elizabeth Barrett Browning was a formidable woman and a formidable artist. She could inhabit if not the true voice at least the persona of a runaway female slave driven to murder her own baby, but able to declare still (and with the same dignity as a Duchess of Malfi) her own identity: 'I am not mad: I am black' (Verse 32, l. 218, p. 226). She could attack gold-driven English capitalists with the powerfully envisaged gush of blood from the downtrodden children they employed in their factories. Yet she could also address a hymn of silly praise to her dog Flush, and write Romaunts and Lays which, however radical in intent, are still Romaunts and Lays. Much of her work is infected by a Victorian rhetoric which veers at one side to sentimentality and at the other to didacticism; but that objection might be made to many of the male poets who occupy far more pages in Ricks's *New Oxford Book of Victorian Verse*. In *Aurora Leigh* we have a truly original epic poem exploring the nature of being a female artist; as many scholarly feminist critics have shown, its range of learned reference both underpins it and subverts the form it borrows. Yet, how widely is it read? *Sonnets from the Portuguese* are more popularly known, but probably only for two or three poems, outside an academic readership.

Behind all this lies the story we all know about Elizabeth Barrett – that she was closely confined by an indefinite illness, that her father dominated her life, that she was carried away (in some versions literally) by Robert Browning, and that they lived happily ever after in Florence. The bones of this story are true. What is missing is that both before her marriage and after it Barrett Browning was a deeply learned, hard-working writer who saw her vocation as a poet as primary, even after an intensely fulfilling marriage and motherhood. Her poetry drove her. Although she was conservative in her opposition to a theorised socialism and feminism, and followed masculine literary models, she constantly subverted those models in her poetry, and proposed far more radical ideas in her poetry than is apparent from its surface. Avery points out a persistent theme of cross-dressing in her letters and in her poetry (Avery and Stott, pp. 92–4). It is there in that image of a man lifting up the skirts of his 'embroidered vanity', where it is used to prick the bubble of masculine pride, but more commonly she uses it to show that women are fully able to occupy the trouser role. At its best, however, it is used to combine the strengths of both femaleness and masculinity within the woman. Here her great idol is George Sand, 'large-brained woman and large-hearted man' ('To George Sand: A Desire', l. 1, p. 15), to whom she wrote two sonnets. In 'To George Sand: A Desire' she envisages some overpowering force 'Drawing two pinions, white as wings of swan, / From thy strong shoulders' (ll. 8–9), an image of angelic cross-gendered power which is a world away from the physical figure of Elizabeth Barrett Browning. But in the second sonnet, 'To George Sand: A Recognition', a familiar trope reappears:

> Thy woman's hair, my sister, all unshorn,
> Floats back dishevelled strength in agony,
>
> [ll. 7–8, p. 15]

A female Samson, unshorn of her strength, precisely by retaining her womanhood in her 'dishevelled' hair; a poetic spirit that can take flight on white wings but powered by 'strong shoulders' – this is the poetic figure that Barrett Browning cuts. Emily Dickinson, a fellow spirit, was inspired by it; and if Dickinson is her poetic descendant, Virginia Woolf is her ideological one. No one could be less like her as a person; but Woolf saw the complications and discomforts of what Barrett Browning had to offer, the messiness of her irruption into the Victorian scene. She is here speaking of *Aurora Leigh*, but she gives us a lead into the 'large-brained' and 'large-hearted' body of Barrett Browning's work:

> We may suspect that Elizabeth Barrett was inspired by a flash of true genius when she rushed into the drawing-room and said that here, where we live and work, is the true place for the poet. At any rate, her courage was justified in her own case. Her bad taste, her tortured ingenuity, her floundering, scrambling, and confused impetuosity have space to spend themselves here without inflicting a deadly wound, while her ardour and abundance, her brilliant descriptive powers, her shrewd and caustic humour, infect us with her own enthusiasm. We laugh, we protest, we complain – it is absurd, it is impossible, we cannot tolerate this exaggeration a moment longer – but, nevertheless, we read to the end enthralled. What more can an author ask? [Woolf, p. 213]

SALLY MINOGUE

Works Cited

Isobel Armstrong, *Victorian Poetry: Poetry, Poetics and Politics*, Routledge, London and New York, 1933

Simon Avery and Rebecca Stott, *Elizabeth Barrett Browning*, Longman, Harlow, 2003

Elizabeth Barrett Browning, *Aurora Leigh and Other Poems*, ed. John R. G. Bolton and Julia Bolton Holloway, Penguin Books, London, 1995

Elizabeth Barrett Browning, *Aurora Leigh and Other Poems*, introduced by Cora Kaplan, The Women's Press, London, 1978

Elizabeth Barrett Browning, *Aurora Leigh and Other Poems*, ed. John R. G. Bolton and Julia Bolton Holloway, Penguin Books, London, 1995

Elizabeth Barrett Browning, *The Works*, Wordsworth Editions, Ware, 1994

Joseph Bristow (ed.), *Victorian Women Poets: Emily Brontë, Elizabeth Barrett Browning, Christina Rossetti*, Macmillan, Basingstoke, 1984

Richard Cronin, Alison Chapman and Antony H. Harrison (eds), *A Companion to Victorian Poetry*, Blackwell, Oxford, 2007

John Donne, *Poetical Works*, Herbert Grierson (ed.), Oxford University Press, London, 1933

John Dryden, *The Poems of John Dryden*, James Kinsley (ed.), The Clarendon Press, Oxford, 1958

Margaret Forster, *Elizabeth Barrett Browning: A Biography*, Chatto and Windus, London, 1988

Daniel Karlin (ed.), *Robert Browning and Elizabeth Barrett: The Courtship Correspondence 1845–1846, A Selection*, Clarendon Press, Oxford, 1989

John Keats, *Selected Poems*, Edmund Blunden (ed.), Collins, London and Glasgow, 1955

Michele C. Martinez, *Elizabeth Barrett Browning's Aurora Leigh: A Reading Guide*, Edinburgh University Press, Edinburgh, 2012

Dorothy Mermin, *Elizabeth Barrett Browning: The Origins of a New Poetry*, University of Chicago Press, Chicago and London, 1989

John Milton, *The Poems of John Milton*, John Carey and Alastair Fowler (eds), Longmans, London, 1968

Christopher Ricks (ed.), *The New Oxford Book of Victorian Verse*, Oxford University Press, Oxford, 1987

Marjorie Stone, *Elizabeth Barrett Browning*, Macmillan, London, 1995

Virginia Woolf, *A Room of One's Own* (1929), in *A Room of One's Own and The Voyage Out*, Wordsworth Editions, Ware, 2012, with an Introduction and Notes by Sally Minogue

Virginia Woolf, *The Common Reader*, Second Series, The Hogarth Press, London, 1932

William Wordsworth, *Poetical Works*, Thomas Hutchinson (ed.), Oxford University Press, London, 1950

Further Reading

Charlotte Brontë, *Jane Eyre* (1847), Wordsworth Editions, Ware, 1999, with an Introduction and Notes by Sally Minogue

Alison Chapman (ed.), *Victorian Women Poets (Essay and Studies)*, Cambridge University Press, Cambridge, 2003

Rod Edmond, *Affairs of the Hearth: Victorian Poetry and Domestic Narrative*, Routledge, London and New York, 1988

Angela Leighton, *Elizabeth Barrett Browning*, Harvester Press, Brighton, 1986

Ellen Moers, *Literary Women*, W. H. Allen, London, 1977

Janet Montefiore, 'Aurora Leigh and the Pure Milk of the Word', in *Arguments of Heart and Mind: Selected Essays 1977–2000*, Manchester University Press, Manchester, 2002

FROM
Poems
published in 1844

The Soul's Expression[1]

With stammering lips and insufficient sound
I strive and struggle to deliver right
That music of my nature, day and night
With dream and thought and feeling interwound,
And inly answering all the senses round   5
With octaves of a mystic depth and height
Which step out grandly to the infinite
From the dark edges of the sensual ground!
This song of soul I struggle to outbear
Through portals of the sense, sublime and whole,   10
And utter all myself into the air.
But if I did it, – as the thunder-roll
Breaks its own cloud, my flesh would perish there,
Before that dread apocalypse of soul.

The Seraph and the Poet

The seraph sings before the manifest
God-One, and in the burning of the Seven,
And with the full life of consummate Heaven
Heaving beneath him, like a mother's breast
Warm with her first-born's slumber in that nest.   5
The poet sings upon the earth grave-riven,
Before the naughty world, soon self-forgiven
For wronging him, – and in the darkness prest
From his own soul by worldly weights. Even so,
Sing, seraph with the glory! heaven is high.   10
Sing, poet with the sorrow! earth is low.
The universe's inward voices cry
'Amen' to either song of joy and woe.
Sing, seraph, – poet, – sing on equally!

On a Portrait of Wordsworth by B. R. Haydon[2]

Wordsworth upon Helvellyn! Let the cloud
Ebb audibly along the mountain-wind,
Then break against the rock, and show behind
The lowland valleys floating up to crowd
The sense with beauty. He with forehead bowed   5
And humble-lidded eyes, as one inclined
Before the sovran thought of his own mind
And very meek with inspirations proud,
Takes here his rightful place as poet-priest
By the high altar, singing prayer and prayer   10
To the higher Heavens. A noble vision free
Our Haydon's hand has flung out from the mist!
No portrait this, with Academic air!
This is the poet and his poetry.

Past and Future

My future will not copy fair my past[3]
On any leaf but Heaven's. Be fully done,
Supernal Will! I would not fain be one
Who, satisfying thirst and breaking fast
Upon the fullness of the heart, at last   5
Says no grace after meat. My wine has run
Indeed out of my cup, and there is none
To gather up the bread of my repast
Scattered and trampled, – yet I find some good
In earth's green herbs, and streams that bubble up   10
Clear from the darkling ground, – content until
I sit with angels before better food.
Dear Christ! when Thy new vintage fills my cup,
This hand shall shake no more, nor that wine spill.

Irreparableness

I have been in the meadows all the day
And gathered there the nosegay that you see,
Singing within myself as bird or bee
When such do field-work on a morn of May.
But now I look upon my flowers, decay   5
Has met them in my hands more fatally
Because more warmly clasped, – and sobs are free
To come instead of songs. What do you say,
Sweet counsellors, dear friends? that I should go
Back straightway to the fields, and gather more?   10
Another, sooth, may do it, – but not I!
My heart is very tired, my strength is low,
My hands are full of blossoms plucked before,
Held dead within them till myself shall die.

Tears

Thank God, bless God, all ye who suffer not
More grief than ye can weep for. That is well –
That is light grieving! lighter, none befell
Since Adam forfeited the primal lot.
Tears! what are tears? The babe weeps in its cot,   5
The mother singing, – at her marriage-bell
The bride weeps, – and before the oracle
Of high-faned hills, the poet has forgot
Such moisture on his cheeks. Thank God for grace,
Ye who weep only! If, as some have done,   10
Ye grope tear-blinded in a desert place
And touch but tombs, – look up! those tears will run
Soon in long rivers down the lifted face,
And leave the vision clear for stars and sun.

Grief

I tell you, hopeless grief is passionless;
That only men incredulous of despair,
Half-taught in anguish, through the midnight air
Beat upward to God's throne in loud access
Of shrieking and reproach. Full desertness,   5
In souls, as countries, lieth silent-bare
Under the blanching, vertical eye-glare
Of the absolute Heavens. Deep-hearted man, express
Grief for thy Dead in silence like to death: –
Most like a monumental statue set   10
In everlasting watch and moveless woe,
Till itself crumble to the dust beneath.
Touch it: the marble eyelids are not wet;
If it could weep, it could arise and go.

Substitution

When some belovèd voice that was to you
Both sound and sweetness, faileth suddenly,
And silence, against which you dare not cry,
Aches round you like a strong disease and new –
What hope? what help? what music will undo   5
That silence to your sense? Not friendship's sigh.
Not reason's subtle count. Not melody
Of viols, nor of pipes that Faunus blew.
Not songs of poets, nor of nightingales,
Whose hearts leap upward through the cypress trees   10
To the clear moon! nor yet the spheric laws
Self-chanted, – nor the angels' sweet All hails,
Met in the smile of God. Nay, none of these.
Speak THOU, availing Christ! – and fill this pause.

Comfort

Speak low to me, my Saviour, low and sweet
From out the hallelujahs, sweet and low,
Lest I should fear and fall, and miss Thee so
Who art not missed by any that entreat.
Speak to me as to Mary at Thy feet!   5
And if no precious gums my hands bestow,
Let my tears drop like amber, while I go
In reach of Thy divinest voice complete
In humanest affection – thus, in sooth,
To lose the sense of losing. As a child,   10
Whose song-bird seeks the wood for evermore,
Is sung to in its stead by mother's mouth,
Till, sinking on her breast, love-reconciled,
He sleeps the faster that he wept before.

Perplexed Music

AFFECTIONATELY INSCRIBED TO E. J.

Experience, like a pale musician, holds
A dulcimer of patience in his hand,
Whence harmonies we cannot understand,
Of God's will in His worlds, the strain unfolds
In sad, perplexèd minors. Deathly colds   5
Fall on us while we hear and countermand
Our sanguine heart back from the fancy-land
With nightingales in visionary wolds.
We murmur, – 'Where is any certain tune
Or measured music, in such notes as these?' –   10
But angels, leaning from the golden seat,
Are not so minded; their fine ear hath won
The issue of completed cadences,
And, smiling down the stars, they whisper – Sweet.

Work

What are we set on earth for? Say, to toil;
Nor seek to leave thy tending of the vines,
For all the heat o' the day, till it declines,
And Death's mild curfew shall from work assoil.
God did anoint thee with His odorous oil,   5
To wrestle, not to reign; and He assigns
All thy tears over, like pure crystallines,
For younger fellow workers of the soil
To wear for amulets. So others shall
Take patience, labour, to their heart and hand,   10
From thy hand, and thy heart, and thy brave cheer,
And God's grace fructify through thee to all.
The least flower, with a brimming cup, may stand,
And share its dewdrop with another near.

Futurity

And, O belovèd voices, upon which
Ours passionately call, because ere long
Ye brake off in the middle of that song
We sang together softly, to enrich
The poor world with the sense of love, and witch   5
The heart out of things evil, – I am strong,
Knowing ye are not lost for ay among
The hills, with last year's thrush. God keeps a niche
In Heaven, to hold our idols: and albeit
He brake them to our faces, and denied   10
That our close kisses should impair their white, –
I know we shall behold them raised, complete,
The dust swept from their beauty, – glorified
New Memnons singing in the great God-light.

The Two Sayings [4]

Two sayings of the Holy Scriptures beat
Like pulses in the Church's brow and breast!
And by them we find rest in our unrest,
And, heart-deep in salt tears, do yet entreat
God's fellowship, as if on heavenly seat.   5
The first is JESUS WEPT, – whereon is prest
Full many a sobbing face that drops its best
And sweetest waters on the record sweet.
And one is, where the Christ, denied and scorned,
LOOKED UPON PETER. Oh, to render plain,   10
By help of having loved a little and mourned,
That look of sovran love and sovran pain
Which HE, who could not sin yet suffered, turned
On him who could reject but not sustain!

The Look [4]

The Saviour looked on Peter. Aye, no word,
No gesture of reproach! the Heavens serene,
Though heavy with armed justice, did not lean
Their thunders that way! the forsaken Lord
Looked only, on the traitor. None record   5
What that look was, none guess; for those who have seen
Wronged lovers loving through a death-pang keen,
Or pale-cheeked martyrs smiling to a sword,
Have missed Jehovah at the judgment-call.
And Peter, from the height of blasphemy –   10
'I never knew this man' – did quail and fall,
As knowing straight THAT GOD, – and turnèd free
And went out speechless from the face of all,
And filled the silence, weeping bitterly.

The Meaning of the Look [4]

I think that look of Christ might seem to say –
'Thou Peter! art thou then a common stone
Which I at last must break My heart upon,
For all God's charge to His high angels may
Guard My foot better? Did I yesterday   5
Wash *thy* feet, My beloved, that they should run
Quick to deny Me 'neath the morning sun?
And do thy kisses, like the rest, betray?
The cock crows coldly. – Go, and manifest
A late contrition, but no bootless fear!   10
For when thy final need is dreariest,
Thou shalt not be denied, as I am here –
My voice, to God and angels, shall attest,
Because I KNOW *this man, let him be clear.'*

A Thought for a Lonely Death-Bed

INSCRIBED TO MY FRIEND E. C.

If God compel thee to this destiny,
To die alone, – with none beside thy bed
To ruffle round with sobs thy last word said,
And mark with tears the pulses ebb from thee, –
Pray then alone – 'O Christ, come tenderly!   5
By Thy forsaken Sonship in the red
Drear wine-press, – by the wilderness outspread, –
And the lone garden where Thine agony
Fell bloody from Thy brow, – by all of those
Permitted desolations, comfort mine!   10
No earthly friend being near me, interpose
No deathly angel 'twixt my face and Thine,
But stoop Thyself to gather my life's rose,
And smile away my mortal to Divine.'

Work and Contemplation

The woman singeth at her spinning-wheel
A pleasant chant, ballad or barcarole:
She thinketh of her song, upon the whole,
Far more than of her flax; and yet the reel
Is full, and artfully her fingers feel   5
With quick adjustment, provident control,
The lines – too subtly twisted to unroll,
Out to a perfect thread. I hence appeal
To the dear Christian Church – that we may do
Our Father's business in these temples mirk,   10
Thus swift and steadfast, – thus, intent and strong;
While, thus, apart from toil, our souls pursue
Some high, calm, spheric tune, and prove our work
The better for the sweetness of our song.

Pain in Pleasure

A thought lay like a flower upon mine heart,
And drew around it other thoughts like bees
For multitude and thirst of sweetnesses, –
Whereat rejoicing, I desired the art
Of the Greek whistler, who to wharf and mart   5
Could lure those insect swarms from orange-trees,
That I might hive with me such thoughts, and please
My soul so, always. Foolish counterpart
Of a weak man's vain wishes! While I spoke,
The thought I called a flower, grew nettle-rough –   10
The thoughts, called bees, stung me to festering.
Oh, entertain (cried Reason, as she woke)
Your best and gladdest thoughts but long enough,
And they will all prove sad enough to sting.

An Apprehension

If all the gentlest-hearted friends I know
Concentred in one heart their gentleness,
That still grew gentler, till its pulse was less
For life than pity, – I should yet be slow
To bring my own heart nakedly below   5
The palm of such a friend, that he should press
Motive, condition, means, appliances,
My false ideal joy and fickle woe,
Out full to light and knowledge; I should fear
Some plait between the brows – some rougher chime   10
In the free voice . . . O angels, let your flood
Of bitter scorn dash on me! do ye hear
What I say, who bear calmly all the time
This everlasting face to face with GOD?

Discontent

Light human nature is too lightly tost
And ruffled without cause, – complaining on,
Restless with rest – until, being overthrown,
It learneth to lie quiet. Let a frost
Or a small wasp have crept to the innermost   5
Of our ripe peach, or let the wilful sun
Shine westward of our window, – straight we run
A furlong's sigh, as if the world were lost.
But what time through the heart and through the brain
God hath transfixed us, – we, so moved before,   10
Attain to a calm. Aye, shouldering weights of pain,
We anchor in deep waters, safe from shore,
And hear, submissive, o'er the stormy main,
God's chartered judgments walk for evermore.

Patience Taught by Nature

'O dreary life,' we cry, 'O dreary life!'
And still the generations of the birds
Sing through our sighing, and the flocks and herds
Serenely live while we are keeping strife
With Heaven's true purpose in us, as a knife   5
Against which we may struggle! ocean girds
Unslackened the dry land, savannah-swards
Unweary sweep, – hills watch, unworn; and rife
Meek leaves drop yearly from the forest-trees,
To show above the unwasted stars that pass   10
In their old glory. O thou God of old,
Grant me some smaller grace than comes to these! –
But so much patience as a blade of grass
Grows by, contented through the heat and cold.

Cheerfulness Taught by Reason

I think we are too ready with complaint
In this fair world of God's. Had we no hope
Indeed beyond the zenith and the slope
Of yon grey blank of sky, we might grow faint
To muse upon eternity's constraint   5
Round our aspirant souls; but since the scope
Must widen early is it well to droop,
For a few days consumed in loss and taint?
O pusillanimous Heart, be comforted, –
And, like a cheerful traveller, take the road,   10
Singing beside the hedge. What if the bread
Be bitter in thine inn, and thou unshod
To meet the flints? – At least it may be said,
'Because the way is *short*, I thank Thee, God!'

Exaggeration

We overstate the ills of life, and take
Imagination (given us to bring down
The choirs of singing angels overshone
By God's clear glory) down our earth to rake
The dismal snows instead, – flake following flake,   5
To cover all the corn. We walk upon
The shadow of hills across a level thrown,
And pant like climbers. Near the alder-brake
We sigh so loud, the nightingale within
Refuses to sing loud, as else she would.   10
O brothers! let us leave the shame and sin
Of taking vainly, in a plaintive mood,
The holy name of GRIEF! – holy herein,
That by the grief of ONE came all our good.

Adequacy

Now by the verdure on thy thousand hills,
Belovèd England, – doth the earth appear
Quite good enough for men to overbear
The will of God in, with rebellious wills!
We cannot say the morning-sun fulfils   5
Ingloriously its course, nor that the clear
Strong stars without significance insphere
Our habitation. We, meantime, our ills
Heap up against this good, and lift a cry
Against this work-day world, this ill-spread feast,   10
As if ourselves were better certainly
Than what we come to. Maker and High Priest,
I ask Thee not my joys to multiply, –
Only to make me worthier of the least.

To George Sand [5]

A DESIRE

Thou large-brained woman and large-hearted man,
Self-called George Sand! whose soul, amid the lions
Of thy tumultuous senses, moans defiance,
And answers roar for roar, as spirits can!
I would some mild miraculous thunder ran   5
Above the applauded circus, in appliance
Of thine own nobler nature's strength and science,
Drawing two pinions, white as wings of swan,
From thy strong shoulders, to amaze the place
With holier light! that thou to woman's claim,   10
And man's, mightst join beside the angel's grace
Of a pure genius sanctified from blame, –
Till child and maiden pressed to thine embrace,
To kiss upon thy lips a stainless fame.

To George Sand

A RECOGNITION

True genius, but true woman! dost deny
Thy woman's nature with a manly scorn,
And break away the gauds and armlets worn
By weaker women in captivity?
Ah, vain denial! that revolted cry   5
Is sobbed in by a woman's voice forlorn! –
Thy woman's hair, my sister, all unshorn,
Floats back dishevelled strength in agony,
Disproving thy man's name! and while before
The world thou burnest in a poet-fire,   10
We see thy woman-heart beat evermore
Through the large flame. Beat purer, heart, and higher,
Till God unsex thee on the heavenly shore,
Where unincarnate spirits purely aspire.

The Prisoner

I count the dismal time by months and years,
Since last I felt the green sward under foot,
And the great breath of all things summer-mute
Met mine upon my lips. Now earth appears
As strange to me as dreams of distant spheres,   5
Or thoughts of Heaven we weep at. Nature's lute
Sounds on behind this door so closely shut,
A strange, wild music to the prisoner's ears,
Dilated by the distance, till the brain
Grows dim with fancies which it feels too fine,   10
While ever, with a visionary pain,
Past the precluded senses, sweep and shine
Streams, forests, glades, – and many a golden train
Of sunlit hills, transfigured to Divine.

Insufficiency

When I attain to utter forth in verse
Some inward thought, my soul throbs audibly
Along my pulses, yearning to be free
And something farther, fuller, higher, rehearse,
To the individual, true, and the universe,   5
In consummation of right harmony.
But, like a wind-exposed, distorted tree,
We are blown against for ever by the curse
Which breathes through nature. Oh, the world is weak –
The effluence of each is false to all,   10
And what we best conceive, we fail to speak.
Wait, soul, until thine ashen garments fall,
And then resume thy broken strains, and seek
Fit peroration without let or thrall.

The Romaunt of the Page[6]

1

A knight of gallant deeds
    And a young page at his side,
From the holy war in Palestine[7]
    Did slow and thoughtful ride,
As each were a palmer and told for beads   5
    The dews of the eventide.

2

'O young page,' said the knight,
    'A noble page art thou!
Thou fearest not to steep in blood
    The curls upon thy brow;   10
And once in the tent, and twice in the fight,
    Didst ward me a mortal blow.'

3

'O brave knight,' said the page,
    'Or ere we hither came,
We talked in tent, we talked in field,   15
    Of the bloody battle-game;
But here, below this greenwood bough,
    I cannot speak the same.

4

'Our troop is far behind,
    The woodland calm is new;   20
Our steeds, with slow grass-muffled hoofs,
    Tread deep the shadows through;
And in my mind some blessing kind
    Is dropping with the dew.

5

'The woodland calm is pure –   25
    I cannot choose but have
A thought from these, o' the beechen-trees
    Which in our England wave,
And of the little finches fine
Which sang there, while in Palestine   30
    The warrior-hilt we drave.

6

'Methinks, a moment gone,
　　I heard my mother pray!
I heard, sir knight, the prayer for *me*
　　Wherein she passed away;　　　　　　　　　35
And I know the heavens are leaning down
　　To hear what I shall say.'

7

The page spake calm and high,
　　As of no mean degree;
Perhaps he felt in nature's broad　　　　　　40
　　Full heart, his own was free:
And the knight looked up to his lifted eye,
　　Then answered smilingly: –

8

'Sir page, I pray your grace!
　　Certes, I meant not so　　　　　　　　　45
To cross your pastoral mood, sir page,
　　With the crook of the battle-bow:
But a knight may speak of a lady's face,
I ween, in any mood or place,
　　If the grasses die or grow.　　　　　　　50

9

'And this I meant to say, –
　　My lady's face shall shine
As ladies' faces use, to greet
　　My page from Palestine;
Or, speak she fair or prank she gay,　　　　55
　　She is no lady of mine.

10

'And this I meant to fear, –
　　Her bower may suit thee ill!
For, sooth, in that same field and tent,
　　Thy *talk* was somewhat still;　　　　　　60
And fitter thy hand for my knightly spear,
　　Than thy tongue for my lady's will.'

11

Slowly and thankfully
  The young page bowed his head:
His large eyes seemed to muse a smile,   65
  Until he blushed instead,
And no lady in her bower, pardiè,
  Could blush more sudden red.
'Sir Knight, – thy lady's bower to me
  Is suited well,' he said.   70

12

Beati, beati, mortui! [8]
From the convent on the sea,
One mile off, or scarce as nigh,
Swells the dirge as clear and high
As if that, over brake and lea,   75
Bodily the wind did carry
The great altar of Saint Mary,
And the fifty tapers burning o'er it,
And the lady Abbess dead before it,
And the chanting nuns whom yesterweek   80
Her voice did charge and bless, –
Chanting steady, chanting meek,
Chanting with a solemn breath
Because that they are thinking less
Upon the Dead than upon death!   85
Beati, beati, mortui!
Now the vision in the sound
Wheeleth on the wind around.
Now it sweepeth back, away –
The uplands will not let it stay   90
To dark the western sun.
Mortui! – away at last, –
Or ere the page's blush is past!
And the knight heard all, and the page heard none.

13

'A boon, thou noble knight,   95
  If ever I servèd thee!
Though thou art a knight and I am a page,

19

Now grant a boon to me;
And tell me sooth, if dark or bright,
If little loved or loved aright   100
  Be the face of thy ladye.'

14

Gloomily looked the knight: –
  'As a son thou hast servèd me,
And would to none I had granted boon
  Except to only thee!   105
For haply then I should love aright,
For then I should know if dark or bright
  Were the face of my ladye.

15

'Yet it ill suits my knightly tongue
  To grudge that granted boon!   110
That heavy price from heart and life
  I paid in silence down.
The hand that claimed it, cleared in fine
My father's fame: I swear by mine,
  That price was nobly won.   115

16

'Earl Walter was a brave old earl, –
  He was my father's friend;
And while I rode the lists at court
  And little guessed the end,
My noble father in his shroud,   120
Against a slanderer lying loud,
  He rose up to defend.

17

'Oh, calm, below the marble grey
  My father's dust was strown!
Oh, meek, above the marble grey   125
  His image prayed alone!
The slanderer lied – the wretch was brave, –
For, looking up the minster-nave,
He saw my father's knightly glaive
  Was changed from steel to stone.   130

18

'Earl Walter's glaive was steel,
   With a brave old hand to wear it,
And dashed the lie back in the mouth
Which lied against the godly truth
   And against the knightly merit!   135
The slanderer, 'neath the avenger's heel,
Struck up the dagger in appeal
From stealthy lie to brutal force –
And out upon the traitor's corse
   Was yielded the true spirit.   140

19

'I would mine hand had fought that fight
   And justified my father!
I would mine heart had caught that wound
   And slept beside him rather!
I think it were a better thing   145
Than murthered friend and marriage-ring
   Forced on my life together.

20

'Wail shook Earl Walter's house;
   His true wife shed no tear;
She lay upon her bed as mute   150
   As the earl did on his bier:
Till – "Ride, ride fast," she said at last,
   "And bring the avengèd's son anear!
Ride fast – ride free, as a dart can flee,
For white of blee with waiting for me   155
   Is the corse in the next chambère."

21

'I came – I knelt beside her bed –
   Her calm was worse than strife;
"My husband, for thy father dear,
Gave freely, when thou wast not here,   160
   His own and eke my life.
A boon! Of that sweet child we make
An orphan for thy father's sake,
   Make thou, for ours, a wife."

22

'I said, "My steed neighs in the court,   165
   My bark rocks on the brine,
And the warrior's vow I am under now
   To free the pilgrim's shrine;
But fetch the ring and fetch the priest
   And call that daughter of thine,   170
And rule she wide from my castle on Nyde
   While I am in Palestine."

23

'In the dark chambère, if the bride was fair,
   Ye wis, I could not see,   174
But the steed thrice neighed, and the priest fast prayed,
   And wedded fast were we.
Her mother smiled upon her bed
As at its side we knelt to wed,
   And the bride rose from her knee
And kissed the smile of her mother dead,   180
   Or ever she kissed me.

24

'My page, my page, what grieves thee so,
   That the tears run down thy face?' –
'Alas, alas! mine own sistèr
   Was in thy lady's case!   185
But *she* laid down the silks she wore
And followed him she wed before,
Disguised as his true servitor,
   To the very battle-place.'

25

And wept the page, but laughed the knight, –   190
   A careless laugh laughed he:
'Well done it were for thy sistèr,
   But not for my ladye!
My love, so please you, shall requite
No woman, whether dark or bright,   195
   Unwomaned if she be.'

26

The page stopped weeping and smiled cold –
  'Your wisdom may declare
That womanhood is proved the best
By golden brooch and glossy vest   200
  The mincing ladies wear;
Yet is it proved, and was of old,
Anear as well, I dare to hold,
  By truth, or by despair.'

27

He smiled no more, he wept no more,   205
  But passionate he spake, –
'Oh, womanly she prayed in tent,
  When none beside did wake!
Oh, womanly she paled in fight,
  For one belovèd's sake! –   210
And her little hand, defiled with blood,
Her tender tears of womanhood
  Most woman-pure did make!'

28

– 'Well done it were for thy sistèr,
  Thou tellest well her tale!   215
But for my lady, she shall pray
  I' the kirk of Nydesdale.
Not dread for me but love for me
  Shall make my lady pale;
No casque shall hide her woman's tear –   220
It shall have room to trickle clear
  Behind her woman's veil.'

29

– 'But what if she mistook thy mind
  And followed thee to strife,
Then kneeling, did entreat thy love,   225
  As Paynims [9] ask for life!'
– 'I would forgive, and evermore
Would love her as my servitor,
  But little as my wife.

30

'Look up – there is a small bright cloud   230
  Alone amid the skies!
So high, so pure, and so apart,
  A woman's honour lies.'
The page looked up – the cloud was sheen –
A sadder cloud did rush, I ween,   235
  Betwixt it and his eyes:

31

Then dimly dropped his eyes away
  From welkin unto hill –
Ha! who rides there? – the page is 'ware,
  Though the cry at his heart is still!   240
And the page seeth all and the knight seeth none,
Though banner and spear do fleck the sun,
  And the Saracens ride at will.

32

He speaketh calm, he speaketh low, –
  'Ride fast, my master, ride,   245
Or ere within the broadening dark
  The narrow shadows hide.'
'Yea, fast, my page, I will do so,
  And keep thou at my side.'

33

'Now nay, now nay, ride on thy way,   250
  Thy faithful page precede,
For I must loose on saddle-bow
My battle-casque that galls, I trow,
  The shoulder of my steed;
And I must pray, as I did vow,   255
  For one in bitter need.

34

'Ere night I shall be near to thee, –
  Now ride, my master, ride!
Ere night, as parted spirits cleave
To mortals too beloved to leave,   260
  I shall be at thy side.'

The knight smiled free at the fantasy,
   And adown the dell did ride.

35

Had the knight looked up to the page's face,
   No smile the word had won: 265
Had the knight looked up to the page's face,
   I ween he had never gone:
Had the knight looked back to the page's geste,
   I ween he had turned anon!
For dread was the woe in the face so young,   270
And wild was the silent geste that flung
Casque, sword to earth – as the boy down-sprung,
   And stood – alone, alone.

36

He clenched his hands as if to hold
   His soul's great agony –   275
'Have I renounced my womanhood,
   For wifehood unto *thee*,
And is this the last, last look of thine
   That ever I shall see?

37

'Yet God thee save, and mayst thou have   280
   A lady to thy mind,
More woman-proud and half as true
   As one thou leav'st behind!
And God me take with Him to dwell –
For HIM I cannot love too well,   285
   As I have loved my kind.'

38

SHE looketh up, in earth's despair,
   The hopeful heavens to seek:
That little cloud still floateth there,
   Whereof her loved did speak.   290
How bright the little cloud appears!
Her eyelids fall upon the tears,
   And the tears down either cheek.

39

The tramp of hoof, the flash of steel –
    The Paynims round her coming!   295
The sound and sight have made her calm, –
    False page, but truthful woman!
She stands amid them all unmoved:
A heart once broken by the loved
    Is strong to meet the foeman.   300

40

'Ho, Christian page! art keeping sheep,
    From pouring wine-cups resting?' –
'I keep my master's noble name,
    For warring, not for feasting;
And if that here Sir Hubert were,   305
My master brave, my master dear,
    Ye would not stay to question.'

41

'Where is thy master, scornful page,
    That we may slay or bind him?' –
'Now search the lea and search the wood,   310
    And see if ye can find him!
Nathless, as hath been often tried,
Your Paynim heroes faster ride
    Before him than behind him.'

42

'Give smoother answers, lying page,   315
    Or perish in the lying.' –
'I trow that if the warrior brand
Beside my foot, were in my hand,
    'Twere better at replying.'
They cursed her deep, they smote her low,   320
They cleft her golden ringlets through;
    The Loving is the Dying.

43

She felt the scimitar gleam down,
   And met it from beneath
With smile more bright in victory   325
   Than any sword from sheath, –
Which flashed across her lip serene,
Most like the spirit-light between
   The darks of life and death.

44

   Ingemisco, ingemisco! [10]   330
From the convent on the sea,
Now it sweepeth solemnly!
As over wood and over lea
Bodily the wind did carry
The great altar of St Mary,   335
And the fifty tapers paling o'er it,
And the Lady Abbess stark before it,
And the weary nuns with hearts that faintly
Beat along their voices saintly –
   Ingemisco, ingemisco!   340
Dirge for abbess laid in shroud
Sweepeth o'er the shroudless dead,
Page or lady, as we said,
With the dews upon her head,
All as sad if not as loud.   345
   Ingemisco, ingemisco!
Is ever a lament begun
By any mourner under sun,
Which, ere it endeth, suits but *one*?

The Lay of the Brown Rosary

'Onora, Onora,' – her mother is calling,
She sits at the lattice and hears the dew falling
Drop after drop from the sycamores laden
With dew as with blossom, and calls home the maiden,
    'Night cometh, Onora.'   5

She looks down the garden-walk caverned with trees,
To the limes at the end where the green arbour is –
'Some sweet thought or other may keep where it found her,
While forgot or unseen in the dreamlight around her
    Night cometh – Onora!'   10

She looks up the forest whose alleys shoot on
Like the mute minster-aisles when the anthem is done,
And the choristers sitting with faces aslant
Feel the silence to consecrate more than the chant –
    'Onora, Onora!'   15

And forward she looketh across the brown heath –
'Onora, art coming?' – what is it she seeth?
Nought, nought, but the grey border-stone that is wist
To dilate and assume a wild shape in the mist –
    'My daughter!' – Then over   20

The casement she leaneth, and as she doth so,
She is 'ware of her little son playing below:
'Now where is Onora?' – He hung down his head
And spake not, then answering blushed scarlet-red, –
    'At the tryst with her lover.'   25

But his mother was wroth. In a sternness quoth she,
'As thou play'st at the ball, art thou playing with me?
When we know that her lover to battle is gone,
And the saints know above that she loveth but one
    And will ne'er wed another?'   30

Then the boy wept aloud. 'Twas a fair sight yet sad
To see the tears run down the sweet blooms he had:
He stamped with his foot, said – 'The saints know I lied
Because truth that is wicked is fittest to hide!
    Must I utter it, mother?'   35

In his vehement childhood he hurried within,
And knelt at her feet as in prayer against sin;
But a child at a prayer never sobbeth as he –
'Oh! she sits with the nun of the brown rosary,
    At nights in the ruin!   40

'The old convent ruin the ivy rots off,
Where the owl hoots by day and the toad is sun-proof;
Where no singing-birds build, and the trees gaunt and grey
As in stormy sea-coasts appear blasted one way –
    But is *this* the wind's doing?   45

'A nun in the east wall was buried alive,
Who mocked at the priest when he called her to shrive, –
And shrieked such a curse, as the stone took her breath,
The old abbess fell backward and swooned unto death
    With an Ave half-spoken.   50

'I tried once to pass it, myself and my hound,
Till, as fearing the lash, down he shivered to ground.
A brave hound, my mother! a brave hound, ye wot!
And the wolf thought the same with his fangs at her throat
    In the pass of the Brocken.   55

'At dawn and at eve, mother, who sitteth there,
With the brown rosary never used for a prayer?
Stoop low, mother, low! If we went there to see,
What an ugly great hole in that east wall must be
    At dawn and at even!   60

'Who meet there, my mother, at dawn and at even?
Who meet by that wall, never looking to heaven?
O sweetest my sister, what doeth with *thee*,
The ghost of a nun with a brown rosary
    And a face turned from heaven?   65

'Saint Agnes[11] o'erwatcheth my dreams, and erewhile
I have felt through mine eyelids the warmth of her smile;
But last night, as a sadness like pity came o'er her,
She whispered – "Say *two* prayers at dawn for Onora!
    The Tempted is sinning." '   70

'Onora, Onora!' they heard her not coming –
Not a step on the grass, not a voice through the gloaming;
But her mother looked up, and she stood on the floor
Fair and still as the moonlight that came there before,
    And a smile just beginning: 75

It touches her lips – but it dares not arise
To the height of the mystical sphere of her eyes;
And the large musing eyes, neither joyous nor sorry,
Sing on like the angels in separate glory
    Between clouds of amber.   80

For the hair droops in clouds amber-coloured, till stirred
Into gold by the gesture that comes with a word;
While – O soft! – her speaking is so interwound
Of the dim and the sweet, 'tis a twilight of sound
    And floats through the chamber.   85

'Since thou shrivest my brother, fair mother,' said she,
'I count on thy priesthood for marrying of me;
And I know by the hills that the battle is done –
That my lover rides on – will be here with the sun,
    'Neath the eyes that behold thee.'   90

Her mother sat silent – too tender, I wis,
Of the smile her dead father smiled dying to kiss;
But the boy started up pale with tears, passion-wrought, –
'O wicked fair sister, the hills utter nought!
    If he cometh, who told thee?'   95

'I know by the hills,' she resumed, calm and clear,
'By the beauty upon them, that HE is anear:
Did they ever look *so* since he bade me adieu?
Oh, love in the waking, sweet brother, is true
    As Saint Agnes in sleeping.'   100

Half-ashamed and half-softened the boy did not speak,
And the blush met the lashes which fell on his cheek:
She bowed down to kiss him: dear saints, did he see
Or feel on her bosom the BROWN ROSARY,
    That he shrank away weeping?   105

SECOND PART

A bed. – ONORA *sleeping. Angels, but not near.*

FIRST ANGEL

    Must we stand so far, and she
    So very fair?

SECOND ANGEL

          As bodies be.

FIRST ANGEL

    And she so mild?

SECOND ANGEL

          As spirits when
They meeken, not to God, but men.

FIRST ANGEL

    And she so young, – that I who bring   110
Good dreams for saintly children, might
Mistake that small soft face tonight,
And fetch her such a blessèd thing,
That at her waking she would weep
For childhood lost anew in sleep.   115
How hath she sinned?

SECOND ANGEL

          In bartering love;
God's love – for man's.

FIRST ANGEL

          We may reprove
The world for this, not only her.
Let me approach to breathe away
This dust o' the heart with holy air.   120

SECOND ANGEL

    Stand off! She sleeps, and did not pray.

FIRST ANGEL

Did none pray for her?

SECOND ANGEL

Aye, a child, –
Who never, praying, wept before:
While, in a mother undefiled,
Prayer goeth on in sleep, as true   125
And pauseless as the pulses do.

FIRST ANGEL

Then I approach.

SECOND ANGEL

It is not WILLED.

FIRST ANGEL

One word: is she redeemed?

SECOND ANGEL

No more!
The place is filled.   [*Angels vanish.*

EVIL SPIRIT (*in a Nun's garb by the bed*).

Forbear that dream – forbear that dream! too near to Heaven it leaned.

ONORA (*in sleep*)

Nay, leave me this – but only this! 'tis but a dream, sweet fiend!   136

EVIL SPIRIT

It is a *thought*.

ONORA (*in sleep*)

A sleeping thought – most innocent of good.
It doth the Devil no harm, sweet fiend! it cannot, if it would.
I say in it no holy hymn, I do no holy work,
I scarcely hear the sabbath-bell that chimeth from the kirk.   135

EVIL SPIRIT

Forbear that dream – forbear that dream!

ONORA (*in sleep*)

Nay, let me dream at least.
That far-off bell, it may be took for viol at a feast.
I only walk among the fields, beneath the autumn-sun,
With my dead father, hand in hand, as I have often done.

EVIL SPIRIT

Forbear that dream – forbear that dream!

ONORA (*in sleep*)

Nay, sweet fiend, let me go:
I never more can walk with *him*, oh, never more but so.   141

32

For they have tied my father's feet beneath the kirkyard stone,
Oh, deep and straight, oh, very straight! they move at nights alone:
And then he calleth through my dreams, he calleth tenderly,
'Come forth, my daughter, my beloved, and walk the fields with me!'

EVIL SPIRIT

Forbear that dream, or else disprove its pureness by a sign.   146

ONORA (*in sleep*)

Speak on, thou shalt be satisfied! my word shall answer thine.
I heard a bird which used to sing when I a child was praying,
I see the poppies in the corn I used to sport away in.
What shall I do – tread down the dew, and pull the blossoms blowing?
Or clap my wicked hands to fright the finches from the rowan?   151

EVIL SPIRIT

Thou shalt do something harder still. Stand up where thou dost stand
Among the fields of Dreamland with thy father hand in hand,
And clear and slow, repeat the vow – declare its cause and kind,
Which, not to break, in sleep or wake, thou bearest on thy mind.   155

ONORA (*in sleep*)

I bear a vow of sinful kind, a vow for mournful cause:
I vowed it deep, I vowed it strong – the spirits laughed applause:
The spirits trailed along the pines low laughter like a breeze,
While, high atween their swinging tops, the stars appeared to freeze.

EVIL SPIRIT

More calm and free, – speak out to me, why such a vow was made.   160

ONORA (*in sleep*)

Because that God decreed my death, and I shrank back afraid.
Have patience, O dead father mine! I did not fear to die; –
I wish I were a young dead child, and had thy company!
I wish I lay beside thy feet, a buried three-year child,
And wearing only a kiss of thine upon my lips that smiled!   165
The linden-tree that covers thee might so have shadowed twain,
For death itself I did not fear – 'tis love that makes the pain.
Love feareth death. I was no child – I was betrothed that day;
I wore a troth-kiss on my lips I could not give away.
How could I bear to lie content and still beneath a stone,   170
And feel mine own betrothed go by – alas! no more mine own, –
Go leading by in wedding pomp some lovely lady brave,
With cheeks that blushed as red as rose, while mine were white in grave?
How could I bear to sit in Heaven, on e'er so high a throne,
And hear him say to her – to *her*! that else he loveth none?   180

Though e'er so high I sat above, though e'er so low he spake,
As clear as thunder I should hear the new oath he might take,
That hers, forsooth, were heavenly eyes – ah, me! while very dim
Some heavenly eyes (indeed of Heaven!) would darken down to *him*.

EVIL SPIRIT

Who told thee thou wast called to death?

ONORA (*in sleep*)

                                    I sat all night beside thee –
The grey owl on the ruined wall shut both his eyes to hide thee,   181
And ever he flapped his heavy wing all brokenly and weak,
And the long grass waved against the sky, around his gasping beak.
I sat beside thee all the night, while the moonlight lay forlorn,
Strewn round us like a dead world's shroud, in ghastly fragments torn.
And through the night, and through the hush, and over the flapping wing,
We heard beside the Heavenly Gate the angels murmuring: –   187
We heard them say, 'Put day to day, and count the days to seven,
And God will draw Onora up the golden stairs of Heaven;
And yet the Evil ones have leave that purpose to defer,   190
For if she has no need of HIM, He has no need of her.' –

EVIL SPIRIT

Speak out to me, speak bold and free.

ONORA (*in sleep*)

                                 And then I heard thee say,
'I count upon my rosary brown the hours thou hast to stay!
Yet God permits us Evil ones to put by that decree,
Since if thou hast no need of HIM, He has no need of thee –   195
And if thou wilt forgo the sight of angels, verily
Thy true love gazing on thy face, shall guess what angels be;
Nor bride shall pass, save thee' . . . Alas! – my father's hand's a-cold,
The meadows seem –

EVIL SPIRIT

                       Forbear the dream, or let the vow be told.

ONORA (*in sleep*)

I vowed upon thy rosary brown, this string of antique beads,   200
By charnel lichens overgrown, and dank among the weeds,
This rosary brown, which is thine own, – lost soul of buried nun,
Who, lost by vow, wouldst render now all souls alike undone, –
I vowed upon thy rosary brown, – and, till such vow should break,
A pledge alwàys of living days, 'twas hung around my neck –   205
I vowed to thee on rosary (dead father, look not so!),

I would not thank God in my weal,[12] *nor seek God in my woe.*
EVIL SPIRIT
    And canst thou prove –
ONORA (*in sleep*)
                    O love – my love! I felt him near again!
I saw his steed on mountain-head, I heard it on the plain!
Was this no weal for me to feel? – is greater weal than this?   210
Yet when he came, I wept his name – and the angels heard but *his.*
EVIL SPIRIT
    Well done, well done!
ONORA (*in sleep*)
                 Aye me! the sun . . . the dreamlight 'gins to pine, –
Aye me! how dread can look the Dead! – Aroint thee,[13] father mine!

She starteth from slumber, she sitteth upright,
And her breath comes in sobs while she stares through the night.   215
There is nought. The great willow, her lattice before,
Large-drawn in the moon, lieth calm on the floor.
But her hands tremble fast as their pulses, and, free
From the death-clasp, close over – the BROWN ROSARY.

THIRD PART

'Tis a morn for a bridal; the merry bride-bell   220
Rings clear through the green-wood that skirts the chapelle,
And the priest at the altar awaiteth the bride,
And the sacristans slyly are jesting aside
    At the work shall be doing;

While down through the wood rides that fair company,   225
The youths with the courtship, the maids with the glee,
Till the chapel-cross opens to sight, and at once
All the maids sigh demurely and think for the nonce,
    'And so endeth a wooing!'

And the bride and the bridegroom are leading the way,   230
With his hand on her rein, and a word yet to say:
Her dropt eyelids suggest the soft answers beneath,
And the little quick smiles come and go with her breath,
    When she sigheth or speaketh.

And the tender bride-mother breaks off unaware 235
From an Ave, to think that her daughter is fair,
Till in nearing the chapel and glancing before
She seeth her little son stand at the door:
    Is it play that he seeketh?

Is it play? when his eyes wander innocent-wild, 240
And sublimed with a sadness unfitting a child?
He trembles not, weeps not – the passion is done,
And calmly he kneels in their midst, with the sun
    On his head like a glory.

'O fair-featured maids, ye are many!' he cried, – 245
'But in fairness and vileness, who matcheth the bride?
O brave-hearted youths, ye are many! but whom,
For the courage and woe, can ye match with the groom,
    As ye see them before ye?'

Out spake the bride's mother, 'The vileness is thine, 250
If thou shame thine own sister, a bride at the shrine!'
Out spake the bride's lover, 'The vileness be mine,
If he shame mine own wife at the hearth or the shrine,
    And the charge be unprovèd.

'Bring the charge, prove the charge, brother! speak it aloud: 255
Let thy father and hers, hear it deep in his shroud!' –
– 'O father, thou seest – for dead eyes can see –
How she wears on her bosom A BROWN ROSARY,
    O my father belovèd!'

Then outlaughed the bridegroom, and outlaughed withal 260
Both maidens and youths, by the old chapel-wall.
'So she weareth no love-gift, kind brother,' quoth he,
'She may wear an she listeth a brown rosary,
    Like a pure-hearted lady.'

Then swept through the chapel the long bridal train. 265
Though he spake to the bride she replied not again:
On, as one in a dream, pale and stately she went
Where the altar-lights burn o'er the great sacrament,
    Faint with daylight, but steady.

But her brother had passed in between them and her,   270
And calmly knelt down on the high-altar stair –
Of an infantine aspect so stern to the view
That the priest could not smile on the child's eyes of blue
    As he would for another.

He knelt like a child marble-sculptured and white,   275
That seems kneeling to pray on the tomb of a knight,
With a look taken up to each iris of stone
From the greatness and death where he kneeleth, but none
    From the face of a mother.

'In your chapel, O priest, ye have wedded and shriven [14]   280
Fair wives for the hearth, and fair sinners for Heaven!
But this fairest my sister, ye think now to wed,
Bid her kneel where she standeth, and shrive her instead:
    O shrive her and wed not!'

In tears, the bride's mother, – 'Sir priest, unto thee   285
Would he lie, as he lied to this fair company.'
In wrath, the bride's lover, – 'The lie shall be clear!
Speak it out, boy! the saints in their niches shall hear:
    Be the charge proved or said not.'

Then serene in his childhood he lifted his face,   290
And his voice sounded holy and fit for the place:
'Look down from your niches, ye still saints, and see
How she wears on her bosom *a brown rosary!*
    Is it used for the praying?'

The youths looked aside – to laugh there were a sin –   295
And the maidens' lips trembled from smiles shut within.
Quoth the priest, 'Thou art wild, pretty boy! Blessed she
Who prefers at her bridal a brown rosary
    To a worldly arraying!'

The bridegroom spake low and led onward the bride,   300
And before the high altar they stood side by side:
The rite-book is opened, the rite is begun,
They have knelt down together to rise up as one.
    Who laughed by the altar?

The maidens looked forward, the youths looked around,   305
The bridegroom's eye flashed from his prayer at the sound;
And each saw the bride, as if no bride she were,
Gazing cold at the priest without gesture of prayer,
    As he read from the psalter.

The priest never knew that she did so, but still   310
He felt a power on him too strong for his will,
And whenever the Great Name was there to be read,
His voice sank to silence – THAT could not be said,
    Or the air could not hold it.

'I have sinnèd,' quoth he, 'I have sinnèd, I wot' –   315
And the tears ran adown his old cheeks at the thought.
They dropped fast on the book, but he read on the same,
And ay was the silence where should be the NAME, –
    As the choristers told it.

The rite-book is closed, and the rite being done   320
They who knelt down togethe arise up as one.
Fair riseth the bride – oh, a fair bride is she, –
But, for all (think the maidens) that brown rosary,
    No saint at her praying!

What aileth the bridegroom? He glares blank and wide –   325
Then suddenly turning he kisseth the bride –
His lip stung her with cold; she glanced upwardly mute:
'Mine own wife,' he said, and fell stark at her foot
    In the word he was saying.

They have lifted him up, – but his head sinks away,   330
And his face showeth bleak in the sunshine and grey.
Leave him now where he lieth – for oh, never more
Will he kneel at an altar or stand on a floor!
    Let his bride gaze upon him.

Long and still was her gaze, while they chafèd him there   335
And breathed in the mouth whose last life had kissed her,
But when they stood up – only *they*! with a start
The shriek from her soul struck her pale lips apart –
    She has lived, and forgone him!

And low on his body she droppeth adown –   340
'Didst call me thine own wife, belovèd – thine own?
Then take thine own with thee! thy coldness is warm
To the world's cold without thee! Come, keep me from harm
    In a calm of thy teaching.'

She looked in his face earnest-long, as in sooth   345
There were hope of an answer, – and then kissed his mouth,
And with head on his bosom, wept, wept bitterly, –
'Now, O God, take pity – take pity on me! –
    God, hear my beseeching!'

She was 'ware of a shadow that crossed where she lay,   350
She was 'ware of a presence that withered the day –
Wild she sprang to her feet, – 'I surrender to *thee*
The broken vow's pledge, the accursed rosary, –
    I am ready for dying!'

She dashed it in scorn to the marble-paved ground   355
Where it fell mute as snow, and a weird music-sound
Crept up, like a chill, up the aisles long and dim, –
As the fiends tried to mock at the choristers' hymn
    And moaned in the trying.

FOURTH PART

Onora looketh listlessly adown the garden walk: 360
'I am weary, O my mother, of thy tender talk;
I am weary of the trees a-waving to and fro,
Of the steadfast skies above, the running brooks below.
All things are the same but I, – only I am dreary,
And, mother, of my dreariness behold me very weary.   365

'Mother, brother, pull the flowers I planted in the spring
And smiled to think I should smile more upon their gathering:
The bees will find out other flowers – oh, pull them, dearest mine,
And carry them and carry me before Saint Agnes' shrine.'
– Whereat they pulled the summer flowers she planted in the spring,
And her and them all mournfully to Agnes' shrine did bring.   371

She looked up to the pictured saint and gently shook her head –
'The picture is too calm for *me* – too calm for *me*,' she said:
'The little flowers we brought with us, before it we may lay,
For those are used to look at heaven, – but *I* must turn away,   375
Because no sinner under sun can dare or bear to gaze
On God's or angel's holiness, except in Jesu's face.'

She spoke with passion after pause – 'And were it wisely done,
If we who cannot gaze above, should walk the earth alone?
If we whose virtue is so weak, should have a will so strong,   380
And stand blind on the rocks, to choose the right path from the wrong?
To choose perhaps a love-lit hearth, instead of love and Heaven, –
A single rose, for a rose-tree, which beareth seven times seven?
A rose that droppeth from the hand, that fadeth in the breast, –
Until, in grieving for the worst, we learn what is the best!'   385
Then breaking into tears, – 'Dear God,' she cried, 'and must we see
All blissful things depart from us or ere we go to THEE?
We cannot guess Thee in the wood, or hear Thee in the wind?
Our cedars must fall round us, ere we see the light behind?
Aye sooth, we feel too strong, in weal, to need Thee on that road,   390
But woe being come, the soul is dumb that crieth not on "God".'

Her mother could not speak for tears; she ever musèd thus,
'*The bees will find out other flowers*, – but what is left for *us*?'
But her young brother stayed his sobs and knelt beside her knee,
– 'Thou sweetest sister in the world, hast never a word for me?'   395
She passed her hand across his face, she pressed it on his cheek,
So tenderly, so tenderly – she needed not to speak.

The wreath which lay on shrine that day, at vespers [15] bloomed no more:
The woman fair who placed it there had died an hour before.
Both perished mute, for lack of root, earth's nourishment to reach.   400
O reader, breathe (the ballad saith) some sweetness out of each!

The Mourning Mother

OF THE DEAD BLIND

1

Dost thou weep, mourning mother,
    For thy blind boy in grave?
That no more with each other
    Sweet counsel ye can have? –
That he, left dark by nature,   5
    Can never more be led
By thee, maternal creature,
    Along smooth paths instead?
That thou canst no more show him
    The sunshine, by the heat;   10
The river's silver flowing,
    By murmurs at his feet?
The foliage, by its coolness;
    The roses, by their smell;
And all creation's fullness,   15
    By Love's invisible?
Weepest thou to behold not
    His meek blind eyes again, –
Closed doorways which were folded,
    And prayed against in vain –   20
And under which sat smiling
    The child-mouth evermore,
As one who watcheth, wiling
    The time by, at a door?
And weepest thou to feel not   25
    His clinging hand on thine –
Which now, at dream-time, will not
    Its cold touch disentwine?
And weepest thou still ofter,
    Oh, never more to mark   30
His low soft words, made softer
    By speaking in the dark?
Weep on, thou mourning mother!

2

But since to him when living
   Thou wast both sun and moon,   35
Look o'er his grave, surviving,
   From a high sphere alone.
Sustain that exaltation,
   Expand that tender light,
And hold in mother-passion   40
   Thy Blessèd in thy sight.
See how he went out straightway
   From the dark world he knew, –
No twilight in the gateway
   To mediate 'twixt the two, –   45
Into the sudden glory,
   Out of the dark he trod,
Departing from before thee
   At once to light and GOD! –
For the first face, beholding   50
   The Christ's in its divine,
For the first place, the golden
   And tideless hyaline;[16]
With trees, at lasting summer,
   That rock to songful sound,   55
While angels, the new-comer,
   Wrap a still smile around.
Oh, in the blessèd psalm now,
   His happy voice he tries,
Spreading a thicker palm-bough,   60
   Than others, o'er his eyes!
Yet still, in all the singing,
   Thinks haply of thy song
Which, in his life's first springing,
   Sang to him all night long;   65
And wishes it beside him,
   With kissing lips that cool
And soft did overglide him,
   To make the sweetness full.
Look up, O mourning mother,   70
   Thy blind boy walks in light!

Ye wait for one another,
    Before God's infinite.
But thou art now the darkest,
    Thou mother left below –   75
Thou, the sole blind, – thou markest,
    Content that it be so, –
Until ye two have meeting
    Where Heaven's pearl-gate is,
And *he* shall lead thy feet in,   80
    As once thou leddest *his*.
Wait on, thou mourning mother.

A Valediction

1

GOD be with thee, my belovèd – GOD be with thee!
    Else alone thou goest forth,
    Thy face unto the north,
Moor and pleasance all around thee and beneath thee,
    Looking equal in one snow;   5
    While I who try to reach thee,
    Vainly follow, vainly follow,
    With the farewell and the hollo,
    And cannot reach thee so.
    Alas, I can but teach thee!   10
GOD be with thee, my belovèd – GOD be with thee.

2

Can I teach thee, my belovèd – can I teach thee?
    If I said, 'Go left or right,'
    The counsel would be light,
The wisdom, poor of all that could enrich thee.   15
    My right would show like left;
    My raising would depress thee,
    My choice of light would blind thee,
    Of way, would leave behind thee,
    Of end, would leave bereft.   20
    Alas, I can but bless thee!
May GOD teach thee, my belovèd – may GOD teach thee.

3

Can I bless thee, my belovèd – can I bless thee?
    What blessing word can I,
    From mine own tears, keep dry?   25
What flowers grow in my field wherewith to dress thee?
    My good reverts to ill;
    My calmnesses would move thee,
    My softnesses would prick thee,
    My bindings up would break thee,   30
    My crownings, curse and kill.
    Alas, I can but love thee!
May GOD bless thee, my belovèd – may GOD bless thee.

4

Can I love thee, my belovèd – can I love thee?
    And is *this* like love, to stand   35
    With no help in my hand,
When strong as death I fain would watch above thee?
    My love-kiss can deny
    No tear that falls beneath it;
    Mine oath of love can swear thee   40
    From no ill that comes near thee, –
    And thou diest while I breathe it,
    And *I* – I can but die!
May GOD love thee, my belovèd – may GOD love thee.

Lady Geraldine's Courtship

A ROMANCE OF THE AGE

A poet writes to his friend
PLACE – *A Room in Wycombe Hall*
TIME – *Late in the evening*

Dear my friend and fellow student, I would lean my spirit o'er you!
Down the purple of this chamber, tears should scarcely run at will.
I am humbled who was humble. Friend, – I bow my head before you:
You should lead me to my peasants, – but their faces are too still.

There's a lady – an earl's daughter, – she is proud and she is noble,   5
And she treads the crimson carpet, and she breathes the perfumed air,
And a kingly blood sends glances up her princely eye to trouble,
And the shadow of a monarch's crown is softened in her hair.

She has halls among the woodlands, she has castles by the breakers,
She has farms and she has manors, she can threaten and command,   10
And the palpitating engines snort in steam across her acres,
As they mark upon the blasted heaven the measure of the land.

There are none of England's daughters who can show a prouder presence;
Upon princely suitors praying, she has looked in her disdain.
She was sprung of English nobles, I was born of English peasants;   15
What was I that I should love her – save for competence to pain?

I was only a poor poet, made for singing at her casement,
As the finches or the thrushes, while she thought of other things.
Oh, she walked so high above me, she appeared to my abasement,
In her lovely silken murmur, like an angel clad in wings!   20

Many vassals bow before her as her carriage sweeps their doorways;
She has blest their little children, – as a priest or queen were she.
Far too tender, or too cruel far, her smile upon the poor was,
For I thought it was the same smile which she used to smile on *me*.

She has voters in the Commons, she has lovers in the palace;   25
And of all the fair court-ladies, few have jewels half as fine;
Oft the prince has named her beauty 'twixt the red wine and the chalice.
Oh, and what was I to love her? my beloved, my Geraldine!

Yet I could not choose but love her. I was born to poet-uses,
To love all things set above me, all of good and all of fair: 30
Nymphs of mountain, not of valley, we are wont to call the Muses
And in nympholeptic [17] climbing, poets pass from mount to star.

And because I was a poet, and because the public praised me,
With a critical deduction for the modern writer's fault,
I could sit at rich men's tables, – though the courtesies that raised me,   35
Still suggested clear between us the pale spectrum of the salt.

And they praised me in her presence; – 'Will your book appear
                                                    this summer?'
Then returning to each other – 'Yes, our plans are for the moors.'
Then with whisper dropped behind me – 'There he is! the latest comer!
Oh, she only likes his verses! what is over, she endures.   40

'Quite low-born! self-educated! somewhat gifted though by nature, –
And we make a point of asking him, – of being very kind.
You may speak, he does not hear you! and besides, he writes no satire, –
All these serpents kept by charmers leave the natural sting behind.'

I grew scornfuller, grew colder, as I stood up there among them,   45
Till as frost intense will burn you, the cold scorning scorched my brow;
When a sudden silver speaking, gravely cadenced, over-rung them,
And a sudden silken stirring touched my inner nature through.

I looked upward and beheld her. With a calm and regnant spirit,
Slowly round she swept her eyelids, and said clear before them all –   50
'Have you such superfluous honour, sir, that able to confer it
You will come down, Mister Bertram, as my guest to Wycombe Hall?'

Here she paused, – she had been paler at the first word of her speaking,
But, because a silence followed it, blushed somewhat, as for shame,
Then, as scorning her own feeling, resumed calmly – 'I am seeking   55
More distinction than these gentlemen think worthy of my claim.

'Ne'ertheless, you see, I seek it – not because I am a woman'
(Here her smile sprang like a fountain and, so, overflowed her mouth),
'But because my woods in Sussex have some purple shades at gloaming
Which are worthy of a king in state, or poet in his youth.   60

'I invite you, Mister Bertram, to no scene for worldly speeches –
Sir, I scarce should dare – but only where God asked the thrushes first –
And if *you* will sing beside them, in the covert of my beeches,
I will thank you for the woodlands, . . . for the human world, at worst.'

Then she smiled around right childly, then she gazed around right queenly,
And I bowed – I could not answer; alternated light and gloom –   66
While as one who quells the lions, with a steady eye serenely,
She, with level fronting eyelids, passed out stately from the room.

Oh, the blessèd woods of Sussex, I can hear them still around me,
With their leafy tide of greenery still rippling up the wind.   70
Oh, the cursèd woods of Sussex! where the hunter's arrow found me,
When a fair face and a tender voice had made me mad and blind!

In that ancient hall of Wycombe, thronged the numerous guests invited,
And the lovely London ladies trod the floors with gliding feet;
And their voices low with fashion, not with feeling, softly freighted   75
All the air about the windows, with elastic laughters sweet.

For at eve, the open windows flung their light out on the terrace,
Which the floating orbs of curtains did with gradual shadow sweep,
While the swans upon the river, fed at morning by the heiress,
Trembled downward through their snowy wings at music in their sleep.   80

And there evermore was music, both of instrument and singing,
Till the finches of the shrubberies grew restless in the dark;
But the cedars stood up motionless, each in a moonlight ringing,
And the deer, half in the glimmer, strewed the hollows of the park.

And though sometimes she would bind me with her silver-corded speeches
To commix my words and laughter with the converse and the jest,   86
Oft I sat apart, and gazing on the river through the beeches,
Heard, as pure the swans swam down it, her pure voice o'erfloat the rest.

In the morning, horn of huntsman, hoof of steed, and laugh of rider,
Spread out cheery from the court-yard till we lost them in the hills,   90
While herself and other ladies, and her suitors left beside her,
Went a-wandering up the gardens through the laurels and abeles.

Thus, her foot upon the new-mown grass, bareheaded, with the flowing
Of the virginal white vesture gathered closely to her throat, –
And the golden ringlets in her neck just quickened by her going,   95
And appearing to breathe sun for air, and doubting if to float, –

With a bunch of dewy maple, which her right hand held above her,
And which trembled a green shadow in betwixt her and the skies,
As she turned her face in going, thus, she drew me on to love her,
And to worship the divineness of the smile hid in her eyes.   100

For her eyes alone smile constantly: her lips have serious sweetness,
And her front is calm – the dimple rarely ripples on the cheek;
But her deep blue eyes smile constantly, as if they in discreetness
Kept the secret of a happy dream she did not care to speak.

Thus she drew me the first morning, out across into the garden,   105
And I walked among her noble friends and could not keep behind.
Spake she unto all and unto me – 'Behold, I am the warden
Of the song-birds in these lindens, which are cages to their mind.

'But within this swarded circle, into which the lime-walk brings us,
Whence the beeches, rounded greenly, stand away in reverent fear,   110
I will let no music enter, saving what the fountain sings us,
Which the lilies round the basin may seem pure enough to hear.

'The live air that waves the lilies waves the slender jet of water
Like a holy thought sent feebly up from soul of fasting saint:
Whereby lies a marble Silence, sleeping! (Lough the sculptor wrought her)
So asleep she is forgetting to say Hush! – a fancy quaint.   116

'Mark how heavy white her eyelids! not a dream between them lingers,
And the left hand's index droppeth from the lips upon the cheek;
While the right hand, – with the symbol rose held slack within the fingers, –
Has fallen backward in the basin – yet this Silence will not speak!   120

'That the essential meaning growing may exceed the special symbol,
Is the thought as I conceive it: it applies more high and low.
Our true noblemen will often through right nobleness grow humble,
And assert an inward honour by denying outward show.'

'Nay, your Silence,' said I, 'truly, holds her symbol rose but slackly,   125
Yet *she holds it* – or would scarcely be a Silence to our ken;
And your nobles wear their ermine on the outside, or walk blackly
In the presence of the social law as mere ignoble men.

'Let the poets dream such dreaming! madam, in these British islands
'Tis the substance that wanes ever, 'tis the symbol that exceeds.   130
Soon we shall have nought but symbol! and, for statues like this Silence,
Shall accept the rose's image – in another case, the weed's.'

'Not so quickly,' she retorted, – 'I confess, where'er you go, you
Find for things, names – shows for actions, and pure gold for honour clear;
But when all is run to symbol in the Social, I will throw you   135
The world's book which now reads dryly, and sit down with Silence here.'

Half in playfulness she spoke, I thought, and half in indignation;
Friends who listened, laughed her words off, while her lovers deemed her fair:
A fair woman, flushed with feeling, in her noble-lighted station
Near the statue's white reposing – and both bathed in sunny air! –   140

With the trees round, not so distant but you heard their vernal murmur,
And beheld in light and shadow the leaves in and outward move,
And the little fountain leaping toward the sun-heart to be warmer,
Then recoiling in a tremble from the too much light above.

'Tis a picture for remembrance. And thus, morning after morning,   145
Did I follow as she drew me by the spirit to her feet.
Why, her greyhound followed also! dogs – we both were dogs for scorning –
To be sent back when she pleased it and her path lay through the wheat.

And thus, morning after morning, spite of vows and spite of sorrow,
Did I follow at her drawing, while the week-days passed along,   150
Just to feed the swans this noontide, or to see the fawns tomorrow,
Or to teach the hill-side echo some sweet Tuscan in a song.

Aye, for sometimes on the hill-side, while we sat down in the gowans,
With the forest green behind us, and its shadow cast before,
And the river running under, and across it from the rowans   155
A brown partridge whirring near us, till we felt the air it bore, –

There, obedient to her praying, did I read aloud the poems
Made to Tuscan flutes, or instruments more various of our own;
Read the pastoral parts of Spenser – or the subtle interflowings   159
Found in Petrarch's sonnets – here's the book – the leaf is folded down!

Or at times a modern volume, – Wordsworth's solemn-thoughted idyl,
Howitt's ballad-verse, or Tennyson's enchanted reverie, –
Or from Browning some 'Pomegranate', which, if cut deep down the middle,
Shows a heart within blood-tinctured, of a veined humanity.

Or at times I read there, hoarsely, some new poem of my making: 165
Poets ever fail in reading their own verses to their worth, –
For the echo in you breaks upon the words which you are speaking,
And the chariot-wheels jar in the gate through which you drive them forth.

After, when we were grown tired of books, the silence round us flinging
A slow arm of sweet compression, felt with beatings at the breast, 170
She would break out, on a sudden, in a gush of woodland singing,
Like a child's emotion in a god – a naiad tired of rest.

Oh, to see or hear her singing! scarce I know which is divinest –
For her looks sing too – she modulates her gestures on the tune;
And her mouth stirs with the song, like song; and when the notes are finest,
'Tis the eyes that shoot out vocal light and seem to swell them on. 176

Then we talked – oh, how we talked! her voice, so cadenced in the talking,
Made another singing – of the soul! a music without bars;
While the leafy sounds of woodlands, humming round
                              where we were walking,
Brought interposition worthy-sweet, – as skies about the stars.   180

And she spake such good thoughts natural, as if she always thought them;
She had sympathies so rapid, open, free as bird on branch,
Just as ready to fly east as west, whichever way besought them,
In the birchen-wood a chirrup, or a cock-crow in the grange.

In her utmost lightness there is truth – and often she speaks lightly,   185
Has a grace in being gay which even mournful souls approve,
For the root of some grave earnest thought is understruck so rightly
As to justify the foliage and the waving flowers above.

And she talked on – *we* talked, rather! upon all things, substance, shadow,
Of the sheep that browsed the grasses, of the reapers in the corn,   190
Of the little children from the schools, seen winding through the meadow –
Of the poor rich world beyond them, still kept poorer by its scorn.

So, of men, and so, of letters – books are men of higher stature,
And the only men that speak aloud for future times to hear;
So, of mankind in the abstract, which grows slowly into nature,   195
Yet will lift the cry of 'progress', as it trod from sphere to sphere.

And her custom was to praise me when I said, – 'The Age culls simples,
With a broad clown's back turned broadly to the glory of the stars.
We are gods by our own reck'ning, and may well shut up the temples,
And wield on, amid the incense-steam, the thunder of our cars.   200

'For we throw out acclamations of self-thanking, self-admiring,
With, at every mile run faster, – "O the wondrous wondrous age!"
Little thinking if we work our SOULS as nobly as our iron,
Or if angels will commend us at the goal of pilgrimage.

'Why, what is this patient entrance into nature's deep resources,   205
But the child's most gradual learning to walk upright without bane?
When we drive out, from the cloud of steam, majestical white horses,
Are we greater than the first men who led black ones by the mane?

'If we trod the deeps of ocean, if we struck the stars in rising,
If we wrapped the globe intensely with one hot electric breath,   210
'Twere but power within our tether, no new spirit-power comprising,
And in life we were not greater men, nor bolder men in death.'

She was patient with my talking; and I loved her, loved her, certes,
As I loved all heavenly objects, with uplifted eyes and hands;
As I loved pure inspirations, loved the graces, loved the virtues,   215
In a Love content with writing his own name on desert sands.

Or at least I thought so, purely! – thought no idiot Hope was raising
Any crown to crown Love's silence – silent Love that sat alone.
Out, alas! the stag is like me – he, that tries to go on grazing
With the great deep gun-wound in his neck, then reels with sudden moan.

It was thus I reeled. I told you that her hand had many suitors;   221
But she smiles them down imperially, as Venus did the waves,
And with such a gracious coldness, that they cannot press their futures
On the present of her courtesy, which yieldingly enslaves.

And this morning, as I sat alone within the inner chamber,   225
With the great saloon beyond it, lost in pleasant thought serene,
For I had been reading Camoëns [18] – that poem you remember,
Which his lady's eyes are praised in, as the sweetest ever seen.

And the book lay open, and my thought flew from it, taking from it
A vibration and impulsion to an end beyond its own,   230
As the branch of a green osier, when a child would overcome it,
Springs up freely from his clasping and goes swinging in the sun.

As I mused I heard a murmur – it grew deep as it grew longer –
Speakers using earnest language – 'Lady Geraldine, you *would*!'
And I heard a voice that pleaded ever on, in accents stronger   235
As a sense of reason gave it power to make its rhetoric good.

Well I knew that voice – it was an earl's, of soul that matched his station,
Soul completed into lordship – might and right read on his brow;
Very finely courteous – far too proud to doubt his domination
Of the common people, he atones for grandeur by a bow.   240

High straight forehead, nose of eagle, cold blue eyes, of less expression
Than resistance, coldly casting off the looks of other men,
As steel, arrows, – unelastic lips, which seem to taste possession,
And be cautious lest the common air should injure or distrain.

For the rest, accomplished, upright, – aye, and standing by his order   245
With a bearing not ungraceful; fond of art and letters too;
Just a good man made a proud man, – as the sandy rocks that border
A wild coast, by circumstances, in a regnant ebb and flow.

Thus, I knew that voice – I heard it, and I could not help the hearkening.
In the room I stood up blindly, and my burning heart within   250
Seemed to seethe and fuse my senses, till they ran on all sides darkening,
And scorched, weighed, like melted metal round my feet that stood therein.

And that voice, I heard it pleading, for love's sake, for wealth, position,
For the sake of liberal uses, and great actions to be done –
And she interrupted gently, 'Nay, my lord, the old tradition   255
Of your Normans, by some worthier hand than mine is, should be won.'

'Ah, that white hand!' he said quickly, – and in his he either drew it
Or attempted – for with gravity and instance she replied,
'Nay, indeed, my lord, this talk is vain, and we had best eschew it,
And pass on, like friends, to other points less easy to decide.'   260

What he said again, I know not. It is likely that his trouble
Worked his pride up to the surface, for she answered in slow scorn,
'And your lordship judges rightly. Whom I marry, shall be noble,
Aye, and wealthy. I shall never blush to think how he was born.'

There, I maddened! her words stung me. Life swept through me into fever,
And my soul sprang up astonished, sprang, full-statured in an hour.   266
Know you what it is when anguish, with apocalyptic *never*,
To a Pythian height dilates you, – and despair sublimes to power?

From my brain, the soul-wings budded, – waved a flame about my body,
Whence conventions coiled to ashes. I felt self-drawn out, as man,   270
From amalgamate false natures, and I saw the skies grow ruddy
With the deepening feet of angels, and I knew what spirits can.

I was mad – inspired – say either! (anguish worketh inspiration)
Was a man, or beast – perhaps so, for the tiger roars, when speared;
And I walked on, step by step, along the level of my passion –   275
Oh my soul! and passed the doorway to her face, and never feared.

He had left her, peradventure, when my footstep proved my coming –
But for *her* – she half arose, then sat – grew scarlet and grew pale.
Oh, she trembled! – 'tis so always with a worldly man or woman
In the presence of true spirits – what else *can* they do but quail? 280

Oh, she fluttered like a tame bird, in among its forest-brothers
Far too strong for it; then drooping, bowed her face upon her hands –
And I spake out wildly, fiercely, brutal truths of her and others:
I, she planted in the desert, swathed her, windlike, with my sands.

I plucked up her social fictions, bloody-rooted though leaf-verdant, –   285
Trod them down with words of shaming, – all the purple and the gold,
All the 'landed stakes' and lordships, all, that spirits pure and ardent
Are cast out of love and honour because chancing not to hold.

'For myself I do not argue,' said I, 'though I love you, madam,
But for better souls that nearer to the height of yours have trod: 290
And this age shows, to my thinking, still more infidels to Adam,
Than directly, by profession, simple infidels to God.

'Yet, O God,' I said, 'O grave,' I said, 'O mother's heart and bosom,
With whom first and last are equal, saint and corpse and little child!
We are fools to your deductions, in these figments of heart-closing;   295
We are traitors to your causes, in these sympathies defiled.

'Learn more reverence, madam, not for rank or wealth –
                                        that needs no learning,
That comes quickly – quick as sin does, aye, and culminates to sin;
But for Adam's seed, MAN! Trust me, 'tis a clay above your scorning,
With God's image stamped upon it, and God's kindling breath within. 300

'What right have you, madam, gazing in your palace mirror daily,
Getting so by heart your beauty which all others must adore,
While you draw the golden ringlets down your fingers, to vow gaily
You will wed no man that's only good to God, and nothing more?

'Why, what right have you, made fair by that same God – the sweetest woman
Of all women He has fashioned – with your lovely spirit-face,   306
Which would seem too near to vanish if its smile were not so human,
And your voice of holy sweetness, turning common words to grace,

'What right *can* you have, God's other works to scorn, despise, revile them
In the gross, as mere men, broadly – not as *noble* men, forsooth, –   310
As mere Pariahs of the outer world, forbidden to assoil them
In the hope of living, dying, near that sweetness of your mouth?

'Have you any answer, madam? If my spirit were less earthly,
If its instrument were gifted with a better silver string,
I would kneel down where I stand, and say – Behold me! I am worthy   315
Of thy loving, for I love thee! I am worthy as a king.

'As it is – your ermined pride, I swear, shall feel this stain upon her,
That *I*, poor, weak, tost with passion, scorned by me and you again,
Love you, madam, dare to love you – to my grief and your dishonour,
To my endless desolation, and your impotent disdain!'   320

More mad words like these – mere madness! friend,
                              I need not write them fuller,
For I hear my hot soul dropping on the lines in showers of tears.
Oh, a woman! friend, a woman! why, a beast had scarce been duller
Than roar bestial loud complaints against the shining of the spheres.

But at last there came a pause. I stood all vibrating with thunder   325
Which my soul had used. The silence drew her face up like a call.
Could you guess what word she uttered? She looked up, as if in wonder,
With tears beaded on her lashes, and said 'Bertram!' – it was all.

If she had cursed me, and she might have – or if even, with queenly bearing
Which at need is used by women, she had risen up and said,   330
'Sir, you are my guest, and therefore I have given you a full hearing,
Now, beseech you, choose a name exacting somewhat less, instead,' –

I had borne it! but that 'Bertram' – why it lies there on the paper
A mere word, without her accent, – and you cannot judge the weight
Of the calm which crushed my passion: I seemed drowning in a vapour, –
And her gentleness destroyed me whom her scorn made desolate.   336

So, struck backward and exhausted by that inward flow of passion
Which had rushed on, sparing nothing, into forms of abstract truth,
By a logic agonising through unseemly demonstration,
And by youth's own anguish turning grimly grey the hairs of youth, –   340

By the sense accursed and instant, that if even I spake wisely
I spake basely – using truth, if what I spake, indeed was true,
To avenge wrong on a woman – *her*, who sat there weighing nicely
A poor manhood's worth, found guilty of such deeds as I could do! –

By such wrong and woe exhausted – what I suffered and occasioned, – 345
As a wild horse through a city runs with lightning in his eyes,
And then dashing at a church's cold and passive wall, impassioned,
Strikes the death into his burning brain, and blindly drops and dies –

So I fell, struck down before her! do you blame me, friend, for weakness?
'Twas my strength of passion slew me! – fell before her like a stone. 350
Fast the dreadful world rolled from me on its roaring wheels of blackness –
When the light came, I was lying in this chamber, and alone.

Oh, of course, she charged her lacqueys to bear out the sickly burden,
And to cast it from her scornful sight – but not *beyond* the gate;
She is too kind to be cruel, and too haughty not to pardon 355
Such a man as I – 'twere something to be level to her hate.

But for me – you now are conscious why, my friend, I write this letter,
How my life is read all backward, and the charm of life undone:
I shall leave her house at dawn; I would tonight, if I were better –
And I charge my soul to hold my body strengthened for the sun. 360

When the sun has dyed the oriel, I depart, with no last gazes,
No weak moanings (one word only, left in writing for her hands),
Out of reach of all derision, and some unavailing praises,
To make front against this anguish in the far and foreign lands.

Blame me not. I would not squander life in grief – I am abstemious: 365
I but nurse my spirit's falcon, that its wing may soar again.
There's no room for tears of weakness in the blind eyes of a Phemius![19]
Into work the poet kneads them, – and he does not die *till then*.

CONCLUSION

Bertram finished the last pages, while along the silence ever
Still in hot and heavy splashes, fell the tears on every leaf: 370
Having ended he leans backward in his chair, with lips that quiver
From the deep unspoken, aye, and deep unwritten thoughts of grief.

Soh! how still the lady standeth! 'Tis a dream – a dream of mercies!
'Twixt the purple lattice-curtains, how she standeth still and pale!
'Tis a vision, sure, of mercies, sent to soften his self-curses –   375
Sent to sweep a patient quiet o'er the tossing of his wail.

'Eyes,' he said, 'now throbbing through me! are ye eyes that did undo me?
Shining eyes, like antique jewels set in Parian statue-stone!
Underneath that calm white forehead, are ye ever burning torrid
O'er the desolate sand-desert of my heart and life undone?'   380

With a murmurous stir uncertain, in the air, the purple curtain
Swelleth in and swelleth out around her motionless pale brows,
While the gliding of the river sends a rippling noise for ever
Through the open casement whitened by the moonlight's slant repose.

Said he – 'Vision of a lady! stand there silent, stand there steady!   385
Now I see it plainly, plainly; now I cannot hope or doubt –
There, the brows of mild repression – there, the lips of silent passion,
Curvèd like an archer's bow to send the bitter arrows out.'

Ever, evermore the while in a slow silence she kept smiling,
And approached him slowly, slowly, in a gliding measured pace;   390
With her two white hands extended, as if praying one offended,
And a look of supplication, gazing earnest in his face.

Said he – 'Wake me by no gesture, – sound of breath, or stir of vesture!
Let the blessèd apparition melt not yet to its divine!
No approaching – hush, no breathing! or my heart must swoon to death in
The too utter life thou bringest – O thou dream of Geraldine!'   396

Ever, evermore the while in a slow silence she kept smiling –
But the tears ran over lightly from her eyes, and tenderly;
'Dost thou, Bertram, truly love me? Is no woman far above me
Found more worthy of thy poet heart than such a one as I?'   400

Said he – 'I would dream so ever, like the flowing of that river,
Flowing ever in a shadow greenly onward to the sea!
So, thou vision of all sweetness – princely to a full completeness –
Would my heart and life flow onward – deathward – through this
                                        dream of THEE!'

Ever, evermore the while in a slow silence she kept smiling,   405
While the silver tears ran faster down the blushing of her cheeks;
Then with both her hands enfolding both of his, she softly told him,
'Bertram, if I say I love thee, . . . 'tis the vision only speaks.'

Softened, quickened to adore her, on his knee he fell before her –
And she whispered low in triumph, 'It shall be as I have sworn!   410
Very rich he is in virtues, – very noble – noble, certes;
And I shall not blush in knowing that men call him lowly born.'

A Vision of Poets

O Sacred Essence, lighting me this hour,
How may I lightly stile thy great power?
Echo.   Power.
Power! but of whence? under the greenwood spraye?
Or liv'st in Heaven? saye.
Echo.   In Heavens aye.
In Heavens aye! tell, may I it obtayne
By alms, by fasting, prayer, – by paine?
Echo.   By paine.
Show me the paine, it shall be undergone:
I to mine end will still go on.
Echo.   Go on.'

Britannia's Pastorals

A poet could not sleep aright,
For his soul kept up too much light
Under his eyelids for the night.

And thus he rose disquieted
With sweet rimes ringing through his head,   5
And in the forest wanderèd,

Where, sloping up the darkest glades,
The moon had drawn long colonnades,
Upon whose floor the verdure fades

To a faint silver, – pavement fair   10
The antique wood-nymphs scarce would dare
To foot-print o'er, had such been there,

And rather sit by breathlessly,
With fear in their large eyes, to see
The consecrated sight. But HE   15

The poet, who with spirit-kiss
Familiar, had long claimed for his
Whatever earthly beauty is, –

Who also in his spirit bore
A Beauty passing the earth's store,   20
Walked calmly onward evermore.

His aimless thoughts in metre went,
Like a babe's hand without intent
Drawn down a seven-stringed instrument.

Nor jarred it with his humour as,   25
With a faint stirring of the grass,
An apparition fair did pass.

He might have feared another time,
But all things fair and strange did chime
With his thoughts then, as rime to rime.   30

An angel had not startled him,
Alighted from Heaven's burning rim
To breathe from glory in the Dim;

Much less a lady riding slow
Upon a palfrey white as snow,   35
And smooth as a snow-cloud could go.

Full upon his she turned her face, –
'What, ho, sir poet! dost thou pace
Our woods at night, in ghostly chace

'Of some fair Dryad of old tales,   40
Who chaunts between the nightingales,
And over sleep by song prevails?'

She smiled; but he could see arise
Her soul from far adown her eyes,
Prepared as if for sacrifice.   45

She looked a queen who seemeth gay
From royal grace alone. 'Now, nay,'
He answered, – 'slumber passed away

'Compelled by instincts in my head
That I should see tonight, instead   50
Of a fair nymph, some fairer Dread.'

She looked up quickly to the sky
And spake: – 'The moon's regality
Will hear no praise; she is as I.

'She is in heaven, and I on earth;   55
This is my kingdom – I come forth
To crown all poets to their worth.'

He brake in with a voice that mourned:
'To their worth, lady? They are scorned
By men they sing for, till inurned.   60

'To their worth? Beauty in the mind
Leaves the hearth cold, – and love-refined
Ambitions make the world unkind.

'The boor who ploughs the daisy down,
The chief whose mortgage of renown   65
Fixed upon graves, has bought a crown –

'Both these are happier, more approved
Than poets! – why should I be moved
In saying . . . both are more beloved?'

'The south can judge not of the north,'   70
She resumed calmly; 'I come forth
To crown all poets to their worth.

'Yea, verily, to anoint them all
With blessèd oils which surely shall
Smell sweeter as the ages fall.'   75

'As sweet,' the poet said, and rung
A low sad laugh, 'as flowers are, sprung
Out of their graves when they die young.

'As sweet as window eglantine,
Some bough of which, as they decline,   80
The hired nurse gathers at their sign.

'As sweet, in short, as perfumed shroud
Which the gay Roman maidens sewed
For English Keats,[20] singing aloud.'

The lady answered, 'Yea, as sweet!   85
The things thou namest being complete
In fragrance as I measure it.

'Since sweet the death-clothes and the knell
Of him who having lived, dies well –
And holy sweet the asphodel   90

'Stirred softly by that foot of his,
When he treads brave on all that is,
Into the world of souls, from this.

'Since sweet the tears, dropped at the door
Of tearless Death, – and even before.   95
Sweet, consecrated evermore.

'What, dost thou judge it a strange thing,
That poets, crowned for vanquishing,
Should bear some dust from out the ring?

'Come on with me, come on with me,   100
And learn in coming! let me free
Thy spirit into verity.'

She ceased: her palfrey's paces sent
No separate noises as she went;
'Twas a bee's hum, a little spent.   105

And while the poet seemed to tread
Along the drowsy noise so made,
The forest heaved up overhead

Its billowy foliage through the air,
And the calm stars did far and spare   110
O'erswim the masses everywhere;

Save when the overtopping pines
Did bar their tremulous light with lines
All fixed and black. Now the moon shines

A broader glory. You may see   115
The trees grow rarer presently:
The air blows up more fresh and free:

Until they come from dark to light,
And from the forest to the sight
Of the large Heaven-heart, bare with night, –   120

A fiery throb in every star,
Those burning arteries that are
The conduits of God's life afar!

A wild brown moorland underneath,
And four pools breaking up the heath   125
With white low gleamings, blank as death.

Beside the first pool, near the wood,
A dead tree in set horror stood,
Peeled and disjointed, stark as rood,

Since thunder-stricken, years ago,   130
Fixed in the spectral strain and throe
Wherewith it struggled from the blow:

A monumental tree, alone,
That will not bend in storms, nor groan,
But break off sudden like a stone.   135

Its lifeless shadow lies oblique
Upon the pool, – where, javelin-like,
The star-rays quiver while they strike.

'Drink,' said the lady, very still –
'Be holy and cold.' He did her will,   140
And drank the starry water chill.

The next pool they came near unto
Was bare of trees: there, only grew
Straight flags and lilies, just a few,

Which sullen on the water sat   145
And leant their faces on the flat,
As weary of the starlight-state.

'Drink,' said the lady, grave and slow,
'*World's use* behoveth thee to know.'
He drank the bitter wave below.   150

The third pool, girt with thorny bushes,
And flaunting weeds, and reeds and rushes
That winds sang through in mournful gushes,

Was whitely smeared in many a round
By a slow slime; the starlight swound   155
Over the ghastly light it found.

'Drink,' said the lady, sad and slow,
'*World's love* behoveth thee to know.'
He looked to her, commanding so.

Her brow was troubled, but her eye   160
Struck clear to his soul. For all reply
He drank the water suddenly, –

Then, with a deathly sickness, passed
Beside the fourth pool and the last,
Where weights of shadow were downcast   165

From yew and alder, and rank trails
Of nightshade clasping the trunk-scales,
And flung across the intervals

From yew to yew. Who dares to stoop
Where those dank branches overdroop,   170
Into his heart the chill strikes up;

He hears a silent gliding coil,
The snakes strain hard against the soil,
His foot slips in their slimy oil,

And toads seem crawling on his hand,   175
And clinging bats, but dimly scanned,
Full in his face their wings expand.

A paleness took the poet's cheek:
'Must I drink *here*?' he seemed to seek
The lady's will with utterance meek.   180

'Aye, aye,' she said, 'it so must be'
(And this time she spake cheerfully)
'Behoves thee know *World's cruelty*.'

He bowed his forehead till his mouth
Curved in the wave, and drank unloath,   185
As if from rivers of the south.

His lips sobbed through the water rank,
His heart paused in him while he drank,
His brain beat heart-like, rose and sank,

And he swooned backward to a dream,   190
Wherein he lay 'twixt gloom and gleam,
With Death and Life at each extreme.

And spiritual thunders, born of soul
Not cloud, did leap from mystic pole
And o'er him roll and counter-roll,   195

Crushing their echoes reboant
With their own wheels. Did Heaven so grant
His spirit a sign of covenant?

At last came silence. A slow kiss
Did crown his forehead after this: 200
His eyelids flew back for the bliss.

The lady stood beside his head,
Smiling a thought, with hair dispread.
The moonshine seemed dishevellèd

In her sleek tresses manifold,   205
Like Danaë's in the rain of old,
That dripped with melancholy gold.

But SHE was holy, pale, and high,
As one who saw an ecstasy
Beyond a foretold agony.   210

'Rise up!' said she, with voice where song
Eddied through speech – 'rise up! be strong!
And learn how right avenges wrong.'

The poet rose up on his feet:
He stood before an altar set   215
For sacrament, with vessels meet;

And mystic altar-lights which shine
As if their flames were crystalline
Carved flames, that would not shrink or pine.

The altar filled the central place   220
Of a great church, and toward its face
Long aisles did shoot and interlace,

And from it a continuous mist
Of incense (round the edges kissed
By a yellow light of amethyst)   225

Wound upward slowly and throbbingly,
Cloud within cloud, right silverly,
Cloud above cloud, victoriously, –

Broke full against the archèd roof,
And, thence refracting, eddied off, 230
And floated through the marble woof

Of many a fine-wrought architrave,
Then, poising its white masses brave,
Swept solemnly down aisle and nave;

Where now in dark, and now in light, 235
The countless columns, glimmering white,
Seemed leading out to the Infinite.

Plunged halfway up the shaft they showed,
In that pale shifting incense-cloud,
Which flowed them by, and overflowed, 240

Till mist and marble seemed to blend,
And the whole temple, at the end,
With its own incense to distend, –

The arches, like a giant's bow,
To bend and slacken, – and below, 245
The nichèd saints to come and go.

Alone, amid the shifting scene,
That central altar stood serene
In its clear steadfast taper-sheen.

Then first, the poet was aware 250
Of a chief angel standing there
Before that altar, in the glare.

His eyes were dreadful, for you saw
That *they* saw God – his lips and jaw,
Grand-made and strong, as Sinai's Law 255

They could enunciate and refrain
From vibratory after-pain,
And his brow's height was sovereign.

On the vast background of his wings
Rises his image, and he flings,   260
From each plumed arc, pale glitterings

And fiery flakes (as beateth more
Or less, the angel-heart) before
And round him, upon roof and floor,

Edging with fire the shifting fumes;   265
While at his side, 'twixt lights and glooms,
The phantasm of an organ booms.

Extending from which instrument
And angel, right and left-way bent,
The poet's sight grew sentient   270

Of a strange company around
And toward the altar, – pale and bound
With bay above the eyes profound.

Deathful their faces were, and yet
The power of life was in them set –   275
Never forgot, nor to forget.

Sublime significance of mouth,
Dilated nostril full of youth,
And forehead royal with the truth.

These faces were not multiplied   280
Beyond your count, but side by side
Did front the altar, glorified.

Still as a vision, yet exprest
Full as an action – look and geste
Of buried saint in risen rest.   285

The poet knew them. Faint and dim
His spirits seemed to sink in him,
Then, like a dolphin, change and swim

The current. These were poets true,
Who died for Beauty, as martyrs do   290
For Truth – the ends being scarcely two.

God's prophets of the Beautiful
These poets were; of iron rule
The rugged cilix, serge of wool.

Here, Homer,[21] with the broad suspense,   295
Of thunderous brows, and lips intense
Of garrulous god-innocence.

There, Shakespeare, on whose forehead climb
The crowns o' the world. Oh, eyes sublime,
With tears and laughters for all time!   300

Here, Aeschylus, the women swooned
To see so awful, when he frowned
As the gods did – he standeth crowned.

Euripides, with close and mild
Scholastic lips, – that could be wild,   305
And laugh or sob out like a child

Even in the classes. Sophocles,
With that king's look which, down the trees,
Followed the dark effigies

Of the lost Theban. Hesiod old,   310
Who, somewhat blind and deaf and cold,
Cared most for gods and bulls. And bold

Electric Pindar, quick as fear,
With race-dust on his cheeks, and clear
Slant startled eyes that seem to hear   315

The chariot rounding the last goal,
To hurtle past it in his soul.
And Sappho, with that gloriole

Of ebon hair on calmèd brows.
O poet-woman! None forgoes   320
The leap, attaining the repose!

Theocritus, with glittering locks
Dropt sideway, as betwixt the rocks
He watched the visionary flocks.

And Aristophanes, who took   325
The world with mirth, and laughter-struck
The hollow caves of Thought and woke

The infinite echoes hid in each.
And Virgil: shade of Mantuan beech
Did help the shade of bay to reach   330

And knit around his forehead high:
For his gods wore less majesty
Than his brown bees hummed deathlessly.

Lucretius – nobler than his mood;
Who dropped his plummet down the broad   335
Deep universe, and said 'No God,'

Finding no bottom: he denied
Divinely the divine, and died
Chief poet on the Tiber-side

By grace of God! his face is stern,   340
As one compelled, in spite of scorn,
To teach a truth he would not learn.

And Ossian, dimly seen or guessed
Once counted greater than the rest,
When mountain-winds blew out his vest.   345

And Spenser drooped his dreaming head
(With languid sleep-smile you had said
From his own verse engenderèd)

On Ariosto's, till they ran
Their curls in one. The Italian   350
Shot nimbler heat of bolder man

From his fine lids. And Dante stern
And sweet, whose spirit was an urn
For wine and milk poured out in turn.

Hard-souled Alfieri; and fancy-willed   355
Boiardo, – who with laughter filled
The pauses of the jostled shield.

And Berni, with a hand stretched out
To sleek that storm. And, not without
The wreath he died in, and the doubt   360

He died by, Tasso! bard and lover,
Whose visions were too thin to cover
The face of a false woman over.

And soft Racine, – and grave Corneille,
The orator of rimes, whose wail   365
Scarce shook his purple. And Petrarch pale,

From whose brain-lighted heart were thrown
A thousand thoughts beneath the sun,
Each lucid with the name of One.

And Camoens, with that look he had,   370
Compelling India's Genius sad
From the wave through the Lusiad, –

The murmurs of the storm-cape ocean
Indrawn in vibrative emotion
Along the verse. And, while devotion   375

In his wild eyes fantastic shone
Under the tonsure blown upon
By airs celestial, – Calderon.

And bold De Vega, – who breathed quick
Verse after verse, till death's old trick   380
Put pause to life and rhetoric.

And Goethe – with that reaching eye
His soul reached out from, far and high,
And fell from inner entity.

And Schiller, with heroic front,   385
Worthy of Plutarch's kiss upon 't,
Too large for wreath of modern wont.

And Chaucer, with his infantine
Familiar clasp of things divine:
That mark upon his lip is wine.   390

Here, Milton's eyes strike piercing-dim:
The shapes of suns and stars did swim
Like clouds from them, and granted him

God for sole vision. Cowley, there;
Whose active fancy debonair   395
Drew straws like amber – foul to fair.

Drayton and Browne, –with smiles they drew
From outward nature, still kept new
From their own inward nature true.

And Marlowe, Webster, Fletcher, Ben –   400
Whose fire-hearts sowed our furrows when
The world was worthy of such men.

And Burns, with pungent passionings
Set in his eyes. Deep lyric springs
Are of the fire-mount's issuings.   405

And Shelley, in his white ideal,
All statue-blind! And Keats the real
Adonis, with the hymeneal

Fresh vernal buds half sunk between
His youthful curls, kissed straight and sheen   410
In his Rome-grave, by Venus queen.

And poor, proud Byron, – sad as grave,
And salt as life: forlornly brave,
And quivering with the dart he drave.

And visionary Coleridge, who   415
Did sweep his thoughts as angels do
Their wings, with cadence up the Blue.

These poets faced, and many more,
The lighted altar looming o'er
The clouds of incense dim and hoar: 420

And all their faces, in the lull
Of natural things, looked wonderful
With life and death and deathless rule.

All, still as stone, and yet intense;
As if by spirit's vehemence   425
That stone were carved, and not by sense.

But where the heart of each should beat,
There seemed a wound instead of it,
From whence the blood dropped to their feet,

Drop after drop – dropped heavily,   430
As century follows century
Into the deep eternity.

Then said the lady – and her word
Came distant, as wide waves were stirred
Between her and the ear that heard,   435

'World's use is cold, world's love is vain,
World's cruelty is bitter bane,
But pain is not the fruit of pain.

'Hearken, O poet, whom I led
From the dark wood. Dismissing dread,   440
Now hear this angel in my stead.

'His organ's clavier strikes along
These poets' hearts, sonorous, strong,
They gave him without count of wrong, –

'A diapason whence to guide   445
Up to God's feet, from these who died,
An anthem fully glorified.

'Whereat God's blessing . . . Y'VAREKH (יברך)[22]
Breathes back this music – folds it back
About the earth in vapoury rack,   450

'And men walk in it, crying "Lo
The world is wider, and we know
The very heavens look brighter so.

"The stars move statelier round the edge
Of the silver spheres, and give in pledge   455
Their light for nobler privilege.

"No little flower but joys or grieves,
Full life is rustling in the sheaves,
Full spirit sweeps the forest-leaves."

'So works this music on the earth,   460
God so admits it, sends it forth,
To add another worth to worth –

'A new creation-bloom that rounds
The old creation, and expounds
His Beautiful in tuneful sounds.   465

'Now hearken!' Then the poet gazed
Upon the angel glorious-faced,
Whose hand, majestically raised,

Floated across the organ-keys,
Like a pale moon o'er murmuring seas,   470
With no touch but with influences.

Then rose and fell (with swell and swound
Of shapeless noises wandering round
A concord which at last they found)

Those mystic keys – the tones were mixed,   475
Dim, faint, and thrilled and throbbed betwixt
The incomplete and the unfixed:

And therein mighty minds were heard
In mighty musings, inly stirred,
And struggling outward for a word.   480

Until these surges, having run
This way and that, gave out as one
An Aphrodite[23] of sweet tune, –

A harmony, that, finding vent,
Upward in grand ascension went,   485
Winged to a heavenly argument –

Up, upward! like a saint who strips
The shroud back from his eyes and lips,
And rises in apocalypse.

A harmony sublime and plain,   490
Which cleft (as flying swan, the rain, –
Throwing the drops off with a strain

Of her white wing) those undertones
Of perplext chords, and soared at once
And struck out from the starry thrones   495

Their several silver octaves as
It passed to God. The music was
Of divine stature – strong to pass.

And those who heard it, understood
Something of life in spirit and blood –   500
Something of nature's fair and good.

And while it sounded, those great souls
Did thrill as racers at the goals,
And burn in all their aureoles.

But she, the lady, as vapour-bound,   505
Stood calmly in the joy of sound, –
Like Nature with the showers around:

And when it ceased, the blood which fell,
Again, alone grew audible,
Tolling the silence as a bell.   510

The sovran angel lifted high
His hand, and spake out sovranly:
'Tried poets, hearken and reply!

'Give me true answers. If we grant
That not to suffer, is to want   515
The conscience of the jubilant, –

'If ignorance of anguish is
But ignorance, – and mortals miss
Far prospects, by a level bliss, –

'If, as two colours must be viewed   520
In a visible image, mortals should
Need good and evil, to see good, –

'If to speak nobly, comprehends
To feel profoundly – if the ends
Of power and suffering, Nature blends, –   525

'If poets on the tripod must
Writhe like the Pythian, to make just
Their oracles, and merit trust, –

'If every vatic word that sweeps
To change the world, must pale their lips,   530
And leave their own souls in eclipse, –

'If to search deep the universe
Must pierce the searcher with the curse, –
Because that bolt (in man's reverse)

'Was shot to the heart o' the wood, and lies   535
Wedged deepest in the best, – if eyes
That look for visions and surprise

'From influent angels, must shut down
Their lids first, upon sun and moon,
The head asleep upon a stone, –   540

'If ONE who did redeem you back,
By His own loss, from final wrack,
Did consecrate by touch and track

'Those temporal sorrows, till the taste
Of brackish waters of the waste   545
Is salt with tears He dropt too fast, –

'If all the crowns of earth must wound
With prickings of the thorns He found, –
If saddest sighs swell sweetest sound, –

'What say ye unto this? – refuse   550
This baptism in salt water? – choose
Calm breasts, mute lips, and labour loose?

'Or, O ye gifted givers! ye
Who give your liberal hearts to me,
To make the world this harmony,   555

'Are ye resigned that they be spent
To such world's help?'
                              The Spirits bent
Their awful brows and said – 'Content.'

Content! it sounded like *amen*,
Said by a choir of mourning men;   560
An affirmation full of pain

And patience, – aye, of glorying
And adoration, – as a king
Might seal an oath for governing.

Then said the angel – and his face   565
Lightened abroad, until the place
Grew larger for a moment's space, –

The long aisles flashing out in light,
And nave and transept, columns white
And arches crossed, being clear to sight   570

As if the roof were off, and all
Stood in the noon-sun, – 'Lo, I call
To other hearts as liberal.

'This pedal strikes out in the air:
My instrument has room to bear   575
Still fuller strains and perfecter.

'Herein is room, and shall be room
While Time lasts, for new hearts to come
Consummating while they consume.

'What living man will bring a gift   580
Of his own heart, and help to lift
The tune? – The race is to the swift.'

So asked the angel. Straight the while,
A company came up the aisle
With measured step and sorted smile;

Cleaving the incense-clouds that rise,   585
With winking unaccustomed eyes,
And love-locks smelling sweet of spice.

One bore his head above the rest,
As if the world were dispossessed;   590
And One did pillow chin on breast,

Right languid – an as he should faint.
One shook his curls across his paint,
And moralised on worldly taint.

One, slanting up his face, did wink   595
The salt rheum to the eyelid's brink,
To think – O gods! or – not to think!

Some trod out stealthily and slow,
As if the sun would fall in snow
If they walked to instead of fro.   600

And some, with conscious ambling free,
Did shake their bells right daintily
On hand and foot, for harmony.

And some, composing sudden sighs
In attitudes of point-device,   605
Rehearsed impromptu agonies.

And when this company drew near
The spirits crowned, it might appear,
Submitted to a ghastly fear.

As a sane eye in master-passion   610
Constrains a maniac to the fashion
Of hideous maniac imitation

In the least geste – the dropping low
O' the lid, the wrinkling of the brow,
Exaggerate with mock and mow, –   615

So mastered was that company
By the crowned vision utterly,
Swayed to a maniac mockery.

One dulled his eyeballs, as they ached
With Homer's forehead, though he lacked   620
An inch of any. And one racked

His lower lip with restless tooth,
As Pindar's rushing words forsooth
Were pent behind it. One, his smooth

Pink cheeks, did rumple passionate,   625
Like Aeschylus, and tried to prate
On trolling tongue, of fate and fate.

One set her eyes like Sappho's – or
Any light woman's! one forbore
Like Dante, or any man as poor   630

In mirth, to let a smile undo
His hard-shut lips. And one that drew
Sour humours from his mother, blew

His sunken cheeks out to the size
Of most unnatural jollities,   635
Because Anacreon looked jest-wise.

So with the rest. – It was a sight
A great world-laughter would requite,
Or great world-wrath, with equal right.

Out came a speaker from that crowd   640
To speak for all – in sleek and proud
Exordial periods, while he bowed

His knee before the angel. – 'Thus,
O angel who hast called for us,
We bring thee service emulous, –   645

'Fit service from sufficient soul,
Hand-service, to receive world's dole,
Lip-service, in world's ear to roll

'Adjusted concords – soft enow
To hear the wine-cups passing, through,   650
And not too grave to spoil the show.

'Thou, certes, when thou askest more,
O sapient angel, leanest o'er
The window-sill of metaphor.

'To give our hearts up? fie! – that rage   655
Barbaric antedates the age:
It is not done on any stage.

'Because your scald or gleeman went
With seven- or nine-stringed instrument
Upon his back, – must ours be bent?   660

'We are not pilgrims, by your leave;
No, nor yet martyrs! if we grieve,
It is to rime to . . . summer eve.

'And if we labour, it shall be,
As suiteth best with our degree,   665
In after-dinner reverie.'

More yet that speaker would have said,
Poising, between his smiles fair-fed,
Each separate phrase till finishèd.

But all the foreheads of those born   670
And dead true poets flashed with scorn
Betwixt the bay leaves round them worn –

Aye, jetted such brave fire, that they,
The new-come, shrank and paled away,
Like leaden ashes when the day   675

Strikes on the hearth. A spirit-blast,
A presence known by power, at last
Took them up mutely – they had passed.

And *he*, our pilgrim-poet, saw
Only their places, in deep awe, –   680
What time the angel's smile did draw

His gazing upward. Smiling on,
The angel in the angel shone,
Revealing glory in benison.

Till, ripened in the light which shut   685
The poet in, his spirit mute
Dropped sudden, as a perfect fruit.

He fell before the angel's feet,
Saying – 'If what is true is sweet,
In something I may compass it.   690

'For, where my worthiness is poor,
My will stands richly at the door,
To pay shortcomings evermore.

'Accept me therefore. Not for price,
And not for pride, my sacrifice   695
Is tendered! for my soul is nice

'And will beat down those dusty seeds
Of bearded corn, if she succeeds
In soaring while the covey feeds.

'I soar – I am drawn up like the lark   700
To its white cloud. So high my mark,
Albeit my wing is small and dark.

'I ask no wages – seek no fame.
Sew me, for shroud round face and name,
God's banner of the oriflamme.   705

'I only would have leave to loose
(In tears and blood, if so He choose)
Mine inward music out to use,

'I only would be spent – in pain
And loss, perchance – but not in vain,   710
Upon the sweetness of that strain!

'Only project, beyond the bound
Of mine own life, so lost and found,
My voice, and live on in its sound!

'Only embrace and be embraced   715
By fiery ends, – whereby to waste,
And light God's future with my past.'

The angel's smile grew more divine,
The mortal speaking – aye, its shine
Swelled fuller, like a choir-note fine,   720

Till the broad glory round his brow
Did vibrate with the light below;
But what he said, I do not know.

Nor know I if the man who prayed,
Rose up accepted, unforbade,   725
From the church-floor where he was laid, –

Nor if a listening life did run
Through the king-poets, one by one
Rejoicing in a worthy son.

My soul, which might have seen, grew blind   730
By what it looked on: I can find
No certain count of things behind.

I saw alone, dim, white, and grand
As in a dream, the angel's hand
Stretched forth in gesture of command   735

Straight through the haze. And so, as erst,
A strain more noble than the first
Mused in the organ, and outburst.

With giant march, from floor to roof
Rose the full notes, – now parted off   740
In pauses massively aloof

Like measured thunders, – now rejoined
In concords of mysterious kind
Which fused together sense and mind, –

Now flashing sharp on sharp along   745
Exultant, in a mounting throng, –
Now dying off to a low song

Fed upon minors! – wavelike sounds
Re-eddying into silver rounds,
Enlarging liberty with bounds.   750

And every rhythm that seemed to close
Survived in confluent underflows
Symphonious with the next that rose.

Thus the whole strain being multiplied
And greatened, – with its glorified   755
Wings shot abroad from side to side, –

Waved backward (as a wind might wave
A Brocken[24] mist, and with as brave
Wild roaring) arch and architrave,

Aisle, transept, column, marble wall, –   760
Then swelling outward, prodigal
Of aspiration beyond thrall,

Soared, – and drew up with it the whole
Of this said vision – as a soul
Is raised by a thought. And as a scroll   765

Of bright devices is unrolled
Still upward, with a gradual gold, –
So rose the vision manifold,

Angel and organ, and the round
Of spirits, solemnised and crowned, –   770
While the freed clouds of incense wound

Ascending, following in their track,
And glimmering faintly, like the rack
O' the moon in her own light cast back.

And as that solemn Dream withdrew,   775
The lady's kiss did fall anew
Cold on the poet's brow as dew.

And that same kiss which bound him first
Beyond the senses, now reversed
Its own law, and most subtly pierced   780

His spirit with the sense of things
Sensual and present. Vanishings
Of glory, with Aeolian wings

Struck him and passed: the lady's face
Did melt back in the chrysopras   785
Of the orient morning sky that was

Yet clear of lark, – and there and so
She melted, as a star might do,
Still smiling as she melted – slow.

Smiling so slow, he seemed to see   790
Her smile the last thing, gloriously,
Beyond her – far as memory.

Then he looked round: he was alone.
He lay before the breaking sun,
As Jacob at the Bethel stone.[25]   795

And thought's entangled skein being wound,
He knew the moorland of his swound,
And the pale pools that smeared the ground;

The far wood-pines, like offing ships –
The fourth pool's yew anear him drips, 800
World's cruelty attaints his lips,

And still he tastes it – bitter still –
Through all that glorious possible
He had the sight of present ill.

Yet rising calmly up and slowly 805
With such a cheer as scorneth folly,
A mild delightsome melancholy,

He journeyed homeward through the wood
And prayed along the solitude,
Betwixt the pines, – 'O God, my God!' 810

The golden morning's open flowings
Did sway the trees to murmurous bowings,
In metric chant of blessed poems.

And passing homeward through the wood,
He prayed along the solitude, – 815
'THOU, Poet-God, art great and good!

'And though we must have, and have had
Right reason to be earthly sad, –
THOU, Poet-God, art great and glad!'

CONCLUSION

Life treads on life, and heart on heart: 820
We press too close in church and mart
To keep a dream or grave apart.

And I was 'ware of walking down
That same green forest where had gone
The poet-pilgrim. One by one   825

I traced his footsteps. From the east
A red and tender radiance pressed
Through the near trees, until I guessed

The sun behind shone full and round;
While up the leafiness profound   830
A wind scarce old enough for sound

Stood ready to blow on me when
I turned that way; and now and then
The birds sang and brake off again

To shake their pretty feathers dry   835
Of the dew sliding droppingly
From the leaf-edges, and apply

Back to their song. 'Twixt dew and bird
So sweet a silence ministered,
God seemed to use it for a word.   840

Yet morning souls did leap and run
In all things, as the least had won
A joyous insight of the sun.

And no one looking round the wood
Could help confessing as he stood,   845
This Poet-God is glad and good.

But hark! a distant sound that grows!
A heaving, sinking of the boughs –
A rustling murmur, not of those!

A breezy noise, which is not breeze!   850
And white-clad children by degrees
Steal out in troops among the trees,

Fair little children, morning-bright,
With faces grave, yet soft to sight,
Expressive of restrained delight.   855

Some plucked the palm-boughs within reach,
And others leapt up high to catch
The upper boughs, and shake from each

A rain of dew, till, wetted so,
The child who held the branch let go,   860
And it swang backward with a flow

Of faster drippings. Then I knew
The children laughed – but the laugh flew
From its own chirrup, as might do

A frightened song-bird; and a child   865
Who seemed the chief, said very mild,
'Hush! keep this morning undefiled.'

His eyes rebuked them from calm spheres;
His soul upon his brow appears
In waiting for more holy years.   870

I called the child to me, and said,
'What are your palms for?' – 'To be spread,'
He answered, 'on a poet dead.

'The poet died last month, and now
The world which had been somewhat slow   875
In honouring his living brow,

'Commands the palms – they must be strown
On his new marble very soon,
In a procession of the town.'

I sighed and said, 'Did he foresee   880
Any such honour?' 'Verily
I cannot tell you,' answered he.

'But this I know. – I fain would lay
Mine own head down, another day,
As *he* did, – with the fame away.   885

'A lily, a friend's hand had plucked,
Lay by his death-bed, which he looked
As deep down as a bee had sucked,

'Then, turning to the lattice, gazed
O'er hill and river, and upraised   890
His eyes illumined and amazed

'With the world's beauty, up to God,
Re-offering on their iris broad
The images of things bestowed

'By the chief Poet. – "God!" he cried,   895
"Be praised for anguish, which has tried;
For beauty, which has satisfied: –

' "For this world's presence, half within
And half without me – thought and scene –
This sense of Being and Having been.   900

' "I thank Thee that my soul hath room
For Thy grand world. Both guests may come –
Beauty, to soul – Body, to tomb.

' "I am content to be so weak:
Put strength into the words I speak,   905
And I am strong in what I seek.

89

' "I am content to be so bare
Before the archers, everywhere
My wounds being stroked by heavenly air.

' "I laid my soul before Thy feet,   910
That Images of fair and sweet
Should walk to other men on it.

' "I am content to feel the step
Of each pure Image! – let those keep
To mandragore who care to sleep.   915

' "I am content to touch the brink
Of the other goblet, and I think
My bitter drink a wholesome drink.

' "Because my portion was assigned
Wholesome and bitter – Thou art kind,   920
And I am blessèd to my mind.

' "Gifted for giving, I receive
The maythorn, and its scent outgive:
I grieve not that I once did grieve.

' "In my large joy of sight and touch   925
Beyond what others count for such,
I am content to suffer much.

' "*I know* – is all the mourner saith,
Knowledge by suffering entereth,
And Life is perfected by Death." '   930

The child spake nobly. Strange to hear,
His infantine soft accents clear
Charged with high meanings, did appear;

And fair to see, his form and face,
Winged out with whiteness and pure grace   935
From the green darkness of the place.

Behind his head a palm-tree grew:
An orient beam which pierced it through
Transversely on his forehead drew

The figure of a palm-branch brown   940
Traced on its brightness up and down
In fine fair lines, – a shadow-crown.

Guido [26] might paint his angels so –
A little angel, taught to go
With holy words to saints below.   945

Such innocence of action yet
Significance of object met
In his whole bearing strong and sweet.

And all the children, the whole band,
Did round in rosy reverence stand,   950
Each with a palm-bough in his hand.

'And so he died,' I whispered. – 'Nay,
Not *so*,' the childish voice did say –
'That poet turned him, first, to pray

'In silence, and God heard the rest   955
'Twixt the sun's footsteps down the west.
Then he called one who loved him best,

'Yea, he called softly through the room
(His voice was weak yet tender) – "Come,"
He said, "come nearer! Let the bloom   960

' "Of Life grow over, undenied,
This bridge of Death, which is not wide –
I shall be soon at the other side.

' "Come, kiss me!" So the one in truth
Who loved him best – in love, not ruth,   965
Bowed down and kissed him mouth to mouth.

'And, in that kiss of Love, was won
Life's manumission. All was done –
The mouth that kissed last, kissed *alone*.

'But in the former, confluent kiss,   970
The same was sealed, I think, by His,
To words of truth and uprightness.'

The child's voice trembled, – his lips shook
Like a rose leaning o'er a brook,
Which vibrates though it is not struck.   975

'And who,' I asked, a little moved
Yet curious-eyed, 'was this that loved
And kissed him last, as it behoved?'

'*I*,' softly said the child; and then,
'*I*,' said he louder, once again;   980
'*His son*, – my rank is among men.

'And now that men exalt his name
I come to gather palms with them,
That holy Love may hallow Fame.

'He did not die alone, nor should   985
His memory live so, 'mid these rude
World-praisers – a worse solitude.

'Me, a voice calleth to that tomb
Where these are strewing branch and bloom,
Saying, *come nearer!* – and I come.   990

'Glory to God!' resumèd he,
And his eyes smiled for victory
O'er their own tears which I could see

Fallen on the palm, down cheek and chin –
'That poet now has entered in   995
The place of rest which is not sin.

'And while he rests, his songs in troops
Walk up and down our earthly slopes,
Companioned by diviner Hopes.'

'But *thou*,' I murmured, – to engage   1000
The child's speech farther – 'hast an age
Too tender for this orphanage.'

'Glory to God – to God!' he saith,
'KNOWLEDGE BY SUFFERING ENTERETH,
AND LIFE IS PERFECTED BY DEATH.'   1005

Rime of the Duchess May

1

To the belfry, one by one, went the ringers from the sun,
Toll slowly.
And the oldest ringer said, 'Ours is music for the Dead,
When the rebecks are all done.'

2

Six abeles i' the churchyard grow on the northside in a row,   5
Toll slowly.
And the shadows of their tops rock across the little slopes
Of the grassy graves below.

3

On the south side and the west, a small river runs in haste,
Toll slowly.   10
And, between the river flowing and the fair green trees a-growing
Do the dead lie at their rest.

4

On the east I sat that day, up against a willow grey.
Toll slowly.
Through the rain of willow-branches, I could see the low hill-ranges,
And the river on its way.   16

5

There I sat beneath the tree, and the bell tolled solemnly,
Toll slowly.
While the trees' and river's voices flowed between
the solemn noises, –
Yet death seemed more loud to me.   20

6

There, I read this ancient rime, while the bell did all the time
Toll slowly.
And the solemn knell fell in with the tale of life and sin,
Like a rhythmic fate sublime.

THE RIME

1

Broad the forests stood (I read) on the hills of Linteged –   25
  Toll slowly.
And three hundred years had stood mute adown each hoary wood,
  Like a full heart having prayed.

2

And the little birds sang east, and the little birds sang west,
  Toll slowly.   30
And but little thought was theirs of the silent antique years,
  In the building of their nest.

3

Down the sun dropt large and red, on the towers of Linteged, –
  Toll slowly.
Lance and spear upon the height, bristling strange in fiery light,   35
  While the castle stood in shade.

4

There, the castle stood up black, with the red sun at its back, –
  Toll slowly.
Like a sullen smouldering pyre, with a top that flickers fire
  When the wind is on its track.   40

5

And five hundred archers tall did besiege the castle wall,
  Toll slowly.
And the castle, seethed in blood, fourteen days and nights had stood,
  And tonight was near its fall.

6

Yet thereunto, blind to doom, three months since, a bride did come, –
  Toll slowly.   46
One who proudly trod the floors, and softly whispered in the doors,
  'May good angels bless our home.'

7

Oh, a bride of queenly eyes, with a front of constancies!
    Toll slowly.   50
Oh, a bride of cordial mouth, – where the untired smile of youth
    Did light outward its own sighs.

8

'Twas a Duke's fair orphan-girl, and her uncle's ward – the Earl;
    Toll slowly.
Who betrothed her twelve years old, for the sake of dowry gold,   55
    To his son Lord Leigh, the churl.

9

But what time she had made good all her years of womanhood,
    Toll slowly.
Unto both these lords of Leigh, spake she out right sovranly,
    'My will runneth as my blood.   60

10

'And while this same blood makes red this same right hand's veins,'
                        she said, –
    Toll slowly.
' 'Tis my will as lady free, not to wed a lord of Leigh,
    But Sir Guy of Linteged.'

11

The old Earl he smilèd smooth, then he sighed for wilful youth, –   65
    Toll slowly.
'Good my niece, that hand withal looketh somewhat soft and small
    For so large a will, in sooth.'

12

She, too, smiled by that same sign, – but her smile was cold and fine, –
    Toll slowly.   70
'Little hand clasps muckle[27] gold, or it were not worth the hold
    Of thy son, good uncle mine!'

13

Then the young lord jerked his breath, and sware thickly in his teeth,
    Toll slowly.
'He would wed his own betrothed, an she loved him an she loathed,
    Let the life come or the death.'   76

14

Up she rose with scornful eyes, as her father's child might rise, –
Toll slowly.
'Thy hound's blood, my lord of Leigh, stains thy knightly heel,' quoth she,
'And he moans not where he lies. 80

15

'But a woman's will dies hard, in the hall or on the sward!' –
Toll slowly.
'By that grave, my lords, which made me orphaned girl and dowered lady,
I deny you wife and ward.'

16

Unto each she bowed her head, and swept past with lofty tread. 85
Toll slowly.
Ere the midnight-bell had ceased, in the chapel had the priest
Blessed her, bride of Linteged.

17

Fast and fain the bridal train along the night-storm rode amain.
Toll slowly. 90
Hard the steeds of lord and serf struck their hoofs out on the turf,
In the pauses of the rain.

18

Fast and fain the kinsmen's train along the storm pursued amain –
Toll slowly.
Steed on steed-track, dashing off – thickening, doubling, hoof on hoof,
In the pauses of the rain. 96

19

And the bridegroom led the flight on his red-roan steed of might,
Toll slowly.
And the bride lay on his arm, still, as if she feared no harm,
Smiling out into the night. 100

20

'Dost thou fear?' he said at last. – 'Nay,' she answered him in haste, –
Toll slowly.
'Not such death as we could find – only life with one behind –
Ride on fast as fear – ride fast!'

21

Up the mountain wheeled the steed – girth to ground, and fetlocks spread,
      Toll slowly.   106
Headlong bounds, and rocking flanks, – down he staggered, down the banks,
    To the towers of Linteged.

22

High and low the serfs looked out, red the flambeaus tossed about, –
      Toll slowly.   110
In the courtyard rose the cry – 'Live the Duchess and Sir Guy!'
    But she never heard them shout.

23

On the steed she dropt her cheek, kissed his mane and kissed his neck, –
      Toll slowly.
'I had happier died by thee, than lived on, a Lady Leigh,'   115
    Were the first words she did speak.

24

But a three months' joyaunce lay 'twixt that moment and today,
      Toll slowly.
When five hundred archers tall stand beside the castle wall,
    To recapture Duchess May.   120

25

And the castle standeth black, with the red sun at its back, –
      Toll slowly.
And a fortnight's siege is done – and, except the duchess, none
    Can misdoubt the coming wrack.

26

Then the captain, young Lord Leigh, with his eyes so grey of blee,[28] 125
      Toll slowly.
And thin lips that scarcely sheath the cold white gnashing of his teeth,
    Gnashed in smiling, absently,

27

Cried aloud, 'So goes the day, bridegroom fair of Duchess May!' –
      Toll slowly.   130
'Look thy last upon that sun! if thou seest tomorrow's one,
    'Twill be through a foot of clay.

28

'Ha, fair bride! dost hear no sound, save that moaning of the hound?' –
　　　　Toll slowly.
'Thou and I have parted troth, – yet I keep my vengeance-oath,　　135
　　And the other may come round.

29

'Ha! thy will is brave to dare, and thy new love past compare,' –
　　　　Toll slowly.
'Yet thine old love's faulchion[29] brave is as strong a thing to have
　　As the will of lady fair.　　　　140

30

'Peck on blindly, netted dove! – If a wife's name thee behove,'
　　　　Toll slowly.
'Thou shalt wear the same tomorrow, ere the grave has hid the sorrow
　　Of thy last ill-mated love.

31

'O'er his fixed and silent mouth, thou and I will call back troth.'　　145
　　　　Toll slowly.
'He shall altar be and priest, – and he will not cry at least
　　"I forbid you – I am loath!" '

32

'I will wring thy fingers pale in the gauntlet of my mail.'
　　　　Toll slowly.　　　　150
' "Little hand and muckle gold" close shall lie within my hold,
　　As the sword did, to prevail.'

33

Oh, the little birds sang east, and the little birds sang west,
　　　　Toll slowly.
Oh, and laughed the Duchess May, and her soul did put away　　155
　　All his boasting, for a jest.

34

In her chamber did she sit, laughing low to think of it, –
　　　　Toll slowly.
'Tower is strong and will is free – thou canst boast, my lord of Leigh,
　　But thou boastest little wit.'　　　　160

35

In her tire-glass gazèd she, and she blushed right womanly.
  Toll slowly.
She blushed half from her disdain – half, her beauty was so plain,
  – 'Oath for oath, my lord of Leigh!'

36

Straight she called her maidens in – 'Since ye gave me blame herein,'
  Toll slowly.   166
'That a bridal such as mine should lack gauds to make it fine,
  Come and shrive me from that sin.

37

'It is three months gone today since I gave mine hand away.'
  Toll slowly.   170
'Bring the gold and bring the gem, we will keep bride-state in them,
  While we keep the foe at bay.

38

'On your arms I loose mine hair! – comb it smooth and crown it fair.'
  Toll slowly.
'I would look in purple pall from this lattice down the wall,   175
  And throw scorn to one that's there!'

39

Oh, the little birds sang east, and the little birds sang west.
  Toll slowly.
On the tower the castle's lord leant in silence on his sword,
  With an anguish in his breast.   180

40

With a spirit-laden weight, did he lean down passionate.
  Toll slowly.
They have almost sapped the wall, – they will enter therewithal,
  With no knocking at the gate.

41

Then the sword he leant upon, shivered, snapped upon the stone, –
  Toll slowly.   186
'Sword,' he thought, with inward laugh, 'ill thou servest for a staff
  When thy nobler use is done!

42

'Sword, thy nobler use is done! – tower is lost, and shame begun!' –
        Toll slowly.   190
'If we met them in the breach, hilt to hilt or speech to speech,
    We should die there, each for one.

43

'If we met them at the wall, we should singly, vainly fall,' –
        Toll slowly.
'But if *I* die here alone, – then I die, who am but one,   195
    And die nobly for them all.

44

'Five true friends lie for my sake, in the moat and in the brake,' –
        Toll slowly.
'Thirteen warriors lie at rest, with a black wound in the breast,
    And not one of these will wake.   200

45

'So no more of this shall be! – heart-blood weighs too heavily,' –
        Toll slowly.
'And I could not sleep in grave, with the faithful and the brave
    Heaped around and over me.

46

'Since young Clare a mother hath, and young Ralph a plighted faith,' –
        Toll slowly.   206
'Since my pale young sister's cheeks blush like rose when Ronald speaks,
    Albeit never a word she saith –

47

'These shall never die for me – life-blood falls too heavily':
        Toll slowly.   210
'And if *I* die here apart, – o'er my dead and silent heart
    They shall pass out safe and free.

48

'When the foe hath heard it said – "Death holds Guy of Linteged," '
        Toll slowly.
'That new corse[30] new peace shall bring, and a blessèd, blessèd thing
    Shall the stone be at its head.   216

49

'Then my friends shall pass out free, and shall bear my memory,' –
    Toll slowly.
'Then my foes shall sleek their pride, soothing fair my widowed bride,
    Whose sole sin was love of me.   220

50

'With their words all smooth and sweet, they will front her and entreat,'
    Toll slowly.
'And their purple pall will spread underneath her fainting head
    While her tears drop over it.

51

'She will weep her woman's tears, she will pray her woman's prayers,' –
    Toll slowly.   226
'But her heart is young in pain, and her hopes will spring again
    By the suntime of her years.

52

'Ah, sweet May! ah, sweetest grief! – once I vowed thee my belief,'
    Toll slowly.   230
'That thy name expressed thy sweetness, – May of poets, in completeness!
    Now my May-day seemeth brief.'

53

All these silent thoughts did swim o'er his eyes grown strange and dim, –
    Toll slowly.
Till his true men in the place, wished they stood there face to face   235
    With the foe instead of him.

54

'One last oath, my friends that wear faithful hearts to do and dare!' –
    Toll slowly.
'Tower must fall and bride be lost! – swear me service worth the cost!'
    – Bold they stood around to swear.   240

55

'Each man clasp my hand and swear, by the deed we failed in there,'
    Toll slowly.
'Not for vengeance, not for right, will ye strike one blow tonight!'
    – Pale they stood around to swear.

56

'One last boon, young Ralph and Clare! faithful hearts to do and dare!' –
       Toll slowly.   246
'Bring that steed up from his stall, which she kissed before you all!
    Guide him up the turret-stair.

57

'Ye shall harness him aright, and lead upward to this height.'
       Toll slowly.   250
'Once in love and twice in war hath he borne me strong and far:
    He shall bear me far tonight.'

58

Then his men looked to and fro, when they heard him speaking so.
       Toll slowly.
' 'Las! the noble heart,' they thought, – 'he in sooth is grief-distraught:
    Would we stood here with the foe!'   256

59

But a fire flashed from his eye, 'twixt their thought and their reply, –
       Toll slowly.
'Have ye so much time to waste? We who ride here, must ride fast,
    As we wish our foes to fly.'   260

60

They have fetched the steed with care, in the harness he did wear,
       Toll slowly.
Past the court, and through the doors, across the rushes of the floors,
    But they goad him up the stair.

61

Then from out her bower chambère, did the Duchess May repair.   265
       Toll slowly.
'Tell me now what is your need,' said the lady, 'of this steed,
    That ye goad him up the stair?'

62

Calm she stood; unbodkined through, fell her dark hair to her shoe, –
       Toll slowly.   270
And the smile upon her face, ere she left the tiring-glass,
    Had not time enough to go.

63

'Get thee back, sweet Duchess May! hope is gone like yesterday,' –
  Toll slowly.
'One half-hour completes the breach; and thy lord grows wild of speech!
  Get thee in, sweet lady, and pray.   276

64

'In the east tower, high'st of all, loud he cries for steed from stall.'
  Toll slowly.
'He would ride as far,' quoth he, 'as for love and victory,
  Though he rides the castle-wall.'   280

65

'And we fetch the steed from stall, up where never a hoof did fall.' –
  Toll slowly.
'Wifely prayer meets deathly need! may the sweet Heavens hear thee plead
  If he rides the castle-wall.'

66

Low she dropt her head, and lower, till her hair coiled on the floor, –   285
  Toll slowly.
And tear after tear you heard fall distinct as any word
  Which you might be listening for.

67

'Get thee in, thou soft ladye! – here is never a place for thee!' –
  Toll slowly.   290
'Braid thine hair and clasp thy gown, that thy beauty in its moan
  May find grace with Leigh of Leigh.'

68

She stood up in bitter case, with a pale yet steady face,
  Toll slowly.
Like a statue thunderstruck, which, though quivering, seems to look   295
  Right against the thunder-place.

69

And her foot trod in, with pride, her own tears i' the stone beside. –
  Toll slowly.
'Go to, faithful friends, go to! – judge no more what ladies do, –
  No, nor how their lords may ride!'   300

70

Then the good steed's rein she took, and his neck did kiss and stroke:
Toll slowly.
Soft he neighed to answer her, and then followed up the stair,
For the love of her sweet look.

71

Oh, and steeply, steeply wound up the narrow stair around! 305
Toll slowly.
Oh, and closely, closely speeding, step by step beside her treading,
Did he follow, meek as hound.

72

On the east tower, high'st of all, – there, where never a hoof did fall, –
Toll slowly. 310
Out they swept, a vision steady, noble steed and lovely lady,
Calm as if in bower or stall.

73

Down she knelt at her lord's knee, and she looked up silently, –
Toll slowly.
And he kissed her twice and thrice, for that look within her eyes 315
Which he could not bear to see.

74

Quoth he, 'Get thee from this strife, – and the sweet saints
bless thy life!' –
Toll slowly.
'In this hour, I stand in need of my noble red-roan steed,
But no more of my noble wife.' 320

75

Quoth she, 'Meekly have I done all thy biddings under sun;'
Toll slowly.
'But by all my womanhood, which is proved so, true and good,
I will never do this one.

76

'Now by womanhood's degree and by wifehood's verity,' 325
Toll slowly.
'In this hour if thou hast need of thy noble red-roan steed,
Thou hast also need of *me*.

77

'By this golden ring ye see on this lifted hand, pardiè,'
   Toll slowly.   330
'If, this hour, on castle-wall can be room for steed from stall,
  Shall be also room for *me*.

78

'So the sweet saints with me be' (did she utter solemnly)
   Toll slowly.
'If a man, this eventide, on this castle-wall will ride, 335
  He shall ride the same with *me*.'

79

Oh, he sprang up in the selle,[31] and he laughed out bitter-well, –
   Toll slowly.
'Wouldst thou ride among the leaves, as we used on other eves,
  To hear chime a vesper-bell?'   340

80

She clung closer to his knee – 'Aye, beneath the cypress-tree!' –
   Toll slowly.
'Mock me not, for otherwhere than along the greenwood fair
  Have I ridden fast with thee.

81

'Fast I rode with new-made vows, from my angry kinsman's house.'
   Toll slowly.   346
'What, and would you men should reck that I dared more for love's sake
  As a bride than as a spouse?

82

'What, and would you it should fall, as a proverb, before all,'
   Toll slowly.   350
'That a bride may keep your side while through castle-gate you ride,
  Yet eschew the castle-wall?'

83

Ho! the breach yawns into ruin, and roars up against her suing,
   Toll slowly.
With the inarticulate din, and the dreadful falling in – 355
  Shrieks of doing and undoing!

84

Twice he wrung her hands in twain, but the small hands closed again.
Toll slowly.
Back he reined the steed – back, back! but she trailed along his track
With a frantic clasp and strain.   360

85

Evermore the foemen pour through the crash of window and door, –
Toll slowly.
And the shouts of Leigh and Leigh, and the shrieks of 'kill!' and 'flee!'
Strike up clear amid the roar.

86

Thrice he wrung her hands in twain, – but they closed and clung again, –
Toll slowly.   366
While she clung, as one, withstood, clasps a Christ upon the rood,
In a spasm of deathly pain.

87

She clung wild and she clung mute, with her shuddering lips half-shut.
Toll slowly.   370
Her head fallen as half in swound, – hair and knee swept on the ground,
She clung wild to stirrup and foot.

88

Back he reined his steed back-thrown on the slippery coping-stone:
Toll slowly.
Back the iron hoofs did grind on the battlement behind   375
Whence a hundred feet went down.

89

And his heel did press and goad on the quivering flank bestrode, –
Toll slowly.
'Friends and brothers, save my wife! – Pardon, sweet, in change for life, –
But I ride alone to God.'   380

90

Straight as if the Holy name had upbreathed her like a flame,
Toll slowly.
She upsprang, she rose upright, – in his selle she sat in sight,
By her love she overcame.

91

And her head was on his breast, where she smiled as one at rest, – 385
     Toll slowly.
'Ring,' she cried, 'O vesper-bell, in the beechwood's old chapelle!
    But the passing-bell rings best.'

92

They have caught out at the rein, which Sir Guy threw loose – in vain, –
     Toll slowly.   390
For the horse in stark despair, with his front hoofs poised in air,
    On the last verge rears amain.

93

Now he hangs, he rocks between, and his nostrils curdle in! –
     Toll slowly.
Now he shivers head and hoof – and the flakes of foam fall off,   395
    And his face grows fierce and thin!

94

And a look of human woe from his staring eyes did go,
     Toll slowly.
And a sharp cry uttered he, in a foretold agony
    Of the headlong death below, –   400

95

And, 'Ring, ring, thou passing-bell,' still she cried, 'i' the old chapelle!' –
     Toll slowly.
Then, back-toppling, crashing back – a dead weight flung out to wrack,
    Horse and riders overfell.

*   *   *

1

Oh, the little birds sang east, and the little birds sang west,   405
      Toll slowly.
And I read this ancient Rime, in the churchyard, while the chime
  Slowly tolled for one at rest.

2

The abeles moved in the sun, and the river smooth did run,
      Toll slowly.   410
And the ancient Rime rang strange, with its passion and its change,
  Here, where all done lay undone.

3

And beneath a willow tree, I a little grave did see,
      Toll slowly.
Where was graved, – HERE UNDEFILED, LIETH MAUD,
            A THREE-YEAR CHILD,
EIGHTEEN HUNDRED, FORTY-THREE.   416

4

Then, O spirits, did I say, ye who rode so fast that day, –
      Toll slowly.
Did star-wheels and angel wings, with their holy winnowings,
  Keep beside you all the way?   420

5

Though in passion ye would dash, with a blind and heavy crash,
      Toll slowly.
Up against the thick-bossed shield of God's judgment in the field, –
  Though your heart and brain were rash, –

6

Now, your will is all unwilled – now, your pulses are all stilled!   425
      Toll slowly.
Now, ye lie as meek and mild (whereso laid) as Maud the child,
  Whose small grave was lately filled.

7

Beating heart and burning brow, ye are very patient now,
      Toll slowly.   430
And the children might be bold to pluck the kingcups from your mould
  Ere a month had let them grow.

8

And you let the goldfinch sing in the alder near in spring,
      Toll slowly.
Let her build her nest and sit all the three weeks out on it,   435
  Murmuring not at anything.

9

In your patience ye are strong; cold and heat ye take not wrong.
      Toll slowly.
When the trumpet of the angel blows eternity's evangel,
  Time will seem to you not long.   440

10

Oh, the little birds sang east, and the little birds sang west,
      Toll slowly.
And I said in underbreath, – All our life is mixed with death,
  And who knoweth which is best?

11

Oh, the little birds sang east, and the little birds sang west,   445
      Toll slowly.
And I smiled to think God's greatness flowed
                   around our incompleteness, –
  Round our restlessness, His rest.

The Lady's Yes

1

'Yes,' I answered you last night;
  'No,' this morning, sir, I say.
Colours seen by candle-light
  Will not look the same by day.

2

When the viols played their best,   5
  Lamps above, and laughs below,
Love me sounded like a jest,
  Fit for *yes* or fit for *no*.

3

Call me false or call me free –
  Vow, whatever light may shine,   10
No man on your face shall see
  Any grief, for change on mine.

4

Yet the sin is on us both;
  Time to dance is not to woo;
Wooing light makes fickle troth,   15
  Scorn of *me* recoils on *you*.

5

Learn to win a lady's faith
  Nobly, as the thing is high,
Bravely, as for life and death –
  With a loyal gravity.   20

6

Lead her from the festive boards,
  Point her to the starry skies,
Guard her, by your truthful words,
  Pure from courtship's flatteries.

6

By your truth she shall be true,   25
    Ever true, as wives of yore;
And her *yes*, once said to you,
    SHALL be Yes for evermore.

The Poet and the Bird

A FABLE

1

Said a people to a poet – 'Go out from among us straightway!
    While we are thinking earthly things, thou singest of divine.
There's a little fair brown nightingale, who, sitting in the gateway,
    Makes fitter music to our ear than any song of thine!'

2

The poet went out weeping – the nightingale ceased chanting,   5
    'Now, wherefore, O thou nightingale, is all thy sweetness done?'
– 'I cannot sing my earthly things, the heavenly poet wanting,
    Whose highest harmony includes the lowest under sun.'

3

The poet went out weeping, – and died abroad, bereft there:
    The bird flew to his grave and died amid a thousand wails.   10
And, when I last came by the place, I swear the music left there
    Was only of the poet's song, and not the nightingale's.

The Lost Bower

1

In the pleasant orchard-closes,
'God bless all our gains,' say we;
But 'May God bless all our losses,'
Better suits with our degree.
Listen, gentle – aye, and simple! listen, children on the knee!   5

2

Green the land is where my daily
Steps in jocund childhood played,
Dimpled close with hill and valley,
Dappled very close with shade;
Summer-snow of apple blossoms running up from glade to glade.   10

3

There is one hill I see nearer
In my vision of the rest;
And a little wood seems clearer
As it climbeth from the west,
Sideway from the tree-locked valley, to the airy upland crest.   15

4

Small the wood is, green with hazels,
And, completing the ascent,
Where the wind blows and sun dazzles
Thrills in leafy tremblement,
Like a heart that, after climbing, beateth quickly through content.   20

5

Not a step the wood advances
O'er the open hill-top's bound;
There, in green arrest, the branches
See their image on the ground:
You may walk beneath them smiling, glad with sight and
                                        glad with sound.   25

6

For you hearken on your right hand,
How the birds do leap and call
In the greenwood, out of sight and
Out of reach and fear of all;
And the squirrels crack the filberts through their cheerful madrigal. 30

7

On your left, the sheep are cropping
The slant grass and daisies pale,
And five apple-trees stand dropping
Separate shadows toward the vale,
Over which, in choral silence, the hills look you their 'All hail!' 35

8

Far out, kindled by each other,
Shining hills on hills arise,
Close as brother leans to brother
When they press beneath the eyes
Of some father praying blessings from the gifts of paradise. 40

9

While beyond, above them mounted,
And above their woods alsò,
Malvern hills, for mountains counted
Not unduly, loom a-row –
Keepers of Piers Plowman's [32] visions through the sunshine
and the snow. 45

10

Yet, in childhood, little prized I
That fair walk and far survey:
'Twas a straight walk unadvised by
The least mischief worth a nay;
Up and down – as dull as grammar on the eve of holiday. 50

11

But the wood, all close and clenching
Bough in bough and root in root, –
No more sky (for over-branching)
At your head than at your foot, –
Oh, the wood drew me within it, by a glamour past dispute. 55

12

Few and broken paths showed through it,
Where the sheep had tried to run, –
Forced with snowy wool to strew it
Round the thickets, when anon
They, with silly thorn-pricked noses, bleated back into the sun.   60

13

But my childish heart beat stronger
Than those thickets dared to grow:
I could pierce them! I could longer
Travel on, methought, than so.
Sheep for sheep-paths! braver children climb and creep
                                            where they would go.   65

14

And the poets wander, said I,
Over places all as rude:
Bold Rinaldo's [33] lovely lady
Sat to meet him in a wood:
Rosalinda, like a fountain, laughed out pure with solitude.   70

15

And if Chaucer had not travelled
Through a forest by a well,
He had never dreamt nor marvelled
At those ladies fair and fell
Who lived smiling without loving in their island-citadel.   75

16

Thus I thought of the old singers,
And took courage from their song,
Till my little struggling fingers
Tore asunder gyve and thong
Of the brambles which entrapped me, and the barrier branches strong.

17

On a day, such pastime keeping,   81
With a fawn's heart debonair,
Under-crawling, overleaping
Thorns that prick and boughs that bear,
I stood suddenly astonied – I was gladdened unaware.   85

18

From the place I stood in, floated
Back the covert dim and close,
And the open ground was coated
Carpet-smooth with grass and moss,
And the blue-bell's purple presence signed it worthily across.   90

19

Here a linden-tree stood, bright'ning
All adown its silver rind;
For as some trees draw the lightning,
So this tree, unto my mind,
Drew to earth the blessèd sunshine from the sky where it was shrined.

20

Tall the linden-tree, and near it   96
An old hawthorn also grew;
And wood-ivy like a spirit
Hovered dimly round the two,
Shaping thence that bower of beauty which I sing of thus to you.   100

21

'Twas a bower for garden fitter
Than for any woodland wide;
Though a fresh and dewy glitter
Struck it through from side to side,
Shaped and shaven was the freshness, as by garden-cunning plied.

22

Oh, a lady might have come there,   106
Hooded fairly like her hawk,
With a book or lute in summer,
And a hope of sweeter talk, –
Listening less to her own music than for footsteps on the walk.   110

23

But that bower appeared a marvel
In the wildness of the place;
With such seeming art and travail,
Finely fixed and fitted was
Leaf to leaf, the dark-green ivy, to the summit from the base.   115

24

And the ivy veined and glossy
Was enwrought with eglantine;
And the wild hop fibred closely,
And the large-leaved columbine,
Arch of door and window mullion, did right sylvanly entwine.   120

25

Rose-trees either side the door were
Growing lithe and growing tall,
Each one set a summer warder
For the keeping of the hall, –
With a red rose and a white rose, leaning, nodding at the wall.   125

26

As I entered – mosses hushing
Stole all noises from my foot;
And a green elastic cushion,
Clasped within the linden's root,
Took me in a chair of silence very rare and absolute.   130

27

All the floor was paved with glory,
Greenly, silently inlaid
(Through quick motions made before me),
With fair counterparts in shade
Of the fair serrated ivy-leaves which slanted overhead.   135

28

'Is such pavement in a palace?'
So I questioned in my thought.
The sun, shining through the chalice
Of the red rose hung without,
Threw within a red libation, like an answer to my doubt.   140

29

At the same time, on the linen
Of my childish lap there fell
Two white may-leaves, downward winning
Through the ceiling's miracle,
From a blossom, like an angel, out of sight yet blessing well.   145

30

Down to floor and up to ceiling
Quick I turned my childish face,
With an innocent appealing
For the secret of the place
To the trees, which surely knew it, in partaking of the grace.   150

31

Where's no foot of human creature,
How could reach a human hand?
And if this be work of nature,
Why has nature turned so bland,
Breaking off from other wild work? It was hard to understand.   155

32

Was she weary of rough-doing, –
Of the bramble and the thorn?
Did she pause in tender rueing
Here of all her sylvan scorn?
Or in mock of art's deceiving, was the sudden mildness worn?   160

33

Or could this same bower (I fancied)
Be the work of Dryad[34] strong,
Who, surviving all that chancèd
In the world's old pagan wrong,
Lay hid, feeding in the woodland on the last true poet's song?   165

34

Or was this the house of fairies,
Left, because of the rough ways,
Unassoiled by Ave Marys
Which the passing pilgrim prays,
And beyond Saint Catherine's chiming on the blessèd Sabbath days?

35

So, young muser, I sat listening   171
To my fancy's wildest word.
On a sudden, through the glistening
Leaves around, a little stirred,
Came a sound, a sense of music, which was rather felt than heard.

36

Softly, finely, it enwound me;   176
From the world it shut me in, –
Like a fountain, falling round me,
Which with silver waters thin
Clips a little water Naiad[35] sitting smilingly within.   180

37

Whence the music came, who knoweth?
I know nothing. But indeed
Pan or Faunus[36] never bloweth
So much sweetness from a reed
Which has sucked the milk of waters at the oldest river-head.   185

38

Never lark the sun can waken
With such sweetness! when the lark,
The high planets overtaking
In the half-evanished Dark,
Casts his singing to their singing, like an arrow to the mark.   190

39

Never nightingale so singeth:
Oh, she leans on thorny tree,
And her poet-song she flingeth
Over pain to victory!
Yet she never sings such music, – or she sings it not to me.   195

40

Never blackbirds, never thrushes,
Nor small finches sing as sweet,
When the sun strikes through the bushes
To their crimson clinging feet,
And their pretty eyes look sideways to the summer heavens complete.

41

If it *were* a bird, it seemèd,   201
Most like Chaucer's, which, in sooth,
He of green and azure dreamèd,
While it sat in spirit-ruth
On that bier of a crowned lady, singing nigh her silent mouth.   205

42

If it *were* a bird! – ah, sceptic,
Give me 'yea' or give me 'nay' –
Though my soul were nympholeptic,
As I heard that virèlay,
You may stoop your pride to pardon, for my sin is far away.   210

43

I rose up in exaltation
And an inward trembling heat,
And (it seemed) in geste of passion
Dropped the music to my feet
Like a garment rustling downwards! – such a silence followed it.

44

Heart and head beat through the quiet   216
Full and heavily, though slower.
In the song, I think, and by it,
Mystic Presences of power
Had up-snatched me to the Timeless, then returned me to the Hour.

45

In a child-abstraction lifted,   221
Straightway from the bower I past,
Foot and soul being dimly drifted
Through the greenwood, till, at last,
In the hill-top's open sunshine I all consciously was cast.   225

46

Face to face with the true mountains
I stood silently and still,
Drawing strength from fancy's dauntings,
From the air about the hill,
And from Nature's open mercies, and most debonair goodwill.   230

47

Oh, the golden-hearted daisies
Witnessed there, before my youth,
To the truth of things, with praises
Of the beauty of the truth,
And I woke to Nature's real, laughing joyfully for both.   235

48

And I said within me, laughing,
I have found a bower today,
A green lusus [37] – fashioned half in
Chance, and half in Nature's play –
And a little bird sings nigh it, I will never more missay.   240

49

Henceforth, *I* will be the fairy
Of this bower not built by one;
I will go there, sad or merry,
With each morning's benison,
And the bird shall be my harper in the dream-hall I have won.   245

50

So I said. But the next morning,
(– Child, look up into my face –
'Ware, O sceptic, of your scorning!
This is truth in its pure grace!)
The next morning, all had vanished, or my wandering missed the place.

51

Bring an oath most sylvan holy,   251
And upon it swear me true –
By the wind-bells swinging slowly
Their mute curfews in the dew,
By the advent of the snowdrop, by the rosemary and rue, –   255

52

I affirm by all or any,
Let the cause be charm or chance,
That my wandering searches many
Missed the bower of my romance –
That I nevermore, upon it, turned my mortal countenance.   260

53

I affirm that, since I lost it,
Never bower has seemed so fair;
Never garden-creeper crossed it
With so deft and brave an air –
Never bird sung in the summer, as I saw and heard them there.   265

54

Day by day, with new desire,
Toward my wood I ran in faith,
Under leaf and over brier,
Through the thickets, out of breath –
Like the prince who rescued Beauty from the sleep as long as death.

55

But his sword of mettle clashèd,   271
And his arm smote strong, I ween,
And her dreaming spirit flashèd
Through her body's fair white screen,
And the light thereof might guide him up the cedar alleys green.

56

But for me, I saw no splendour –   276
All my sword was my child-heart;
And the wood refused surrender
Of that bower it held apart,
Safe as Oedipus's grave-place,[38] 'mid Colonos' olives swart.   280

57

As Aladdin[39] sought the basements
His fair palace rose upon,
And the four-and-twenty casements
Which gave answers to the sun;
So, in 'wilderment of gazing I looked up, and I looked down.   285

58

Years have vanished since as wholly
As the little bower did then;
And you call it tender folly
That such thoughts should come again?
Ah, I cannot change this sighing for your smiling, brother men! 290

59

For this loss it did prefigure
Other loss of better good,
When my soul, in spirit-vigour,
And in ripened womanhood,
Fell from visions of more beauty than an arbour in a wood.   295

60

I have lost – oh, many a pleasure,
Many a hope, and many a power –
Studious health, and merry leisure,
The first dew on the first flower!
But the first of all my losses was the losing of the bower.   300

61

I have lost the dream of Doing,
And the other dream of Done,
The first spring in the pursuing,
The first pride in the Begun, –
First recoil from incompletion, in the face of what is won –   305

62

Exaltations in the far light
Where some cottage only is;
Mild dejections in the starlight,
Which the sadder-hearted miss;
And the child-cheek blushing scarlet for the very shame of bliss.

63

I have lost the sound child-sleeping   311
Which the thunder could not break;
Something too of the strong leaping
Of the staglike heart awake,
Which the pale is low for keeping in the road it ought to take.   315

64

Some respect to social fictions
Has been also lost by me;
And some generous genuflexions,
Which my spirit offered free
To the pleasant old conventions of our false humanity.   320

65

All my losses did I tell you,
Ye, perchance, would look away; –
Ye would answer me, 'Farewell! you
Make sad company today,
And your tears are falling faster than the bitter words you say.'   325

66

For God placed me like a dial
In the open ground with power,
And my heart had for its trial
All the sun and all the shower!
And I suffered many losses, – and my first was of the bower.   330

67

Laugh you? If that loss of mine be
Of no heavy-seeming weight –
When the cone falls from the pine tree
The young children laugh thereat;
Yet the wind that struck it, riseth, and the tempest shall be great.

68

One who knew me in my childhood   336
In the glamour and the game,
Looking on me long and mild, would
Never know me for the same.
Come, unchanging recollections, where those changes overcame.

69

By this couch I weakly lie on,   341
While I count my memories, –
Through the fingers which, still sighing,
I press closely on mine eyes, –
Clear as once beneath the sunshine, I behold the bower arise.   345

70

Springs the linden-tree as greenly,
Stroked with light adown its rind;
And the ivy-leaves serenely
Each in either intertwined;
And the rose-trees at the doorway, they have neither grown nor pined.

71

From those overblown faint roses   351
Not a leaf appeareth shed,
And that little bud discloses
Not a thorn's-breadth more of red
For the winters and the summers which have passed me overhead.

72

And that music overfloweth,   356
    Sudden sweet, the sylvan eaves:
    Thrush or nightingale – who knoweth?
    Fay or Faunus – who believes?
But my heart still trembles in me to the trembling of the leaves.   360

73

Is the bower lost, then? who sayeth
    That the bower indeed is lost?
    Hark! my spirit in it prayeth
    Through the sunshine and the frost, –
And the prayer preserves it greenly, to the last and uttermost.   365

74

Till another open for me
    In God's Eden-land unknown,
    With an angel at the doorway,
    White with gazing at His Throne;
And a saint's voice in the palm-trees, singing – 'All is lost . . . and *won*!'
                                                               370

A Child Asleep

1

How he sleepeth, having drunken
    Weary childhood's mandragore![40]
From its pretty eyes have sunken
    Pleasures to make room for more –
Sleeping near the withered nosegay which he pulled the day before.   5

2

Nosegays! leave them for the waking;
    Throw them earthward where they grew;
Dim are such, beside the breaking
    Amaranths he looks unto:
Folded eyes see brighter colours than the open ever do.   10

3

Heaven-flowers, rayed by shadows golden
    From the palms they sprang beneath,
Now perhaps divinely holden,
    Swing against him in a wreath:
We may think so from the quickening of his bloom and of his breath.

4

Vision unto vision calleth,   16
    While the young child dreameth on;
Fair, O dreamer, thee befalleth
    With the glory thou hast won!
Darker wert thou in the garden, yestermorn by summer sun.   20

5

We should see the spirits ringing
    Round thee, were the clouds away;
'Tis the child-heart draws them, singing
    In the silent-seeming clay:
Singing! – stars that seem the mutest, go in music all the way.   25

6

As the moths around a taper,
    As the bees around a rose,
As the gnats around a vapour,
    So the spirits group and close
Round about a holy childhood, as if drinking its repose.   30

7

Shapes of brightness overlean thee,
    Flash their diadems of youth
On the ringlets which half screen thee,
    While thou smilest . . . not in sooth
Thy smile, but the overfair one, dropt from some ethereal mouth.   35

8

Haply it is angels' duty,
    During slumber, shade by shade
To fine down this childish beauty
    To the thing it must be made,
Ere the world shall bring it praises, or the tomb shall see it fade.   40

9

Softly, softly! make no noises!
    Now he lieth dead and dumb;
Now he hears the angels' voices
    Folding silence in the room:
Now he muses deep the meaning of the Heaven-words as they come.

10

Speak not! he is consecrated;   46
    Breathe no breath across his eyes:
Lifted up and separated
    On the hand of God he lies,
In a sweetness beyond touching, – held in cloistral sanctities.   50

11

Could ye bless him – father – mother,
    Bless the dimple in his cheek?
Dare ye look at one another,
    And the benediction speak?
Would ye not break out in weeping, and confess yourselves too weak?

12

He is harmless – ye are sinful;   56
    Ye are troubled – he at ease;
From his slumber, virtue winful
    Floweth outward with increase.
Dare not bless him! but be blessèd by his peace – and go in peace.   60

The Cry of the Children [41]

Φεῦ, φεῦ· τί προσδέρκεσθέ μ' ὄμμασιν, τέκνα;
                              Medea

[Alas, alas, why do you gaze at me with your eyes, my children]

1

Do ye hear the children weeping, O my brothers,
    Ere the sorrow comes with years?
They are leaning their young heads against their mothers,
    And *that* cannot stop their tears.
The young lambs are bleating in the meadows,   5
    The young birds are chirping in the nest,
The young fawns are playing with the shadows,
    The young flowers are blowing toward the west –
But the young, young children, O my brothers,
    They are weeping bitterly!   10
They are weeping in the playtime of the others,
    In the country of the free.

2

Do you question the young children in the sorrow,
    Why their tears are falling so?
The old man may weep for his tomorrow   15
    Which is lost in Long Ago;
The old tree is leafless in the forest,
    The old year is ending in the frost,
The old wound, if stricken, is the sorest,
    The old hope is hardest to be lost.   20

But the young, young children, O my brothers,
    Do you ask them why they stand
Weeping sore before the bosoms of their mothers,
    In our happy Fatherland?

3

They look up with their pale and sunken faces,   25
    And their looks are sad to see,
For the man's hoary anguish draws and presses
    Down the cheeks of infancy;
'Your old earth,' they say, 'is very dreary;
    Our young feet,' they say, 'are very weak!   30
Few paces have we taken, yet are weary –
    Our grave-rest is very far to seek.
Ask the aged why they weep, and not the children;
    For the outside earth is cold;
And we young ones stand without, in our bewildering,   35
    And the graves are for the old.'

4

'True,' say the children, 'it may happen
    That we die before our time:
Little Alice died last year – her grave is shapen
    Like a snowball, in the rime.   40
We looked into the pit prepared to take her:
    Was no room for any work in the close clay!
From the sleep wherein she lieth none will wake her,
    Crying, "Get up, little Alice! it is day."
If you listen by that grave, in sun and shower,   45
    With your ear down, little Alice never cries;
Could we see her face, be sure we should not know her,
    For the smile has time for growing in her eyes:
And merry go her moments, lulled and stilled in
    The shroud by the kirk-chime!   50
It is good when it happens,' say the children,
    'That we die before our time.'

5

Alas, alas, the children! they are seeking
    Death in life, as best to have;
They are binding up their hearts away from breaking,   55

With a cerement[42] from the grave.
Go out, children, from the mine and from the city,
    Sing out, children, as the little thrushes do;
Pluck your handfuls of the meadow cowslips pretty,
    Laugh aloud, to feel your fingers let them through!   60
But they answer, 'Are your cowslips of the meadows
    Like our weeds anear the mine?
Leave us quiet in the dark of the coal-shadows,
    From your pleasures fair and fine!

6

'For oh,' say the children, 'we are weary,   65
    And we cannot run or leap;
If we cared for any meadows, it were merely
    To drop down in them and sleep.
Our knees tremble sorely in the stooping,
    We fall upon our faces, trying to go;   70
And, underneath our heavy eyelids drooping,
    The reddest flower would look as pale as snow;
For, all day, we drag our burden tiring
    Through the coal-dark, underground –
Or, all day, we drive the wheels of iron   75
    In the factories, round and round.

7

'For all day the wheels are droning, turning, –
    Their wind comes in our faces, –
Till our hearts turn, – our heads, with pulses burning,
    And the walls turn in their places: 80
Turns the sky in the high window blank and reeling,
    Turns the long light that drops adown the wall,
Turn the black flies that crawl along the ceiling:
    All are turning, all the day, and we with all.
And all day, the iron wheels are droning,   85
    And sometimes we could pray,
"O ye wheels" (breaking out in a mad moaning),
    "Stop! be silent for today!" '

8

Aye, be silent! Let them hear each other breathing
    For a moment, mouth to mouth!   90

Let them touch each other's hands, in a fresh wreathing
    Of their tender human youth!
Let them feel that this cold metallic motion
    Is not all the life God fashions or reveals:
Let them prove their living souls against the notion   95
   That they live in you, or under you, O wheels! –
Still, all day, the iron wheels go onward,
    Grinding life down from its mark;
And the children's souls, which God is calling sunward,
    Spin on blindly in the dark.   100

9

Now tell the poor young children, O my brothers,
    To look up to Him and pray;
So the blessèd One who blesseth all the others,
    Will bless them another day.
They answer, 'Who is God that He should hear us,   105
   While the rushing of the iron wheels is stirred?
When we sob aloud, the human creatures near us
   Pass by, hearing not, or answer not a word.
And we hear not (for the wheels in their resounding)
    Strangers speaking at the door: 110
Is it likely God, with angels singing round Him,
    Hears our weeping any more?

10

'Two words, indeed, of praying we remember,
    And at midnight's hour of harm,
"Our Father," looking upward in the chamber,   115
    We say softly for a charm.
We know no other words except "Our Father,"
   And we think that, in some pause of angels' song,
God may pluck them with the silence sweet to gather,
   And hold both within His right hand which is strong.   120
"Our Father!" If He heard us, He would surely
    (For they call Him good and mild)
Answer, smiling down the steep world very purely,
    "Come and rest with Me, My child."

11

'But, no!' say the children, weeping faster,   125
    'He is speechless as a stone:
And they tell us, of His image is the master
    Who commands us to work on.
Go to!' say the children, – 'up in Heaven,
    Dark, wheel-like, turning clouds are all we find.   130
Do not mock us; grief has made us unbelieving –
    We look up for God, but tears have made us blind.'
Do you hear the children weeping and disproving,
    O my brothers, what ye preach?
For God's possible is taught by His world's loving,   135
    And the children doubt of each.

12

And well may the children weep before you!
    They are weary ere they run;
They have never seen the sunshine, nor the glory
    Which is brighter than the sun.   140
They know the grief of man, without its wisdom;
    They sink in man's despair, without its calm;
Are slaves, without the liberty in Christdom,
    Are martyrs, by the pang without the palm, –
Are worn, as if with age, yet unretrievingly   145
    The harvest of its memories cannot reap, –
Are orphans of the earthly love and heavenly.
    Let them weep! let them weep!

13

They look up, with their pale and sunken faces,
    And their look is dread to see,   150
For they mind you of their angels in high places,
    With eyes turned on Deity! –
'How long,' they say, 'how long, O cruel nation,
    Will you stand, to move the world, on a child's heart, –
Stifle down with a mailed heel its palpitation,   155
    And tread onward to your throne amid the mart?
Our blood splashes upward, O gold-heaper,
    And your purple shows your path!
But the child's sob in the silence curses deeper
    Than the strong man in his wrath.'   160

Crowned and Wedded 43

1

When last before her people's face her own fair face she bent,
Within the meek projection of that shade she was content
To erase the child-smile from her lips, which seemed as if it might
Be still kept holy from the world to childhood still in sight –
To erase it with a solemn vow, – a princely vow – to rule;   5
A priestly vow – to rule by grace of God the pitiful;
A very godlike vow – to rule in right and righteousness,
And with the law and for the land! – so God the vower bless!

2

The minster was alight that day, but not with fire, I ween,
And long-drawn glitterings swept adown that mighty aislèd scene;   10
The priests stood stolèd in their pomp, the sworded chiefs in theirs,
And so, the collared knights, and so, the civil ministers,
And so, the waiting lords and dames – and little pages best
At holding trains – and legates so, from countries east and west.
So, alien princes, native peers, and highborn ladies bright,   15
Along whose brows the Queen's, new crowned, flashed coronets to light.
And so, the people at the gates, with priestly hands on high,
Which bring the first anointing to all legal majesty.
And so the DEAD – who lie in rows beneath the minster floor,
There, verily an awful state maintaining evermore;   20
The statesman whose clean palm will kiss no bribe, whate'er it be,
The courtier who, for no fair queen, will rise up to his knee;
The court-dame who, for no court-tire, will leave her shroud behind;
The laureate who no courtlier rime than 'dust to dust' can find;
The kings and queens who having made that vow and worn that crown,   25
Descended unto lower thrones and darker, deep adown!
Dieu et mon droit – what is 't to them? – what meaning can it have? –
The King of kings, the right of death – God's judgment and the grave.
And when betwixt the quick and dead, the young fair queen had vowed,
The living shouted 'May she live! Victoria, live!' aloud.   30
And as the loyal shouts went up, true spirits prayed between,
'The blessings happy monarchs have be thine, O crownèd queen!'

3

But now before her people's face she bendeth hers anew,
And calls them, while she vows, to be her witness thereunto.
She vowed to rule, and, in that oath, her childhood put away: 35
She doth maintain her womanhood, in vowing love today.
O lovely lady! – let her vow! – such lips become such vows,
And fairer goeth bridal wreath than crown with vernal brows.
O lovely lady! – let her vow! – yea, let her vow to love! –
And though she be no less a queen – with purples hung above,   40
The pageant of a court behind, the royal kin around,
And woven gold to catch her looks turned maidenly to ground,
Yet may the bride-veil hide from her a little of that state,
While loving hopes, for retinues, about her sweetness wait.
SHE vows to love who vowed to rule – (the chosen at her side)   45
Let none say, 'God preserve the queen!' – but rather, 'Bless the bride!'
None blow the trump, none bend the knee, none violate the dream
Wherein no monarch but a wife, she to herself may seem.
Or if ye say, 'Preserve the queen!' – oh, breathe it inward low –
She is a *woman*, and *beloved!* – and 'tis enough but so.   50
Count it enough, thou noble prince, who tak'st her by the hand,
And claimest for thy lady-love, our lady of the land!
And since, Prince Albert, men have called thy spirit high and rare,
And true to truth and brave for truth, as some at Augsburg were, –
We charge thee by thy lofty thoughts, and by thy poet-mind   55
Which not by glory and degree takes measure of mankind,
Esteem that wedded hand less dear for sceptre than for ring,
And hold her uncrowned womanhood to be the royal thing.

4

And now, upon our queen's last vow, what blessings shall we pray?
None, straitened to a shallow crown, will suit our lips today.   60
Behold, they must be free as love – they must be broad as free,
Even to the borders of heaven's light and earth's humanity.
Long live she! – send up loyal shouts – and true hearts pray between, –
'The blessings happy PEASANTS have, be thine, O crownèd queen!'

Crowned and Buried

1

Napoleon![44] – years ago, and that great word
Compàct of human breath in hate and dread
And exultation, skied us overhead –
An atmosphere whose lightning was the sword
Scathing the cedars of the world, – drawn down   5
In burnings, by the metal of a crown.

2

Napoleon! nations, while they cursed that name,
Shook at their own curse; and while others bore
Its sound, as of a trumpet, on before,
Brass-fronted legions justified its fame;   10
And dying men, on trampled battle-sods,
Near their last silence, uttered it for God's.

3

Napoleon! sages, with high foreheads drooped,
Did use it for a problem: children small
Leapt up to greet it, as at manhood's call: 15
Priests blessed it from their altars overstooped
By meek-eyed Christs, – and widows with a moan
Spake it, when questioned why they sat alone.

4

That name consumed the silence of the snows
In Alpine keeping, holy and cloud-hid;   20
The mimic eagles dared what Nature's did,
And over-rushed her mountainous repose
In search of eyries; and the Egyptian river
Mingled the same word with its grand 'For ever.'

5

That name was shouted near the pyramidal   25
Nilotic tombs, whose mummied habitants,
Packed to humanity's significance,
Motioned it back with stillness! shouts as idle
As hireling artists' work of myrrh and spice
Which swathed last glories round the Ptolemies.   30

6

The world's face changed to hear it. Kingly men
Came down in chidden babes' bewilderment
From autocratic places, each content
With sprinkled ashes for anointing. – Then
The people laughed, or wondered for the nonce,   35
To see one throne a composite of thrones.

7

Napoleon! even the torrid vastitude
Of India felt in throbbings of the air
That name which scattered by disastrous blare
All Europe's bound-lines, – drawn afresh in blood.   40
Napoleon – from the Russias, west to Spain!
And Austria trembled – till ye heard her chain.

8

And Germany was 'ware; and Italy
Oblivious of old fames – her laurel-locked,
High-ghosted Caesars passing uninvoked –   45
Did crumble her own ruins with her knee,
To serve a newer. Aye! but Frenchmen cast
A future from them nobler than her past:

9

For, verily, though France augustly rose
With that raised NAME, and did assume by such   50
The purple of the world, none gave so much
As she, in purchase – to speak plain, in loss –
Whose hands, toward freedom stretched, dropped paralysed
To wield a sword or fit an undersized

10

King's crown to a great man's head. And though along   55
Her Paris' streets, did float on frequent streams
Of triumph, pictured or emmarbled dreams
Dreamt right by genius in a world gone wrong, –
No dream, of all so won, was fair to see
As the lost vision of her liberty.   60

11

Napoleon! 'twas a high name lifted high!
It met at last God's thunder sent to clear
Our compassing and covering atmosphere
And open a clear sight beyond the sky
Of supreme empire; this of earth's was done –   65
And kings crept out again to feel the sun.

12

The kings crept out – the peoples sat at home,
And finding the long-invocated peace
(A pall embroidered with worn images
Of rights divine) too scant to cover doom   70
Such as they suffered, – cursed the corn that grew
Rankly, to bitter bread, on Waterloo.

13

A deep gloom centred in the deep repose;
The nations stood up mute to count their dead.
And *he* who owned the NAME which vibrated   75
Through silence, – trusting to his noblest foes
When earth was all too grey for chivalry,
Died of their mercies 'mid the desert sea.

14

O wild St Helen! very still she kept him,
With a green willow for all pyramid, –   80
Which stirred a little if the low wind did,
A little more, if pilgrims overwept him,
Disparting the little boughs to see the clay
Which seemed to cover his for judgment-day.

15

Nay, not so long! – France kept her old affection   85
As deeply as the sepulchre the corse,
Until, dilated by such love's remorse
To a new angel of the resurrection,
She cried, 'Behold, thou England! I would have
The dead whereof thou wottest, from that grave.'   90

16

And England answered in the courtesy
Which, ancient foes turned lovers, may befit, –
'Take back thy dead! and when thou buriest it,
Throw in all former strifes 'twixt thee and me.'
Amen, mine England! 'tis a courteous claim –   95
But ask a little room too . . . for thy shame!

17

Because it was not well, it was not well,
Nor tuneful with thy lofty-chanted part
Among the Oceanides, – that Heart
To bind and bare and vex with vulture fell.   100
I would, my noble England! men might seek
All crimson stains upon thy breast – not cheek!

18

I would that hostile fleets had scarred Torbay,
Instead of the lone ship which waited moored
Until thy princely purpose was assured,   105
Then left a shadow, not to pass away –
Not for tonight's moon, nor tomorrow's sun!
Green watching hills, ye witnessed what was done!*

19

But since it *was* done, – in sepulchral dust
We fain would pay back something of our debt   110
To France, if not to honour, and forget
How through much fear we falsified the trust
Of a fallen foe and exile. – We return
Orestes to Electra[45] . . . in his urn.

20

A little urn – a little dust inside,   115
Which once outbalanced the large earth, albeit
Today a four-years child might carry it
Sleek-browed and smiling, 'Let the burden 'bide!'
Orestes to Electra! – O fair town
Of Paris, how the wild tears will run down   120

---

* Written at Torquay.

21

And run back in the chariot-marks of time,
When all the people shall come forth to meet
The passive victor, death-still in the street
He rode through 'mid the shouting and bell-chime
And martial music, under eagles which   125
Dyed their rapacious beaks at Austerlitz.

22

Napoleon! he hath come again – borne home
Upon the popular ebbing heart, – a sea
Which gathers its own wrecks perpetually,
Majestically moaning. Give him room! –   130
Room for the dead in Paris! welcome solemn
And grave-deep, 'neath the cannon-moulded column!*

23

There, weapon spent and warrior spent may rest
From roar of fields, – provided Jupiter
Dare trust Saturnus[46] to lie down so near   135
His bolts! – and this he may. For, dispossessed
Of any godship lies the godlike arm –
The goat, Jove sucked, as likely to do harm.

24

And yet . . . Napoleon! – the recovered name
Shakes the old casements of the world! and we   140
Look out upon the passing pageantry,
Attesting that the Dead makes good his claim
To a French grave, – another kingdom won,
The last, of few spans – by Napoleon.

25

Blood fell like dew beneath his sunrise – sooth;   145
But glittered dew-like in the covenanted
Meridian light. He was a despot – granted!
But the αὐτός [self] of his autocratic mouth
Said yea i' the people's French; he magnified
The image of the freedom he denied.   150

---

* It was the first intention to bury him under the column.

26

And if they asked for rights, he made reply
'Ye have my glory!' – and so, drawing round them
His ample purple, glorified and bound them
In an embrace that seemed identity.
He ruled them like a tyrant – true! but none   155
Were ruled like slaves: each felt Napoleon.

27

I do not praise this man: the man was flawed
For Adam – much more, Christ! – his knee unbent,
His hand unclean, his aspiration pent
Within a sword-sweep – pshaw! – but since he had   160
The genius to be loved, why, let him have
The justice to be honoured in his grave.

28

I think this nation's tears thus poured together
Better than shouts. I think this funeral
Grander than crownings, though a Pope bless all.   165
I think this grave stronger than thrones. But whether
The crowned Napoleon or the buried clay
Be worthier, I discern not. Angels may.

To Flush, My Dog [47]

1

Loving friend, the gift of one
Who her own true faith has run
   Through thy lower nature,
Be my benediction said
With my hand upon thy head,   5
   Gentle fellow creature!

2

Like a lady's ringlets brown,
Flow thy silken ears adown
   Either side demurely
Of thy silver-suited breast,   10
Shining out from all the rest
   Of thy body purely.

3

Darkly brown thy body is,
Till the sunshine striking this
   Alchemise its dullness,   15
When the sleek curls manifold
Flash all over into gold,
   With a burnished fullness.

4

Underneath my stroking hand,
Startled eyes of hazel bland   20
   Kindling, growing larger,
Up thou leapest with a spring,
Full of prank and curveting,
   Leaping like a charger.

5

Leap! thy broad tail waves a light,   25
Leap! thy slender feet are bright,
   Canopied in fringes;
Leap – those tasselled ears of thine
Flicker strangely, fair and fine,
   Down their golden inches.   30

6

Yet, my pretty, sportive friend,
Little is 't to such an end
    That I praise thy rareness!
Other dogs may be thy peers
Haply in these drooping ears,   35
    And this glossy fairness.

7

But of *thee* it shall be said,
This dog watched beside a bed
    Day and night unweary, –
Watched within a curtained room,   40
Where no sunbeam brake the gloom
    Round the sick and dreary.

8

Roses, gathered for a vase,
In that chamber died apace,
    Beam and breeze resigning;   45
This dog only, waited on,
Knowing that when light is gone
    Love remains for shining.

9

Other dogs in thymy dew
Tracked the hares and followed through   50
    Sunny moor or meadow;
This dog only, crept and crept
Next a languid cheek that slept,
    Sharing in the shadow.

10

Other dogs of loyal cheer   55
Bounded at the whistle clear,
    Up the woodside hieing;
This dog only, watched in reach
Of a faintly uttered speech,
    Or a louder sighing.   60

11

And if one or two quick tears
Dropped upon his glossy ears,
 Or a sigh came double, –
Up he sprang in eager haste,
Fawning, fondling, breathing fast,   65
 In a tender trouble.

12

And this dog was satisfied
If a pale thin hand would glide
 Down his dewlaps sloping, –
Which he pushed his nose within,   70
After, – platforming his chin
 On the palm left open.

13

This dog, if a friendly voice
Call him now to blither choice
 Than such chamber-keeping,   75
'Come out!' praying from the door, –
Presseth backward as before,
 Up against me leaping.

14

Therefore to this dog will I,
Tenderly not scornfully,   80
 Render praise and favour:
With my hand upon his head,
Is my benediction said
 Therefore, and for ever.

15

And because he loves me so,   85
Better than his kind will do
 Often, man or woman,
Give I back more love again
Than dogs often take of men,
 Leaning from my Human.   90

16

Blessings on thee, dog of mine,
Pretty collars make thee fine,
   Sugared milk make fat thee!
Pleasures wag on in thy tail,
Hands of gentle motion fail   95
   Nevermore, to pat thee!

17

Downy pillow take thy head,
Silken coverlid bestead,
   Sunshine help thy sleeping!
No fly's buzzing wake thee up,   100
No man break thy purple cup,
   Set for drinking deep in.

18

Whiskered cats arointed flee,
Sturdy stoppers keep from thee
   Cologne distillations;   105
Nuts lie in thy path for stones,
And thy feast-day macaroons
   Turn to daily rations!

19

Mock I thee, in wishing weal? –
Tears are in my eyes to feel   110
   Thou art made so straitly,
Blessing needs must straiten too, –
Little canst thou joy or do,
   Thou who lovest *greatly*.

20

Yet be blessèd to the height   115
Of all good and all delight
   Pervious to thy nature;
Only *loved* beyond that line,
With a love that answers thine,
   Loving fellow creature!   120

The Fourfold Aspect

When ye stood up in the house
    With your little childish feet,
And, in touching Life's first shows,
    First the touch of Love did meet, –
Love and Nearness seeming one,   5
    By the heartlight cast before,
And, of all Beloveds, none
    Standing farther than the door!
Not a name being dear to thought,
    With its owner beyond call;   10
Nor a face, unless it brought
    Its own shadow to the wall;
When the worst recorded change
    Was of apple dropt from bough,
When love's sorrow seemed more strange   15
    Than love's treason can seem now, –
Then, the Loving took you up
    Soft, upon their elder knees, –
Telling why the statues droop
    Underneath the churchyard trees,   20
And how ye must lie beneath them
    Through the winters long and deep,
Till the last trump overbreathe them,
    And ye smile out of your sleep . . .
Oh, ye lifted up your head, and it seemed as if they said   25
    A tale of fairy ships
    With a swan-wing for a sail! –
Oh, ye kissed their loving lips
    For the merry, merry tale! –
So carelessly ye thought upon the Dead.   30

Soon ye read in solemn stories
    Of the men of long ago –
Of the pale bewildering glories
    Shining farther than we know;

Of the heroes with the laurel,   35
    Of the poets with the bay,
Of the two worlds' earnest quarrel
    For that beauteous Helena;
How Achilles at the portal
    Of the tent, heard footsteps nigh,   40
And his strong heart, half-immortal,
    Met the *keitai* with a cry;
How Ulysses left the sunlight
    For the pale eidola race
Blank and passive through the dun light,   45
    Staring blindly in his face;
How that true wife said to Paetus,
    With calm smile and wounded heart,
'Sweet, it hurts not!' – how Admetus
    Saw his blessèd one depart;   50
How King Arthur proved his mission,
    And Sir Roland wound his horn,
And at Sangreal's moony vision
    Swords did bristle round like corn.
Oh, ye lifted up your head, and it seemed the while ye read,
    That this Death, then, must be found   56
    A Valhalla for the crowned,
The heroic who prevail:
None, be sure, can enter in
    Far below a paladin   60
Of a noble, noble tale! –
So awfully ye thought upon the Dead.

3

Aye, but soon ye woke up shrieking, –
    As a child that wakes at night
From a dream of sisters speaking   65
    In a garden's summer-light, –
That wakes, starting up and bounding,
    In a lonely, lonely bed,
With a wall of darkness round him,
    Stifling black about his head! –   70
And the full sense of your mortal
    Rushed upon you deep and loud,

And ye heard the thunder hurtle
From the silence of the cloud!
Funeral-torches at your gateway 75
Threw a dreadful light within.
All things changed! you rose up straightway,
And saluted Death and Sin.
Since, – your outward man has rallied,
And your eye and voice grown bold – 80
Yet the Sphinx of Life stands pallid,
With her saddest secret told.
Happy places have grown holy:
If ye went where once ye went,
Only tears would fall down slowly, 85
As at solemn sacrament.
Merry books, once read for pastime,
If ye dared to read again,
Only memories of the last time
Would swim darkly up the brain. 90
Household names, which used to flutter
Through your laughter unawares, –
God's Divinest ye could utter
With less trembling in your prayers!
Ye have dropt adown your head, and it seems as if ye tread
On your own hearts in the path 96
Ye are called to in His wrath, –
And your prayers go up in wail!
– 'Dost Thou see, then, all our loss,
O Thou agonised on cross? 100
Art thou reading all its tale?'
So mournfully ye think upon the Dead.

4

Pray, pray, thou who also weepest,
And the drops will slacken so.
Weep, weep, – and the watch thou keepest 105
With a quicker count will go.
Think. – the shadow on the dial
For the nature most undone,
Marks the passing of the trial,

Proves the presence of the sun.   110
Look, look up, in starry passion,
 To the throne above the spheres!
Learn, – the spirit's gravitation
 Still must differ from the tear's.
Hope, – with all the strength thou usest   115
 In embracing thy despair,
Love, – the earthly love thou losest
 Shall return to thee more fair.
Work, – make clear the forest-tangles
 Of the wildest stranger-land.   120
Trust, – the blessèd deathly angels
 Whisper, 'Sabbath hours at hand!'
By the heart's wound when most gory,
 By the longest agony,
Smile! – Behold, in sudden glory   125
 The TRANSFIGURED smiles on *thee*!
And ye lifted up your head, and it seemed as if He said,
 'My Belovèd, is it so?
 Have ye tasted of my woe?
 Of my Heaven ye shall not fail!' –   130
He stands brightly where the shade is,
With the keys of Death and Hades,
 And there, ends the mournful tale. –
So hopefully ye think upon the Dead.

A Flower in a Letter

1

My lonely chamber next the sea[48]
Is full of many flowers set free
  By summer's earliest duty:
Dear friends upon the garden-walk
Might stop amid their fondest talk   5
  To pull the least in beauty.

2

A thousand flowers – each seeming one
That learnt by gazing on the sun
  To counterfeit his shining;
Within whose leaves the holy dew   10
That falls from heaven, has won anew
  A glory, in declining.

3

Red roses, used to praises long,
Contented with the poet's song,
  The nightingale's being over;   15
And lilies white, prepared to touch
The whitest thought, nor soil it much,
  Of dreamer turned to lover.

4

Deep violets, you liken to
The kindest eyes that look on you,   20
  Without a thought disloyal;
And cactuses a queen might don,
If weary of a golden crown,
  And still appear as royal.

5

Pansies for ladies all – (wis   25
That none who wear such brooches, miss
  A jewel in the mirror);
And tulips, children love to stretch
Their fingers down, to feel in each
  Its beauty's secret nearer.   30

6

Love's language may be talked with these;
To work out choicest sentences
    No blossoms can be meeter;
And, such being used in Eastern bowers,
Young maids may wonder if the flowers   35
    Or meanings be the sweeter.

7

And such being strewn before a bride,
Her little foot may turn aside,
    Their longer bloom decreeing,
Unless some voice's whispered sound   40
Should make her gaze upon the ground
    Too earnestly – for seeing.

8

And such being scattered on a grave,
Whoever mourneth there, may have
    A type which seemeth worthy   45
Of that fair body hid below,
Which bloomed on earth a time ago,
    Then perished as the earthy.

9

And such being wreathed for worldly feast,
Across the brimming cup some guest   50
    Their rainbow colours viewing,
May feel them, with a silent start,
The covenant, his childish heart
    With nature made, – renewing.

10

No flowers our gardened England hath   55
To match with these, in bloom and breath,
    Which from the world are hiding,
In sunny Devon moist with rills, –
A nunnery of cloistered hills,
    The elements presiding.   60

11

By Loddon's stream the flowers are fair
That meet one gifted lady's care
   With prodigal rewarding
(For Beauty is too used to run
To Mitford's bower[49] – to want the sun   65
   To light her through the garden).

12

But, here, all summers are comprised –
The nightly frosts shrink exorcised
   Before the priestly moonshine;
And every wind with stolèd feet,   70
In wandering down the alleys sweet,
   Steps lightly on the sunshine,

13

And (having promised Harpocrate[50]
Among the nodding roses, that
   No harm shall touch his daughters)   75
Gives quite away the rushing sound,
He dares not use upon such ground,
   To ever-trickling waters.

14

Yet, sun and wind! what can ye do
But make the leaves more brightly show   80
   In posies newly gathered?
I look away from all your best,
To one poor flower unlike the rest,
   A little flower half-withered.

15

I do not think it ever was   85
A pretty flower, – to make the grass
   Look greener where it reddened;
And now it seems ashamed to be
Alone, in all this company,
   Of aspect shrunk and saddened.   90

16

A chamber-window was the spot
It grew in, from a garden-pot,
   Among the city shadows.
If any, tending it, might seem
To smile, 'twas only in a dream   95
   Of nature in the meadows.

17

How coldly on its head did fall
The sunshine, from the city wall
   In pale refraction driven!
How sadly, plashed upon its leaves,   100
The raindrops, losing in the eaves
   The first sweet news of heaven!

18

And those who planted, gathered it
In gamesome or in loving fit,
   And sent it as a token   105
Of what their city pleasures be, –
For one, in Devon by the sea
   And garden-blooms, to look on.

19

But SHE, for whom the jest was meant,
With a grave passion innocent   110
   Receiving what was given, –
Oh, if her face she turnèd then,
Let none say 'twas to gaze again
   Upon the flowers of Devon!

20

Because, whatever virtue dwells   115
In genial skies, warm oracles
   For gardens brightly springing, –
The flower which grew beneath your eyes,
Belovèd friends, to mine supplies
   A beauty worthier singing!   120

The Cry of the Human [51]

1

'There is no God,' the foolish saith,
    But none 'There is no sorrow,'
And nature oft the cry of faith
    In bitter need will borrow:
Eyes, which the preacher could not school,   5
    By wayside graves are raisèd,
And lips say 'God be pitiful,'
    Who ne'er said 'God be praisèd.'
          Be pitiful, O God!

2

The tempest stretches from the steep   10
    The shadow of its coming,
The beasts grow tame, and near us creep,
    As help were in the human;
Yet, while the cloud-wheels roll and grind,
    We spirits tremble under! –   15
The hills have echoes, but we find
    No answer for the thunder.
          Be pitiful, O God!

3

The battle hurtles on the plains,
    Earth feels new scythes upon her;   20
We reap our brothers for the wains,
    And call the harvest – honour:
Draw face to face, front line to line,
    One image all inherit, –
Then kill, curse on, by that same sign,   25
    Clay, clay, – and spirit, spirit.
          Be pitiful, O God!

4

The plague runs festering through the town,
    And never a bell is tolling,
And corpses, jostled 'neath the moon,   30
    Nod to the dead-cart's rolling.

The young child calleth for the cup,
    The strong man brings it weeping;
The mother from her babe looks up,
    And shrieks away its sleeping.   35
               Be pitiful, O God!

5

The plague of gold strikes far and near,
    And deep and strong it enters;
This purple chimar which we wear
    Makes madder than the centaur's: 40
Our thoughts grow blank, our words grow strange,
    We cheer the pale gold-diggers –
Each soul is worth so much on 'Change,[52]
    And marked, like sheep, with figures.
               Be pitiful, O God!   45

6

The curse of gold upon the land
    The lack of bread enforces;
The rail-cars snort from strand to strand,
    Like more of Death's white horses:
The rich preach 'rights' and future days,   50
    And hear no angel scoffing, –
The poor die mute – with starving gaze
    On corn-ships in the offing.
               Be pitiful, O God!

7

We meet together at the feast,   55
    To private mirth betake us;
We stare down in the winecup, lest
    Some vacant chair should shake us.
We name delight, and pledge it round –
    'It shall be ours tomorrow!'   60
God's seraphs, do your voices sound
    As sad in naming sorrow?
               Be pitiful, O God!

8

We sit together, with the skies,
   The steadfast skies, above us,   65
We look into each other's eyes,
   'And how long will you love us?' –
The eyes grow dim with prophecy,
   The voices, low and breathless, –
'Till death us part!' – O words, to be   70
   Our *best*, for love the deathless!
           Be pitiful, O God!

9

We tremble by the harmless bed
   Of one loved and departed:
Our tears drop on the lips that said   75
   Last night, 'Be stronger-hearted!'
O God, – to clasp those fingers close,
   And yet to feel so lonely! –
To see a light upon such brows,
   Which is the daylight only!   80
           Be pitiful, O God!

10

The happy children come to us,
   And look up in our faces:
They ask us – 'Was it thus, and thus,
   When we were in their places?' –   85
We cannot speak; – we see anew
   The hills we used to live in,
And feel our mother's smile press through
   The kisses she is giving.
           Be pitiful, O God!   90

11

We pray together at the kirk,
   For mercy, mercy, solely:
Hands weary with the evil work,
   We lift them to the Holy.
The corpse is calm below our knee,   95
   Its spirit, bright before Thee –

Between them, worse than either, we –
    Without the rest of glory!
            Be pitiful, O God!

12

We leave the communing of men,   100
    The murmur of the passions,
And live alone, to live again
    With endless generations.
Are we so brave? – The sea and sky
    In silence lift their mirrors,   105
And, glassed therein, our spirits high
    Recoil from their own terrors.
            Be pitiful, O God!

13

We sit on hills our childhood wist,
    Woods, hamlets, streams, beholding: 110
The sun strikes through the farthest mist,
    The city's spire to golden.
The city's golden spire it was,
    When hope and health were strongest,
But now it is the churchyard grass   115
    We look upon the longest.
            Be pitiful, O God!

14

And soon all vision waxeth dull –
    Men whisper, 'He is dying':
We cry no more 'Be pitiful!'   120
    We have no strength for crying.
No strength, no need. Then, soul of mine,
    Look up and triumph rather –
Lo, in the depth of God's Divine,
    The Son adjures the Father,   125
           BE PITIFUL, O GOD!

A Lay of the Early Rose [53]

– discordance that can accord.

Romaunt of the Rose [54]

A rose once grew within
A garden April-green,
In her loneness, in her loneness,
And the fairer for that oneness.

A white rose delicate   5
On a tall bough and straight:
Early comer, early comer,
Never waiting for the summer.

Her pretty gestes did win
South winds to let her in,   10
In her loneness, in her loneness,
All the fairer for that oneness.

'For if I wait,' said she,
'Till time for roses be, –
For the moss-rose and the musk-rose,   15
Maiden-blush and royal-dusk rose, –

'What glory then for me
In such a company? –
Roses plenty, roses plenty,
And one nightingale for twenty!   20

'Nay, let me in,' said she,
'Before the rest are free, –
In my loneness, in my loneness,
All the fairer for that oneness.

'For I would lonely stand   25
Uplifting my white hand,
On a mission, on a mission,
To declare the coming vision.

'Upon which lifted sign,
  What worship will be mine?
What addressing, what caressing,
And what thanks and praise and blessing!   30

'A windlike joy will rush
  Through every tree and bush,
Bending softly in affection
And spontaneous benediction.   35

'Insects, that only may
  Live in a sunbright ray,
To my whiteness, to my whiteness,
Shall be drawn, as to a brightness, –   40

'And every moth and bee,
  Approach me reverently,
Wheeling o'er me, wheeling o'er me
Coronals of motioned glory.

'Three larks shall leave a cloud,   45
  To my whiter beauty vowed,
Singing gladly all the moontide,
Never waiting for the suntide.

'Ten nightingales shall flee
  Their woods for love of me,   50
Singing sadly all the suntide,
Never waiting for the moontide.

'I ween the very skies
  Will look down with surprise,
When low on earth they see me   55
With my starry aspect dreamy.

'And earth will call her flowers
  To hasten out of doors;
By their curtsies and sweet-smelling
To give grace to my foretelling.'   60

So praying, did she win
South winds to let her in,
In her loneness, in her loneness,
And the fairer for that oneness.

But ah, – alas for her!   65
No thing did minister
To her praises, to her praises,
More than might unto a daisy's.

No tree nor bush was seen
To boast a perfect green,   70
Scarcely having, scarcely having
One leaf broad enough for waving.

The little flies did crawl
Along the southern wall,
Faintly shifting, faintly shifting   75
Wings scarce long enough for lifting.

The lark, too high or low,
I ween, did miss her so,
With his nest down in the gorses,
And his song in the star-courses.   80

The nightingale did please
To loiter beyond seas:
Guess him in the Happy Islands,
Learning music from the silence.

Only the bee, forsooth,   85
Came in the place of both,
Doing honour, doing honour
To the honey-dews upon her.

The skies looked coldly down
As on a royal crown;   90
Then with drop for drop, at leisure,
They began to rain for pleasure.

Whereat the Earth did seem
To waken from a dream,
Winter-frozen, winter-frozen,   95
Her unquiet eyes unclosing –

Said to the Rose, 'Ha, Snow!
And art thou fallen so?
Thou, who wast enthronèd stately
All along my mountains lately?   100

'Holla, thou world-wide snow!
And art thou wasted so?
With a little bough to catch thee,
And a little bee to watch thee?'

– Poor Rose, to be misknown!   105
Would she had ne'er been blown,
In her loneness, in her loneness,
All the sadder for that oneness!

Some word she tried to say,
Some no . . . ah, wellaway!   110
But the passion did o'ercome her,
And the fair frail leaves dropped from her.

Dropped from her, fair and mute,
Close to a poet's foot,
Who beheld them, smiling slowly,   115
As at something sad yet holy, –

Said, 'Verily and thus
It chances too with us
Poets, singing sweetest snatches
While that deaf men keep the watches: 120

'Vaunting to come before
Our own age evermore,
In a loneness, in a loneness,
And the nobler for that oneness.

'Holy in voice and heart,   125
    To high ends, set apart!
All unmated, all unmated,
Just because so consecrated.

'But if alone we be,
    Where is our empery?   130
And if none can reach our stature,
Who can mete our lofty nature?

'What bell will yield a tone,
    Swung in the air alone?
If no brazen clapper bringing,   135
Who can hear the chimèd ringing?

'What angel, but would seem
    To sensual eyes, ghost-dim?
And without assimilation,
Vain is interpenetration.   140

'And thus, what can we do,
    Poor rose and poet too,
Who both antedate our mission
In an unpreparèd season?

'Drop, leaf – be silent song!   145
    Cold things we come among:
We must warm them, we must warm them,
Ere we ever hope to charm them.

'Howbeit' (here his face
    Lightened around the place, –   150
So to mark the outward turning
Of his spirit's inward burning)

'Something it is, to hold
    In God's worlds manifold,
First revealed to creature-duty,   155
Some new form of His mild Beauty.

'Whether that form respect
   The sense or intellect,
Holy be, in mood or meadow,
The Chief Beauty's sign and shadow!   160

'Holy, in me and thee,
   Rose fallen from the tree, –
Though the world stand dumb around us,
All unable to expound us.

'Though none us deign to bless,   165
   Blessèd are we, nathless;
Blessèd still and consecrated,
In that, rose, we were created.

'Oh, shame to poet's lays,
   Sung for the dole of praise, –   170
Hoarsely sung upon the highway
With that *obolum da mihi*![55]

'Shame, shame to poet's soul
   Pining for such a dole,
When Heaven-chosen to inherit   175
The high throne of a chief spirit!

'Sit still upon your thrones,
   O ye poetic ones!
And if, sooth, the world decry you,
Let it pass unchallenged by you!   180

'Ye to yourselves suffice,
   Without its flatteries.
Self-contentedly approve you
Unto HIM who sits above you, –

'In prayers – that upward mount   185
   Like to a fair-sunned fount
Which, in gushing back upon you,
Hath an upper music won you.

'In faith – that still perceives
No rose can shed her leaves,
Far less, poet fall from mission,
With an unfulfilled fruition.

'In hope – that apprehends
An end beyond these ends,
And great uses rendered duly
By the meanest song sung truly.

'In thanks – for all the good
By poets understood –
For the sound of seraphs moving
Down the hidden depths of loving, –

'For sights of things away
Through fissures of the clay,
Promised things which *shall* be given
And sung over, up in Heaven, –

'For life, so lovely-vain,
For death, which breaks the chain, –
For this sense of present sweetness, –
And this yearning to completeness!'

190

195

200

205

Bertha in the Lane

1

Put the broidery-frame away,
　　For my sewing is all done:
The last thread is used today,
　　And I need not join it on.
　　Though the clock stands at the noon
　　I am weary. I have sewn,
　　Sweet, for thee, a wedding-gown.

2

Sister, help me to the bed,
　　And stand near me, Dearest-sweet.
Do not shrink nor be afraid,
　　Blushing with a sudden heat!
　　No one standeth in the street? –
　　By God's love I go to meet,
　　Love I thee with love complete.

3

Lean thy face down! drop it in
　　These two hands, that I may hold
'Twixt their palms thy cheek and chin,
　　Stroking back the curls of gold.
　　'Tis a fair, fair face, in sooth –
　　Larger eyes and redder mouth
　　Than mine were in my first youth.

4

Thou art younger by seven years –
　　Ah! – so bashful at my gaze,
That the lashes, hung with tears,
　　Grow too heavy to upraise?
　　I would wound thee by no touch
　　Which thy shyness feels as such:
　　Dost thou mind me, Dear, so much?

5

Have I not been nigh a mother
    To thy sweetness – tell me, Dear?   30
Have we not loved one another
    Tenderly, from year to year,
    Since our dying mother mild
    Said with accents undefiled,
    'Child, be mother to this child'!   35

6

Mother, mother, up in heaven,
    Stand up on the jasper sea,
And be witness I have given
    All the gifts required of me, –
    Hope that blessed me, bliss that crowned,   40
    Love that left me with a wound,
    Life itself, that turneth round!

7

Mother, mother, thou art kind,
    Thou art standing in the room,
In a molten glory shrined,   45
    That rays off into the gloom!
    But thy smile is bright and bleak
    Like cold waves – I cannot speak,
    I sob in it, and grow weak.

8

Ghostly mother, keep aloof   50
    One hour longer from my soul –
For I still am thinking of
    Earth's warm-beating joy and dole!
    On my finger is a ring
    Which I still see glittering,   55
    When the night hides everything

9

Little sister, thou art pale!
    Ah, I have a wandering brain –
But I lose that fever-bale,

And my thoughts grow calm again.   60
Lean down closer – closer still!
I have words thine ear to fill, –
And would kiss thee at my will.

10

Dear, I heard thee in the spring,
   Thee and Robert – through the trees, –   65
When we all went gathering
   Boughs of May-bloom for the bees.
   Do not start so! think instead
   How the sunshine overhead
   Seemed to trickle through the shade.   70

11

What a day it was, that day!
   Hills and vales did openly
Seem to heave and throb away
   At the sight of the great sky;
   And the Silence, as it stood   75
   In the Glory's golden flood,
   Audibly did bud – and bud.

12

Through the winding hedgerows green,
   How we wandered, I and you, –
With the bowery tops shut in,   80
   And the gates that showed the view!
   How we talked there! thrushes soft
   Sang our praises out – or oft
   Bleatings took them from the croft:

13

Till the pleasure grown too strong   85
   Left me muter evermore,
And, the winding road being long,
   I walked out of sight, before,
   And so, wrapt in musings fond,
   Issued (past the wayside pond)   90
   On the meadow-lands beyond.

14

I sat down beneath the beech
   Which leans over to the lane,
And the far sound of your speech
   Did not promise any pain;   95
   And I blessed you full and free,
   With a smile stooped tenderly
   O'er the May-flowers on my knee.

15

But the sound grew into word
   As the speakers drew more near –   100
Sweet, forgive me that I heard
   What you wished me not to hear.
   Do not weep so – do not shake –
   Oh, – I heard thee, Bertha, make
   Good true answers for my sake.   105

16

Yes, and HE too! let him stand
   In thy thoughts, untouched by blame.
Could he help it, if my hand
   He had claimed with hasty claim?
   That was wrong perhaps – but then   110
   Such things be – and will, again.
   Women cannot judge for men.

17

Had he seen thee, when he swore
   He would love but me alone?
Thou wert absent – sent before   115
   To our kin in Sidmouth town.
   When he saw thee who art best
   Past compare, and loveliest,
   He but judged thee as the rest.

18

Could we blame him with grave words,   120
   Thou and I, Dear, if we might?
Thy brown eyes have looks like birds,

Flying straightway to the light:
Mine are older. – Hush! – look out –
Up the street! Is none without? 125
How the poplar swings about.

19

And that hour – beneath the beech,
When I listened in a dream,
And he said in his deep speech,
That he owed me all *esteem*, – 130
Each word swam in on my brain
With a dim, dilating pain,
Till it burst with that last strain.

20

I fell flooded with a dark,
In the silence of a swoon. 135
When I rose, still cold and stark,
There was night, – I saw the moon.
And the stars, each in its place,
And the May-blooms on the grass,
Seemed to wonder what I was. 140

21

And I walked as if apart
From myself, when I could stand –
And I pitied my own heart,
As if I held it in my hand,
Somewhat coldly, – with a sense 145
Of fulfilled benevolence,
And a 'Poor thing' negligence.

22

And I answered coldly too,
When you met me at the door;
And I only *heard* the dew 150
Dripping from me to the floor;
And the flowers I bade you see
Were too withered for the bee, –
As my life, henceforth, for me.

23

Do not weep so – Dear – heart-warm!　　　　155
　　All was best as it befell:
If I say he did me harm,
　　I speak wild, – I am not well.
　　All his words were kind and good –
　　He esteemed me! Only, blood　　　　160
　　Runs so faint in womanhood!

24

Then I always was too grave, –
　　Like the saddest ballad sung, –
With that look, besides, we have
　　In our faces, who die young.　　　　165
　　I had died, Dear, all the same;
　　Life's long, joyous, jostling game
　　Is too loud for my meek shame.

25

We are so unlike each other,
　　Thou and I, that none could guess　　　　170
We were children of one mother,
　　But for mutual tenderness.
　　Thou art rose-lined from the cold,
　　And meant, verily, to hold
　　Life's pure pleasures manifold.　　　　175

26

I am pale as crocus grows
　　Close beside a rose-tree's root;
Whosoe'er would reach the rose,
　　Treads the crocus underfoot.
　　I, like May-bloom on thorn-tree –　　　　180
　　Thou, like merry summer-bee!
　　Fit, that I be plucked for thee.

27

Yet who plucks me? – no one mourns,
　　I have lived my season out,
And now die of my own thorns　　　　185

Which I could not live without.
Sweet, be merry! How the light
Comes and goes! If it be night,
Keep the candles in my sight.

28

Are there footsteps at the door?   190
    Look out quickly. Yea, or nay?
Some one might be waiting for
    Some last word that I might say.
    Nay? So best! – so angels would
    Stand off clear from deathly road,   195
    Not to cross the sight of God.

29

Colder grow my hands and feet.
    When I wear the shroud I made,
Let the folds lie straight and neat,
    And the rosemary be spread,   200
    That if any friend should come
    (To see *thee*, Sweet!) all the room
    May be lifted out of gloom.

30

And, dear Bertha, let me keep
    On my hand this little ring,   205
Which at nights, when others sleep,
    I can still see glittering:
    Let me wear it out of sight,
    In the grave, – where it will light
    All the dark up, day and night.   210

31

On that grave, drop not a tear!
    Else, though fathom-deep the place,
Through the woollen shroud I wear
    I shall feel it on my face.
    Rather smile there, blessèd one,   215
    Thinking of me in the sun,
    Or forget me – smiling on!

32

Art thou near me? nearer! so!
    Kiss me close upon the eyes,
That the earthly light may go   220
    Sweetly, as it used to rise,
    When I watched the morning-grey
    Strike, betwixt the hills, the way
    He was sure to come that day.

33

So, – no more vain words be said! –   225
    The hosannas nearer roll.
Mother, smile now on thy Dead,
    I am death-strong in my soul.
    Mystic Dove alit on cross,
    Guide the poor bird of the snows   230
    Through the snow-wind above loss!

34

Jesus, Victim, comprehending
    Love's divine self-abnegation,
Cleanse my love in its self-spending,
    And absorb the poor libation!   235
    Wind my thread of life up higher,
    Up, through angels' hands of fire! –
    I aspire while I expire.

That Day

I stand by the river where both of us stood,
And there is but one shadow to darken the flood;
And the path leading to it, where both used to pass,
Has the step but of one, to take dew from the grass, –
One forlorn since that day.

2

The flowers of the margin are many to see;
None stoops at my bidding to pluck them for me.
The bird in the alder sings loudly and long, –
My low sound of weeping disturbs not his song,
As thy vow did that day.

3

I stand by the river – I think of the vow –
Oh, calm as the place is, vow-breaker, be thou!
I leave the flower growing, the bird unreproved; –
Would I trouble *thee* rather than *them*, my beloved,
And my lover that day?

4

Go, be sure of my love – by that treason forgiven;
Of my prayers – by the blessings they win thee from Heaven;
Of my grief – (guess the length of the sword by the sheath's)
By the silence of life, more pathetic than death's!
Go, – be clear of that day!

Loved Once

1

I classed, appraising once,
Earth's lamentable sounds, – the welladay,
   The jarring yea and nay,
The fall of kisses on unanswering clay,
The sobbed farewell, the welcome mournfuller, –   5
   But all did leaven the air
With a less bitter leaven of sure despair
   Than these words – 'I loved ONCE.'

2

And who saith 'I loved ONCE'?
Not angels, – whose clear eyes, love, love foresee,   10
   Love, through eternity,
And by To Love do apprehend To Be.
Not God, called LOVE, His noble crown-name, casting
   A light too broad for blasting!
The great God changing not from everlasting,   15
   Saith never 'I loved ONCE.'

3

Oh, never is 'Loved ONCE'
Thy word, Thou Victim-Christ, misprizèd friend!
   Thy cross and curse may rend,
But having loved Thou lovest to the end.   20
This is man's saying – man's. Too weak to move
   One spherèd star above,
Man desecrates the eternal God-word Love
   By his No More, and Once.

4

How say ye 'We loved once,'   25
Blasphemers? Is your earth not cold enow,
   Mourners, without that snow?
Ah, friends! and would ye wrong each other so?
And could ye say of some whose love is known,
   Whose prayers have met your own,   30
Whose tears have fallen for you, whose smiles have shone
   So long, – 'We loved them ONCE'?

5

Could ye 'We loved her once'
Say calm of me, sweet friends, when out of sight?
  When hearts of better right   35
Stand in between me and your happy light?
Or when, as flowers kept too long in the shade,
  Ye find my colours fade,
And all that is not love in me, decayed?
  Such words – Ye loved me ONCE!   40

6

Could ye 'We loved her once'
Say cold of me when further put away
  In earth's sepulchral clay, –
When mute the lips which deprecate today?
Not so! not then – least then. When life is shriven,   45
  And death's full joy is given, –
Of those who sit and love you up in heaven,
  Say not 'We loved them once.'

7

Say never, ye loved ONCE.
God is too near above, the grave, beneath,   50
  And all our moments breathe
Too quick in mysteries of life and death,
For such a word. The eternities avenge
  Affections light of range.
There comes no change to justify that change,   55
  Whatever comes – Loved ONCE!

8

And yet that same word ONCE
Is humanly acceptive. Kings have said,
  Shaking a discrowned head,
'We ruled once,' – dotards, 'We once taught and led.'   60
Cripples once danced i' the vines – and bards approved
  Were once by scornings moved:
But love strikes one hour – LOVE! those *never* loved
  Who dream that they loved ONCE.

A Rhapsody of Life's Progress

Fill all the stops of life with tuneful breath.

CORNELIUS MATHEWS, *Poems of Man*

1

We are borne into life – it is sweet, it is strange.
We lie still on the knee of a mild Mystery,
    Which smiles with a change!
But we doubt not of changes, we know not of spaces,
The Heavens seem as near as our own mother's face is,   5
And we think we could touch all the stars that we see;
And the milk of our mother is white on our mouth;
And, with small childish hands, we are turning around
The apple of Life which another has found;
It is warm with our touch, not with sun of the south,   10
And we count, as we turn it, the red side for four.
    O Life, O Beyond,
      Thou art sweet, thou art strange evermore!

2

Then all things look strange in the pure golden ether:
We walk through the gardens with hands linked together,   15
    And the lilies look large as the trees;
And as loud as the birds sing the bloom-loving bees,
And the birds sing like angels, so mystical-fine,
And the cedars are brushing the archangels' feet,
And time is eternity, love is divine,   20
    And the world is complete.
Now, God bless the child, – father, mother, respond!
    O Life, O Beyond,
      Thou art strange, thou art sweet.

3

Then we leap on the earth with the armour of youth,   25
    And the earth rings again,
And we breathe out, 'O beauty', – we cry out, 'O truth,'
And the bloom of our lips drops with wine,
And our blood runs amazed 'neath the calm hyaline,
The earth cleaves to the foot, the sun burns to the brain, –   30

What is this exultation? and what this despair? –
The strong pleasure is smiting the nerves into pain,
And we drop from the Fair as we climb to the Fair,
   And we lie in a trance at its feet;
And the breath of an angel cold-piercing the air   35
   Breathes fresh on our faces in swoon,
And we think him so near he is this side the sun,
And we wake to a whisper self-murmured and fond,
       O Life, O Beyond,
      Thou art strange, thou art sweet!   40

4

And the winds and the waters in pastoral measures
Go winding around us, with roll upon roll,
Till the soul lies within in a circle of pleasures
   Which hideth the soul.
And we run with the stag, and we leap with the horse,   45
And we swim with the fish through the broad water-course,
And we strike with the falcon, and hunt with the hound,
And the joy which is in us flies out by a wound.
And we shout so aloud, 'We exult, we rejoice,'
That we lose the low moan of our brothers around;   50
And we shout so adeep down creation's profound,
   We are deaf to God's voice.
And we bind the rose-garland on forehead and ears
   Yet we are not ashamed,
And the dew of the roses that runneth unblamed   55
  Down our cheeks, is not taken for tears.
Help us, God, trust us, man! love us, woman! 'I hold
Thy small head in my hands, – with its grapelets of gold
Growing bright through my fingers, – like altar for oath,
'Neath the vast golden spaces like witnessing faces   60
That watch the eternity strong in the troth –
   I love thee, I leave thee,
   Live for thee, die for thee!
   I prove thee, deceive thee,
   Undo evermore thee!   65
Help me, God! slay me, man! – one is mourning for both.'
And we stand up, though young, near the funeral-sheet
Which covers the Caesar and old Pharamond,

And death is so nigh us, life cools from its heat.
  O Life, O Beyond,   70
  Art thou fair, – *art* thou sweet?

5

Then we act to a purpose – we spring up erect:
We will tame the wild mouths of the wilderness-steeds,
We will plough up the deep in the ships double-decked,
We will build the great cities, and do the great deeds,   75
Strike the steel upon steel, strike the soul upon soul,
Strike the dole on the weal, overcoming the dole,
Let the cloud meet the cloud in a grand thunder-roll!
'While the eagle of Thought rides the tempest in scorn,
Who cares if the lightning is burning the corn?   80
  Let us sit on the thrones
   In a purple sublimity,
  And grind down men's bones
   To a pale unanimity.
Speed me, God! – serve me, man! – I am god over men;   85
When I speak in my cloud, none shall answer again,
  'Neath the stripe and the bond,
   Lie and mourn at my feet!' –
  O Life, O Beyond,
   Thou art strange, thou art sweet!   90

6

Then we grow into thought, – and with inward ascensions
  Touch the bounds of our Being.
We lie in the dark here, swathed doubly around
With our sensual relations and social conventions,
Yet are 'ware of a sight, yet are 'ware of a sound   95
  Beyond Hearing and Seeing, –
Are aware that a Hades rolls deep on all sides
  With its infinite tides
About and above us, – until the strong arch
Of our life creaks and bends as if ready for falling,   100
And through the dim rolling we hear the sweet calling
Of spirits that speak in a soft under-tongue
  The sense of the mystical march.
And we cry to them softly, 'Come nearer, come nearer,

And lift up the lap of this Dark, and speak clearer, 105
    And teach us the song that ye sung!'
And we smile in our thought if they answer or no,
For to dream of a sweetness is sweet as to know.
    Wonders breathe in our face
      And we ask not their name; 110
    Love takes all the blame
Of the world's prison-place.
And we sing back the songs as we guess them, aloud;
And we send up the lark of our music that cuts
    Untired through the cloud, 115
To beat with its wings at the lattice Heaven shuts;
Yet the angels look down and the mortals look up
    As the little wings beat,
And the poet is blessed with their pity or hope.
'Twixt the heavens and the earth *can* a poet despond? 120
      O Life, O Beyond,
    Thou art strange, thou art sweet!

7

Then we wring from our souls their applicative strength,
And bend to the cord the strong bow of our ken,
And bringing our lives to the level of others 125
Hold the cup we have filled, to their uses at length.
'Help me, God! love me, man! I am man among men,
    And my life is a pledge
    Of the ease of another's!'
From the fire and the water we drive out the steam 130
With a rush and a roar and the speed of a dream;
And the car without horses, the car without wings,
    Roars onward and flies
    On its grey iron edge,
'Neath the heat of a Thought sitting still in our eyes: 135
And our hand knots in air, with the bridge that it flings,
Two peaks far disrupted by ocean and skies,
And, lifting a fold of the smooth-flowing Thames,
Draws under the world with its turmoils and pothers,
While the swans float on softly, untouched in their calms 140
By humanity's hum at the root of the springs.
And with reachings of Thought we reach down to the deeps

Of the souls of our brothers, –
We teach them full words with our slow-moving lips,
'God,' 'Liberty,' 'Truth,' – which they hearken and think   145
And work into harmony, link upon link,
Till the silver meets round the earth gelid and dense,
Shedding sparks of electric responding intense
  On the dark of eclipse.
Then we hear through the silence and glory afar,   150
  As from shores of a star
In aphelion, the new generations that cry
Disenthralled by our voice to harmonious reply,
  'God,' 'Liberty', 'Truth!'
  We are glorious forsooth –   155
  And our name has a seat,
 Though the shroud should be donned.
   O Life, O Beyond,
 Thou art strange, thou art sweet!

8

Help me, God – help me, man! I am low, I am weak –   160
Death loosens my sinews and creeps in my veins:
My body is cleft by these wedges of pains
  From my spirit's serene,
And I feel the externe and insensate creep in
  On my organised clay.   165
  I sob not, nor shriek,
  Yet I faint fast away!
I am strong in the spirit, – deep-thoughted, clear-eyed, –
I could walk, step for step, with an angel beside,
  On the heaven-heights of truth.   170
  Oh, the soul keeps its youth,
But the body faints sore, it is tired in the race,
It sinks from the chariot ere reaching the goal,
  It is weak, it is cold,
  The rein drops from its hold –   175
It sinks back, with the death in its face.
  On, chariot – on, soul,
  Ye are all the more fleet –
  Be alone at the goal
 Of the strange and the sweet!   180

9

Love us, God, love us, man! we believe, we achieve –
    Let us love, let us live,
    For the acts correspond;
    We are glorious – and DIE!
And again on the knee of a mild Mystery   185
    That smiles with a change,
      Here we lie.
      O DEATH, O BEYOND,
    Thou art sweet, thou art strange!

L. E. L.'s Last Question [56]

Do you think of me as I think of you?
From her poem written during
the voyage to the Cape

1

'Do you think of me as I think of you,
My friends, my friends?' – She said it from the sea,
The English minstrel in her minstrelsy,
While, under brighter skies than erst she knew,
Her heart grew dark, and groped there as the blind,   5
To reach across the waves friends left behind –
'Do you think of me as I think of you?'

2

It seemed not much to ask – as *I* of *you*?
We all do ask the same. No eyelids cover
Within the meekest eyes, that question over.   10
And little in the world the Loving do
But sit (among the rocks?) and listen for
The echo of their own love evermore –
'Do you think of me as I think of you?'

3

Love-learnèd she had sung of love and love, –   15
And like a child that, sleeping with dropt head
Upon the fairy-book he lately read,
Whatever household noises round him move,
Hears in his dream some elfin turbulence, –
Even so, suggestive to her inward sense,   20
All sounds of life assumed one tune of love.

4

And when the glory of her dream withdrew,
When knightly gestes and courtly pageantries
Were broken in her visionary eyes
By tears the solemn seas attested true. –   25
Forgetting that sweet lute beside her hand
She asked not, – 'Do you praise me, O my land?' –
But, 'Think ye of me, friends, as I of you?'

5

Hers was the hand that played for many a year
Love's silver phrase for England, – smooth and well.   30
Would God, her heart's more inward oracle
In that lone moment might confirm her dear!
For when her questioned friends in agony
Made passionate response, 'We think of thee,'
Her place was in the dust, too deep to hear.   35

6

Could she not wait to catch their answering breath?
Was she content, content, with ocean's sound,
Which dashed its mocking infinite around
One thirsty for a little love? – beneath
Those stars content, where last her song had gone, –   40
They mute and cold in radiant life, – as soon
Their singer was to be, in darksome death?

7

Bring your vain answers – cry, 'We think of thee!'
How think ye of her? warm in long ago
Delights? – or crowned with budding bays? Not so.   45
None smile and none are crowned where lieth she,
With all her visions unfulfilled save one,
Her childhood's – of the palm-trees in the sun –
And lo! their shadow on her sepulchre!

8

'Do ye think of me as I think of you?' –   50
O friends, O kindred, O dear brotherhood
Of all the world! what are we, that we should
For covenants of long affection sue?
Why press so near each other when the touch
Is barred by graves? Not much, and yet too much,   55
Is this 'Think of me as I think of you.'

9

But while on mortal lips I shape anew
A sigh to mortal issues, – verily
Above the unshaken stars that see us die,
A vocal pathos rolls; and HE who drew   60
All life from dust, and for all, tasted death,
By death and life and love, appealing, saith,
Do you think of Me as I think of you?

The House of Clouds

1

I would build a cloudy House
    For my thoughts to live in,
When for earth too fancy-loose,
    And too low for heaven.
Hush! I talk my dream aloud;   5
    I build it bright to see, –
I build it on the moonlit cloud
    To which I looked with *thee*.

2

Cloud-walls of the morning's grey,
    Faced with amber column,   10
Crowned with crimson cupola
    From a sunset solemn:
May-mists, for the casements, fetch,
    Pale and glimmering,
With a sunbeam hid in each,   15
    And a smell of spring.

3

Build the entrance high and proud,
    Darkening and then brightening,
Of a riven thunder-cloud,
    Veinèd by the lightning: 20

Use one with an iris-stain
    For the door within,
Turning to a sound like rain
    As I enter in.

4

Build a spacious hall thereby,   25
    Boldly, never fearing;
Use the blue place of the sky
    Which the wind is clearing;
Branched with corridors sublime,
    Flecked with winding stairs,   30
Such as children wish to climb,
    Following their own prayers.

5

In the mutest of the house,
    I will have my chamber:
Silence at the door shall use   35
    Evening's light of amber;
Solemnising every mood,
    Softening in degree,
Turning sadness into good
    As I turn the key.   40

6

Be my chamber tapestried
    With the showers of summer,
Close, but soundless, – glorified
    When the sunbeams come here;
Wandering harpers, harping on   45
    Waters stringed for such,
Drawing colour, for a tune,
    With a vibrant touch.

7

Bring a shadow green and still
    From the chestnu forest,   50
Bring a purple from the hill,
    When the heat is sorest;

Spread them out from wall to wall,
   Carpet-wove around,
Whereupon the foot shall fall   55
   In light instead of sound.

8

Bring fantastic cloudlets home
   From the noontide zenith,
Ranged for sculptures round the room,
   Named as Fancy weeneth.   60
Some be Junos, without eyes,
   Naiads, without sources;
Some be birds of paradise,
   Some, Olympian horses.

9

Bring the dews the birds shake off,   65
   Waking in the hedges, –
Those too, perfumed, for a proof,
   From the lilies' edges;
From our England's field and moor,
   Bring them calm and white in,   70
Whence to form a mirror pure
   For Love's self-delighting.

10

Bring a grey cloud from the east
   Where the lark is singing
(Something of the song at least   75
   Unlost in the bringing):
That shall be a morning-chair
   Poet-dream may sit in,
When it leans out on the air,
   Unrimed and unwritten.   80

11

Bring the red cloud from the sun!
   While he sinketh, catch it:
That shall be a couch, – with one
   Sidelong star to watch it, –

Fit for Poet's finest thought 85
    At the curfew-sounding;
Things unseen being nearer brought
    Than the seen, around him.

12

Poet's thought, – not poet's sigh.
    'Las, they come together! 90
Cloudy walls divide and fly,
    As in April weather!
Cupola and column proud,
    Structure bright to see,
Gone! except that moonlit cloud 95
    To which I looked with *thee*.

13

Let them. Wipe such visionings
    From the fancy's cartel:
Love secures some fairer things,
    Dowered with his immortal. 100
The sun may darken, heaven be bowed,
    But still unchanged shall be, –
Here, in my soul, – that moonlit cloud,
    To which I looked with THEE!

Catarina to Camoëns[57]

DYING IN HIS ABSENCE ABROAD,
AND REFERRING TO THE
POEM IN WHICH HE RECORDED
THE SWEETNESS OF HER EYES

1

On the door you will not enter,
  I have gazed too long – adieu!
Hope withdraws her peradventure –
  Death is near me, – and not *you*.
      Come, O lover,   5
      Close and cover
These poor eyes, you called, I ween,
'Sweetest eyes, were ever seen.'

2

When I heard you sing that burden
  In my vernal days and bowers,   10
Other praises disregarding,
  I but hearkened that of yours –
      Only saying
      In heart-playing,
'Blessed eyes mine eyes have been,   15
If the sweetest, HIS have seen!'

3

But all changes. At this vesper,
  Cold the sun shines down the door.
If you stood there, would you whisper
  'Love, I love you,' as before, –   20
      Death pervading
      Now, and shading
Eyes you sang of, that yestreen,
As the sweetest ever seen?

4

Yes, I think, were you beside them,   25
   Near the bed I die upon, –
Though their beauty you denied them,
   As you stood there, looking down,
      You would truly
      Call them duly,   30
For the love's sake found therein, –
'Sweetest eyes, were ever seen.'

5

And if *you* looked down upon them,
   And if *they* looked up to *you*,
All the light which has foregone them   35
   Would be gathered back anew.
      They would truly
      Be as duly
Love-transformed to beauty's sheen, –
'Sweetest eyes, were ever seen.'   40

6

But, ah me! you only see me,
   In your thoughts of loving man,
Smiling soft perhaps and dreamy
   Through the wavings of my fan, –
      And unweeting   45
      Go repeating,
In your reverie serene,
'Sweetest eyes, were ever seen.'

7

While my spirit leans and reaches
   From my body still and pale,   50
Fain to hear what tender speech is
   In your love to help my bale –
      O my poet,
      Come and show it!
Come, of latest love, to glean   55
'Sweetest eyes, were ever seen.'

8

O my poet, O my prophet,
   When you praised their sweetness so,
Did you think, in singing of it,
   That it might be near to go?   60
      Had you fancies
      From their glances,
That the grave would quickly screen
'Sweetest eyes, were ever seen'?

9

No reply! The fountain's warble   65
   In the courtyard sounds alone.
As the water to the marble
   So my heart falls with a moan
      From love-sighing
      To this dying.   70
Death forerunneth Love to win
'Sweetest eyes, were ever seen.'

10

Will you come? When I'm departed
   Where all sweetnesses are hid;
Where thy voice, my tender-hearted,   75
   Will not lift up either lid.
      Cry, O lover,
      Love is over!
Cry beneath the cypress green –
'Sweetest eyes, were ever seen.'   80

11

When the angelus is ringing,
   Near the convent will you walk,
And recall the choral singing
   Which brought angels down our talk?
      Spirit-shriven   85
      I viewed Heaven,
Till you smiled – 'Is earth unclean,
Sweetest eyes, were ever seen?'

12

When beneath the palace-lattice,
   You ride slow as you have done,   90
And you see a face there – that is
   Not the old familiar one, –
      Will you oftly
      Murmur softly,
'Here, ye watched me morn and e'en,   95
Sweetest eyes, were ever seen'?

13

When the palace-ladies, sitting
   Round your gittern, shall have said,
'Poet, sing those verses written
   For the lady who is dead,'   100
      Will you tremble,
      Yet dissemble, –
Or sing hoarse, with tears between,
'Sweetest eyes, were ever seen'?

14

'Sweetest eyes!' how sweet in flowings   105
   The repeated cadence is!
Though you sang a hundred poems,
   Still the best one would be this.
      I can hear it
      'Twixt my spirit   110
And the earth-noise intervene –
'Sweetest eyes, were ever seen!'

15

But the priest waits for the praying,
   And the choir are on their knees,
And the soul must pass away in   115
   Strains more solemn high than these.
      Miserere
      For the weary!
Oh, no longer for Catrine,
'Sweetest eyes, were ever seen!'   120

16

Keep my ribbon, take and keep it
   (I have loosed it from my hair),*
Feeling, while you overweep it,
   Not alone in your despair,
      Since with saintly   125
      Watch unfaintly
Out of heaven shall o'er you lean
'Sweetest eyes, were ever seen.'

17

But – but *now* – yet unremovèd
   Up to Heaven, they glisten fast.   130
You may cast away, Belovèd,
   In your future all my past.
      Such old phrases
      May be praises
For some fairer bosom-queen –   135
'Sweetest eyes, were ever seen!'

18

Eyes of mine, what are ye doing?
   Faithless, faithless, – praised amiss
If a tear be of your showing,
   Dropt for any hope of HIS!   140
      Death has boldness
      Besides coldness,
If unworthy tears demean
'Sweetest eyes, were ever seen.'

19

I will look out to his future;   145
   I will bless it till it shine.
Should he ever be a suitor
   Unto sweeter eyes than mine,
      Sunshine gild them,
      Angels shield them,   150
Whatsoever eyes terrene
Be the sweetest HIS have seen!

---

* She left him the ribbon from her hair.

A Portrait

'One name is Elizabeth.'

– BEN JONSON

I will paint her as I see her.
   Ten times have the lilies blown,
   Since she looked upon the sun.

And her face is lily-clear,
   Lily-shaped, and dropped in duty   5
   To the law of its own beauty.

Oval cheeks encoloured faintly,
   Which a trail of golden hair
   Keeps from fading off to air:

And a forehead fair and saintly,   10
   Which two blue eyes undershine,
   Like meek prayers before a shrine.

Face and figure of a child, –
   Though too calm, you think, and tender,
   For the childhood you would lend her.   15

Yet child-simple, undefiled,
   Frank, obedient, – waiting still
   On the turnings of your will.

Moving light, as all young things,
   As young birds, or early wheat,   20
   When the wind blows over it.

Only, free from flutterings
   Of loud mirth that scorneth measure –
   Taking love for her chief pleasure.

Choosing pleasures, for the rest,   25
   Which come softly – just as she,
   When she nestles at your knee.

Quiet talk she liketh best,
  In a bower of gentle looks, –
  Watering flowers, or reading books.   30

And her voice, it murmurs lowly,
  As a silver stream may run,
  Which yet feels, you feel, the sun.

And her smile, it seems half holy,
  As if drawn from thoughts more far   35
  Than our common jestings are.

And if any poet knew her,
  He would sing of her with falls
  Used in lovely madrigals.

And if any painter drew her,   40
  He would paint her unaware
  With a halo round the hair.

And if reader read the poem,
  He would whisper – 'You have done a
  Consecrated little Una.'[58]   45

And a dreamer (did you show him
  That same picture) would exclaim,
  ' 'Tis my angel, with a name!'

And a stranger, when he sees her
  In the street even – smileth stilly,   50
  Just as you would at a lily.

And all voices that address her,
  Soften, sleeken every word,
  As if speaking to a bird.

And all fancies yearn to cover   55
  The hard earth whereon she passes,
  With the thymy scented grasses.

And all hearts do pray – 'God love her!'
  Aye, and always, in good sooth,
  We may all be sure HE DOTH.   60

Sleeping and Watching

1

Sleep on, baby, on the floor,
  Tired of all the playing!
Sleep with smile the sweeter for
  That, you dropped away in!
On your curls' full roundness, stand   5
  Golden lights serenely;
One cheek, pushed out by the hand,
  Folds the dimple inly.
Little head and little foot
  Heavy laid for pleasure,   10
Underneath the lids half shut,
  Slants the shining azure. –
Open-soul in noonday sun,
  So, you lie and slumber!
Nothing evil having done,   15
  Nothing can encumber.

2

I, who cannot sleep as well,
  Shall I sigh to view you?
Or sigh further to foretell
  All that may undo you?   20
Nay, keep smiling, little child,
  Ere the sorrow neareth:
I will smile too! patience mild
  Pleasure's token weareth.
Nay, keep sleeping before loss: 25
  I shall sleep though losing!
As by cradle, so by cross,
  Sure is the reposing.

3

And God knows who sees us twain,
  Child at childish leisure,   30
I am near as tired of pain
  As you seem of pleasure.

Very soon too, by His grace
   Gently wrapt around me,
Shall I show as calm a face,   35
   Shall I sleep as soundly.
Differing in this, that you
   Clasp your playthings, sleeping,
While my hand shall drop the few
   Given to my keeping: 40
Differing in this, that I
   Sleeping shall be colder,
And in waking presently,
   Brighter to beholder:
Differing in this beside   45
   (Sleeper, have you heard me?
Do you move, and open wide
   Eyes of wonder toward me?) –
That while you, I thus recall
   From your sleep, I solely,   50
Me from mine an angel shall,
   With reveillie holy,

Wine of Cyprus

GIVEN TO ME BY H. S. BOYD,[59]
AUTHOR OF 'SELECT PASSAGES
FROM THE GREEK FATHERS,' ETC.,
TO WHOM THESE STANZAS
ARE ADDRESSED

1

If old Bacchus [60] were the speaker
   He would tell you with a sigh,
Of the Cyprus in this beaker
   I am sipping like a fly, –
Like a fly or gnat on Ida   5
   At the hour of goblet-pledge,
By queen Juno [61] brushed aside, a
   Full white arm-sweep, from the edge.

2

Sooth, the drinking should be ampler
   When the drink is so divine,   10
And some deep-mouthed Greek exampler
   Would become your Cyprus wine:
Cyclops' [62] mouth might plunge aright in,
   While his one eye over-leered –
Nor too large were mouth of Titan,   15
   Drinking rivers down his beard.

3

Pan might dip his head so deep in
   That his ears alone pricked out,
Fauns around him, pressing, leaping,
   Each one pointing to his throat: 20
While the Naiads, like Bacchantes,[63]
   Wild, with urns thrown out to waste,
Cry, 'O earth, that thou wouldst grant us
   Springs to keep, of such a taste!'

4

But for me, I am not worthy   25
   After gods and Greeks to drink,
And my lips are pale and earthy
   To go bathing from this brink:
Since you heard them speak the last time
   They have faded from their blooms,   30
And the laughter of my pastime
   Has learnt silence at the tombs.

5

Ah, my friend! the antique drinkers
   Crowned the cup and crowned the brow.
Can I answer the old thinkers   35
   In the forms they thought of, now?
Who will fetch from garden-closes
   Some new garlands while I speak,
That the forehead, crowned with roses,
   May strike scarlet down the cheek?   40

6

Do not mock me! with my mortal
   Suits no wreath again, indeed!
I am sad-voiced as the turtle
   Which Anacreon[64] used to feed:
Yet as that same bird demurely   45
   Wet her beak in cup of his,
So, without a garland, surely
   I may touch the brim of this.

7

Go, – let others praise the Chian![65] –
   This is soft as Muses' string,   50
This is tawny as Rhea's lion,
   This is rapid as his spring,
Bright as Paphia's[66] eyes e'er met us,
   Light as ever trod her feet!
And the brown bees of Hymettus[67]   55
   Make their honey not so sweet.

8

Very copious are my praises,
    Though I sip it like a fly! –
Ah – but, sipping, – times and places
    Change before me suddenly: 60
As Ulysses'[68] old libation
    Drew the ghosts from every part,
So your Cyprus wine, dear Grecian,
    Stirs the Hades of my heart.

9

And I think of those long mornings   65
    Which my thought goes far to seek,
When, betwixt the folio's turnings,
    Solemn flowed the rhythmic Greek:
Past the pane the mountain spreading,
    Swept the sheep-bell's tinkling noise,   70
While a girlish voice was reading,
    Somewhat low for αι's and οι's.

10

Then, what golden hours were for us! –
    While we sat together there,
How the white vests of the chorus   75
    Seemed to wave up a live air!
How the cothurns trod majestic
    Down the deep iambic lines,
And the rolling anapaestic
    Curled like vapour over shrines!   80

11

Oh, our Aeschylus, the thunderous!
    How he drove the bolted breath
Through the cloud, to wedge it ponderous
    In the gnarlèd oak beneath.
Oh, our Sophocles, the royal,   85
    Who was born to monarch's place,
And who made the whole world loyal,
    Less by kingly power than grace.

12

Our Euripides, the human,
    With his droppings of warm tears,   90
And his touches of things common
    Till they rose to touch the spheres!
Our Theocritus, our Bion,[69]
    And our Pindar's shining goals! –
These were cup-bearers undying,   95
    Of the wine that's meant for souls:

13

And my Plato, the divine one,
    If men know the gods aright
By their motions as they shine on
    With a glorious trail of light! –   100
And your noble Christian bishops,
    Who mouthed grandly the last Greek!
Though the sponges on their hyssops
    Were distent with wine – too weak.

14

Yet, your Chrysostom,[70] you praised him   105
    As a liberal mouth of gold;
And your Basil,[71] you upraised him
    To the height of speakers old.
And we both praised Heliodorus [72]
    For his secret of pure lies, –   110
Who forged first his linkèd stories
    In the heat of lady's eyes.

15

And we both praised your Synesius [73]
    For the fire shot up his odes,
Though the Church was scarce propitious   115
    As he whistled dogs and gods.
And we both praised Nazianzen [74]
    For the fervid heart and speech:
Only I eschewed his glancing
    At the lyre hung out of reach.   120

16

Do you mind that deed of Atè [75]
    Which you bound me to so fast, –
Reading 'De Virginitate,' [76]
    From the first line to the last?
How I said at ending, solemn,   125
    As I turned and looked at you,
That Saint Simeon [77] on the column
    Had had somewhat less to do?

17

For we sometimes gently wrangled,
    Very gently, be it said,   130
Since our thoughts were disentangled
    By no breaking of the thread!
And I charged you with extortions
    On the nobler fames of old –
Aye, and sometimes thought your Porsons   135
    Stained the purple they would fold.

18

For the rest – a mystic moaning
    Kept Cassandra [78] at the gate,
With wild eyes the vision shone in,
    And wide nostrils scenting fate.   140
And Prometheus, [79] bound in passion
    By brute Force to the blind stone,
Showed us looks of invocation
    Turned to ocean and the sun.

19

And Medea [80] we saw burning   145
    At her nature's planted stake:
And proud Oedipus fate-scorning
    While the cloud came on to break –
While the cloud came on slow – slower,
    Till he stood discrowned, resigned! –   150
But the reader's voice dropped lower
    When the poet called him BLIND.

20

Ah, my gossip! you were older,
    And more learned, and a man! –
Yet that shadow, the enfolder   155
    Of your quiet eyelids, ran
Both our spirits to one level,
    And I turned from hill and lea
And the summer-sun's green revel,
    To your eyes that could not see.   160

21

Now Christ bless you with the one light
    Which goes shining night and day!
May the flowers which grow in sunlight
    Shed their fragrance in your way!
Is it not right to remember   165
    All your kindness, friend of mine,
When we two sat in the chamber,
    And the poets poured us wine?

22

So, to come back to the drinking
    Of this Cyprus, – it is well,   170
But those memories, to my thinking,
    Make a better oenomel;
And whoever be the speaker,
    None can murmur with a sigh,
That, in drinking from *that* beaker,   175
    I am sipping like a fly.

The Romance of the Swan's Nest

So the dreams depart,
So the fading phantoms flee,
And the sharp reality
Now must act its part.

WESTWOOD'S Beads from a Rosary

1

Little Ellie sits alone
'Mid the beeches of a meadow,
  By a stream-side on the grass,
  And the trees are showering down
Doubles of their leaves in shadow,   5
  On her shining hair and face.

2

She has thrown her bonnet by,
And her feet she has been dipping
  In the shallow water's flow;
  Now she holds them nakedly   10
In her hands, all sleek and dripping,
  While she rocketh to and fro.

3

Little Ellie sits alone,
And the smile she softly uses
  Fills the silence like a speech,   15
  While she thinks what shall be done, –
And the sweetest pleasure chooses
  For her future within reach.

4

Little Ellie in her smile
Chooses . . . 'I will have a lover,   20
  Riding on a steed of steeds!
  He shall love me without guile,
And to *him* I will discover
  The swan's nest among the reeds.

5

'And the steed shall be red-roan,   25
And the lover shall be noble,
  With an eye that takes the breath;
  And the lute he plays upon,
Shall strike ladies into trouble,
  As his sword strikes men to death.   30

6

'And the steed it shall be shod
All in silver, housed in azure,
  And the mane shall swim the wind;
  And the hoofs along the sod
Shall flash onward and keep measure,   35
  Till the shepherds look behind.

7

'But my lover will not prize
All the glory that he rides in,
  When he gazes in my face.
  He will say, "O Love, thine eyes   40
Build the shrine my soul abides in,
  And I kneel here for thy grace."

8

'Then, aye, then – he shall kneel low,
With the red-roan steed anear him,
  Which shall seem to understand,   45
  Till I answer, "Rise and go!
For the world must love and fear him
  Whom I gift with heart and hand."

9

'Then he will arise so pale,
I shall feel my own lips tremble   50
  With a *yes* I must not say,
  Nathless maiden-brave, "Farewell,"
I will utter, and dissemble –
  "Light tomorrow with today!"

10

'Then he'll ride among the hills   55
To the wide world past the river,
    There to put away all wrong,
    To make straight distorted wills,
And to empty the broad quiver
    Which the wicked bear along.   60

11

'Three times shall a young foot-page
Swim the stream and climb the mountain
    And kneel down beside my feet –
    "Lo, my master sends this gage,
Lady, for thy pity's counting!   65
    What wilt thou exchange for it?"

12

'And the first time, I will send
A white rosebud for a guerdon, –
    And the second time, a glove;
    But the third time – I may bend   70
From my pride, and answer – "Pardon,
    If he comes to take my love."

13

'Then the young foot-page will run –
Then my lover will ride faster,
    Till he kneeleth at my knee: 75
    "I am a duke's eldest son!
Thousand serfs do call me master, –
    But, O Love, I love but *thee*!"

14

'He will kiss me on the mouth
Then, and lead me as a lover   80
    Through the crowds that praise his deeds;
    And, when soul-tied by one troth,
Unto *him* I will discover
    That swan's nest among the reeds.'

15

Little Ellie, with her smile 85
Not yet ended, rose up gaily,
   Tied the bonnet, donned the shoe,
   And went homeward, round a mile,
Just to see, as she did daily,
   What more eggs were with the two. 90

16

Pushing through the elm-tree copse,
Winding up the stream, light-hearted,
   Where the osier pathway leads –
   Past the boughs she stoops – and stops.
Lo, the wild swan had deserted, 95
   And a rat had gnawed the reeds.

17

Ellie went home sad and slow.
If she found the lover ever,
   With his red-roan steed of steeds,
   Sooth I know not! but I know 100
She could never show him – never,
   That swan's nest among the reeds!

Lessons from the Gorse

To win the secret of a weed's plain heart.

LOWELL

1

Mountain gorses, ever-golden,
Cankered not the whole year long!
Do ye teach us to be strong,
Howsoever pricked and holden
Like your thorny blooms, and so   5
Trodden on by rain and snow,
Up the hillside of this life, as bleak as where ye grow?

2

Mountain blossoms, shining blossoms,
Do ye teach us to be glad
When no summer can be had,   10
Blooming in our inward bosoms?
Ye, whom God preserveth still, –
Set as lights upon a hill,
Tokens to the wintry earth that Beauty liveth still!

3

Mountain gorses, do ye teach us   15
From that academic chair,
Canopied with azure air,
That the wisest word man reaches
Is the humblest he can speak?
Ye, who live on mountain peak,   20
Yet live low along the ground, beside the grasses meek!

4

Mountain gorses, since Linnaeus[81]
Knelt beside you on the sod,
For your beauty thanking God, –
For your teaching, ye should see us   25
Bowing in prostration new!
Whence arisen, – if one or two
Drops be on our cheeks – O world, they are not tears but dew.

The Dead Pan [82]

1

Gods of Hellas, gods of Hellas,
Can ye listen in your silence?
Can your mystic voices tell us
Where ye hide? In floating islands,
With a wind that evermore   5
Keeps you out of sight of shore?
                    Pan, Pan is dead.

2

In what revels are ye sunken,
In old Ethiopia?
Have the Pygmies made you drunken,   10
Bathing in mandragora
Your divine pale lips, that shiver
Like the lotus in the river?
                    Pan, Pan is dead.

3

Do ye sit there still in slumber,   15
In gigantic Alpine rows?
The black poppies out of number
Nodding, dripping from your brows
To the red lees of your wine,
And so kept alive and fine?   20
                    Pan, Pan is dead.

4

Or lie crushed your stagnant corses
Where the silver spheres roll on,
Stung to life by centric forces
Thrown like rays out from the sun? –   25
While the smoke of your old altars
Is the shroud that round you welters?
                    Great Pan is dead.

5

'Gods of Hellas, gods of Hellas,
Said the old Hellenic tongue!   30
Said the hero-oaths, as well as
Poets' songs the sweetest sung!
Have ye grown deaf in a day?
Can ye speak not yea or nay –
    Since Pan is dead?   35

6

Do ye leave your rivers flowing
All alone, O Naiades,
While your drenchèd locks dry slow in
This cold feeble sun and breeze? –
Not a word the Naiads say,   40
Though the rivers run for ay.
    For Pan is dead.

7

From the gloaming of the oak-wood,
O ye Dryads, could ye flee?
At the rushing thunderstroke, would   45
No sob tremble through the tree? –
Not a word the Dryads say,
Though the forests wave for ay.
    For Pan is dead.

8

Have ye left the mountain places,   50
Oreads[83] wild, for other tryst?
Shall we see no sudden faces
Strike a glory through the mist?
Not a sound the silence thrills
Of the everlasting hills.   55
    Pan, Pan is dead.

9

O twelve gods of Plato's[84] vision,
Crowned to starry wanderings, –
With your chariots in procession,

And your silver clash of wings!   60
Very pale ye seem to rise,
Ghosts of Grecian deities, –
           Now Pan is dead!

10

Jove, that right hand is unloaded,
Whence the thunder did prevail,   65
While in idiocy of godhead
Thou art staring the stars pale!
And thine eagle, blind and old,
Roughs his feathers in the cold.
           Pan, Pan is dead.   70

11

Where, O Juno, is the glory
Of thy regal look and tread?
Will they lay, for evermore, thee,
On thy dim, straight, golden bed?
Will thy queendom all lie hid   75
Meekly under either lid?
           Pan, Pan is dead.

12

Ha, Apollo![85] floats his golden
Hair all mist-like where he stands,
While the Muses hang enfolding   80
Knee and foot with faint wild hands?
'Neath the clanging of thy bow,
Niobe looked lost as thou!
           Pan, Pan is dead.

13

Shall the casque with its brown iron,   85
Pallas' broad blue eyes, eclipse,
And no hero take inspiring
From the god-Greek of her lips?
'Neath her olive dost thou sit,
Mars the mighty, cursing it?   90
           Pan, Pan is dead.

14

Bacchus, Bacchus! on the panther
He swoons, – bound with his own vines;
And his Maenads slowly saunter,
Head aside, among the pines,   95
While they murmur dreamingly,
'Evohe! – ah – evohe – !
             Ah, Pan is dead!'

15

Neptune[86] lies beside the trident,
Dull and senseless as a stone;   100
And old Pluto[87] deaf and silent
Is cast out into the sun:
Ceres smileth stern thereat,
'We *all* now are desolate –
             Now Pan is dead.'   105

16

Aphrodite! dead and driven
As thy native foam, thou art;
With the cestus long done heaving
On the white calm of thine heart!
Ai Adonis! at that shriek,   110
Not a tear runs down her cheek –
             Pan, Pan is dead.

17

And the Loves, we used to know from
One another, huddled lie,
Frore as taken in a snow-storm,   115
Close beside her tenderly, –
As if each had weakly tried
Once to kiss her as he died.
             Pan, Pan is dead.

18

What, and Hermes?[88] Time enthralleth   120
All thy cunning, Hermes, thus, –
And the ivy blindly crawleth

Round thy brave caduceus?
Hast thou no new message for us,
Full of thunder and Jove-glories?   125
    Nay, Pan is dead.

19

Crownèd Cybele's [89] great turret
Rocks and crumbles on her head;
Roar the lions of her chariot
Toward the wilderness, unfed.   130
Scornful children are not mute, –
'Mother, mother, walk afoot,
    Since Pan is dead.'

20

In the fiery-hearted centre
Of the solemn universe,   135
Ancient Vesta,[90] – who could enter
To consume thee with this curse?
Drop thy grey chin on thy knee,
O thou palsied Mystery!
    For Pan is dead.   140

21

Gods, we vainly do adjure you, –
Ye return nor voice nor sign!
Not a votary could secure you
Even a grave for your Divine!
Not a grave, to show thereby,   145
Here these grey old gods do lie.
    Pan, Pan is dead.

22

Even that Greece who took your wages
Calls the obolus outworn;
And the hoarse deep-throated ages   150
Laugh your godships unto scorn;
And the poets do disclaim you,
Or grow colder if they name you –
    And Pan is dead.

23

Gods bereavèd, gods belated,   155
With your purples rent asunder!
Gods discrowned and desecrated,
Disinherited of thunder!
Now, the goats may climb and crop
The soft grass on Ida's top –   160
    Now, Pan is dead.

24

Calm, of old, the bark went onward,
When a cry more loud than wind
Rose up, deepened, and swept sunward,
From the pilèd Dark behind;   165
And the sun shrank and grew pale,
Breathed against by the great wail –
    'Pan, Pan is dead.'

25

And the rowers from the benches
Fell, – each shuddering on his face –   170
While departing Influences
Struck a cold back through the place;
And the shadow of the ship
Reeled along the passive deep –
    'Pan, Pan is dead.'   175

26

And that dismal cry rose slowly
And sank slowly through the air,
Full of spirit's melancholy
And eternity's despair!
And they heard the words it said –   180
'PAN IS DEAD – GREAT PAN IS DEAD –
    PAN, PAN IS DEAD.'

27

'Twas the hour when One in Sion
Hung for love's sake on a cross;
When His brow was chill with dying,   185

And His soul was faint with loss;
When His priestly blood dropped downward,
And His kingly eyes looked throneward –
       Then, Pan was dead.

28

By the love He stood alone in   190
His sole Godhead rose complete,
And the false gods fell down moaning,
Each from off his golden seat;
All the false gods with a cry
Rendered up their deity –   195
       Pan, Pan was dead.

29

Wailing wide across the islands,
They rent, vest-like, their Divine!
And a darkness and a silence
Quenched the light of every shrine;   200
And Dodona's oak[91] swang lonely
Henceforth, to the tempest only,
       Pan, Pan was dead.

30

Pythia[92] staggered, – feeling o'er her,
Her lost god's forsaking look;   205
Straight her eyeballs filmed with horror,
And her crispy fillets shook,
And her lips gasped through their foam
For a word that did not come.
       Pan, Pan was dead.   210

31

O ye vain false gods of Hellas,
Ye are silent evermore!
And I dash down this old chalice,
Whence libations ran of yore.
See, the wine crawls in the dust   215
Wormlike – as your glories must,
       Since Pan is dead.

32

Get to dust, as common mortals,
By a common doom and track!
Let no Schiller from the portals   220
Of that Hades call you back,
Or instruct us to weep all
At your antique funeral.
                 Pan, Pan is dead.

33

By your beauty, which confesses   225
Some chief Beauty conquering you, –
By our grand heroic guesses,
Through your falsehood, at the True, –
We will weep *not* . . . earth shall roll
Heir to each god's aureole –   230
                 And Pan is dead.

34

Earth outgrows the mythic fancies
Sung beside her in her youth;
And those debonair romances
Sound but dull beside the truth.   235
Phoebus' chariot-course is run:
Look up, poets, to the sun!
                 Pan, Pan is dead.

35

Christ hath sent us down the angels;
And the whole earth and the skies   240
Are illumed by altar-candles
Lit for blessèd mysteries;
And a Priest's hand, through creation,
Waveth calm and consecration –
                 And Pan is dead.   245

36

Truth is fair: should we forgo it?
Can we sigh right for a wrong?
God Himself is the best Poet,
And the Real is His song.
Sing His truth out fair and full,   250
And secure His beautiful.
        Let Pan be dead.

37

Truth is large. Our aspiration
Scarce embraces half we be:
Shame, to stand in His creation,   255
And doubt truth's sufficiency! –
To think God's song unexcelling
The poor tales of our own telling –
        When Pan is dead.

38

What is true and just and honest,   260
What is lovely, what is pure –
All of praise that hath admonisht,
All of virtue, shall endure, –
These are themes for poets' uses,
Stirring nobler than the Muses,   265
        Ere Pan was dead.

39

O brave poets, keep back nothing,
Nor mix falsehood with the whole:
Look up Godward; speak the truth in
Worthy song from earnest soul!   270
Hold, in high poetic duty,
Truest Truth the fairest Beauty.
        Pan, Pan is dead.

Poems
published in 1850

The Runaway Slave at Pilgrim's Point [93, 94]

1

I stand on the mark beside the shore
  Of the first white pilgrim's bended knee,
Where exile turned to ancestor,
  And God was thanked for liberty;
I have run through the night, my skin is as dark,   5
I bend my knee down on this mark . . .
  I look on the sky and the sea.

2

O pilgrim-souls, I speak to you!
  I see you come out proud and slow
From the land of the spirits pale as dew,   10
  And round me and round me ye go!
O pilgrims, I have gasped and run
All night long from the whips of one
  Who in your names works sin and woe.

3

And thus I thought that I would come   15
  And kneel here where ye knelt before,
And feel your souls around me hum
  In undertone to the ocean's roar;
And lift my black face, my black hand,
Here, in your names, to curse this land   20
  Ye blessed in freedom's, evermore.

4

I am black, I am black!
  And yet God made me, they say;
But if He did so, smiling back
  He must have cast His work away   25
Under the feet of His white creatures,
With a look of scorn, – that the dusky features
  Might be trodden again to clay.

5

And yet He has made dark things
  To be glad and merry as light: 30
There's a little dark bird sits and sings;
  There's a dark stream ripples out of sight;
And the dark frogs chant in the safe morass,
And the sweetest stars are made to pass
  O'er the face of the darkest night.   35

6

But *we* who are dark, we are dark!
  Ah God, we have no stars!
About our souls in care and cark
  Our blackness shuts like prison-bars;
The poor souls crouch so far behind   40
That never a comfort can they find
  By reaching through the prison-bars.

7

Indeed we live beneath the sky,
  That great smooth Hand of God stretched out
On all His children fatherly,   45
  To save them from the dread and doubt
Which would be, if, from this low place,
All opened straight up to His face
  Into the grand eternity.

8

And still God's sunshine and His frost,
  They make us hot, they make us cold,   50
As if we were not black and lost:
  And the beasts and birds, in wood and fold,
Do fear and take us for very men!
Could the whip-poor-will or the cat of the glen   . 55
  Look into my eyes and be bold?

9

I am black, I am black! –
  But, once, I laughed in girlish glee,
For one of my colour stood in the track

Where the drivers drove, and looked at me,   60
And tender and full was the look he gave –
Could a slave look so at another slave? –
    I look at the sky and the sea.

10

And from that hour our spirits grew
    As free as if unsold, unbought: 65
Oh, strong enough, since we were two,
    To conquer the world, we thought!
The drivers drove us day by day:
We did not mind, we went one way,
    And no better a freedom sought.   70

11

In the sunny ground between the canes,
    He said 'I love you' as he passed:
When the shingle-roof rang sharp with the rains,
    I heard how he vowed it fast;
While others shook he smiled in the hut,   75
As he carved me a bowl of the cocoa-nut
    Through the roar of the hurricanes.

12

I sang his name instead of a song,
    Over and over I sang his name –
Upward and downward I drew it along   80
    My various notes, – the same, the same!
I sang it low, that the slave-girls near
Might never guess from aught they could hear,
    It was only a name – a name.

13

I look on the sky and the sea.   85
    We were two to love, and two to pray. –
Yes, two, O God, who cried to Thee,
    Though nothing didst Thou say.
Coldly Thou sat'st behind the sun!
And now I cry who am but one,   90
    Thou wilt not speak today. –

14

We were black, we were black,
   We had no claim to love and bliss,
What marvel, if each went to wrack?
   They wrung my cold hands out of his, –   95
They dragged him . . . where? . . . I crawled to touch
His blood's mark in the dust! . . . not much,
   Ye pilgrim-souls, . . . though plain as *this*!

15

Wrong, followed by a deeper wrong!
   Mere grief's too good for such as I;   100
So the white men brought the shame ere long
   To strangle the sob of my agony.
They would not leave me for my dull
Wet eyes! – it was too merciful
   To let me weep pure tears and die.   105

16

I am black, I am black!
   I wore a child upon my breast . . .
An amulet that hung too slack,
   And, in my unrest, could not rest.
Thus we went moaning, child and mother,   110
One to another, one to another,
   Until all ended for the best.

17

For hark! I will tell you low . . . low . . .
   I am black, you see, –
And the babe who lay on my bosom so,   115
   Was far too white . . . too white for me;
As white as the ladies who scorned to pray
Beside me at church but yesterday,
   Though my tears had washed a place for my knee.

18

My own, own child! I could not bear   120
   To look in his face, it was so white;
I covered him up with a kerchief there;

I covered his face in close and tight:
And he moaned and struggled, as well might be,
For the white child wanted his liberty –					125
   Ha, ha! he wanted the master-right.

19

He moaned and beat with his head and feet,
   His little feet that never grew –
He struck them out, as it was meet,
   Against my heart to break it through.					130
I might have sung and made him mild –
But I dared not sing to the white-faced child
   The only song I knew.

20

I pulled the kerchief very close:
   He could not see the sun, I swear,					135
More, then, alive, than now he does
   From between the roots of the mango . . . where?
. . . I know where. Close! A child and mother
Do wrong to look at one another
   When one is black and one is fair.					140

21

Why, in that single glance I had
   Of my child's face, . . . I tell you all,
I saw a look that made me mad!
   The *master's* look, that used to fall
On my soul like his lash . . . or worse! –					145
And so, to save it from my curse,
   I twisted it round in my shawl.

22

And he moaned and trembled from foot to head,
   He shivered from head to foot;
Till after a time, he lay instead					150
   Too suddenly still and mute.
I felt, beside, a stiffening cold:
I dared to lift up just a fold, . . .
   As in lifting a leaf of the mango-fruit.

23

But *my* fruit . . . ha, ha! – there, had been 155
   (I laugh to think on 't at this hour!)
Your fine white angels (who have seen
   Nearest the secret of God's power)
And plucked my fruit to make them wine,
And sucked the soul of that child of mine, 160
   As the humming-bird sucks the soul of the flower.

24

Ha, ha, the trick of the angels white!
   They freed the white child's spirit so.
I said not a word, but, day and night,
   I carried the body to and fro, 165
And it lay on my heart like a stone . . . as chill.
– The sun may shine out as much as he will:
   I am cold, though it happened a month ago.

25

From the white man's house, and the black man's hut,
   I carried the little body on; 170
The forest's arms did round us shut,
   And silence through the trees did run.
They asked no question as I went, –
They stood too high for astonishment, –
   They could see God sit on His throne. 175

26

My little body, kerchiefed fast,
   I bore it on through the forest . . . on;
And when I felt it was tired at last,
   I scooped a hole beneath the moon.
Through the forest-tops the angels far, 180
With a white sharp finger from every star,
   Did point and mock at what was done.

27

Yet when it was all done aright, . . .
   Earth, 'twixt me and my baby, strewed, . . .
All, changed to black earth, . . . nothing white . . . 185

A dark child in the dark! – ensued
Some comfort, and my heart grew young;
I sat down smiling there and sung
    The song I learnt in my maidenhood.

28

And thus we two were reconciled,   190
    The white child and black mother, thus;
For as I sang it soft and wild,
    The same song, more melodious,
Rose from the grave whereon I sat:
It was the dead child singing that,   195
    To join the souls of both of us.

29

I look on the sea and the sky!
    Where the pilgrims' ships first anchored lay
The free sun rideth gloriously,
    But the pilgrim-ghosts have slid away   200
Through the earliest streaks of the morn:
My face is black, but it glares with a scorn
    Which they dare not meet by day.

30

Ah! – in their 'stead, their hunter sons!
    Ah, ah! they are on me – they hunt in a ring –   205
Keep off! I brave you all at once –
    I throw off your eyes like snakes that sting!
You have killed the black eagle at nest, I think:
Did you never stand still in your triumph, and shrink
    From the stroke of her wounded wing?   210

31

(Man, drop that stone you dared to lift! –)
    I wish you who stand there five abreast,
Each, for his own wife's joy and gift,
    A little corpse as safely at rest
As mine in the mangos! Yes, but *she*   215
May keep live babies on her knee,
    And sing the song she likes the best.

32

I am not mad: I am black.
   I see you staring in my face –
I know you staring, shrinking back,   220
   Ye are born of the Washington-race,
And this land is the free America,
And this mark on my wrist . . . (I prove what I say)
   Ropes tied me up here to the flogging-place.

33

You think I shrieked then? Not a sound!   225
   I hung, as a gourd hangs in the sun;
I only cursed them all around
   As softly as I might have done
My very own child. – From these sands
Up to the mountains, lift your hands,   230
   O slaves, and end what I begun!

34

Whips, curses; these must answer those!
   For in this UNION [95] you have set
Two kinds of men in adverse rows,
   Each loathing each: and all forget   235
The seven wounds in Christ's body fair,
While HE sees gaping everywhere
   Our countless wounds that pay no debt.

35

Our wounds are different. Your white men
   Are, after all, not gods indeed,   240
Nor able to make Christs again
   Do good with bleeding. *We* who bleed
(Stand off!) we help not in our loss!
We are too heavy for our cross,
   And fall and crush you and your seed.   245

36

I fall, I swoon! I look at the sky:
  The clouds are breaking on my brain:
I am floated along, as if I should die
  Of liberty's exquisite pain.
In the name of the white child waiting for me   250
In the death-dark where we may kiss and agree,
White men, I leave you all curse-free
  In my broken heart's disdain!

Hector in the Garden

1

Nine years old! The first of any
  Seem the happiest years that come:
Yet when *I* was nine, I said
  No such word! – I thought instead
That the Greeks had used as many   5
  In besieging Ilium.

2

Nine green years had scarcely brought me
  To my childhood's haunted spring:
I had life, like flowers and bees,
  In betwixt the country trees,   10
And the sun the pleasure taught me
  Which he teacheth every thing.

3

If the rain fell, there was sorrow,
  Little head leant on the pane,
  Little finger drawing down it   15
  The long trailing drops upon it,
And the 'Rain, rain, come tomorrow,'
  Said for charm against the rain.

4

Such a charm was right Canidian,
    Though you meet it with a jeer!   20
    If I said it long enough,
    Then the rain hummed dimly off,
And the thrush with his pure Lydian[96]
    Was left only to the ear;

5

And the sun and I together   25
    Went a-rushing out of doors!
    We, our tender spirits, drew
    Over hill and dale in view,
Glimmering hither, glimmering thither,
    In the footsteps of the showers.   30

6

Underneath the chestnuts dripping,
    Through the grasses wet and fair,
    Straight I sought my garden-ground
    With the laurel on the mound,
And the pear-tree oversweeping   35
    A side-shadow of green air.

7

In the garden lay supinely
    A huge giant wrought of spade!
    Arms and legs were stretched at length
    In a passive giant strength, –   40
The fine meadow turf, cut finely,
    Round them laid and interlaid.

8

Call him Hector, son of Priam![97]
    Such his title and degree:
    With my rake I smoothed his brow,   45
    Both his cheeks I weeded through,
But a rimer such as I am
    Scarce can sing his dignity.

9

Eyes of gentianellas azure,
 Staring, winking at the skies;   50
 Nose of gillyflowers and box;
 Scented grasses put for locks,
Which a little breeze, at pleasure,
 Set a-waving round his eyes.

10

Brazen helm of daffodillies,   55
 With a glitter toward the light;
 Purple violets for the mouth,
 Breathing perfumes west and south;
And a sword of flashing lilies,
 Holden ready for the fight.   60

11

And a breastplate made of daisies,
 Closely fitting, leaf on leaf;
 Periwinkles interlaced
 Drawn for belt about the waist;
While the brown bees, humming praises,   65
 Shot their arrows round the chief.

12

And who knows (I sometimes wondered)
 If the disembodied soul
 Of old Hector, once of Troy,
 Might not take a dreary joy   70
Here to enter – if it thundered,
 Rolling up the thunder-roll?

13

Rolling this way from Troy-ruin,
 In this body rude and rife
 Just to enter, and take rest   75
 'Neath the daisies of the breast –
They, with tender roots, renewing
 His heroic heart to life?

14

Who could know? I sometimes started
　At a motion or a sound!　　　　　　　　　　　80
　Did his mouth speak – naming Troy,
　With an ὀτοτοτοτοῖ?*
Did the pulse of the Strong-hearted
　Make the daisies tremble round?

15

It was hard to answer, often:　　　　　　　　　85
　But the birds sang in the tree –
　But the little birds sang bold
　In the pear-tree green and old,
And my terror seemed to soften
　Through the courage of their glee.　　　　　　90

16

Oh, the birds, the tree, the ruddy
　And white blossoms, sleek with rain!
　Oh, my garden, rich with pansies!
　Oh, my childhood's bright romances!
All revive, like Hector's body,　　　　　　　　95
　And I see them stir again!

17

And despite life's changes – chances,
　And despite the deathbell's toll,
　They press on me in full seeming!
　Help, some angel! stay this dreaming!　　　　100
As the birds sang in the branches,
　Sing God's patience through my soul!

18

That no dreamer, no neglecter
　Of the present's work unsped,
　I may wake up and be doing,　　　　　　　　105
　Life's heroic ends pursuing,
Though my past is dead as Hector,
　And though Hector is twice dead.

* 　Greek expression of pain or grief.

Flush or Faunus

You see this dog. It was but yesterday
I mused forgetful of his presence here
Till thought on thought drew downward tear on tear,
When from the pillow, where wet-cheeked I lay,
A head as hairy as Faunus, thrust its way   5
Right sudden against my face, – two golden-clear
Great eyes astonished mine, – a drooping ear
Did flap me on either cheek to dry the spray!
I started first, as some Arcadian,
Amazed by goatly god in twilight grove;   10
But, as the bearded vision closelier ran
My tears off, I knew Flush, and rose above
Surprise and sadness, – thanking the true PAN
Who, by low creatures, leads to heights of love.

Finite and Infinite

The wind sounds only in opposing straits,
The sea, beside the shore; man's spirit rends
Its quiet only up against the ends
Of wants and oppositions, loves and hates,
Where, worked and worn by passionate debates,   5
And losing by the loss it apprehends,
The flesh rocks round, and every breath it sends
Is ravelled to a sigh. All tortured states
Suppose a straitened place. Jehovah Lord,
Make room for rest, around me! out of sight   10
Now float me, of the vexing land abhorred,
Till in deep calms of space my soul may right
Her nature, – shoot large sail on lengthening cord,
And rush exultant on the Infinite.

Two Sketches

H. B.

The shadow of her face upon the wall
May take your memory to the perfect Greek,
But when you front her, you would call the cheek
Too full, sir, for your models, if withal
That bloom it wears could leave you critical,   5
And that smile reaching toward the rosy streak;
For one who smiles so, has no need to speak
To lead your thoughts along, as steed to stall.
A smile that turns the sunny side o' the heart
On all the world, as if herself did win   10
By what she lavished on an open mart!
Let no man call the liberal sweetness, sin, –
For friends may whisper, as they stand apart,
'Methinks there's still some warmer place within.'

A. B.

Her azure eyes, dark lashes hold in fee;
Her fair superfluous ringlets, without check,
Drop after one another down her neck,
As many to each cheek as you might see
Green leaves to a wild rose! this sign outwardly,   5
And a like woman-covering seems to deck
Her inner nature. For she will not fleck
World's sunshine with a finger. Sympathy
Must call her in Love's name! and then, I know,
She rises up, and brightens as she should,   10
And lights her smile for comfort, and is slow
In nothing of high-hearted fortitude.
To smell this flower, come near it! such can grow
In that sole garden where Christ's brow dropped blood.

Mountaineer and Poet

The simple goatherd, between Alp and sky,
Seeing his shadow, in that awful tryst,
Dilated to a giant's on the mist,
Esteems not his own stature larger by
The apparent image, but more patiently   5
Strikes his staff down beneath his clenching fist,
While the snow-mountains lift their amethyst
And sapphire crowns of splendour, far and nigh,
Into the air around him. Learn from hence
Meek morals, all ye poets that pursue   10
Your way still onward up to eminence!
Ye are not great because creation drew
Large revelations round your earliest sense,
Nor bright because God's glory shines for you.

The Poet

The poet hath the child's sight in his breast,
And sees all *new*. What oftenest he has viewed,
He views with the first glory. Fair and good
Pall never on him, at the fairest, best,
But stand before him holy and undressed   5
In week-day false conventions, such as would
Drag other men down from the altitude
Of primal types, too early dispossessed.
Why, God would tire of all His heavens, as soon
As thou, O godlike, childlike poet, didst,   10
Of daily and nightly sights of sun and moon!
And therefore hath He set thee in the midst,
Where men may hear thy wonder's ceaseless tune,
And praise His world for ever, as thou bidst.

Hiram Power's Greek Slave

They say Ideal beauty cannot enter
The house of anguish. On the threshold stands
An alien Image with enshackled hands,
Called the Greek Slave! as if the artist meant her
(That passionless perfection which he lent her, 5
Shadowed not darkened where the sill expands)
To, so, confront man's crimes in different lands
With man's ideal sense. Pierce to the centre,
Art's fiery finger! – and break up ere long
The serfdom of this world! appeal, fair stone, 10
From God's pure heights of beauty against man's wrong!
Catch up in thy divine face, not alone
East griefs but west, – and strike and shame the strong,
By thunders of white silence, overthrown.

Life

Each creature holds an insular point in space;
Yet what man stirs a finger, breathes a sound,
But all the multitudinous beings round
In all the countless worlds, with time and place
For their conditions, down to the central base, 5
Thrill, haply, in vibration and rebound,
Life answering life across the vast profound,
In full antiphony, by a common grace?
I think, this sudden joyaunce which illumes
A child's mouth sleeping, unaware may run 10
From some soul newly loosened from earth's tombs.
I think, this passionate sigh, which half-begun
I stifle back, may reach and stir the plumes
Of God's calm angel standing in the sun.

Love

We cannot live, except thus mutually
We alternate, aware or unaware,
The reflex act of life; and when we bear
Our virtue outward most impulsively,
Most full of invocation, and to be   5
Most instantly compellant, certes, there
We live most life, whoever breathes most air,
And counts his dying years by sun and sea.
But when a soul, by choice and conscience, doth
Throw out her full force on another soul,   10
The conscience and the concentration both
Make mere life, Love. For Life in perfect whole
And aim consummated, is Love in sooth,
As nature's magnet-heat rounds pole with pole.

Heaven and Earth

And there was silence in heaven about the space of half an hour.
Revelation 8:1

God, who, with thunders and great voices kept
Beneath Thy throne, and stars most silver-paced
Along the inferior gyres, and open-faced
Melodious angels round, canst intercept   5
Music with music, – yet, at will, has swept
All back, all back (said he in Patmos placed),
To fill the heavens with silence of the waste
Which lasted half an hour! – lo, I who have wept
All day and night, beseech Thee by my tears,   10
And by that dread response of curse and groan
Men alternate across these hemispheres,
Vouchsafe us such a half-hour's hush alone,
In compensation for our stormy years!
As heaven has paused from song, let earth, from moan.

The Prospect

Methinks we do as fretful children do,
Leaning their faces on the window-pane
To sigh the glass dim with their own breath's stain,
And shut the sky and landscape from their view.
And thus, alas! since God the maker drew   5
A mystic separation 'twixt those twain,
The life beyond us, and our souls in pain,
We miss the prospect which we are called unto
By grief we are fools to use. Be still and strong,
O man, my brother! hold thy sobbing breath,   10
And keep thy soul's large window pure from wrong, –
That so, as life's appointment issueth,
Thy vision may be clear to watch along
The sunset consummation-lights of death.

Hugh Stuart Boyd

HIS BLINDNESS

God would not let the spheric Lights accost
This God-loved man, and bade the earth stand off
With all her beckoning hills, whose golden stuff
Under the feet of the royal sun is crossed.
Yet such things were to him not wholly lost, –   5
Permitted, with his wandering eyes light-proof,
To catch fair visions, rendered full enough
By many a ministrant accomplished ghost, –
Still seeing, to sounds of softly-turned book-leaves,
Sappho's crown-rose, and Meleager's spring,   10
And Gregory's starlight on Greek-burnished eves!
Till Sensuous and Unsensuous seemed one thing,
Viewed from one level, – earth's reapers at the sheaves
Scarce plainer than Heaven's angels on the wing!

Hugh Stuart Boyd

HIS DEATH, 1848

Belovèd friend, who living many years
With sightless eyes raised vainly to the sun,
Didst learn to keep thy patient soul in tune
To visible nature's elemental cheers!
God has not caught thee to new hemispheres   5
Because thou wast aweary of this one; –
I think thine angel's patience first was done,
And that he spake out with celestial tears,
'Is it enough, dear God? then lighten so
This soul that smiles in darkness!' Steadfast friend,   10
Who never didst my heart or life misknow,
Nor either's faults too keenly apprehend, –
How can I wonder when I see thee go
To join the Dead found faithful to the end?

Hugh Stuart Boyd

LEGACIES

Three gifts the Dying left me, – Aeschylus,
And Gregory Nazianzen, and a clock,
Chiming the gradual hours out like a flock
Of stars whose motion is melodious.
The books were those I used to read from, thus   5
Assisting my dear teacher's soul to unlock
The darkness of his eyes. Now, mine they mock,
Blinded in turn, by tears! now, murmurous
Sad echoes of my young voice, years agone
Intoning from these leaves the Grecian phrase,   10
Return and choke my utterance. Books, lie down
In silence on the shelf there, within gaze;
And thou, clock, striking the hour's pulses on,
Chime in the day which ends these parting days!

Confessions

1

Face to face in my chamber, my silent chamber, I saw her:
God and she and I only . . . there, I sat down to draw her
Soul through the clefts of confession . . . Speak, I am holding thee fast,
As the angels of resurrection shall do it at the last.
     'My cup is blood-red   5
      With my sin,' she said,
  'And I pour it out to the bitter lees,
As if the angels of judgment stood over me strong at the last,
     Or as thou wert as these!'

2

When God smote His hands together, and struck out thy soul as a spark 10
Into the organised glory of things, from deeps of the dark, –
Say, didst thou shine, didst thou burn, didst thou honour the
                            power in the form,
As the star does at night, or the fire-fly, or even the little ground-worm?
     'I have sinned,' she said,
      'For my seed-light shed   15
  Has smouldered away from His first decrees!
The cypress praiseth the fire-fly, the ground-leaf praiseth the worm, –
     I am viler than these!'

3

When God on that sin had pity, and did not trample thee straight
With His wild rains beating and drenching thy light found inadequate; 20
When He only sent thee the north-winds, a little searching and chill,
To quicken thy flame . . . didst thou kindle and flash to the heights
                            of His will?
     'I have sinned,' she said,
      'Unquickened, unspread,
  My fire dropt down, and I wept on my knees!   25
I only said of His winds of the north as I shrank from their chill, . . .
     What delight is in these?'

4

When God on that sin had pity, and did not meet it as such,
But tempered the wind to thy uses, and softened the world to thy touch,
At least thou wast moved in thy soul, though unable to prove it afar,   30
Thou couldst carry thy light like a jewel, not giving it out like a star?
  'I have sinned,' she said,
  'And not merited
 The gift He gives, by the grace He sees!
The mine-cave praiseth the jewel, the hillside praiseth the star;   35
  I am viler than these.'

5

Then I cried aloud in my passion, . . . Unthankful and impotent creature,
To throw up thy scorn unto God through the rents in thy beggarly nature!
If He, the all-giving and loving, is served so unduly, what then
Hast thou done to the weak and the false, and the changing, . . .
      thy fellows of men?   40
  'I have *loved*,' she said,
  (Words bowing her head
 As the wind the wet acacia-trees!)
'I saw God sitting above me, – but I . . . I sat among men,
  And I have loved these.'   45

6

Again with a lifted voice, like a choral trumpet that takes
The lowest note of a viol that trembles, and triumphing breaks
On the air with it solemn and clear, – 'Behold! I have sinned not in this!
Where I loved, I have loved much and well, – I have verily loved not amiss.
  Let the living,' she said,   50
  'Inquire of the Dead,
 In the house of the pale-fronted Images:
My own true dead will answer for me, that I have not loved amiss
  In my love for all these.

7

'The least touch of their hands in the morning, I keep it by day and by night;
Their least step on the stair, at the door, still throbs through me,
                                                   if ever so light;   56
Their least gift, which they left to my childhood, far off,
                                                   in the long-ago years,
Is now turned from a toy to a relic, and seen through the crystals of tears.
        Dig the snow,' she said,
        'For my churchyard bed,   60
    Yet I, as I sleep, shall not fear to freeze,
If one only of these my beloveds, shall love me with heart-warm tears,
        As I have loved these!

8

'If I angered any among them, from thenceforth my own life was sore;
If I fell by chance from their presence, I clung to their memory more.   65
Their tender I often felt holy, their bitter I sometimes called sweet;
And whenever their heart has refused me, I fell down straight at their feet.
        I have loved,' she said, –
        'Man is weak, God is dread,
    Yet the weak man dies with his spirit at ease,   70
Having poured such an unguent of love but once on the Saviour's feet,
        As I lavished for these.'

9

'Go,' I cried, 'thou hast chosen the Human, and left the Divine!
Then, at least, have the Human shared with thee their wild-berry wine?
Have they loved back thy love, and when strangers approached
                                                   thee with blame,   75
Have they covered thy fault with their kisses, and loved thee the same?'
        But she shrunk and said
        'God, over my head,
    Must sweep in the wrath of His judgment-seas,
If *He* shall deal with me sinning, but only indeed the same   80
        And no gentler than these.'

A Sabbath Morning at Sea

1

The ship went on with solemn face;
  To meet the darkness on the deep,
    The solemn ship went onward.
I bowed down weary in the place,
  For parting tears and present sleep   5
    Had weighed mine eyelids downward.

2

Thick sleep which shut all dreams from me,
  And kept my inner self apart
    And quiet from emotion,
Then brake away and left me free,   10
  Made conscious of a human heart
    Betwixt the heaven and ocean.

3

The new sight, the new wondrous sight!
  The waters round me, turbulent, –
    The skies impassive o'er me,   15
Calm, in a moonless, sunless light,
  Half glorified by that intent
    Of holding the day-glory!

4

Two pale thin clouds did stand upon
  The meeting line of sea and sky,   20
    With aspect still and mystic.
I think they did foresee the sun,
  And rested on their prophecy
    In quietude majestic,

5

Then flushed to radiance where they stood,   25
  Like statues by the open tomb
    Of shining saints half risen. –
The sun! – he came up to be viewed,
  And sky and sea made mighty room
    To inaugurate the vision.   30

6

I oft had seen the dawnlight run,
  As red wine, through the hills, and break
    Through many a mist's inurning;
But, here, no earth profaned the sun!
  Heaven, ocean, did alone partake   35
    The sacrament of morning.

7

Away with thoughts fantastical!
  I would be humble to my worth,
    Self-guarded as self-doubted:
Though here no earthly shadows fall,   40
  I, joying, grieving without earth,
    May desecrate without it.

8

God's sabbath morning sweeps the waves;
  I would not praise the pageant high,
    Yet miss the dedicature.   45
I, carried toward the sunless graves
  By force of natural things, – should I
    Exult in only nature?

9

And could I bear to sit alone
  'Mid nature's fixed benignities,   50
    While my warm pulse was moving?
Too dark thou art, O glittering sun,
  Too strait ye are, capacious seas,
    To satisfy the loving!

10

It seems a better lot than so,   55
  To sit with friends beneath the beech,
    And feel them dear and dearer;
Or follow children as they go
  In pretty pairs, with softened speech,
    As the church-bells ring nearer.   60

11

Love me, sweet friends, this sabbath day!
   The sea sings round me while ye roll
     Afar the hymn unaltered,
And kneel, where once I knelt to pray,
   And bless me deeper in the soul,   65
     Because the voice has faltered.

12

And though this sabbath comes to me
   Without the stolèd minister
     Or chanting congregation,
God's Spirit brings communion, HE   70
   Who brooded soft on waters drear,
     Creator on creation.

13

Himself, I think, shall draw me higher,
   Where keep the saints with harp and song
     An endless sabbath morning,   75
And on that sea commixed with fire
   Oft drop their eyelids, raised too long
     To the full Godhead's burning.

The Mask

1

I have a smiling face, she said,
   I have a jest for all I meet,
I have a garland for my head
   And all its flowers are sweet, –
And so you call me gay, she said.   5

2

Grief taught to me this smile, she said,
   And Wrong did teach this jesting bold;
These flowers were plucked from garden-bed
   While a death-chime was tolled.
And what now will you say? – she said.   10

3

Behind no prison-grate, she said,
   Which slurs the sunshine half a mile,
Live captives so uncomforted
   As souls behind a smile.
God's pity let us pray, she said.   15

4

I know my face is bright, she said, –
   Such brightness, dying suns diffuse;
I bear upon my forehead shed
   The sign of what I lose, –
The ending of my day, she said.   20

5

If I dared leave this smile, she said,
   And take a moan upon my mouth,
And tie a cypress round my head,
   And let my tears run smooth, –
It were the happier way, she said.   25

6

And since that must not be, she said,
  I fain your bitter world would leave.
How calmly, calmly, smile the Dead,
  Who do not, therefore, grieve!
The yea of Heaven is yea, she said.   30

7

But in your bitter world, she said,
  Face-joy's a costly mask to wear.
'Tis bought with pangs long nourishèd,
  And rounded to despair.
Grief's earnest makes life's play, she said.   35

8

Ye weep for those who weep? she said –
  Ah fools! I bid you pass them by.
Go, weep for those hearts have bled
  What time their eyes were dry.
Whom sadder can I say? she said   40

Calls on the Heart

1

Free Heart, that singest today,
Like a bird on the first green spray,
Wilt thou go forth to the world,
Where the hawk hath his wing unfurled
    To follow, perhaps, thy way?   5
Where the tamer, thine own will bind,
And, to make thee sing, will blind,
While the little hip grows for the free behind?
      Heart, wilt thou go?
        – 'No, no!   10
    Free hearts are better so.'

2

The world, thou hast heard it told,
Has counted its robber-gold,
And the pieces stick to the hand.
The world goes riding it fair and grand,   15
    While the truth is bought and sold!
World-voices east, world-voices west,
    They call thee, Heart, from thine early rest,
'Come hither, come hither and be our guest.'
      Heart, wilt thou go?   20
        – 'No, no!
    Good hearts are calmer so.'

3

Who calleth thee, Heart? World's Strife,
With a golden heft to his knife;
World's Mirth, with a finger fine   25
That draws on a board in wine
    Her blood-red plans of life;
World's Gain, with a brow knit down;
World's Fame, with a laurel crown,
Which rustles most as the leaves turn brown –   30
      Heart, wilt thou go?
        – 'No, no!
    Calm hearts are wiser so.'

4

Hast heard that Proserpina
(Once fooling) was snatched away,   35
To partake the dark king's seat, –
And that the tears ran fast on her feet
    To think how the sun shone yesterday?
With her ankles sunken in asphodel
She wept for the roses of earth which fell   40
From her lap when the wild car drave to hell.
        Heart, wilt thou go?
          – 'No, no!
      Wise hearts are warmer so.'

5

And what is this place not seen,   45
Where Hearts may hide serene?
' 'Tis a fair still house well-kept,
Which humble thoughts have swept,
    And holy prayers made clean.
There, I sit with Love in the sun,   50
And we two never have done
Singing sweeter songs than are guessed by *one*.'
        Heart, wilt thou go?
          – 'No, no!
      Warm hearts are fuller so.'   55

6

O Heart, O Love, – I fear
That Love may be kept too near.
Has heard, O Heart, that tale,
How Love may be false and frail
    To a Heart once holden dear?   60
– 'But this true Love of mine
Clings fast as the clinging vine,
And mingles pure as the grapes in wine.'
        Heart, wilt thou go?
          – 'No, no!   65
      Full hearts beat higher so.'

7

O Heart, O Love, beware! –
Look up, and boast not there.
For who has twirled at the pin?
'Tis the World, between Death and Sin, – 70
   The World, and the world's Despair!
And Death has quickened his pace
To the hearth, with a mocking face,
Familiar as Love, in Love's own place –
       Heart, will thou go? 75
       – 'Still, no!
   High hearts must grieve even so.'

8

The house is waste today, –
The leaf has dropt from the spray,
The thorn, prickt through to the song. 80
If summer doeth no wrong
   The winter will, they say.
Sing, Heart! what heart replies?
In vain we were calm and wise,
If the tears unkissed stand on in our eyes. 85
       Heart, wilt thou go?
       – 'Ah, no!
   Grieved hearts must break even so.'

9

Howbeit all is not lost.
The warm noon ends in frost, 90
And worldly tongues of promise,
Like sheep-bells, die off from us
   On the desert hills cloud-crossed!
Yet, through the silence, shall
Pierce the death-angel's call, 95
And 'Come up hither,' recover all.
       Heart, wilt thou go?
       – 'I go!
   Broken hearts triumph so.'

Wisdom Unapplied

1

If I were thou, O butterfly,
And poised my purple wing to spy
The sweetest flowers that live and die,

2

I would not waste my strength on those,
As thou, – for summer has a close,   5
And pansies bloom not in the snows.

3

If I were thou, O working bee,
And all that honey-gold I see
Could delve from roses easily,

4

I would not hive it at man's door,   10
As thou, – that heirdom of my store
Should make him rich, and leave me poor.

5

If I were thou, O eagle proud,
And screamed the thunder back aloud,
And faced the lightning from the cloud,   15

6

I would not build my eyrie-throne,
As thou, – upon a crumbling stone,
Which the next storm may trample down.

7

If I were thou, O gallant steed,
With pawing hoof, and dancing head,   20
And eye outrunning thine own speed,

8

I would not meeken to the rein,
As thou, – nor smooth my nostril plain
From the glad desert's snort and strain.

9

If I were thou, red-breasted bird,   25
With song at shut-up window heard,
Like Love's sweet yes too long deferred,

10

I would not overstay delight,
As thou, – but take a swallow-flight,
Till the new spring returned to sight.   30

11

While yet I spake, a touch was laid
Upon my brow, whose pride did fade
As thus, methought, an angel said, –

12

'If I were *thou* who sing'st this song,
Most wise for others, and most strong   35
In seeing right while doing wrong,

13

'I would not waste my cares, and choose,
As *thou*, – to seek what thou must lose,
Such gains as perish in the use.

14

'I would not work where none can win,   40
As *thou*, – halfway 'twixt grief and sin,
But look above, and judge within.

15

'I would not let my pulse beat high,
As *thou*, – towards fame's regality,
Nor yet in love's great jeopardy.   45

16

'I would not champ the hard cold bit,
As *thou*, – of what the world thinks fit,
But take God's freedom, using it.

17

'I would not play earth's winter out,
As *thou*, – but gird my soul about,   50
And live for live past death and doubt.

18

'Then sing, O singer! – but allow,
Beast, fly, and bird, called foolish now,
Are wise (for all thy scorn) as thou!'

Human Life's Mystery

1

We sow the glebe, we reap the corn,
    We build the house where we may rest,
And then, at moments, suddenly
We look up to the great wide sky,
Inquiring wherefore we were born . . .   5
    For earnest, or for jest?

2

The senses folding thick and dark
    About the stifled soul within,
We guess diviner things beyond,
And yearn to them with yearning fond;   10
We strike out blindly to a mark
    Believed in, but not seen.

3

We vibrate to the pant and thrill
    Wherewith Eternity has curled
In serpent-twine about God's seat;   15
While, freshening upward to His feet,
In gradual growth His full-leaved will
    Expands from world to world.

4

And, in the tumult and excess
    Of act and passion under sun,   20
We sometimes hear – oh, soft and far,
As silver star did touch with star,
The kiss of Peace and Righteousness
    Through all things that are done.

5

God keeps His holy mysteries   25
    Just on the outside of man's dream.
In diapason slow, we think
To hear their pinions rise and sink,
While they float pure beneath His eyes,
    Like swans adown a stream.   30

6

Abstractions, are they, from the forms
    Of His great beauty? – exaltations
From His great glory? – strong previsions
Of what we shall be? – intuitions
Of what we are – in calms and storms,   35
    Beyond our peace and passions?

7

Things nameless! which, in passing so,
    Do stroke us with a subtle grace.
We say, 'Who passes?' – they are dumb.
We cannot see them go or come: 40
Their touches fall soft – cold – as snow
    Upon a blind man's face.

8

Yet, touching so, they draw above
    Our common thoughts to Heaven's unknown;
Our daily joy and pain, advance   45
To a divine significance, –
Our human love – O mortal love,
    That light is not its own!

9

And, sometimes, horror chills our blood
   To be so near such mystic Things,   50
And we wrap round us, for defence,
Our purple manners, moods of sense –
As angels, from the face of God,
   Stand hidden in their wings.

10

And, sometimes, through life's heavy swound   55
   We grope for them! – with strangled breath
We stretch our hands abroad and try
To reach them in our agony, –
And widen, so, the broad life-wound
   Which soon is large enough for death.   60

A Child's Thought of God

1

They say that God lives very high:
   But if you look above the pines
You cannot see our God; and why?

2

And if you dig down in the mines
   You never see Him in the gold;
Though, from Him, all that's glory shines.

3

God is so good, He wears a fold
   Of heaven and earth across His face –
Like secrets kept, for love, untold.

4

But still I feel that His embrace
   Slides down by thrills, through all things made,
Through sight and sound of every place.

5

As if my tender mother laid
   On my shut lids her kisses' pressure,
Half-waking me at night, and said
   'Who kissed you through the dark, dear guesser?'

The Claim

1

Grief sat upon a rock and sighed one day,
   (Sighing is all her rest!)
'Wellaway, wellaway, ah, wellaway!'
As ocean beat the stone, did she her breast,
'Ah, wellaway! . . . ah me! alas, ah me!'   5
   Such sighing uttered she.

2

A Cloud spake out of heaven, as soft as rain
   That falls on water, – 'Lo,
The Winds have wandered from me! I remain
Alone in the sky-waste, and cannot go   10
To lean my whiteness on the mountain blue
   Till wanted for more dew.

3

'The Sun has struck my brain to weary peace,
   Whereby constrained and pale
I spin for him a larger golden fleece   15
Than Jason's, yearning for as full a sail.
Sweet Grief, when thou hast sighèd to thy mind,
   Give me a sigh for wind,

4

'And let it carry me adown the west.'
   But Love, who, pròstrated,   20
Lay at Grief's foot, his lifted eyes possessed
Of her full image, answered in her stead:
'Now nay, now nay! she shall not give away
What is my wealth, for any Cloud that flieth.
   Where Grief makes moan,   25
   Love claims his own!
And therefore do I lie here night and day,
And eke my life out with the breath she sigheth.'

A Dead Rose

1

O Rose, who dares to name thee?
No longer roseate now, nor soft, nor sweet,
But pale, and hard, and dry, as stubble-wheat, –
    Kept seven years in a drawer – thy titles shame thee.

2

The breeze that used to blow thee
Between the hedgerow thorns, and take away
An odour up the lane to last all day, –
    If breathing now, – unsweetened would forgo thee.

3

The sun that used to smite thee,
And mix his glory in thy gorgeous urn
Till beam appeared to bloom, and flower to burn, –
    If shining now, – with not a hue would light thee.

4

The dew that used to wet thee,
And, white first, grow incarnadined, because
It lay upon thee where the crimson was, –
    If dropping now, – would darken, where it met thee.

5

The fly that 'it upon thee,
To stretch the tendrils of its tiny feet
Along thy leaf's pure edges after heat, –
    If 'ighting now, – would coldly overrun thee.

6

The bee that once did suck thee,
And build thy perfumed ambers up his hive,
And swoon in thee for joy, till scarce alive, –
    If passing now, – would blindly overlook thee.

7

The heart doth recognise thee,   25
Alone, alone! the heart doth smell thee sweet,
Doth view thee fair, doth judge thee most complete,
    Perceiving all those changes that disguise thee.

8

Yes, and the heart doth owe thee
More love, dead rose, than to any roses bold   30
Which Julia wears at dances, smiling cold! –
    Lie still upon this heart – which breaks below thee!

A Woman's Shortcomings

1

She has laughed as softly as if she sighed,
    She has counted six, and over,
Of a purse well filled, and a heart well tried –
    Oh, each a worthy lover!
They 'give her time'; for her soul must slip   5
    Where the world has set the grooving.
She will lie to none with her fair red lip –
    But love seeks truer loving.

2

She trembles her fan in a sweetness dumb,
    As her thoughts were beyond recalling,   10
With a glance for *one*, and a glance for *some*,
    From her eyelids rising and falling;
Speaks common words with a blushful air,
    Hears bold words, unreproving;
But her silence says – what she never will swear –   15
    And love seeks better loving.

3

Go, lady, lean to the night-guitar,
    And drop a smile to the bringer,
Then smile as sweetly, when he is far,
    At the voice of an indoor singer.   20
Bask tenderly beneath tender eyes;
    Glance lightly, on their removing;
And join new vows to old perjuries –
    But dare not call it loving.

4

Unless you can think, when the song is done,   25
    No other is soft in the rhythm;
Unless you can feel, when left by One,
    That all men else go with him;
Unless you can know, when unpraised by his breath,
    That your beauty itself wants proving;   30
Unless you can swear, 'For life, for death!' –
    Oh, fear to call it loving!

5

Unless you can muse in a crowd all day
    On the absent face that fixed you;
Unless you can love, as the angels may,   35
    With the breadth of heaven betwixt you;
Unless you can dream that his faith is fast,
    Through behoving and unbehoving;
Unless you can *die* when the dream is past –
    Oh, never call it loving!   40

A Man's Requirements

1

Love me, sweet, with all thou art,
 Feeling, thinking, seeing, –
Love me in the lightest part,
 Love me in full being.

2

Love me with thine open youth
 In its frank surrender;
With the vowing of thy mouth,
 With its silence tender.

3

Love me with thine azure eyes,
 Made for earnest grantings!
Taking colour from the skies,
 Can Heaven's truth be wanting?

4

Love me with their lids, that fall
 Snow-like at first meeting;
Love me with thine heart, that all
 The neighbours then see beating.

5

Love me with thine hand stretched out
 Freely – open-minded;
Love me with thy loitering foot, –
 Hearing one behind it.

6

Love me with thy voice, that turns
 Sudden faint above me;
Love me with thy blush that burns
 When I murmur, *Love me!*

7

Love me with thy thinking soul –   25
    Break it to love-sighing;
Love me with thy thoughts that roll
    On through living – dying.

8

Love me in thy gorgeous airs,
    When the world has crowned thee!   30
Love me, kneeling at thy prayers,
    With the angels round thee.

9

Love me pure, as musers do,
    Up the woodlands shady;
Love me gaily, fast, and true,   35
    As a winsome lady.

10

Through all hopes that keep us brave,
    Further off or nigher,
Love me for the house and grave, –
    And for something higher.   40

11

Thus, if thou wilt prove me, dear,
    Woman's love no fable,
I will love *thee* – half-a-year –
    As a man is able.

A Year's Spinning

1

He listened at the porch that day,
  To hear the wheel go on, and on;
And then it stopped – ran back away –
  While through the door he brought the sun.
  But now my spinning is all done.   5

2

He sat beside me, with an oath
  That love ne'er ended, once begun.
I smiled – believing for us both,
  What was the truth for only one.
  And now my spinning is all done.   10

3

My mother cursed me that I heard
  A young man's wooing as I spun.
Thanks, cruel mother, for that word, –
  For I have, since, a harder known!
  And now my spinning is all done.   15

4

I thought – O God!—my first-born's cry
  Both voices to mine ear would drown.
I listened in mine agony –
  It was the *silence* made me groan!
  And now my spinning is all done.   20

5

Bury me 'twixt my mother's grave
  (Who cursed me on her death-bed lone)
And my dead baby's (God it save!),
  Who, not to bless me, would not moan.
  And now my spinning is all done.   25

6

A stone upon my heart and head,
　　But no name written on the stone!
Sweet neighbours, whisper low instead,
　　'This sinner was a loving one –
　　And now her spinning is all done.'　　　　　30

7

And let the door ajar remain,
　　In case he should pass by anon;
And leave the wheel out very plain, –
　　That　HE, when passing in the sun,
　　May see the spinning is all done.　　　　　35

Change upon Change

Five months ago the stream did flow,
    The lilies bloomed within the sedge,
And we were lingering to and fro,
Where none will track thee in this snow,
    Along the stream, beside the hedge.   5
Ah, sweet, be free to love and go!
    For if I do not hear thy foot,
    The frozen river is as mute,
    The flowers have dried down to the root.
    And why, since these be changed since May,   10
                Shouldst *thou* change less than *they*?

And slow, slow, as the winter snow,
    The tears have drifted to mine eyes;
And my poor cheeks, five months ago,
Set blushing at thy praises so,   15
    Put paleness on for a disguise.
Ah, sweet, be free to praise and go!
    For if my face is turned too pale,
    It was thine oath that first did fail, –
    It was thy love proved false and frail!   20
    And why, since these be changed enow,
                Should *I* change less than *thou*?

A Reed

1

I am no trumpet, but a reed:
No flattereing breath shall from me lead
   A silver sound, a hollow sound:
I will not ring, for priest or king,
One blast that in re-echoing
    Would leave a bondsman faster bound.

2

I am no trumpet, but a reed, –
A broken reed, the wind indeed
   Left flat upon a dismal shore;
Yet if a little maid, or child,
Should sigh within it, earnest-mild,
    This reed will answer evermore.

3

I am no trumpet, but a reed.
Go, tell the fishers, as they spread
   Their nets along the river's edge,
I will not tear their nets at all,
Nor pierce their hands, if they should fall;
    Then let them leave me in the sedge.

A Child's Grave at Florence

A. A. E. C. Born, July 1848. Died, November 1849

1

Of English blood, of Tuscan birth, . . .
  What country should we give her?
Instead of any on the earth,
  The civic Heavens receive her.

2

And here, among the English tombs,
  In Tuscan ground we lay her,
While the blue Tuscan sky endomes
  Our English words of prayer.

3

A little child! – how long she lived,
  By months, not years, is reckoned:
Born in one July, she survived
  Alone to see a second.

4

Bright-featured, as the July sun
  Her little face still played in,
And splendours, with her birth begun,
  Had had no time for fading.

5

So, LILY, from those July hours,
  No wonder we should call her;
She looked such kinship to the flowers,
  Was but a little taller.

6

A Tuscan Lily, – only white,
  As Dante, in abhorrence
Of red corruption, wished aright
  The lilies of his Florence.

7

We could not wish her whiter, – her   25
    Who perfumed with pure blossom
The house! – a lovely thing to wear
    Upon a mother's bosom!

8

This July creature thought perhaps
    Our speech not worth assuming;   30
She sat upon her parents' laps,
    And mimicked the gnat's humming;

9

Said 'father,' 'mother' – then, left off,
    For tongues celestial, fitter;
Her hair had grown just long enough   35
    To catch heaven's jasper-glitter.

10

Babes! Love could always hear and see
    Behind the cloud that hid them.
'Let little children come to Me,
    And do not thou forbid them.'   40

11

So, unforbidding, have we met,
    And gently here have laid her,
Though winter is no time to get
    The flowers that should o'erspread her:

12

We should bring pansies quick with spring,   45
    Rose, violet, daffodilly,
And also, above everything,
    White lilies for our Lily.

13

Nay, more than flowers, this grave exacts, –
    Glad, grateful attestations   50
Of her sweet eyes and pretty acts,
    With calm renunciations.

14

Her very mother with light feet
    Should leave the place too earthy,
Saying 'The angels have thee, Sweet,   55
    Because we are not worthy.'

15

But winter kills the orange buds,
    The gardens in the frost are,
And all the heart dissolves in floods,
    Remembering we have lost her!   60

16

Poor earth, poor heart, – too weak, too weak,
    To miss the July shining!
Poor heart! – what bitter words we speak
    When God speaks of resigning!

17

Sustain this heart in us that faints,   65
    Thou God, the self-existent!
We catch up wild at parting saints,
    And feel Thy heaven too distant.

18

The wind that swept them out of sin
    Has ruffled all our vesture: 70
On the shut door that let them in,
    We beat with frantic gesture, –

19

To us, us also – open straight!
    The outer life is chilly –
Are *we* too, like the earth, to wait   75
    Till next year for our Lily?

20

– Oh, my own baby on my knees,
    My leaping, dimpled treasure,
At every word I write like these,
    Clasped close, with stronger pressure!   80

21

Too well my own heart understands, –
   At every word beats fuller –
My little feet, my little hands,
   And hair of Lily's colour!

22

– But God gives patience, Love learns strength,   85
   And Faith remembers promise,
And Hope itself can smile at length
   On other hopes gone from us.

23

Love, strong as Death, shall conquer Death,
   Through struggle, made more glorious.   90
This mother stills her sobbing breath,
   Renouncing, yet victorious.

24

Arms, empty of her child, she lifts,
   With spirit unbereaven, –
'God will not all take back His gifts;   95
   My Lily's mine in heaven!

25

'Still mine! maternal rights serene
   Not given to another!
The crystal bars shine faint between
   The souls of child and mother.   100

26

'Meanwhile,' the mother cries, 'content!
   Our love was well divided.
Its sweetness following where she went,
   Its anguish stayed where I did.

27

'Well done of God, to halve the lot,   105
   And give her all the sweetness;
To us, the empty room and cot, –
   To her, the Heaven's completeness.

28

'To us, this grave, – to her, the rows
    The mystic palm-trees spring in;   110
To us, the silence in the house, –
    To her, the choral singing.

29

'For her, to gladden in God's view, –
    For us, to hope and bear on! –
Grow, Lily, in thy garden new   115
    Beside the Rose of Sharon.

30

'Grow fast in heaven, sweet Lily clipped,
    In love more calm than this is, –
And may the angels dewy-lipped
    Remind thee of our kisses!   120

31

'While none shall tell thee of our tears,
    These human tears now falling,
Till, after a few patient years,
    One home shall take us all in.

32

'Child, father, mother – who, left out?   125
    Not mother, and not father! –
And when, our dying couch about,
    The natural mists shall gather,

33

'Some smiling angel close shall stand
    In old Correggio's fashion,   130
And bear a LILY in his hand,
    For death's ANNUNCIATION.'

Life and Love

Fast this Life of mine was dying,
    Blind already and calm as death,
Snowflakes on her bosom lying
    Scarcely heaving with her breath.

Love came by, and having known her   5
    In a dream of fabled lands,
Gently stooped, and laid upon her
    Mystic chrism of holy hands;

Drew his smile across her folded
    Eyelids, as the swallow dips;   10
Breathed as finely as the cold did,
    Through the locking of her lips.

So, when Life looked upward, being
    Warmed and breathed on from above,
What sight could she have for seeing,   15
    Evermore . . . but only LOVE?

A Denial

1

We have met late – it is too late to meet,
  O friend, not more than friend!
Death's forecome shroud is tangled round my feet,
And if I step or stir, I touch the end.
  In this last jeopardy   5
Can I approach thee, I, who cannot move?
How shall I answer thy request for love?
  Look in my face and see.

2

I love thee not, I dare not love thee! go
  In silence; drop my hand.   10
If thou seek roses, seek them where they blow
In garden-alleys, not in desert-sand.
  Can life and death agree,
That thou shouldst stoop thy song to my complaint?
I cannot love thee. If the word is faint,   15
  Look in my face and see.

3

I might have loved thee in some former days.
  Oh, then, my spirits had leapt
As now they sink, at hearing thy love-praise.
Before these faded cheeks were overwept,   20
  Had this been asked of me,
To love thee with my whole strong heart and head, –
I should have said still . . . yes, but *smiled* and said,
  'Look in my face and see!'

4

But now . . . God sees me, God, who took my heart   25
  And drowned it in life's surge.
In all your wide warm earth I have no part –
A light song overcomes me like a dirge.
  Could Love's great harmony

The saints keep step to when their bonds are loose,   30
Not weigh me down? am *I* a wife to choose?
   Look in my face and see.

5

While I behold, as plain as one who dreams,
   Some woman of full worth,
Whose voice, as cadenced as a silver stream's,   35
Shall prove the fountain-soul which sends it forth;
   One younger, more thought-free
And fair and gay, than I, thou must forget,
With brighter eyes than these . . . which are not wet . . .
   Look in my face and see!   40

6

So farewell thou, whom I have known too late
   To let thee come so near.
Be counted happy while men call thee great,
And one belovèd woman feels thee dear! –
   Not I! – that cannot be.   45
I am lost, I am changed, – I must go farther, where
The change shall take me worse, and no one dare
   Look in my face to see.

7

Meantime I bless thee. By these thoughts of mine
   I bless thee from all such!   50
I bless thy lamp to oil, thy cup to wine,
Thy hearth to joy, thy hand to an equal touch
   Of loyal troth. For me,
I love thee not, I love thee not! – away!
Here's no more courage in my soul to say   55
   'Look in my face and see.'

Proof and Disproof

1

Dost thou love me, my belovèd?
  Who shall answer yes or no?
What is provèd or disprovèd
  When my soul inquireth so,
Dost thou love me, my belovèd?   5

2

I have seen thy heart today,
  Never open to the crowd,
While to love me ay and ay
  Was the vow as it was vowed
By thine eyes of steadfast grey.   10

3

Now I sit alone, alone –
  And the hot tears break and burn,
Now, belovèd, thou art gone,
  Doubt and terror have their turn.
Is it love that I have known?   15

4

I have known some bitter things, –
  Anguish, anger, solitude.
Year by year an evil brings,
  Year by year denies a good;
March winds violate my springs.   20

5

I have known how sickness bends,
  I have known how sorrow breaks, –
How quick hopes have sudden ends,
  How the heart thinks till it aches
Of the smile of buried friends.   25

6

Last, I have known *thee*, my brave
  Noble thinker, lover, doer!
The best knowledge last I have.
  But thou comest as the thrower
Of fresh flowers upon a grave.   30

7

Count what feelings used to move me!
  Can this love assort with those?
Thou, who art so far above me,
  Wilt thou stoop so, for repose?
Is it true that thou canst love me?   35

8

Do not blame me if I doubt thee.
  I can call love by its name
When thine arm is wrapt about me;
  But even love seems not the same,
When I sit alone, without thee.   40

9

In thy clear eyes I descried
  Many a proof of love, today;
But tonight, those unbelied
  Speechful eyes being gone away,
There's the proof to seek, beside.   45

10

Dost thou love me, my belovèd?
  Only *thou* canst answer yes!
And, thou gone, the proof's disprovèd,
  And the cry rings answerless –
Dost thou love me, my belovèd?   50

Question and Answer

1

Love you seek for, presupposes
  Summer heat and sunny glow.
Tell me, do you find moss-roses
  Budding, blooming in the snow?
Snow might kill the rose-tree's root –   5
Shake it quickly from your foot,
  Lest it harm you as you go.

2

From the ivy where it dapples
  A grey ruin, stone by stone, –
Do you look for grapes or apples,   10
  Or for sad green leaves alone?
Pluck the leaves off, two or three –
Keep them for morality
  When you shall be safe and gone.

Inclusions

1

Oh, wilt thou have my hand, Dear, to lie along in thine?
As a little stone in a running stream, it seems to lie and pine.
Now drop the poor pale hand, Dear, . . . unfit to plight with thine.

2

Oh, wilt thou have my cheek, Dear, drawn closer to thine own?
My cheek is white, my cheek is worn, by many a tear run down. 5
Now leave a little space, Dear, . . . lest it should wet thine own.

3

Oh, must thou have my soul, Dear, commingled with thy soul? –
Red grows the cheek, and warm the hand, . . . the part is in the whole!
Nor hands nor cheeks keep separate, when soul is joined to soul.

Insufficiency

1

There is no one beside thee and no one above thee,
  Thou standest alone as the nightingale sings!
  And my words that would praise thee are impotent things,
For none can express thee though all should approve thee.
  I love thee so, Dear, that I only can love thee. 5

2

Say, what can I do for thee? weary thee, grieve thee?
  Lean on thy shoulder, new burdens to add?
  Weep my tears over thee, making thee sad?
Oh, hold me not – love me not! let me retrieve thee.
  I love thee so, Dear, that I only can leave thee. 10

Sonnets from the Portuguese

1

I thought once how Theocritus had sung
Of the sweet years, the dear and wished-for years,
Who each one in a gracious hand appears
To bear a gift for mortals, old or young:
And, as I mused it in his antique tongue,   5
I saw, in gradual vision through my tears,
The sweet, sad years, the melancholy years,
Those of my own life, who by turns had flung
A shadow across me. Straightway I was 'ware,
So weeping, how a mystic Shape did move   10
Behind me, and drew me backward by the hair,
And a voice said in mastery while I strove, . . .
'Guess now who holds thee?' – 'Death,' I said. But, there,
The silver answer rang, . . . 'Not Death, but Love.'

2

But only three in all God's universe
Have heard this word thou hast said, – Himself, beside
Thee speaking, and me listening! and replied
One of us . . . *that* was God, . . . and laid the curse
So darkly on my eyelids, as to amerce   5
My sight from seeing thee, – that if I had died,
The deathweights, placed there, would have signified
Less absolute exclusion. 'Nay' is worse
From God than from all others, O my friend!
Men could not part us with their worldly jars,   10
Nor the seas change us, nor the tempests bend;
Our hands would touch for all the mountain-bars, –
And, heaven being rolled between us at the end,
We should but vow the faster for the stars.

3

Unlike are we, unlike, O princely Heart!
Unlike our uses and our destinies.
Our ministering two angels look surprise
On one another, as they strike athwart
Their wings in passing. Thou, bethink thee, art   5
A guest for queens to social pageantries,
With gages from a hundred brighter eyes
Than tears even can make mine, to play thy part
Of chief musician. What hast *thou* to do
With looking from the lattice-lights at me,   10
A poor, tired, wandering singer, . . . singing through
The dark, and leaning up a cypress tree?
The chrism is on thine head, – on mine, the dew, –
And Death must dig the level where these agree.

4

Thou hast thy calling to some palace-floor,
Most gracious singer of high poems! where
The dancers will break footing, from the care
Of watching up thy pregnant lips for more.
And dost thou lift this house's latch too poor   5
For hand of thine? and canst thou think and bear
To let thy music drop here unaware
In folds of golden fullness at my door?
Look up and see the casement broken in,
The bats and owlets builders in the roof!   10
My cricket chirps against thy mandolin.
Hush, call no echo up in further proof
Of desolation! there's a voice within
That weeps . . . as thou must sing . . . alone, aloof.

5

I lift my heavy heart up solemnly,
As once Electra her sepulchral urn,
And, looking in thine eyes, I overturn
The ashes at thy feet. Behold and see
What a great heap of grief lay hid in me, 5
And how the red wild sparkles dimly burn
Through the ashen greyness. If thy foot in scorn
Could tread them out to darkness utterly,
It might be well perhaps. But if instead
Thou wait beside me for the wind to blow 10
The grey dust up, . . . those laurels on thine head,
O my Belovèd, will not shield thee so,
That none of all the fires shall scorch and shred
The hair beneath. Stand further off then! go.

6

Go from me. Yet I feel that I shall stand
Henceforward in thy shadow. Nevermore
Alone upon the threshold of my door
Of individual life, I shall command
The uses of my soul, nor lift my hand 5
Serenely in the sunshine as before,
Without the sense of that which I forbore, . . .
Thy touch upon the palm. The widest land
Doom takes to part us, leaves thy heart in mine
With pulses that beat double. What I do 10
And what I dream include thee, as the wine
Must taste of its own grapes. And when I sue
God for myself, He hears that name of thine,
And sees within my eyes the tears of two.

7

The face of all the world is changed, I think,
Since first I heard the footsteps of thy soul
Move still, oh, still, beside me, as they stole
Betwixt me and the dreadful outer brink
Of obvious death, where I, who thought to sink,   5
Was caught up into love, and taught the whole
Of life in a new rhythm. The cup of dole
God gave for baptism, I am fain to drink,
And praise its sweetness, Sweet, with thee anear.
The names of country, heaven, are changed away   10
For where thou art or shalt be, there or here;
And this . . . this lute and song . . . loved yesterday
(The singing angels know) are only dear,
Because thy name moves right in what they say.

8

What can I give thee back, O liberal
And princely giver, who hast brought the gold
And purple of thine heart, unstained, untold,
And laid them on the outside of the wall
For such as I to take or leave withal,   5
In unexpected largesse? am I cold,
Ungrateful, that for these most manifold
High gifts, I render nothing back at all?
Not so; not cold, – but very poor instead.
Ask God who knows. For frequent tears have run   10
The colours from my life, and left so dead
And pale a stuff, it were not fitly done
To give the same as pillow to thy head.
Go farther! let it serve to trample on.

9

Can it be right to give what I can give?
To let thee sit beneath the fall of tears
As salt as mine, and hear the sighing years
Re-sighing on my lips renunciative
Through those infrequent smiles which fail to live   5
For all thy adjurations? O my fears,
That this can scarce be right! We are not peers,
So to be lovers; and I own, and grieve,
That givers of such gifts as mine are, must
Be counted with the ungenerous. Out, alas!   10
I will not soil thy purple with my dust,
Nor breathe my poison on thy Venice-glass,[98]
Nor give thee any love . . . which were unjust.
Beloved, I only love thee! let it pass.

10

Yet, love, mere love, is beautiful indeed
And worthy of acceptation. Fire is bright,
Let temple burn, or flax. An equal light
Leaps in the flame from cedar-plank or weed.
And love is fire; and when I say at need   5
I love thee . . . mark! . . . . *I love thee!* . . . in thy sight
I stand transfigured, glorified aright,
With conscience of the new rays that proceed
Out of my face toward thine. There's nothing low
In love, when love the lowest: meanest creatures   10
Who love God, God accepts while loving so.
And what I *feel*, across the inferior features
Of what I *am*, doth flash itself, and show
How that great work of Love enhances Nature's.

11

And therefore if to love can be desert,
I am not all unworthy. Cheeks as pale
As these you see, and trembling knees that fail
To bear the burden of a heavy heart, –
This weary minstrel-life that once was girt   5
To climb Aornus,[99] and can scarce avail
To pipe now 'gainst the valley nightingale
A melancholy music, – why advert
To these things? O Belovèd, it is plain
I am not of thy worth nor for thy place!   10
And yet, because I love thee, I obtain
From that same love this vindicating grace,
To live on still in love, and yet in vain, ...
To bless thee, yet renounce thee to thy face.

12

Indeed this very love which is my boast,
And which, when rising up from breast to brow,
Doth crown me with a ruby large enow
To draw men's eyes and prove the inner cost, ...
This love even, all my worth, to the uttermost,   5
I should not love withal, unless that thou
Hadst set me an example, shown me how,
When first thine earnest eyes with mine were crossed,
And love called love. And thus, I cannot speak
Of love even, as a good thing of my own.   10
Thy soul hath snatched up mine all faint and weak,
And placed it by thee on a golden throne, –
And that I love (O soul, we must be meek!)
Is by thee only, whom I love alone.

13

And wilt thou have me fashion into speech
The love I bear thee, finding words enough,
And hold the torch out, while the winds are rough,
Between our faces, to cast light on each? –
I drop it at thy feet. I cannot teach   5
My hand to hold my spirit so far off
From myself . . . me . . . that I should bring thee proof
In words, of love hid in me out of reach.
Nay, let the silence of my womanhood
Commend my woman-love to thy belief, –   10
Seeing that I stand unwon, however wooed,
And rend the garment of my life, in brief,
By a most dauntless, voiceless fortitude,
Lest one touch of this heart convey its grief.

14

If thou must love me, let it be for nought
Except for love's sake only. Do not say
'I love her for her smile . . . her look . . . her way
Of speaking gently, . . . for a trick of thought
That falls in well with mine, and certes brought   5
A sense of pleasant ease on such a day' –
For these things in themselves, Belovèd, may
Be changed, or change for thee, – and love, so wrought,
May be unwrought so. Neither love me for
Thine own dear pity's wiping my cheeks dry, –   10
A creature might forget to weep, who bore
Thy comfort long, and lose thy love thereby!
But love me for love's sake, that evermore
Thou mayst love on, through love's eternity.

15

Accuse me not, beseech thee, that I wear
Too calm and sad a face in front of thine;
For we two look two ways, and cannot shine
With the same sunlight on our brow and hair.
On me thou lookest, with no doubting care,   5
As on a bee shut in a crystalline, –
Since sorrow hath shut me safe in love's divine,
And to spread wing and fly in the outer air
Were most impossible failure, if I strove
To fail so. But I look on thee ... on thee ...   10
Beholding, besides love, the end of love,
Hearing oblivion beyond memory!
As one who sits and gazes from above,
Over the rivers to the bitter sea.

16

And yet, because thou overcomest so,
Because thou art more noble and like a king,
Thou canst prevail against my fears and fling
Thy purple round me, till my heart shall grow
Too close against thine heart, henceforth to know   5
How it shook when alone. Why, conquering
May prove as lordly and complete a thing
In lifting upward, as in crushing low!
And as a vanquished soldier yields his sword
To one who lifts him from the bloody earth, –   10
Even so, Belovèd, I at last record,
Here ends my strife. If *thou* invite me forth,
I rise above abasement at the word.
Make thy love larger to enlarge my worth.

17

My poet, thou canst touch on all the notes
God set between His After and Before,
And strike up and strike off the general roar
Of the rushing worlds, a melody that floats
In a serene air purely. Antidotes   5
Of medicated music, answering for
Mankind's forlornest uses, thou canst pour
From thence into their ears. God's will devotes
Thine to such ends, and mine to wait on thine.
How, Dearest, wilt thou have me for most use?   10
A hope, to sing by gladly? . . . or a fine
Sad memory, with thy songs to interfuse?
A shade, in which to sing . . . of palm or pine?
A grave, on which to rest from singing? . . . Choose.

18

I never gave a lock of hair away
To a man, dearest, except this to thee,
Which now upon my fingers thoughtfully
I ring out to the full brown length and say
'Take it.' My day of youth went yesterday;   5
My hair no longer bounds to my foot's glee,
Nor plant I it from rose or myrtle-tree,
As girls do, any more. It only may
Now shade on two pale cheeks, the mark of tears,
Taught drooping from the head that hangs aside   10
Through sorrow's trick. I thought the funeral-shears
Would take this first, but Love is justified, –
Take it, thou, . . . finding pure, from all those years,
The kiss my mother left here when she died.

19

The soul's Rialto[100] hath its merchandise;
I barter curl for curl upon that mart,
And from my poet's forehead to my heart,
Receive this lock which outweighs argosies,[101] –
As purply black, as erst, to Pindar's eyes,   5
The dim purpureal tresses gloomed athwart
The nine white Muse-brows.[102] For this counterpart, . . .
The bay-crown's shade,[103] Belovèd, I surmise,
Still lingers on thy curl, it is so black!
Thus, with a fillet of smooth-kissing breath,   10
I tie the shadow safe from gliding back,
And lay the gift where nothing hindereth,
Here on my heart, as on thy brow, to lack
No natural heat till mine grows cold in death.

20

Belovèd, my Belovèd, when I think
That thou wast in the world a year ago,
What time I sat alone here in the snow
And saw no footprint, heard the silence sink
No moment at thy voice, . . . but, link by link,   5
Went counting all my chains, as if that so
They never could fall off at any blow
Struck by thy possible hand, ... why, thus I drink
Of life's great cup of wonder! Wonderful,
Never to feel thee thrill the day or night   10
With personal act or speech, – nor ever cull
Some prescience of thee with the blossoms white
Thou sawest growing! Atheists are as dull,
Who cannot guess God's presence out of sight.

21

Say over again, and yet once over again,
That thou dost love me. Though the word repeated
Should seem 'a cuckoo-song', as thou dost treat it.
Remember, never to the hill or plain,
Valley and wood, without her cuckoo-strain,   5
Comes the fresh Spring in all her green completed.
Belovèd, I, amid the darkness greeted
By a doubtful spirit-voice, in that doubt's pain
Cry . . . 'Speak once more . . . thou lovest!' Who can fear
Too many stars, though each in heaven shall roll –   10
Too many flowers, though each shall crown the year?
Say thou dost love me, love me, love me – toll
The silver iterance! – only minding, dear,
To love me also in silence, with thy soul.

22

When our two souls stand up erect and strong,
Face to face, silent, drawing nigh and nigher,
Until the lengthening wings break into fire
At either curvèd point, – what bitter wrong
Can the earth do to us, that we should not long   5
Be here contented? Think. In mounting higher,
The angels would press on us, and aspire
To drop some golden orb of perfect song
Into our deep, dear silence. Let us stay
Rather on earth, Belovèd, – where the unfit   10
Contrarious moods of men recoil away
And isolate pure spirits, and permit
A place to stand and love in for a day,
With darkness and the death-hour rounding it.

23

Is it indeed so? If I lay here dead,
Wouldst thou miss any life in losing mine?
And would the sun for thee more coldly shine,
Because of grave-damps falling round my head?
I marvelled, my Belovèd, when I read 5
Thy thought so in the letter. I am thine –
But . . . *so* much to thee? Can I pour thy wine
While my hands tremble? Then my soul, instead
Of dreams of death, resumes life's lower range.
Then, love me, Love! look on me . . . breathe on me! 10
As brighter ladies do not count it strange,
For love, to give up acres and degree,
I yield the grave for thy sake, and exchange
My near sweet view of Heaven, for earth with thee!

24

Let the world's sharpness like a clasping knife
Shut in upon itself and do no harm
In this close hand of Love, now soft and warm,
And let us hear no sound of human strife
After the click of the shutting. Life to life – 5
I lean upon thee, dear, without alarm,
And feel as safe as guarded by a charm
Against the stab of worldlings, who if rife
Are weak to injure. Very whitely still
The lilies of our lives may reassure 10
Their blossoms from their roots, accessible
Alone to heavenly dews that drop not fewer:
Growing straight, out of man's reach, on the hill.
God only, who made us rich, can make us poor.

25

A heavy heart, Belovèd, have I borne
From year to year until I saw thy face,
And sorrow after sorrow took the place
Of all those natural joys as lightly worn
As the stringed pearls . . . each lifted in its turn   5
By a beating heart at dance-time. Hopes apace
Were changed to long despairs, till God's own grace
Could scarcely lift above the world forlorn
My heavy heart. Then *thou* didst bid me bring
And let it drop adown thy calmly great   10
Deep being! Fast it sinketh, as a thing
Which its own nature doth precipitate,
While thine doth close above it, mediating
Betwixt the stars and the unaccomplished fate.

26

I lived with visions for my company,
Instead of men and women, years ago,
And found them gentle mates, nor thought to know
A sweeter music than they played to me.
But soon their trailing purple was not free   5
Of this world's dust, – their lutes did silent grow,
And I myself grew faint and blind below
Their vanishing eyes. Then THOU didst come . . . to be,
Belovèd, what they seemed. Their shining fronts,
Their songs, their splendours (better, yet the same,   10
As river-water hallowed into fonts),
Met in thee, and from out thee overcame
My soul with satisfaction of all wants –
Because God's gifts put man's best dreams to shame.

27

My own Belovèd, who hast lifted me
From this drear flat of earth where I was thrown,
And, in betwixt the languid ringlets, blown
A life-breath, till the forehead hopefully
Shines out again, as all the angels see,   5
Before thy saving kiss! My own, my own,
Who camest to me when the world was gone,
And I who looked for only God, found *thee*!
I find thee; I am safe, and strong, and glad.
As one who stands in dewless asphodel,[104]   10
Looks backward on the tedious time he had
In the upper life, – so I, with bosom-swell,
Make witness, here, between the good and bad,
That Love, as strong as Death, retrieves as well.

28

My letters![105] all dead paper, . . . mute and white! –
And yet they seem alive and quivering
Against my tremulous hands which loose the string
And let them drop down on my knee tonight.
This said, . . . he wished to have me in his sight   5
Once, as a friend: this fixed a day in spring
To come and touch my hand . . . a simple thing,
Yet I wept for it! – this, . . . the paper's light . . .
Said, *Dear, I love thee*; and I sank and quailed
As if God's future thundered on my past.   10
This said, *I am thine* – and so its ink has paled
With lying at my heart that beat too fast.
And this . . . O Love, thy words have ill availed,
If, what this said, I dared repeat at last!

29

I think of thee! – my thoughts do twine and bud
About thee, as wild vines, about a tree,
Put out broad leaves, and soon there's nought to see
Except the straggling green which hides the wood.
Yet, O my palm-tree, be it understood   5
I will not have my thoughts instead of thee
Who art dearer, better! Rather instantly
Renew thy presence. As a strong tree should,
Rustle thy boughs and set thy trunk all bare,
And let these bands of greenery which insphere thee,   10
Drop heavily down, . . . burst, shattered, everywhere!
Because, in this deep joy to see and hear thee
And breathe within thy shadow a new air,
I do not think of thee – I am too near thee.

30

I see thine image through my tears tonight,
And yet today I saw thee smiling. How
Refer the cause? – Belovèd, is it thou
Or I, who makes me sad? The acolyte
Amid the chanted joy and thankful rite,   5
May so fall flat, with pale insensate brow,
On the altar-stair. I hear thy voice and vow
Perplexed, uncertain, since thou art out of sight,
As he, in his swooning ears, the choir's amen.
Belovèd, dost thou love? or did I see all   10
The glory as I dreamed, and fainted when
Too vehement light dilated my ideal,
For my soul's eyes? Will that light come again,
As now these tears come . . . falling hot and real?

31

Thou comest! all is said without a word.
I sit beneath thy looks, as children do
In the noon-sun, with souls that tremble through
Their happy eyelids from an unaverred
Yet prodigal inward joy. Behold, I erred   5
In that last doubt! and yet I cannot rue
The sin most, but the occasion . . . that we two
Should for a moment stand unministered
By a mutual presence. Ah, keep near and close,
Thou dovelike help! and, when my fears would rise,   10
With thy broad heart serenely interpose.
Brood down with thy divine sufficiencies
These thoughts which tremble when bereft of those,
Like callow birds left desert to the skies.

32

The first time that the sun rose on thine oath
To love me, I looked forward to the moon
To slacken all those bonds which seemed too soon
And quickly tied to make a lasting troth.
Quick-loving hearts, I thought, may quickly loathe;   5
And, looking on myself, I seemed not one
For such man's love! – more like an out-of-tune
Worn viol, a good singer would be wroth
To spoil his song with, and which, snatched in haste,
Is laid down at the first ill-sounding note.   10
I did not wrong myself so, but I placed
A wrong on *thee*. For perfect strains may float
'Neath master-hands, from instruments defaced, –
And great souls, at one stroke, may do and dote.

33

Yes, call me by my pet-name![106] let me hear
The name I used to run at, when a child,
From innocent play, and leave the cowslips piled,
To glance up in some face that proved me dear
With the look of its eyes. I miss the clear   5
Fond voices, which, being drawn and reconciled
Into the music of Heaven's undefiled,
Call me no longer. Silence on the bier,
While I call God . . . call God! – So let thy mouth
Be heir to those who are now exanimate.   10
Gather the north flowers to complete the south,
And catch the early love up in the late.
Yes, call me by that name, – and I, in truth,
With the same heart, will answer and not wait.

34

With the same heart, I said, I'll answer thee
As those, when thou shalt call me by my name –
Lo, the vain promise! is the same, the same,
Perplexed and ruffled by life's strategy?
When called before, I told how hastily   5
I dropped my flowers or brake off from a game,
To run and answer with the smile that came
At play last moment, and went on with me
Through my obedience. When I answer now,
I drop a grave thought – break from solitude;   10
Yet still my heart goes to thee . . . ponder how . . .
Not as to a single good, but all my good!
Lay thy hand on it, best one, and allow
That no child's foot could run fast as this blood.

35

If I leave all for thee, wilt thou exchange
And be all to me? Shall I never miss
Home-talk and blessing and the common kiss
That comes to each in turn, nor count it strange,
When I look up, to drop on a new range   5
Of walls and floors . . . another home than this?
Nay, wilt thou fill that place by me which is
Filled by dead eyes too tender to know change?
That's hardest. If to conquer love, has tried,
To conquer grief, tries more . . . as all things prove;   10
For grief indeed is love and grief beside.
Alas, I have grieved so I am hard to love.
Yet love me – wilt thou? Open thine heart wide,
And fold within, the wet wings of thy dove.

36

When we met first and loved, I did not build
Upon the event with marble. Could it mean
To last, a love set pendulous between
Sorrow and sorrow? Nay, I rather thrilled,
Distrusting every light that seemed to gild   5
The onward path, and feared to overlean
A finger even. And, though I have grown serene
And strong since then, I think that God has willed
A still renewable fear . . . O love, O troth . . .
Lest these enclaspèd hands should never hold,   10
This mutual kiss drop down between us both
As an unowned thing, once the lips being cold.
And Love, be false! if *he*, to keep one oath,
Must lose one joy, by his life's star foretold.

37

Pardon, oh, pardon, that my soul should make,
Of all that strong divineness which I know
For thine and thee, an image only so
Formed of the sand, and fit to shift and break.
It is that distant years which did not take   5
Thy sovranty, recoiling with a blow,
Have forced my swimming brain to undergo
Their doubt and dread, and blindly to forsake
Thy purity of likeness, and distort
Thy worthiest love to a worthless counterfeit.   10
As if a shipwrecked Pagan, safe in port,
His guardian sea-god to commemorate,
Should set a sculptured porpoise, gills a-snort
And vibrant tail, within the temple-gate.

38

First time he kissed me, he but only kissed
The fingers of this hand wherewith I write;
And ever since, it grew more clean and white, . . .
Slow to world-greetings . . . quick with its 'Oh, list,'
When the angels speak. A ring of amethyst   5
I could not wear here, plainer to my sight,
Than that first kiss. The second passed in height
The first, and sought the forehead, and half missed,
Half falling on the hair. O beyond meed!
That was the chrism of love,[107] which love's own crown, 10
With sanctifying sweetness, did precede.
The third upon my lips was folded down
In perfect, purple state; since when, indeed,
I have been proud and said, 'My love, my own.'

39

Because thou hast the power and own'st the grace
To look through and behind this mask of me
(Against which years have beat thus blanchingly
With their rains) and behold my soul's true face,
The dim and weary witness of life's race! –   5
Because thou hast the faith and love to see,
Through that same soul's distracting lethargy,
The patient angel waiting for a place
In the new heavens! because nor sin nor woe,
Nor God's infliction, nor death's neighbourhood,   10
Nor all which others viewing, turn to go, . . .
Nor all which makes me tired of all, self-viewed, . . .
Nothing repels thee, . . . dearest, teach me so
To pour out gratitude, as thou dost, good.

40

Oh, yes! they love through all this world of ours!
I will not gainsay love, called love forsooth.
I have heard love talked in my early youth,
And since, not so long back but that the flowers
Then gathered, smell still. Mussulmans [108] and Giaours [109]   5
Throw kerchiefs at a smile, and have no ruth
For any weeping. Polypheme's [110] white tooth
Slips on the nut, if, after frequent showers,
The shell is over-smooth, – and not so much
Will turn the thing called love, aside to hate,   10
Or else to oblivion. But thou art not such
A lover, my Belovèd! thou canst wait
Through sorrow and sickness, to bring souls to touch,
And think it soon when others cry 'Too late.'

41

I thank all who have loved me in their hearts,
With thanks and love from mine. Deep thanks to all
Who paused a little near the prison-wall,
To hear my music in its louder parts,
Ere they went onward, each one to the mart's   5
Or temple's occupation, beyond call.
But thou, who, in my voice's sink and fall,
When the sob took it, thy divinest Art's
Own instrument didst drop down at thy foot,
To hearken what I said between my tears, . . .   10
Instruct me how to thank thee! – Oh, to shoot
My soul's full meaning into future years,
That *they* should lend it utterance, and salute
Love that endures, from Life that disappears!

42

'*My future will not copy fair my past*'[111] –
I wrote that once; and thinking at my side
My ministering life-angel justified
The word by his appealing look upcast
To the white throne of God, I turned at last,   5
And there, instead, saw thee, not unallied
To angels in thy soul! Then I, long tried
By natural ills, received the comfort fast,
While budding, at thy sight, my pilgrim's staff
Gave out green leaves with morning dews impearled.   10
I seek no copy now of life's first half:
Leave here the pages with long musing curled,
And write me new my future's epigraph,
New angel mine, unhoped for in the world!

43

How do I love thee? Let me count the ways.
I love thee to the depth and breadth and height
My soul can reach, when feeling out of sight
For the ends of Being and ideal Grace.
I love thee to the level of every day's   5
Most quiet need, by sun and candlelight.
I love thee freely, as men strive for Right;
I love thee purely, as they turn from Praise.
I love thee with the passion put to use
In my old griefs, and with my childhood's faith.   10
I love thee with a love I seemed to lose
With my lost saints, – I love thee with the breath,
Smiles, tears, of all my life! – and, if God choose,
I shall but love thee better after death.

44

Belovèd, thou hast brought me many flowers
Plucked in the garden, all the summer through
And winter, and it seemed as if they grew
In this close room, nor missed the sun and showers.
So, in the like name of that love of ours,   5
Take back these thoughts which here unfolded too,
And which on warm and cold days I withdrew
From my heart's ground. Indeed, those beds and bowers
Be overgrown with bitter weeds and rue,
And wait thy weeding; yet here's eglantine,   10
Here's ivy! – take them, as I used to do
Thy flowers, and keep them where they shall not pine.
Instruct thine eyes to keep their colours true,
And tell thy soul, their roots are left in mine.

Aurora Leigh

A Poem, in Nine Books

Aurora Leigh

A Poem, in Nine Books

DEDICATION TO JOHN KENYON, ESQ.

The words 'cousin' and 'friend' are constantly recurring in this poem, the last pages of which have been finished under the hospitality of your roof, my own dearest cousin and friend – cousin and friend, in a sense of less equality and greater disinterestedness than in the case of 'Romney'.

Ending, therefore, and preparing once more to quit England, I venture to leave in your hands this book, the most mature of my works, and the one into which my highest convictions upon Life and Art have entered; that as, through my various efforts in literature and steps in life, you have believed in me, borne with me, and been generous to me, far beyond the common uses of mere relationship or sympathy of mind, so you may kindly accept, in sight of the public, this poor sign of esteem, gratitude, and affection from

Your unforgetting

E. B. B.
39 DEVONSHIRE PLACE,
October 17, 1856.

First Book

Of writing many books there is no end;
And I who have written much in prose and verse
For others' uses, will write now for mine, –
Will write my story for my better self
As when you paint your portrait for a friend,   5
Who keeps it in a drawer and looks at it
Long after he has ceased to love you, just
To hold together what he was and is.

I, writing thus, am still what men call young,
I have not so far left the coasts of life   10
To travel inland, that I cannot hear
That murmur of the outer Infinite

Which unweaned babies smile at in their sleep
When wondered at for smiling; not so far,
But still I catch my mother at her post   15
Beside the nursery-door, with finger up,
'Hush, hush – here's too much noise!' while her sweet eyes
Leap forward, taking part against her word
In the child's riot. Still I sit and feel
My father's slow hand, when she had left us both,   20
Stroke out my childish curls across his knee,
And hear Assunta's daily jest (she knew
He liked it better than a better jest)
Inquire how many golden scudi went
To make such ringlets. O my father's hand,   25
Stroke heavily, heavily, the poor hair down,
Draw, press the child's head closer to thy knee!
I'm still too young, too young, to sit alone.

I write. My mother was a Florentine,
Whose rare blue eyes were shut from seeing me   30
When scarcely I was four years old; my life,
A poor spark snatched up from a failing lamp
Which went out therefore. She was weak and frail;
She could not bear the joy of giving life,
The mother's rapture slew her. If her kiss   35
Had left a longer weight upon my lips
It might have steadied the uneasy breath,
And reconciled and fraternised my soul
With the new order. As it was, indeed,
I felt a mother-want about the world,   40
And still went seeking, like a bleating lamb
Left out at night, in shutting up the fold, –
As restless as a nest-deserted bird
Grown chill through something being away, though what
It knows not. I, Aurora Leigh, was born   45
To make my father sadder, and myself
Not overjoyous, truly. Women know
The way to rear up children (to be just),
They know a simple, merry, tender knack
Of tying sashes, fitting baby-shoes,   50
And stringing pretty words that make no sense,

And kissing full sense into empty words,
Which things are corals to cut life upon,
Although such trifles: children learn by such,
Love's holy earnest in a pretty play   55
And get not over-early solemnised,
But seeing, as in a rose-bush, Love's Divine
Which burns and hurts not, – not a single bloom, –
Become aware and unafraid of Love.
Such good do mothers. Fathers love as well   60
– Mine did, I know, – but still with heavier brains,
And wills more consciously responsible,
And not as wisely, since less foolishly;
So mothers have God's licence to be missed.

My father was an austere Englishman,   65
Who, after a dry life-time spent at home
In college-learning, law, and parish talk,
Was flooded with a passion unaware,
His whole provisioned and complacent past
Drowned out from him that moment. As he stood   70
In Florence, where he had come to spend a month
And note the secret of Da Vinci's drains,
He musing somewhat absently perhaps
Some English question . . . whether men should pay
The unpopular but necessary tax   75
With left or right hand – in the alien sun
In that great square of the Santissima
There drifted past him (scarcely marked enough
To move his comfortable island scorn)
A train of priestly banners, cross and psalm,   80
The white-veiled rose-crowned maidens holding up
Tall tapers, weighty for such wrists, aslant
To the blue luminous tremor of the air,
And letting drop the white wax as they went
To eat the bishop's wafer at the church;   85
From which long trail of chanting priests and girls,
A face flashed like a cymbal on his face
And shook with silent clangour brain and heart,
Transfiguring him to music. Thus, even thus,
He too received his sacramental gift   90

With eucharistic meanings; for he loved.

And thus beloved, she died. I've heard it said
That but to see him in the first surprise
Of widower and father, nursing me,
Unmothered little child of four years old,   95
His large man's hands afraid to touch my curls,
As if the gold would tarnish, – his grave lips
Contriving such a miserable smile
As if he knew needs must, or I should die,
And yet 'twas hard, – would almost make the stones   100
Cry out for pity. There's a verse he set
In Santa Croce to her memory, –
'Weep for an infant too young to weep much
When death removed this mother' – stops the mirth
Today on women's faces when they walk   105
With rosy children hanging on their gowns,
Under the cloister to escape the sun
That scorches in the piazza. After which
He left our Florence and made haste to hide
Himself, his prattling child, and silent grief,   110
Among the mountains above Pelago;
Because unmothered babes, he thought, had need
Of mother nature more than others use,
And Pan's white goats, with udders warm and full
Of mystic contemplations, come to feed   115
Poor milkless lips of orphans like his own –
Such scholar-scraps he talked, I've heard from friends,
For even prosaic men who wear grief long
Will get to wear it as a hat aside
With a flower stuck in 't. Father, then, and child,   120
We lived among the mountains many years,
God's silence on the outside of the house,
And we who did not speak too loud within,
And old Assunta to make up the fire,
Crossing herself whene'er a sudden flame   125
Which lightened from the firewood, made alive
That picture of my mother on the wall.

The painter drew it after she was dead,

And when the face was finished, throat and hands,
Her cameriera carried him, in hate   130
Of the English-fashioned shroud, the last brocade
She dressed in at the Pitti; 'he should paint
No sadder thing than that,' she swore, 'to wrong
Her poor signora.' Therefore very strange
The effect was. I, a little child, would crouch   135
For hours upon the floor with knees drawn up,
And gaze across them, half in terror, half
In adoration, at the picture there, –
That swan-like supernatural white life
Just sailing upward from the red stiff silk   140
Which seemed to have no part in it nor power
To keep it from quite breaking out of bounds.
For hours I sat and stared. Asssunta's awe
And my poor father's melancholy eyes
Still pointed that way. That way went my thoughts   145
When wandering beyond sight. And as I grew
In years, I mixed, confused, unconsciously,
Whatever I last read or heard or dreamed,
Abhorrent, admirable, beautiful,
Pathetical, or ghastly, or grotesque,   150
With still that face . . . which did not therefore change,
But kept the mystic level of all forms,
Hates, fears and admirations, was by turns
Ghost, fiend, and angel, fairy, witch, and sprite,
A dauntless Muse who eyes a dreadful Fate,   155
A loving Psyche [112] who loses sight of Love,
A still Medusa [113] with mild milky brows
All curdled and all clothed upon with snakes
Whose slime falls fast as sweat will; or anon
Our Lady of the Passion, stabbed with swords   160
Where the Babe sucked; or, Lamia [114] in her first
Moonlighted pallor, ere she shrunk and blinked
And shuddering wriggled down to the unclean;
Or my own mother, leaving her last smile
In her last kiss upon the baby-mouth   165
My father pushed down on the bed for that, –
Or my dead mother, without smile or kiss,
Buried at Florence. All which images,

Concentred on the picture, glassed themselves
Before my meditative childhood, as   170
The incoherencies of change and death
Are represented fully, mixed and merged,
In the smooth fair mystery of perpetual Life.

And while I stared away my childish wits
Upon my mother's picture (ah, poor child!)   175
My father, who through love had suddenly
Thrown off the old conventions, broken loose
From chin-bands of the soul, like Lazarus,
Yet had no time to learn to talk and walk
Or grow anew familiar with the sun, –   180
Who had reached to freedom, not to action, lived,
But lived as one entranced, with thoughts, not aims, –
Whom love had unmade from a common man
But not completed to an uncommon man, –
My father taught me what he had learnt the best   185
Before he died and left me, – grief and love.
And, seeing we had books among the hills,
Strong words of counselling souls confederate
With vocal pines and waters, – out of books
He taught me all the ignorance of men,   190
And how God laughs in heaven when any man
Says 'Here I'm learned; this, I understand;
In that, I am never caught at fault or doubt.'
He sent the schools to school, demonstrating
A fool will pass for such through one mistake,   195
While a philosopher will pass for such,
Through said mistakes being ventured in the gross
And heaped up to a system.
                              I am like,
They tell me, my dear father. Broader brows
Howbeit, upon a slenderer undergrowth   200
Of delicate features, – paler, near as grave;
But then my mother's smile breaks up the whole,
And makes it better sometimes than itself.

So, nine full years, our days were hid with God
Among his mountains: I was just thirteen,   205

Still growing like the plants from unseen roots
In tongue-tied Springs, – and suddenly awoke
To full life and life's needs and agonies
With an intense, strong, struggling heart beside
A stone-dead father. Life, struck sharp on death,   210
Makes awful lightning. His last word was, 'Love' –
'Love, my child, love, love!' – (then he had done with grief)
'Love, my child.' Ere I answered he was gone,
And none was left to love in all the world.

There, ended childhood. What succeeded next   215
I recollect as, after fevers, men
Thread back the passage of delirium,
Missing the turn still, baffled by the door;
Smooth endless days, notched here and there with knives;
A weary, wormy darkness, spurred i' the flank   220
With flame, that it should eat and end itself
Like some tormented scorpion. Then at last
I do remember clearly, how there came
A stranger with authority, not right
(I thought not), who commanded, caught me up   225
From old Assunta's neck; how, with a shriek,
She let me go, – while I, with ears too full
Of my father's silence to shriek back a word,
In all a child's astonishment at grief
Stared at the wharfedge where she stood and moaned,   230
My poor Assunta, where she stood and moaned!
The white walls, the blue hills, my Italy,
Drawn backward from the shuddering steamer-deck,
Like one in anger drawing back her skirts
Which suppliants catch at. Then the bitter sea   235
Inexorably pushed between us both,
And sweeping up the ship with my despair
Threw us out as a pasture to the stars.

Ten nights and days we voyaged on the deep;
Ten nights and days, without the common face   240
Of any day or night; the moon and sun
Cut off from the green reconciling earth,
To starve into a blind ferocity

And glare unnatural; the very sky
(Dropping its bell-net down upon the sea   245
As if no human heart should 'scape alive,)
Bedraggled with the desolating salt,
Until it seemed no more than holy heaven
To which my father went. All new and strange;
The universe turned stranger, for a child.   250

Then, land! – then, England! oh, the frosty cliffs
Looked cold upon me. Could I find a home
Among those mean red houses through the fog?
And when I heard my father's language first
From alien lips which had no kiss for mine   255
I wept aloud, then laughed, then wept, then wept,
And some one near me said the child was mad
Through much sea-sickness. The train swept us on.
Was this my father's England? the great isle?
The ground seemed cut up from the fellowship   260
Of verdure, field from field, as man from man;
The skies themselves looked low and positive,
As almost you could touch them with a hand,
And dared to do it they were so far off
From God's celestial crystals; all things blurred   265
And dull and vague. Did Shakespeare and his mates
Absorb the light here? – not a hill or stone
With heart to strike a radiant colour up
Or active outline on the indifferent air.

I think I see my father's sister stand   270
Upon the hall-step of her country-house
To give me welcome. She stood straight and calm,
Her somewhat narrow forehead braided tight
As if for taming accidental thoughts
From possible pulses; brown hair pricked with grey   275
By frigid use of life (she was not old
Although my father's elder by a year),
A nose drawn sharply, yet in delicate lines;
A close mild mouth, a little soured about
The ends, through speaking unrequited loves   280
Or peradventure niggardly half-truths;

Eyes of no colour, – once they might have smiled,
But never, never have forgot themselves
In smiling; cheeks, in which was yet a rose
Of perished summers, like a rose in a book,   285
Kept more for ruth than pleasure, – if past bloom,
Past fading also.
              She had lived, we'll say,
A harmless life, she called a virtuous life,
A quiet life, which was not life at all
(But that, she had not lived enough to know),   290
Between the vicar and the county squires,
The lord-lieutenant looking down sometimes
From the empyrean, to assure their souls
Against chance-vulgarisms, and, in the abyss
The apothecary, looked on once a year   295
To prove their soundness of humility.
The poor-club exercised her Christian gifts
Of knitting stockings, stitching petticoats,
Because we are of one flesh after all
And need one flannel (with a proper sense   300
Of difference in the quality) – and still
The book-club, guarded from your modern trick
Of shaking dangerous questions from the crease,
Preserved her intellectual. She had lived
A sort of cage-bird life, born in a cage,   305
Accounting that to leap from perch to perch
Was act and joy enough for any bird.
Dear heaven, how silly are the things that live
In thickets, and eat berries!
                   I, alas,
A wild bird scarcely fledged, was brought to her cage,   310
And she was there to meet me. Very kind.
Bring the clean water, give out the fresh seed.

She stood upon the steps to welcome me,
Calm, in black garb. I clung about her neck, –
Young babes, who catch at every shred of wool   315
To draw the new light closer, catch and cling
Less blindly. In my ears, my father's word
Hummed ignorantly, as the sea in shells,

'Love, love, my child.' She, black there with my grief,
Might feel my love – she was his sister once,   320
I clung to her. A moment she seemed moved,
Kissed me with cold lips, suffered me to cling,
And drew me feebly through the hall into
The room she sat in.

           There, with some strange spasm
Of pain and passion, she wrung loose my hands   325
Imperiously, and held me at arm's length,
And with two grey-steel naked-bladed eyes
Searched through my face, – ay, stabbed it through and through,
Through brows and cheeks and chin, as if to find
A wicked murderer in my innocent face,   330
If not here, there perhaps. Then, drawing breath,
She struggled for her ordinary calm
And missed it rather, – told me not to shrink,
As if she had told me not to lie or swear, –
'She loved my father and would love me too   335
As long as I deserved it.' Very kind.

I understood her meaning afterward;
She thought to find my mother in my face,
And questioned it for that. For she, my aunt,
Had loved my father truly, as she could,   340
And hated, with the gall of gentle souls,
My Tuscan mother who had fooled away
A wise man from wise courses, a good man
From obvious duties, and, depriving her,
His sister, of the household precedence,   345
Had wronged his tenants, robbed his native land,
And made him mad, alike by life and death,
In love and sorrow. She had pored for years
What sort of woman could be suitable
To her sort of hate, to entertain it with,   350
And so, her very curiosity
Became hate too, and all the idealism
She ever used in life, was used for hate,
Till hate, so nourished, did exceed at last
The love from which it grew, in strength and heat,   355
And wrinkled her smooth conscience with a sense

Of disputable virtue (say not, sin)
When Christian doctrine was enforced at church.

And thus my father's sister was to me
My mother's hater. From that day, she did   360
Her duty to me (I appreciate it
In her own word as spoken to herself),
Her duty, in large measure, well-pressed out,
But measured always. She was generous, bland,
More courteous than was tender, gave me still   365
The first place, – as if fearful that God's saints
Would look down suddenly and say, 'Herein
You missed a point, I think, through lack of love.'
Alas, a mother never is afraid
Of speaking angrily to any child,   370
Since love, she knows, is justified of love.

And I, I was a good child on the whole,
A meek and manageable child. Why not?
I did not live, to have the faults of life:
There seemed more true life in my father's grave   375
Than in all England. Since *that* threw me off
Who fain would cleave (his latest will, they say,
Consigned me to his land), I only thought
Of lying quiet there where I was thrown
Like sea-weed on the rocks, and suffering her   380
To prick me to a pattern with her pin
Fibre from fibre, delicate leaf from leaf,
And dry out from my drowned anatomy
The last sea-salt left in me.
                                    So it was.
I broke the copious curls upon my head   385
In braids, because she liked smooth-ordered hair.
I left off saying my sweet Tuscan words
Which still at any stirring of the heart
Came up to float across the English phrase
As lilies (*Bene* . . . . or *Che che*), because   390
She liked my father's child to speak his tongue.
I learnt the collects and the catechism,
The creeds, from Athanasius back to Nice,[115]

313

The Articles, the Tracts *against* the times
(By no means Buonaventure's 'Prick of Love'),   395
And various popular synopses of
Inhuman doctrines never taught by John,
Because she liked instructed piety.
I learnt my complement of classic French
(Kept pure of Balzac and neologism)   400
And German also, since she liked a range
Of liberal education, – tongues, not books.
I learnt a little algebra, a little
Of the mathematics, – brushed with extreme flounce
The circle of the sciences, because   405
She misliked women who are frivolous.
I learnt the royal genealogies
Of Oviedo, the internal laws
Of the Burmese Empire – by how many feet
Mount Chimborazo outsoars Teneriffe,   410
What navigable river joins itself
To Lara, and what census of the year five
Was taken at Klagenfurt, – because she liked
A general insight into useful facts.
I learnt much music, – such as would have been   415
As quite impossible in Johnson's day
As still it might be wished – fine sleights of hand
And unimagined fingering, shuffling off
The hearer's soul through hurricanes of notes
To a noisy Tophet; and I drew . . . costumes   420
From French engravings, nereids neatly draped,
(With smirks of simmering godship) – I washed in
Landscapes from nature (rather say, washed out).
I danced the polka and Cellarius,
Spun glass, stuffed birds, and modelled flowers in wax,   425
Because she liked accomplishments in girls.
I read a score of books on womanhood
To prove, if women do not think at all,
They may teach thinking (to a maiden-aunt
Or else the author), – books that boldy assert   430
Their right of comprehending husband's talk
When not too deep, and even of answering
With pretty 'may it please you,' or 'so it is,' –

Their rapid insight and fine aptitude,
Particular worth and general missionariness,   435
As long as they keep quiet by the fire
And never say 'no' when the world says 'aye,'
For that is fatal, – their angelic reach
Of virtue, chiefly used to sit and darn,
And fatten household sinners, – their, in brief,   440
Potential faculty in everything
Of abdicating power in it: she owned
She liked a woman to be womanly,
And English women, she thanked God and sighed
(Some people always sigh in thanking God),   445
Were models to the universe. And last
I learnt cross-stitch, because she did not like
To see me wear the night with empty hands
A-doing nothing. So, my shepherdess
Was something after all (the pastoral saints   450
Be praised for 't), leaning lovelorn with pink eyes
To match her shoes, when I mistook the silks;
Her head uncrushed by that round weight of hat
So strangely similar to the tortoise-shell
Which slew the tragic poet.

       By the way,   455
The works of women are symbolical.
We sew, sew, prick our fingers, dull our sight,
Producing what? A pair of slippers, sir,
To put on when you're weary – or a stool
To stumble over and vex you . . . 'curse that stool!'   460
Or else at best, a cushion, where you lean
And sleep, and dream of something we are not
But would be for your sake. Alas, alas!
This hurts most, this – that, after all, we are paid
The worth of our work, perhaps.

        In looking down   465
Those years of education (to return)
I wondered if Brinvilliers suffered more
In the water-torture . . . flood succeeding flood
To drench the incapable throat and split the veins . . .
Than I did. Certain of your feebler souls   470
Go out in such a process; many pine

To a sick, inodorous light; my own endured:
I had relations in the Unseen, and drew
The elemental nutriment and heat
From nature, as earth feels the sun at nights,   475
Or as a babe sucks surely in the dark.
I kept the life thrust on me, on the outside
Of the inner life with all its ample room
For heart and lungs, for will and intellect,
Inviolable by conventions. God,   480
I thank thee for that grace of thine!
                                        At first
I felt no life which was not patience, – did
The thing she bade me, without heed to a thing
Beyond it, sat in just the chair she placed,
With back against the window, to exclude   485
The sight of the great lime-tree on the lawn,
Which seemed to have come on purpose from the woods
To bring the house a message, – aye, and walked
Demurely in her carpeted low rooms,
As if I should not, hearkening my own steps,   490
Misdoubt I was alive. I read her books,
Was civil to her cousin, Romney Leigh,
Gave ear to her vicar, tea to her visitors,
And heard them whisper, when I changed a cup
(I blushed for joy at that), – 'The Italian child,   495
For all her blue eyes and her quiet ways,
Thrives ill in England: she is paler yet
Than when we came the last time; she will die.'

'Will die.' My cousin, Romney Leigh, blushed too,
With sudden anger, and approaching me   500
Said low between his teeth, 'You're wicked now?
You wish to die and leave the world a-dusk
For others, with your naughty light blown out?'
I looked into his face defyingly;
He might have known that, being what I was,   505
'Twas natural to like to get away
As far as dead folk can: and then indeed
Some people make no trouble when they die.
He turned and went abruptly, slammed the door

And shut his dog out.
Romney, Romney Leigh.   515

I have not named my cousin hitherto,
And yet I used him as a sort of friend;
My elder by few years, but cold and shy
And absent . . . tender, when he thought of it,
Which scarcely was imperative, grave betimes,   515
As well as early master of Leigh Hall,
Whereof the nightmare sat upon his youth
Repressing all its seasonable delights
And agonising with a ghastly sense
Of universal hideous want and wrong   520
To incriminate possession. When he came
From college to the country, very oft
He crossed the hill on visits to my aunt,
With gifts of blue grapes from the hothouses,
A book in one hand, – mere statistics (if   525
I chanced to lift the cover), count of all
The goats whose beards grow sprouting down toward hell
Against God's separative judgment-hour.
And she, she almost loved him, – even allowed
That sometimes he should seem to sigh my way;   530
It made him easier to be pitiful,
And sighing was his gift. So, undisturbed
At whiles she let him shut my music up
And push my needles down, and lead me out
To see in that south angle of the house   535
The figs grow black as if by a Tuscan rock,
On some light pretext. She would turn her head
At other moments, go to fetch a thing,
And leave me breath enough to speak with him,
For his sake; it was simple.
Sometimes too   540

He would have saved me utterly, it seemed,
He stood and looked so.
Once, he stood so near

He dropped a sudden hand upon my head
Bent down on woman's work, as soft as rain –
But then I rose and shook it off as fire,   545
The stranger's touch that took my father's place

317

Yet dared seem soft.
                 I used him for a friend
Before I ever knew him for a friend.
'Twas better, 'twas worse also, afterward:
We came so close, we saw our differences   550
Too intimately. Always Romney Leigh
Was looking for the worms, I for the gods.
A godlike nature his; the gods look down,
Incurious of themselves; and certainly
'Tis well I should remember, how, those days,   555
I was a worm too and he looked on me.

A little by his act perhaps, yet more
By something in me, surely not my will,
I did not die. But slowly, as one in swoon,
To whom life creeps back in the form of death,   560
With a sense of separation, a blind pain
Of blank obstruction, and a roar i' the ears
Of visionary chariots which retreat
As earth grows clearer . . . slowly, by degrees,
I woke, rose up . . . where was I? in the world;   565
For uses therefore I must count worth while.

I had a little chamber in the house,
As green as any privet-hedge a bird
Might choose to build in, though the nest itself
Could show but dead-brown sticks and straws; the walls 570
Were green, the carpet was pure green, the straight
Small bed was curtained greenly, and the folds
Hung green about the window, which let in
The outdoor world with all its greenery.
You could not push your head out and escape   575
A dash of dawn-dew from the honeysuckle,
But so you were baptised into the grace
And privilege of seeing . . .
                    First, the lime
(I had enough there, of the lime, be sure, –
My morning-dream was often hummed away   580
By the bees in it), past the lime, the lawn,
Which, after sweeping broadly round the house,

Went trickling through the shrubberies in a stream
Of tender turf, and wore and lost itself
Among the acacias, over which you saw   585
The irregular line of elms by the deep lane
Which stopped the grounds and dammed the overflow
Of arbutus and laurel. Out of sight
The lane was; sunk so deep, no foreign tramp
Nor drover of wild ponies out of Wales   590
Could guess if lady's hall or tenant's lodge
Dispensed such odours, – though his stick well-crooked
Might reach the lowest trail of blossoming brier
Which dipped upon the wall. Behind the elms,
And through their tops, you saw the folded hills   595
Striped up and down with hedges (burly oaks
Projecting from the line to show themselves),
Through which my cousin Romney's chimneys smoked
As still as when a silent mouth in frost
Breathes, showing where the woodlands hid Leigh Hall;   600
While, far above, a jut of table-land,
A promontory without water, stretched, –
You could not catch it if the days were thick,
Or took it for a cloud; but, otherwise,
The vigorous sun would catch it up at eve   605
And use it for an anvil till he had filled
The shelves of heaven with burning thunderbolts,
Protesting against night and darkness: – then,
When all his setting trouble was resolved
To a trance of passive glory, you might see   610
In apparition on the golden sky
(Alas, my Giotto's [116] background!) the sheep run
Along the fine clear outline, small as mice
That run along a witch's scarlet thread.

Not a grand nature. Not my chestnut-woods   615
Of Vallombrosa, cleaving by the spurs
To the precipices. Not my headlong leaps
Of waters, that cry out for joy or fear
In leaping through the palpitating pines,
Like a white soul tossed out to eternity   620
With thrills of time upon it. Not indeed

My multitudinous mountains, sitting in
The magic circle, with the mutual touch
Electric, panting from their full deep hearts
Beneath the influent heavens, and waiting for   625
Communion and commission. Italy
Is one thing, England one.

                 On English ground
You understand the letter – ere the fall
How Adam lived in a garden. All the fields
Are tied up fast with hedges, nosegay-like;   630
The hills are crumpled plains, the plains parterres,
The trees, round, woolly, ready to be clipped,
And if you seek for any wilderness
You find, at best, a park. A nature tamed
And grown domestic like a barn-door fowl,   635
Which does not awe you with its claws and beak
Nor tempt you to an eyrie too high up,
But which, in cackling, sets you thinking of
Your eggs tomorrow at breakfast, in the pause
Of finer meditation.

                 Rather say,   640
A sweet familiar nature, stealing in
As a dog might, or child, to touch your hand
Or pluck your gown, and humbly mind you so
Of presence and affection, excellent
For inner uses, from the things without.   645

I could not be unthankful, I who was
Entreated thus and holpen. In the room
I speak of, ere the house was well awake,
And also after it was well asleep,
I sat alone, and drew the blessing in   650
Of all that nature. With a gradual step,
A stir among the leaves, a breath, a ray,
It came in softly, while the angels made
A place for it beside me. The moon came,
And swept my chamber clean of foolish thoughts.   655
The sun came, saying, 'Shall I lift this light
Against the lime-tree, and you will not look?
I make the birds sing – listen! but, for you,

God never hears your voice, excepting when
You lie upon the bed at nights and weep.'   660

Then, something moved me. Then, I wakened up
More slowly than I verily write now,
But wholly, at last, I wakened, opened wide
The window and my soul, and let the airs .
And outdoor sights sweep gradual gospels in,   665
Regenerating what I was. O Life,
How oft we throw it off and think, – 'Enough,
Enough of life in so much! – here's a cause
For rupture; – herein we must break with Life,
Or be ourselves unworthy; here we are wronged,   670
Maimed, spoiled for aspiration: farewell Life!'
And so, as froward babes, we hide our eyes
And think all ended. – Then, Life calls to us
In some transformed, apocalyptic voice,
Above us, or below us, or around: 675
Perhaps we name it Nature's voice, or Love's,
Tricking ourselves, because we are more ashamed
To own our compensations than our griefs:
Still, Life's voice! – still, we make our peace with Life.

And I, so young then, was not sullen. Soon   680
I used to get up early, just to sit
And watch the morning quicken in the grey,
And hear the silence open like a flower
Leaf after leaf, – and stroke with listless hand
The woodbine through the window, till at last   685
I came to do it with a sort of love,
At foolish unaware: whereat I smiled, –
A melancholy smile, to catch myself
Smiling for joy.
                    Capacity for joy
Admits temptation. It seemed, next, worth while   690
To dodge the sharp sword set against my life;
To slip downstairs through all the sleepy house,
As mute as any dream there, and escape
As a soul from the body, out of doors,
Glide through the shrubberies, drop into the lane,   695

And wander on the hills an hour or two,
Then back again before the house should stir.

Or else I sat on in my chamber green,
And lived my life, and thought my thoughts, and prayed
My prayers without the vicar; read my books,   700
Without considering whether they were fit
To do me good. Mark, there. We get no good
By being ungenerous, even to a book,
And calculating profits, – so much help
By so much reading. It is rather when   705
We gloriously forget ourselves and plunge
Soul-forward, headlong, into a book's profound,
Impassioned for its beauty and salt of truth –
'Tis then we get the right good from a book.

I read much. What my father taught before   710
From many a volume, Love re-emphasised
Upon the self-same pages: Theophrast [117]
Grew tender with the memory of his eyes,
And Aelian [118] made mine wet. The trick of Greek
And Latin, he had taught me, as he would   715
Have taught me wrestling or the game of fives
If such he had known, – most like a shipwrecked man
Who heaps his single platter with goats' cheese
And scarlet berries; or like any man
Who loves but one, and so gives all at once,   720
Because he has it, rather than because
He counts it worthy. Thus, my father gave;
And thus, as did the women formerly
By young Achilles, when they pinned a veil
Across the boy's audacious front, and swept   725
With tuneful laughs the silver-fretted rocks,
He wrapt his little daughter in his large
Man's doublet, careless did it fit or no.

But, after I had read for memory,
I read for hope. The path my father's foot   730
Had trod me out (which suddenly broke off
What time he dropped the wallet of the flesh

And passed) alone I carried on, and set
My child-heart 'gainst the thorny underwood,
To reach the grassy shelter of the trees.   735
Ah, babe i' the wood, without a brother-babe!
My own self-pity, like the red-breast bird,
Flies back to cover all that past with leaves.

Sublimest danger, over which none weeps,
When any young wayfaring soul goes forth   740
Alone, unconscious of the perilous road,
The day-sun dazzling in his limpid eyes,
To thrust his own way, he an alien, through
The world of books! Ah, you! – you think it fine,
You clap hands – 'A fair day!' – you cheer him on,   745
As if the worst, could happen, were to rest
Too long beside a fountain. Yet, behold,
Behold! – the world of books is still the world,
And worldlings in it are less merciful
And more puissant. For the wicked there   750
Are winged like angels; every knife that strikes
Is edged from elemental fire to assail
A spiritual life; the beautiful seems right
By force of beauty, and the feeble wrong
Because of weakness; power is justified   755
Though armed against Saint Michael; many a crown
Covers bald foreheads. In the book-world, true,
There's no lack, neither, of God's saints and kings,
That shake the ashes of the grave aside
From their calm locks and undiscomfited   760
Look steadfast truths against Time's changing mask.
True, many a prophet teaches in the roads;
True, many a seer pulls down the flaming heavens
Upon his own head in strong martyrdom
In order to light men a moment's space.   765
But stay! – who judges? – who distinguishes
'Twixt Saul and Nahash[119] justly, at first sight,
And leaves king Saul precisely at the sin,
To serve king David? who discerns at once
The sound of the trumpets, when the trumpets blow   770
For Alaric[120] as well as Charlemagne?[121]

323

Who judges wizards, and can tell true seers
From conjurors? the child, there? Would you leave
That child to wander in a battle-field
And push his innocent smile against the guns;   775
Or even in a catacomb – his torch
Grown ragged in the fluttering air, and all
The dark a-mutter round him? not a child.

I read books bad and good – some bad and good
At once (good aims not always make good books: 780
Well-tempered spades turn up ill-smelling soils
In digging vineyards even); books that prove
God's being so definitely, that man's doubt
Grows self-defined the other side the line,
Made atheist by suggestion; moral books,   785
Exasperating to licence; genial books,
Discounting from the human dignity;
And merry books, which set you weeping when
The sun shines, – aye, and melancholy books,
Which make you laugh that any one should weep   790
In this disjointed life for one wrong more.

The world of books is still the world, I write,
And both worlds have God's providence, thank God,
To keep and hearten: with some struggle, indeed,
Among the breakers, some hard swimming through   795
The deeps – I lost breath in my soul sometimes
And cried, 'God save me if there's any God,'
But, even so, God saved me; and, being dashed
From error on to error, every turn
Still brought me nearer to the central truth.   800

I thought so. All this anguish in the thick
Of men's opinions . . . press and counterpress,
Now up, now down, now underfoot, and now
Emergent . . . all the best of it, perhaps,
But throws you back upon a noble trust   805
And use of your own instinct, – merely proves
Pure reason stronger than bare inference
At strongest. Try it, – fix against heaven's wall

The scaling-ladders of school logic – mount
Step by step! – sight goes faster; that still ray   810
Which strikes out from you, how, you cannot tell,
And why, you know not (did you eliminate,
That such as you indeed should analyse?),
Goes straight and fast as light, and high as God.
The cygnet finds the water, but the man   815
Is born in ignorance of his element
And feels out blind at first, disorganised
By sin i' the blood, – his spirit-insight dulled
And crossed by his sensations. Presently
He feels it quicken in the dark sometimes,   820
When, mark, be reverent, be obedient,
For such dumb motions of imperfect life
Are oracles of vital Deity
Attesting the Hereafter. Let who says
'The soul's a clean white paper,' rather say,   825
A palimpsest, a prophet's holograph
Defiled, erased and covered by a monk's, –
The apocalypse, by a Longus! poring on
Which obscene text, we may discern perhaps
Some fair, fine trace of what was written once,   830
Some upstroke of an alpha and omega
Expressing the old scripture.
                          Books, books, books!
I had found the secret of a garret-room
Piled high with cases in my father's name,
Piled high, packed large, – where, creeping in and out   835
Among the giant fossils of my past,
Like some small nimble mouse between the ribs
Of a mastodon, I nibbled here and there
At this or that box, pulling through the gap,
In heats of terror, haste, victorious joy,   840
The first book first. And how I felt it beat
Under my pillow, in the morning's dark,
An hour before the sun would let me read!
My books! At last because the time was ripe,
I chanced upon the poets.
                          As the earth   845
Plunges in fury, when the internal fires

Have reached and pricked her heart, and, throwing flat
The marts and temples, the triumphal gates
And towers of observation, clears herself
To elemental freedom – thus, my soul,   850
At poetry's divine first finger-touch,
Let go conventions and sprang up surprised,
Convicted of the great eternities
Before two worlds.
     What's this, Aurora Leigh,
You write so of the poets, and not laugh?   855
Those virtuous liars, dreamers after dark,
Exaggerators of the sun and moon,
And soothsayers in a tea-cup?
       I write so
Of the only truth-tellers now left to God,
The only speakers of essential truth,   860
Opposed to relative, comparative,
And temporal truths; the only holders by
His sun-skirts, through conventional grey glooms;
The only teachers who instruct mankind
From just a shadow on a charnel-wall   865
To find man's veritable stature out
Erect, sublime, – the measure of a man,
And that's the measure of an angel, says
The apostle. Aye, and while your common men
Lay telegraphs, gauge railroads, reign, reap, dine,   870
And dust the flaunty carpets of the world
For kings to walk on, or our president,
The poet suddenly will catch them up
With his voice like a thunder, – 'This is soul,
This is life, this word is being said in heaven,   875
Here's God down on us! what are you about?'
How all those workers start amid their work,
Look round, look up, and feel, a moment's space,
That carpet-dusting, though a pretty trade,
Is not the imperative labour after all.   880

My own best poets, am I one with you,
That thus I love you, – or but one through love?
Does all this smell of thyme about my feet

Conclude my visit to your holy hill
In personal presence, or but testify   885
The rustling of your vesture through my dreams
With influent odours? When my joy and pain,
My thought and aspiration, like the stops
Of pipe or flute, are absolutely dumb
Unless melodious, do you play on me   890
My pipers, – and if, sooth, you did not blow,
Would no sound come? or is the music mine,
As a man's voice or breath is called his own,
Inbreathed by the Life-breather? There's a doubt
For cloudy seasons!
             But the sun was high   895
When first I felt my pulses set themselves
For concord; when the rhythmic turbulence
Of blood and brain swept outward upon words,
As wind upon the alders, blanching them
By turning up their under-natures till   900
They trembled in dilation. O delight
And triumph of the poet, who would say
A man's mere 'yes,' a woman's common 'no,'
A little human hope of that or this,
And says the word so that it burns you through   905
With a special revelation, shakes the heart
Of all the men and women in the world,
As if one came back from the dead and spoke,
With eyes too happy, a familiar thing
Become divine i' the utterance! while for him   910
The poet, speaker, he expands with joy;
The palpitating angel in his flesh
Thrills inly with consenting fellowship
To those innumerous spirits who sun themselves
Outside of time.
            O life, O poetry,   915
– Which means life in life! cognisant of life
Beyond this blood-beat, – passionate for truth
Beyond these senses! – poetry, my life,
My eagle, with both grappling feet still hot
From Zeus's thunder, who hast ravished me   920
Away from all the shepherds, sheep, and dogs,

And set me in the Olympian roar and round
Of luminous faces for a cup-bearer,
To keep the mouths of all the godheads moist
For everlasting laughters, – I myself   925
Half drunk across the beaker with their eyes!
How those gods look!
    Enough so, Ganymede,[122]
We shall not bear above a round or two.
We drop the golden cup at Heré's [123] foot
And swoon back to the earth, – and find ourselves   930
Face-down among the pine-cones, cold with dew,
While the dogs bark, and many a shepherd scoffs,
'What's come now to the youth?' Such ups and downs
Have poets.
    Am I such indeed? The name
Is royal, and to sign it like a queen,   935
Is what I dare not, – though some royal blood
Would seem to tingle in me now and then,
With sense of power and ache, – with imposthumes
And manias usual to the race. Howbeit
I dare not: 'tis too easy to go mad   940
And ape a Bourbon in a crown of straws;
The thing's too common.
    Many fervent souls
Strike rime on rime, who would strike steel on steel
If steel had offered, in a restless heat
Of doing something. Many tender souls   945
Have strung their losses on a riming thread,
As children, cowslips: – the more pains they take,
The work more withers. Young men, aye, and maids,
Too often sow their wild oats in tame verse,
Before they sit down under their own vine   950
And live for use. Alas, near all the birds
Will sing at dawn, – and yet we do not take
The chaffering swallow for the holy lark.

In those days, though, I never analysed,
Not even myself. Analysis comes late.   955
You catch a sight of Nature, earliest,
In full front sun-face, and your eyelids wink

And drop before the wonder of 't; you miss
The form, through seeing the light. I lived, those days,
And wrote because I lived – unlicensed else;   960
My heart beat in my brain. Life's violent flood
Abolished bounds, – and, which my neighbour's field,
Which mine, what mattered? it is thus in youth!
We play at leap-frog over the god Term;
The love within us and the love without   965
Are mixed, confounded; if we are loved or love,
We scarce distinguish: thus, with other power;
Being acted on and acting seem the same:
In that first onrush of life's chariot-wheels,
We know not if the forests move or we.   970

And so, like most young poets, in a flush
Of individual life I poured myself
Along the veins of others, and achieved
Mere lifeless imitations of life verse,
And made the living answer for the dead,   975
Profaning nature. 'Touch not, do not taste,
Nor handle,' – we're too legal, who write young:
We beat the phorminx [124] till we hurt our thumbs,
As if still ignorant of counterpoint;
We call the Muse, – 'O Muse, benignant Muse,' –   980
As if we had seen her purple-braided head.
With the eyes in it, start between the boughs
As often as a stag's. What make-believe,
With so much earnest! what effete results,
From virile efforts! what cold wire-drawn odes,   985
From such white heats! – bucolics, where the cows
Would scare the writer if they splashed the mud
In lashing off the flies, – didactics, driven
Against the heels of what the master said;
And counterfeiting epics, shrill with trumps   990
A babe might blow between two straining cheeks
Of bubbled rose, to make his mother laugh;
And elegiac griefs, and songs of love,
Like cast-off nosegays picked up on the road,
The worse for being warm: all these things, writ   995
On happy mornings, with a morning heart,

That leaps for love, is active for resolve,
Weak for art only. Oft, the ancient forms
Will thrill, indeed, in carrying the young blood.
The wine-skins, now and then, a little warped,   1000
Will crack even, as the new wine gurgles in.
Spare the old bottles! – spill not the new wine.

By Keats's soul, the man who never stepped
In gradual progress like another man,
But, turning grandly on his central self,   1005
Ensphered himself in twenty perfect years
And died, not young (the life of a long life
Distilled to a mere drop, falling like a tear
Upon the world's cold cheek to make it burn
For ever); by that strong excepted soul,   1010
I count it strange and hard to understand
That nearly all young poets should write old,
That Pope was sexagenary at sixteen,
And beardless Byron academical,
And so with others. It may be perhaps   1015
Such have not settled long and deep enough
In trance, to attain to clairvoyance, – and still
The memory mixes with the vision, spoils,
And works it turbid.
                            Or perhaps, again,
In order to discover the Muse-Sphinx,   1020
The melancholy desert must sweep round,
Behind you as before. –
                            For me, I wrote
False poems, like the rest, and thought them true
Because myself was true in writing them.
I peradventure have writ true ones since   1025
With less complacence.
                            But I could not hide
My quickening inner life from those at watch.
They saw a light at a window now and then,
They had not set there: who had set it there?
My father's sister started when she caught   1030
My soul agaze in my eyes. She could not say
I had no business with a sort of soul,

But plainly she objected, – and demurred
That souls were dangerous things to carry straight
Through all the spilt saltpetre of the world.   1035
She said sometimes, 'Aurora, have you done
Your task this morning? have you read that book?
And are you ready for the crochet here?' –
As if she said, 'I know there's something wrong;
I know I have not ground you down enough   1040
To flatten and bake you to a wholesome crust
For household uses and proprieties,
Before the rain has got into my barn
And set the grains a-sprouting. What, you're green
With outdoor impudence? you almost grow?'   1045
To which I answered, 'Would she hear my task,
And verify my abstract of the book?
And should I sit down to the crochet work?
Was such her pleasure?' Then I sat and teased
The patient needle till it split the thread,   1050
Which oozed off from it in meandering lace
From hour to hour. I was not, therefore, sad;
My soul was singing at a work apart
Behind the wall of sense, as safe from harm
As sings the lark when sucked up out of sight   1055
In vortices of glory and blue air.
And so, through forced work and spontaneous work,
The inner life informed the outer life,
Reduced the irregular blood to a settled rhythm,
Made cool the forehead with fresh-sprinkling dreams,   1060
And, rounding to the spheric soul the thin,
Pined body, struck a colour up the cheeks,
Though somewhat faint. I clenched my brows across
My blue eyes greatening in the looking-glass,
And said, 'We'll live, Aurora! we'll be strong.   1065
The dogs are on us – but we will not die.'

Whoever lives true life, will love true love.
I learnt to love that England. Very oft,
Before the day was born, or otherwise
Through secret windings of the afternoons,   1070
I threw my hunters off and plunged myself

331

Among the deep hills, as a hunted stag
Will take the waters, shivering with the fear
And passion of the course. And when at last
Escaped, so many a green slope built on slope   1075
Betwixt me and the enemy's house behind,
I dared to rest, or wander, in a rest
Made sweeter for the step upon the grass,
And view the ground's most gentle dimplement
(As if God's finger touched but did not press   1080
In making England), such an up and down
Of verdure, – nothing too much up or down,
A ripple of land; such little hills, the sky
Can stoop to tenderly and the wheatfields climb;
Such nooks of valleys lined with orchises,   1085
Fed full of noises by invisible streams;
And open pastures where you scarcely tell
White daisies from white dew, – at intervals
The mythic oaks and elm-trees standing out
Self-poised upon their prodigy of shade, –   1090
I thought my father's land was worthy too
Of being my Shakespeare's.

      Very oft alone,
Unlicensed; not unfrequently with leave
To walk the third with Romney and his friend
The rising painter, Vincent Carrington,   1095
Whom men judge hardly as bee-bonneted,
Because he holds that, paint a body well,
You paint a soul by implication, like
The grand first Master. Pleasant walks! for if
He said, 'When I was last in Italy,'   1100
It sounded as an instrument that's played
Too far off for the tune – and yet it's fine
To listen.

    Often we walked only two,
If cousin Romney pleased to walk with me.
We read, or talked, or quarrelled, as it chanced.   1105
We were not lovers, nor even friends well-matched:
Say rather, scholars upon different tracks,
And thinkers disagreed; he, overfull
Of what is, and I, haply, overbold

For what might be.

                But then the thrushes sang,   1110
And shook my pulses and the elms' new leaves;
At which I turned, and held my finger up,
And bade him mark that, howsoe'er the world
Went ill, as he related, certainly
The thrushes still sang in it. At the word   1115
His brow would soften, – and he bore with me
In melancholy patience, not unkind,
While breaking into voluble ecstasy
I flattered all the beauteous country round,
As poets use, the skies, the clouds, the fields,   1120
The happy violets hiding from the roads
The primroses run down to, carrying gold;
The tangled hedgerows, where the cows push out
Impatient horns and tolerant churning mouths
'Twixt dripping ash-boughs, – hedgerows all alive   1125
With birds and gnats and large white butterflies
Which look as if the May-flower had caught life
And palpitated forth upon the wind;
Hills, vales, woods, netted in a silver mist,
Farms, granges, doubled up among the hills;   1130
And cattle grazing in the watered vales,
And cottage-chimneys smoking from the woods,
And cottage-gardens smelling everywhere,
Confused with smell of orchards. 'See,' I said,
'And see! is God not with us on the earth?   1135
And shall we put Him down by aught we do?
Who says there's nothing for the poor and vile
Save poverty and wickedness? behold!'
And ankle-deep in English grass I leaped
And clapped my hands, and called all very fair.   1140

In the beginning when God called all good,
Even then was evil near us, it is writ;
But we indeed who call things good and fair,
The evil is upon us while we speak;
Deliver us from evil, let us pray.   1145

Second Book

Times followed one another. Came a morn
I stood upon the brink of twenty years,
And looked before and after, as I stood
Woman and artist, – either incomplete,
Both credulous of completion. There I held   5
The whole creation in my little cup,
And smiled with thirsty lips before I drank
'Good health to you and me, sweet neighbour mine,
And all these peoples.'
              I was glad, that day;
The June was in me, with its multitudes   10
Of nightingales all singing in the dark,
And rosebuds reddening where the calyx split.
I felt so young, so strong, so sure of God!
So glad, I could not choose be very wise!
And, old at twenty, was inclined to pull   15
My childhood backward in a childish jest
To see the face of 't once more, and farewell!
In which fantastic mood I bounded forth
At early morning, – would not wait so long
As even to snatch my bonnet by the strings,   20
But, brushing a green trail across the lawn
With my gown in the dew, took will and way
Among the acacias of the shrubberies,
To fly my fancies in the open air
And keep my birthday, till my aunt awoke   25
To stop good dreams. Meanwhile I murmured on
As honeyed bees keep humming to themselves,
'The worthiest poets have remained uncrowned
Till death has bleached their foreheads to the bone;
And so with me it must be unless I prove   30
Unworthy of the grand adversity,
And certainly I would not fail so much.
What, therefore, if I crown myself today
In sport, not pride, to learn the feel of it,
Before my brows be numbed as Dante's own   35

To all the tender pricking of such leaves?
Such leaves! what leaves?'
                            I pulled the branches down,
To choose from.
                    'Not the bay! I choose no bay
(The fates deny us if we are overbold),
Nor myrtle – which means chiefly love; and love   40
Is something awful which one dares not touch
So early o' mornings. This verbena strains
The point of passionate fragrance; and hard by,
This guelder-rose, at far too slight a beck
Of the wind, will toss about her flower-apples.   45
Ah – there's my choice, – that ivy on the wall,
That headlong ivy! not a leaf will grow
But thinking of a wreath. Large leaves, smooth leaves,
Serrated like my vines, and half as green.
I like such ivy, bold to leap a height   50
'Twas strong to climb; as good to grow on graves
As twist about a thyrsus; pretty too
(And that's not ill) when twisted round a comb.'

Thus speaking to myself, half singing it,
Because some thoughts are fashioned like a bell   55
To ring with once being touched, I drew a wreath
Drenched, blinding me with dew, across my brow,
And fastening it behind so, turning faced
. . . My public! – cousin Romney – with a mouth
Twice graver than his eyes.
                            I stood there fixed, –   60
My arms up, like the caryatid, sole
Of some abolished temple, helplessly
Persistent in a gesture which derides
A former purpose. Yet my blush was flame,
As if from flax, not stone.
                            'Aurora Leigh,   65
The earliest of Auroras!'
                            Hand stretched out
I clasped, as shipwrecked men will clasp a hand,
Indifferent to the sort of palm. The tide
Had caught me at my pastime, writing down

My foolish name too near upon the sea   70
Which drowned me with a blush as foolish. 'You,
My cousin!'
          The smile died out in his eyes
And dropped upon his lips, a cold dead weight,
For just a moment, 'Here's a book I found!
No name writ on it – poems, by the form;   75
Some Greek upon the margin, – lady's Greek
Without the accents. Read it? Not a word.
I saw at once the thing had witchcraft in 't,
Whereof the reading calls up dangerous spirits:
I rather bring it to the witch.'
                    'My book!   80
You found it.' . . .
               'In the hollow by the stream
That beech leans down into – of which you said
The Oread in it has a Naiad's heart
And pines for waters.'
              'Thank you.'
                    Thanks to *you*,
My cousin! that I have seen you not too much   85
Witch, scholar, poet, dreamer and the rest,
To be a woman also.'
               With a glance
The smile rose in his eyes again and touched
The ivy on my forehead, light as air.
I answered gravely, 'Poets needs must be   90
Or men or women – more's the pity.'
                   'Ah,
But men, and still less women, happily,
Scarce need be poets. Keep to the green wreath,
Since even dreaming of the stone and bronze
Brings headaches, pretty cousin, and defiles   95
The clean white morning dresses.'
                   'So you judge!
Because I love the beautiful I must
Love pleasure chiefly, and be overcharged
For ease and whiteness! well, you know the world,
And only miss your cousin, 'tis not much.   100
But learn this; I would rather take my part

336

With God's Dead, who afford to walk in white
Yet spread His glory, than keep quiet here
And gather up my feet from even a step
For fear to soil my gown in so much dust.　　　　　105
I choose to walk at all risks. – Here, if heads
That hold a rhythmic thought must ache perforce,
For my part I choose headaches, – and today's
My birthday.'
　　　　　　　'Dear Aurora, choose instead
To cure them. You have balsams.'
　　　　　　　　　　　　　'I perceive.　　　　　110
The headache is too noble for my sex.
You think the heartache would sound decenter,
Since that's the woman's special, proper ache,
And altogether tolerable, except
To a woman.'
　　　　　　　Saying which, I loosed my wreath,　　　115
And swinging it beside me as I walked,
Half petulant, half playful, as we walked,
I sent a sidelong look to find his thought, –
As falcon set on falconer's finger may,
With sidelong head, and startled, braving eye,　　　120
Which means, 'You'll see – you'll see! I'll soon take flight,
You shall not hinder.' He, as shaking out
His hand and answering 'Fly then,' did not speak,
Except by such a gesture. Silently
We paced, until, just coming into sight　　　　　125
Of the house-windows, he abruptly caught
At one end of the swinging wreath, and said
'Aurora!' There I stopped short, breath and all.

'Aurora, let's be serious, and throw by
This game of head and heart. Life means, be sure,　　130
Both heart and head, – both active, both complete,
And both in earnest. Men and women make
The world, as head and heart make human life.
Work man, work woman, since there's work to do
In this beleaguered earth, for head and heart,　　　135
And thought can never do the work of love:
But work for ends, I mean for uses, not

For such sleek fringes (do you call them ends,
Still less God's glory?) as we sew ourselves
Upon the velvet of those baldaquins   140
Held 'twixt us and the sun. That book of yours,
I have not read a page of; but I toss
A rose up – it falls calyx down, you see!
The chances are that, being a woman, young
And pure, with such a pair of large, calm eyes,   145
You write as well . . . and ill . . . upon the whole,
As other women. If as well, what then?
If even a little better . . . still, what then?
We want the Best in art now, or no art.
The time is done for facile settings up   150
Of minnow gods, nymphs here and tritons there;
The polytheists have gone out in God,
That unity of Bests. No best, no God!
And so with art, we say. Give art's divine,
Direct, indubitable, real as grief,   155
Or leave us to the grief we grow ourselves
Divine by overcoming with mere hope
And most prosaic patience. You, you are young
As Eve with nature's daybreak on her face,
But this same world you are come to, dearest coz,   160
Has done with keeping birthdays, saves her wreaths
To hang upon her ruins, – and forgets
To rime the cry with which she still beats back
Those savage, hungry dogs that hunt her down
To the empty grave of Christ. The world's hard pressed;   165
The sweat of labour in the early curse
Has (turning acrid in six thousand years)
Become the sweat of torture. Who has time,
An hour's time . . . think! – to sit upon a bank
And hear the cymbal tinkle in white hands?   170
When Egypt's slain, I say, let Miriam sing! –
Before – where's Moses?'
                          'Ah, exactly that.
Where's Moses? – is a Moses to be found?
You'll sink him vainly in the bulrushes,
While I in vain touch cymbals. Yet concede,   175
Such sounding brass has done some actual good

(The application in a woman's hand,
If that were credible, being scarcely spoilt)
In colonising beehives.'

'There it is! –
You play beside a death-bed like a child,   180
Yet measure to yourself a prophet's place
To teach the living. None of all these things,
Can women understand. You generalise
– Oh, nothing, – not even grief! Your quick-breathed hearts,
So sympathetic to the personal pang,   185
Close on each separate knife-stroke, yielding up
A whole life at each wound, incapable
Of deepening, widening a large lap of life
To hold the world-full woe. The human race
To you means, such a child, or such a man,   190
You saw one morning waiting in the cold,
Beside that gate, perhaps. You gather up
A few such cases, and when strong sometimes
Will write of factories and of slaves, as if
Your father were a negro, and your son   195
A spinner in the mills. All's yours and you,
All, coloured with your blood, or otherwise
Just nothing to you. Why, I call you hard
To general suffering. Here's the world half blind
With intellectual light, half brutalised   200
With civilisation, having caught the plague
In silks from Tarsus, shrieking east and west
Along a thousand railroads, mad with pain
And sin too! . . . does one woman of you all
(You who weep easily) grow pale to see   205
This tiger shake his cage? – does one of you
Stand still from dancing, stop from stringing pearls,
And pine and die because of the great sum
Of universal anguish? – Show me a tear
Wet as Cordelia's, in eyes bright as yours,   210
Because the world is mad. You cannot count,
That you should weep for this account, not you!
You weep for what you know. A red-haired child
Sick in a fever, if you touch him once,
Though but so little as with a finger-tip,   215

Will set you weeping; but a million sick . . .
You could as soon weep for the rule of three
Or compound fractions. Therefore this same world,
Uncomprehended by you, must remain
Uninfluenced by you. – Women as you are,   220
Mere women, personal and passionate,
You give us doting mothers, and perfect wives,
Sublime Madonnas, and enduring saints!
We get no Christ from you, – and verily
We shall not get a poet, in my mind.'   225

'With which conclusion you conclude' . . .
                                        'But this:
That you, Aurora, with the large live brow
And steady eyelids, cannot condescend
To play at art, as children play at swords,
To show a pretty spirit, chiefly admired   230
Because true action is impossible.
You never can be satisfied with praise
Which men give women when they judge a book
Not as mere work but as mere woman's work,
Expressing the comparative respect   235
Which means the absolute scorn. "Oh, excellent!
What grace! what facile turns, what fluent sweeps,
What delicate discernment . . . almost thought!
The book does honour to the sex, we hold.
Among our female authors we make room   240
For this fair writer, and congratulate
The country that produces in these times
Such women, competent to . . . spell." '
                                        'Stop there!'
I answered, burning through his thread of talk
With a quick flame of emotion, – 'You have read   245
My soul, if not my book, and argue well.
I would not condescend . . . we will not say
To such a kind of praise (a worthless end
Is praise of all kinds), but to such a use
Of holy art and golden life. I am young,   250
And peradventure weak – you tell me so –
Through being a woman. And, for all the rest,

Take thanks for justice. I would rather dance
At fairs on tight-rope, till the babies dropped
Their gingerbread for joy, – than shift the types   255
For tolerable verse, intolerable
To men who act and suffer. Better far
Pursue a frivolous trade by serious means,
Than a sublime art frivolously.'
                                        'You,
Choose nobler work than either, O moist eyes   260
And hurrying lips and heaving heart! We are young,
Aurora, you and I. The world, – look round, –
The world, we're come to late, is swollen hard
With perished generations and their sins:
The civiliser's spade grinds horribly   265
On dead men's bones, and cannot turn up soil
That's otherwise than fetid. All success
Proves partial failure; all advance implies
What's left behind; all triumph, something crushed
At the chariot-wheels; all government, some wrong: 270
And rich men make the poor, who curse the rich,
Who agonise together, rich and poor,
Under and over, in the social spasm
And crisis of the ages. Here's an age
That makes its own vocation! here we have stepped   275
Across the bounds of time! here's nought to see,
But just the rich man and just Lazarus,
And both in torments, with a mediate gulf,
Though not a hint of Abraham's bosom. Who
Being man, Aurora, can stand calmly by   280
And view these things, and never tease his soul
For some great cure? No physic for this grief,
In all the earth and heavens too?'
                                        'You believe
In God, for your part? – aye? that He who makes,
Can make good things from ill things, best from worst,   285
As men plant tulips upon dunghills when
They wish them finest?'
                                        'True. A death-heat is
The same as life-heat, to be accurate,
And in all nature is no death at all,

341

As men account of death, so long as God   290
Stands witnessing for life perpetually,
By being just God. That's abstract truth, I know,
Philosophy, or sympathy with God:
But I, I sympathise with man, not God
(I think I was a man for chiefly this),   295
And when I stand beside a dying bed,
'Tis death to me. Observe, – it had not much
Consoled the race of mastodons to know,
Before they went to fossil, that anon
Their place would quicken with the elephant: 300
They were not elephants but mastodons;
And I, a man, as men are now, and not
As men may be hereafter, feel with men
In the agonising present.'
                          'Is it so,'
I said, 'my cousin? is the world so bad,   305
While I hear nothing of it through the trees?
The world was always evil, – but so bad?'

'So bad, Aurora. Dear, my soul is grey
With poring over the long sum of ill;
So much for vice, so much for discontent,   310
So much for the necessities of power,
So much for the connivances of fear,
Coherent in statistical despairs
With such a total of distracted life . . .
To see it down in figures on a page,   315
Plain, silent, clear, as God sees through the earth
The sense of all the graves, – that's terrible
For one who is not God, and cannot right
The wrong he looks on. May I choose indeed
But vow away my years, my means, my aims,   320
Among the helpers, if there's any help
In such a social strait? The common blood
That swings along my veins is strong enough
To draw me to this duty.'
                          Then I spoke.
'I have not stood long on the strand of life,   325
And these salt waters have had scarcely time

To creep so high up as to wet my feet:
I cannot judge these tides – I shall, perhaps.
A woman's always younger than a man
At equal years, because she is disallowed   330
Maturing by the outdoor sun and air,
And kept in long-clothes past the age to walk.
Ah well, I know you men judge otherwise!
You think a woman ripens as a peach,
In the cheeks, chiefly. Pass it to me now;   335
I'm young in age, and younger still, I think,
As a woman. But a child may say amen
To a bishop's prayer and feel the way it goes,
And I, incapable to loose the knot
Of social questions, can approve, applaud   340
August compassion, Christian thoughts that shoot
Beyond the vulgar white of personal aims.
Accept my reverence.'
             There he glowed on me
With all his face and eyes. 'No other help?'
Said he – 'no more than so?'
                'What help?' I asked.   345
'You'd scorn my help, – as Nature's self, you say,
Has scorned to put her music in my mouth
Because a woman's. Do you now turn round
And ask for what a woman cannot give?'

'For what she only can, I turn and ask,'   350
He answered, catching up my hands in his,
And dropping on me from his high-eaved brow
The full weight of his soul, – 'I ask for love,
And that, she can; for life in fellowship
Through bitter duties – that, I know she can;   355
For wifehood – will she?'
               'Now,' I said, 'may God
Be witness 'twixt us two!' and with the word,
Meseemed I floated into a sudden light
Above his stature, – 'am I proved too weak
To stand alone, yet strong enough to bear   360
Such leaners on my shoulder? poor to think,
Yet rich enough to sympathise with thought?

Incompetent to sing, as blackbirds can,
Yet competent to love, like HIM?'
                  I paused;
Perhaps I darkened, as the lighthouse will   365
That turns upon the sea. 'It's always so.
Anything does for a wife.'
                 'Aurora, dear,
And dearly honoured, – he pressed in at once
With eager utterance, – 'you translate me ill.
I do not contradict my thought of you   370
Which is most reverent, with another thought
Found less so. If your sex is weak for art
(And I who said so, did but honour you
By using truth in courtship), it is strong
For life and duty. Place your fecund heart   375
In mine, and let us blossom for the world
That wants love's colour in the grey of time.
My talk, meanwhile, is arid to you, aye,
Since all my talk can only set you where
You look down coldly on the arena-heaps   380
Of headless bodies, shapeless, indistinct!
The Judgment-Angel scarce would find his way
Through such a heap of generalised distress
To the individual man with lips and eyes,
Much less Aurora. Ah, my sweet, come down,   385
And hand in hand we'll go where yours shall touch
These victims, one by one! till, one by one,
The formless, nameless trunk of every man
Shall seem to wear a head with hair you know,
And every woman catch your mother's face   390
To melt you into passion.'
                 'I am a girl,'
I answered slowly; 'you do well to name
My mother's face. Though far too early, alas,
God's hand did interpose 'twixt it and me,
I know so much of love as used to shine   395
In that face and another. Just so much;
No more indeed at all. I have not seen
So much love since, I pray you pardon me,
As answers even to make a marriage with

In this cold land of England. What you love,   400
Is not a woman, Romney, but a cause:
You want a helpmate, not a mistress, sir.
A wife to help your ends, – in her no end!
Your cause is noble, your ends excellent,
But I, being most unworthy of these and that,   405
Do otherwise conceive of love. Farewell.'

'Farewell, Aurora? you reject me thus?'
He said.
        'Sir, you were married long ago.
You have a wife already whom you love,
Your social theory. Bless you both, I say.   410
For my part, I am scarcely meek enough
To be the handmaid of a lawful spouse.
Do I look a Hagar,[125] think you?'
                                'So you jest.'

'Nay, so, I speak in earnest,' I replied.
'You treat of marriage too much like, at least,   415
A chief apostle: you would bear with you
A wife . . . a sister . . . shall we speak it out?
A sister of charity.'
                'Then, must it be
Indeed farewell? And was I so far wrong
In hope and in illusion, when I took   420
The woman to be nobler than the man,
Yourself the noblest woman, in the use
And comprehension of what love is, – love,
That generates the likeness of itself
Through all heroic duties? so far wrong,   425
In saying bluntly, venturing truth on love,
"Come, human creature, love and work with me," –
Instead of, "Lady, thou art wondrous fair,
And, where the Graces walk before, the Muse
Will follow at the lighting of their eyes,   430
And where the Muse walks, lovers need to creep:
Turn round and love me, or I die of love." '

With quiet indignation I broke in.
'You misconceive the question like a man,

Who sees a woman as the complement 435
Of his sex merely. You forget too much
That every creature, female as the male,
Stands single in responsible act and thought
As also in birth and death. Whoever says
To a loyal woman, "Love and work with me," 440
Will get fair answers if the work and love,
Being good themselves, are good for her – the best
She was born for. Women of a softer mood,
Surprised by men when scarcely awake to life,
Will sometimes only hear the first word, love, 445
And catch up with it any kind of work,
Indifferent, so that dear love go with it.
I do not blame such women, though, for love,
They pick much oakum;[126] earth's fanatics make
Too frequently heaven's saints. But *me* your work 450
Is not the best for, – nor your love the best,
Nor able to commend the kind of work
For love's sake merely. Ah, you force me, sir,
To be over-bold in speaking of myself:
I too have my vocation, – work to do, 455
The heavens and earth have set me since I changed
My father's face for theirs, and, though your world
Were twice as wretched as you represent,
Most serious work, most necessary work
As any of the economists'. Reform, 460
Make trade a Christian possibility,
And individual right no general wrong;
Wipe out earth's furrows of the Thine and Mine,
And leave one green for men to play at bowls,
With innings for them all! . . . what then, indeed, 465
If mortals are not greater by the head
Than any of their prosperities? what then,
Unless the artist keep up open roads
Betwixt the seen and unseen, – bursting through
The best of your conventions with his best, 470
The speakable, imaginable best
God bids him speak, to prove what lies beyond
Both speech and imagination? A starved man
Exceeds a fat beast: we'll not barter, sir,

The beautiful for barley. – And, even so,   475
I hold you will not compass your poor ends
Of barley-feeding and material ease,
Without a poet's individualism
To work your universal. It takes a soul
To move a body: it takes a high-souled man   480
To move the masses, even to a cleaner sty:
It takes the ideal to blow a hair's-breadth off
The dust of the actual. – Ah, your Fouriers[127] failed,
Because not poets enough to understand
That life develops from within. – For me,   485
Perhaps I am not worthy, as you say,
Of work like this: perhaps a woman's soul
Aspires, and not creates: yet we aspire,
And yet I'll try out your perhapses, sir;
And if I fail . . . why, burn me up my straw   490
Like other false works – I'll not ask for grace;
Your scorn is better, cousin Romney. I,
Who love my art, would never wish it lower
To suit my stature. I may love my art.
You'll grant that even a woman may love art,   495
Seeing that to waste true love on anything
Is womanly, past question.'
                              I retain
The very last word which I said that day,
As you the creaking of the door, years past,
Which let upon you such disabling news   500
You ever after have been graver. He,
His eyes, the motions in his silent mouth,
Were fiery points on which my words were caught,
Transfixed for ever in my memory
For his sake, not their own. And yet I know   505
I did not love him . . . nor he me . . . that's sure . . .
And what I said is unrepented of,
As truth is always. Yet . . . a princely man! –
If hard to me, heroic for himself!
He bears down on me through the slanting years,   510
The stronger for the distance. If he had loved,
Aye, loved me, with that retributive face . . .
I might have been a common woman now

347

And happier, less known and less left alone,
Perhaps a better woman after all,   515
With chubby children hanging on my neck
To keep me low and wise. Ah me, the vines
That bear such fruit are proud to stoop with it.
The palm stands upright in a realm of sand.

And I, who spoke the truth then, stand upright,   520
Still worthy of having spoken out the truth;
By being content I spoke it, though it set
Him there, me here. – O woman's vile remorse,
To hanker after a mere name, a show,
A supposition, a potential love!   525
Does every man who names love in our lives,
Become a power for that? Is love's true thing
So much best to us, that what personates love
Is next best? A potential love, forsooth!
I'm not so vile. No, no – he cleaves, I think,   530
This man, this image, – chiefly for the wrong
And shock he gave my life, in finding me
Precisely where the devil of my youth
Had set me, on those mountain-peaks of hope
All glittering with the dawn-dew, all erect   535
And famished for the noon, – exclaiming while
I looked for empire and much tribute, 'Come,
I have some worthy work for thee below.
Come, sweep my barns and keep my hospitals,
And I will pay thee with a current coin   540
Which men give women.'
                                    As we spoke, the grass
Was trod in haste beside us, and my aunt,
With smile distorted by the sun, – face, voice
As much at issue with the summer-day
As if you brought a candle out of doors, –   545
Broke in with, 'Romney, here! – My child, entreat
Your cousin to the house, and have your talk,
If girls must talk upon their birthdays. Come.'

He answered for me calmly, with pale lips
That seemed to motion for a smile in vain,   550

'The talk is ended, madam, where we stand.
Your brother's daughter has dismissed me here;
And all my answer can be better said
Beneath the trees, than wrong by such a word
Your house's hospitalities. Farewell.'   555

With that he vanished. I could hear his heel
Ring bluntly in the lane, as down he leapt
The short way from us. – Then a measured speech
Withdrew me. 'What means this, Aurora Leigh?
My brother's daughter has dismissed my guests?'   560

The lion in me felt the keeper's voice;
Through all its quivering dewlaps: I was quelled
Before her, – meekened to the child she knew:
I prayed her pardon, said, 'I had little thought
To give dismissal to a guest of hers,   565
In letting go a friend of mine who came
To take me into service as a wife, –
No more than that, indeed.'
                              'No more, no more?
Pray Heaven,' she answered, 'that I was not mad.
I could not mean to tell her to her face   570
That Romney Leigh had asked me for a wife,
And I refused him?'
                      'Did he ask?' I said;
'I think he rather stooped to take me up
For certain uses which he found to do
For something called a wife. He never asked.'   575

'What stuff!' she answered; 'are they queens, these girls?
They must have mantles, stitched with twenty silks,
Spread out upon the ground, before they'll step
One footstep for the noblest lover born.'

'But I am born,' I said with firmness, 'I,   580
To walk another way than his, dear aunt.'

'You walk, you walk! A babe at thirteen months
Will walk as well as you,' she cried in haste,
'Without a steadying finger. Why, you child,
God help you, you are groping in the dark,   585

For all this sunlight. You suppose, perhaps,
That you, sole offspring of an opulent man,
Are rich and free to choose a way to walk?
You think, and it's a reasonable thought,
That I, beside, being well to do in life,   590
Will leave my handful in my niece's hand
When death shall paralyse these fingers? Pray,
Pray, child, albeit I know you love me not,
As if you loved me, that I may not die!
For when I die and leave you, out you go   595
(Unless I make room for you in my grave),
Unhoused, unfed, my dear, poor brother's lamb
(Ah heaven, – that pains!) – without a right to crop
A single blade of grass beneath these trees,
Or cast a lamb's small shadow on the lawn,   600
Unfed, unfolded! Ah, my brother, here's
The fruit you planted in your foreign loves! –
Aye, there's the fruit he planted! never look
Astonished at me with your mother's eyes,
For it was they who set you where you are,   605
An undowered orphan. Child, your father's choice
Of that said mother, disinherited
His daughter, his and hers. Men do not think
Of sons and daughters, when they fall in love,
So much more than of sisters; otherwise   610
He would have paused to ponder what he did,
And shrunk before that clause in the entail[128]
Excluding offspring by a foreign wife
(The clause set up a hundred years ago
By a Leigh who wedded a French dancing-girl   615
And had his heart danced over in return);
But this man shrank at nothing, never thought
Of you, Aurora, any more than me –
Your mother must have been a pretty thing,
For all the coarse Italian blacks and browns,   620
To make a good man, which my brother was,
Unchary of the duties to his house;
But so it fell indeed. Our cousin Vane,
Vane Leigh, the father of this Romney, wrote
Directly on your birth, to Italy,   625

"I ask your baby daughter for my son
In whom the entail now merges by the law.
Betroth her to us out of love, instead
Of colder reasons, and she shall not lose
By love or law from henceforth" – so he wrote;   630
A generous cousin, was my cousin Vane.
Remember how he drew you to his knee
The year you came here, just before he died,
And hollowed out his hands to hold your cheeks,
And wished them redder, – you remember Vane?   635
And now his son who represents our house
And holds the fiefs and manors in his place,
To whom reverts my pittance when I die
(Except a few books and a pair of shawls),
The boy is generous like him, and prepared   640
To carry out his kindest word and thought
To you, Aurora. Yes, a fine young man
Is Romney Leigh; although the sun of youth
Has shone too straight upon his brain, I know,
And fevered him with dreams of doing good   645
To good-for-nothing people. But a wife
Will put all right, and stroke his temples cool
With healthy touches' . . .

              I broke in at that.
I could not lift my heavy heart to breathe
Till then, but then I raised it, and it fell   650
In broken words like these – 'No need to wait;
The dream of doing good to . . . me, at least,
Is ended, without waiting for a wife
To cool the fever for him. We've escaped
That danger, – thank Heaven for it.'

                'You,' she cried,   655
'Have got a fever. What, I talk and talk
An hour long to you, – I instruct you how
You cannot eat or drink or stand or sit
Or even die, like any decent wretch
In all this unroofed and unfurnished world,   660
Without your cousin, – and you still maintain
There's room 'twixt him and you, for flirting fans
And running knots in eyebrows! You must have

A pattern lover sighing on his knee?
You do not count enough, a noble heart   665
(Above book-patterns) which this very morn
Unclosed itself in two dear fathers' names
To embrace your orphaned life? fie, fie! But stay,
I write a word, and counteract this sin.'

She would have turned to leave me, but I clung.   670
'O sweet my father's sister, hear my word
Before you write yours. Cousin Vane did well,
And Romney well, – and I well too,
In casting back with all my strength and will
The good they meant me. O my God, my God!   675
God meant me good, too, when he hindered me
From saying "yes" this morning. If you write
A word, it shall be "no." I say no, no!
I tie up "no" upon His altar-horns,
Quite out of reach of perjury! At least   680
My soul is not a pauper; I can live
At least my soul's life, without alms from men;
And if it must be in heaven instead of earth,
Let heaven look to it, – I am not afraid.'

She seized my hands with both hers, strained them fast, 685
And drew her probing and unscrupulous eyes
Right through me, body and heart. 'Yet, foolish Sweet,
You love this man. I've watched you when he came,
And when he went, and when we've talked of him:
I am not old for nothing; I can tell   690
The weather-signs of love: you love this man.'

Girls blush sometimes because they are alive,
Half wishing they were dead to save the shame.
The sudden blush devours them, neck and brow;
They have drawn too near the fire of life, like gnats,   695
And flare up bodily, wings and all. What then?
Who's sorry for a gnat . . . or girl?
                              I blushed.
I feel the brand upon my forehead now
Strike hot, sear deep, as guiltless men may feel
The felon's iron, say, and scorn the mark   700

Of what they are not. Most illogical
Irrational nature of our womanhood,
That blushes one way, feels another way,
And prays, perhaps, another! After all,
We cannot be the equal of the male   705
Who rules his blood a little.

                  For although
I blushed indeed, as if I loved the man,
And her incisive smile, accrediting
That treason of false witness in my blush,
Did bow me downward like a swathe of grass   710
Below its level that struck me, – I attest
The conscious skies and all their daily suns,
I think I loved him not, – nor then, nor since,
Nor ever. Do we love the schoolmaster,
Being busy in the woods? much less, being poor,   715
The overseer of the parish? Do we keep
Our love to pay our debts with?

                    White and cold
I grew next moment. As my blood recoiled
From that imputed ignominy, I made
My heart great with it. Then, at last, I spoke,   720
Spoke veritable words but passionate,
Too passionate perhaps . . . ground up with sobs
To shapeless endings. She let fall my hands
And took her smile off, in sedate disgust,
As peradventure she had touched a snake, –   725
A dead snake, mind! – and turning round, replied,
'We'll leave Italian manners, if you please.
I think you had an English father, child,
And ought to find it possible to speak
A quiet "yes" or "no," like English girls,   730
Without convulsions. In another month
We'll take another answer – no, or yes.'
With that, she left me in the garden-walk.

I had a father! yes, but long ago –
How long it seemed that moment. Oh, how far,   735
How far and safe, God, dost Thou keep Thy saints
When once gone from us! We may call against

The lighted windows of Thy fair June-heaven
Where all the souls are happy, – and not one,
Not even my father, look from work or play   740
To ask, 'Who is it that cries after us,
Below there, in the dusk?' Yet formerly
He turned his face upon me quick enough,
If I said 'father.' Now I might cry loud;
The little lark reached higher with his song   745
Than I with crying. Oh, alone, alone, –
Not troubling any in heaven, nor any on earth,
I stood there in the garden, and looked up
The deaf blue sky that brings the roses out
On such June mornings.
                              You who keep account   750
Of crisis and transition in this life,
Set down the first time Nature says plain 'no'
To some 'yes' in you, and walks over you
In gorgeous sweeps of scorn. We all begin
By singing with the birds, and running fast   755
With June-days, hand in hand: but once, for all,
The birds must sing against us, and the sun
Strike down upon us like a friend's sword caught
By an enemy to slay us, while we read
The dear name on the blade which bites at us! –   760
That's bitter and convincing: after that,
We seldom doubt that something in the large
Smooth order of creation, though no more
Than haply a man's footstep, has gone wrong.

Some tears fell down my cheeks, and then I smiled,   765
As those smile who have no face in the world
To smile back to them. I had lost a friend
In Romney Leigh; the thing was sure – a friend,
Who had looked at me most gently now and then,
And spoken of my favourite books, 'our books,'   770
With such a voice! Well, voice and look were now
More utterly shut out from me, I felt,
Than even my father's. Romney now was turned
To a benefactor, to a generous man,
Who had tied himself to marry . . . me, instead   775

Of such a woman, with low timorous lids
He lifted with a sudden word one day,
And left, perhaps, for my sake. – Ah, self-tied
By a contract, – male Iphigenia bound
At a fatal Aulis[129] for the winds to change   780
(But loose him, they'll not change), he well might seem
A little cold and dominant in love!
He had a right to be dogmatical,
This poor, good Romney. Love, to him, was made
A simple law-clause. If I married him,   785
I should not dare to call my soul my own
Which so he had bought and paid for: every thought
And every heart-beat down there in the bill;
Not one found honestly deductible
From any use that pleased him! He might cut   790
My body into coins to give away
Among his other paupers; change my sons,
While I stood dumb as Griseld,[130] for black babes
Or piteous foundlings; might unquestioned set
My right hand teaching in the Ragged Schools,   795
My left hand washing in the Public Baths,
What time my angel of the Ideal stretched
Both his to me in vain. I could not claim
The poor right of a mouse in a trap, to squeal,
And take so much as pity from myself.   800

Farewell, good Romney! if I loved you even,
I could but ill afford to let you be
So generous to me. Farewell, friend, since friend
Betwixt us two, forsooth, must be a word
So heavily overladen. And, since help   805
Must come to me from those who love me not,
Farewell, all helpers – I must help myself,
And am alone from henceforth. – Then I stooped
And lifted the soiled garland from the earth,
And set it on my head as bitterly   810
As when the Spanish monarch crowned the bones
Of his dead love. So be it. I preserve
That crown still, – in the drawer there! 'twas the first.
The rest are like it; – those Olympian crowns,

We run for, till we lose sight of the sun   815
In the dust of the racing chariots!
                    After that,
Before the evening fell, I had a note,
Which ran, – 'Aurora, sweet Chaldean,[131] you read
My meaning backward like your eastern books,
While I am from the west, dear. Read me now   820
A little plainer. Did you hate me quite
But yesterday? I loved you for my part;
I love you. If I spoke untenderly
This morning, my belovèd, pardon it;
And comprehend me that I loved you so   825
I set you on the level of my soul,
And overwashed you with the bitter brine
Of some habitual thoughts. Henceforth, my flower,
Be planted out of reach of any such,
And lean the side you please, with all your leaves!   830
Write woman's verses and dream woman's dreams;
But let me feel your perfume in my home
To make my sabbath after working-days.
Bloom out your youth beside me, – be my wife.'

I wrote in answer – 'We Chaldeans discern   835
Still farther than we read. I know your heart,
And shut it like the holy book it is,
Reserved for mild-eyed saints to pore upon
Betwixt their prayers at vespers. Well, you're right,
I did not surely hate you yesterday;   840
And yet I do not love you enough today
To wed you, cousin Romney. Take this word,
And let it stop you as a generous man
From speaking farther. You may tease, indeed,
And blow about my feelings, or my leaves,   845
And here's my aunt will help you with east winds
And break a stalk, perhaps, tormenting me;
But certain flowers grow near as deep as trees,
And, cousin, you'll not move my root, not you,
With all your confluent storms. Then let me grow   850
Within my wayside hedge, and pass your way!
This flower has never as much to say to you

As the antique tomb which said to travellers, "Pause,"
"Siste, viator." '¹³² Ending thus, I signed.

The next week passed in silence, so the next,   855
And several after: Romney did not come
Nor my aunt chide me. I lived on and on,
As if my heart were kept beneath a glass,
And everybody stood, all eyes and ears,
To see and hear it tick. I could not sit,   860
Nor walk, nor take a book, nor lay it down,
Nor sew on steadily, nor drop a stitch,
And a sigh with it, but I felt her looks
Still cleaving to me, like the sucking asp
To Cleopatra's breast, persistently   865
Through the intermittent pantings. Being observed,
When observation is not sympathy,
Is just being tortured. If she said a word,
A 'thank you,' or an 'if it please you, dear,'
She meant a commination, or, at best,   870
An exorcism against the devildom
Which plainly held me. So with all the house.
Susannah could not stand and twist my hair,
Without such glancing at the looking-glass
To see my face there, that she missed the plait.   875
And John, – I never sent my plate for soup,
Or did not send it, but the foolish John
Resolved the problem, 'twixt his napkined thumbs,
Of what was signified by taking soup
Or choosing mackerel. Neighbours who dropped in   880
On morning visits, feeling a joint wrong,
Smiled admonition, sat uneasily,
And talked with measured, emphasised reserve,
Of parish news, like doctors to the sick,
When not called in, – as if, with leave to speak,   885
They might say something. Nay, the very dog
Would watch me from his sun-patch on the floor,
In alternation with the large black fly
Not yet in reach of snapping. So I lived.

A Roman died so; smeared with honey, teased   890
By insects, stared to torture by the noon:

And many patient souls 'neath English roofs
Have died like Romans. I, in looking back,
Wish only, now, I had borne the plague of all
With meeker spirits than were rife in Rome.   895

For, on the sixth week, the dead sea broke up,
Dashed suddenly through beneath the heel of Him
Who stands upon the sea and earth and swears
Time shall be nevermore. The clock struck nine
That morning too, – no lark was out of tune,   900
The hidden farms among the hills breathed straight
Their smoke toward heaven, the lime-trees scarcely stirred
Beneath the blue weight of the cloudless sky,
Though still the July air came floating through
The woodbine at my window, in and out,   905
With touches of the outdoor country-news
For a bending forehead. There I sat, and wished
That morning-truce of God would last till eve,
Or longer. 'Sleep,' I thought, 'late sleepers, – sleep,
And spare me yet the burden of your eyes.'   910

Then, suddenly, a single ghastly shriek
Tore upward from the bottom of the house.
Like one who wakens in a grave and shrieks,
The still house seemed to shriek itself alive,
And shudder through its passages and stairs   915
With slam of doors and clash of bells. – I sprang,
I stood up in the middle of the room,
And there confronted at my chamber-door,
A white face, – shivering, ineffectual lips.

'Come, come,' they tried to utter, and I went: 920
As if a ghost had drawn me at the point
Of a fiery finger through the uneven dark,
I went with reeling footsteps down the stair,
Nor asked a question.
                    There she sat, my aunt, –
Bolt upright in the chair beside her bed,   925
Whose pillow had no dint! she had used no bed
For that night's sleeping, yet slept well. My God,
The dumb derision of that grey, peaked face

Concluded something grave against the sun,
Which filled the chamber with its July burst   930
When Susan drew the curtains ignorant
Of who sat open-eyed behind her. There
She sat . . . it sat . . . we said 'she' yesterday . . .
And held a letter with unbroken seal,
As Susan gave it to her hand last night: 935
All night she had held it. If its news referred
To duchies or to dunghills, not an inch
She'd budge, 'twas obvious, for such worthless odds:
Nor, though the stars were suns and overburned
Their spheric limitations, swallowing up   940
Like wax the azure spaces, could they force
Those open eyes to wink once. What last sight
Had left them blank and flat so, – drawing out
The faculty of vision·from the roots,
As nothing more, worth seeing, remained behind?   945

Were those the eyes that watched me, worried me?
That dogged me up and down the hours and days,
A beaten, breathless, miserable soul?
And did I pray, a half-hour back, but so,
To escape the burden of those eyes . . . those eyes?   950
'Sleep late,' I said? –

      Why now, indeed, they sleep.
God answers sharp and sudden on some prayers,
And thrusts the thing we have prayed for in our face,
A gauntlet with a gift in 't. Every wish
Is like a prayer, with God.

        I had my wish,   955
To read and meditate the thing I would,
To fashion all my life upon my thought,
And marry or not marry. Henceforth none
Could disapprove me, vex me, hamper me.
Full ground-room, in this desert newly made,   960
For Babylon or Balbec,[133] – when the breath,
Now choked with sand, returns, for building towns.

The heir came over on the funeral day,
And we two cousins met before the dead,

With two pale faces. Was it death or life   965
That moved us? When the will was read and done,
The official guest and witnesses withdrawn,
We rose up in a silence almost hard,
And looked at one another. Then I said,
'Farewell, my cousin.'

              But he touched, just touched   970
My hatstrings tied for going (at the door
The carriage stood to take me), and said low,
His voice a little unsteady through his smile,
'Siste, viator.'

           'Is there time,' I asked,
'In these last days of railroads, to stop short   975
Like Caesar's chariot (weighing half a ton)
On the Appian road for morals?'

                    'There is time,'
He answered grave, 'for necessary words,
Inclusive, trust me, of no epitaph
On man or act, my cousin. We have read   980
A will, which gives you all the personal goods
And funded moneys of your aunt.'

                      'I thank
Her memory for it. With three hundred pounds
We buy in England even, clear standing-room
To stand and work in. Only two hours since,   985
I fancied I was poor.'

              'And cousin, still
You're richer than you fancy. The will says,
*Three hundred pounds, and any other sum
Of which the said testatrix dies possessed.*
I say she died possessed of other sums.'   990

'Dear Romney, need we chronicle the pence?
I'm richer than I thought – that's evident.
Enough so.'

           'Listen rather. You've to do
With business and a cousin,' he resumed,
'And both, I fear, need patience. Here's the fact.   995
The other sum (there *is* another sum,
Unspecified in any will which dates

After possession, yet bequeathed as much
And clearly as those said three hundred pounds)
Is thirty thousand. You will have it paid   1000
When? . . . where? My duty troubles you with words.'

He struck the iron when the bar was hot;
No wonder if my eyes sent out some sparks.
'Pause there! I thank you. You are delicate
In glosing gifts; – but I, who share your blood,   1005
Am rather made for giving, like yourself,
Than taking, like your pensioners. Farewell.'

He stopped me with a gesture of calm pride.
'A Leigh,' he said, 'gives largesse and gives love,
But gloses never: if a Leigh could glose,   1010
He would not do it, moreover, to a Leigh,
With blood trained up along nine centuries
To hound and hate a lie from eyes like yours.
And now we'll make the rest as clear; your aunt
Possessed these moneys.'
                            'You will make it clear,   1015
My cousin, as the honour of us both,
Or one of us speaks vainly! that's not I.
My aunt possessed this sum, – inherited
From whom, and when? bring documents, prove dates.'

'Why now indeed you throw your bonnet off   1020
As if you had time left for a logarithm!
The faith's the want. Dear cousin, give me faith,
And you shall walk this road with silken shoes,
As clean as any lady of our house
Supposed the proudest. Oh, I comprehend   1025
The whole position from your point of sight.
I oust you from your father's halls and lands
And make you poor by getting rich – that's law;
Considering which, in common circumstance,
You would not scruple to accept from me   1030
Some compensation, some sufficiency
Of income – that were justice; but, alas,
I love you, – that's mere nature; you reject

My love, – that's nature also; and at once
You cannot, from a suitor disallowed,   1035
A hand thrown back as mine is, into yours
Receive a doit, a farthing, – not for the world!
That's woman's etiquette, and obviously
Exceeds the claim of nature, law, and right,
Unanswerable to all. I grant, you see,   1040
The case as you conceive it, – leave you room
To sweep your ample skirts of womanhood,
While, standing humbly squeezed against the wall,
I own myself excluded from being just,
Restrained from paying indubitable debts,   1045
Because denied from giving you my soul.
That's my misfortune! – I submit to it
As if, in some more reasonable age,
'Twould not be less inevitable. Enough.
You'll trust me, cousin, as a gentleman,   1050
To keep your honour, as you count it, pure,
Your scruples (just as if I thought them wise)
Safe and inviolate from gifts of mine.'

I answered mild but earnest. 'I believe
In no one's honour which another keeps,   1055
Nor man's nor woman's. As I keep, myself,
My truth and my religion, I depute
No father, though I had one this side death,
Nor brother, though I had twenty, much less you,
Though twice my cousin, and once Romney Leigh,   1060
To keep my honour pure. You face, today,
A man who wants instruction, mark me, not
A woman who wants protection. As to a man,
Show manhood, speak out plainly, be precise
With facts and dates. My aunt inherited   1065
This sum, you say – '
                       'I said she died possessed
Of this, dear cousin.'
                       'Not by heritage.
Thank you: we're getting to the facts at last.
Perhaps she played at commerce with a ship
Which came in heavy with Australian gold?   1070

Or touched a lottery with her finger-end,
Which tumbled on a sudden into her lap
Some old Rhine tower or principality?
Perhaps she had to do with a marine
Sub-transatlantic railroad, which pre-pays   1075
As well as pre-supposes? or perhaps
Some stale ancestral debt was after-paid
By a hundred years, and took her by surprise? –
You shake your head, my cousin; I guess ill.'

'You need not guess, Aurora, nor deride;   1080
The truth is not afraid of hurting you.
You'll find no cause, in all your scruples, why
Your aunt should cavil at a deed of gift
'Twixt her and me.'
                    'I thought so – ah! a gift.'

'You naturally thought so,' he resumed.   1085
'A very natural gift.'
                    'A gift, a gift!
Her individual life being stranded high
Above all want, approaching opulence,
Too haughty was she to accept a gift
Without some ultimate aim: ah, ah, I see, –   1090
A gift intended plainly for her heirs,
And so accepted . . . if accepted . . . ah,
Indeed that might be; I am snared perhaps
Just so. But, cousin, shall I pardon you,
If thus you have caught me with a cruel springe?'   1095

He answered gently, 'Need you tremble and pant
Like a netted lioness? is't my fault, mine,
That you're a grand wild creature of the woods
And hate the stall built for you? Any way,
Though triply netted, need you glare at me?   1100
I do not hold the cords of such a net;
You're free from me, Aurora!'
                    'Now may God
Deliver me from this strait! This gift of yours
Was tendered . . . when? accepted . . . when?' I asked.
'A month . . . a fortnight since? Six weeks ago   1105

363

It was not tendered; by a word she dropped
I know it was not tendered nor received.
When was it? bring your dates.'
                    'What matters when?
A half-hour ere she died, or a half-year,
Secured the gift, maintains the heritage   1110
Inviolable with law. As easy pluck
The golden stars from heaven's embroidered stole
To pin them on the grey side of this earth,
As make you poor again, thank God.'
                        'Not poor
Nor clean again from henceforth, you thank God?   1115
Well, sir – I ask you – I insist at need, –
Vouchsafe the special date, the special date.'

'The day before her death-day,' he replied,
'The gift was in her hands. We'll find that deed,
And certify that date to you.'
                      As one   1120
Who has climbed a mountain-height and carried up
His own heart climbing, panting in his throat
With the toil of the ascent, takes breath at last,
Looks back in triumph – so I stood and looked.
'Dear cousin Romney, we have reached the top   1125
Of this steep question, and may rest, I think.
But first – I pray you pardon, that the shock
And surge of natural feeling and event
Had made me oblivious of acquainting you
That this, this letter (unread, mark, still sealed),   1130
Was found enfolded in the poor dead hand:
That spirit of hers had gone beyond the address,
Which could not find her though you wrote it clear, –
I know your writing, Romney, – recognise
The open-hearted A, the liberal sweep   1135
Of the G. Now listen, – let us understand:
You will not find that famous deed of gift,
Unless you find it in the letter here,
Which, not being mine, I give you back. – Refuse
To take the letter? well then – you and I,   1140
As writer and as heiress, open it

Together, by your leave. – Exactly so:
The words in which the noble offering's made,
Are nobler still, my cousin; and, I own,
The proudest and most delicate heart alive,   1145
Distracted from the measure of the gift
By such a grace in giving, might accept
Your largesse without thinking any more
Of the burthen of it, than King Solomon[134]
Considered, when he wore his holy ring   1150
Charactered over with the ineffable spell,
How many carats of fine gold made up
Its money-value: so, Leigh gives to Leigh!
Or rather, might have given, observe, – for that's
The point we come to. Here's a proof of gift,   1155
But here's no proof, sir, of acceptancy,
But rather, disproof. Death's black dust, being blown,
Infiltrated through every secret fold
Of this sealed letter by a puff of fate,
Dried up for ever the fresh-written ink,   1160
Annulled the gift, disutilised the grace,
And left these fragments.'
                              As I spoke, I tore
The paper up and down, and down and up
And crosswise, till it fluttered from my hands,
As forest-leaves, stripped suddenly and rapt   1165
By a whirlwind on Valdarno, drop again,
Drop slow, and strew the melancholy ground
Before the amazed hills . . . why, so, indeed,
I'm writing like a poet, somewhat large
In the type of the image, and exaggerate   1170
A small thing with a great thing, topping it: –
But then I'm thinking how his eyes looked, his,
With what despondent and surprised reproach!
I think the tears were in them as he looked;
I think the manly mouth just trembled. Then   1175
He broke the silence.
                        'I may ask, perhaps,
Although no stranger . . . only Romney Leigh,
Which means still less . . . than Vincent Carrington,
Your plans in going hence, and where you go.

This cannot be a secret.'

                    'All my life   1080
Is open to you, cousin. I go hence
To London, to the gathering-place of souls,
To live mine straight out, vocally, in books;
Harmoniously for others, if indeed
A woman's soul, like man's, be wide enough   1185
To carry the whole octave (that's to prove)
Or, if I fail, still purely for myself.
Pray God be with me, Romney.'

                       'Ah, poor child,
Who fight against the mother's 'tiring hand,
And choose the headsman's! May God change His world 1190
For your sake, sweet, and make it mild as heaven,
And juster than I have found you.'

                     But I paused.
'And you, my cousin?' –

               'I,' he said, – 'you ask?
You care to ask? Well, girls have curious minds
And fain would know the end of everything,   1195
Of cousins therefore with the rest. For me,
Aurora, I've my work; you know my work;
And, having missed this year some personal hope,
I must beware the rather that I miss
No reasonable duty. While you sing   1200
Your happy pastorals of the meads and trees,
Bethink you that I go to impress and prove
On stifled brains and deafened ears, stunned deaf,
Crushed dull with grief, that nature sings itself,
And needs no mediate poet, lute or voice,   1205
To make it vocal. While you ask of men
Your audience, I may get their leave perhaps
For hungry orphans to say audibly
"We're hungry, see," – for beaten and bullied wives
To hold their unweaned babies up in sight,   1210
Whom orphanage would better, and for all
To speak and claim their portion . . . by no means
Of the soil, . . . but of the sweat in tilling it;
Since this is nowadays turned privilege,
To have only God's curse on us, and not man's.   1215

Such work I have for doing, elbow-deep
In social problems, – as you tie your rimes,
To draw my uses to cohere with needs
And bring the uneven world back to its round,
Or, failing so much, fill up, bridge at least   1220
To smoother issues some abysmal cracks
And feuds of earth, intestine heats have made
To keep men separate, – using sorry shifts
Of hospitals, almshouses, infant schools,
And other practical stuff of partial good   1225
You lovers of the beautiful and whole
Despise by system.'
                              'I despise? The scorn
Is yours, my cousin. Poets become such
Through scorning nothing. You decry them for
The good of beauty sung and taught by them,   1230
While they respect your practical partial good
As being a part of beauty's self. Adieu!
When God helps all the workers for His world,
The singers shall have help of Him, not last.'

He smiled as men smile when they will not speak   1235
Because of something bitter in the thought;
And still I feel his melancholy eyes
Look judgment on me. It is seven years since:
I know not if 'twas pity or 'twas scorn
Has made them so far-reaching: judge it ye   1240
Who have had to do with pity more than love,
And scorn than hatred. I am used, since then,
To other ways, from equal men. But so,
Even so, we let go hands, my cousin and I,
And, in between us, rushed the torrent-world   1245
To blanch our faces like divided rocks,
And bar for ever mutual sight and touch
Except through swirl of spray and all that roar.

Third Book

'Today thou girdest up thy loins thyself
And goest where thou wouldest: presently
Others shall gird thee,' said the Lord, 'to go
Where thou wouldst not.' He spoke to Peter thus,
To signify the death which he should die   5
When crucified head downward

       If He spoke
To Peter then, He speaks to us the same;
The word suits many different martyrdoms,
And signifies a multiform of death,
Although we scarcely die apostles, we,   10
And have mislaid the keys of heaven and earth.

For 'tis not in mere death that men die most,
And, after our first girding of the loins
In youth's fine linen and fair broidery,
To run up hill and meet the rising sun,   15
We are apt to sit tired, patient as a fool,
While others gird us with the violent bands
Of social figments, feints, and formalisms,
Reversing our straight nature, lifting up
Our base needs, keeping down our lofty thoughts,   20
Head downward on the cross-sticks of the world.
Yet He can pluck us from that shameful cross.
God, set our feet low and our forehead high,
And show us how a man was made to walk!

Leave the lamp, Susan, and go up to bed.   25
The room does very well; I have to write
Beyond the stroke of midnight. Get away;
Your steps, for ever buzzing in the room,
Tease me like gnats. Ah, letters! throw them down
At once, as I must have them, to be sure,   30
Whether I bid you never bring me such
At such an hour, or bid you. No excuse;
You choose to bring them, as I choose perhaps

To throw them in the fire. Now get to bed,
And dream, if possible, I am not cross.   35

Why what a pettish, petty thing I grow, –
A mere, mere woman, a mere flaccid nerve,
A kerchief left out all night in the rain,
Turned soft so, – overtasked and overstrained
And overlived in this close London life!   40
And yet I should be stronger.
                                  Never burn
Your letters, poor Aurora! for they stare
With red seals from the table, saying each,
'Here's something that you know not.' Out alas,
'Tis scarcely that the world's more good and wise   45
Or even straighter and more consequent
Since yesterday at this time – yet, again,
If but one angel spoke from Ararat
I should be very sorry not to hear:
So open all the letters! let me read.   50
Blanche Ord, the writer in the 'Lady's Fan,'
Requests my judgement on . . . that, afterwards.
Kate Ward desires the model of my cloak,
And signs, 'Elisha to you.' Pringle Sharpe
Presents his work on 'Social Conduct,' craves   55
A little money for his pressing debts . . .
From me, who scarce have money for my needs;
Art's fiery chariot which we journey in
Being apt to singe our singing-robes to holes
Although you ask me for my cloak, Kate Ward!   60
Here's Rudgely knows it, – editor and scribe;
He's 'forced to marry where his heart is not,
Because the purse lacks where he lost his heart.'
Ah, – lost it because no one picked it up;
That's really loss, – (and passable impudence.)   65
My critic Hammond flatters prettily,
And wants another volume like the last.
My critic Belfair wants another book
Entirely different, which will sell (and live?),
A striking book, yet not a startling book,   70
The public blames originalities

(You must not pump spring-water unawares
Upon a gracious public full of nerves),
Good things, not subtle, new yet orthodox,
As easy reading as the dog-eared page   75
That's fingered by said public fifty years,
Since first taught spelling by its grandmother,
And yet a revelation in some sort:
That's hard, my critic Belfair. So – what next?
My critic Stokes objects to abstract thoughts;   80
'Call a man, John, a woman, Joan,' says he,
'And do not prate so of *humanities*:'
Whereat I call my critic simply, Stokes.
My critic Jobson recommends more mirth
Because a cheerful genius suits the times,   85
And all true poets laugh unquenchably
Like Shakespeare and the gods. That's very hard.
The gods may laugh, and Shakespeare; Dante smiled
With such a needy heart on two pale lips,
We cry, 'Weep rather, Dante.' Poems are   90
Men, if true poems: and who dares exclaim
At any man's door, 'Here, 'tis understood
The thunder fell last week and killed a wife
And scared a sickly husband – what of that?
Get up, be merry, shout and clap your hands,   95
Because a cheerful genius suits the times – '?
None says so to the man, – and why indeed
Should any to the poem? A ninth seal;
The apocalypse is drawing to a close.
Ha, – this from Vincent Carrington, – 'Dear friend,   100
I want good counsel. Will you lend me wings
To raise me to the subject, in a sketch
I'll bring tomorrow – may I? at eleven?
A poet's only born to turn to use:
So save you! for the world . . . and Carrington.'   105
'(Writ after.) Have you heard of Romney Leigh,
Beyond what's said of him in newspapers,
His phalansteries[135] there, his speeches here,
His pamphlets, pleas, and statements, everywhere?
He dropped *me* long ago, but no one drops   110
A golden apple – though indeed one day

You hinted that, but jested. Well, at least
You know Lord Howe who sees him . . . whom he sees
And *you* see and I hate to see, – for Howe
Stands high upon the brink of theories,   115
Observes the swimmers and cries "Very fine,"
But keeps dry linen equally, – unlike
That gallant breaster, Romney. Strange it is,
Such sudden madness seizing a young man
To make earth over again, – while I'm content   120
To make the pictures. Let me bring the sketch.
A tiptoe Danae,[136] overbold and hot,
Both arms a-flame to meet her wishing Jove
Halfway, and burn him faster down; the face
And breasts upturned and straining, the loose locks   125
All glowing with the anticipated gold.
Or here's another on the self-same theme.
She lies here – flat upon her prison-floor,
The long hair swathed about her to the heel
Like wet sea-weed. You dimly see her through   130
The glittering haze of that prodigious rain,
Half blotted out of nature by a love
As heavy as fate. I'll bring you either sketch.
I think, myself, the second indicates
More passion.'   135
                Surely. Self is put away,
And calm with abdication. She is Jove,
And no more Danae – greater thus. Perhaps
The painter symbolises unaware
Two states of the recipient artist-soul,
One, forward, personal, wanting reverence,   140
Because aspiring only. We'll be calm,
And know that, when indeed our Joves come down,
We all turn stiller than we have ever been.

Kind Vincent Carrington. I'll let him come.
He talks of Florence, – and may say a word   145
Of something as it chanced seven years ago,
A hedgehog in the path, or a lame bird,
In those green country walks, in that good time
When certainly I was so miserable . . .

371

I seem to have missed a blessing ever since.   150

The music soars within the little lark,
And the lark soars. It is not thus with men.
We do not make our places with our strains, –
Content, while they rise, to remain behind
Alone on earth instead of so in heaven.   155
No matter; I bear on my broken tale.

When Romney Leigh and I had parted thus,
I took a chamber up three flights of stairs
Not far from being as steep as some larks climb,
And there in a certain house in Kensington,   160
Three years I lived and worked. Get leave to work
In this world, – 'tis the best you get at all;
For God, in cursing, gives us better gifts
Than men in benediction. God says, 'Sweat
For foreheads,' men say 'crowns,' and so we are crowned,   165
Aye, gashed by some tormenting circle of steel
Which snaps with a secret spring. Get work, get work;
Be sure 'tis better than what you work to get.

Serene and unafraid of solitude
I worked the short days out, – and watched the sun   170
On lurid morns or monstrous afternoons
(Like some Druidic idol's fiery brass
With fixed unflickering outline of dead heat,
From which the blood of wretches pent inside
Seems oozing forth to incarnadine the air)   175
Push out through fog with his dilated disk,
And startle the slant roofs and chimney-pots
With splashes of fierce colour. Or I saw
Fog only, the great tawny weltering fog
Involve the passive city, strangle it   180
Alive, and draw it off into the void,
Spires, bridges, streets, and squares, as if a sponge
Had wiped out London, – or as noon and night
Had clapped together and utterly struck out
The intermediate time, undoing themselves   185
In the act. Your city poets see such things

Not despicable. Mountains of the south,
When drunk and mad with elemental wines
They rend the seamless mist and stand up bare,
Make fewer singers, haply. No one sings,   190
Descending Sinai: on Parnassus-mount[137]
You take a mule to climb and not a muse
Except in fable and figure: forests chant
Their anthems to themselves, and leave you dumb.
But sit in London at the day's decline,   195
And view the city perish in the mist
Like Pharaoh's armaments in the deep Red Sea,
The chariots, horsemen, footmen, all the host,
Sucked down and choked to silence – then, surprised
By a sudden sense of vision and of tune,   200
You feel as conquerors though you did not fight,
And you and Israel's other singing girls,
Aye, Miriam[138] with them, sing the song you chose.

I worked with patience, which means almost power:
I did some excellent things indifferently,   205
Some bad things excellently. Both were praised,
The latter loudest. And by such a time
That I myself had set them down as sins
Scarce worth the price of sackcloth, week by week
Arrived some letter through the sedulous post,   210
Like these I've read, and yet dissimilar,
With pretty maiden seals, – initials twined
Of lilies, or a heart marked *Emily*,
(Convicting Emily of being all heart);
Or rarer tokens from young bachelors,   215
Who wrote from college with the same goosequill,
Suppose, they had just been plucked of, and a snatch
From Horace, 'Collegisse juvat,'[139] set
Upon the first page. Many a letter, signed
Or unsigned, showing the writers at eighteen   220
Had lived too long, though a muse should help
Their dawn by holding candles, – compliments
To smile or sigh at. Such could pass with me
No more than coins from Moscow circulate
At Paris: would ten roubles buy a tag   225

Of ribbon on the boulevard, worth a sou?
I smiled that all this youth should love me, – sighed
That such a love could scarcely raise them up
To love what was more worthy than myself;
Then sighed again, again, less generously,⁣ 230
To think the very love they lavished so
Proved me inferior. The strong loved me not,
And he . . . my cousin Romney . . . did not write.
I felt the silent finger of his scorn
Prick every bubble of my frivolous fame⁣ 235
As my breath blew it, and resolve it back
To the air it came from. Oh, I justified
The measure he had taken of my height:
The thing was plain – he was not wrong a line;
I played at art, made thrusts with a toy-sword,⁣ 240
Amused the lads and maidens.
                 Came a sigh
Deep, hoarse with resolution, – I would work
To better ends, or play in earnest. 'Heavens,
I think I should be almost popular
If this went on!' – I ripped my verses up,⁣ 245
And found no blood upon the rapier's point;
The heart in them was just an embryo's heart
Which never yet had beat, that it should die;
Just gasps of make-believe galvanic life;
Mere tones, inorganised to any tune.⁣ 250

And yet I felt it in me where it burnt,
Like those hot fire-seeds of creation held
In Jove's clenched palm[140] before the worlds were sown, –
But I – I was not Juno even! my hand
Was shut in weak convulsion, woman's ill,⁣ 255
And when I yearned to loose a finger – lo,
The nerve revolted. 'Tis the same even now:
This hand may never, haply, open large,
Before the spark is quenched, or the palm charred,
To prove the power not else than by the pain.⁣ 260

It burns, it burnt – my whole life burnt with it,
And light, not sunlight and not torchlight, flashed

My steps out through the slow and difficult road.
I had grown distrustful of too forward Springs,
The season's books in drear significance   265
Of morals, dropping round me. Lively books?
The ash has livelier verdure than the yew;
And yet the yew's green longer, and alone
Found worthy of the holy Christmas time:
We'll plant more yews if possible, albeit   270
We plant the graveyards with them.
                                    Day and night
I worked my rhythmic thought, and furrowed up
Both watch and slumber with long lines of life
Which did not suit their season. The rose fell
From either cheek, my eyes globed luminous   275
Through orbits of blue shadow, and my pulse
Would shudder along the purple-veinèd wrist
Like a shot bird. Youth's stern, set face to face
With youth's ideal: and when people came
And said, 'You work too much, you are looking ill,'   280
I smiled for pity of them who pitied me,
And thought I should be better soon perhaps
For those ill looks. Observe – 'I,' means in youth
Just *I*, the conscious and eternal soul
With all its ends, and not the outside life,   285
The parcel-man, the doublet of the flesh,
The so much liver, lung, integument,
Which make the sum of 'I' hereafter when
World-talkers talk of doing well or ill.
I prosper if I gain a step, although   290
A nail then pierced my foot: although my brain
Embracing any truth froze paralysed,
I prosper: I but change my instrument;
I break the spade off, digging deep for gold,
And catch the mattock up.
                            I worked on, on.   295
Through all the bristling fence of nights and days
Which hedges time in from the eternities,
I struggled, – never stopped to note the stakes
Which hurt me in my course. The midnight oil
Would stink sometimes; there came some vulgar needs: 300

I had to live that therefore I might work,
And, being but poor, I was constrained, for life,
To work with one hand for the booksellers
While working with the other for myself
And art: you swim with feet as well as hands,   305
Or make small way. I apprehended this, –
In England no one lives by verse that lives;
And, apprehending, I resolved by prose
To make a space to sphere my living verse.
I wrote for cyclopaedias, magazines,   310
And weekly papers, holding up my name
To keep it from the mud. I learnt the use
Of the editorial 'we' in a review
As courtly ladies the fine trick of trains,
And swept it grandly through the open doors   315
As if one could not pass through doors at all
Save so encumbered. I wrote tales beside,
Carved many an article on cherry-stones
To suit light readers, – something in the lines
Revealing, it was said, the mallet-hand,   320
But that, I'll never vouch for: what you do
For bread, will taste of common grain, not grapes,
Although you have a vineyard in Champagne;
Much less in Nephelococcygia [141]
As mine was, peradventure.
                              Having bread   325
For just so many days, just breathing-room
For body and verse, I stood up straight and worked
My veritable work. And as the soul
Which grows within a child makes the child grow, –
Or as the fiery sap, the touch from God,   330
Careering through a tree, dilates the bark
And roughs with scale and knob, before it strikes
The summer foliage out in a green flame –
So life, in deepening with me, deepened all
The course I took, the work I did. Indeed   335
The academic law convinced of sin;
The critics cried out on the falling off,
Regretting the first manner. But I felt
My heart's life throbbing in my verse to show

It lived, it also – certes incomplete,   340
Disordered with all Adam in the blood,
But even its very tumours, warts and wens
Still organised by and implying life.

A lady called upon me on such a day.
She had the low voice of your English dames,   345
Unused, it seems, to need rise half a note
To catch attention, – and their quiet mood,
As if they lived too high above the earth
For that to put them out in anything:
So gentle, because verily so proud;   350
So wary and afraid of hurting you,
By no means that you are not really vile,
But that they would not touch you with their foot
To push you to your place; so self-possessed
Yet gracious and conciliating, it takes   355
An effort in their presence to speak truth:
You know the sort of woman, – brilliant stuff,
And out of nature. 'Lady Waldemar.'
She said her name quite simply, as if it meant
Not much indeed, but something, – took my hands,   360
And smiled as if her smile could help my case,
And dropped her eyes on me and let them melt.
'Is this,' she said, 'the Muse?'
                                  'No sibyl even,'
I answered, 'since she fails to guess the cause
Which taxed you with this visit, madam.'
                                          'Good,'   365
She said, 'I value what's sincere at once.
Perhaps if I had found a literal Muse,
The visit might have taxed me. As it is,
You wear your blue so chiefly in your eyes,
My fair Aurora, in a frank good way,   370
It comforts me entirely for your fame,
As well as for the trouble of ascent
To this Olympus.'
                  There, a silver laugh
Ran rippling through her quickened little breaths
The steep stair somewhat justified.

                   'But still   375
Your ladyship has left me curious why
You dared the risk of finding the said Muse?'

'Ah, – keep me, notwithstanding, to the point,
Like any pedant? Is the blue in eyes
As awful as in stockings, after all,   380
I wonder, that you'd have my business out
Before I breathe – exact the epic plunge
In spite of gasps? Well, naturally you think
I've come here, as the lion-hunters go
To deserts, to secure you with a trap   385
For exhibition in my drawing-rooms
On zoologic soirées? not in the least.
Roar softly at me; I am frivolous,
I dare say; I have played at wild-beast shows
Like other women of my class, – but now   390
I meet my lion simply as Androcles[142]
Met his . . . when at his mercy.'
                     So, she bent
Her head, as queens may mock, – then lifting up
Her eyelids with a real grave queenly look,
Which ruled and would not spare, not even herself, –   395
'I think you have a cousin: – Romney Leigh.'

'You bring a word from *him*?' – my eyes leapt up
To the very height of hers, – 'a word from *him*?'

'I bring a word about him, actually.
But first' (she pressed me with her urgent eyes)   400
'You do not love him, – you?'
                     'You're frank at least
In putting questions, madam,' I replied;
'I love my cousin cousinly – no more.'

'I guessed as much. I'm ready to be frank
In answering also, if you'll question me,   405
Or even for something less. You stand outside,
You artist women, of the common sex;
You share not with us, and exceed us so

Perhaps by what you're mulcted in, your hearts
Being starved to make your heads: so run the old   410
Traditions of you. I can therefore speak
Without the natural shame which creatures feel
When speaking on their level, to their like.
There's many a papist she, would rather die
Than own to her maid she put a ribbon on   415
To catch the indifferent eye of such a man,
Who yet would count adulteries on her beads
At holy Mary's shrine, and never blush;
Because the saints are so far off, we lose
All modesty before them. Thus, today.   420
'Tis I, love Romney Leigh.'
                              'Forbear,' I cried.
'If here's no muse, still less is any saint;
Nor even a friend, that Lady Waldemar
Should make confessions' . . .
                              'That's unkindly said.
If no friend, what forbids to make a friend   425
To join to our confession ere we have done?
I love your cousin. If it seems unwise
To say so, it's still foolisher (we're frank)
To feel so. My first husband left me young,
And pretty enough, so please you, and rich enough,   430
To keep my booth in May-fair with the rest
To happy issues. There are marquises
Would serve seven years to call me wife, I know,
And, after seven, I might consider it,
For there's some comfort in a marquisate   435
When all's said, – yes, but after the seven years;
I, now, love Romney. You put up your lip,
So like a Leigh! so like him! – Pardon me,
I am well aware I do not derogate
In loving Romney Leigh. The name is good,   440
The means are excellent, but the man, the man –
Heaven help us both, – I am near as mad as he,
In loving such an one.'
                              She slowly swung
Her heavy ringlets till they touched her smile,
As reasonably sorry for herself,   445

And thus continued.
                  'Of a truth, Miss Leigh,
I have not, without a struggle, come to this.
I took a master in the German tongue,
I gamed a little, went to Paris twice;
But, after all, this love! . . . . you eat of love,   450
And do as vile a thing as if you ate
Of garlic – which, whatever else you eat,
Tastes uniformly acrid, till your peach
Reminds you of your onion. Am I coarse?
Well, love's coarse, nature's coarse – ah, there's the rub!   455
We fair fine ladies, who park out our lives
From common sheep-paths, cannot help the crows
From flying over, – we're as natural still
As Blowsalinda.[143] Drape us perfectly
In Lyons' velvet, – we are not, for that,   460
Lay-figures, look you: we have hearts within,
Warm, live, improvident, indecent hearts, ·
As ready for outrageous ends and acts
As any distressed sempstress of them all
That Romney groans and toils for. We catch love   465
And other fevers, in the vulgar way:
Love will not be outwitted by our wit,
Nor outrun by our equipages: – mine
Persisted, spite of efforts. All my cards
Turned up but Romney Leigh; my German stopped   470
At germane Wertherism; my Paris rounds
Returned me from the Champs Elysées just
A ghost, and sighing like Dido's.[144] I came home
Uncured, – convicted rather to myself
Of being in love . . . in love! That's coarse, you'll say.   475
I'm talking garlic.'
            Coldly I replied.
'Apologise for atheism, not love!
For me, I do believe in love, and God.
I know my cousin: Lady Waldemar
I know not: yet I say as much as this;   480
Whoever loves him, let her not excuse
But cleanse herself, that, loving such a man,
She may not do it with such unworthy love

He cannot stoop and take it.'
       'That is said
Austerely, like a youthful prophetess,   485
Who knits her brows across her pretty eyes
To keep them back from following the grey flight
Of doves between the temple-columns. Dear,
Be kinder with me; let us two be friends.
I'm a mere woman – the more weak perhaps   490
Through being so proud; you're better; as for him,
He's best. Indeed he builds his goodness up
So high, it topples down to the other side
And makes a sort of badness; there's the worst
I have to say against your cousin's best!   495
And so be mild, Aurora, with my worst
For his sake, if not mine.'
       'I own myself
Incredulous of confidence like this
Availing him or you.'
      'And I, myself,
Of being worthy of him with any love: 500
In your sense I am not so – let it pass.
And yet I save him if I marry him;
Let that pass too.'
      'Pass, pass! we play police
Upon my cousin's life, to indicate
What may or may not pass?' I cried. 'He knows   505
What's worthy of him; the choice remains with *him*;
And what he chooses, act or wife, I think
I shall not call unworthy, I, for one.'

' 'Tis somewhat rashly said,' she answered slow;
'Now let's talk reason, though we talk of love.   510
Your cousin Romney Leigh's a monster; there,
The word's out fairly, let me prove the fact.
We'll take, say, that most perfect of antiques
They call the Genius of the Vatican,
(Which seems too beauteous to endure itself   515
In this mixed world), and fasten it for once
Upon the torso of the Dancing Fawn,
(Who might limp surely, if he did not dance,)

Instead of Buonarroti's mask: what then?
We show the sort of monster Romney is,   520
With god-like virtues and heroic aims
Subjoined to limping possibilities
Of mismade human nature. Grant the man
Twice god-like, twice heroic, – still he limps,
And here's the point we come to.'
                                 'Pardon me,   525
But, Lady Waldemar, the point's the thing
We never come to.'
                    'Caustic, insolent
At need! I like you' – (there, she took my hands)
'And now my lioness, help Androcles,
For all your roaring. Help me! for myself   530
I would not say so – but for him. He limps
So certainly, he'll fall into the pit
A week hence, – so I lose him – so he is lost!
And when he's fairly married, he a Leigh,
To a girl of doubtful life, undoubtful birth,   535
Starved out in London till her coarse-grained hands
Are whiter than her morals, – even you
May call his choice unworthy.'
                         'Married! lost!
He, . . . Romney!'
                  'Ah, you're moved at last,' she said.
'These monsters, set out in the open sun,   540
Of course throw monstrous shadows: those who think
Awry, will scarce act straightly. Who but he?
And who but you can wonder? He has been mad,
The whole world knows, since first, a nominal man,
He soured the proctors, tried the gownsmen's wits,   545
With equal scorn of triangles and wine,
And took no honours, yet was honourable.
They'll tell you he lost count of Homer's ships
In Melbourne's poor-bills, Ashley's factory bills, –
Ignored the Aspasia [145] we all dare to praise,   550
For other women, dear, we could not name
Because we're decent. Well, he had some right
On his side probably; men always have,
Who go absurdly wrong. The living boor

Who brews your ale, exceeds in vital worth   555
Dead Caesar who "stops bungholes" in the cask;
And also, to do good is excellent,
For persons of his income, even to boors:
I sympathise with all such things. But he
Went mad upon them . . . madder and more mad   560
From college times to these, – as, going down hill,
The faster still, the farther. You must know
Your Leigh by heart: he has sown his black young curls
With bleaching cares of half a million men
Already. If you do not starve, or sin,   565
You're nothing to him: pay the income-tax
And break your heart upon 't , he'll scarce be touched;
But come upon the parish, qualified
For the parish stocks, and Romney will be there
To call you brother, sister, or perhaps   570
A tenderer name still. Had I any chance
With Mister Leigh, who am Lady Waldemar
And never committed felony?'
                              'You speak
Too bitterly,' I said, 'for the literal truth.'

'The truth is bitter. Here's a man who looks   575
For ever on the ground! you must be low,
Or else a pictured ceiling overhead,
Good painting thrown away. For me, I've done
What women may, we're somewhat limited,
We modest women, but I've done my best.   580
– How men are perjured when they swear our eyes
Have meaning in them! they're just blue or brown,
They just can drop their lids a little. And yet
Mine did more, for I read half Fourier through,
Proudhon, Considérant, and Louis Blanc,[146]   585
With various others of his socialists,
And, if I had been a fathom less in love,
Had cured myself with gaping. As it was,
I quoted from them prettily enough
Perhaps, to make them sound half rational   590
To a saner man than he whene'er we talked,
(For which I dodged occasion) – learnt by heart

His speeches in the Commons and elsewhere
Upon the social question; heaped reports
Of wicked women and penitentiaries   595
On all my tables (with a place for Sue),
And gave my name to swell subscription-lists
Toward keeping up the sun at nights in heaven,
And other possible ends. All things I did,
Except the impossible . . . such as wearing gowns   600
Provided by the Ten Hours' movement:[147] there,
I stopped – we must stop somewhere. He, meanwhile,
Unmoved as the Indian tortoise 'neath the world,
Let all that noise go on upon his back:
He would not disconcert or throw me out,   605
'Twas well to see a woman of my class
With such a dawn of conscience. For the heart,
Made firewood for his sake, and flaming up
To his face, – he merely warmed his feet at it:
Just deigned to let my carriage stop him short   610
In park or street, – he leaning on the door
With news of the committee which sat last
On pickpockets at suck.'

                                    'You jest – you jest.'

'As martyrs jest, dear (if you read their lives),
Upon the axe which kills them. When all's done   615
By me, . . . for him – you'll ask him presently
The colour of my hair – he cannot tell,
Or answers "dark" at random; while, be sure,
He's absolute on the figure, five or ten,
Of my last subscription. Is it bearable,   620
And I a woman?'
                        'Is it reparable,
Though I were a man?'
                                'I know not. That's to prove.
But first, this shameful marriage?'
                                        'Aye?' I cried,
'Then really there's a marriage?'
                                        'Yesterday
I held him fast upon it. "Mister Leigh,"   625

                            384

Said I, "shut up a thing, it makes more noise.
The boiling town keeps secrets ill; I've known
Yours since last week. Forgive my knowledge so:
You feel I'm not the woman of the world
The world thinks; you have borne with me before,   630
And used me in your noble work, our work,
And now you shall not cast me off because
You're at the difficult point, the *join*. 'Tis true
Even if I can scarce admit the cogency
Of such a marriage . . . where you do not love   635
(Except the class), yet marry and throw your name
Down to the gutter, for a fire-escape
To future generations! 'tis sublime,
A great example, a true Genesis
Of the opening social era. But take heed,   640
This virtuous act must have a patent weight,
Or loses half its virtue. Make it tell,
Interpret it, and set it in the light,
And do not muffle it in a winter-cloak
As a vulgar bit of shame, – as if, at best,   645
A Leigh had made a misalliance and blushed
A Howard should know it." Then, I pressed him more:
"He would not choose," I said, "that even his kin, . . .
Aurora Leigh, even . . . should conceive his act
Less sacrifice, more fantasy." At which   650
He grew so pale, dear, . . . to the lips, I knew
I had touched him. "Do you know her," he enquired,
"My cousin Aurora?" "Yes," I said, and lied,
(But truly we all know you by your books)
And so I offered to come straight to you,   655
Explain the subject, justify the cause,
And take you with me to St Margaret's Court
To see this miracle, this Marian Erle,
This drover's daughter (she's not pretty, he swears)
Upon whose finger, exquisitely pricked   660
By a hundred needles, we're to hang the tie
'Twixt class and class in England, – thus indeed
By such a presence, yours and mine, to lift
The match up from the doubtful place. At once
He thanked me sighing, murmured to himself   665

385

"She'll do it perhaps, she's noble," – thanked me twice,
And promised, as my guerdon, to put off
His marriage for a month.'
                  I answered then.
'I understand your drift imperfectly.
You wish to lead me to my cousin's betrothed, 670
To touch her hand if worthy, and hold her hand
If feeble, thus to justify his match.
So be it then. But how this serves your ends,
And how the strange confession of your love
Serves this, I have to learn – I cannot see.' 675

She knit her restless forehead. 'Then, despite,
Aurora, that most radiant morning name,
You're dull as any London afternoon.
I wanted time, – and gained it, – wanted *you*,
And gain you! you will come and see the girl 680
In whose most prodigal eyes the lineal pearl
And pride of all your lofty race of Leighs
Is destined to solution. Authorised
By sight and knowledge, then, you'll speak your mind,
And prove to Romney, in your brilliant way, 685
He'll wrong the people and posterity,
(Say such a thing is bad for me and you,
And you fail utterly,) by concluding thus
An execrable marriage. Break it up,
Disroot it – peradventure presently 690
We'll plant a better fortune in its place.
Be good to me, Aurora, scorn me less
For saying the thing I should not. Well I know
I should not. I have kept, as others have,
The iron rule of womanly reserve 695
In lip and life, till now: I wept a week
Before I came here.' – Ending, she was pale;
The last words, haughtily said, were tremulous.
This palfrey pranced in harness, arched her neck,
And, only by the foam upon the bit, 700
You saw she champed against it.
                     Then I rose.
'I love love: truth's no cleaner thing than love.

I comprehend a love so fiery hot
It burns its natural veil of august shame,
And stands sublimely in the nude, as chaste   705
As Medicean Venus. But I know,
A love that burns through veils will burn through masks
And shrivel up treachery. What, love and lie!
Nay – go to the opera! your love's curable.'

'I love and lie!' she said – 'I lie, forsooth?'   710
And beat her taper foot upon the floor,
And smiled against the shoe, – 'You're hard, Miss Leigh,
Unversed in current phrases. – Bowling-greens
Of poets are fresher than the world's highways:
Forgive me that I rashly blew the dust,   715
Which dims our hedges even, in your eyes,
And vexed you so much. You find, probably,
No evil in this marriage, – rather good
Of innocence, to pastoralise in song:
You'll give the bond your signature, perhaps,   720
Beneath the lady's mark, – indifferent
That Romney chose a wife could write her name,
In witnessing he loved her.'
                                             'Loved!' I cried;
'Who tells you that he wants a wife to love?
He gets a horse to use, not love, I think: 725
There's work for wives as well, – and after, straw,
When men are liberal. For myself, you err
Supposing power in me to break this match.
I could not do it, to save Romney's life,
And would not, to save mine.'
                                             'You take it so,'   730
She said, 'farewell, then. Write your books in peace,
As far as may be for some secret stir
Now obvious to me, – for, most obviously,
In coming hither I mistook the way.'
Whereat she touched my hand and bent her head,   735
And floated from me like a silent cloud
That leaves the sense of thunder.
                                             I drew breath,
Oppressed in my deliverance. After all

This woman breaks her social system up
For love, so counted – the love possible   740
To such, – and lilies are still lilies, pulled
By smutty hands, though spotted from their white;
And thus she is better haply, of her kind,
Than Romney Leigh, who lives by diagrams,
And crosses out the spontaneities   745
Of all his individual, personal life
With formal universals. As if man
Were set upon a high stool at a desk
To keep God's books for Him in red and black,
And feel by millions! What, if even God   750
Were chiefly God by living out Himself
To an individualism of the Infinite,
Eterne, intense, profuse, – still throwing up
The golden spray of multitudinous worlds
In measure to the proclive weight and rush   755
Of his inner nature, – the spontaneous love
Still proof and outflow of spontaneous life?
Then live, Aurora.
          Two hours afterward,
Within St Margaret's Court I stood alone,
Close-veiled. A sick child, from an ague-fit,   760
Whose wasted right hand gambled 'gainst his left
With an old brass button in a blot of sun,
Jeered weakly at me as I passed across
The uneven pavement; while a woman, rouged
Upon the angular cheek-bones, kerchief torn,   765
Thin dangling locks, and flat lascivious mouth,
Cursed at a window both ways, in and out,
By turns some bed-rid creature and myself, –
'Lie still there, mother! liker the dead dog
You'll be tomorrow. What, we pick our way,   770
Fine madam, with those damnable small feet!
We cover up our face from doing good,
As if it were our purse! What brings you here,
My lady? is 't to find my gentleman
Who visits his tame pigeon in the eaves?   775
Our cholera catch you with its cramps and spasms,
And tumble up your good clothes, veil and all,

And turn your whiteness dead-blue.' I looked up;
I think I could have walked through hell that day,
And never flinched. 'The dear Christ comfort you,'   780
I said, 'you must have been most miserable,
To be so cruel,' – and I emptied out
My purse upon the stones: when, as I had cast
The last charm in the cauldron, the whole court
Went boiling, bubbling up, from all its doors   785
And windows, with a hideous wail of laughs
And roar of oaths, and blows perhaps . . . I passed
Too quickly for distinguishing . . . and pushed
A little side-door hanging on a hinge,
And plunged into the dark, and groped and climbed   790
The long, steep, narrow stair 'twixt broken rail
And mildewed wall that let the plaster drop
To startle me in the blackness. Still, up, up!
So high lived Romney's bride. I paused at last
Before a low door in the roof, and knocked;   795
There came an answer like a hurried dove –
'So soon? can that be Mister Leigh? so soon?'
And, as I entered, an ineffable face
Met mine upon the threshold. 'Oh, not you,
Not you!' – the dropping of the voice implied,   800
'Then, if not you, for me not any one.'
I looked her in the eyes, and held her hands,
And said, 'I am his cousin, – Romney Leigh's;
And here I'm come to see my cousin too.'
She touched me with her face and with her voice,   805
This daughter of the people. Such soft flowers,
From such rough roots? the people, under there,
Can sin so, curse so, look so, smell so . . . . faugh!
Yet have such daughters?
                 Nowise beautiful
Was Marian Erle. She was not white nor brown,   810
But could look either, like a mist that changed
According to being shone on more or less:
The hair, too, ran its opulence of curls
In doubt 'twixt dark and bright, nor left you clear
To name the colour. Too much hair perhaps   815
(I'll name a fault here) for so small a head,

Which seemed to droop on that side and on this,
As a full-blown rose uneasy with its weight
Though not a wind should trouble it. Again,
The dimple in the cheek had better gone   820
With redder, fuller rounds; and somewhat large
The mouth was, though the milky little teeth
Dissolved it to so infantine a smile.
For soon it smiled at me; the eyes smiled too,
But 'twas as if remembering they had wept,   825
And knowing they should, some day, weep again.

We talked. She told me all her story out,
Which I'll re-tell with fuller utterance,
As coloured and confirmed in aftertimes
By others and herself too. Marian Erle   830
Was born upon the ledge of Malvern Hill
To eastward, in a hut built up at night
To evade the landlord's eye, of mud and turf,
Still liable, if once he looked that way,
To being straight levelled, scattered by his foot, 835
Like any other anthill. Born, I say;
God sent her to His world, commissioned right,
Her human testimonials fully signed,
Not scant in soul – complete in lineaments;
But others had to swindle her a place   840
To wail in when she had come. No place for her,
By man's law! born an outlaw, was this babe;
Her first cry in our strange and strangling air,
When cast in spasms out by the shuddering womb,
Was wrong against the social code, – forced wrong: –   845
What business had the baby to cry there?

I tell her story and grow passionate.
She, Marian, did not tell it so, but used
Meek words that made no wonder of herself
For being so sad a creature. 'Mister Leigh   850
Considered truly that such things should change.
They *will*, in heaven – but meantime, on the earth,
There's none can like a nettle as a pink,
Except himself. We're nettles, some of us,

And give offence by the act of springing up;   855
And, if we leave the damp side of the wall,
The hoes, of course, are on us.' So she said.
Her father earned his life by random jobs
Despised by steadier workmen – keeping swine
On commons, picking hops, or hurrying on   860
The harvest at wet seasons, or, at need,
Assisting the Welsh drovers, when a drove
Of startled horses plunged into the mist
Below the mountain-road, and sowed the wind
With wandering neighings. In between the gaps   865
Of such irregular work, he drank and slept,
And cursed his wife because, the pence being out,
She could not buy more drink. At which she turned
(The worm), and beat her baby in revenge
For her own broken heart. There's not a crime   870
But takes its proper change out still in crime
If once rung on the counter of this world:
Let sinners look to it.
                 Yet the outcast child,
For whom the very mother's face forewent
The mother's special patience, lived and grew;   875
Learnt early to cry low, and walk alone,
With that pathetic vacillating roll
Of the infant body on the uncertain feet
(The earth being felt unstable ground so soon),
At which most women's arms unclose at once   880
With irrepressive instinct. Thus, at three,
This poor weaned kid would run off from the fold,
This babe would steal off from the mother's chair,
And, creeping through the golden walls of gorse,
Would find some keyhole toward the secrecy   885
Of Heaven's high blue, and, nestling down, peer out –
Oh, not to catch the angels at their games,
She had never heard of angels, – but to gaze
She knew not why, to see she knew not what,
A-hungering outward from the barren earth   890
For something like a joy. She liked, she said,
To dazzle black her sight against the sky,
For then, it seemed, some grand blind Love came down,

And groped her out, and clasped her with a kiss;
She learnt God that way, and was beat for it   895
Whenever she went home, – yet came again,
As surely as the trapped hare, getting free,
Returns to his form. This grand blind Love, she said,
This skyey father and mother both in one,
Instructed her and civilised her more   900
Than even the Sunday-school did afterward,
To which a lady sent her to learn books
And sit upon a long bench in a row
With other children. Well, she laughed sometimes
To see them laugh and laugh and maul their texts;   905
But ofter she was sorrowful with noise
And wondered if their mothers beat them hard
That ever they should laugh so. There was one
She loved indeed, – Rose Bell, a seven years' child
So pretty and clever, who read syllables   910
When Marian was at letters; *she* would laugh
At nothing – hold your finger up, she laughed,
Then shook her curls down over eyes and mouth
To hide her make-mirth from the schoolmaster:
And Rose's pelting glee, as frank as rain   915
On cherry-blossoms, brightened Marian too,
To see another merry whom she loved.
She whispered once (the children side by side,
With mutual arms entwined about their necks)
'Your mother lets you laugh so?' 'Aye,' said Rose,   920
'She lets me. She was dug into the ground
Six years since, I being but a yearling wean.
Such mothers let us play and lose our time,
And never scold nor beat us! don't you wish
You had one like that?' There, Marian, breaking off   925
Looked suddenly in my face. 'Poor Rose,' said she,
'I heard her laugh last night in Oxford Street.
I'd pour out half my blood to stop that laugh.
Poor Rose, poor Rose!' said Marian.
                                        She resumed.
It tried her, when she had learnt at Sunday-school   930
What God was, what He wanted from us all,
And how in choosing sin we vexed the Christ,

To go straight home and hear her father pull
The Name down on us from the thunder-shelf,
Then drink away his soul into the dark   935
From seeing judgment. Father, mother, home,
Were God and heaven reversed to her: the more
She knew of Right, the more she guessed their wrong;
Her price paid down for knowledge, was to know
The vileness of her kindred: through her heart,   940
Her filial and tormented heart, henceforth,
They struck their blows at virtue. Oh, 'tis hard
To learn you have a father up in heaven
By a gathering certain sense of being, on earth,
Still worse than orphaned: 'tis too heavy a grief,   945
The having to thank God for such a joy!

And so passed Marian's life from year to year.
Her parents took her with them when they tramped,
Dodged lanes and heaths, frequented towns and fairs,
And once went farther and saw Manchester,   950
And once the sea, that blue end of the world,
That fair scroll-finis of a wicked book, –
And twice a prison, – back at intervals,
Returning to the hills. Hills draw like heaven,
And stronger sometimes, holding out their hands   955
To pull you from the vile flats up to them.
And though perhaps these strollers still strolled back,
As sheep do, simply that they knew the way,
They certainly felt bettered unaware
Emerging from the social smut of towns   960
To wipe their feet clean on the mountain turf.
In which long wanderings, Marian lived and learned,
Endured and learned. The people on the roads
Would stop and ask her why her eyes outgrew
Her cheeks, and if she meant to lodge the birds   965
In all that hair; and then they lifted her,
The miller in his cart, a mile or twain,
The butcher's boy on horseback. Often too
The pedlar stopped, and tapped her on the head
With absolute forefinger, brown and ringed,   970
And asked if peradventure she could read,

And when she answered 'aye,' would toss her down
Some stray odd volume from his heavy pack,
A Thomson's Seasons, mulcted of the Spring,
Or half a play of Shakespeare's, torn across,   975
(She had to guess the bottom of a page
By just the top sometimes, – as difficult,
As, sitting on the moon, to guess the earth!)
Or else a sheaf of leaves (for that small Ruth's
Small gleanings) torn out from the heart of books,   980
From Churchyard Elegies and Edens Lost,
From Burns, and Bunyan, Selkirk, and Tom Jones, –
'Twas somewhat hard to keep the things distinct,
And oft the jangling influence jarred the child
Like looking at a sunset full of grace   985
Through a pothouse window while the drunken oaths
Went on behind her. But she weeded out
Her book-leaves, threw away the leaves that hurt
(First tore them small, that none should find a word),
And made a nosegay of the sweet and good   990
To fold within her breast, and pore upon
At broken moments of the noontide glare,
When leave was given her to untie her cloak
And rest upon the dusty highway's bank
From the road dust: or oft, the journey done,   995
Some city friend would lead her by the hand
To hear a lecture at an institute.
And thus she had grown, this Marian Erle of ours,
To no book-learning, – she was ignorant
Of authors, – not in earshot of the things   1000
Outspoken o'er the heads of common men
By men who are uncommon, – but within
The cadenced hum of such, and capable
Of catching from the fringes of the wind
Some fragmentary phrases, here and there,   1005
Of that fine music, which, being carried in
To her soul, had reproduced itself afresh
In finer motions of the lips and lids.

She said, in speaking of it, 'If a flower
Were thrown you out of heaven at intervals,   1010

You'd soon attain to a trick of looking up, –
And so with her.' She counted me her years,
Till *I* felt old; and then she counted me
Her sorrowful pleasures, till I felt ashamed.
She told me she was fortunate and calm   1015
On such and such a season, sat and sewed,
With no one to break up her crystal thoughts,
While rimes from lovely poems span around
Their ringing circles of ecstatic tune,
Beneath the moistened finger of the Hour.   1020
Her parents called her a strange, sickly child,
Not good for much, and given to sulk and stare,
And smile into the hedges and the clouds,
And tremble if one shook her from her fit
By any blow, or word even. Out-door jobs   1025
Went ill with her, and household quiet work
She was not born to. Had they kept the north,
They might have had their pennyworth out of her
Like other parents, in the factories,
(Your children work for you, not you for them,   1030
Or else they better had been choked with air
The first breath drawn;) but, in this tramping life,
Was nothing to be done with such a child
But tramp and tramp. And yet she knitted hose
Not ill, and was not dull at needlework;   1035
And all the country people gave her pence
For darning stockings past their natural age,
And patching petticoats from old to new,
And other light work done for thrifty wives.

One day, said Marian, – the sun shone that day –   1040
Her mother had been badly beat, and felt
The bruises sore about her wretched soul
(That must have been): she came in suddenly,
And snatching in a sort of breathless rage
Her daughter's headgear comb, let down the hair   1045
Upon her like a sudden waterfall,
Then drew her drenched and passive by the arm
Outside the hut they lived in. When the child
Could clear her blinded face from all that stream

Of tresses . . . there, a man stood, with beasts' eyes   1050
That seemed as they would swallow her alive
Complete in body and spirit, hair and all, –
With burning stertorous breath that hurt her cheek,
He breathed so near. The mother held her tight,
Saying hard between her teeth – 'Why wench, why wench, 1055
The squire speaks to you now – the squire's too good;
He means to set you up and comfort us.
Be mannerly at least.' The child turned round
And looked up piteous in the mother's face
(Be sure that mother's death-bed will not want   1060
Another devil to damn, than such a look),
'Oh, mother!' then, with desperate glance to heaven,
'God, free me from my mother,' she shrieked out,
'These mothers are too dreadful.' And, with force
As passionate as fear, she tore her hands   1065
Like lilies from the rocks, from hers and his,
And sprang down, bounded headlong down the steep,
Away from both – away, if possible,
As far as God, – away! They yelled at her,
As famished hounds at a hare. She heard them yell;   1070
She felt her name hiss after her from the hills,
Like shot from guns. On, on. And now she had cast
The voices off with the uplands. On. Mad fear
Was running in her feet and killing the ground;
The white roads curled as if she burnt them up,   1075
The green fields melted, wayside trees fell back
To make room for her. Then her head grew vexed;
Trees, fields, turned on her and ran after her;
She heard the quick pants of the hills behind,
Their keen air pricked her neck: she had lost her feet, 1080
Could run no more, yet somehow went as fast,
The horizon red 'twixt steeples in the east
So sucked her forward, forward, while her heart
Kept swelling, swelling, till it swelled so big
It seemed to fill her body, – when it burst   1085
And overflowed the world and swamped the light;
'And now I am dead and safe,' thought Marian Erle –
She had dropped, she had fainted.
                                As the sense returned,

The night had passed – not life's night. She was 'ware
Of heavy tumbling motions, creaking wheels,   1090
The driver shouting to the lazy team
That swung their rankling bells against her brain,
While, through the waggon's coverture and chinks,
The cruel yellow morning pecked at her
Alive or dead upon the straw inside, –   1095
At which her soul ached back into the dark
And prayed, 'no more of that.' A waggoner
Had found her in a ditch beneath the moon,
As white as moonshine save for the oozing blood.
At first he thought her dead; but when he had wiped   1100
The mouth and heard it sigh, he raised her up,
And laid her in his waggon in the straw,
And so conveyed her to the distant town
To which his business called himself, and left
That heap of misery at the hospital.   1105

She stirred; – the place seemed new and strange as death.
The white strait bed, with others strait and white,
Like graves dug side by side at measured lengths,
And quiet people walking in and out
With wonderful low voices and soft steps   1110
And apparitional equal care for each,
Astonished her with order, silence, law.
And when a gentle hand held out a cup,
She took it, as you do at sacrament,
Half awed, half melted, – not being used, indeed,   1115
To so much love as makes the form of love
And courtesy of manners. Delicate drinks
And rare white bread, to which some dying eyes
Were turned in observation. O my God,
How sick we must be, ere we make men just!   1120
I think it frets the saints in heaven to see
How many desolate creatures on the earth
Have learnt the simple dues of fellowship
And social comfort, in a hospital,
As Marian did. She lay there, stunned, half tranced,   1125
And wished, at intervals of growing sense,
She might be sicker yet, if sickness made

The world so marvellous kind, the air so hushed,
And all her wake-time quiet as a sleep;
For now she understood (as such things were)   1130
How sickness ended very oft in heaven
Among the unspoken raptures: – yet more sick,
And surelier happy. Then she dropped her lids,
And, folding up her hands as flowers at night,
Would lose no moment of the blessed time.   1135

She lay and seethed in fever many weeks,
But youth was strong and overcame the test;
Revolted soul and flesh were reconciled
And fetched back to the necessary day
And daylight duties. She could creep about   1140
The long bare rooms, and stare out drearily
From any narrow window on the street,
Till some one who had nursed her as a friend
Said coldly to her, as an enemy,
'She had leave to go next week, being well enough,'   1145
(While only her heart ached). 'Go next week,' thought she,
'Next week! how would it be with her next week,
Let out into that terrible street alone
Among the pushing people, . . . to go . . . where?'

One day, the last before the dreaded last,   1150
Among the convalescents, like herself
Prepared to go next morning, she sat dumb,
And heard half absently the women talk, –
How one was famished for her baby's cheeks,
'The little wretch would know her! a year old   1155
And lively, like his father!' – one was keen
To get to work, and fill some clamorous mouths;
And one was tender for her dear goodman
Who had missed her sorely, – and one, querulous . . .
'Would pay backbiting neighbours who had dared   1160
To talk about her as already dead,' –
And one was proud . . . 'and if her sweetheart Luke
Had left her for a ruddier face than hers,
(The gossip would be seen through at a glance)
Sweet riddance of such sweethearts – let him hang!   1165

'Twere good to have been as sick for such an end.'

And while they talked, and Marian felt the worse
For having missed the worst of all their wrongs,
A visitor was ushered through the wards
And paused among the talkers. 'When he looked,   1170
It was as if he spoke, and when he spoke
He sang perhaps,' said Marian; 'could she tell?
She only knew' (so much she had chronicled,
As seraphs might the making of the sun)
'That he who came and spake, was Romney Leigh,   1175
And then and there she saw and heard him first.'

And when it was her turn to have the face
Upon her, all those buzzing pallid lips
Being satisfied with comfort – when he changed
To Marian, saying, 'And *you*? you're going, where?' –   1180
She, moveless as a worm beneath a stone
Which some one's stumbling foot has spurned aside,
Writhed suddenly, astonished with the light,
And breaking into sobs cried, 'Where I go?
None asked me till this moment. Can I say   1185
Where *I* go, – when it has not seemed worth while
To God Himself, who thinks of every one,
To think of me and fix where I shall go?'

'So young,' he gently asked her, 'you have lost
Your father and your mother?'
                              'Both,' she said,   1190
'Both lost! My father was burnt up with gin
Or ever I sucked milk, and so is lost.
My mother sold me to a man last month,
And so my mother's lost, 'tis manifest.
And I, who fled from her for miles and miles,   1195
As if I had caught sight of the fire of hell
Through some wild gap (she was my mother, sir),
It seems I shall be lost too, presently,
And so we end, all three of us.'
                              'Poor child,'
He said, – with such a pity in his voice,   1200

It soothed her more than her own tears, – 'poor child!
'Tis simple that betrayal by mother's love
Should bring despair of God's too. Yet be taught
He's better to us than many mothers are,
And children cannot wander beyond reach   1205
Of the sweep of His white raiment. Touch and hold!
And if you weep still, weep where John was laid
While Jesus loved him.'
                   'She could say the words,'
She told me, 'exactly as he uttered them
A year back, since in any doubt or dark   1210
They came out like the stars, and shone on her
With just their comfort. Common words, perhaps;
The ministers in church might say the same;
But *he*, he made the church with what he spoke, –
The difference was the miracle,' said she.   1215

Then catching up her smile to ravishment,
She added quickly, 'I repeat his words,
But not his tones: can any one repeat
The music of an organ, out of church?
And when he said "poor child," I shut my eyes   1220
To feel how tenderly his voice broke through,
As the ointment-box broke on the Holy feet
To let out the rich medicative nard.'

She told me how he had raised and rescued her
With reverent pity, as, in touching grief,   1225
He touched the wounds of Christ, – and made her feel
More self-respecting. Hope, he called, belief
In God, – work, worship, – therefore let us pray!
And thus, to snatch her soul from atheism,
And keep it stainless from her mother's face,   1230
He sent her to a famous sempstress-house
Far off in London, there to work and hope.

With that, they parted. She kept sight of Heaven,
But not of Romney. He had good to do
To others: through the days and through the nights   1235
She sewed and sewed and sewed. She drooped sometimes,

And wondered, while along the tawny light
She struck the new thread into her needle's eye,
How people without mothers on the hills
Could choose the town to live in! – then she drew   1240
The stitch, and mused how Romney's face would look,
And if 'twere likely he'd remember hers
When they two had their meeting after death.

Fourth Book

They met still sooner. 'Twas a year from thence
That Lucy Gresham, the sick semptress girl,
Who sewed by Marian's chair so still and quick,
And leant her head upon its back to cough
More freely, when, the mistress turning round,   5
The others took occasion to laugh out,
Gave up at last. Among the workers, spoke
A bold girl with black eyebrows and red lips;
'You know the news? Who's dying, do you think?
Our Lucy Gresham. I expected it   10
As little as Nell Hart's wedding. Blush not, Nell,
Thy curls be red enough without thy cheeks,
And, some day, there'll be found a man to dote
On red curls. – Lucy Gresham swooned last night,
Dropped sudden in the street while going home;   15
And now the baker says, who took her up
And laid her by her grandmother in bed,
He'll give her a week to die in. Pass the silk.
Let's hope he gave her a loaf too, within reach,
For otherwise they'll starve before they die,   20
That funny pair of bedfellows! Miss Bell,
I'll thank you for the scissors. The old crone
Is paralytic – that's the reason why
Our Lucy's thread went faster than her breath,
Which went too quick, we all know. Marian Erle!   25
Why, Marian Erle, you're not the fool to cry?
Your tears spoil Lady Waldemar's new dress,
You piece of pity!'
                        Marian rose up straight,
And, breaking through the talk and through the work,
Went outward, in the face of their surprise,   30
To Lucy's home, to nurse her back to life
Or down to death. She knew, by such an act,
All place and grace were forfeit in the house,
Whose mistress would supply the missing hand
With necessary, not inhuman haste,   35

402

And take no blame. But pity, too, had dues:
She could not leave a solitary soul
To founder in the dark, while she sat still
And lavished stitches on a lady's hem
As if no other work were paramount.   40
'Why, God,' thought Marian, 'has a missing hand
This moment; Lucy wants a drink, perhaps.
Let others miss me! never miss me, God!'

So Marian sat by Lucy's bed, content
With duty, and was strong, for recompense,   45
To hold the lamp of human love arm-high
To catch the death-strained eyes and comfort them,
Until the angels, on the luminous side
Of death, had got theirs ready. And she said,
If Lucy thanked her sometimes, called her kind,   50
It touched her strangely. 'Marian Erle, called kind!
What, Marian, beaten and sold, who could not die!
'Tis verily good fortune to be kind.
Ah, you,' she said, 'who are born to such a grace,
Be sorry for the unlicensed class, the poor,   55
Reduced to think the best good fortune means
That others, simply, should be kind to them.'

From sleep to sleep while Lucy slid away
So gently, like a light upon a hill,
Of which none names the moment that it goes   60
Though all see when 'tis gone, – a man came in
And stood beside the bed. The old idiot wretch
Screamed feebly, like a baby overlain,
'Sir, sir, you won't mistake me for the corpse?
Don't look at *me*, sir! never bury *me*!   65
Although I lie here, I'm alive as you,
Except my legs and arms, – I eat and drink
And understand, – (that you're the gentleman
Who fits the funerals up, Heaven speed you, sir,)
And certainly I should be livelier still   70
If Lucy here . . . sir, Lucy is the corpse . . .
Had worked more properly to buy me wine:
But Lucy, sir, was always slow at work,

I shan't lose much by Lucy. Marian Erle,
Speak up and show the gentleman the corpse.'   75

And then a voice said, 'Marian Erle.' She rose;
It was the hour for angels – there, stood hers!
She scarcely marvelled to see Romney Leigh.
As light November snows to empty nests,
As grass to graves, as moss to mildewed stones,   80
As July suns to ruins, through the rents,
As ministering spirits to mourners, through a loss,
As Heaven itself to men, through pangs of death,
He came uncalled wherever grief had come.
'And so,' said Marian Erle, 'we met anew,'   85
And added softly, 'so, we shall not part.'

He was not angry that she had left the house
Wherein he placed her. Well – she had feared it might
Have vexed him. Also, when he found her set
On keeping, though the dead was out of sight,   90
That half-dead, half-live body left behind
With cankerous heart and flesh, – which took your best
And cursed you for the little good it did,
(Could any leave the bed-rid wretch alone,
So joyless, she was thankless even to God,   95
Much more to you?) he did not say 'twas well,
Yet Marian thought he did not take it ill, –
Since day by day he came, and, every day,
She felt within his utterance and his eyes
A closer, tenderer presence of the soul,   100
Until at last he said, 'We shall not part.'

On that same day, was Marian's work complete:
She had smoothed the empty bed, and swept the floor
Of coffin sawdust, set the chairs anew
The dead had ended gossip in, and stood   105
In that poor room so cold and orderly,
The door-key in her hand, prepared to go
As *they* had, howbeit not their way. He spoke.

'Dear Marian, of one clay God made us all,

And though men push and poke and paddle in't 110
(As children play at fashioning dirt-pies)
And call their fancies by the name of facts,
Assuming difference, lordship, privilege,
When all's plain dirt, – they come back to it at last,
The first grave-digger proves it with a spade, 115
And pats all even. Need we wait for this,
You, Marian, and I, Romney?'
     She, at that,
Looked blindly in his face, as when one looks
Through driving autumn-rains to find the sky.
He went on speaking.
      'Marian, I being born 120
What men call noble, and you, issued from
The noble people, – though the tyrannous sword
Which pierced Christ's heart, has cleft the world in twain
'Twixt class and class, opposing rich to poor,
Shall *we* keep parted? Not so. Let us lean 125
And strain together rather, each to each,
Compress the red lips of this gaping wound,
As far as two souls can, – aye, lean and league,
I, from my superabundance, – from your want
You, – joining in a protest 'gainst the wrong 130
On both sides.'
    All the rest, he held her hand
In speaking, which confused the sense of much.
Her heart against his words beat out so thick,
They might as well be written on the dust
Where some poor bird, escaping from hawk's beak, 135
Has dropped and beats its shuddering wings, – the lines
Are rubbed so, – yet 'twas something like to this,
– 'That they two, standing at the two extremes
Of social classes, had received one seal,
Been dedicate and drawn beyond themselves 140
To mercy and ministration, – he, indeed,
Through what he knew, and she, through what she felt,
He, by man's conscience, she, by woman's heart,
Relinquishing their several 'vantage posts
Of wealthy ease and honourable toil, 145
To work with God at love. And since God willed

That putting out his hand to touch this ark,
He found a woman's hand there, he'd accept
The sign too, hold the tender fingers fast,
And say, "My fellow-worker, be my wife!" '   150

She told the tale with simple, rustic turns, –
Strong leaps of meaning in her sudden eyes
That took the gaps of any imperfect phrase
Of the unschooled speaker; I have rather writ
The thing I understood so, than the thing   155
I heard so. And I cannot render right
Her quick gesticulation, wild yet soft,
Self-startled from the habitual mood she used,
Half sad, half languid, – like dumb creatures (now
A rustling bird, and now a wandering deer,   160
Or squirrel 'gainst the oak-gloom flashing up
His sidelong burnished head, in just her way
Of savage spontaneity), that stir
Abruptly the green silence of the woods,
And make it stranger, holier, more profound;   165
As Nature's general heart confessed itself
Of life, and then fell backward on repose.

I kissed the lips that ended. – 'So indeed
He loves you, Marian?'
                       'Loves me!' She looked up
With a child's wonder when you ask him first   170
Who made the sun – a puzzled blush, that grew,
Then broke off in a rapid radiant smile
Of sure solution. 'Loves me! he loves all, –
And me, of course. He had not asked me else
To work with him for ever, and be his wife.'   175

Her words reproved me. This perhaps was love –
To have its hands too full of gifts to give,
For putting out a hand to take a gift;
To love so much, the perfect round of love
Includes, in strict conclusion, being loved;   180
As Eden-dew went up and fell again,
Enough for watering Eden. Obviously

She had not thought about his love at all:
The cataracts of her soul had poured themselves,
And risen self-crowned in rainbow: would she ask   185
Who crowned her? – it sufficed that she was crowned.
With women of my class 'tis otherwise:
We haggle for the small change of our gold,
And so much love accord for so much love,
Rialto-prices. Are we therefore wrong?   190
If marriage be a contract, look to it then,
Contracting parties should be equal, just,
Bit if, a simple fealty on one side,
A mere religion, – right to give, is all,
And certain brides of Europe duly ask   195
To mount the pile as Indian widows do,
The spices of their tender youth heaped up,
The jewels of their gracious virtues worn,
More gems, more glory, – to consume entire
For a living husband: as the man's alive,   200
Not dead, the woman's duty by so much
Advanced in England beyond Hindostan.

I sat there musing, till she touched my hand
With hers, as softly as a strange white bird
She feared to startle in touching. 'You are kind.   205
But are you, peradventure, vexed at heart
Because your cousin takes me for a wife?
I know I am not worthy – nay, in truth,
I'm glad on 't, since, for that, he chooses me.
He likes the poor things of the world the best;   210
I would not therefore, if I could, be rich.
It pleasures him to stoop for buttercups;
I would not be a rose upon the wall
A queen might stop at, near the palace-door,
To say to a courtier, "Pluck that rose for me,   215
It's prettier than the rest." O Romney Leigh!
I'd rather far be trodden by his foot,
Than lie in a great queen's bosom.'

                          Out of breath
She paused.
             'Sweet Marian, do you disavow

The roses with that face?'
                       She dropt her head   220
As if the wind had caught that flower of her,
And bent it in the garden, – then looked up
With grave assurance. 'Well, you think me bold!
But so we all are, when we're praying God.
And if I'm bold – yet, lady, credit me,   225
That, since I know myself for what I am
Much fitter for his handmaid than his wife,
I'll prove the handmaid and the wife at once,
Serve tenderly, and love obediently,
And be a worthier mate, perhaps, than some   230
Who are wooed in silk among their learned books;
While I shall set myself to read his eyes,
Till such grow plainer to me than the French
To wisest ladies. Do you think I'll miss
A letter, in the spelling of his mind?   235
No more than they do when they sit and write
Their flying words with flickering wild-fowl tails,
Nor ever pause to ask how many *t*s,
Should that be *y* or *i*, they know't so well:
I've seen them writing, when I brought a dress   240
And waited, – floating out their soft white hands
On shining paper. But they're hard sometimes,
For all those hands! – we've used out many nights,
And worn the yellow daylight into shreds
Which flapped and shivered down our aching eyes   245
Till night appeared more tolerable, just
That pretty ladies might look beautiful,
Who said at last . . . "You're lazy in that house!
You're slow in sending home the work, – I count
I've waited near an hour for't." Pardon me,   250
I do not blame them, madam, nor misprize;
They are fair and gracious; aye, but not like you,
Since none but you has Mister Leigh's own blood
Both noble and gentle, – and, without it . . . well,
They are fair, I said; so fair, it scarce seems strange   255
That, flashing out in any looking-glass
The wonder of their glorious brows and breasts,
They're charmed so, they forget to look behind

And mark how pale we've grown, we pitiful
Remainders of the world. And so perhaps   260
If Mister Leigh had chosen a wife from these,
She might, although he's better than her best
And dearly she would know it, steal a thought
Which should be all his, an eye-glance from his face,
To plunge into the mirror opposite   265
In search of her own beauty's pearl; while I . . .
Ah, dearest lady, serge will outweigh silk
For winter-wear when bodies feel a-cold,
And I'll be a true wife to your cousin Leigh.'

Before I answered he was there himself.   270
I think he had been standing in the room
And listened probably to half her talk,
Arrested, turned to stone, – as white as stone.
Will tender sayings make men look so white?
He loves her then profoundly.

                              'You are here,   275
Aurora? Here I meet you!' – We clasped hands.

'Even so, dear Romney. Lady Waldemar
Has sent me in haste to find a cousin of mine
Who shall be.'

                    'Lady Waldemar is good.'

'Here's one, at least, who is good,' I sighed, and touched 280
Poor Marian's happy head, as doglike she,
Most passionately patient, waited on,
A-tremble for her turn of greeting words;
'I've sat a full hour with your Marian Erle,
And learnt the thing by heart, – and from my heart   285
Am therefore competent to give you thanks
For such a cousin.'
                    'You accept at last
A gift from me, Aurora, without scorn?
At last I please you?' – How his voice was changed.

'You cannot please a woman against her will,   290

409

And once you vexed me. Shall we speak of that?
We'll say, then, you were noble in it all
And I not ignorant – let it pass. And now
You please me, Romney, when you please yourself;
So, please you, be fanatical in love,   295
And I'm well pleased. Ah, cousin! at the old hall,
Among the gallery portraits of our Leighs,
We shall not find a sweeter signory
Than this pure forehead's.'
                        Not a word he said.
How arrogant men are! – Even philanthropists,   300
Who try to take a wife up in the way
They put down a subscription-cheque, – if once
She turns and says, 'I will not tax you so,
Most charitable sir,' – feel ill at ease,
As though she had wronged them somehow. I suppose   305
We women should remember what we are,
And not throw back an obolus inscribed
With Caesar's image,[148] lightly. I resumed.

'It strikes me, some of those sublime Vandykes
Were not too proud to make good saints in heaven;   310
And if so, then they're not too proud today,
To bow down (now the ruffs are off their necks)
And own this good, true, noble Marian, yours,
And mine, I'll say! – For poets (bear the word),
Half-poets even, are still whole democrats, –   315
Oh, not that we're disloyal to the high,
But loyal to the low, and cognisant
Of the less scrutable majesties. For me,
I comprehend your choice, I justify
Your right in choosing.'
                  'No, no, no,' he sighed,   320
With a sort of melancholy impatient scorn,
As some grown man who never had a child
Puts by some child who plays at being a man,
'You did not, do not, cannot comprehend
My choice, my ends, my motives, nor myself: 325
No matter now; we'll let it pass, you say.
I thank you for your generous cousinship

410

Which helps this present; I accept for her
Your favourable thoughts. We're fallen on days,
We two who are not poets, when to wed   330
Requires less mutual love than common love
For two together to bear out at once
Upon the loveless many. Work in pairs,
In galley-couplings or in marriage-rings,
The difference lies in the honour, not the work, –   335
And such we're bound to, I and she. But love
(You poets are benighted in this age,
The hour's too late for catching even moths,
You've gnats instead), love! – love's fool-paradise
Is out of date, like Adam's. Set a swan   340
To swim the Trenton, rather than true love
To float its fabulous plumage safely down
The cataracts of this loud transition-time, –
Whose roar for ever henceforth in my ears
Must keep me deaf to music.'
                    There, I turned   345
And kissed poor Marian, out of discontent.
The man had baffled, chafed me, till I flung
For refuge to the woman, – as, sometimes,
Impatient of some crowded room's close smell,
You throw a window open and lean out   350
To breathe a long breath in the dewy night
And cool your angry forehead. She, at least,
Was not built up as walls are, brick by brick,
Each fancy squared, each feeling ranged by line,
The very heat of burning youth applied   355
To indurate form and system! excellent bricks,
A well-built wall, – which stops you on the road,
And, into which, you cannot see an inch
Although you beat your head against it – pshaw!

'Adieu,' I said, 'for this time, cousins both,   360
And, cousin Romney, pardon me the word,
Be happy! – oh, in some esoteric sense
Of course! – I mean no harm in wishing well.
Adieu, my Marian: – may she come to me,
Dear Romney, and be married from my house?   365

It is not part of your philosophy
To keep your bird upon the blackthorn?'

                                     'Aye,'

He answered, 'but it is. I take my wife
Directly from the people, – and she comes,
As Austria's daughter to imperial France,   370
Betwixt her eagles, blinking not her race,
From Margaret's Court at garret-height, to meet
And wed me at St James's, nor put off
Her gown of serge for that. The things we do,
We do: we'll wear no mask, as if we blushed.'   375

'Dear Romney, you're the poet,' I replied.
But felt my smile too mournful for my word,
And turned and went. Aye, masks, I thought, – beware
Of tragic masks we tie before the glass,
Uplifted on the cothurn half a yard   380
Above the natural stature! we would play
Heroic parts to ourselves, – and end, perhaps,
As impotently as Athenian wives
Who shrieked in fits at the Eumenides.[149]

His foot pursued me down the stair. 'At least   385
You'll suffer me to walk with you beyond
These hideous streets, these graves, where men alive
Packed close with earthworms, burr unconsciously
About the plague that slew them; let me go.
The very women pelt their souls in mud   390
At any woman who walks here alone.
How came you here alone? – you are ignorant.'

We had a strange and melancholy walk:
The night came drizzling downward in dark rain,
And, as we walked, the colour of the time,   395
The act, the presence, my hand upon his arm,
His voice in my ear, and mine to my own sense,
Appeared unnatural. We talked modern books
And daily papers, Spanish marriage-schemes
And English climate – was't so cold last year?   400
And will the wind change by tomorrow morn?

Can Guizot stand? is London full? is trade
Competitive? has Dickens turned his hinge
A-pinch upon the fingers of the great?
And are potatoes to grow mythical   405
Like moly? will the apple die out too?
Which way is the wind tonight? south-east? due east?
We talked on fast, while every common word
Seemed tangled with the thunder at one end,
And ready to pull down upon our heads   410
A terror out of sight. And yet to pause
Were surelier mortal: we tore greedily up
All silence, all the innocent breathing-points,
As if, like pale conspirators in haste,
We tore up papers where our signatures   415
Imperilled us to an ugly shame or death.

I cannot tell you why it was. 'Tis plain
We had not loved nor hated: wherefore dread
To spill gunpowder on ground safe from fire?
Perhaps we had lived too closely, to diverge   420
So absolutely: leave two clocks, they say,
Wound up to different hours, upon one shelf,
And slowly, through the interior wheels of each,
The blind mechanic motion sets itself
A-throb to feel out for the mutual time.   425
It was not so with us, indeed: while he
Struck midnight, I kept striking six at dawn,
While he marked judgment, I, redemption-day;
And such exception to a general law
Imperious upon inert matter even,   430
Might make us, each to either, insecure,
A beckoning mystery or a troubling fear.

I mind me, when we parted at the door,
How strange his good-night sounded, – like good-night
Beside a deathbed, where the morrow's sun   435
Is sure to come too late for more good days:
And all that night I thought . . . ' "Good-night," said he.'

And so, a month passed. Let me set it down
At once, – I have been wrong, I have been wrong.

We are wrong always when we think too much   440
Of what we think or are: albeit our thoughts
Be verily bitter as self-sacrifice,
We're no less selfish. If we sleep on rocks
Or roses, sleeping past the hour of noon
We're lazy. This I write against myself.   445
I had done a duty in the visit paid
To Marian, and was ready otherwise
To give the witness of my presence and name
Whenever she should marry. – Which, I thought,
Sufficed. I even had cast into the scale   450
An overweight of justice toward the match;
The Lady Waldemar had missed her tool,
Had broken it in the lock as being too straight
For a crooked purpose, while poor Marian Erle
Missed nothing in my accents or my acts: 455
I had not been ungenerous on the whole,
Nor yet untender; so, enough. I felt
Tired, overworked: this marriage somewhat jarred;
Or, if it did not, all the bridal noise,
The pricking of the map of life with pins,   460
In schemes of . . . 'Here we'll go,' and 'There we'll stay,'
And 'Everywhere we'll prosper in our love,'
Was scarce my business: let them order it;
Who else should care? I threw myself aside,
As one who had done her work and shuts her eyes   465
To rest the better.
                    I, who should have known,
Forereckoned mischief! Where we disavow
Being keeper to our brother we're his Cain.

I might have held that poor child to my heart
A little longer! 'twould have hurt me much   470
To have hastened by its beats the marriage day,
And kept her safe meantime from tampering hands
Or, peradventure, traps. What drew me back
From telling Romney plainly the designs
Of Lady Waldemar, as spoken out   475
To me . . . me? had I any right, aye, right,
With womanly compassion and reserve

To break the fall of woman's impudence? –
To stand by calmly, knowing what I knew,
And hear him call her *good*?
                        Distrust that word. 480
'There is none good save God,' said Jesus Christ.
If He once, in the first creation-week,
Called creatures good, – for ever, afterward,
The Devil only has done it, and his heirs.
The knaves who win so, and the fools who lose; 485
The world's grown dangerous. In the middle age,
I think they called malignant fays and imps
Good people. A good neighbour, even in this,
Is fatal sometimes, – cuts your morning up
To mince-meat of the very smallest talk, 490
Then helps to sugar her bohea at night
With your reputation. I have known good wives,
As chaste, or nearly so, as Potiphar's;[150]
And good, good mothers, who would use a child
To better an intrigue; good friends, beside 495
(Very good), who hung succinctly round your neck
And sucked your breath, as cats are fabled to do
By sleeping infants. And we all have known
Good critics who have stamped out poet's hopes;
Good statesmen who pulled ruin on the state, 500
Good patriots who for a theory risked a cause,
Good kings who disembowelled for a tax,
Good popes who brought all good to jeopardy,
Good Christians who sat still in easy chairs
And damned the general world for standing up. – 505
Now may the good God pardon all good men!

How bitterly I speak, – how certainly
The innocent white milk in us is turned,
By much persistent shining of the sun! –
Shake up the sweetest in us long enough 510
With men, it drops to foolish curd, too sour
To feed the most untender of Christ's lambs.

I should have thought, – a woman of the world
Like her I'm meaning, centre to herself,
Who has wheeled on her own pivot half a life 515

In isolated self-love and self-will,
As a windmill seen at distance radiating
Its delicate white vans against the sky,
So soft and soundless, simply beautiful,
Seen nearer, – what a roar and tear it makes,   520
How it grinds and bruises! – if she loves at last,
Her love's a readjustment of self-love,
No more, – a need felt of another's use
To her one advantage, as the mill wants grain,
The fire wants fuel, the very wolf wants prey,   525
And none of these is more unscrupulous
Than such a charming woman when she loves.
She'll not be thwarted by an obstacle
So trifling as . . . her soul is, . . . much less yours! –
Is God a consideration? – she loves you,   530
Not God; she will not flinch for Him indeed:
She did not for the Marchioness of Perth,
When wanting tickets for the fancy ball.
She loves you, sir, with passion, to lunacy,
She loves you like her diamonds . . . almost.

                                                     Well,   535
A month passed so, and then the notice came,
On such a day the marriage at the church.
I was not backward.
                   Half Saint Giles in frieze
Was bidden to meet Saint James in cloth of gold,
And, after contract at the altar, pass   540
To eat a marriage-feast on Hampstead Heath.
Of course the people came in uncompelled,
Lame, blind, and worse – sick, sorrowful, and worse,
The humours of the peccant social wound
All pressed out, poured down upon Pimlico,   545
Exasperating the unaccustomed air
With a hideous interfusion. You'd suppose
A finished generation, dead of plague,
Swept outward from their graves into the sun,
The moil of death upon them. What a sight!   550
A holiday of miserable men
Is sadder than a burial-day of kings.

*

They clogged the streets, they oozed into the church
In a dark slow stream, like blood. To see that sight,
The noble ladies stood up in their pews,   555
Some pale for fear, a few as red for hate,
Some simply curious, some just insolent,
And some in wondering scorn, – 'What next? what next?'
These crushed their delicate rose-lips from the smile
That misbecame them in a holy place,   560
With broidered hems of perfumed handkerchiefs;
Those passed the salts, with confidence of eyes
And simultaneous shiver of moiré silk:
While all the aisles, alive and black with heads,
Crawled slowly toward the altar from the street,   565
As bruised snakes crawl and hiss out of a hole
With shuddering involution, swaying slow
From right to left, and then from left to right,
In pants and pauses. What an ugly crest
Of faces rose upon you everywhere   570
From that crammed mass! you did not usually
See faces like them in the open day:
They hide in cellars, not to make you mad
As Romney Leigh is. – Faces! – O my God,
We call those, faces? men's and women's . . . aye,   575
And children's; – babies, hanging like a rag
Forgotten on their mother's neck, – poor mouths,
Wiped clean of mother's milk by mother's blow
Before they are taught her cursing. Faces? . . . phew,
We'll call them vices, festering to despairs,   580
Or sorrows, petrifying to vices: not
A finger-touch of God left whole on them,
All ruined, lost – the countenance worn out
As the garment, the will dissolute as the act,
The passions loose and draggling in the dirt   585
To trip a foot up at the first free step! –
Those, faces! 'twas as if you had stirred up hell
To heave its lowest dreg-fiends uppermost
In fiery swirls of slime, – such strangled fronts,
Such obdurate jaws were thrown up constantly   590
To twit you with your race, corrupt your blood,
And grind to devilish colours all your dreams

417

Henceforth, – though, haply, you should drop asleep
By clink of silver waters, in a muse
On Raffael's mild Madonna of the Bird.[151]   595

I've waked and slept through many nights and days
Since then, – but still that day will catch my breath
Like a nightmare. There are fatal days, indeed,
In which the fibrous years have taken root
So deeply, that they quiver to their tops   600
Whene'er you stir the dust of such a day.

My cousin met me with his eyes and hand,
And then, with just a word, . . . that 'Marian Erle
Was coming with her bridesmaids presently,'
Made haste to place me by the altar-stair   605
Where he and other noble gentlemen
And high-born ladies, waited for the bride.

We waited. It was early: there was time
For greeting, and the morning's compliment,
And gradually a ripple of women's talk   610
Arose and fell and tossed about a spray
Of English ss, soft as a silent hush,
And, notwithstanding, quite as audible
As louder phrases thrown out by the men.
– 'Yes, really, if we need to wait in church   615
We need to talk there.' – 'She? 'tis Lady Ayr,
In blue – not purple! that's the dowager.'
– 'She looks as young' – 'She flirts as young, you mean.
Why if you had seen her upon Thursday night,
You'd call Miss Norris modest.' – '*You* again!   620
I waltzed with you three hours back. Up at six,
Up still at ten; scarce time to change one's shoes:
I feel as white and sulky as a ghost,
So pray don't speak to me, Lord Belcher.' – 'No,
I'll look at you instead, and it's enough   625
While you have that face.' 'In church, my lord! fie, fie!'
– 'Adair, you stayed for the Division?' – 'Lost
By one.' 'The devil it is! I'm sorry for 't.
And if I had not promised Mistress Grove' . . .

– 'You might have kept your word to Liverpool.'   630
– 'Constituents must remember, after all,
We're mortal.' – 'We remind them of it.' – 'Hark,
The bride comes! here she comes, in a stream of milk!'
– 'There? Dear, you are asleep still; don't you know
The five Miss Granvilles? always dressed in white   635
To show they're ready to be married.' – 'Lower!
The aunt is at your elbow.' – 'Lady Maud,
Did Lady Waldemar tell you she had seen
This girl of Leigh's?' 'No, – wait! 'twas Mistress Brookes,
Who told me Lady Waldemar told her –   640
No, 'twasn't Mistress Brookes.' – 'She's pretty?' – 'Who?
Mistress Brookes? Lady Waldemar?' – 'How hot!
Pray is't the law today we're not to breathe?
You're treading on my shawl – I thank you, sir.'
– 'They say the bride's a mere child, who can't read,   645
But knows the things she shouldn't, with wide-awake
Great eyes. I'd go through fire to look at her.'
– 'You do, I think.' – 'And Lady Waldemar
(You see her; sitting close to Romney Leigh.
How beautiful she looks, a little flushed!)   650
Has taken up the girl, and methodised
Leigh's folly. Should I have come here, you suppose,
Except she'd asked me?' – 'She'd have served him more
By marrying him herself.'

                         'Ah – there she comes,
The bride, at last!'

                         'Indeed, no. Past eleven.   655
She puts off her patched petticoat today
And puts on May-fair manners, so begins
By setting us to wait.' – 'Yes, yes, this Leigh
Was always odd; it's in the blood, I think;
His father's uncle's cousin's second son   660
Was, was . . . you understand me; and for him,
He's stark, – has turned quite lunatic upon
This modern question of the poor – the poor.
An excellent subject when you're moderate;
You've seen Prince Albert's model lodging-house?   665
Does honour to his Royal Highness. Good!
But would he stop his carriage in Cheapside

To shake a common fellow by the fist
Whose name was . . . Shakespeare? no. We draw a line,
And if we stand not by our order, we   670
In England, we fall headlong. Here's a sight!
A hideous sight, a most indecent sight!
My wife would come, sir, or I had kept her back.
By heaven, sir, when poor Damiens' trunk and limbs
Were torn by horses, women of the court   675
Stood by and stared, exactly as today
On this dismembering of society,
With pretty, troubled faces.'
                                   'Now, at last.
She comes now.'
                        'Where? who sees? you push me, sir,
Beyond the point of what is mannerly.   680
You're standing, madam, on my second flounce.
I do beseech you . . . '
                         'No – it's not the bride.
Half-past eleven. How late. The bridegroom, mark,
Gets anxious and goes out.'
                                   'And as I said,
These Leighs! our best blood running in the rut!   685
It's something awful. We had pardoned him
A simple misalliance got up aside
For a pair of sky-blue eyes; the House of Lords
Has winked at such things, and we've all been young.
But here's an intermarriage reasoned out,   690
A contract (carried boldly to the light
To challenge observation, pioneer
Good acts by a great example) 'twixt the extremes
Of martyrised society, – on the left
The well-born, – on the right the merest mob,   695
To treat as equals! – 'tis anarchical;
It means more than it says; 'tis damnable.
Why, sir, we can't have even our coffee good,
Unless we strain it.'
                        'Here, Miss Leigh!'
                                          'Lord Howe,
You're Romney's friend. What's all this waiting for?'   700
                            *

420

'I cannot tell. The bride has lost her head
(And way, perhaps!) to prove her sympathy
With the bridegroom.'
                    'What, – you also, disapprove!'

'Oh, I approve of nothing in the world,'
He answered, 'not of you, still less of me,   705
Nor even of Romney, though he's worth us both.
We're all gone wrong. The tune in us is lost;
And whistling down back alleys to the moon
Will never catch it.'
                    Let me draw Lord Howe.
A born aristocrat, bred radical,   710
And educated socialist, who still
Goes floating, on traditions of his kind,
Across the theoretic flood from France,
Though, like a drenched Noah on a rotten deck,
Scarce safer for his place there. He, at least,   715
Will never land on Ararat, he knows,
To recommence the world on the new plan:
Indeed, he thinks, said world had better end,
He sympathises rather with the fish
Outside, than with the drowned paired beasts within   720
Who cannot couple again or multiply, –
And that's the sort of Noah he is, Lord Howe.
He never could be anything complete,
Except a loyal, upright gentleman,
A liberal landlord, graceful diner-out,   725
And entertainer more than hospitable,
Whom authors dine with and forget the hock.
Whatever he believes, and it is much,
But nowise certain, now here and now there,
He still has sympathies beyond his creed   730
Diverting him from action. In the House,
No party counts upon him, while for all
His speeches have a noticeable weight.
Men like his books too (he has written books),
Which, safe to lie beside a bishop's chair,   735
At times outreach themselves with jets of fire
At which the foremost of the progressists

421

May warm audacious hands in passing by.
Of stature over-tall, lounging for ease;
Light hair, that seems to carry a wind in it,   740
And eyes that, when they look on you, will lean
Their whole weight, half in indolence, and half
In wishing you unmitigated good,
Until you know not if to flinch from him
Or thank him. – 'Tis Lord Howe.

                    'We're all gone wrong,'   745
Said he, 'and Romney, that dear friend of ours,
Is nowise right. There's one true thing on earth,
That's love! he takes it up, and dresses it,
And acts a play with it, as Hamlet[152] did,
To show what cruel uncles we have been,   750
And how we should be uneasy in our minds
While he, Prince Hamlet, weds a pretty maid
(Who keeps us too long waiting, we'll confess)
By symbol, to instruct us formally
To fill the ditches up 'twixt class and class,   755
And live together in phalansteries.
What then? – he's mad, our Hamlet! clap his play,
And bind him.'

              'Ah, Lord Howe, this spectacle
Pulls stronger at us than the Dane's. See there!
The crammed aisles heave and strain and steam with life.   760
Dear Heaven, what life!'

              'Why, yes, – a poet sees;
Which makes him different from a common man.
I, too, see somewhat, though I cannot sing;
I should have been a poet, only that
My mother took fright at the ugly world,   765
And bore me tongue-tied. If you'll grant me now
That Romney gives us a fine actor-piece
To make us merry on his marriage-morn,
The fable's worse than Hamlet's I'll concede.
The terrible people, old and poor and blind,   770
Their eyes eat out with plague and poverty
From seeing beautiful and cheerful sights,
We'll liken to a brutalised King Lear,
Led out, – by no means to clear scores with wrongs –

His wrongs are so far back, he has forgot 775
(All's past like youth); but just to witness here
A simple contract, – he, upon his side,
And Regan with her sister Goneril
And all the dappled courtiers and court-fools
On their side. Not that any of these would say 780
They're sorry, neither. What is done, is done,
And violence is now turned privilege,
As cream turns cheese, if buried long enough.
What could such lovely ladies have to do
With the old man there, in those ill-odorous rags, 785
Except to keep the wind-side of him? Lear
Is flat and quiet, as a decent grave;
He does not curse his daughters in the least:
Be these his daughters? Lear is thinking of
His porridge chiefly . . . is it getting cold 790
At Hampstead? will the ale be served in pots?
Poor Lear, poor daughters! Bravo, Romney's play.'

A murmur and a movement drew around,
A naked whisper touched us. Something wrong.
What's wrong! The black crowd, as an overstrained 795
Cord, quivered in vibration, and I saw . . .
Was that *his* face I saw? . . . his . . . Romney Leigh's . . .
Which tossed a sudden horror like a sponge
Into all eyes, – while himself stood white upon
The topmost altar-stair and tried to speak, 800
And failed, and lifted higher above his head
A letter, . . . as a man who drowns and gasps.

'My brothers, bear with me! I am very weak.
I meant but only good. Perhaps I meant
Too proudly, and God snatched the circumstance 805
And changed it therefore. There's no marriage – none.
She leaves me, – she departs, – she disappears,
I lose her. Yet I never forced her "ay",
To have her "no" so cast into my teeth
In manner of an accusation, thus. 810
My friends, you are dismissed. Go, eat and drink
According to the programme, – and farewell!'

*

He ended. There was silence in the church.
We heard a baby sucking in its sleep
At the farthest end of the aisle. Then spoke a man,   815
'Now, look to it, coves, that all the beef and drink
Be not filched from us like the other fun,
For beer's spilt easier than a woman's lost!
This gentry is not honest with the poor;
They bring us up, to trick us.' – 'Go it, Jim,'   820
A woman screamed back, – 'I'm a tender soul,
I never banged a child at two years old
And drew blood from him, but I sobbed for it
Next moment, – and I've had a plague of seven.
I'm tender; I've no stomach even for beef,   825
Until I know about the girl that's lost,
That's killed, mayhap. I did misdoubt, at first,
The fine lord meant no good by her or us.
He, maybe, got the upper hand of her
By holding up a wedding-ring, and then . . .   830
A choking finger on her throat last night,
And just a clever tale to keep us still,
As she is, poor lost innocent. "Disappear!"
Who ever disappears except a ghost?
And who believes a story of a ghost?   835
I ask you, – would a girl go off, instead
Of staying to be married? a fine tale!
A wicked man, I say, a wicked man!
For my part I would rather starve on gin
Than make my dinner on his beef and beer.' –   840
At which a cry rose up – 'We'll have our rights.
We'll have the girl, the girl! Your ladies there
Are married safely and smoothly every day,
And *she* shall not drop through into a trap
Because she's poor and of the people: shame!   845
We'll have no tricks played off by gentlefolks;
We'll see her righted.'
                         Through the rage and roar
I heard the broken words which Romney flung
Among the turbulent masses, from the ground
He held still with his masterful pale face, –   850
As huntsmen throw the ration to the pack,

Who, falling on it headlong, dog on dog
In heaps of fury, rend it, swallow it up
With yelling hound-jaws, – his indignant words,
His suppliant words, his most pathetic words,   855
Whereof I caught the meaning here and there
By his gesture . . . torn in morsels, yelled across,
And so devoured. From end to end, the church
Rocked round us like the sea in storm, and then
Broke up like the earth in earthquake. Men cried out   860
'Police' – and women stood and shrieked for God,
Or dropt and swooned; or, like a herd of deer
(For whom the black woods suddenly grow alive,
Unleashing their wild shadows down the wind
To hunt the creatures into corners, back   865
And forward) madly fled, or blindly fell,
Trod screeching underneath the feet of those
Who fled and screeched.
                The last sight left to me
Was Romney's terrible calm face above
The tumult! – the last sound was 'Pull him down!   870
Strike – kill him!' Stretching my unreasoning arms,
As men in dreams, who vainly interpose
'Twixt gods and their undoing, with a cry
I struggled to precipitate myself
Head-foremost to the rescue of my soul   875
In that white face, . . . till some one caught me back,
And so the world went out, – I felt no more.

What followed was told after by Lord Howe,
Who bore me senseless from the strangling crowd
In church and street, and then returned alone   880
To see the tumult quelled. The men of law
Had fallen as thunder on a roaring fire,
And made all silent, – while the people's smoke
Passed eddying slowly from the emptied aisles.

Here's Marian's letter, which a ragged child   885
Brought running, just as Romney at the porch
Looked out expectant of the bride. He sent
The letter to me by his friend Lord Howe

Some two hours after, folded in a sheet
On which his well-known hand had left a word.   890
Here's Marian's letter.
                'Noble friend, dear saint,
Be patient with me. Never think me vile,
Who might tomorrow morning be your wife
But that I loved you more than such a name.
Farewell, my Romney. Let me write it once, –   895
My Romney.
          'Tis so pretty a coupled word,
I have no heart to pluck it with a blot.
We say "my God" sometimes, upon our knees,
Who is not therefore vexed: so bear with it . . .
And me. I know I'm foolish, weak, and vain;   900
Yet most of all I'm angry with myself
For losing your last footstep on the stair,
The last time of your coming, – yesterday!
The very first time I lost step of yours
(Its sweetness comes the next to what you speak),   905
But yesterday sobs took me by the throat
And cut me off from music.
              'Mister Leigh,
You'll set me down as wrong in many things.
You've praised me, sir, for truth, – and now you'll learn
I had not courage to be rightly true.   910
I once began to tell you how she came,
The woman . . . and you stared upon the floor
In one of your fixed thoughts . . . which put me out
For that day. After, some one spoke of me,
So wisely, and of you, so tenderly,   915
Persuading me to silence for your sake . . .
Well, well! it seems this moment I was wrong
In keeping back from telling you the truth:
There might be truth betwixt us two, at least,
If nothing else. And yet 'twas dangerous.   920
Suppose a real angel came from heaven
To live with men and women! he'd go mad,
If no considerate hand should tie a blind
Across his piercing eyes. 'Tis thus with you:
You see us too much in your heavenly light;   925

I always thought so, angel, – and indeed
There's danger that you beat yourself to death
Against the edges of this alien world,
In some divine and fluttering pity.

               'Yes,
It would be dreadful for a friend of yours,   930
To see all England thrust you out of doors
And mock you from the windows. You might say,
Or think (that's worse), "There's some one in the house
I miss and love still." Dreadful!

              'Very kind,
I pray you mark, was Lady Waldemar.   935
She came to see me nine times, rather ten –
So beautiful, she hurts one like the day
Let suddenly on sick eyes.

              'Most kind of all,
Your cousin! – ah, most like you! Ere you came
She kissed me mouth to mouth: I felt her soul   940
Dip through her serious lips in holy fire.
God help me, but it made me arrogant;
I almost told her that you would not lose
By taking me to wife: though ever since
I've pondered much a certain thing she asked . . .   945
"He loves you, Marian?" . . . in a sort of mild
Derisive sadness . . . as a mother asks
Her babe, "You'll touch that star, you think?"

                 'Farewell!
I know I never touched it.

            'This is worst:
Babes grow and lose the hope of things above;   950
A silver threepence sets them leaping high –
But no more stars! mark that.

            'I've writ all night
Yet told you nothing. God, if I could die,
And let this letter break off innocent
Just here! But no – for your sake . . .

             'Here's the last: 955
I never could be happy as your wife,
I never could be harmless as your friend,
I never will look more into your face

Till God says, "Look!" I charge you, seek me not,
Nor vex yourself with lamentable thoughts   960
That peradventure I have come to grief;
Be sure I'm well, I'm merry, I'm at ease,
But such a long way, long way, long way off,
I think you'll find me sooner in my grave,
And that's my choice, observe. For what remains,   965
An over-generous friend will care for me
And keep me happy . . . happier . . .
        'There's a blot!
This ink runs thick . . . we light girls lightly weep . . .
And keep me happier . . . was the thing to say,
Than as your wife I could be. – O, my star,   970
My saint, my soul! for surely you're my soul,
Through whom God touched me! I am not so lost
I cannot thank you for the good you did,
The tears you stopped, which fell down bitterly,
Like these – the times you made me weep for joy   975
At hoping I should learn to write your notes
And save the tiring of your eyes, at night;
And most for that sweet thrice you kissed my lips
And said "Dear Marian."
      ' 'Twould be hard to read,
This letter, for a reader half as learn'd;   980
But you'll be sure to master it in spite
Of ups and downs. My hand shakes, I am blind;
I'm poor at writing at the best, – and yet
I tried to make my gs the way you showed.
Farewell. Christ love you. – Say "poor Marian" now.'   985

Poor Marian! – wanton Marian! – was it so,
Or so? For days, her touching, foolish lines
We mused on with conjectural fantasy,
As if some riddle of a summer-cloud
On which one tries unlike similitudes   990
Of now a spotted Hydra-skin[153] cast off,
And now a screen of carven ivory
That shuts the heaven's conventual secrets up
From mortals over-bold. We sought the sense:
She loved him so perhaps (such words mean love),   995

That, worked on by some shrewd perfidious tongue
(And then I thought of Lady Waldemar),
She left him, not to hurt him; or perhaps
She loved one in her class, – or did not love,
But mused upon her wild bad tramping life   1000
Until the free blood fluttered at her heart,
And black bread eaten by the roadside hedge
Seemed sweeter than being put to Romney's school
Of philanthropical self-sacrifice
Irrevocably. – Girls are girls, beside,   1005
Thought I, and like a wedding by one rule.
You seldom catch these birds except with chaff:
They feel it almost an immoral thing
To go out and be married in broad day,
Unless some winning special flattery should   1010
Excuse them to themselves for 't, . . . 'No one parts
Her hair with such a silver line as you,
One moonbeam from the forehead to the crown!'
Or else . . . 'You bite your lip in such a way,
It spoils me for the smiling of the rest,'   1015
And so on. Then a worthless gaud or two
To keep for love, – a ribbon for the neck,
Or some glass pin, – they have their weight with girls.

And Romney sought her many days and weeks:
He sifted all the refuse of the town,   1020
Explored the trains, enquired among the ships,
And felt the country through from end to end;
No Marian! – Though I hinted what I knew, –
A friend of his had reasons of her own
For throwing back the match – he would not hear: 1025
The lady had been ailing ever since,
The shock had harmed her. Something in his tone
Repressed me; something in me shamed my doubt
To a sigh repressed too. He went on to say
That, putting questions where his Marian lodged,   1030
He found she had received for visitors,
Besides himself and Lady Waldemar
And, that once, me – a dubious woman dressed
Beyond us both: the rings upon her hands

Had dazed the children when she threw them pence;   1035
'She wore her bonnet as the queen might hers,
To show the crown,' they said, – 'a scarlet crown
Of roses that had never been in bud.'

When Romney told me that, – for now and then
He came to tell me how the search advanced,   1040
His voice dropped: I bent forward for the rest:
The woman had been with her, it appeared,
At first from week to week, then day by day,
And last, 'twas sure . . .
                              I looked upon the ground
To escape the anguish of his eyes, and asked   1045
As low as when you speak to mourners new
Of those they cannot bear yet to call dead,
If Marian had as much as named to him
A certain Rose, an early friend of hers,
A ruined creature.'
                          'Never.' – Starting up   1050
He strode from side to side about the room,
Most like some prisoned lion sprung awake,
Who has felt the desert sting him through his dreams.
'What was I to her, that she should tell me aught?
A friend! Was I a friend? I see all clear.   1055
Such devils would pull angels out of heaven,
Provided they could reach them; 'tis their pride;
And that's the odds 'twixt soul and body-plague!
The veriest slave who drops in Cairo's street,
Cries, "Stand off from me," to the passengers;   1060
While these blotched souls are eager to infect,
And blow their bad breath in a sister's face
As if they got some ease by it.'
                                  I broke through.
'Some natures catch no plagues. I've read of babes
Found whole and sleeping by the spotted breast   1065
Of one a full day dead. I hold it true,
As I'm a woman and know womanhood,
That Marian Erle, however lured from place,
Deceived in way, keeps pure in aim and heart
As snow that's drifted from the garden-bank   1070

To the open road.'
                    'twas hard to hear him laugh.
'The figure's happy. Well – a dozen carts
And trampers will secure you presently
A fine white snow-drift. Leave it there, your snow!
'Twill pass for soot ere sunset. Pure in aim?   1075
She's pure in aim, I grant you, – like myself,
Who thought to take the world upon my back
To carry it o'er a chasm of social ill,
And end by letting slip through impotence
A single soul, a child's weight in a soul,   1080
Straight down the pit of hell! yes, I and she
Have reason to be proud of our pure aims.'
Then softly, as the last repenting drops
Of a thunder shower, he added, 'The poor child,
Poor Marian! 'twas a luckless day for her,   1085
When first she chanced on my philanthropy.'

He drew a chair beside me, and sat down;
And I, instinctively, as women use
Before a sweet friend's grief, – when, in his ear,
They hum the tune of comfort though themselves   1090
Most ignorant of the special words of such,
And quiet so and fortify his brain
And give it time and strength for feeling out
To reach the availing sense beyond that sound, –
Went murmuring to him what, if written here,   1095
Would seem not much, yet fetched him better help
Than peradventure if it had been more.

I've known the pregnant thinkers of our time
And stood by breathless, hanging on their lips,
When some chromatic sequence of fine thought   1100
In learned modulation phrased itself
To an unconjectured harmony of truth:
And yet I've been more moved, more raised, I say,
By a simple word . . . a broken easy thing at need
A three-years infant might repeat,   1105
A look, a sigh, a touch upon the palm,
Which meant less than 'I love you', than by all

431

The full-voiced rhetoric of those master-mouths.

'Ah, dear Aurora,' he began at last,
His pale lips fumbling for a sort of smile,   1110
'Your printer's devils[154] have not spoilt your heart:
That's well. And who knows but, long years ago,
When you and I talked, you were somewhat right
In being so peevish with me? You, at least,
Have ruined no one through your dreams! Instead,   1115
You've helped the facile youth to live youth's day
With innocent distraction, still perhaps
Suggestive of things better than your rimes.
The little shepherd-maiden, eight years old,
I've seen upon the mountains of Vaucluse,   1120
Asleep i' the sun, her head upon her knees,
The flocks all scattered, – is more laudable
Than any sheep-dog trained imperfectly,
Who bites the kids through too much zeal.'
         'I look
As if I had slept, then?'
       He was touched at once   1125
By something in my face. Indeed 'twas sure
That he and I, – despite a year or two
Of younger life on my side, and on his
The heaping of the years' work on the days,
The three-hour speeches from the member's seat,   1130
The hot committees in and out of doors,
The pamphlets, 'Arguments,' 'Collective Views,'
Tossed out as straw before sick houses, just
To show one's sick and so be trod to dirt
And no more use, – through this world's underground   1135
The burrowing, groping effort, whence the arm
And heart come torn, – 'twas sure that he and I
Were, after all, unequally fatigued;
That he, in his developed manhood, stood
A little sunburnt by the glare of life,   1140
While I . . . it seemed no sun had shone on me,
So many seasons I had missed my Springs,
My cheeks had pined and perished from their orbs.
And all the youth-blood in them had grown white

As dew on autumn cyclamens: alone   1145
My eyes and forehead answered for my face.
He said, 'Aurora, you are changed – are ill!'

'Not so, my cousin, – only not asleep,'
I answered, smiling gently. 'Let it be.
You scarcely found the poet of Vaucluse   1150
As drowsy as the shepherds. What is art
But life upon the larger scale, the higher,
When, graduating up in a spiral line
Of still expanding and ascending gyres,
It pushes toward the intense significance   1155
Of all things, hungry for the Infinite?
Art's life, – and where we live, we suffer and toil.'

He seemed to sift me with his painful eyes.
'You take it gravely, cousin; you refuse
Your dreamland's right of common, and green rest.   1160
You break the mythic turf where danced the nymphs,
With crooked ploughs of actual life, – let in
The axes to the legendary woods,
To pay the poll-tax. You are fallen indeed
On evil days, you poets, if yourselves   1165
Can praise that art of yours no otherwise;
And, if you cannot, . . . better take a trade
And be of use: 'twere cheaper for your youth.'

'Of use!' I softly echoed, 'there's the point
We sweep about for ever in an argument,   1170
Like swallows which the exasperate, dying year
Sets spinning in black circles, round and round,
Preparing for far flights o'er unknown seas.
And we, where tend we?'
                              'Where?' he said, and sighed.
'The whole creation, from the hour we are born,   1175
Perplexes us with questions. Not a stone
But cries behind us, every weary step,
"Where, where?" I leave stones to reply to stones.
Enough for me and for my fleshly heart
To hearken the invocations of my kind,   1180

When men catch hold upon my shuddering nerves
And shriek, "What help? what hope? what bread i' the house,
What fire i' the frost?" There must be some response,
Though mine fail utterly. This social Sphinx
Who sits between the sepulchres and stews,   1185
Makes mock and mow against the crystal heavens,
And bullies God, – exacts a word at least
From each man standing on the side of God,
However paying a sphinx-price for it.
We pay it also if we hold our peace,   1190
In pangs and pity. Let me speak and die.
Alas, you'll say I speak and kill instead.'

I pressed in there. 'The best men, doing their best,
Know peradventure least of what they do:
Men usefullest i' the world are simply used;   1195
The nail that holds the wood, must pierce it first,
And He alone who wields the hammer sees
The work advanced by the earliest blow. Take heart.'

'Ah, if I could have taken yours!' he said,
'But that's past now.' Then rising, – 'I will take   1200
At least your kindness and encouragement.
I thank you. Dear, be happy. Sing your songs,
If that's your way! but sometimes slumber too,
Nor tire too much with following, out of breath,
The rimes upon your mountains of Delight.   1205
Reflect, if Art be in truth the higher life,
You need the lower life to stand upon
In order to reach up into that higher:
And none can stand a-tiptoe in the place
He cannot stand in with two stable feet.   1210
Remember then! – for Art's sake, hold your life.'

We parted so. I held him in respect.
I comprehended what he was in heart
And sacrificial greatness. Aye, but he
Supposed me a thing too small, to deign to know: 1215
He blew me, plainly, from the crucible
As some intruding, interrupting fly

Not worth the pains of his analysis
Absorbed on nobler subjects. Hurt a fly,
He would not for the world: he's pitiful   1220
To flies even. 'Sing,' says he, 'and tease me still,
If that's your way, poor insect.' That's your way!

Fifth Book

Aurora Leigh, be humble. Shall I hope
To speak my poems in mysterious tune
With man and nature? – with the lava-lymph
That trickles from successive galaxies
Still drop by drop adown the finger of God   5
In still new worlds? – with summer-days in this
That scarce dare breathe they are so beautiful?
With spring's delicious trouble in the ground,
Tormented by the quickened blood of roots,
And softly pricked by golden crocus-sheaves   10
In token of the harvest-time of flowers?
With winters and with autumns, – and beyond
With the human heart's large seasons, when it hopes
And fears, joys, grieves, and loves? – with all that strain
Of sexual passion, which devours the flesh   15
In a sacrament of souls? with mother's breasts
Which, round the new-made creatures hanging there,
Throb luminous and harmonious like pure spheres? –
With multitudinous life, and finally
With the great escapings of ecstatic souls,   20
Who, in a rush of too long prisoned flame,
Their radiant faces upward, burn away
This dark of the body, issuing on a world
Beyond our mortal? – can I speak my verse
So plainly in tune to these things and the rest,   25
That men shall feel it catch them on the quick,
As having the same warrant over them
To hold and move them if they will or no,
Alike imperious as the primal rhythm
Of that theurgic nature? – I must fail,   30
Who fail at the beginning to hold and move
One man, – and he my cousin, and he my friend,
And he born tender, made intelligent,
Inclined to ponder the precipitous sides
Of difficult questions; yet, obtuse to *me*,   35
Of *me*, incurious! likes me very well,

And wishes me a paradise of good,
Good looks, good means, and good digestion, – aye,
But otherwise evades me, puts me off
With kindness, with a tolerant gentleness, –   40
Too light a book for a grave man's reading! Go,
Aurora Leigh: be humble.
          There it is,
We women are too apt to look to one,
Which proves a certain impotence in art.
We strain our natures at doing something great,   45
Far less because it's something great to do,
Than haply that we, so, commend ourselves
As being not small, and more appreciable
To some one friend. We must have mediators
Betwixt our highest conscience and the judge;   50
Some sweet saint's blood must quicken in our palms,
Or all the life in heaven seems slow and cold:
Good only being perceived as the end of good,
And God alone pleased, – that's too poor, we think,
And not enough for us by any means.   55
Aye – Romney, I remember, told me once
We miss the abstract when we comprehend. –
We miss it most when we aspire, – and fail.

Yet, so, I will not. – This vile woman's way
Of trailing garments, shall not trip me up: 60
I'll have no traffic with the personal thought
In art's pure temple. Must I work in vain,
Without the approbation of a man?
It cannot be; it shall not. Fame itself,
That approbation of the general race,   65
Presents a poor end (though the arrow speed,
Shot straight with vigorous finger to the white),
And the highest fame was never reached except
By what was aimed above it. Art for art,
And good for God Himself, the essential Good!   70
We'll keep our aims sublime, our eyes erect,
Although our woman-hands should shake and fail;
And if we fail . . . But must we? –
                    Shall I fail?

The Greeks said grandly in their tragic phrase,
'Let no one be called happy till his death.'   75
To which I add, – Let no one till his death
Be called unhappy. Measure not the work
Until the day's out and the labour done,
Then bring your gauges. If the day's work's scant,
Why, call it scant; affect no compromise;   80
And, in that we have nobly striven at least,
Deal with us nobly, women though we be,
And honour us with truth if not with praise.

My ballads prospered; but the ballad's race
Is rapid for a poet who bears weights   85
Of thought and golden image. He can stand
Like Atlas, in the sonnet, – and support
His own heavens pregnant with dynastic stars;
But then he must stand still, nor take a step.

In that descriptive poem called 'The Hills,'   90
The prospects were too far and indistinct.
'Tis true my critics said, 'A fine view, that!'
The public scarcely cared to climb my book
For even the finest and the public's right;
A tree's mere firewood, unless humanised, –   95
Which well the Greeks knew when they stirred its bark
With close-pressed bosoms of subsiding nymphs,
And made the forest-rivers garrulous
With babble of gods. For us, we are called to mark
A still more intimate humanity   100
In this inferior nature, or ourselves
Must fall like dead leaves trodden underfoot
By veritable artists. Earth (shut up
By Adam, like a fakir in a box
Left too long buried) remained stiff and dry,   105
A mere dumb corpse, till Christ the Lord came down,
Unlocked the doors, forced opened the blank eyes,
And used his kingly chrisms to straighten out
The leathery tongue turned back into the throat;
Since when, she lives, remembers, palpitates   110
In every limb, aspires in every breath,

Embraces infinite relations. Now
We want no half-gods, Panomphaean Joves,
Fauns, Naiads, Tritons, Oreads and the rest,
To take possession of a senseless world   115
To unnatural vampire-uses. See the earth,
The body of our body, the green earth,
Indubitably human like this flesh
And these articulated veins through which
Our heart drives blood. There's not a flower of spring   120
That dies ere June, but vaunts itself allied
By issue and symbol, by significance
And correspondence, to that spirit-world
Outside the limits of our space and time,
Whereto we are bound. Let poets give it voice   125
With human meanings, – else they miss the thought,
And henceforth step down lower, stand confessed
Instructed poorly for interpreters,
Thrown out by an easy cowslip in the text.

Even so my pastoral failed: it was a book   130
Of surface-pictures – pretty, cold, and false
With literal transcript, – the worse done, I think,
For being not ill-done: let me set my mark
Against such doings, and do otherwise.
This strikes me. – If the public whom we know   135
Could catch me at such admissions, I should pass
For being right modest. Yet how proud we are,
In daring to look down upon ourselves!

The critics say that epics have died out
With Agamemnon and the goat-nursed gods;   140
I'll not believe it. I could never deem
As Payne Knight[155] did (the mythic mountaineer
Who travelled higher than he was born to live,
And showed sometimes the goitre in his throat
Discoursing of an image seen through fog),   145
That Homer's heroes measured twelve feet high.
They were but men: – his Helen's hair turned grey
Like any plain Miss Smith's who wears a front;
And Hector's[156] infant blubbered at a plume

As yours last Friday at a turkey-cock. 150
All actual heroes are essential men,
And all men possible heroes: every age,
Heroic in proportions, double-faced,
Looks backward and before, expects a morn
And claims an epos.

     Aye, but every age 155
Appears to souls who live in 't (ask Carlyle)
Most unheroic. Ours, for instance, ours:
The thinkers scout it, and the poets abound
Who scorn to touch it with a finger-tip:
A pewter age, – mixed metal, silver-washed; 160
An age of scum, spooned off the richer past,
An age of patches for old gaberdines,
An age of mere transition, meaning nought
Except that what succeeds must shame it quite
If God please. That's wrong thinking, to my mind, 165
And wrong thoughts make poor poems.

       Every age,
Through being beheld too close, is ill-discerned
By those who have not lived past it. We'll suppose
Mount Athos carved, as Alexander schemed,
To some colossal statue of a man. 170
The peasants, gathering brushwood in his ear,
Had guessed as little as the browsing goats
Of form or feature of humanity.
Up there, – in fact, to travel ten miles off
Or ere the giant image broke on them, 175
Full human profile, nose and chin distinct,
Mouth, muttering rhythms of silence up the sky,
And fed at evening with the blood of suns;
Grand torso, – hand, that flung perpetually
The largesse of a silver river down 180
To all the country pastures. 'Tis even thus
With times we live in, – evermore too great
To be apprehended near.

      But poets should
Exert a double vision; should have eyes
To see near things as comprehensively 185
As if afar they took their point of sight,

And distant things, as intimately deep,
As if they touched them. Let us strive for this.
I do distrust the poet who discerns
No character or glory in his times,   190
And trundles back his soul five hundred years,
Past moat and drawbridge, into a castle-court,
To sing – oh, not of lizard or of toad
Alive i' the ditch there, – 'twere excusable,
But of some black chief, half knight, half sheep-lifter,   195
Some beauteous dame, half chattel and half queen,
As dead as must be, for the greater part,
The poems made on their chivalric bones;
And that's no wonder: death inherits death.

Nay, if there's room for poets in this world   200
A little overgrown (I think there is),
Their sole work is to represent the age,
Their age, not Charlemagne's, – this live, throbbing age,
That brawls, cheats, maddens, calculates, aspires,
And spends more passion, more heroic heat,   205
Betwixt the mirrors of its drawing-rooms,
Than Roland with his knights at Roncesvalles.[157]
To flinch from modern varnish, coat or flounce,
Cry out for togas and the picturesque,
Is fatal, – foolish too. King Arthur's self   210
Was commonplace to Lady Guenever;
And Camelot to minstrels seemed as flat
As Fleet Street to our poets.
                                Never flinch,
But still, unscrupulously epic, catch
Upon a burning lava of a song   215
The full-veined, heaving, double-breasted Age:
That, when the next shall come, the men of that
May touch the impress with reverent hand, and say
'Behold, – behold the paps we all have sucked!
This bosom seems to beat still, or at least   220
It sets ours beating: this is living art,
Which thus presents, and thus records true life.'

What form is best for poems? Let me think

Of forms less, and the external. Trust the spirit,
As sovran nature does, to make the form;   225
For otherwise we only imprison spirit
And not embody. Inward evermore
To outward, – so in life, and so in art
Which still is life.
                              Five acts to make a play.
And why not fifteen? why not ten? or seven?   230
What matter for the number of the leaves,
Supposing the tree lives and grows? exact
The literal unities of time and place,
When 'tis the essence of passion to ignore
Both time and place? Absurd. Keep up the fire,   235
And leave the generous flames to shape themselves.

'Tis true the stage requires obsequiousness
To this or that convention; 'exit' here
And 'enter' there; the points for clapping, fixed,
Like Jacob's white-peeled rods before the rams,   240
And all the close-curled imagery clipped
In manner of their fleece at shearing-time.
Forget to prick the galleries to the heart
Precisely at the fourth act, – culminate
Our five pyramidal acts with one act more, –   245
We're lost so: Shakespeare's ghost could scarcely plead
Against our just damnation. Stand aside;
We'll muse for comfort that, last century,
On this same tragic stage on which we have failed,
A wigless Hamlet would have failed the same.   250
And whosoever writes good poetry,
Looks just to art. He does not write for you
Or me, – for London or for Edinburgh;
He will not suffer the best critic known
To step into his sunshine of free thought   255
And self-absorbed conception and exact
An inch-long swerving of the holy lines.
If virtue done for popularity
Defiles like vice, can art, for praise or hire,
Still keep its splendour and remain pure art?   260
Eschew such serfdom. What the poet writes,

He writes: mankind accepts it if it suits,
And that's success: if not, the poem's passed
From hand to hand, and yet from hand to hand,
Until the unborn snatch it, crying out   265
In pity on their fathers' being so dull,
And that's success too.

                      I will write no plays;
Because the drama, less sublime in this,
Makes lower appeals, submits more menially,
Adopts the standard of the public taste   270
To chalk its height on, wears a dog-chain round
Its regal neck, and learns to carry and fetch
The fashions of the day to please the day,
Fawns close on pit and boxes, who clap hands
Commending chiefly its docility   275
And humour in stage-tricks, or else indeed
Gets hissed at, howled at, stamped at like a dog,
Or worse, we'll say. For dogs, unjustly kicked,
Yell, bite at need; but if your dramatist
(Being wronged by some five hundred nobodies   280
Because their grosser brains most naturally
Misjudge the fineness of his subtle wit)
Shows teeth an almond's breadth, protests the length
Of a modest phrase, – 'My gentle countrymen,
There's something in it haply of your fault,' –   285
Why then, besides five hundred nobodies,
He'll have five thousand and five thousand more
Against him, – the whole public, – all the hoofs
Of King Saul's father's asses, in full drove,
And obviously deserve it. He appealed   290
To these, – and why say more if they condemn,
Than if they praise him? – Weep, my Aeschylus,
But low and far, upon Sicilian shores!
For since 'twas Athens (so I read the myth)
Who gave commission to that fatal weight   295
The tortoise, cold and hard, to drop on thee
And crush thee, – better cover thy bald head;
She'll hear the softest hum of Hyblan bee
Before thy loudest protestation!
                         Then

The risk's still worse upon the modern stage: 300
I could not, for so little, accept success,
Nor would I risk so much, in ease and calm,
For manifester gains: let those who prize,
Pursue them: I stand off. And yet, forbid,
That any irreverent fancy or conceit 305
Should litter in the Drama's throne-room where
The rulers of our art, in whose full veins
Dynastic glories mingle, sit in strength
And do their kingly work, – conceive, command,
And, from the imagination's crucial heat, 310
Catch up their men and women all aflame
For action, all alive and forced to prove
Their life by living out heart, brain, and nerve,
Until mankind makes witness, 'These be men
As we are,' and vouchsafes the greeting due 315
To Imogen and Juliet [158] – sweetest kin
On art's side.
       'Tis that, honouring to its worth
The drama, I would fear to keep it down
To the level of the footlights. Dies no more
The sacrificial goat, for Bacchus slain, 320
His filmed eyes fluttered by the whirling white
Of choral vestures, – troubled in his blood,
While tragic voices that clanged keen as swords,
Leapt high together with the altar-flame
And made the blue air wink. The waxen mask, 325
Which set the grand still front of Themis' [159] son
Upon the puckered visage of a player, –
The buskin,[160] which he rose upon and moved,
As some tall ship first conscious of the wind
Sweeps slowly past the piers, – the mouthpiece, where 330
The mere man's voice with all its breaths and breaks
Went sheathed in brass, and clashed on even heights
Its phrasèd thunders, – these things are no more,
Which once were. And concluding, which is clear,
The growing drama has outgrown such toys 335
Of simulated stature, face, and speech,
It also peradventure may outgrow
The simulation of the painted scene,

Boards, actors, prompters, gaslight, and costume,
And take for a worthier stage the soul itself,   340
Its shifting fancies and celestial lights,
With all its grand orchestral silences
To keep the pauses of its rhythmic sounds.

Alas, I still see something to be done,
And what I do, falls short of what I see,   345
Though I waste myself on doing. Long green days,
Worn bare of grass and sunshine, – long calm nights,
From which the silken sleeps were fretted out,
Be witness for me, with no amateur's
Irreverent haste and busy idleness   350
I myself to art! What then? what's done?
What's done, at last?
                          Behold, at last, a book.
If life-blood's necessary, which it is
(By that blue vein athrob on Mahomet's brow,
Each prophet-poet's book must show man's blood!), –   355
If life-blood's fertilising, I wrung mine
On every leaf of this, – unless the drops
Slid heavily on one side and left it dry.
That chances often: many a fervid man
Writes books as cold and flat as graveyard stones   360
From which the lichen's scraped; and if Saint Preux[161]
Had written his own letters, as he might,
We had never wept to think of the little mole
'Neath Julie's drooping eyelid. Passion is
But something suffered, after all.
                              While Art   365
Sets action on the top of suffering:
The artist's part is both to be and do,
Transfixing with a special, central power
The flat experience of the common man,
And turning outward, with a sudden wrench,   370
Half agony, half ecstasy, the thing
He feels the inmost, – never felt the less
Because he sings it. Does a torch less burn
For burning next reflectors of blue steel,
That *he* should be the colder for his place   375

'Twixt two incessant fires, – his personal life's
And that intense refraction which burns back
Perpetually against him from the round
Of crystal conscience he was born into
If artist-born? O sorrowful great gift   380
Conferred on poets, of a twofold life,
When one life has been found enough for pain!
We, staggering 'neath our burden as mere men,
Being called to stand up straight as demi-gods,
Support the intolerable strain and stress   385
Of the universal, and send clearly up
With voices broken by the human sob,
Our poems to find rimes among the stars!
But soft! – a 'poet' is a word soon said,
A book's a thing soon written. Nay, indeed,   390
The more the poet shall be questionable,
The more unquestionably comes his book.
And this of mine, – well, granting to myself
Some passion in it, – furrowing up the flats,
Mere passion will not prove a volume worth   395
Its gall and rags even. Bubbles round a keel
Mean nought, excepting that the vessel moves.
There's more than passion goes to make a man,
Or book, which is a man too.
                        I am sad.
I wonder if Pygmalion[162] had these doubts   400
And, feeling the hard marble first relent,
Grow supple to the straining of his arms,
And tingle through its cold to his burning lip,
Supposed his senses mocked, supposed the toil
Of stretching past the known and seen to reach   405
The archetypal Beauty out of sight,
Had made his heart beat fast enough for two,
And with his own life dazed and blinded him!
Not so; Pygmalion loved, – and whoso loves
Believes the impossible.
                     But I am sad: 410
I cannot thoroughly love a work of mine,
Since none seems worthy of my thought and hope
More highly mated. He has shot them down,

My Phoebus Apollo,[163] soul within my soul,
Who judges, by the attempted, what's attained,   415
And with the silver arrow from his height
Has struck down all my works before my face
While I said nothing. Is there aught to say?
I called the artist but a greatened man.
He may be childless also, like a man.   420

I laboured on alone. The wind and dust
And sun of the world beat blistering in my face;
And hope, now for me, now against me, dragged
My spirits onward, as some fallen balloon,
Which, whether caught by blossoming tree or bare,   425
Is torn alike. I sometimes touched my aim,
Or seemed, – and generous souls cried out, 'Be strong,
Take courage; now you're on our level, – now!
The next step saves you!' I was flushed with praise,
But, pausing just a moment to draw breath,   430
I could not choose but murmur to myself
'Is this all? all that's done? and all that's gained?
If this then be success, 'tis dismaller
Than any failure.'
                O my God, my God,
O supreme Artist, who as sole return   435
For all the cosmic wonder of Thy work,
Demandest of us just a word . . . a name,
'My Father!' Thou hast knowledge, only Thou,
How dreary 'tis for women to sit still
On winter nights by solitary fires   440
And hear the nations praising them far off,
Too far! aye, praising our quick sense of love,
Our very heart of passionate womanhood,
Which could not beat so in the verse without
Being present also in the unkissed lips   445
And eyes undried because there's none to ask
The reason they grew moist.
                To sit alone
And think for comfort how, that very night,
Affianced lovers, leaning face to face
With sweet half-listenings for each other's breath,   450

Are reading haply from a page of ours,
To pause with a thrill (as if their cheeks had touched)
When such a stanza, level to their mood,
Seems floating their own thought out – 'So I feel
For thee,' – 'And I, for thee: this poet knows   455
What everlasting love is!' – how, that night,
Some father, issuing from the misty roads
Upon the luminous round of lamp and hearth
And happy children, having caught up first
The youngest there until it shrink and shriek   460
To feel the cold chin prick its dimples through
With winter from the hills, may throw i' the lap
Of the eldest (who has learnt to drop her lids
To hide some sweetness newer than last year's),
Our book and cry, . . . 'Ah you, you care for rimes;   465
So here be rimes to pore on under trees,
When April comes to let you! I've been told
They are not idle as so many are,
But set hearts beating pure as well as fast.
'Tis yours, the book; I'll write your name in it,   470
That so you may not lose, however lost
In poet's lore and charming reverie,
The thought of how your father thought of *you*
In riding from the town.'
                To have our books
Appraised by love, associated with love,   475
While *we* sit loveless! is it hard, you think?
At least 'tis mournful. Fame, indeed, 'twas said,
Means simply love. It was a man said that:
And then, there's love and love: the love of all
(To risk in turn a woman's paradox),   480
Is but a small thing to the love of one.
You bid a hungry child be satisfied
With a heritage of many cornfields: nay,
He says he's hungry, – he would rather have
That little barley-cake you keep from him   485
While reckoning up his harvests. So with us
(Here, Romney, too, we fail to generalise!);
We're hungry.
            Hungry! but it's pitiful

To wail like unweaned babes and suck our thumbs
Because we're hungry. Who, in all this world,   490
(Wherein we are haply set to pray and fast,
And learn what good is by its opposite),
Has never hungered? Woe to him who has found
The meal enough! if Ugolino's [164] full,
His teeth have crunched some foul unnatural thing: 495
For here satiety proves penury
More utterly irremediable. And since
We needs must hunger, – better, for man's love,
Than God's truth! better, for companions sweet,
Than great convictions! let us bear our weights,   500
Preferring dreary hearths to desert souls.
Well, well! they say we're envious, we who rime;
But I, because I am a woman perhaps
And so rime ill, am ill at envying.
I never envied Graham his breadth of style,   505
Which gives you, with a random smutch or two,
(Near-sighted critics analyse to smutch)
Such delicate perspectives of full life:
Nor Belmore, for the unity of aim
To which he cuts his cedarn poems, fine   510
As sketchers do their pencils: nor Mark Gage,
For that caressing colour and trancing tone
Whereby you're swept away and melted in
The sensual element, which with a back wave
Restores you to the level of pure souls   515
And leaves you with Plotinus. None of these,
For native gifts or popular applause,
I've envied; but for this, – that when by chance
Says some one, – 'There goes Belmore a great man!
He leaves clean work behind him, and requires   520
No sweeper-up of the chips,' . . . a girl I know,
Who answers nothing, save with her brown eyes,
Smiles unaware as if a guardian saint
Smiled in her: – for this, too, – that Gage comes home
And lays his last book's prodigal review   525
Upon his mother's knee, where, years ago,
He laid his childish spelling-book and learned
To chirp and peck the letters from her mouth,

As young birds must. 'Well done,' she murmured then;
She will not say it now more wonderingly: 530
And yet the last 'Well done' will touch him more,
As catching up today and yesterday
In a perfect chord of love: and so, Mark Gage,
I envy you your mother! – and you, Graham,
Because you have a wife who loves you so,   535
She half forgets, at moments, to be proud
Of being Graham's wife, until a friend observes,
'The boy here, has his father's massive brow,
Done small in wax . . . if we push back the curls.'

Who loves me? Dearest father, – mother sweet, –   540
I speak the names out sometimes by myself,
And make the silence shiver. They sound strange,
As Hindostanee to an Ind-born man
Accustomed many years to English speech;
Or lovely poet-words grown obsolete,   545
Which will not leave off singing. Up in heaven
I have my father, – with my mother's face
Beside him in a blotch of heavenly light;
No more for earth's familiar, household use,
No more. The best verse written by this hand,   550
Can never reach them where they sit, to seem
Well-done to *them*. Death quite unfellows us,
Sets dreadful odds betwixt the live and dead,
And makes us part as those at Babel did
Through sudden ignorance of a common tongue.   555
A living Caesar would not dare to play
At bowls with such as my dead father is.

And yet this may be less so than appears,
This change and separation. Sparrows five
For just two farthings, and God cares for each.   560
If God is not too great for little cares,
Is any creature, because gone to God?
I've seen some men, veracious, nowise mad,
Who have thought or dreamed, declared and testified,
They heard the Dead a-ticking like a clock   565
Which strikes the hours of the eternities,

Beside them, with their natural ears, – and known
That human spirits feel the human way
And hate the unreasoning awe which waves them off
From possible communion. It may be.   570

At least, earth separates as well as heaven.
For instance, I have not seen Romney Leigh
Full eighteen months . . . add six, you get two years.
They say he's very busy with good works, –
Has parted Leigh Hall into almshouses.   575
He made one day an almshouse of his heart,
Which ever since is loose upon the latch
For those who pull the string. – I never did.

It always makes me sad to go abroad,
And now I'm sadder that I went tonight   580
Among the lights and talkers at Lord Howe's.
His wife is gracious, with her glossy braids,
And even voice, and gorgeous eyeballs, calm
As her other jewels. If she's somewhat cold,
Who wonders, when her blood has stood so long   585
In the ducal reservoir she calls her line
By no means arrogantly? she's not proud;
Not prouder than the swan is of the lake
He has always swum in; – 'tis her element;
And so she takes it with a natural grace,   590
Ignoring tadpoles. She just knows, perhaps,
There *are* who travel without outriders,
Which isn't her fault. Ah, to watch her face,
When good Lord Howe expounds his theories
Of social justice and equality!   595
'Tis curious, what a tender, tolerant bend
Her neck takes: for she loves him, likes his talk,
'Such clever talk – that dear, odd Algernon!'
She listens on, exactly as if he talked
Some Scandinavian myth of Lemures,   600
Too pretty to dispute, and too absurd.

She's gracious to me as her husband's friend,
And would be gracious, were I not a Leigh,

Being used to smile just so, without her eyes,
On Joseph Strangways, the Leeds mesmerist, 605
And Delia Dobbs, the lecturer from 'the States'
Upon the 'Woman's question.' Then, for him,
I like him; he's my friend. And all the rooms
Were full of crinkling silks that swept about
The fine dust of most subtle courtesies. 610
What then? – why then, we come home to be sad.

How lovely, One I love not looked tonight!
She's very pretty, Lady Waldemar.
Her maid must use both hands to twist that coil
Of tresses, then be careful lest the rich 615
Bronze rounds should slip: – she missed, though, a grey hair,
A single one, – I saw it; otherwise
The woman looked immortal. How they told,
Those alabaster shoulders and bare breasts,
On which the pearls, drowned out of sight in milk, 620
Were lost, excepting for the ruby-clasp!
They split the amaranth velvet-bodice down
To the waist or nearly, with the audacious press
Of full-breathed beauty. If the heart within
Were half as white! – but, if it were, perhaps 625
The breast were closer covered and the sight
Less aspectable, by half, too.
                              I heard
The young man with the German student's look –
A sharp face, like a knife in a cleft stick,
Which shot up straight against the parting line 630
So equally dividing the long hair, –
Say softly to his neighbour, (thirty-five
And mediaeval), 'Look that way, Sir Blaise.
She's Lady Waldemar – to the left, – in red –
Whom Romney Leigh, our ablest man just now, 635
Is soon about to marry.'
                        Then replied
Sir Blaise Delorme, with quiet, priest-like voice,
Too used to syllable damnations round
To make a natural emphasis worth while:
'Is Leigh your ablest man? the same, I think, 640

Once jilted by a recreant pretty maid
Adopted from the people? Now, in change,
He seems to have plucked a flower from the other side
Of the social hedge.'
    'A flower, a flower,' exclaimed
My German student, – his own eyes full-blown   645
Bent on her. He was twenty, certainly.

Sir Blaise resumed with gentle arrogance,
As if he had dropped his alms into a hat,
And gained the right to counsel, – 'My young friend,
I doubt your ablest man's ability   650
To get the least good or help meet for him,
For pagan phalanstery or Christian home,
From such a flowery creature.'
     'Beautiful!'
My student murmured, rapt, – 'Mark how she stirs!
Just waves her head, as if a flower indeed,   655
Touched far off by the vain breath of our talk.'

At which that bilious Grimwald (he who writes
For the Renovator), who had seemed absorbed
Upon the table-book of autographs
(I dare say mentally he crunched the bones   660
Of all those writers, wishing them alive
To feel his tooth in earnest), turned short round
With low carnivorous laugh, – 'A flower, of course!
She neither sews nor spins, – and takes no thought
Of her garments . . . falling off.'
     The student flinched; 665
Sir Blaise, the same; then both, drawing back their chairs
As if they spied black-beetles on the floor,
Pursued their talk, without a word being thrown
To the critic.
   Good Sir Blaise's brow is high
And noticeably narrow: a strong wind,   670
You fancy, might unroof him suddenly,
And blow that great top attic off his head
So piled with feudal relics. You admire
His nose in profile, though you miss his chin;

But, though you miss his chin, you seldom miss   675
His ebon cross worn innermostly (carved
For penance by a saintly Styrian monk
Whose flesh was too much with him), slipping through
Some unaware unbuttoned casualty
Of the under-waistcoat. With an absent air   680
Sir Blaise sat fingering it and speaking low,
While I, upon the sofa, heard it all.

'My dear young friend, if we could bear our eyes,
Like blessedest Saint Lucy,[165] on a plate,
They would not trick us into choosing wives,   685
As doublets, by the colour. Otherwise
Our fathers chose, – and therefore, when they had hung
Their household keys about a lady's waist,
The sense of duty gave her dignity;
She kept her bosom holy to her babes,   690
And, if a moralist reproved her dress,
'Twas, "Too much starch!" – and not, "Too little lawn!"

'Now, pshaw!' returned the other in a heat,
A little fretted by being called 'young friend,'
Or so I took it, – 'for Saint Lucy's sake,   695
If she's the saint to swear by, let us leave
Our fathers, – plagued enough about our sons!'
(He stroked his beardless chin), 'yes, plagued, sir, plagued:
The future generations lie on us
As heavy as the nightmare of a seer;   700
Our meat and drink grow painful prophecy:
I ask you, – have we leisure, if we liked,
To hollow out our weary hands to keep
Your intermittent rushlight of the past
From draughts in lobbies? Prejudice of sex   705
And marriage-law . . . the socket drops them through
While we two speak, – however may protest
Some over-delicate nostrils like your own,
'Gainst odours thence arising.'
                              'You are young,'
Sir Blaise objected.
                    'If I am,' he said   710

With fire, – 'though somewhat less so than I seem,
The young run on before, and see the thing
That's coming. Reverence for the young, I cry.
In that new church for which the world's near ripe,
You'll have the younger in the Elder's chair,   715
Presiding with his ivory front of hope
O'er foreheads clawed by cruel carrion-birds
Of life's experience.'
                     'Pray your blessing, sir,'
Sir Blaise replied good-humouredly, – 'I plucked
A silver hair this morning from my beard,   720
Which left me your inferior. Would I were
Eighteen and worthy to admonish you!
If young men of your order run before
To see such sights as sexual prejudice
And marriage-law dissolved, – in plainer words,   725
A general concubinage expressed
In a universal pruriency, – the thing
Is scarce worth running fast for, and you'd gain
By loitering with your elders.'
                  'Ah,' he said,
'Who, getting to the top of Pisgah-hill,[166]   730
Can talk with one at the bottom of the view,
To make it comprehensible? Why, Leigh
Himself, although our ablest man, I said,
Is scarce advanced to see as far as this,
Which some are: he takes up imperfectly   735
The social question – by one handle – leaves
The rest to trail. A Christian socialist
Is Romney Leigh, you understand.'
                      'Not I.
I disbelieve in Christian-pagans, much
As you in women-fishes. If we mix   740
Two colours, we lose both, and make a third
Distinct from either. Mark you! to mistake
A colour is the sign of a sick brain,
And mine, I thank the saints, is clear and cool;
A neutral tint is here impossible.   745
The church, – and by the church, I mean of course
The catholic, apostolic, mother-church, –

Draws lines as plain and straight as her own wall;
Inside of which, are Christians, obviously,
And outside . . . dogs.'

        'We thank you. Well I know   750
The ancient mother-church would fain still bite,
For all her toothless gums, – as Leigh himself
Would fain be a Christian still, for all his wit.
Pass that; you two may settle it, for me.
You're slow in England. In a month I learnt   755
At Göttingen enough philosophy
To stock your English schools for fifty years;
Pass that, too. Here alone, I stop you short,
– Supposing a true man like Leigh could stand
Unequal in the stature of his life   760
To the height of his opinions. Choose a wife
Because of a smooth skin? – not he, not he!
He'd rail at Venus' self for creaking shoes,
Unless she walked his way of righteousness:
And if he takes a Venus Meretrix [167]   765
(No imputation on the lady there),
Be sure that, by some sleight of Christian art,
He has metamorphosed and converted her
To a Blessed Virgin.'

        'Soft!' Sir Blaise drew breath
As if it hurt him, – 'Soft! no blasphemy,   770
I pray you!'

        'The first Christians did the thing:
Why not the last?' asked he of Göttingen,
With just that shade of sneering on the lip,
Compensates for the lagging of the beard, –
'And so the case is. If that fairest fair   775
Is talked of as the future wife of Leigh,
She's talked of too, at least as certainly,
As Leigh's disciple. You may find her name
On all his missions and commissions, schools,
Asylums, hospitals, – he has had her down,   780
With other ladies whom her starry lead
Persuaded from their spheres, to his country-place
In Shropshire, to the famed phalanstery
At Leigh Hall, christianised from Fourier's own

(In which he has planted out his sapling stocks   785
Of knowledge into social nurseries),
And there, they say, she has tarried half a week,
And milked the cows, and churned, and pressed the curd,
And said "my sister" to the lowest drab
Of all the assembled castaways; such girls!   790
Aye, sided with them at the washing-tub –
Conceive, Sir Blaise, those naked perfect arms,
Round glittering arms, plunged elbow-deep in suds,
Like wild swans hid in lilies all a-shake.'

Lord Howe came up. 'What, talking poetry   795
So near the image of the unfavouring Muse?
That's you, Miss Leigh: I've watched you half an hour,
Precisely as I watched the statue called
A Pallas in the Vatican; – you mind
The face, Sir Blaise? – intensely calm and sad,   800
As wisdom cut it off from fellowship, –
But *that* spoke louder. Not a word from *you*!
And these two gentlemen were bold, I marked,
And unabashed by even your silence.'
                                              'Ah,'
Said I, 'my dear Lord Howe, you shall not speak   805
To a printing woman who has lost her place
(The sweet safe corner of the household fire
Behind the heads of children), compliments,
As if she were a woman. We who have clipt
The curls before our eyes, may see at least   810
As plain as men do. Speak out, man to man;
No compliments, beseech you.'
                                    'Friend to friend,
Let that be. We are sad tonight, I saw
(– Good night, Sir Blaise! ah, Smith – he has slipped away),
I saw you across the room, and stayed, Miss Leigh,   815
To keep a crowd of lion-hunters off,
With faces toward your jungle. There were three;
A spacious lady, five feet ten and fat,
Who has the devil in her (and there's room),
For walking to and fro upon the earth,   820
From Chipewa to China; she requires

Your autograph upon a tinted leaf
'Twixt Queen Pomare's and Emperor Soulouque's.
Pray give it; she has energies, though fat:
For me, I'd rather see a rick on fire   825
Than such a woman angry. Then a youth
Fresh from the backwoods, green as the underboughs,
Asks modestly, Miss Leigh, to kiss your shoe,
And adds, he has an epic in twelve parts,
Which when you've read, you'll do it for his boot: 830
All which I saved you, and absorb next week
Both manuscript and man, – because a lord
Is still more potent that a poetess
With any extreme republican. Ah, ah,
You smile, at last, then.'
                              'Thank you.'
                                        'Leave the smile,   835
I'll lose the thanks for 't, – aye, and throw you in
My transatlantic girl, with golden eyes,
That draw you to her splendid whiteness as
The pistil of a water-lily draws,
Adust with gold. Those girls across the sea   840
Are tyrannously pretty, – and I swore
(She seemed to me an innocent, frank girl)
To bring her to you for a woman's kiss,
Not now, but on some other day or week:
– We'll call it perjury; I give her up.'   845

'No, bring her.'
                  'Now,' said he, 'you make it hard
To touch such goodness with a grimy palm.
I thought to tease you well, and fret you cross,
And steel myself, when rightly vexed with you,
For telling you a thing to tease you more.'   850

'Of Romney?'
              'No, no; nothing worse,' he cried,
'Of Romney Leigh than what is buzzed about, –
That *he* is taken in an eye-trap too,
Like many half as wise. The thing I mean

Refers to you, not him.'
                       'Refers to me,'   855

He echoed, – 'Me! You sound it like a stone
Dropped down a dry well very listlessly
By one who never thinks about the toad
Alive at the bottom. Presently perhaps
You'll sound your "me" more proudly – till I shrink.'   860

'Lord Howe's the toad, then, in this question?'
                               'Brief,
We'll take it graver. Give me sofa-room,
And quiet hearing. You know Eglinton,
John Eglinton, of Eglinton in Kent?'

'Is *he* the toad? – he's rather like the snail,   865
Known chiefly for the house upon his back:
Divide the man and house – you kill the man;
That's Eglinton of Eglinton, Lord Howe.'

He answered grave. 'A reputable man,
An excellent landlord of the olden stamp   870
If somewhat slack in new philanthropies,
Who keeps his birthdays with a tenants' dance,
Is hard upon them when they miss the church
Or hold their children back from catechism,
But not ungentle when the aged poor   875
Pick sticks at hedge-sides: nay, I've heard him say,
"The old dame has a twinge because she stoops:
That's punishment enough for felony." '
'O tender-hearted landlord! may I take
My long lease with him, when the time arrives   880
For gathering winter-faggots!'
                           'He likes art,
Buys books and pictures . . . of a certain kind;
Neglects no patient duty; a good son' . . .

'To a most obedient mother. Born to wear
His father's shoes, he wears her husband's too: 885
Indeed, I've heard it's touching. Dear Lord Howe,

You shall not praise *me* so against your heart,
When I'm at worst for praise and faggots.'
                                        'Be
Less bitter with me, for . . . in short,' he said,
'I have a letter, which he urged me so   890
To bring you . . . I could scarcely choose but yield;
Insisting that a new love, passing through
The hand of an old friendship, caught from it
Some reconciling odour.'
                              'Love, you say?
My lord, I cannot love: I only find   895
The rime for love, – and that's not love, my lord.
Take back your letter.'
                          'Pause: you'll read it first?'

'I will not read it: it is stereotyped;
The same he wrote to, – anybody's name,
Anne Blythe, the actress, when she died so true,   900
A duchess fainted in a private box:
Pauline the dancer, after the great *pas*
In which her little feet winked overhead
Like other fire-flies, and amazed the pit:
Or Baldinacci, when her F in alt   905
Had touched the silver tops of heaven itself
With such a pungent spirit-dart, the Queen
Laid softly, each to each, her white-gloved palms,
And sighed for joy: or else (I thank your friend)
Aurora Leigh, – when some indifferent rimes,   910
Like those the boys sang round the holy ox
On Memphis-highway, chance perhaps to set
Our Apis-public lowing. Oh, he wants,
Instead of any worthy wife at home,
A star upon his stage of Eglinton?   915
Advise him that he is not overshrewd
In being so little modest: a dropped star
Makes bitter waters, says a Book I've read, –
And there's his unread letter,'
                                  'My dear friend,'
Lord Howe began . . .

                              *

In haste I tore the phrase.　　920
'You mean your friend of Eglinton, or me?'

'I mean you, you,' he answered with some fire.
'A happy life means prudent compromise;
The tare runs through the farmer's garnered sheaves,
And though the gleaner's apron holds pure wheat　　925
We count her poorer. Tare with wheat, we cry,
And good with drawbacks. You, you love your art,
And, certain of vocation, set your soul
On utterance. Only, in this world we have made
(They say God made it first, but if He did　　930
'Twas so long since, and, since, we have spoiled it so,
He scarce would know it, if He looked this way,
From hells we preach of, with the flames blown out)'
– In this bad, twisted, topsy-turvy world
Where all the heaviest wrongs get uppermost, –　　935
In this uneven, unfostering England here,
Where ledger-strokes and sword-strokes count indeed,
But soul-strokes merely tell upon the flesh
They strike from, – it is hard to stand for art,
Unless some golden tripod from the sea　　940
Be fished up, by Apollo's divine chance,
To throne such feet as yours, my prophetess,
At Delphi.[168] Think, – the god comes down as fierce
As twenty bloodhounds, shakes you, strangles you,
Until the oracular shriek shall ooze in froth!　　945
At best 'tis not all ease, – at worst too hard:
A place to stand on is a 'vantage gained,
And here's your tripod. To be plain, dear friend,
You're poor, except in what you richly give;
You labour for your own bread painfully,　　950
Or ere you pour our wine. For art's sake, pause.'

I answered slow, – as some wayfaring man,
Who feels himself at night too far from home
Makes steadfast face against the bitter wind.
'Is art so less a thing than virtue is,　　955
That artists first must cater for their ease
Or ever they make issue past themselves

461

To generous use? alas, and is it so,
That we who would be somewhat clean, must sweep
Our ways as well as walk them, and no friend   960
Confirm us nobly, – "Leave results to God,
But you, be clean?" What! "prudent compromise
Makes acceptable life," you say instead,
You, you, Lord Howe? – in things indifferent, well.
For instance, compromise the wheaten bread   965
For rye, the meat for lentils, silk for serge,
And sleep on down, if needs, for sleep on straw;
But there, end compromise. I will not bate
One artist-dream, on straw or down, my lord,
Nor pinch my liberal soul, though I be poor,   970
Nor cease to love high, though I live thus low.'

So speaking, with less anger in my voice
Than sorrow, I rose quickly to depart;
While he, thrown back upon the noble shame
Of such high-stumbling natures, murmured words,   975
The right words after wrong ones. Ah, the man
Is worthy, but so given to entertain
Impossible plans of superhuman life, –
He sets his virtues on so raised a shelf,
To keep them at the grand millennial height,   980
He has to mount a stool to get at them;
And, meantime, lives on quite the common way,
With everybody's morals.
                              As we passed,
Lord Howe insisting that his friendly arm
Should oar me across the sparkling brawling stream   985
Which swept from room to room, – we fell at once
On Lady Waldemar. 'Miss Leigh,' she said,
And gave me such a smile, so cold and bright,
As if she tried it in a 'tiring glass
And liked it; 'all tonight I've strained at you   990
As babes at baubles held up out of reach
By spiteful nurses, ("Never snatch," they say),
And there you sat, most perfectly shut in
By good Sir Blaise and clever Mister Smith
And then our dear Lord Howe! at last indeed   995

I almost snatched. I have a world to speak
About your cousin's place in Shropshire, where
I've been to see his work . . . our work, – you heard
I went? . . . and of a letter yesterday,
In which if I should read a page or two   1000
You might feel interest, though you're locked of course
In literary toil. – You'll like to hear
Your last book lies at the phalanstery,
As judged innocuous for the elder girls
And younger women who still care for books.   1005
We all must read, you see, before we live,
Till slowly the ineffable light comes up
And, as it deepens, drowns the written word, –
So said your cousin, while we stood and felt
A sunset from his favorite beech-tree seat.   1010
He might have been a poet if he would,
But then he saw the higher thing at once
And climbed to it. I think he looks well now,
Has quite got over that unfortunate . . .
Ah, ah . . . I know it moved you. Tender-heart!   1015
You took a liking to the wretched girl.
Perhaps you thought the marriage suitable,
Who knows? a poet hankers for romance,
And so on. As for Romney Leigh, 'tis sure
He never loved her, – never. By the way,   1020
You have not heard of *her* . . .? quite out of sight,
And out of saving? lost in every sense?'

She might have gone on talking half an hour
And I stood still, and cold, and pale, I think,
As a garden-statue a child pelts with snow   1025
For pretty pastime. Every now and then
I put in 'yes' or 'no,' I scarce knew why;
The blind man walks wherever the dog pulls,
And so I answered. Till Lord Howe broke in;
'What penance takes the wretch who interrupts   1030
The talk of charming women? I, at last,
Must brave it. Pardon, Lady Waldemar!
The lady on my arm is tired, unwell,
And loyally I've promised she may say

Nor harder word this evening, than . . . good-night;   1035
The rest her face speaks for her.' – Then we went.

And I breathe large at home. I drop my cloak,
Unclasp my girdle, loose the band that ties
My hair . . . now could I but unloose my soul!
We are sepulchred alive in this close world,   1040
And want more room.
                              The charming woman there –
This reckoning up and writing down her talk
Affects me singularly. How she talked
To pain me! woman's spite. – You wear steel-mail;
A woman takes a housewife from her breast   1045
And plucks the delicatest needle out
As 'twere a rose, and pricks you carefully
'Neath nails, 'neath eyelids, in your nostrils, – say,
A beast would roar so tortured, – but a man,
A human creature, must not, shall not flinch,   1050
No, not for shame.
                              What vexes, after all,
Is just that such as she, with such as I,
Knows how to vex. Sweet heaven, she takes me up
As if she had fingered me and dog-eared me
And spelled me by the fireside half a life!   1055
She knows my turns, my feeble points. – What then?
The knowledge of a thing implies the thing;
Of course, she found *that* in me, she saw *that*,
Her pencil underscored *this* for a fault,
And I, still ignorant. Shut the book up, close!   1060
And crush that beetle in the leaves.
                                       O heart,
At last we shall grow hard too, like the rest,
And call it self-defence because we are soft.

And after all, now, . . . why should I be pained
That Romney Leigh, my cousin, should espouse   1065
This Lady Waldemar? And, say, she held
Her newly-blossomed gladness in my face, . . .
'Twas natural surely, if not generous,
Considering how, when winter held her fast,

464

I helped the frost with mine, and pained her more 1070
Than she pains me. Pains me! – but wherefore pained?
'Tis clear my cousin Romney wants a wife, –
So, good! – The man's need of the woman, here,
Is greater than the woman's of the man,
And easier served; for where the man discerns 1075
A sex (ah, ah, the man can generalise,
Said he), we see but one, ideally
And really: where we yearn to lose ourselves
And melt like white pearls in another's wine,
He seeks to double himself by what he loves, 1080
And make his drink more costly by our pearls.
At board, at bed, at work and holiday,
It is not good for man to be alone,
And that's his way of thinking, first and last,
And thus my cousin Romney wants a wife. 1085

But then my cousin sets his dignity
On personal virtue. If he understands
By love, like others, self-aggrandisement,
It is that he may verily be great
By doing rightly and kindly. Once he thought, 1090
For charitable ends set duly forth
In Heaven's white judgment-book, to marry . . . ah,
We'll call her name Aurora Leigh, although
She's changed since then! – and once, for social ends,
Poor Marian Erle, my sister Marian Erle, 1095
My woodland sister, sweet maid Marian,
Whose memory moans on in me like the wind
Through ill-shut casements, making me more sad
Than ever I find reasons for. Alas,
Poor pretty plaintive face, embodied ghost! 1100
He finds it easy then, to clap thee off
From pulling at his sleeve and book and pen, –
He locks thee out at night into the cold,
Away from butting with thy horny eyes
Against his crystal dreams, that now he's strong 1105
To love anew? that Lady Waldemar
Succeeds my Marian?
                    After all, why not?

He loved not Marian, more than once he loved
Aurora. If he loves at last that Third,
Albeit she prove as slippery as spilt oil   1110
On marble floors, I will not augur him
Ill-luck for that. Good love, howe'er ill-placed,
Is better for a man's soul in the end,
Than if he loved ill what deserves love well.
A pagan, kissing for a step of Pan   1115
The wild-goat's hoof-print on the loamy down,
Exceeds our modern thinker who turns back
The strata . . . granite, limestone, coal, and clay,
Concluding coldly with, 'Here's law! where's God?'

And then at worse, – if Romney loves her not, –   1120
At worst, – if he's incapable of love,
Which may be – then indeed, for such a man
Incapable of love, she's good enough;
For she, at worst too, is a woman still
And loves him . . . as the sort of woman can.   1125

My loose long hair began to burn and creep,
Alive to the very ends, about my knees:
I swept it backward as the wind sweeps flame,
With the passion of my hands. Ah, Romney laughed
One day . . . (how full the memories come up!)   1130
' – Your Florence fire-flies live on in your hair,'
He said, 'it gleams so.' Well, I wrung them out,
My fire-flies; made a knot as hard as life
Of those loose, soft, impracticable curls,
And then sat down and thought . . . 'She shall not think   1135
Her thought of me,' – and drew my desk and wrote.

'Dear Lady Waldemar, I could not speak
With people round me, nor can sleep tonight
And not speak, after the great news I heard
Of you and of my cousin. May you be   1140
Most happy; and the good he meant the world,
Replenish his own life. Say what I say,
And let my word be sweeter for your mouth,
As you are *you* . . . I only Aurora Leigh.'

*

That's quiet, guarded: though she hold it up 1145
Against the light, she'll not see through it more
Than lies there to be seen. So much for pride;
And now for peace, a little. Let me stop
All writing back . . . 'Sweet thanks, my sweetest friend,
'You've made more joyful my great joy itself.' 1150
– No, that's too simple! she would twist it thus,
'My joy would still be as sweet as thyme in drawers,
However shut up in the dark and dry;
But violets, aired and dewed by love like yours,
Out-smell all thyme: we keep that in our clothes, 1155
But drop the other down our bosoms till
They smell like' . . . ah, I see her writing back
Just so. She'll make a nosegay of her words,
And tie it with blue ribbons at the end
To suit a poet; – pshaw!

             And then we'll have 1160
The call to church, the broken, sad, bad dream
Dreamed out at last, the marriage-vow complete
With the marriage breakfast; praying in white gloves,
Drawn off in haste for drinking pagan toasts
In somewhat stronger wine than any sipped 1165
By gods since Bacchus had his way with grapes.

A postscript stops all that and rescues me.
'You need not write. I have been overworked,
And think of leaving London, England even,
And hastening to get nearer to the sun 1170
Where men sleep better. So, adieu.' – I fold
And seal, – and now I'm out of all the coil;
I breathe now, I spring upward like a branch
A ten-years schoolboy with a crooked stick
May pull down to his level in search of nuts, 1175
But cannot hold a moment. How we twang
Back on the blue sky, and assert our height,
While he stares after! Now, the wonder seems
That I could wrong myself by such a doubt.
We poets always have uneasy hearts, 1180
Because our hearts, large-rounded as the globe,
Can turn but one side to the sun at once.

We are used to dip our artist-hands in gall
And potash, trying potentialities
Of alternated colour, till at last   1185
We get confused, and wonder for our skin
How nature tinged it first. Well – here's the true
Good flesh-colour; I recognise my hand, –
Which Romney Leigh may clasp as just a friend's,
And keep his clean.

          And now, my Italy.   1190
Alas, if we could ride with naked souls
And make no noise and pay no price at all,
I would have seen thee sooner, Italy,
For still I have heard thee crying through my life,
Thou piercing silence of ecstatic graves,   1195
Men call that name!

          But even a witch today
Must melt down golden pieces in the nard
Wherewith to anoint her broomstick ere she rides;
And poets evermore are scant of gold,
And if they find a piece behind the door   1200
It turns by sunset to a withered leaf.
The Devil himself scarce trusts his patented
Gold-making art to any who make rimes,
But culls his Faustus from philosophers
And not from poets. 'Leave my Job,' said God;   1205
And so the Devil leaves him without pence,
And poverty proves plainly special grace.
In these new, just, administrative times
Men clamour for an order of merit: why?
Here's black bread on the table and no wine!   1210

At least I am a poet in being poor,
Thank God. I wonder if the manuscript
Of my long poem, if 'twere sold outright,
Would fetch enough to buy me shoes to go
Afoot (thrown in, the necessary patch   1215
For the other side the Alps)? It cannot be.
I fear that I must sell this residue
Of my father's books, although the Elsevirs[169]
Have fly-leaves over-written by his hand

In faded notes as thick and fine and brown   1220
As cobwebs on a tawny monument
Of the old Greeks – *conferenda haec cum his*[170] –
Corruptè citat[171] – *lege potius*,[172]
And so on, in the scholar's regal way
Of giving judgment on the parts of speech,   1225
As if he sat on all twelve thrones up-piled,
Arraigning Israel. Aye, but books and notes
Must go together. And this Proclus[173] too,
In these dear quaint contracted Grecian types,
Fantastically crumpled like his thoughts   1230
Which would not seem too plain; you go round twice
For one step forward, then you take it back
Because you're somewhat giddy; there's the rule
For Proclus. Ah, I stained this middle leaf
With pressing in 't my Florence iris-bell,   1235
Long stalk and all: my father chided me
For that stain of blue blood, – I recollect
The peevish turn his voice took, – 'Silly girls,
Who plant their flowers in our philosophy
To make it fine, and only spoil the book!   1240
No more of it, Aurora.' Yes – no more!
Ah, blame of love, that's sweeter than all praise
Of those who love not! 'tis so lost to me,
I cannot, in such beggared life, afford
To lose my Proclus, – not for Florence, even.   1245

The kissing Judas, Wolff,[174] shall go instead,
Who builds us such a royal book as this
To honour a chief-poet, folio-built,
And writes above, 'The house of Nobody!'
Who floats in cream, as rich as any sucked   1250
From Juno's breasts,[175] the broad Homeric lines,
And, while with their spondaic prodigious mouths
They lap the lucent margins as babe-gods,
Proclaims them bastards. Wolff's an atheist;
And if the Iliad fell out, as he says,   1255
By mere fortuitous concourse of old songs,
Conclude as much too for the universe.

*

469

That Wolff, those Platos: sweep the upper shelves
As clean as this, and so I am almost rich,
Which means, not forced to think of being poor   1260
In sight of ends. Tomorrow: no delay.
I'll wait in Paris till good Carrington
Dispose of such and, having chaffered for
My book's price with the publisher, direct
All proceeds to me. Just a line to ask   1265
His help.
       And now I come, my Italy,
My own hills! are you 'ware of me, my hills,
How I burn toward you? do you feel tonight
The urgency and yearning of my soul,
As sleeping mothers feel the sucking babe   1270
And smile? – Nay, not so much as when in heat
Vain lightnings catch at your inviolate tops
And tremble while ye are steadfast. Still ye go
Your own determined, calm, indifferent way
Toward sunrise, shade by shade, and light by light,   1275
Of all the grand progression nought left out,
As if God verily made you for yourselves
And would not interrupt your life with ours.

Sixth Book

The English have a scornful insular way
Of calling the French light. The levity
Is in the judgement only, which yet stands,
For say a foolish thing but oft enough
(And here's the secret of a hundred creeds,   5
Men get opinions as boys learn to spell,
By reiteration chiefly), the same thing
Shall pass at least for absolutely wise,
And not with fools exclusively. And so
We say the French are light, as if we said   10
The cat mews or the milch-cow gives us milk:
Say rather, cats are milked and milch-cows mew;
For what is lightness but inconsequence,
Vague fluctuation 'twixt effect and cause
Compelled by neither? Is a bullet light,   15
That dashes from the gun-mouth, while the eye
Winks and the heart beats one, to flatten itself
To a wafer on the white speck on a wall
A hundred paces off? Even so direct,
So sternly undivertible of aim,   20
Is this French people.
                    All, idealists
Too absolute and earnest, with them all
The idea of a knife cuts real flesh;
And still, devouring the safe interval
Which Nature placed between the thought and act   25
With those too fiery and impatient souls,
They threaten conflagration to the world,
And rush with most unscrupulous logic on
Impossible practice. Set your orators
To blow upon them with loud windy mouths   30
Through watchword phrases, jest or sentiment,
Which drive our burly brutal English mobs
Like so much chaff, whichever way they blow, –
This light French people will not thus be driven.
They turn indeed, – but then they turn upon   35

Some central pivot of their thought and choice,
And veer out by the force of holding fast.
That's hard to understand, for Englishmen
Unused to abstract questions, and untrained
To trace the involutions, valve by valve,   40
In each orbed bulb-root of a general truth,
And mark what subtly fine integument
Divides opposed compartments. Freedom's self
Comes concrete to us, to be understood,
Fixed in a feudal form incarnately   45
To suit our ways of thought and reverence,
The special form, with us, being still the thing.
With us, I say, though I'm of Italy
My mother's birth and grave, by father's grave
And memory; let it be; – a poet's heart   50
Can swell to a pair of nationalities,
However ill-lodged in a woman's breast.

And so I am strong to love this noble France,
This poet of the nations, who dreams on
And wails on (while the household goes to wreck)   55
For ever, after some ideal good, –
Some equal poise of sex, some unvowed love
Inviolate, some spontaneous brotherhood,
Some wealth that leaves none poor and finds none tired,
Some freedom of the many hat respects   60
The wisdom of the few. Heroic dreams!
Sublime, to dream so; natural, to wake:
And sad, to use such lofty scaffoldings,
Erected for the building of a church,
To build instead a brothel or a prison –   65
May God save France!
                    And if at last she sighs
Her great soul up into a great man's face,
To flush his temples out so gloriously
That few dare carp at Caesar for being bald,
What then? – this Caesar represents, not reigns,   70
And is no despot, though twice absolute:
This Head has all the people for a heart;
This purple's lined with the democracy, –

Now let him see to it! for a rent within
Must leave irreparable rags without.   75

A serious riddle: find such anywhere
Except in France; and when 'tis found in France,
Be sure to read it rightly. So, I mused
Up and down, up and down, the terraced streets,
The glittering boulevards, the white colonnades   80
Of fair fantastic Paris who wears trees
Like plumes, as if a man made them, spire and tower
As if they had grown by nature, tossing up
Her fountains in the sunshine of the squares,
As if in beauty's game she tossed the dice,   85
Or blew the silver down-balls of her dreams
To sow futurity with seeds of thought
And count the passage of her festive hours.

The city swims in verdure, beautiful
As Venice on the waters, the sea-swan.   90
What bosky gardens dropped in close-walled courts
Like plums in ladies' laps who start and laugh:
What miles of streets that run on after trees,
Still carrying the necessary shops,
Those open caskets with the jewels seen!   95
And trade is art, and art's philosophy,
In Paris. There's a silk for instance, there,
As worth an artist's study for the folds,
As that bronze opposite! nay, the bronze has faults,
Art's here too artful, – conscious as a maid   100
Who leans to mark her shadow on the wall
Until she lose a 'vantage in her step.
Yet Art walks forward, and knows where to walk;
The artists also are idealists,
Too absolute for nature, logical   105
To austerity in the application of
The special theory – not a soul content
To paint a crooked pollard and an ass,
As the English will because they find it so
And like it somehow. – There the old Tuileries[176]   110
Is pulling its high cap down on its eyes,
Confounded, conscience-stricken, and amazed

By the apparition of a new fair face
In those devouring mirrors. Through the grate
Within the gardens, what a heap of babes,   115
Swept up like leaves beneath the chestnut-trees
From every street and alley of the town,
By ghosts perhaps that blow too bleak this way
A-looking for their heads! dear pretty babes,
I wish them luck to have their ball-play out   120
Before the next change. Here the air is thronged
With statues poised upon their columns fine
As if to stand a moment were a feat,
Against that blue! What squares, – what breathing-room
For a nation that runs fast, – aye, runs against   125
The dentist's teeth at the corner in pale rows,
Which grin at progress in an epigram.

I walked the day out, listening to the chink
Of the first Napoleon's dry bones in his second grave
By victories guarded 'neath the golden dome   130
That caps all Paris like a bubble. 'Shall
These dry bones live,' thought Louis Philippe[177] once,
And lived to know. Herein is argument
For kings and politicians, but still more
For poets, who bear buckets to the well   135
Of ampler draught.
     These crowds are very good
For meditation (when we are very strong),
Though love of beauty makes us timorous,
And draws us backward from the coarse town-sights
To count the daisies upon dappled fields   140
And hear the streams bleat on among the hills
In innocent and indolent repose,
While still with silken elegiac thoughts
We wind out from us the distracting world
And die into the chrysalis of a man,   145
And leave the best that may, to come of us,
In some brown moth. I would be bold and bear
To look into the swarthiest face of things,
For God's sake who has made them.

Six days' work;

The last day shutting 'twixt its dawn and eve 150
The whole work bettered of the previous five!
Since God collected and resumed in man
The firmaments, the strata, and the lights,
Fish, fowl, and beast, and insect, – all their trains
Of various life caught back upon His arm, 155
Reorganised, and constituted MAN,
The microcosm, the adding up of works, –
Within whose fluttering nostrils, then at last
Consummating Himself the Maker sighed,
As some strong winner at the foot-race sighs 160
Touching the goal.
Humanity is great;

And, if I would not rather pore upon
An ounce of common, ugly, human dust,
An artisan's palm, or a peasant's brow,
Unsmooth, ignoble, save to me and God, 165
Than track old Nilus to his silver roots,
And wait on all the changes of the moon
Among the mountain-peaks of Thessaly
(Until her magic crystal round itself
For many a witch to see in) – set it down 170
As weakness, – strength by no means. How is this
That men of science, osteologists
And surgeons, beat some poets in respect
For nature, – count nought common or unclean,
Spend raptures upon perfect specimens 175
Of indurated veins, distorted joints,
Or beautiful new cases of curved spine,
While we, we are shocked at nature's falling off,
We dare to shrink back from her warts and blains,
We will not, when she sneezes, look at her, 180
Not even to say 'God bless her'? That's our wrong;
For that, she will not trust us often with
Her larger sense of beauty and desire,
But tethers us to a lily or a rose
And bids us diet on the dew inside, 185
Left ignorant that the hungry beggar-boy
(Who stares unseen against our absent eyes,

475

And wonders at the gods that we must be,
To pass so careless for the oranges!)
Bears yet a breastful of a fellow-world   190
To this world, undisparaged, undespoiled,
And (while we scorn him for a flower or two,
As being, Heaven help us, less poetical)
Contains himself both flowers and firmaments
And surging seas and aspectable stars,   195
And all that we would push him out of sight
In order to see nearer. Let us pray
God's grace to keep God's image in repute,
That so, the poet and philanthropist
(Even I and Romney) may stand side by side,   200
Because we both stand face to face with men,
Contemplating the people in the rough,
Yet each so follow a vocation, his
And mine.
                    I walked on, musing with myself
On life and art, and whether after all,   205
A larger metaphysics might not help
Our physics, a completer poetry
Adjust our daily life and vulgar wants
More fully than the special outside plans,
Phalansteries, material institutes,   210
The civil conscriptions and lay monasteries
Preferred by modern thinkers, as they thought
The bread of man indeed made all his life,
And washing seven times in the 'People's Baths'
Were sovereign for a people's leprosy,   215
Still leaving out the essential prophet's word
That comes in power. On which, we thunder down,
We prophets, poets, – Virtue's in the *word*!
The maker burnt the darkness up with His,
To inaugurate the use of vocal life;   220
And, plant a poet's word even, deep enough
In any man's breast, looking presently
For offshoots, you have done more for the man
Than if you dressed him in a broadcloth coat
And warmed his Sunday potage at your fire.   225
Yet Romney leaves me . . .

                    God! what face is that?
O Romney, O Marian!
                    Walking on the quays
And pulling thoughts to pieces leisurely,
As if I caught at grasses in a field
And bit them slow between my absent lips   230
And shred them with my hands . . .
                              What face is that?
What a face, what a look, what a likeness! Full on mine
The sudden blow of it came down, till all
My blood swam, my eyes dazzled. Then I sprang . . .

It was as if a meditative man   235
Were dreaming out a summer afternoon
And watching gnats a-prick upon a pond,
When something floats up suddenly, out there,
Turns over . . . a dead face, known once alive . . .
So old, so new! It would be dreadful now.   240
To lose the sight and keep the doubt of this:
He plunges – ha! he has lost it in the splash.

I plunged – I tore the crowd up, either side,
And rushed on, forward, forward, after her.
Her? whom?
                    A woman sauntered slow in front,   245
Munching an apple, – she left off amazed
As if I had snatched it: that's not she, at least.
A man walked arm linked with a lady veiled,
Both heads dropped closer than the need of talk:
They started; he forgot her with his face,   250
And she, herself, and clung to him as if
My look were fatal. Such a stream of folk,
And all with cares and business of their own!
I ran the whole quay down against their eyes;
No Marian; nowhere Marian. Almost, now,   255
I could call Marian, Marian, with the shriek
Of desperate creatures calling for the Dead.
Where is she, was she? was she anywhere?
I stood still, breathless, gazing, straining out
In every uncertain distance, till at last   260

A gentleman abstracted as myself
Came full against me, then resolved the clash
In voluble excuses, – obviously
Some learned member of the Institute
Upon his way there, walking, for his health,   265
While meditating on the last 'Discourse';
Pinching the empty air 'twixt finger and thumb,
From which the snuff being ousted by that shock
Defiled his snow-white waistcoat duly pricked
At the button-hole with honourable red;   270
'Madame, your pardon,' – there he swerved from me
A metre, as confounded as he had heard
That Dumas[178] would be chosen to fill up
The next chair vacant, by his 'men *in us*,'
Since when was genius found respectable?   275
It passes in its place, indeed, – which means
The seventh floor back, or else the hospital:
Revolving pistols are ingenious things,
But prudent men (Academicians[179] are)
Scare keep them in the cupboard, next the prunes.   280

And so, abandoned to a bitter mirth,
I loitered to my inn. O world, O world,
O jurists, rimers, dreamers, what you please,
We play a weary game of hide-and-seek!
We shape a figure of our fantasy,   285
Call nothing something, and run after it
And lose it, lose ourselves too in the search,
Till clash against us comes a somebody
Who also has lost something and is lost,
Philosopher against philanthropist,   290
Academician against poet, man
Against woman, against the living the dead, –
Then home, with a bad headache and worse jest!

To change the water for my heliotropes
And yellow roses. Paris has such flowers,   295
But England, also. 'Twas a yellow rose,
By that south window of the little house,
My cousin Romney gathered with his hand
On all my birthdays for me, save the last;

And then I shook the tree too rough, too rough,   300
For roses to stay after.

               Now, my maps.
I must not linger here from Italy
Till the last nightingale is tired of song,
And the last fire-fly dies off in the maize.
My soul's in haste to leap into the sun   305
And scorch and seethe itself to a finer mood,
Which here, in this chill north, is apt to stand
Too stiffly in former moulds.

                  That face persists.
It floats up, it turns over in my mind,
As like to Marian, as one dead is like   310
That same alive. In very deed a face
And not a fancy, though it vanished so;
The small fair face between the darks of hair,
I used to liken, when I saw her first,
To a point of moonlit water down a well: 315
The low brow, the frank space between the eyes,
Which always had the brown pathetic look
Of a dumb creature who had been beaten once
And never since was easy with the world.
Ah, ah, – now I remember perfectly   320
Those eyes, today, – how overlarge they seemed,
As if some patient passionate despair
(Like a coal dropt and forgot on tapestry,
Which slowly burns a widening circle out)
Had burnt them larger, larger. And those eyes,   325
Today, I do remember, saw me too,
As I saw them, with conscious lids astrain
In recognition. Now a fantasy,
A simple shade or image of the brain,
Is merely passive, does not retro-act,   330
Is seen, but sees not.

             'Twas a real face,
Perhaps a real Marian.

             Which being so,
I ought to write to Romney, 'Marian's here;
Be comforted for Marian.'

              My pen fell,

My hands struck sharp together, as hands do   335
Which hold at nothing. Can I write to *him*
A half-truth? can I keep my own soul blind
To the other half, . . . the worse? What are our souls,
If still, to run on straight a sober pace
Nor start at every pebble or dead leaf,   340
They must wear blinkers, ignore facts, suppress
Six tenths of the road? Confront the truth, my soul!
And oh, as truly as that was Marian's face,
The arms of that same Marian clasped a thing
. . . Not hid so well beneath the scanty shawl,   345
I cannot name it now for what it was.

A child. Small business has a castaway
Like Marian with that crown of prosperous wives
At which the gentlest she grows arrogant
And says, 'my child.' Who finds an emerald ring   350
On a beggar's middle finger and requires
More testimony to convict a thief?
A child's too costly for so mere a wretch;
She filched it somewhere, and it means, with her,
Instead of honour, blessing, merely shame.   355

I cannot write to Romney, 'Here she is,
Here's Marian found! I'll set you on her track:
I saw her here, in Paris, . . . and her child.
She put away your love two years ago,
But, plainly, not to starve. You suffered then;   360
And, now that you've forgot her utterly
As any lost year's annual, in whose place
You've planted a thick flowering evergreen,
I choose, being kind, to write and tell you this
To make you wholly easy – she's not dead,   365
But only . . . damned.'
                          Stop there: I go too fast;
I'm cruel like the rest, – in haste to take
The first stir in the arras for a rat,
And set my barking, biting thoughts upon 't.
– A child! what then? Suppose a neighbour's sick   370
And asked her, 'Marian, carry out my child

In this Spring air,' – I punish her for that?
Or say, the child should hold her round the neck
For good child-reasons, that he liked it so
And would not leave her – she had winning ways –   375
I brand her therefore that she took the child?
Not so.
            I will not write to Romney Leigh.
For now he's happy, – and she may indeed
Be guilty, – and the knowledge of her fault
Would draggle his smooth time. But I, whose days   380
Are not so fine they cannot bear the rain,
And who moreover having seen her face
Must see it again, . . . *will* see it, by my hopes
Of one day seeing heaven too. The police
Shall track her, hound her, ferret their own soil;   385
We'll dig this Paris to its catacombs
But certainly we'll find her, have her out,
And save her, if she will or will not – child
Or no child, – if a child, then one to save!

The long weeks passed on without consequence.   390
As easy find a footstep on the sand
The morning after spring-tide, as the trace
Of Marian's feet between the incessant surfs
Of this live flood. She may have moved this way, –
But so the star-fish does, and crosses out   395
The dent of her small shoe. The foiled police
Renounced me. 'Could they find a girl and child,
No other signalment but girl and child?
No data shown, but noticeable eyes
And hair in masses, low upon the brow,   400
As if it were an iron crown and pressed?
Friends heighten, and suppose they specify:
Why, girls with hair and eyes are everywhere
In Paris; they had turned me up in vain
No Marian Erle indeed, but certainly   405
Mathildes, Justines, Victoires, . . . or, if I sought
The English, Betsis, Saras, by the score.
They might as well go out into the fields
To find a speckled bean, that's somehow specked,

And somewhere in the pod.' – They left me so.   410
Shall I leave Marian? have I dreamed a dream?

– I thank God I have found her! I must say
'Thank God,' for finding her, although 'tis true
I find the world more sad and wicked for 't.
But she –

    I'll write about her, presently.   410
My hand's a-tremble, as I had just caught up
My heart to write with, in the place of it.
At least you'd take these letters to be writ
At sea, in storm! – wait now . . .

       A simple chance
Did all. I could not sleep last night, and, tired   420
Of turning on my pillow and harder thoughts,
Went out at early morning, when the air
Is delicate with some last starry touch,
To wander through the Market-place of Flowers
(The prettiest haunt in Paris), and make sure   425
At worst that there were roses in the world.
So wandering, musing, with the artist's eye,
That keeps the shade-side of the thing it loves,
Half-absent, whole-observing, while the crowd
Of young vivacious and black-braided heads   430
Dipped, quick as finches in a blossomed tree,
Among the nosegays, cheapening this and that
In such a cheerful twitter of rapid speech, –
My heart leapt in me, startled by a voice
That slowly, faintly, with long breaths that marked   435
The interval between the wish and word,
Inquired in stranger's French, 'Would *that* be much,
That branch of flowering mountain-gorse?' – 'So much?
Too much for me, then!' turning the face round
So close upon me that I felt the sigh   440
It turned with.

    'Marian, Marian!' – face to face –
'Marian! I find you. Shall I let you go?'
I held her two slight wrists with both my hands;
'Ah, Marian, Marian, can I let you go?'
– She fluttered from me like a cyclamen,   445

As white, which taken in a sudden wind
Beats on against the palisade. – 'Let pass,'
She said at last. 'I will not,' I replied;
'I lost my sister Marian many days,
And sought her ever in my walks and prayers,   450
And now I find her . . . do we throw away
The bread we worked and prayed for, – crumble it
And drop it, . . . to do even so by thee
Whom still I've hungered after more than bread,
My sister Marian? – can I hurt thee, dear?   455
Then why distrust me? Never tremble so.
Come with me rather where we'll talk and live
And none shall vex us. I've a home for you
And me and no one else' . . .

                She shook her head.
'A home for you and me and no one else   460
Ill-suits one of us: I prefer to such,
A roof of grass on which a flower might spring,
Less costly to me than the cheapest here;
And yet I could not, at this hour, afford
A like home even. That you offer yours,   465
I thank you. You are good as heaven itself –
As good as one I knew before . . . Farewell.'

I loosed her hands. 'In *his* name, no farewell!'
(She stood as if I held her.) 'For his sake,
For his sake, Romney's! by the good he meant,   470
Aye, always! by the love he pressed for once, –
And by the grief, reproach, abandonment,
He took in change' . . .

             'He, Romney! who grieved *him*?
Who had the heart for 't? what reproach touched *him*?
Be merciful, – speak quickly.'

                'Therefore come,'   475
I answered with authority. – 'I think
We dare to speak such things and name such names
In the open squares of Paris!'

                Not a word
She said, but in a gentle humbled way
(As one who had forgot herself in grief)   480

Turned round and followed closely where I went,
As if I led her by a narrow plank
Across devouring waters, step by step;
And so in silence we walked on a mile.

And then she stopped: her face was white as wax.   485
'We go much farther?'
                        'You are ill,' I asked,
'Or tired?'
              She looked the whiter for her smile.
'There's one at home,' she said, 'has need of me
By this time, – and I must not let him wait.'

'Not even,' I asked, 'to hear of Romney Leigh?'   490

'Not even,' she said, 'to hear of Mister Leigh.'

'In that case,' I resumed, 'I go with you,
And we can talk the same thing there as here.
None waits for me: I have my day to spend.'

Her lips moved in a spasm without a sound, –   495
But then she spoke. 'It shall be as you please;
And better so – 'tis shorter seen than told:
And though you will not find me worth your pains,
That, even, may be worth some pains to know
For one as good as you are.'
                            Then she led   500
The way, and I, as by a narrow plank
Across devouring waters, followed her,
Stepping by her footsteps, breathing by her breath,
And holding her with eyes that would not slip;
And so, without a word, we walked a mile,   505
And so, another mile, without a word.

Until the peopled streets being all dismissed,
House-rows and groups all scattered like a flock,
The market-gardens thickened, and the long
White walls beyond, like spiders' outside threads,   510
Stretched, feeling blindly toward the country-fields
Through half-built habitations and half-dug

Foundations, – intervals of trenchant chalk
That bit betwixt the grassy uneven turfs
Where goats (vine-tendrils trailing from their mouths)   515
Stood perched on edges of the cellarage
Which should be, staring as about to leap
To find their coming Bacchus. All the place
Seemed less a cultivation than a waste.
Men work here, only, – scarce begin to live: 520
All's sad, the country struggling with the town,
Like an untamed hawk upon a strong man's fist,
That beats its wings and tries to get away,
And cannot choose be satisfied so soon
To hop through court-yards with its right foot tied,   525
The vintage plains and pastoral hills in sight.

We stopped beside a house too high and slim
To stand there by itself, but waiting till
Five others, two on this side, three on that,
Should grow up from the sullen second floor   530
They pause at now, to build it to a row.
The upper windows partly were unglazed
Meantime, – a meagre, unripe house: a line
Of rigid poplars elbowed it behind,
And, just in front, beyond the lime and bricks   535
That wronged the grass between it and the road,
A great acacia with its slender trunk
And overpoise of multitudinous leaves
(In which a hundred fields might spill their dew
And intense verdure, yet find room enough)   540
Stood reconciling all the place with green.

I followed up the stair upon her step.
She hurried upward, shot across a face,
A woman's, on the landing, – 'How now, now!
Is no one to have holidays but you?   545
You said an hour, and stay three hours, I think,
And Julie waiting for your betters here!
Why if he had waked he might have waked, for me.'
 – Just murmuring an excusing word she passed
And shut the rest out with the chamber-door,   550

Myself shut in beside her.
     'Twas a room
Scarce larger than a grave, and near as bare;
Two stools, a pallet-bed; I saw the room:
A mouse could find no sort of shelter in 't,
Much less a greater secret; curtainless, –   555
The window fixed you with its torturing eye,
Defying you to take a step apart
If peradventure you would hide a thing.
I saw the whole room, I and Marian there
Alone.
   Alone? She threw her bonnet off,   560
Then, sighing as 'twere sighing the last time,
Approached the bed, and drew a shawl away:
You could not peel a fruit you fear to bruise
More calmly and more carefully than so, –
Nor would you find within, a rosier flushed   565
Pomegranate –
     There he lay upon his back,
The yearling creature, warm and moist with life
To the bottom of his dimples, – to the ends
Of the lovely tumbled curls about his face;
For since he had been covered over-much   570
To keep him from the light-glare, both his cheeks
Were hot and scarlet as the first live rose
The shepherd's heart-blood ebbed away into
The faster for his love. And love was here
As instant; in the pretty baby-mouth,   575
Shut close as if for dreaming that it sucked,
The little naked feet, drawn up the way
Of nestled birdlings; everything so soft
And tender, – to the little holdfast hands,
Which, closing on a finger into sleep,   580
Had kept the mould of 't.
     While we stood there dumb,
For oh, that it should take such innocence
To prove just guilt, I thought, and stood there dumb,
The light upon his eyelids pricked them wide,
And, staring out at us with all their blue,   585
As half perplexed between the angelhood

He had been away to visit in his sleep,
And our most mortal presence, gradually
He saw his mother's face, accepting it
In change for heaven itself with such a smile   590
As might have well been learnt there, – never moved,
But smiled on, in a drowse of ecstasy,
So happy (half with her and half with heaven)
He could not have the trouble to be stirred,
But smiled and lay there. Like a rose, I said?   595
As red and still indeed as any rose,
That blows in all the silence of its leaves,
Content in blowing to fulfil its life.

She leaned above him (drinking him as wine)
In that extremity of love, 'twill pass   600
For agony or rapture, seeing that love
Includes the whole of nature, rounding it
To love . . . no more, – since more can never be
Than just love. Self-forgot, cast out of self,
And drowning in the transport of the sight,   605
Her whole pale passionate face, mouth, forehead, eyes,
One gaze, she stood: then, slowly as he smiled
She smiled too, slowly, smiling unaware,
And drawing from his countenance to hers
A fainter red, as if she watched a flame   610
And stood in it a-glow. 'How beautiful,'
Said she.
          I answered, trying to be cold.
(Must sin have compensations, was my thought,
As if it were a holy thing like grief?
And is a woman to be fooled aside   615
From putting vice down, with that woman's toy
A baby?) – 'Aye! the child is well enough'
I answered. 'If his mother's palms are clean,
They need be glad of course in clasping such;
But if not, I would rather lay my hand,   620
Were I she, on God's brazen altar-bars
Red-hot with burning sacrificial lambs,
Than touch the sacred curls of such a child.'

*

She plunged her fingers in his clustering locks,
As one who would not be afraid of fire;   625
And then with indrawn steady utterance said,
'My lamb, my lamb! although, through such as thou,
The most unclean got courage and approach
To God, once, – now they cannot, even with men,
Find grace enough for pity and gentle words.'   630

'My Marian,' I made answer, grave and sad,
'The priest who stole a lamb to offer him,
Was still a thief. And if a woman steals
(Through God's own barrier-hedges of true love,
Which fence out licence in securing love)   635
A child like this, that smiles so in her face,
She is no mother but a kidnapper,
And he's a dismal orphan . . . not a son,
Whom all her kisses cannot feed so full
He will not miss hereafter a pure home   640
To live in, a pure heart to lean against,
A pure good mother's name and memory
To hope by, when the world grows thick and bad
And he feels out for virtue.'
                              'Oh,' she smiled
With bitter patience, 'the child takes his chance;   645
Not much worse off in being fatherless
Than I was, fathered. He will say, belike,
His mother was the saddest creature born;
He'll say his mother lived so contrary
To joy, that even the kindest, seeing her,   650
Grew sometimes almost cruel: he'll not say
She flew contrarious in the face of God
With bat-wings of her vices. Stole my child, –
My flower of earth, my only flower on earth,
My sweet, my beauty!' . . . Up she snatched the child,   655
And, breaking on him in a storm of tears,
Drew out her long sobs from their shivering roots,
Until he took it for a game, and stretched
His feet and flapped his eager arms like wings
And crowed and gurgled through his infant laugh: 660
'Mine, mine,' she said. 'I have as sure a right

As any glad pround mother in the world,
Who sets her darling down to cut his teeth
Upon her church-ring. If she talks of law,
I talk of law! I claim my mother-dues   665
By law, – the law which now is paramount, –
The common law, by which the poor and weak
Are trodden underfoot by vicious men,
And loathed for ever after by the good.
Let pass! I did not filch, – I found the child.'   670

'You found him, Marian?'
                                    'Aye, I found him where
I found my curse, – in the gutter, with my shame!
What have you, any of you, to say to that,
Who all are happy, and sit safe and high,
And never spoke before to arraign my right   675
To grief itself? What, what, . . . being beaten down
By hoofs of maddened oxen into a ditch,
Half-dead, whole mangled, when a girl at last
Breathes, sees . . . and finds there, bedded in her flesh
Because of the extremity of the shock,   680
Some coin of price! . . . and when a good man comes
(That's God! the best men are not quite as good)
And says, "I dropped the coin there: take it you,
And keep it, – it shall pay you for the loss," –
You all put up your finger – "See the thief!   685
Observe what precious thing she has come to filch.
How bad those girls are!" Oh, my flower, my pet,
I dare forget I have you in my arms
And fly off to be angry with the world,
And fright you, hurt you with my tempers, till   690
You double up your lip. Why, that indeed
Is bad: a naughty mother!'
                                    'You mistake,'
I interrupted; if I loved you not,
I should not, Marian, certainly be here.'

'Alas,' she said, 'you are so very good;   695
And yet I wish indeed you had never come
To make me sob until I vex the child.
It is not wholesome for these pleasure-plats

To be so early watered by our brine.
And then, who knows? he may not like me now   700
As well, perhaps, as ere he saw me fret, –
One's ugly fretting! he has eyes the same
As angels, but he cannot see as deep,
And so I've kept for ever in his sight
A sort of smile to please him, – as you place   705
A green thing from the garden in a cup,
To make believe it grows there. Look, my sweet,
My cowslip-ball! we've done with that cross face,
And here's the face come back you used to like.
And, ah! he laughs! he likes me. Ah, Miss Leigh,   710
You're great and pure; but were you purer still, –
As if you had walked, we'll say, no otherwhere
Than up and down the new Jerusalem,
And held your trailing lutestring up yourself
From brushing the twelve stones, for fear of some   715
Small speck as little as a needle prick,
White stitched on white, – the child would keep to *me*,
Would choose his poor lost Marian, like me best,
And, though you stretched your arms, cry back and cling,
As we do, when God says it's time to die   720
And bids us go up higher. Leave us, then;
We two are happy. Does *he* push me off?
He's satisfied with me, as I with him.'

'So soft to one, so hard to others! Nay.'
I cried, more angry that she melted me,   725
'We make henceforth a cushion of our faults
To sit and practise easy virtues on?
I thought a child was given to sanctify
A woman, – set her in the sight of all
The clear-eyed heavens, a chosen minister   730
To do their business and lead spirits up
The difficult blue heights. A woman lives,
Not bettered, quickened toward the truth and good
Through being a mother? . . . then she's none! although
She damps her baby's cheeks by kissing them,   735
As we kill roses.'

                    'Kill! O Christ,' she said,

And turned her wild sad face from side to side
With most despairing wonder in it, 'What,
What have you in your souls against me then,
All of you? am I wicked, do you think?   740
God knows me, trusts me with the child; but you,
You think me really wicked?'

                  'Complaisant,'
I answered softly, 'to a wrong you've done,
Because of certain profits, – which is wrong
Beyond the first wrong, Marian. When you left   745
The pure place and the noble heart, to take
The hand of a seducer' . . .

                'Whom? whose hand?
I took the hand of' . . .

              Springing up erect
And lifting up the child at full arm's length,
As if to bear him like an oriflamme   750
Unconquerable to armies of reproach, –
'By *him*,' she said, 'my child's head and its curls,
By these blue eyes no woman born could dare
A perjury on, I make my mother's oath,
That if I left that Heart, to lighten it,   755
The blood of mine was still, except for grief!
No cleaner maid than I was, took a step
To a sadder end, – no matron-mother now
Looks backward to her early maidenhood
Through chaster pulses. I speak steadily: 760
And if I lie so, . . . if, being fouled in will
And paltered with in soul by devil's lust,
I dare to bid this angel take my part, . . .
Would God sit quiet, let us think, in heaven,
Nor strike me dumb with thunder? Yet I speak: 765
He clears me therefore. What, "seduced"'s your word?
Do wolves seduce a wandering fawn in France?
Do eagles, who have pinched a lamb with claws,
Seduce it into carrion? So with me.
I was not ever, as you say, seduced,   770
But simply, murdered.'

             There she paused, and sighed,
With such a sigh as drops from agony

To exhaustion, – sighing while she let the babe
Slide down upon her bosom from her arms,
And all her face's light fell after him   775
Like a torch quenched in falling. Down she sank,
And sat upon the bedside with the child.

But I, convicted, broken utterly,
With woman's passion clung about her waist
And kissed her hair and eyes, – 'I have been wrong,   780
Sweet Marian' . . . (weeping in a tender rage)
'Sweet holy Marian! And now, Marian, now,
I use your oath although my lips are hard,
And by the child, my Marian, by the child,
I swear his mother shall be innocent   785
Before my conscience, as in the open Book
Of Him who reads for judgment. Innocent,
My sister! let the night be ne'er so dark;
The moon is surely somewhere in the sky:
So surely is your whiteness to be found   790
Through all dark facts. But pardon, pardon me,
And smile a little, Marian, – for the child,
If not for me, my sister.'
                                        The poor lip
Just motioned for the smile and let it go:
And then, with scarce a stirring of the mouth,   795
As if a statue spoke that could not breathe,
But spoke on calm between its marble lips, –
'I'm glad, I'm very glad you clear me so.
I should be sorry that you set me down
With harlots, or with even a better name   800
Which misbecomes his mother. For the rest,
I am not on a level with your love,
Nor ever was, you know, – but now am worse,
Because that world of yours has dealt with me
As when the hard sea bites and chews a stone   805
And changes the first form of it. I've marked
A shore of pebbles bitten to one shape
From all the various life of madrepores;
And so, that little stone, called Marian Erle,
Picked up and dropped by you and another friend,   810

Was ground and tortured by the incessant sea
And bruised from what she was, – changed! death's a change,
And she, I said, was murdered; Marian's dead.
What can you do with people when they are dead,
But, if you are pious, sing a hymn and go,   815
Or, if you are tender, heave a sigh and go,
But go by all means, – and permit the grass
To keep its green feud up 'twixt them and you?
Then leave me, – let me rest. I'm dead, I say.
And if, to save the child from death as well,   820
The mother in me has survived the rest,
Why, that's God's miracle you must not tax,
I'm not less dead for that: I'm nothing more
But just a mother. Only for the child
I'm warm, and cold, and hungry, and afraid,   825
And smell the flowers a little and see the sun,
And speak still, and am silent, – just for him!
I pray you therefore to mistake me not
And treat me haply as I were alive;
For though you ran a pin into my soul,   830
I think it would not hurt nor trouble me.
Here's proof, dear lady, – in the market-place
But now, you promised me to say a word
About . . . a friend, who once, long years ago,
Took God's place toward me, when He leans and loves   835
And does not thunder, . . . whom at last I left,
As all of us leave God. You thought perhaps
I seemed to care for hearing of that friend?
Now, judge me! we have sat here half an hour
And talked together of the child and me,   840
And I not asked as much as, "What's the thing
You had to tell me of the friend . . . the friend?"
He's sad, I think you said, – he's sick perhaps?
'Tis nought to Marian if he's sad or sick.
Another would have crawled beside your foot   845
And prayed your words out. Why, a beast, a dog,
A starved cat, if he had fed it once with milk,
Would show less hardness. But I'm dead, you see,
And that explains it.'

                    Poor, poor thing, she spoke

And shook her head, as white and calm as frost   850
On days too cold for raining any more,
But still with such a face, so much alive,
I could not choose but take it on my arm
And stroke the placid patience of its cheeks, –
Then told my story out, of Romney Leigh,   855
How, having lost her, sought her, missed her still,
He, broken-hearted for himself and her,
Had drawn the curtains of the world awhile
As if he had done with morning. There I stopped,
For when she gasped, and pressed me with her eyes,   860
'And now . . . how is it with him? tell me now,'
I felt the shame of compensated grief,
And chose my words with scruple – slowly stepped
Upon the slippery stones set here and there
Across the sliding water. 'Certainly,   865
As evening empties morning into night,
Another morning takes the evening up
With healthful, providential interchange;
And, though he thought still of her,' –
                      'Yes, she knew,
She understood: she had supposed indeed   870
That, as one stops a hole upon a flute,
At which a new note comes and shapes the tune,
Excluding her would bring a worthier in,
And, long ere this, that Lady Waldemar
He loved so' . . .
                'Loved,' I started, – 'loved her so!   875
Now tell me' . . .
                'I will tell you,' she replied:
'But, since we're taking oaths, you'll promise first
That he in England, he, shall never learn
In what a dreadful trap his creature here,
Round whose unworthy neck he had meant to tie   880
The honourable ribbon of his name,
Fell unaware and came to butchery:
Because, – I know him, – as he takes to heart
The grief of every stranger, he's not like
To banish mine as far as I should choose   885
In wishing him most happy. Now he leaves

To think of me, perverse, who went my way,
Unkind, and left him, – but if once he knew . . .
Ah, then, the sharp nail of my cruel wrong
Would fasten me for ever in his sight,   890
Like some poor curious bird, through each spread wing
Nailed high up over a fierce hunter's fire,
To spoil the dinner of all tenderer folk
Come in by chance. Nay, since your Marian's dead,
You shall not hang her up, but dig a hole   895
And bury her in silence! ring no bells.'

I answered gaily, though my whole voice wept,
'We'll ring the joy-bells, not the funeral-bells,
Because we have her back, dead or alive.'

She never answered that, but shook her head;   900
Then low and calm, as one who, safe in heaven,
Shall tell a story of his lower life,
Unmoved by shame or anger, – so she spoke.
She told me she had loved upon her knees,
As others pray, more perfectly absorbed   905
In the act and inspiration. She felt his
For just his uses, not her own at all,
His stool, to sit on or put up his foot,
His cup, to fill with wine or vinegar,
Whichever drink might please him at the chance   910
For that should please her always: let him write
His name upon her . . . it seemed natural;
It was most precious, standing on his shelf,
To wait until he chose to lift his hand.
Well, well, – I saw her then, and must have seen   915
How bright her life went floating on her love,
Like wicks the housewives send afloat on oil
Which feeds them to a flame that lasts the night.

To do good seemed so much his business,
That, having done it, she was fain to think,   920
Must fill up his capacity for joy.
At first she never mooted with herself
If *he* was happy, since he made her so,
Or if he loved her, being so much beloved.

Who thinks of asking if the sun is light,   925
Observing that it lightens? who's so bold,
To question God of his felicity?
Still less. And thus she took for granted first
What first of all she should have put to proof,
And sinned against him so, but only so.   930
'What could you hope,' she said, 'of such as she?
You take a kid you like, and turn it out
In some fair garden: though the creature's fond
And gentle, it will leap upon the beds
And break your tulips, bite your tender trees; 935
The wonder would be if such innocence
Spoiled less: a garden is no place for kids.'

And, by degrees, when he who had chosen her
Brought in his courteous and benignant friends
To spend their goodness on her, which she took 940
So very gladly, as a part of his, –
By slow degrees it broke on her slow sense
That she too in that Eden of delight
Was out of place, and, like the silly kid,
Still did most mischief where she meant most love. 945
A thought enough to make a woman mad
(No beast in this, but she may well go mad),
That, saying, 'I am thine to love and use'
May blow the plague in her protesting breath
To the very man for whom she claims to die, – 950
That, clinging round his neck, she pulls him down
And drowns him, – and that, lavishing her soul,
She hales perdition on him. 'So, being mad,'
Said Marian . . .
     'Ah – who stirred such thoughts, you ask?
Whose fault it was, that she should have such thoughts? 955
None's fault, none's fault. The light comes, and we see:
But if it were not truly for our eyes,
There would be nothing seen, for all the light.
And so with Marian: if she saw at last,
The sense was in her, – Lady Waldemar   960
Had spoken all in vain else.'
       'O my heart,

O prophet in my heart,' I cried aloud,
'Then Lady Waldemar spoke!'
                              '*Did* she speak,'
Mused Marian softly, 'or did she only sign?
Or did she put a word into her face   965
And look, and so impress you with the word?
Or leave it in the foldings of her gown,
Like rosemary smells a movement will shake out
When no one's conscious? who shall say, or guess?
One thing alone was certain – from the day   970
The gracious lady paid a visit first,
She, Marian, saw things different, – felt distrust
Of all that sheltering roof of circumstance
Her hopes were building into with clay nests:
Her heart was restless, pacing up and down   975
And fluttering, like dumb creatures before storms,
Not knowing wherefore she was ill at ease.'

'And still the lady came,' said Marian Erle,
'Much oftener than *he* knew it, Mister Leigh.
She bade me never tell him she had come,   980
She liked to love me better than he knew,
So very kind was Lady Waldemar:'
And every time she brought with her more light,
And every light made sorrow clearer . . . Well,
Ah, well! we cannot give her blame for that;   985
'Twould be the same thing if an angel came,
Whose right should prove our wrong. And every time
The lady came, she looked more beautiful
And spoke more like a flute among green trees,
Until at last, as one, whose heart being sad   990
On hearing lovely music, suddenly
Dissolves in weeping, I brake out in tears
Before her . . . asked her counsel, – "Had I erred
In being too happy? would she set me straight?
For she, being wise and good and born above   995
The flats I had never climbed from, could perceive
If such as I, might grow upon the hills;
And whether such poor herb sufficed to grow,
For Romney Leigh to break his fast upon 't, –

Or would he pine on such, or haply starve?"   1000
She wrapt me in her generous arms at once,
And let me dream a moment how it feels
To have a real mother, like some girls:
But when I looked, her face was younger . . . aye,
Youth's too bright not to be a little hard,   1005
And beauty keeps itself still uppermost,
That's true! – Though Lady Waldemar was kind
She hurt me, hurt, as if the morning-sun
Should smite us on the eyelids when we sleep,
And wake us up with headache. Aye, and soon   1010
Was light enough to make my heart ache too:
She told me truths I asked for, – 'twas my fault, –
"That Romney could not love me, if he would,
As men call loving: there are bloods that flow
Together like some rivers and not mix,   1015
Through contraries of nature. He indeed
Was set to wed me, to espouse my class,
Act out a rash opinion, – and, once wed,
So just a man and gentle could not choose
But make my life as smooth as marriage-ring,   1020
Bespeak me mildly, keep me a cheerful house,
With servants, brooches, all the flowers I liked,
And pretty dresses, silk the whole year round" . . .
At which I stopped her, – "This for me. And now
For *him*." – She hesitated, – truth grew hard;   1025
She owned, " 'Twas plain a man like Romney Leigh
Required a wife more level to himself.
If day by day he had to bend his height
To pick up sympathies, opinions, thoughts,
And interchange the common talk of life   1030
Which helps a man to live as well as talk,
His days were heavily taxed. Who buys a staff
To fit the hand, that reaches but the knee?
He'd feel it bitter to be forced to miss
The perfect joy of married suited pairs,   1035
Who, bursting through the separating hedge
Of personal dues with that sweet eglantine
Of equal love, keep saying, 'So *we* think,
It strikes *us*, – that's *our* fancy.' " – When I asked

If earnest will, devoted love, employed   1040
In youth like mine, would fail to raise me up
As two strong arms will always raise a child
To a fruit hung overhead, she sighed and sighed . . .
"That could not be," she feared. "You take a pink,
You dig about its roots and water it   1045
And so improve it to a garden-pink,
But will not change it to a heliotrope,
The kind remains. And then, the harder truth –
This Romney Leigh, so rash to leap a pale,
So bold for conscience, quick for martyrdom,   1050
Would suffer steadily and never flinch,
But suffer surely and keenly, when his class
Turned shoulder on him for a shameful match,
And set him up as ninepin in their talk
To bowl him down with jestings." – There, she paused;   1055
And when I used the pause in doubting that
We wronged him after all in what we feared –
"Suppose such things should never touch him more
In his high conscience (if the things should be)
Than, when the queen sits in an upper room,   1060
The horses in the street can spatter her!" –
A moment, hope came, – but the lady closed
That door and nicked the lock and shut it out,
Observing wisely that, "the tender heart
Which made him over-soft to a lower class,   1065
Would scarcely fail to make him sensitive
To a higher, – how they thought and what they felt."

'Alas, alas!' said Marian, rocking slow
The pretty baby who was near asleep,
The eyelids creeping over the blue balls, –   1070
'She made it clear, too clear – I saw the whole!
And yet who knows if I had seen my way
Straight out of it by looking, though 'twas clear,
Unless the generous lady, 'ware of this,
Had set her own house all afire for me   1075
To light me forwards? Leaning on my face
Her heavy agate eyes which crushed my will,
She told me tenderly (as when men come

To a bedside to tell people they must die),
"She knew of knowledge, – aye, of knowledge knew, 1080
That Romney Leigh had loved *her* formerly.
And *she* loved *him*, she might say, now the chance
Was past, – but that, of course, he never guessed, –
For something came between them, something thin
As a cobweb, catching every fly of doubt 1085
To hold it buzzing at the window-pane
And help to dim the daylight. Ah, man's pride
Or woman's – which is greatest? most averse
To brushing cobwebs? Well, but she and he
Remained fast friends; it seemed not more than so, 1090
Because he had bound his hands and could not stir.
An honourable man, if somewhat rash;
And she, not even for Romney, would she spill
A blot . . . as little even as a tear . . .
Upon his marriage-contract, – not to gain 1095
A better joy for two than came by that:
For, though I stood between her heart and heaven,
She loved me wholly." '
                    Did I laugh or curse?
I think I sat there silent, hearing all,
Aye, hearing double, – Marian's tale, at once, 1100
And Romney's marriage-vow, '*I'll keep to* THEE,'
Which means that woman-serpent. Is it time
For church now?
                    'Lady Waldemar spoke more,'
Continued Marian, 'but, as when a soul
Will pass out through the sweetness of a song 1105
Beyond it, voyaging the uphill road,
Even so mine wandered from the things I heard
To those I suffered. It was afterward
I shaped the resolution to the act.
For many hours we talked. What need to talk? 1110
The fate was clear and close; it touched my eyes;
But still the generous lady tried to keep
The case afloat, and would not let it go,
And argued, struggled upon Marian's side,
Which was not Romney's! though she little knew 1115
What ugly monster would take up the end, –

What griping death within the drowning death
Was ready to complete my sum of death.'

I thought, – Perhaps he's sliding now the ring
Upon that woman's finger . . .
                    She went on: 1120
'The lady, failing to prevail her way,
Up-gathered my torn wishes from the ground
And pieced them with her strong benevolence;
And, as I thought I could breathe freer air
Away from England, going without pause,   1125
Without farewell, just breaking with a jerk
The blossomed offshoot from my thorny life, –
She promised kindly to provide the means,
With instant passage to the colonies
And full protection, – "would commit me straight   1130
To one who once had been her waiting-maid
And had the customs of the world, intent
On changing England for Australia
Herself, to carry out her fortune so."
For which I thanked the Lady Waldemar,   1135
As men upon their death-beds thank last friends
Who lay the pillow straight: it is not much,
And yet 'tis all of which they are capable,
This lying smoothly in a bed to die.
And so, 'twas fixed; – and so, from day to day,   1140
The woman named came in to visit me.'

Just then the girl stopped speaking, – sat erect,
And stared at me as if I had been a ghost
(Perhaps I looked as white as any ghost)
With large-eyed horror. 'Does God make,' she said,   1145
'All sorts of creatures really, do you think?
Or is it that the Devil slavers them
So excellently, that we come to doubt
Who's stronger, He who makes, or he who mars?
I never liked the woman's face or voice   1150
Or ways: it made me blush to look at her;
It made me tremble if she touched my hand;
And when she spoke a fondling word I shrank

As if one hated me who had power to hurt;
And, every time she came, my veins ran cold   1155
As somebody were walking on my grave.
At last I spoke to Lady Waldemar:
"Could such an one be good to trust?" I asked.
Whereat the lady stroked my cheek and laughed
Her silver-laugh (one must be born to laugh,   1160
To put such music in it), – "Foolish girl,
Your scattered wits are gathering wool beyond
The sheep-walk reaches! – leave the thing to me."
And therefore, half in trust, and half in scorn
That I had heart still for another fear   1165
In such a safe despair, I left the thing.

'The rest is short. I was obedient:
I wrote my letter which delivered *him*
From Marian to his own prosperities,
And followed that bad guide. The lady? – hush,   1170
I never blame the lady. Ladies who
Sit high, however willing to look down,
Will scarce see lower than their dainty feet;
And Lady Waldemar saw less than I,
With what a Devil's daughter I went forth   1175
Along the swine's road, down the precipice,
In such a curl of hell-foam caught and choked,
No shriek of soul in anguish could pierce through
To fetch some help. They say there's help in heaven
For all such cries. But if one cries from hell . . .   1180
What then? – the heavens are deaf upon that side.

'A woman . . . hear me, let me make it plain, . . .
A woman . . . not a monster . . . both her breasts
Made right to suckle babes . . . she took me off
A woman also, young and ignorant   1185
And heavy with my grief, my two poor eyes
Near washed away with weeping, till the trees,
The blessed unaccustomed trees and fields
Ran either side the train like stranger dogs
Unworthy of any notice, – took me off   1190
So dull, so blind, so only half alive,

Not seeing by what road, nor by what ship,
Nor toward what place, nor to what end of all.
Men carry a corpse thus, – past the doorway, past
The garden-gate, the children's playground, up   1195
The green lane, – then they leave it in the pit,
To sleep and find corruption, cheek to cheek
With him who stinks since Friday.

                        'But suppose;
To go down with one's soul into the grave,
To go down half dead, half alive, I say,   1200
And wake up with corruption, . . . cheek to cheek
With him who stinks since Friday! There it is,
And that's the horror of 't, Miss Leigh.

                           'You feel?
You understand? – no, do not look at me,
But understand. The blank, blind, weary way,   1205
Which led, where'er it led, away at least;
The shifted ship, to Sydney or to France,
Still bound, wherever else, to another land;
The swooning sickness on the dismal sea,
The foreign shore, the shameful house, the night,   1210
The feeble blood, the heavy-headed grief, . . .
No need to bring their damnable drugged cup,
And yet they brought it. Hell's so prodigal
Of devil's gifts, hunts liberally in packs,
Will kill no poor small creature of the wilds   1215
But fifty red wide throats must smoke at it,
As HIS at me . . . when waking up at last . . .
I told you that I waked up in the grave.

'Enough so! – it is plain enough so. True,
We wretches cannot tell out all our wrong   1220
Without offence to decent happy folk.
I know that we must scrupulously hint
With half-words, delicate reserves, the thing
Which no one scrupled we should feel in full.
Let pass the rest, then; only leave my oath   1225
Upon this sleeping child, – man's violence,
Not man's seduction, made me what I am,
As lost as . . . I told *him* I should be lost.

When mothers fail us, can we help ourselves?
That's fatal! – And you call it being lost,   1230
That down came next day's noon and caught me there
Half gibbering and half raving on the floor,
And wondering what had happened up in heaven,
That suns should dare to shine when God Himself
Was certainly abolished.

               'I was mad,   1235
How many weeks, I know not, – many weeks.
I think they let me go when I was mad,
They feared my eyes and loosed me, as boys might
A mad dog which they had tortured. Up and down
I went, by road and village, over tracts   1240
Of open foreign country, large and strange,
Crossed everywhere by long thin poplar-lines
Like fingers of some ghastly skeleton Hand
Through sunlight and through moonlight evermore
Pushed out from hell itself to pluck me back,   1245
And resolute to get me, slow and sure;
While every roadside Christ upon his cross
Hung reddening through his gory wounds at me,
And shook his nails in anger, and came down
To follow a mile after, wading up   1250
The low vines and green wheat, crying "Take the girl!
She's none of mine from henceforth." Then I knew
(But this is somewhat dimmer than the rest)
The charitable peasants gave me bread
And leave to sleep in straw: and twice they tied,   1255
At parting, Mary's image round my neck –
How heavy it seemed! as heavy as a stone;
A woman has been strangled with less weight:
I threw it in a ditch to keep it clean
And ease my breath a little, when none looked;   1260
I did not need such safeguards: – brutal men
Stopped short, Miss Leigh, in insult, when they had seen
My face, – I must have had an awful look.
And so I lived: the weeks passed on, – I lived.
'Twas living my old tramp-life o'er again,   1265
But, this time, in a dream, and hunted round
By some prodigious Dream-fear at my back,

Which ended yet: my brain cleared presently;
And there I sat, one evening, by the road,
I, Marian Erle, myself, alone, undone,   1270
Facing a sunset low upon the flats
As if it were the finish of all time,
The great red stone upon my sepulchre,
Which angels were too weak to roll away.

Seventh Book

'The woman's motive? shall we daub ourselves
With finding roots for nettles? 'tis soft clay
And easily explored. She had the means,
The moneys, by the lady's liberal grace,
In trust for that Australian scheme and me,　　　　　5
Which so, that she might clutch with both her hands
And chink to her naughty uses undisturbed,
She served me (after all it was not strange,
'Twas only what my mother would have done)
A motherly, right damnable, good turn.　　　　　10

'Well, after. There are nettles everywhere,
But smooth green grasses are more common still;
The blue of heaven is larger than the cloud;
A miller's wife at Clichy took me in
And spent her pity on me, – made me calm　　　　　15
And merely very reasonably sad.
She found me a servant's place in Paris, where
I tried to take the cast-off life again,
And stood as quiet as a beaten ass
Who, having fallen through overloads, stands up　　　　　20
To let them charge him with another pack.

'A few months, so. My mistress, young and light,
Was easy with me, less for kindness than
Because she led, herself, an easy time
Betwixt her lover and her looking-glass,　　　　　25
Scarce knowing which way she was praised the most.
She felt so pretty and so pleased all day
She could not take the trouble to be cross,
But sometimes, as I stooped to tie her shoe,
Would tap me softly with her slender foot　　　　　30
Still restless with the last night's dancing in 't,
And say "Fie, pale-face! are you English girls
All grave and silent? mass-book still, and Lent?
And first-communion palloron your cheeks,

Worn past the time for 't? little fool, be gay!"   35
At which she vanished like a fairy, through
A gap of silver laughter.
                              'Came an hour
When all went otherwise. She did not speak,
But clenched her brows, and clipped me with her eyes
As if a viper with a pair of tongs,   40
Too far for any touch, yet near enough
To view the writhing creature, – then at last,
"Stand still there, in the holy Virgin's name,
Thou Marian; thou'rt no reputable girl,
Although sufficient dull for twenty saints!   45
I think thou mock'st me and my house,' she said;
"Confess thou'lt be a mother in a month,
Thou mask of saintship."
                              'Could I answer her?
The light broke in so. It meant *that* then, *that*?
I had not thought of that, in all my thoughts,   50
Through all the cold, numb aching of my brow,
Through all the heaving of impatient life
Which threw me on death at intervals, – through all
The upbreak of the fountains of my heart
The rains had swelled too large: it could mean *that*?   55
Did God make mothers out of victims, then,
And set such pure amens to hideous deeds?
Why not? He overblows an ugly grave
With violets which blossom in the spring.
And *I* could be a mother in a month?   60
I hope it was not wicked to be glad.
I lifted up my voice and wept, and laughed,
To heaven, not her, until it tore my throat.
"Confess, confess!" – what was there to confess,
Except man's cruelty, except my wrong?   65
Except this anguish, or this ecstasy?
This shame or glory? The light woman there
Was small to take it in: an acorn-cup
Would take the sea in sooner.
                              ' "Good," she cried;
"Unmarried and a mother, and she laughs!   70
These unchaste girls are always impudent.

Get out, intriguer! leave my house and trot.
I wonder you should look me in the face,
With such a filthy secret."
                'Then I rolled
My scanty bundle up, and went my way,   75
Washed white with weeping, shuddering head and foot
With blind hysteric passion, staggering forth
Beyond those doors, 'Twas natural of course
She should not ask me where I meant to sleep;
I might sleep well beneath the heavy Seine,   80
Like others of my sort; the bed was laid
For us. By any woman, womanly,
Had thought of him who should be in a month,
The sinless babe that should be in a month,
And if by chance he might be warmer housed   85
Than underneath such dreary dripping eaves.'

I broke on Marian there. 'Yet she herself,
A wife, I think, had scandals of her own,
A lover not her husband.'
                'Aye,' she said,
'But gold and meal are measured otherwise;   90
I learnt so much at school,' said Marian Erle.

'O crooked world,' I cried, 'ridiculous
If not so lamentable! 'Tis the way
With these light women of a thrifty vice,
My Marian, – always hard upon the rent   95
In any sister's virtue! while they keep
Their own so darned and patched with perfidy,
That, though a rag itself, it looks as well
Across a street, in balcony or coach,
As any perfect stuff might. For my part,   100
I'd rather take the wind-side of the stews
Than touch such women with my finger-end!
They top the poor street-walker by their lie
And look the better for being so much worse:
The devil's most devilish when respectable.   105
But you, dear, and your story.'
                'All the rest
Is here,' she said, and sighed upon the child.

'I found a mistress-sempstress who was kind
And let me sew in peace among her girls.
And what was better than to draw the threads   110
All day and half the night for him and him?
And so I lived for him, and so he lives,
And so I know, by this time, God lives too.'

She smiled beyond the sun and ended so,
And all my soul rose up to take her part   115
Against the world's successes, virtues, fames.
'Come with me, sweetest sister,' I returned,
'And sit within my house and do me good
From henceforth, thou and thine! ye are my own
From henceforth. I am lonely in the world,   120
And thou art lonely, and the child is half
An orphan. Come, – and, henceforth thou and I
Being still together will not miss a friend,
Nor he a father, since two mothers shall
Make that up to him. I am journeying south,   125
And in my Tuscan home I'll find a niche
And set thee there, my saint, the child and thee,
And burn the lights of love before thy face,
And ever at thy sweet look cross myself
From mixing with the world's prosperities;   130
That so, in gravity and holy calm,
We too may live on toward the truer life.'

She looked me in the face and answered not,
Nor signed she was unworthy, nor gave thanks,
But took the sleeping child and held it out   135
To meet my kiss, as if requiting me
And trusting me at once. And thus, at once,
I carried him and her to where I live;
She's there now, in the little room, asleep,
I hear the soft child-breathing through the door,   140
And all three of us, at tomorrow's break,
Pass onward, homeward, to our Italy.
Oh, Romney Leigh, I have your debts to pay,
And I'll be just and pay them.
                              But yourself!
To pay your debts is scarcely difficult,   145

To buy your life is nearly impossible,
Being sold away to Lamia. My head aches,
I cannot see my road along this dark;
Nor can I creep and grope, as fits the dark,
For these foot-catching robes of womanhood: 150
A man might walk a little . . . but I! – He loves
The Lamia-woman, – and I, write to him
What stops his marriage, and destroys his peace, –
Or what perhaps shall simply trouble him,
Until she only need to touch his sleeve   155
With just a finger's tremulous white flame,
Saying, 'Ah, – Aurora Leigh! a pretty tale,
A very pretty poet! I can guess
The motive' – then, to catch his eyes in hers
And vow she does not wonder, – and they two   160
To break in laughter as the sea along
A melancholy coast, and float up higher,
In such a laugh, their fatal weeds of love!
Aye, fatal, aye. And who shall answer me
Fate has not hurried tides, – and if tonight   165
My letter would not be a night too late,
An arrow shot into a man that's dead,
To prove a vain intention? Would I show
The new wife vile, to make the husband mad?
No, Lamia! shut the shutters, bar the doors   170
From every glimmer on thy serpent-skin!
I will not let thy hideous secret out
To agonise the man I love – I mean
The friend I love . . . as friends love.

                                        It is strange,
Today while Marian told her story like   175
To absorb most listeners, how I listened chief
To a voice not hers, nor yet that enemy's,
Nor God's in wrath, . . . but one that mixed with mine
Long years ago among the garden-trees,
And said to *me*, to *me* too, 'Be my wife,   180
Aurora!' It is strange with what a swell
Of yearning passion, as a snow of ghosts
Might beat against the impervious door of heaven,
I thought, 'Now, if I had been a woman, such

As God made women, to save men by love, – 185
By just my love I might have saved this man,
And made a nobler poem for the world
Than all I have failed in.' But I failed besides
In this; and now he's lost! through me alone!
And, by my only fault, his empty house 190
Sucks in, at this same hour, a wind from hell
To keep his hearth cold, make his casements creak
For ever to the tune of plague and sin –
O Romney, O my Romney, O my friend,
My cousin and friend! my helper, when I would, 195
My love, that might be! mine!
                                        Why, how one weeps
When one's too weary! Were a witness by,
He'd say some folly . . . that I loved the man,
Who knows? . . . and make me laugh again for scorn.
At strongest, women are as weak in flesh, 200
As men, at weakest, vilest are in soul:
So, hard for women to keep pace with men!
As well give up at once, sit down at once,
And weep as I do. Tears, tears! *why* we weep?
'Tis worth enquiry? – that we've shamed a life, 205
Or lost a love, or missed a world, perhaps?
By no means. Simply, that we've walked too far,
Or talked too much, or felt the wind i' the east, –
And so we weep, as if both body and soul
Broke up in water – this way.
                                        Poor mixed rags 210
Forsooth we're made of, like those other dolls
That lean with pretty faces into fairs.
It seems as if I had a man in me,
Despising such a woman.
                                        Yet indeed,
To see a wrong or suffering moves us all 215
To undo it though we should undo ourselves,
Aye, all the more, that we undo ourselves;
That's womanly, past doubt, and not ill-moved.
A natural movement therefore, on my part,
To fill the chair up of my cousin's wife, 220
And save him from a devil's company!

We're all so, – made so – 'tis our woman's trade
To suffer torment for another's ease.
The world's male chivalry has perished out,
But women are knights-errant to the last;   225
And, if Cervantes had been Shakesperean too,
He had made his Don a Donna.
                    So it clears,
And so we rain our skies blue.
                    Put away
This weakness. If, as I have just now said,
A man's within me, – let him act himself,   230
Ignoring the poor conscious trouble of blood
That's called the woman merely. I will write
Plain words to England, – if too late, too late,
If ill-accounted, then accounted ill;
We'll trust the heavens with something.
                      'Dear Lord Howe,   235
You'll find a story on another leaf
Of Marian Erle, – what noble friend of yours
She trusted once, through what flagitious [180] means,
To what disastrous ends; – the story's true.
I found her wandering on the Paris quays,   240
A babe upon her breast, – unnatural,
Unseasonable outcast on such snow
Unthawed to this time. I will tax in this
Your friendship, friend, if that convicted She
Be not his wife yet, to denounce the facts   245
To himself, – but, otherwise, to let them pass
On tip-toe like escaping murderers,
And tell my cousin merely – Marian lives,
Is found, and finds her home with such a friend,
Myself, Aurora. Which good news, "She's found,"   250
Will help to make him merry in his love:
I send it, tell him, for my marriage-gift,
As good as orange-water for the nerves,
Or perfumed gloves for headache, – though aware
That he, except of love, is scarcely sick: 255
I mean the new love this time, . . . since last year.
Such quick forgetting on the part of men!
Is any shrewder trick upon the cards

To enrich them? pray instruct me how 'tis done.
First, clubs, – and while you look at clubs, 'tis spades;   260
That's prodigy. The lightning strikes a man,
And when we think to find him dead and charred . . .
Why, there he is on a sudden, playing pipes
Beneath the splintered elm-tree! Crime and shame
And all their hoggery trample your smooth world,   265
Nor leave more foot-marks than Apollo's kine
Whose hoofs were muffled by the thieving god
In tamarisk-leaves and myrtle. I'm so sad,
So weary and sad tonight, I'm somewhat sour, –
Forgive me. To be blue and shrew at once,   270
Exceeds all toleration except yours,
But yours, I know, is infinite. Farewell.
Tomorrow we take train for Italy.
Speak gently of me to your gracious wife,
As one, however far, shall yet be near   275
In loving wishes to your house.'
                                    I sign.
And now I loose my heart upon a page,
This –
              'Lady Waldemar, I'm very glad
I never liked you; which you knew so well
You spared me, in your turn, to like me much: 280
Your liking surely had done worse for me
Than has your loathing, though the last appears
Sufficiently unscrupulous to hurt,
And not afraid of judgement. Now, there's space
Between our faces, – I stand off, as if   285
I judged a stranger's portrait and pronounced
Indifferently the type was good or bad.
What matter to me that the lines are false,
I ask you? did I ever ink my lips
By drawing your name through them as a friend's,   290
Or touch your hands as lovers do? Thank God
I never did: and since you're proved so vile,
Aye, vile, I say, – we'll show it presently, –
I'm not obliged to nurse my friend in you,
Or wash out my own blots, in counting yours,   295
Or even excuse myself to honest souls

Who seek to press my lip or clasp my palm, –
"Alas, but Lady Waldemar came first!"

' 'Tis true, by this time you may near me so
That you're my cousin's wife. You've gambled deep   300
As Lucifer, and won the morning-star
In that case, – and the noble house of Leigh
Must henceforth with its good roof shelter you:
I cannot speak and burn you up between
Those rafters, I who am born a Leigh, – nor speak   305
And pierce your breast through Romney's, I who live
His friend and cousin, – so, you're safe. You two
Must grow together like the tares and wheat
Till God's great fire. – But make the best of time.

'And hide this letter: let it speak no more   310
Than I shall, how you tricked poor Marian Erle,
And set her own love digging its own grave
Within her green hope's pretty garden-ground –
Aye, sent her forth with some one of your sort
To a wicked house in France, from which she fled   315
With curses in her eyes and ears and throat,
Her whole soul choked with curses, – mad in short,
And madly scouring up and down for weeks
The foreign hedgeless country, lone and lost, –
So innocent, male-fiends might slink within   320
Remote hell-corners, seeing her so defiled.

'But you, – you are a woman and more bold.
To do you justice, you'd not shrink to face . . .
We'll say, the unfledged life in the other room,
Which, treading down God's corn, you trod in sight   325
Of all the dogs, in reach of all the guns, –
Aye, Marian's babe, her poor unfathered child,
Her yearling babe! – you'd face him when he wakes
And opens up his wonderful blue eyes:
You'd meet them and not wink perhaps, nor fear   330
God's triumph in them and supreme revenge
When righting His creation's balance-scale
(You pulled as low as Tophet)[181] to the top

Of most celestial innocence. For me
Who am not as bold, I own those infant eyes   335
Have set me praying.
             'While they look at heaven,
No need of protestation in my words
Against the place you've made them! let them look.
They'll do your business with the heavens, be sure:
I spare you common curses.
              'Ponder this;   340
If haply you're the wife of Romney Leigh
(For which inheritance beyond your birth
You sold that poisonous porridge called your soul),
I charge you, be his faithful and true wife!
Keep warm his hearth and clean his board, and, when   345
He speaks, be quick with your obedience;
Still grind your paltry wants and low desires
To dust beneath his heel; though, even thus,
The ground must hurt him, – it was writ of old,
"Ye shall not yoke together ox and ass,"   350
The nobler and ignobler. Aye, but you
Shall do your part as well as such ill things
Can do aught good. You shall not vex him, – mark,
You shall not vex him, jar him when he's sad,
Or cross him when he's eager. Understand   355
To trick him with apparent sympathies,
Nor let him see thee in the face too near
And unlearn thy sweet seeming. Pay the price
Of lies, by being constrained to lie on still:
'Tis easy for thy sort: a million more   360
Will scarcely damn thee deeper.
                  'Doing which
You are very safe from Marian and myself;
We'll breathe as softly as the infant here,
And stir no dangerous embers. Fail a point,
And show our Romney wounded, ill-content,   365
Tormented in his home, we open mouth,
And such a noise will follow, the last trump's
Will scarcely seem more dreadful, even to you;
You'll have no pipers after: Romney will
(I know him) push you forth as none of his,   370

All other men declaring it well done,
While women, even the worst, your like, will draw
Their skirts back, not to brush you in the street,
And so I warn you. I'm . . . . Aurora Leigh.'

The letter written I felt satisfied.   375
The ashes, smouldering in me, were thrown out
By handfuls from me: I had writ my heart
And wept my tears, and now was cool and calm;
And, going straightway to the neighbouring room,
I lifted up the curtains of the bed   380
Where Marian Erle, the babe upon her arm,
Both faces leaned together like a pair
Of folded innocences self-complete,
Each smiling from the other, smiled and slept.
There seemed no sin, no shame, no wrath, no grief.   385
I felt she too had spoken words that night,
But softer certainly, and said to God,
Who laughs in heaven perhaps that such as I
Should make ado for such as she. – 'Defiled'
I wrote? 'defiled' I thought her? Stoop,   390
Stoop lower, Aurora! get the angels' leave
To creep in somewhere, humbly, on your knees,
Within this round of sequestration white
In which they have wrapt earth's foundlings, heaven's elect.

The next day we took train to Italy   395
And fled on southward in the roar of steam.
The marriage-bells of Romney must be loud,
To sound so clear through all: I was not well,
And truly, though the truth is like a jest,
I could not choose but fancy, half the way,   400
I stood alone i' the belfry, fifty bells
Of naked iron, mad with merriment
(As one who laughs and cannot stop himself),
All clanking at me, in me, over me,
Until I shrieked a shriek I could not hear,   405
And swooned with noise, – but still, along my swoon,
Was 'ware the baffled changes backward rang,
Prepared, at each emerging sense, to beat

And crash it out with clangour. I was weak;
I struggled for the posture of my soul   410
In upright consciousness of place and time,
But evermore, 'twixt waking and asleep,
Slipped somehow, staggered, caught at Marian's eyes
A moment (it is very good for strength
To know that some one needs you to be strong),   415
And so recovered what I called myself,
For that time.
          I just knew it when we swept
Above the old roofs of Dijon; Lyons dropped
A spark into the night, half trodden out
Unseen. But presently the winding Rhone   420
Washed out the moonlight large along his banks
Which strained their yielding curves out clear and clean
To hold it, – shadow of town and castle blurred
Upon the hurrying river. Such an air
Blew thence upon the forehead, – half an air   425
And half a water, – that I leaned and looked,
Then, turning back on Marian, smiled to mark
That she looked only on her child, who slept,
His face toward the moon too.
                So we passed
The liberal open country and the close,   430
And shot through tunnels, like a lightning-wedge
By great Thor-hammers driven through the rock,
Which, quivering through the intestine blackness, splits,
And lets it in at once: the train swept in
Athrob with effort, trembling with resolve,   435
The fierce denouncing whistle wailing on
And dying off smothered in the shuddering dark,
While we, self-awed, drew troubled breath, oppressed
As other Titans underneath the pile
And nightmare of the mountains. Out, at last,   440
To catch the dawn afloat upon the land!
– Hills, slung forth broadly and gauntly everywhere,
Not crampt in their foundations, pushing wide
Rich outspreads of the vineyards and the corn
(As if they entertained i' the name of France),   445
While, down their straining sides, streamed manifest

A soil as red as Charlemagne's knightly blood,
To consecrate the verdure. Some one said,
'Marseilles!' And lo, the city of Marseilles,
With all her ships behind her, and beyond,   450
The scimitar of ever-shining sea
For right-hand use, bared blue against the sky!

That night we spent between the purple heaven
And purple water: I think Marian slept;
But I, as a dog a-watch for his master's foot,   455
Who cannot sleep or eat before he hears,
I sat upon the deck and watched the night
And listened through the stars for Italy.
Those marriage-bells I spoke of, sounded far,
As some child's go-cart in the street beneath   460
To a dying man who will not pass the day,
And knows it, holding by a hand he loves.
I too sat quiet, satisfied with death,
Sat silent: I could hear my own soul speak,
And had my friend, – for Nature comes sometimes   465
And says, 'I am ambassador for God.'
I felt the wind soft from the land of souls;
The old miraculous mountains heaved in sight,
One straining past another along the shore,
The way of grand dull Odyssean ghosts,   470
Athirst to drink the cool blue wine of seas
And stare on voyagers. Peak pushing peak
They stood: I watched, beyond that Tyrian belt
Of intense sea betwixt them and the ship,
Down all their sides the misty olive-woods   475
Dissolving in the weak congenial moon
And still disclosing some brown convent-tower
That seems as if it grew from some brown rock,
Or many a little lighted village, dropt
Like a fallen star upon so high a point,   480
You wonder what can keep it in its place
From sliding headlong with the waterfalls
Which powder all the myrtle and orange groves
With spray of silver. Thus my Italy
Was stealing on us. Genoa broke with day,   485

The Doria's long pale palace striking out,
From green hills in advance of the white town,
A marble finger dominant to ships,
Seen glimmering through the uncertain grey of dawn.

But then I did not think, 'my Italy,'   490
I thought, 'my father!' O my father's house,
Without his presence! – Places are too much
Or else too little, for immortal man, –
Too little, when love's May o'ergrows the ground,
Too much, when that luxuriant robe of green   495
Is rustling to our ankles in dead leaves.
'Tis only good to be or here or there,
Because we had a dream on such a stone,
Or this or that, – but, once being wholly waked
And come back to the stone without the dream,   500
We trip upon 't, – alas, and hurt ourselves;
Or else it falls on us and grinds us flat,
The heaviest grave-stone on this buying earth.
– But while I stood and mused, a quiet touch
Fell light upon my arm, and turning round,   505
A pair of moistened eyes convicted mine.
'What, Marian! is the babe astir so soon?'
'He sleeps,' she answered; 'I have crept up thrice,
And seen you sitting, standing, still at watch.
I thought it did you good till now, but now' . . .   510
'But now,' I said, 'you leave the child alone.'
'And you're alone,' she answered, – and she looked
As if I too were something. Sweet the help
Of one we have helped! Thanks, Marian, for such help.

I found a house at Florence[182] on the hill   515
Of Bellosguardo. 'Tis a tower which keeps
A post of double-observation o'er
The valley of Arno (holding as a hand
The outspread city) straight toward Fiesole
And Mount Morello and the setting sun,   520
The Vallombrosan mountains opposite,
Which sunrise fills as full as crystal cups
Turned red to the brim because their wine is red.

No sun could die nor yet be born unseen
By dwellers at my villa: morn and eve   525
Were magnified before us in the pure
Illimitable space and pause of sky,
Intense as angels' garments blanched with God,
Less blue than radiant. From the outer wall
Of the garden drops the mystic floating grey   530
Of olive trees (with interruptions green
From maize and vine), until 'tis caught and torn
Upon the abrupt black line of cypresses
Which signs the way to Florence. Beautiful
The city lies along the ample vale,   535
Cathedral, tower and palace, piazza and street,
The river trailing like a silver cord
Through all, and curling loosely, both before
And after, over the whole stretch of land
Sown whitely up and down its opposite slopes   540
With farms and villas.
               Many weeks had passed,
No word was granted. – Last, a letter came
From Vincent Carrington: – 'My dear Miss Leigh,
You've been as silent as a poet should,
When any other man is sure to speak.   545
If sick, if vexed, if dumb, a silver piece
Will split a man's tongue, – straight he speaks and says,
"Received that cheque." But you! . . . I send you funds
To Paris, and you make no sign at all.
Remember I'm responsible and wait   550
A sign of you, Miss Leigh.
               'Meantime your book
Is eloquent as if you were not dumb;
And common critics, ordinarily deaf
To such fine meanings, and, like deaf men, loath
To seem deaf, answering chance-wise, yes or no,   555
"It must be," or "it must not," (most pronounced
When least convinced), pronounce for once aright:
You'd think they really heard, – and so they do . . .
The burr of three or four who really hear
And praise your book aright: Fame's smallest trump   560
Is a great ear-trumpet for the deaf as posts,

No other being effective. Fear not, friend;
We think here you have written a good book,
And you, a woman! It was in you – yes,
I felt 'twas in you: yet I doubted half   565
If that od-force of German Reichenbach,
Which still from female finger-tips burns blue,
Could strike out as our masculine white heats
To quicken a man. Forgive me. All my heart
Is quick with yours since, just a fortnight since,   570
I read your book and loved it.
                'Will you love
My wife, too? Here's my secret I might keep
A month more from you! but I yield it up
Because I know you'll write the sooner for 't,
Most women (of your height even) counting love   575
Life's only serious business. Who's my wife
That shall be in a month, you ask? nor guess?
Remember what a pair of topaz eyes
You once detected, turned against the wall,
That morning in my London painting-room;   580
The face half-sketched, and slurred; the eyes alone!
But you . . . you caught them up with yours, and said
"Kate Ward's eyes, surely." – Now I own the truth:
I had thrown them there to keep them safe from Jove,
They would so naughtily find out their way   585
To both the heads of both my Danaës
Where just it made me mad to look at them.
Such eyes! I could not paint or think of eyes
But those, – and so I flung them into paint
And turned them to the wall's care. Aye, but now   590
I've let them out, my Kate's: I've painted her,
(I'll change my style and leave mythologies)
The whole sweet face; it looks upon my soul
Like a face on water, to beget itself.
A half-length portrait, in a hanging cloak   595
Like one you wore once; 'tis a little frayed, –
I pressed too for the nude harmonious arm –
But she, she'd have her way, and have her cloak;
She said she could be like you only so,
And would not miss the fortune. Ah, my friend,   600

You'll write and say she shall not miss your love
Through meeting mine? in faith, she would not change.
She has your books by heart more than my words,
And quotes you up against me till I'm pushed
Where, three months since, her eyes were: nay, in fact,   605
Nought satisfied her but to make me paint
Your last book folded in her dimpled hands
Instead of my brown palette as I wished,
And, grant me, the presentment had been newer;
She'd grant me nothing: I compounded for   610
The naming of the wedding-day next month,
And gladly too. 'Tis pretty, to remark
How women can love women of your sort,
And tie their hearts with love-knots to your feet,
Grow insolent about you against men   615
And put us down by putting up the lip,
As if a man, – there *are* such, let us own,
Who write not ill, – remains a man, poor wretch,
While you – ! Write weaker than Aurora Leigh,
And there'll be women who believe of you   620
(Besides my Kate) that if you walked on sand
You would not leave a footprint.

                  'Are you put
To wonder by my marriage, like poor Leigh?
"Kate Ward!" he said. "Kate Ward!" he said anew.
"I thought . . . ." he said, and stopped, – "I did not think . . . "
And then he dropped to silence.

                  'Ah, he's changed.   626
I had not seen him, you're aware, for long,
But went of course. I have not touched on this
Through all this letter, – conscious of your heart,
And writing lightlier for the heavy fact,   630
As clocks are voluble with lead.

                'How poor,
To say I'm sorry! dear Leigh, dearest Leigh.
In those old days of Shropshire, – pardon me, –
When he and you fought many a field of gold
On what you should do, or you should not do,   635
Make bread or verses (it just came to that),
I thought you'd one day draw a silken peace

Through a golden ring. I thought so: foolishly,
The event proved, – for you went more opposite
To each other, month by month, and year by year,   640
Until this happened. God knows best, we say,
But hoarsely. When the fever took him first,
Just after I had writ to you in France,
They tell me Lady Waldemar mixed drinks
And counted grains, like any salaried nurse,   645
Excepting that she wept too. Then Lord Howe,
You're right about Lord Howe, Lord Howe's a trump,
And yet, with such in his hand, a man like Leigh
May lose as *he* does. There's an end to all,
Yes, even this letter, though this second sheet   650
May find you doubtful. Write a word for Kate:
She reads my letters always, like a wife,
And if she sees her name, I'll see her smile
And share the luck. So, bless you, friend of two!
I will not ask you what your feeling is   655
At Florence with my pictures; I can hear
Your heart a-flutter over the snow-hills:
And, just to pace the Pitti [183] with you once,
I'd give a half-hour of tomorrow's walk
With Kate . . . I think so. Vincent Carrington.'   660

The noon was hot; the air scorched like the sun
And was shut out. The closed persiani threw
Their long-scored shadows on my villa-floor,
And interlined the golden atmosphere
Straight, still, – across the pictures on the wall,   665
The statuette on the console (of young Love
And Psyche made one marble by a kiss),
The low couch where I leaned, the table near,
The vase of lilies Marian pulled last night
(Each green leaf and each white leaf ruled in black   670
As if for writing some new text of fate),
And the open letter, rested on my knee,
But there the lines swerved, trembled, though I sat
Untroubled, plainly, reading it again
And three times. Well, he's married; that is clear.   675
No wonder that he's married, nor much more

That Vincent's therefore 'sorry.' Why, of course
The lady nursed him when he was not well,
Mixed drinks, – unless nepenthe[184] was the drink
'Twas scarce worth telling. But a man in love   680
Will see the whole sex in his mistress' hood,
The prettier for its lining of fair rose,
Although he catches back and says at last,
'I'm sorry.' Sorry. Lady Waldemar
At prettiest, under the said hood, preserved   685
From such a light as I could hold to her face
To flare its ugly wrinkles out to shame,
Is scarce a wife for Romney, as friends judge,
Aurora Leigh or Vincent Carrington,
That's plain. And if he's 'conscious of my heart' . . . 690
It may be natural, though the phrase is strong
(One's apt to use strong phrases, being in love);
And even that stuff of 'fields of gold,' 'gold rings,'
And what he 'thought,' poor Vincent! what he 'thought,'
May never mean enough to ruffle me.   695
– Why, this room stifles. Better burn than choke;
Best have air, air, although it comes with fire, –
Throw open blinds and windows to the noon
And take a blister on my brow instead
Of this dead weight! best, perfectly be stunned   700
By those insufferable cicale, sick
And hoarse with rapture of the summer-heat,
That sing, like poets, till their hearts break, – sing
Till men say, 'It's too tedious.'
                              Books succeed,
And lives fail. Do I feel it so, at last?   705
Kate loves a worn-out cloak for being like mine,
While I live self-despised for being myself,
And yearn toward some one else, who yearns away
From what he is, in his turn. Strain a step
For ever, yet gain no step? Are we such,   710
We cannot, with our admirations even,
Our tip-toe aspirations, touch a thing
That's higher than we? is all a dismal flat,
And God alone above each, as the sun
O'er level lagunes, to make them shine and stink, –   715

Laying stress upon us with immediate flame,
While we respond with our miasmal fog
And call it mounting higher because we grow
More highly fatal?
            Tush, Aurora Leigh!
You wear your sackcloth looped in Caesar's way   720
And brag your failings as mankind's. Be still.
There *is* what's higher, in this very world,
Than you can live, or catch at. Stand aside,
And look at others – instance little Kate!
She'll make a perfect wife for Carrington.   725
She always has been looking round the earth
For something good and green to alight upon
And nestle into, with those soft-winged eyes,
Subsiding now beneath his manly hand
'Twixt trembling lids of inexpressive joy.   730
I will not scorn her, after all, too much,
That so much she should love me: a wise man
Can pluck a leaf, and find a lecture in 't;
And I, too, . . . God has made me, – I've a heart
That's capable of worship, love, and loss;   735
We say the same of Shakespeare's. I'll be meek
And learn to reverence, even this poor myself.

The book, too – pass it. 'A good book,' says he,
'And you a woman.' I had laughed at that,
But long since. I'm a woman, – it is true;   740
Alas, and woe to us, when we feel it most!
Then, least care have we for the crowns and goals
And compliments on writing our good books.

The book has some truth in it, I believe,
And truth outlives pain, as the soul does life.   745
I know we talk our Phaedons[185] to the end,
Through all the dismal faces that we make,
O'er-wrinkled with dishonouring agony
From decomposing drugs. I have written truth,
And I a woman, – feebly – partially,   750
Inaptly in presentation, Romney'll add,
Because a woman. For the truth itself,

That's neither man's nor woman's, but just God's,
None else has reason to be proud of truth:
Himself will see it sifted, disenthralled,   755
And kept upon the height and in the light,
As far as and no farther than 'tis truth;
For, now He has left off calling firmaments
And strata, flowers and creatures, very good,
He says it still of truth, which is His own.   760

Truth, so far, in my book; – the truth which draws
Through all things upwards, – that a twofold world
Must go to a perfect cosmos. Natural things
And spiritual, – who separates those two
In art, in morals, or the social drift,   765
Tears up the bond of nature and brings death,
Paints futile pictures, writes unreal verse,
Leads vulgar days, deals ignorantly with men,
Is wrong, in short, at all points. We divide
This apple of life, and cut it through the pips, –   770
The perfect round which fitted Venus' hand
Has perished utterly as if we ate
Both halves: without the spiritual, observe,
The natural's impossible, – no form,
No motion: without sensuous, spiritual   775
Is inappreciable, – no beauty or power:
And in this twofold sphere the twofold man
(For still the artist is intensely a man)
Holds firmly by the natural, to reach
The spiritual beyond it, – fixes still   780
The type with mortal vision, to pierce through,
With eyes immortal, to the antetype
Some call the ideal, – better called the real,
And certain to be called so presently
When things shall have their names. Look long enough   785
On any peasant's face here, coarse and lined,
You'll catch Antinous[186] somewhere in that clay,
As perfect featured as he yearns at Rome
From marble pale with beauty; then persist,
And, if your apprehension's competent,   790
You'll find some fairer angel at his back,

526

As much exceeding him as he the boor,
And pushing him with empyreal disdain
For ever out of sight. Aye, Carrington
Is glad of such a creed: an artist must, 795
Who paints a tree, a leaf, a common stone
With just his hand, and finds it suddenly
A-piece with and conterminous to his soul.
Why else do these things move him, leaf, or stone?
The bird's not moved, that pecks at a spring-shoot; 800
Nor yet the horse, before a quarry a-graze:
But man, the twofold creature, apprehends
The twofold manner, in and outwardly,
And nothing in the world comes single to him,
A mere itself, – cup, column, or candlestick, 805
All patterns of what shall be in the Mount;
The whole temporal show related royally,
And built up to eterne significance
Through the open arms of God. 'There's nothing great
Nor small,' has said a poet of our day, 810
Whose voice will ring beyond the curfew of eve
And not be thrown out by the matin's bell:
And truly, I reiterate, nothing's small!
No lily-muffled hum of a summer-bee,
But finds some coupling with the spinning stars; 815
No pebble at your foot, but proves a sphere;
No chaffinch, but implies the cherubim;
And (glancing on my own thin, veinèd wrist),
In such a little tremor of the blood
The whole strong clamour of a vehement soul 820
Doth utter itself distinct. Earth's crammed with heaven,
And every common bush afire with God;
But only he who sees, takes off his shoes,
The rest sit round it and pluck blackberries,
And daub their natural faces unaware 825
More and more from the first similitude.

Truth, so far, in my book! a truth which draws
From all things upward. I, Aurora, still
Have felt it hound me through the wastes of life
As Jove did Io; and, until that Hand 830

Shall overtake me wholly and, on my head
Lay down its large unfluctuating peace,
The feverish gad-fly pricks me up and down.
It must be. Art's the witness of what Is
Behind this show. If this world's show were all,   835
Then imitation would be all in Art;
There, Jove's hand gripes us! – For we stand here, we,
If genuine artists, witnessing for God's
Complete, consummate, undivided work;
– That every natural flower which grows on earth   840
Implies a flower upon the spiritual side,
Substantial, archetypal, all a-glow
With blossoming causes, – not so far away,
But we, whose spirit-sense is somewhat cleared,
May catch at something of the bloom and breath, –   845
Too vaguely apprehended, though indeed
Still apprehended, consciously or not,
And still transferred to picture, music, verse,
For thrilling audient and beholding souls
By signs and touches which are known to souls.   850
How known, they know not, – why, they cannot find,
So straight call out on genius, say, 'A man
Produced this,' – when much rather they should say,
' 'Tis insight and he saw this.'
                                        Thus is Art
Self-magnified in magnifying a truth   855
Which, fully recognised, would change the world
And shift its morals. If a man could feel,
Not one day, in the artist's ecstasy,
But every day, feast, fast, or working-day,
The spiritual significance burn through   860
The hieroglyphic of material shows,
Henceforward he would paint the globe with wings,
And reverence fish and fowl, the bull, the tree,
And even his very body as a man, –
Which now he counts so vile, that all the towns   865
Make offal of their daughters for its use,
On summer-nights, when God is sad in heaven
To think what goes on in his recreant world
He made quite other; while that moon He made

To shine there, at the first love's covenant,⠀⠀⠀⠀⠀⠀870
Shines still, convictive as a marriage-ring
Before adulterous eyes.
⠀⠀⠀⠀⠀⠀⠀⠀⠀⠀⠀⠀How sure it is,
That, if we say a true word, instantly
We feel 'tis God's, not ours, and pass it on
As bread at sacrament we taste and pass⠀⠀⠀⠀⠀⠀875
Nor handle for a moment, as indeed
We dared to set up any claim to such!
And I – my poem, – let my readers talk.
I'm closer to it – I can speak as well:
I'll say with Romney, that the book is weak,⠀⠀⠀⠀⠀⠀880
The range uneven, the points of sight obscure,
The music interrupted.
⠀⠀⠀⠀⠀⠀⠀⠀⠀⠀⠀⠀Let us go.
The end of woman (or of man, I think)
Is not a book. Alas, the best of books
Is but a word in Art, which soon grows cramped,⠀⠀⠀⠀⠀⠀885
Stiff, dubious-statured with the weight of years,
And drops an accent or digamma[187] down
Some cranny of unfathomable time,
Beyond the critic's reaching. Art itself,
We've called the larger life, must feel the soul⠀⠀⠀⠀⠀⠀890
Live past it. For more's felt than is perceived,
And more's perceived than can be interpreted,
And Love strikes higher with his lambent flame
Than Art can pile the faggots.
⠀⠀⠀⠀⠀⠀⠀⠀⠀⠀⠀⠀Is it so?
When Jove's hand meets us with composing touch,⠀⠀⠀⠀⠀⠀895
And when at last we are hushed and satisfied,
Then Io does not call it truth, but love?
Well, well! my father was an Englishman:
My mother's blood in me is not so strong
That I should bear this stress of Tuscan noon⠀⠀⠀⠀⠀⠀900
And keep my wits. The town, there, seems to seethe
In this Medaean boil-pot of the sun,[188]
And all the patient hills are bubbling round
As if a prick would leave them flat. Does heaven
Keep far off, not to set us in a blaze?⠀⠀⠀⠀⠀⠀905
Not so, – let drag your fiery fringes, heaven,

And burn us up to quiet. Ah, we know
Too much here, not to know what's best for peace;
We have too much light here, not to want more fire
To purify and end us. We talk, talk, 910
Conclude upon divine philosophies,
And get the thanks of men for hopeful books,
Whereat we take our own life up, and . . . pshaw!
Unless we piece it with another's life
(A yard of silk to carry out our lawn) 915
As well suppose my little handkerchief
Would cover Samminiato, church and all,
If out I threw it past the cypresses,
As, in this ragged, narrow life of mine,
Contain my own conclusions.

                       But at least 920
We'll shut up the persiani and sit down,
And when my head's done aching, in the cool,
Write just a word to Kate and Carrington.
May joy be with them! she has chosen well,
And he not ill.

                I should be glad, I think, 925
Except for Romney. Had *he* married Kate,
I surely, surely, should be very glad.
This Florence sits upon me easily,
With native air and tongue. My graves are calm,
And do not too much hurt me. Marian's good, 930
Gentle and loving, – lets me hold the child,
Or drags him up the hills to find me flowers
And fill these vases ere I'm quite awake, –
The grandiose red tulips, which grow wild,
Or Dante's purple lilies, which he blew 935
To a larger bubble with his prophet breath,
Or one of those tall flowering reeds that stand
In Arno, like a sheaf of sceptres left
By some remote dynasty of dead gods
To suck the stream for ages and get green, 940
And blossom wheresoe'er a hand divine
Had warmed the place with ichor. Such I find
At early morning laid across my bed,
And wake up pelted with a childish laugh

Which even Marian's low precipitous 'hush'   945
Has vainly interposed to put away, –
While I, with shut eyes, smile and motion for
The dewy kiss that's very sure to come
From mouth and cheeks, the whole child's face at once
Dissolved on mine, – as if a nosegay burst   950
Its string with the weight of roses overblown,
And dropt upon me. Surely I should be glad.
The little creature almost loves me now,
And calls my name, 'Alola,' stripping off
The rs like thorns, to make it smooth enough   955
To take between his dainty, milk-fed lips,
God love him! I should certainly be glad,
Except, God help me, that I'm sorrowful
Because of Romney.
                    Romney, Romney! Well,
This grows absurd! – too like a tune that runs   960
I' the head, and forces all things in the world,
Wind, rain, the creaking gnat, or stuttering fly,
To sing itself and vex you,   yet perhaps
A paltry tune you never fairly liked,
Some 'I'd be a butterfly,' or 'C'est l'amour':   965
We're made so, – not such tyrants to ourselves
But still we are slaves to nature. Some of us
Are turned, too, overmuch like some poor verse
With a trick of ritournelle: the same thing goes
And comes back ever.
                    Vincent Carrington   970
Is 'sorry,' and I'm sorry; but *he's* strong
To mount from sorrow to his heaven of love,
And when he says at moments, 'Poor, poor Leigh,
Who'll never call his own so true a heart,
So fair a face even,' – he must quickly lose   975
The pain of pity, in the blush he makes
By his very pitying eyes. The snow, for him,
Has fallen in May and finds the whole earth warm,
And melts at the first touch of the green grass.

But Romney, – he has chosen, after all.   980
I think he has as excellent a sun

To see by, as most others, and perhaps
Has scarce seen really worse than some of us
When all's said. Let him pass. I'm not too much
A woman, not to be a man for once   985
And bury all my Dead like Alaric,
Depositing the treasures of my soul
In this drained water-course, then letting flow
The river of life again with commerce-ships
And pleasure-barges full of silks and songs.   990
Blow, winds, and help us.
                              Ah, we mock ourselves
With talking of the winds; perhaps as much
With other resolutions. How it weighs,
This hot, sick air! and how I covet here
The Dead's provision on the river-couch,   995
With silver curtains drawn on tinkling rings!
Or else their rest in quiet crypts, – laid by
From heat and noise; – from those cicale, say,
And this more vexing heart-beat.
                                  So it is:
We covet for the soul, the body's part,   1000
To die and rot. Even so, Aurora, ends
Our aspiration who bespoke our place
So far in the east. The occidental flats
Had fed us fatter, therefore? we have climbed
Where herbage ends? we want the beast's part now   1005
And tire of the angel's? – Men define a man,
The creature who stands front-ward to the stars,
The creature who looks inward to himself,
The tool-wright, laughing creature. 'Tis enough:
We'll say instead, the inconsequent creature, man,   1010
For that's his specialty. What creature else
Conceives the circle, and then walks the square?
Loves things proved bad, and leaves a thing proved good?
You think the bee makes honey half a year,
To loathe the comb in winter and desire   1015
The little ant's food rather? But a man –
Note men! – they are but women after all,
As women are but Auroras! – there are men
Born tender, apt to pale at a trodden worm,

Who paint for pastime, in their favourite dream,   1020
Spruce auto-vestments flowered with crocus-flames.
There are, too, who believe in hell, and lie;
There are, too, who believe in heaven, and fear:
There are, who waste their souls in working out
Life's problem on these sands betwixt two tides,   1025
Concluding, – 'Give us the oyster's part, in death.'

Alas, long-suffering and most patient God,
Thou needst be surelier God to bear with us
Than even to have made us! Thou aspire, aspire
From henceforth for me! Thou who hast Thyself,   1030
Endured this fleshhood, knowing how as a soaked
And sucking vesture, it can drag us down
And choke us in the melancholy Deep,
Sustain me, that with Thee I walk these waves,
Resisting! – breathe me upward, Thou in me   1035
Aspiring who art the way, the truth, the life, –
That no truth henceforth seem indifferent,
No way to truth laborious, and no life,
Not even this life I live, intolerable!

The days went by. I took up the old days,   1040
With all their Tuscan pleasures worn and spoiled,
Like some lost book we dropped in the long grass
On such a happy summer-afternoon
When last we read it with a loving friend,
And find in autumn when the friend is gone,   1045
The grass cut short, the weather changed, too late,
And stare at, as at something wonderful
For sorrow, – thinking how two hands before
Had held up what is left to only one,
And how we smiled when such a vehement nail   1050
Impressed the tiny dint here which presents
This verse in fire for ever. Tenderly
And mournfully I lived. I knew the birds
And insects, – which look fathered by the flowers
And emulous of their hues: I recognised   1055
The moths, with that great overpoise of wings
Which makes a mystery of them how at all

533

They can stop flying: butterflies, that bear
Upon their blue wings such red embers round,
They seem to scorch the blue air into holes   1060
Each flight they take: and fire-flies, that suspire
In short soft lapses of transported flame
Across the tingling Dark, while overhead
The constant and inviolable stars
Outburn those light-of-love: melodious owls   1065
(If music had but one note and was sad,
'Twould sound just so); and all the silent swirl
Of bats that seem to follow in the air
Some grand circumference of a shadowy dome
To which we are blind: and then the nightingales,   1070
Which pluck our heart across a garden-wall
(When walking in the town) and carry it
So high into the bowery almond-trees
We tremble and are afraid, and feel as if
The golden flood of moonlight unaware   1075
Dissolved the pillars of the steady earth
And made it less substantial. And I knew
The harmless opal snakes, the large-mouthed frogs,
(Those noisy vaunters of their shallow streams);
And lizards, the green lightnings of the wall,   1080
Which, if you sit down quiet, nor sigh loud,
Will flatter you and take you for a stone,
And flash familiarly about your feet
With such prodigious eyes in such small heads! –
I knew them (though they had somewhat dwindled from   1085
My childish imagery), and kept in mind
How last I sat among them equally,
In fellowship and mateship, as a child
Feels equal still toward insect, beast, and bird,
Before the Adam in him has forgone   1090
All privilege of Eden, – making friends
And talk with such a bird or such a goat,
And buying many a two-inch-wide rush-cage
To let out the caged cricket on a tree,
Saying, 'Oh, my dear grillino, were you cramped?   1095
And are you happy with the ilex-leaves?
And do you love me who have let you go?

Say *yes* in singing, and I'll understand.'

But now the creatures all seemed farther off,
No longer mine, nor like me, only *there*,   1100
A gulf between us. I could yearn indeed,
Like other rich men, for a drop of dew
To cool this heat, – a drop of the early dew,
The irrecoverable child-innocence
(Before the heart took fire and withered life)   1105
When childhood might pair equally with birds;
But now . . . the birds were grown too proud for us!
Alas, the very sun forbids the dew.

And I, I had come back to an empty nest,
Which every bird's too wise for. How I heard   1110
My father's step on that deserted ground,
His voice along that silence, as he told
The names of bird and insect, tree and flower,
And all the presentations of the stars
Across Valdarno, interposing still   1115
'My child,' 'my child.' When fathers say 'my child,'
'Tis easier to conceive the universe,
And life's transitions down the steps of law.

I rode once to the little mountain-house
As fast as if to find my father there,   1120
But, when in sight of 't, within fifty yards,
I dropped my horse's bridle on his neck
And paused upon his flank. The house's front
Was cased with lingots of ripe Indian corn
In tesselated order and device   1125
Of golden patterns, not a stone of wall
Uncovered – not an inch of room to grow
A vine-leaf. The old porch had disappeared;
And right in the open doorway sat a girl
At plaiting straws, her black hair strained away   1130
To a scarlet kerchief caught beneath her chin
In Tuscan fashion, – her full ebon eyes,
Which looked too heavy to be lifted so,
Still dropped and lifted toward the mulberry-tree

On which the lads were busy with their staves   1135
In shout and laughter, stripping every bough
As bare as winter, of those summer leaves
My father had not changed for all the silk
In which the ugly silkworms hide themselves.
Enough. My horse recoiled before my heart;   1140
I turned the rein abruptly. Back we went
As fast, to Florence.
                    That was trial enough
Of graves. I would not visit, if I could,
My father's, or my mother's any more,
To see if stone-cutter or lichen beat   1145
So early in the race, or throw my flowers,
Which could not out-smell heaven or sweeten earth.
They live too far above, that I should look
So far below to find them: let me think
That rather they are visiting my grave,   1150
Called life here (undeveloped yet to life),
And that they drop upon me, now and then,
For token or for solace, some small weed
Least odorous of the growths of paradise,
To spare such pungent scents as kill with joy.   1155

My old Assunta, too, was dead, was dead –
O land of all men's past! for me alone,
It would not mix its tenses. I was past,
It seemed, like others, – only not in heaven.
And many a Tuscan eve I wandered down   1160
The cypress alley like a restless ghost
That tries its feeble ineffectual breath
Upon its own charred funeral-brands put out
Too soon, – where black and stiff stood up the trees
Against the broad vermilion of the skies.   1165
Such skies! – all clouds abolished in a sweep
Of God's skirt, with a dazzle to ghosts and men,
As down I went, saluting on the bridge
The hem of such before 'twas caught away
Beyond the peaks of Lucca. Underneath,   1170
The river, just escaping from the weight
Of that intolerable glory, ran

In acquiescent shadow murmurously;
While up beside it, streamed the festa-folk
With fellow-murmurs from their feet and fans,   1175
And *issimo* and *ino* and sweet poise
Of vowels in their pleasant scandalous talk;
Returning from the grand-duke's dairy-farm
Before the trees grew dangerous at eight
(For, 'trust no tree by moonlight,' Tuscans say),   1180
To eat their ice at Donay's tenderly, –
Each lovely lady close to a cavalier
Who holds her dear fan while she feeds her smile
On meditative spoonfuls of vanille
And listens to his hot breathed vows of love   1185
Enough to thaw her cream and scorch his beard.

'Twas little matter. I could pass them by
Indifferently, not fearing to be known.
No danger of being wrecked upon a friend,
And forced to take an iceberg for an isle!   1190
The very English, here, must wait and learn
To hang the cobweb of their gossip out
To catch a fly. I'm happy. It's sublime,
This perfect solitude of foreign lands!
To be, as if you had not been till then,   1195
And were then, simply that you chose to be:
To spring up, not be brought forth from the ground,
Like grasshoppers at Athens, and skip thrice
Before a woman makes a pounce on you
And plants you in her hair! – possess, yourself,   1200
A new world all alive with creatures new,
New sun, new moon, new flowers, new people – ah,
And be possessed by none of them! no right
In one, to call your name, enquire your where,
Or what you think of Mister Some-one's book,   1205
Or Mister Other's marriage or decease,
Or how's the headache which you had last week,
Or why you look so pale still, since it's gone?
– Such most surprising riddance of one's life
Comes next one's death; 'tis disembodiment   1210
Without the pang. I marvel, people choose

To stand stock-still like fakirs, till the moss
Grows on them and they cry out, self-admired,
'How verdant and how virtuous!' Well, I'm glad:
Or should be, if grown foreign to myself   1215
As surely as to others.
              Musing so,
I walked the narrow unrecognising streets,
Where many a palace-front peers gloomily
Through stony vizors iron-barred (prepared
Alike, should foe or lover pass that way,   1220
For guest or victim), and came wandering out
Upon the churches with mild open doors
And plaintive wail of vespers, where a few,
Those chiefly women, sprinkled round in blots
Upon the dusky pavement, knelt and prayed   1225
Toward the altar's silver glory. Oft a ray
(I liked to sit and watch) would tremble out,
Just touch some face more lifted, more in need
(Of course a woman's), – while I dreamed a tale
To fit its fortunes. There was one who looked   1230
As if the earth had suddenly grown too large
For such a little humpbacked thing as she;
The pitiful black kerchief round her neck
Sole proof she had had a mother. One, again,
Looked sick for love, – seemed praying some soft saint   1235
To put more virtue in the new fine scarf
She spent a fortnight's meals on, yesterday,
That cruel Gigi might return his eyes
From Giuliana. There was one, so old,
So old, to kneel grew easier than to stand, –   1240
So solitary, she accepts at last
Our Lady for her gossip, and frets on
Against the sinful world which goes its rounds
In marrying and being married, just the same
As when 'twas almost good and had the right   1245
(Her Gian alive, and she herself eighteen).
And yet, now even, if Madonna willed,
She'd win a tern in Thursday's lottery
And better all things. Did she dream for nought,
That, boiling cabbage for the fast-day's soup,   1250

It smelt like blessed entrails? such a dream
For nought? would sweetest Mary cheat her so,
And lose that certain candle, straight and white
As any fair grand-duchess in her teens,
Which otherwise should flare here in a week?   1255
Benigna sis,[189] thou beauteous Queen of heaven!'

I sat there musing, and imagining
Such utterance from such faces: poor blind souls
That writhe toward heaven along the devil's trail, –
Who knows, I thought, but He may stretch His hand   1260
And pick them up? 'tis written in the Book
He heareth the young ravens when they cry,
And yet they cry for carrion. – O my God,
And we, who make excuses for the rest,
We do it in our measure. Then I knelt,   1265
And dropped my head upon the pavement too,
And prayed, since I was foolish in desire
Like other creatures, craving offal-food,
That He would stop His ears to what I said,
And only listen to the run and beat   1270
Of this poor, passionate, helpless blood –
                                        And then
I lay, and spoke not: but He heard in heaven.

So many Tuscan evenings passed the same.
I could not lose a sunset on the bridge,
And would not miss a vigil in the church,   1275
And liked to mingle with the outdoor crowd
So strange and gay and ignorant of my face,
For men you know not, are as good as trees.
And only once, at the Santissima,
I almost chanced upon a man I knew,   1280
Sir Blaise Delorme. He saw me certainly,
And somewhat hurried, as he crossed himself,
The smoothness of the action, – then half bowed,
But only half, and merely to my shade,
I slipped so quick behind the porphyry plinth   1285
And left him dubious if 'twas really I,
Or peradventure Satan's usual trick

To keep a mounting saint uncanonised.
But he was safe for that time, and I too;
The argent angels in the altar-flare   1290
Absorbed his soul next moment. The good man!
In England we were scarce acquaintances,
That here in Florence he should keep my thought
Beyond the image on his eye, which came
And went: and yet his thought disturbed my life: 1295
For, after that, I oftener sat at home
On evenings, watching how they fined themselves
With gradual conscience to a perfect night,
Until the moon, diminished to a curve,
Lay out there like a sickle for His hand   1300
Who cometh down at last to reap the earth.
At such times, ended seemed my trade of verse;
I feared to jingle bells upon my robe
Before the four-faced silent cherubim:
With God so near me, could I sing of God?   1305
I did not write, nor read, nor even think,
But sat absorbed amid the quickening glooms,
Most like some passive broken lump of salt
Dropped in by chance to a bowl of oenomel,
To spoil the drink a little and lose itself,   1310
Dissolving slowly, slowly, until lost.

Eighth Book

One eve it happened, when I sat alone,
Alone, upon the terrace of my tower,
A book upon my knees to counterfeit
The reading that I never read at all,
While Marian, in the garden down below,   5
Knelt by the fountain I could just hear thrill
The drowsy silence of the exhausted day,
And peeled a new fig from that purple heap
In the grass beside her, turning out the red
To feed her eager child (who sucked at it   10
With vehement lips across a gap of air
As he stood opposite, face and curls a-flame
With that last sun-ray, crying, 'give me, give,'
And stamping with imperious baby-feet,
We're all born princes) – something startled me, –   15
The laugh of sad and innocent souls, that breaks
Abruptly, as if frightened at itself.
'Twas Marian laughed. I saw her glance above
In sudden shame that I should hear her laugh,
And straightway dropped my eyes upon my book,   20
And knew, the first time, 'twas Boccaccio's [190] tale,
The Falcon's, of the lover who for love
Destroyed the best that loved him. Some of us
Do it still, and then we sit and laugh no more.
Laugh *you*, sweet Marian, – you've the right to laugh,   25
Since God Himself is for you, and a child!
For me there's somewhat less, – and so I sigh.

The heavens were making room to hold the night,
The sevenfold heavens unfolding all their gates
To let the stars out slowly (prophesied   30
In close-approaching advent, not discerned),
While still the cue-owls from the cypresses
Of the Poggio called and counted every pulse
Of the skyey palpitation. Gradually
The purple and transparent shadows slow   35

541

Had filled up the whole valley to the brim,
And flooded all the city, which you saw
As some drowned city in some enchanted sea,
Cut off from nature, – drawing you who gaze,
With passionate desire, to leap and plunge   40
And find a sea-king with a voice of waves,
And treacherous soft eyes, and slippery locks
You cannot kiss but you shall bring away
Their salt upon your lips. The duomo-bell
Strikes ten, as if it struck ten fathoms down,   45
So deep; and twenty churches answer it
The same, with twenty various instances.
Some gaslights tremble along squares and streets:
The Pitti's palace-front is drawn in fire;
And, past the quays, Maria Novella Place,   50
In which the mystic obelisks stand up
Triangular, pyramidal, each based
Upon its four-square brazen tortoises,
To guard that fair church, Buonarroti's Bride,
That stares out from her large blind dial-eyes,   55
(Her quadrant and armillary dials, black
With rhythms of many suns and moons), in vain
Enquiry for so rich a soul as his.
Methinks I have plunged, I see it all so clear . . .
And, O my heart, . . . the sea-king!
                         In my ears   60
The sound of waters. There he stood, my king!

I felt him, rather than beheld him. Up
I rose, as if he were my king indeed,
And then sat down, in trouble at myself,
And struggling for my woman's empery.   65
'Tis pitiful; but women are so made:
We'll die for you perhaps, – 'tis probable;
But we'll not spare you an inch of our full height:
We'll have our whole just stature, – five feet four,
Though laid out in our coffins: pitiful.   70
– 'You, Romney! – Lady Waldemar is here?'

He answered in a voice which was not his.
'I have her letter; you shall read it soon.

But first, I must be heard a little, I,
Who have waited long and travelled far for that,   75
Although you thought to have shut a tedious book
And farewell. Ah, you dog-eared such a page,
And here you find me.'
                    Did he touch my hand,
Or but my sleeve? I trembled, hand and foot, –
He must have touched me. – 'Will you sit?' I asked,   80
And motioned to a chair; but down he sat,
A little slowly, as a man in doubt,
Upon the couch beside me, – couch and chair
Being wheeled upon the terrace.
                    'You are come,
My cousin Romney? – this is wonderful.   85
But all is wonder on such summer-nights;
And nothing should surprise us any more,
Who see that miracle of stars. Behold.'

I signed above, where all the stars were out,
As if an urgent heat had started there   90
A secret writing from a sombre page,
A blank, last moment, crowded suddenly
With hurrying splendours.
                    'Then you do not know' –
He murmured.
                    'Yes, I know,' I said, 'I know.
I had the news from Vincent Carrington.   95
And yet I did not think you'd leave the work
In England, for so much even, – though of course
You'll make a work-day of your holiday,
And turn it to our Tuscan people's use, –
Who much need helping since the Austrian boar[191]   100
(So bold to cross the Alp to Lombardy
And dash his brute front unabashed against
The steep snow-bosses of that shield of God
Who soon shall rise in wrath and shake it clear),
Came hither also, raking up our grape   105
And olive-gardens with his tyrannous tusk,
And rolling on our maize with all his swine.'

*

'You had the news from Vincent Carrington,'
He echoed, – picking up the phrase beyond,
As if he knew the rest was merely talk   110
To fill a gap and keep out a strong wind;
'You had, then, Vincent's personal news?'

                                        'His own,
I answered. 'All that ruined world of yours
Seems crumbling into marriage. Carrington
Has chosen wisely.'

                        'Do you take it so?'   115
He cried, 'and is it possible at last' . . .
He paused there, – and then, inward to himself,
'Too much at last, too late! – yet certainly' . . .
(And there his voice swayed as an Alpine plank
That feels a passionate torrent underneath)   120
'The knowledge, had I known it first or last,
Could scarce have changed the actual case for *me*.
And best for *her*, at this time.'

                                Nay, I thought,
He loves Kate Ward, it seems, now, like a man,
Because he has married Lady Waldemar!   125
Ah, Vincent's letter said how Leigh was moved
To hear that Vincent was betrothed to Kate.
With what cracked pitchers go we to deep wells
In this world! Then I spoke, – 'I did not think,
My cousin, you had ever known Kate Ward.'   130

'In fact I never knew her. 'Tis enough
That Vincent did, and therefore he chose his wife
For other reasons than those topaz eyes
We've heard of. Not to undervalue them,
For all that. One takes up the world with eyes.'   135

– Including Romney Leigh, I thought again,
Albeit he knows them only by repute.
How vile must all men be, since *he*'s a man.

His deep pathetic voice, as if he guessed
I did not surely love him, took the word;   140
'You never got a letter from Lord Howe

A month back, dear Aurora?'

'None,' I said.

'I felt it was so,' he replied: 'yet, strange!
Sir Blaise Delorme has passed through Florence?'

'Aye,
By chance I saw him in Our Lady's church   145
(I saw him, mark you, but he saw not me),
Clean-washed in holy water from the count
Of things terrestrial, – letters, and the rest;
He had crossed us out together with his sins.
Aye, strange; but only strange that good Lord Howe   150
Preferred him to the post because of pauls.
For me I'm sworn never to trust a man –
At least with letters.'

'There were facts to tell,
To smooth with eye and accent. Howe supposed . . .
Well, well, no matter! there was dubious need;   155
You heard the news from Vincent Carrington.
And yet perhaps you had been startled less
To see me, dear Aurora, if you had read
That letter.'
– Now he sets me down as vexed.
I think I've draped myself in woman's pride   160
To a perfect purpose. Oh, I'm vexed, it seems!
My friend Lord Howe deputes his friend Sir Blaise
To break as softly as a sparrow's egg
That lets a bird out tenderly, the news
Of Romney's marriage to a certain saint;   165
To *smooth with eye and accent*, – indicate
His possible presence. Excellently well
You've played your part, my Lady Waldemar, –
As I've played mine.
'Dear Romney,' I began,
'You did not use, of old, to be so like   170
A Greek king coming from a taken Troy,
'Twas needful that precursors spread your path
With three-piled carpets, to receive your foot

And dull the sound of 't. For myself, be sure,
Although it frankly grinds the gravel here,   175
I still can bear it. Yet I'm sorry too
To lose this famous letter, which Sir Blaise
Has twisted to a lighter absently
To fire some holy taper: dear Lord Howe
Writes letters good for all things but to lose;   180
And many a flower of London gossipry
Has dropped wherever such a stem broke off.
Of course I feel that, lonely among my vines,
Where nothing's talked of, save the blight again,
And no more Chianti! Still the letter's use   185
As preparation . . . Did I start indeed?
Last night I started at a cochchafer,
And shook a half-hour after. Have you learnt
No more of women, 'spite of privilege,
Than still to take account too seriously   190
Of such weak flutterings? Why, we like it, sir,
We get our powers and our effects that way:
The trees stand stiff and still at time of frost,
If no wind tears them; but, let summer come,
When trees are happy, – and a breath avails   195
To set them trembling through a million leaves
In luxury of emotion. Something less
It takes to move a woman: let her start
And shake at pleasure, – nor conclude at yours,
The winter's bitter, – but the summer's green.'   200

He answered, 'Be the summer ever green
With you, Aurora! – though you sweep your sex
With somewhat bitter gusts from where you live
Above them, – whirling downward from your heights
Your very own pine-cones, in a grand disdain   205
Of the lowland burrs with which you scatter them.
So high and cold to others and yourself,
A little less to Romney were unjust,
And thus, I would not have you. Let it pass:
I feel content so. You can bear indeed   210
My sudden step beside you: but for me,
'Twould move me sore to hear your softened voice, –

Aurora's voice, – if softened unaware
In pity of what I am.'

           Ah friend, I thought,
As husband of the Lady Waldemar   215
You're granted very sorely pitiable!
And yet Aurora Leigh must guard her voice
From softening in the pity of your case,
As if from lie or licence. Certainly
We'll soak up all the slush and soil of life   220
With softened voices, ere we come to *you*.

At which I interrupted my own thought
And spoke out calmly. 'Let us ponder, friend,
Whate'er our state we must have made it first;
And though the thing displease us, aye, perhaps   225
Displease us warrantably, never doubt
That other states, thought possible once, and then
Rejected by the instinct of our lives,
If then adopted had displeased us more
Than this in which the choice, the will, the love,   230
Has stamped the honour of a patent act
From henceforth. What we choose may not be good,
But, that we choose it, proves it good for *us*
Potentially, fantastically, now
Or last year, rather than a thing we saw,   235
And saw no need for choosing. Moths will burn
Their wings, – which proves that light is good for moths,
Who else had flown not where they agonise.'

'Aye, light is good,' he echoed, and there paused;
And then abruptly, . . . 'Marian. Marian's well?'   240

I bowed my head but found no word. 'Twas hard
To speak of *her* to Lady Waldemar's
New husband. How much did he know, at last?
How much? how little? – He would take no sign,
But straight repeated, – 'Marian. Is she well?'   245

'She's well,' I answere.

She was there in sight
An hour back, but the night had drawn her home,
Where still I heard her in an upper room,
Her low voice singing to the child in bed,
Who restless with the summer-heat and play   250
And slumber snatched at noon, was long sometimes
In falling off, and took a score of songs
And mother-hushes, ere she saw him sound.

'She's well,' I answered.

      'Here?' he asked.

            'Yes, here.'

He stopped and sighed. 'That shall be presently,   255
But now this must be. I have words to say,
And would be alone to say them, I with you,
And no third troubling.'

       'Speak then,' I returned,
'She will not vex you.'

       At which, suddenly,
He turned his face upon me with its smile   260
As if to crush me. 'I have read your book,
Aurora.'

   'You have read it,' I replied,
'And I have writ it, – we have done with it.
And now the rest?'

     'The rest is like the first,'
He answered, – 'for the book is in my heart,   265
Lives in me, wakes in me, and dreams in me:
My daily bread tastes of it, – and my wine
Which has no smack of it, I pour it out,
It seems unnatural drinking.'

      Bitterly
I took the word up; 'Never waste your wine.   270
The book lived in me ere it lived in you;
I know it closer than another does,
And how it's foolish, feeble, and afraid,
And all unworthy so much compliment.
Beseech you, keep your wine, – and, when you drink,   275
Still wish some happier fortune to a friend,

Than even to have written a far better book.'

He answered gently, 'That is consequent:
The poet looks beyond the book he has made,
Or else he had not made it. If a man   280
Could make a man, he'd henceforth be a god
In feeling what a little thing is man:
It is not my case. And this special book,
I did not make it, to make light of it:
It stands above my knowledge, draws me up;   285
'Tis high to me. It may be that the book
Is not so high, but I so low, instead;
Still high to me. I mean no compliment:
I will not say there are not, young or old,
Male writers, aye, or female, let it pass,   290
Who'll write us richer and completer books.
A man may love a woman perfectly,
And yet by no means ignorantly maintain
A thousand women have not larger eyes:
Enough that she alone has looked at him   295
With eyes that, large or small, have won his soul.
And so, this book, Aurora, – so, your book.'

'Alas,' I answered, 'is it so, indeed?'
And then was silent.

              'Is it so, indeed,'
He echoed, 'that *alas* is all your word?'   300
I said, – 'I'm thinking of a far-off June,
When you and I, upon my birthday once,
Discoursed of life and art, with both untried.
I'm thinking, Romney, how 'twas morning then,
And now 'tis night.'

                 'And now,' he said, ' 'tis night.'   305

'I'm thinking,' I resumed, ''tis somewhat sad,
That if I had known, that morning in the dew,
My cousin Romney would have said such words
On such a night at close of many years,
In speaking of a future book of mine,   310
It would have pleased me better as a hope,

Than as an actual grace it can at all:
That's sad, I'm thinking.'

              'Aye,' he said, ' 'tis night.'

'And there,' I added lightly, 'are the stars!
And here, we'll talk of stars and not of books.'   315

'You have the stars,' he murmured, – 'it is well:
Be like them! shine, Aurora, on my dark,
Though high and cold and only like star,
And for this short night only, – you, who keep
The same Aurora of the bright June day   320
That withered up the flowers before my face,
And turned me from the garden evermore
Because I was not worthy. Oh, deserved,
Deserved! that I, who verily had not learnt
God's lesson half, attaining as a dunce   325
To obliterate good words with fractious thumbs
And cheat myself of the context, – I should push
Aside, with male ferocious impudence,
The world's Aurora who had conned her part
On the other side the leaf! ignore her so,   330
Because she was a woman and a queen,
And had no beard to bristle through her song,
My teacher, who has taught me with a book,
My Miriam, whose sweet mouth, when nearly drowned
I still heard singing on the shore! Deserved,   335
That here I should look up into the stars
And miss the glory' . . .

             'Can I understand?'
I broke in. 'You speak wildly, Romney Leigh,
Or I hear wildly. In that morning-time
We recollect, the roses were too red,   340
The trees too green, reproach too natural
If one should see not what the other saw:
And now, it's night, remember; we have shades
In place of colours; we are now grown cold,
And old, my cousin Romney. Pardon me, –   345
I'm very happy that you like my book,
And very sorry that I quoted back
A ten years' birthday. 'Twas so mad a thing

In any woman, I scarce marvel much
You took it for a venturous piece of spite,   350
Provoking such excuses as indeed
I cannot call you slack in.'
                          'Understand,'
He answered sadly, 'something, if but so.
This night is softer than an English day,
And men may well come hither when they're sick,   355
To draw in easier breath from larger air.
'Tis thus with me; I've come to you, – to you,
My Italy of women, just to breathe
My soul out once before you, ere I go,
As humble as God makes me at the last   360
(I thank Him), quite out of the way of men
And yours, Aurora, – like a punished child,
His cheeks all blurred with tears and naughtiness,
To silence in a corner. I am come
To speak, beloved' . . .
                          'Wisely, cousin Leigh,   365
And worthily of us both!'
                          'Yes, worthily;
For this time I must speak out and confess
That I, so truculent in assumption once,
So absolute in dogma, proud in aim,
And fierce in expectation, – I, who felt   370
The whole world tugging at my skirts for help,
As if no other man than I, could pull,
Nor woman, but I led her by the hand,
Nor cloth hold, but I had it in my coat,
Do know myself tonight for what I was   375
On that June-day, Aurora. Poor bright day,
Which meant the best . . . a woman and a rose,
And which I smote upon the cheek with words
Until it turned and rent me! Young you were,
That birthday, poet, but you talked the right: 380
While I, . . . I built up follies like a wall
To intercept the sunshine and your face.
Your face! that's worse.'
                          'Speak wisely, cousin Leigh.'

*

'Yes, wisely, dear Aurora, though too late:
But then, not wisely. I was heavy then,   385
And stupid, and distracted with the cries
Of tortured prisoners in the polished brass
Of that Phalarian bull,[192] society,
Which seems to bellow bravely like ten bulls
But, if you listen, moans and cries instead   390
Despairingly, like victims tossed and gored
And trampled by their hoofs. I heard the cries
Too close: I could not hear the angels lift
A fold of rustling air, nor what they said
To help my pity. I beheld the world   395
As one great famishing carnivorous mouth, –
A huge, deserted, callow, blind, bird Thing,
With piteous open beak that hurt my heart,
Till down upon the filthy ground I dropped,
And tore the violets up to get the worms.   400
Worms, worms, was all my cry: an open mouth,
A gross want, bread to fill it to the lips,
No more. That poor men narrowed their demands
To such an end, was virtue, I supposed,
Adjudicating that to see it so   405
Was reason. Oh, I did not push the case
Up higher, and ponder how it answers when
The rich take up the same cry for themselves,
Professing equally, – "An open mouth,
A gross need, food to fill us, and no more."   410
Why that's so far from virtue, only vice
Finds reason for 't! that makes libertines,
And slurs our cruel streets from end to end
With eighty thousand women in one smile,
Who only smile at night beneath the gas.   415
The body's satisfaction and no more,
Is used for argument against the soul's,
Here too; the want, here too, implies the right.
– How dark I stood that morning in the sun,
My best Aurora (though I saw your eyes),   420
When first you told me . . . oh, I recollect
The sound, and how you lifted your small hand,
And how your white dress and your burnished curls

Went greatening round you in the still blue air,
As if an inspiration from within   425
Had blown them all out when you spoke the words,
Even these, – "You will not compass your poor ends
Of barley-feeding and material ease,
Without the poet's individualism
To work your universal. It takes a soul,   430
To move a body, – it takes a high-souled man,
To move the masses, even to a cleaner sty:
It takes the ideal, to blow an inch inside
The dust of the actual: and your Fouriers failed,
Because not poets enough to understand   435
"That life develops from within." I say
Your words, – I could say other words of yours,
For none of all your words will let me go;
Like sweet verbena which, being brushed against,
Will hold us three hours after by the smell   440
In spite of long walks upon windy hills.
But these words dealt in sharper perfume, – these
Were ever on me, stinging through my dreams,
And saying themselves for ever o'er my acts
Like some unhappy verdict. That I failed,   445
Is certain. Sty or no sty, to contrive
The swine's propulsion toward the precipice,
Proved easy and plain. I subtly organised
And ordered, built the cards up high and higher,
Till, some one breathing, all fell flat again;   450
In setting right society's wide wrong,
Mere life's so fatal. So I failed indeed,
Once, twice, and oftener, – hearing through the rents
Of obstinate purpose, still those words of yours,
"You will not compass your poor ends, not you!"   455
But harder than you said them; every time
Still farther from your voice, until they came
To overcrow me with triumphant scorn
Which vexed me to resistance. Set down this
For condemnation, – I was guilty here;   460
I stood upon my deed and fought my doubt,
As men will, – for I doubted, – till at last
My deed gave way beneath me suddenly,

And left me what I am: – the curtain dropped,
My part quite ended, all the footlights quenched,   465
My own soul hissing at me through the dark,
I ready for confession, – I was wrong,
I've sorely failed, I've slipped the ends of life,
I yield, you have conquered.'
                                'Stay,' I answered him;
'I've something for your hearing, also. I   470
Have failed too.'
                                'You!' he said, 'you're very great;
The sadness of your greatness fits you well:
As if the plume upon a hero's casque
Should nod a shadow upon his victor face.'

I took him up austerely, – 'You have read   475
My book, but not my heart; for recollect,
'Tis writ in Sanscrit[193] which you bungle at.
I've surely failed, I know, if failure means
To look back sadly on work gladly done, –
To wander on my mountains of Delight,   480
So called (I can remember a friend's words
As well as you, sir), weary and in want
Of even a sheep-path, thinking bitterly . . .
Well, well! no matter. I but say so much,
To keep you, Romney Leigh, from saying more,   485
And let you feel I am not so high indeed,
That I can bear to have you at my foot, –
Or safe, that I can help you. That June-day,
Too deeply sunk in craterous sunsets now
For you or me to dig it up alive, –   490
To pluck it out all bleeding with spent flame
At the roots, before those moralising stars
We have got instead, – that poor lost day, you said
Some words as truthful as the thing of mine
You cared to keep in memory; and I hold   495
If I, that day, and, being the girl I was,
Had shown a gentler spirit, less arrogance,
It had not hurt me. You will scarce mistake
The point here: I but only think, you see,
More justly, that's more humbly, of myself,   500

Than when I tried a crown on and supposed . . .
Nay, laugh, sir, – I'll laugh with you! – pray you, laugh.
I've had so many birthdays since that day
I've learnt to prize mirth's opportunities,
Which come too seldom. Was it you who said   505
I was not changed? the same Aurora? Ah,
We could laugh there, too! Why, Ulysses' dog
Knew *him*, and wagged his tail and died: but if
I had owned a dog, I too, before my Troy,
And if you brought him here, . . . I warrant you   510
He'd look into my face, bark lustily,
And live on stoutly, as the creatures will
Whose spirits are not troubled by long loves.
A dog would never know me, I'm so changed,
Much less a friend . . . except that you're misled   515
By the colour of the hair, the trick of the voice,
Like that Aurora Leigh's.'
                              'Sweet trick of voice!
I would be a dog for this, to know it at last,
And die upon the falls of it. O love,
O best Aurora! are you then so sad,   520
You scarcely had been sadder as my wife?'

'Your wife, sir! I must certainly be changed,
If I, Aurora, can have said a thing
So light, it catches at the knightly spurs
Of a noble gentleman like Romney Leigh   525
And trips him from his honourable sense
Of what befits' . . .
                              'You wholly misconceive,'
He answered.
                    I returned, – 'I'm glad of it.
But keep from misconception, too, yourself:
I am not humbled to so low a point,   530
Nor so far saddened. If I am sad at all,
Ten layers of birthdays on a woman's head,
Are apt to fossilise her girlish mirth,
Though ne'er so merry: I'm perforce more wise,
And that, in truth, means sadder. For the rest,   535
Look here, sir: I was right upon the whole

That birthday morning. 'Tis impossible
To get at men excepting through their souls,
However open their carnivorous jaws;
And poets get directlier at the soul,   540
Than any of your economists: – for which
You must not overlook the poet's work
When scheming for the world's necessities.
The soul's the way. Not even Christ Himself
Can save man else than as He hold man's soul;   545
And therefore did He come into our flesh,
As some wise hunter creeping on his knees
With a torch, into the blackness of a cave,
To face and quell the beast there, – take the soul,
And so possess the whole man, body and soul.   550
I said, so far, right, yes; not farther, though:
We both were wrong that June-day, – both as wrong
As an east wind had been. I who talked of art,
And you who grieved for all men's griefs . . . what then?
We surely made too small a part for God   555
In these things. What we are, imports us more
Than what we eat; and life, you've granted me,
Develops from within. But innermost
Of the inmost, most interior of the interne,
God claims His own, Divine humanity   560
Renewing nature, – or the piercingest verse,
Pressed in by subtlest poet, still must keep
As much upon the outside of a man
As the very bowl in which he dips his beard.
– And then, . . . the rest; I cannot surely speak: 565
Perhaps I doubt more than you doubted then,
If I, the poet's veritable charge,
Have borne upon my forehead. If I have,
It might feel somewhat liker to a crown,
The foolish green one even. – Ah, I think,   570
And chiefly when the sun shines, that I've failed.
But what then, Romney? Though we fail indeed,
You . . . I . . . a score of such weak workers, . . . He
Fails never. If He cannot work by us,
He will work over us. Does He want a man,   575
Much less a woman, think you? Every time

The star winks there, so many souls are born,
Who all shall work too. Let our own be calm.
We should be ashamed to sit beneath those stars,
Impatient that we're nothing.'
                      'Could we sit   580
Just so for ever, sweetest friend,' he said,
'My failure would seem better than success.
And yet indeed your book has dealt with me
More gently, cousin, than you ever will!
The book brought down entire the bright June-day,   585
And set me wandering in the garden-walks,
And let me watch the garland in a place
You blushed so . . . nay, forgive me, do not stir, –
I only thank the book for what it taught,
And what permitted. Poet, doubt yourself,   590
But never doubt that you're a poet to me
From henceforth. You have written poems, sweet,
Which moved me in secret, as the sap is moved
In still March-branches, signless as a stone:
But this last book o'ercame me like soft rain   595
Which falls at midnight, when the tightened bark
Breaks out into unhesitating buds
And sudden protestations of the spring.
In all your other books, I saw but *you*:
A man may see the moon so, in a pond,   600
And not be nearer therefore to the moon,
Nor use the sight . . . except to drown himself:
And so I forced my heart back from the sight,
For what had *I*, I thought, to do with *her*,
Aurora . . . Romney? But, in this last book,   605
You showed me something separate from yourself,
Beyond you, and I bore to take it in
And let it draw me. You have shown me truths,
O June-day friend, that help me now at night
When June is over! truths not yours, indeed,   610
But set within my reach by means of you,
Presented by your voice and verse the way
To take them clearest. Verily I was wrong;
And verily many thinkers of this age,
Aye, many Christian teachers, half in heaven,   615

Are wrong in just my sense who understood
Our natural world too insularly, as if
No spiritual counterpart completed it,
Consummating its meaning, rounding all
To justice and perfection, line by line,   620
Form by form, nothing single nor alone,
The great below clenched by the great above,
Shade here authenticating substance there,
The body proving spirit, as the effect
The cause: we meantime being too grossly apt   625
To hold the natural, as dogs a bone
(Though reason and nature beat us in the face),
So obstinately, that we'll break our teeth
Or ever we let go. For everywhere
We're too materialistic, – eating clay   630
(Like men of the west) instead of Adam's corn
And Noah's wine, clay by handfuls, clay by lumps,
Until we're filled up to the throat with clay,
And grow the grimy colour of the ground
On which we are feeding. Aye, materialist   635
The age's name is. God Himself, with some,
Is apprehended as the bare result
Of what His hand materially has made,
Expressed in such an algebraic sign
Called God; – that is, to put it otherwise.   640
They add up nature to a nought of God
And cross the quotient. There are many even,
Whose names are written in the Christian church
To no dishonour, diet still on mud
And splash the altars with it. You might think   645
The clay, Christ laid upon their eyelids when,
Still blind, He called them to the use of sight,
Remained there to retard its exercise
With clogging incrustations. Close to heaven,
They see for mysteries, through the open doors,   650
Vague puffs of smoke from pots of earthenware;
And fain would enter, when their time shall come,
With quite another than Saint Paul
Has promised, – husk and chaff, the whole barley-corn,
Or where's the resurrection?'

                'Thus it is,'   655
I sighed. And he resumed with mournful face:
'Beginning so, and filling up with clay
The wards of this great key, the natural world,
And fumbling vainly therefore at the lock
Of the spiritual, we feel ourselves shut in   660
With all the wild-beast roar of struggling life,
The terrors and compunctions of our souls.
As saints with lions, – we who are not saints,
And have no heavenly lordship in our stare
To awe them backward. Aye, we are forced, so pent,   665
To judge the whole too partially, . . . confound
Conclusions. Is there any common phrase
Significant, with the adverb heard alone,
The verb being absent, and the pronoun out?
But we, distracted in the roar of life,   670
Still insolently at God's adverb snatch,
And bruit against Him that His thought is void,
His meaning hopeless, – cry, that everywhere
The government is slipping from His hand,
Unless some other Christ (say Romney Leigh)   675
Come up and toil and moil and change the world,
Because the First has proved inadequate,
However we talk bigly of His work
And piously of His person. We blaspheme
At last, to finish our doxology,   680
Despairing on the earth for which He died.'

'So now,' I asked, 'you have more hope of men?'

'I hope,' he answered. 'I am come to think
That God will have His work done, as you said,
And that we need not be disturbed too much   685
For Romney Leigh or others having failed
With this or that quack nostrum,[194] – recipes
For keeping summits by annulling depths,
For wrestling with luxurious lounging sleeves,
And acting heroism without a scratch.   690
We fail, – what then? Aurora, if I smiled
To see you, in your lovely morning-pride,

Try on the poet's wreath which suits the noon
(Sweet cousin, walls must get the weather-stain
Before they grow the ivy!), certainly   695
I stood myself there worthier of contempt,
Self-rated, in disastrous arrogance,
As competent to sorrow for mankind
And even their odds. A man may well despair,
Who counts himself so needful to success.   700
I failed: I throw the remedy back on God,
And sit down here beside you, in good hope.'

'And yet take heed,' I answered, 'lest we lean
Too dangerously on the other side,
And so fail twice. Be sure, no earnest work   705
Of any honest creature, howbeit weak,
Imperfect, ill-adapted, fails so much,
It is not gathered as a grain of sand
To enlarge the sum of human action used
For carrying out God's end. No creature works   710
So ill, observe, that therefore he's cashiered.[195]
The honest earnest man must stand and work,
The woman also – otherwise she drops
At once below the dignity of man,
Accepting serfdom. Free men freely work.   715
Whoever fears God, fears to sit at ease.'

He cried, 'True. After Adam, work was curse;
The natural creature labours, sweats, and frets.
But, after Christ, work turns to privilege,
And henceforth, one with our humanity,   720
The Six-day Worker working still in us
Has called us freely to work on with Him
In high companionship. So, happiest!
I count that Heaven itself is only work
To a surer issue. Let us work, indeed,   725
But no more work as Adam, – nor as Leigh
Erewhile, as if the only man on earth,
Responsible for all the thistles blown
And tigers couchant, struggling in amaze
Against disease and winter, snarling on   730

For ever, that the world's not paradise.
Oh, cousin, let us be content, in work,
To do the thing we can, and not presume
To fret because it's little. 'Twill employ
Seven men, they say, to make a perfect pin; 735
Who makes the head, content to miss the point,
Who makes the point, agreed to leave the join:
And if a man should cry, "I want a pin,
And I must make it straightway, head and point,"
His wisdom is not worth the pin he wants. 740
Seven men to a pin, – and not a man too much!
Seven generations, haply, to this world,
To right it visibly a finger's breadth,
And mend its rents a little. Oh, to storm
And say, "This world here is intolerable; 745
I will not eat this corn, nor drink this wine,
Nor love this woman, flinging her my soul
Without a bond for 't as a lover should,
Nor use the generous leave of happiness
As not too good for using generously" – 750
(Since virtue kindles at the touch of joy
Like a man's cheek laid on a woman's hand,
And God, who knows it, looks for quick returns
From joys) – to stand and claim to have a life
Beyond the bounds of the individual man, 755
And raze all personal cloisters of the soul
To build up public stores and magazines,
As if God's creatures otherwise were lost,
The builder surely saved by any means!
To think, – I have a pattern on my nail, 760
And I will carve the world new after it
And solve so these hard social questions, – nay,
Impossible social questions, – since their roots
Strike deep in Evil's own existence here
Which God permits because the question's hard 765
To abolish evil nor attaint free-will.
Aye, hard to God, but not to Romney Leigh!
For Romney has a pattern on his nail
(Whatever may be lacking on the Mount),
And, not being overnice to separate 770

What's element from what's convention, hastes
By line on line, to draw you out a world,
Without your help indeed, unless you take
His yoke upon you and will learn of Him,
So much He has to teach! so good a world!   775
The same, the whole creation's groaning for!
No rich nor poor, no gain nor loss nor stint;
No potage in it able to exclude
A brother's birthright, and no right of birth,
The potage, – both secured to every man,   780
And perfect virtue dealt out like the rest
Gratuitously, with the soup at six,
To whoso does not seek it.'

       'Softly, sir,'
I interrupted, – 'I had a cousin once
I held in reverence. If he strained too wide,   785
It was not to take honour but give help;
The gesture was heroic. If his hand
Accomplished nothing . . . (well, it is not proved)
That empty hand thrown impotently out
Were sooner caught, I think, by One in heaven,   790
Than many a hand that reaped a harvest in
And keeps the scythe's glow on it. Pray you, then,
For my sake merely, use less bitterness
In speaking of my cousin.'

       'Ah,' he said,
'Aurora! when the prophet beats the ass,   795
The angel intercedes.' He shook his head –
'And yet to mean so well and fail so foul,
Expresses ne'er another beast than man;
The antithesis is human. Hearken, dear;
There's too much abstract willing, purposing,   800
In this poor world. We talk by aggregates,
And think by systems, and, being used to face
Our evils in statistics, are inclined
To cap them with unreal remedies
Drawn out in haste on the other side the slate.'

              805

'That's true,' I answered, fain to throw up thought
And make a game of 't; 'Yes, we generalise

Enough to please you. If we pray at all,
We pray no longer for our daily bread
But next centenary's harvests. If we give,   810
Our cup of water is not tendered till
We lay down pipes and found a Company
With Branches. Ass or angel, 'tis the same:
A woman cannot do the thing she ought,
Which means whatever perfect thing she can,   815
In life, in art, in science, but she fears
To let the perfect action take her part,
And rest there: she must prove what she can do
Before she does it, – prate of woman's rights,
Of woman's mission, woman's function, till   820
The men (who are prating too on their side) cry,
"A woman's function plainly is . . . to talk."
Poor souls, they are very reasonably vexed;
They cannot hear each other talk.'

                       'And you,
An artist, judge so?'

                  'I, an artist, – yes: 825
Because, precisely, I'm an artist, sir,
And woman, if another sat in sight,
I'd whisper, – Soft, my sister! not a word!
By speaking we prove only we can speak,
Which he, the man here, never doubted. What   830
He doubts is, whether we can *do* the thing
With decent grace we've not yet done at all.
Now, do it; bring your statue, – you have room!
He'll see it even by the starlight here;
And if 'tis e'er so little like the god   835
Who looks out from the marble silently
Along the track of his own shining dart
Through the dusk of ages, there's no need to speak;
The universe shall henceforth speak for you,
And witness, "She who did this thing, was born   840
To do it, – claims her licence in her work."
And so with more works. Whoso cures the plague,
Though twice a woman, shall be called a leech:
Who rights a land's finances, is excused
For touching coppers, though her hands be white, –   845

But we, we talk!'
            'It is the age's mood,'
He said; 'we boast, and do not. We put up
Hostelry signs where'er we lodge a day,
Some red colossal cow with mighty paps
A Cyclops' fingers could not strain to milk, –   850
Then bring out presently our saucerful
Of curds. We want more quiet in our works,
More knowledge of the bounds in which we work;
More knowledge that each individual man
Remains an Adam to the general race,   855
Constrained to see, like Adam, that he keep
His personal state's condition honestly,
Or vain all thoughts of his to help the world,
Which still must be developed from its *one*
If bettered in its many. We indeed,   860
Who think to lay it out new like a park,
We take a work on us which is not man's,
For God alone sits far enough above
To speculate so largely. None of us
(Not Romney Leigh) is mad enough to say,   865
We'll have a grove of oaks upon that slope
And sink the need of acorns. Government,
If veritable and lawful, is not given
By imposition of the foreign hand,
Nor chosen from a pretty pattern-book   870
Of some domestic idealogue who sits
And coldly chooses empire, where as well
He might republic. Genuine government
Is but the expression of a nation, good
Or less good, – even as all society,   875
Howe'er unequal, monstrous, crazed, and cursed,
Is but the expression of men's single lives,
The loud sum of the silent units. What,
We'd change the aggregate and yet retain
Each separate figure? whom do we cheat by that?   880
Now, not even Romney.'
                'Cousin, you are sad.
Did all your social labour at Leigh Hall
And elsewhere, come to nought then?'

                      'It *was* nought,'
He answered mildly. 'There is room indeed
For statues still, in this large world of God's,   885
But not for vacuums, – so I am not sad;
Not sadder than is good for what I am.
My vain phalanstery dissolved itself;
My men and women of disordered lives,
I brought in orderly to dine and sleep,   890
Broke up those waxen masks I made them wear,
With fierce contortions of the natural face, –
And cursed me for my tyrannous constraint
In forcing crooked creatures to live straight;
And set the country hounds upon my back   895
To bite and tear me for my wicked deed
Of trying to do good without the church
Or even the squires, Aurora. Do you mind
Your ancient neighbours? The great book-club teems
With "sketches," "summaries," and "last tracts" but twelve, 900
On socialistic troublers of close bonds
Betwixt the generous rich and grateful poor.
The vicar preached from "Revelations," (till
The doctor woke), and found me with "the frogs"
On three successive Sundays; aye, and stopped   905
To weep a little (for he's getting old)
That such perdition should o'ertake a man
Of such fair acres, – in the parish, too!
He printed his discourses "by request,"
And if your book shall sell as his did, then   910
Your verses are less good than I suppose.
The women of the neighbourhood subscribed,
And sent me a copy bound in scarlet silk,
Tooled edges, blazoned with the arms of Leigh:
I own that touched me.'
                      'What, the pretty ones?   915
Poor Romney!'
                'Otherwise the effect was small:
I had my windows broken once or twice
By liberal peasants naturally incensed
At such a vexer of Arcadian peace,[196]
Who would not let men call their wives their own   920

565

To kick like Britons, and made obstacles
When things went smoothly as a baby drugged,
Toward freedom and starvation, – bringing down
The wicked London tavern-thieves and drabs
To affront the blessed hillside drabs and thieves   925
With mended morals, quotha, – fine new lives! –
My windows paid for 't. I was shot at, once,
By an active poacher who had hit a hare
From the other barrel (tired of springeing game
So long upon my acres, undisturbed,   930
And restless for the country's virtue, – yet
He missed me) – aye, and pelted very oft
In riding through the village. "There he goes
Who'd drive away our Christian gentlefolks,
To catch us undefended in the trap   935
He baits with poisonous cheese, and locks us up
In that pernicious prison of Leigh Hall
With all his murderers! Give another name
And say Leigh Hell, and burn it up with fire."
And so they did, at last, Aurora.'

              'Did?'   940

'You never heard it, cousin? Vincent's news
Came stinted, then.'

                  'They did? they burnt Leigh Hall?'

'You're sorry, dear Aurora? Yes indeed,
They did it perfectly: a thorough work,
And not a failure, this time. Let us grant   945
'Tis somewhat easier, though, to burn a house
Than build a system; – yet that's easy, too,
In a dream. Books, pictures, – aye, the pictures! what,
You think your dear Vandykes would give them pause?
Our proud ancestral Leighs, with those peaked beards, 950
Or bosoms white as foam thrown up on rocks
From the old-spent wave. Such calm defiant looks
They flared up with! now nevermore to twit
The bones in the family-vault with ugly death.
Not one was rescued, save the Lady Maud,   955
Who threw you down, that morning you were born,
The undeniable lineal mouth and chin

To wear for ever for her gracious sake,
For which good deed I saved her; the rest went:
And you, you're sorry, cousin. Well, for me,   960
With all my phalansterians safely out
(Poor hearts, they helped the burners, it was said,
And certainly a few clapped hands and yelled),
The ruin did not hurt me as it might, –
As when for instance I was hurt one day   965
A certain letter being destroyed. In fact,
To see the great house flare so . . . oaken floors,
Our fathers made so fine with rushes once
Before our mothers furbished them with trains,
Carved wainscots, panelled walls, the favourite slide   970
For draining off a martyr (or a rogue),
The echoing galleries, half a half-mile long,
And all the various stairs that took you up
And took you down, and took you round about
Upon their slippery darkness, recollect,   975
All helping to keep up one blazing jest!
The flames through all the casements pushing forth
Like red-hot devils crinkled into snakes,
All signifying, – "Look you, Romney Leigh,
We save the people from your saving, here,   980
Yet so as by fire! we make a pretty show
Besides, – and that's the best you've ever done."
– To see this, almost moved myself to clap!
The "vale et plaude" came too with effect
When, in the roof fell, and the fire that paused,   985
Stunned momently beneath the stroke of slates
And tumbling rafters, rose at once and roared,
And wrapping the whole house (which disappeared
In a mounting whirlwind of dilated flame),
Blew upward, straight, its drift of fiery chaff   990
In the face of Heaven, which blenched and ran up higher.'

'Poor Romney!'

         'Sometimes when I dream,' he said,
'I hear the silence after; 'twas so still.
For all those wild beasts, yelling, cursing round,
Were suddenly silent, while you counted five,   995

So silent, that you heard a young bird fall
From the top-nest in the neighbouring rookery,
Through edging over-rashly toward the light.
The old rooks had already fled too far,
To hear the screech they fled with, though you saw   1000
Some flying still, like scatterings of dead leaves
In autumn-gusts, seen dark against the sky, –
All flying, – ousted, like the House of Leigh.'

'Dear Romney!'
                'Evidently 'twould have been
A fine sight for a poet, sweet, like you,   1005
To make the verse blaze after. I myself,
Even I, felt something in the grand old trees,
Which stood that moment like brute Druid gods,[197]
Amazed upon the rim of ruin, where,
As into a blackened socket, the great fire   1010
Had dropped, – still throwing up splinters now and then,
To show them grey with all their centuries,
Left there to witness that on such a day
The house went out.'
            'Ah!'
                  'While you counted five
I seemed to feel a little like a Leigh, –   1015
But then it passed, Aurora. A child cried,
And I had enough to think of what to do
With all those houseless wretches in the dark,
And ponder where they'd dance the next time, they
Who had burnt the viol.'
                  'Did you think of that?   1020
Who burns his viol will not dance, I know,
To cymbals, Romney.'
                'O my sweet sad voice,'
He cried, – 'O voice that speaks and overcomes!
The sun is silent, but Aurora speaks.'

'Alas,' I said, 'I speak I know not what: 1025
I'm back in childhood, thinking as a child,
A foolish fancy – will it make you smile?
I shall not from the window of my room

Catch sight of those old chimneys any more.'

'No more,' he answered. 'If you pushed one day   1030
Through all the green hills to our fathers' house,
You'd come upon a great charred circle, where
The patient earth was singed an acre round;
With one stone-stair, symbolic of my life,
Ascending, winding, leading up to nought!   1035
'Tis worth a poet's seeing. Will you go?'

I made no answer. Had I any right
To weep with this man, that I dared to speak?
A woman stood between his soul and mine,
And waved us off from touching evermore,   1040
With those unclean white hands of hers. Enough.
We had burnt our viols and were silent.
                        So,
The silence lengthened till it pressed. I spoke,
To breathe: 'I think you were ill afterward.'

'More ill,' he answered, 'had been scarcely ill.   1045
I hoped this feeble tumbling at life's knot
Might end concisely, – but I failed to die,
As formerly I failed to live, – and thus
Grew willing, having tried all other ways,
To try just God's. Humility's so good,   1050
When pride's impossible. Mark us, how we make
Our virtues, cousin, from our worn-out sins,
Which smack of them from henceforth. Is it right,
For instance, to wed here while you love there?
And yet because a man sins once, the sin   1055
Cleaves to him, in necessity to sin,
That if he sin not *so*, to damn himself,
He sins *so*, to damn others with himself:
And thus, to wed here, loving there, becomes
A duty. Virtue buds a dubious leaf   1060
Round mortal brows; your ivy's better, dear.
– Yet she, 'tis certain, is my very wife,
The very lamb left mangled by the wolves
Through my own bad shepherding: and could I choose
But take her on my shoulder past this stretch   1065

Of rough, uneasy wilderness, poor lamb,
Poor child, poor child? – Aurora, my beloved,
I will not vex you any more tonight,
But, having spoken what I came to say,
The rest shall please you. What she can, in me, –   1070
Protection, tender liking, freedom, ease,
She shall have surely, liberally, for her
And hers, Aurora. Small amends they'll make
For hideous evils which she had not known
Except by me, and for this imminent loss.   1075
This forfeit presence of a gracious friend,
Which also she must forfeit for my sake,
Since, . . . drop your hand in mine a moment, sweet,
We're parting! – ah, my snowdrop, what a touch,
As if the wind had swept it off! you grudge   1080
Your gelid sweetness on my palm but so,
A moment? angry, that I could not bear
You . . . speaking, breathing, living, side by side
With some one called my wife . . . and live, myself?
Nay, be not cruel – you must understand!   1085
Your lightest footfall on a floor of mine
Would shake the house, my lintel being uncrossed
'Gainst angels: henceforth it is night with me,
And so, henceforth, I put the shutters up:
Auroras must not come to spoil my dark.'   1090

He smiled so feebly, with an empty hand
Stretched sideway from me, – as indeed he looked
To any one but me to give him help;
And, while the moon came suddenly out full,
The double-rose of our Italian moons,   1095
Sufficient plainly for the heaven and earth
(The stars struck dumb and washed away in dews
Of golden glory, and the mountains steeped
In divine languor), he, the man, appeared
So pale and patient, like the marble man   1100
A sculptor puts his personal sadness in
To join his grandeur of ideal thought, –
As if his mallet struck me from my height
Of passionate indignation, I who had risen

Pale, – doubting, paused, . . . Was Romney mad indeed?
Had all this wrong of heart made sick the brain? 1106

Then quiet, with a sort of tremulous pride,
'Go, cousin,' I said coldly; 'a farewell
Was sooner spoken 'twixt a pair of friends
In those old days, than seems to suit you now. 1110
Howbeit, since then, I've writ a book or two,
I'm somewhat dull still in the manly art
Of phrase and metaphrase. Why, any man
Can carve a score of white Loves out of snow,
As Buonarroti[198] in my Florence there, 1115
And set them on the wall in some safe shade,
As safe, sir, as your marriage! very good;
Though if a woman took one from the ledge
To put it on the table by her flowers
And let it mind her of a certain friend, 1120
'Twould drop at once (so better), would not bear
Her nail-mark even, where she took it up
A little tenderly, – so best, I say:
For me, I would not touch the fragile thing
And risk to spoil it half an hour before 1125
The sun shall shine to melt it: leave it there.
I'm plain at speech, direct in purpose: when
I speak, you'll take the meaning as it is,
And not allow for puckerings in the silk
By clever stitches: – I'm a woman, sir, 1130
I use the woman's figures naturally,
As you the male licence. So, I wish you well.
I'm simply sorry for the griefs you've had,
And not for your sake only, but mankind's.
This race is never grateful: from the first, 1135
One fills their cup at supper with pure wine,
Which back they give at cross-time on a sponge,
In vinegar and gall.'[199]
                              'If gratefuller,'
He murmured, 'by so much less pitiable!
God's self would never have come down to die, 1140
Could man have thanked him for it.'
                              'Happily

571

'Tis patent that, whatever,' I resumed,
'You suffered from this thanklessness of men,
You sink no more than Moses' bulrush-boat[200]
When once relieved of Moses, – for you're light,   1145
You're light, my cousin! which is well for you,
And manly. For myself, – now mark me, sir,
They burnt Leigh Hall; but if, consummated
To devils, heightened beyond Lucifers,
They had burnt instead, a star or two of those   1150
We saw above there just a moment back,
Before the moon abolished them, – destroyed
And riddled them in ashes through a sieve
On the head of the foundering universe, – what then?
If you and I remained still you and I,   1155
It would not shift our places as mere friends,
Nor render decent you should toss a phrase
Beyond the point of actual feeling! – nay,
You shall not interrupt me: as you said,
We're parting. Certainly, not once nor twice   1160
Tonight you've mocked me somewhat, or yourself,
And I, at least, have not deserved it so
That I should meet it unsurprised. But now,
Enough: we're parting . . . parting. Cousin Leigh,
I wish you well through all the acts of life   1165
And life's relations, wedlock not the least,
And it shall "please me," in your words, to know
You yield your wife, protection, freedom, ease,
And very tender liking. May you live
So happy with her, Romney, that your friends   1170
Shall praise her for it. Meantime some of us
Are wholly dull in keeping ignorant
Of what she has suffered by you, and what debt
Of sorrow your rich love sits down to pay:
But if 'tis sweet for love to pay its debt,   1175
'Tis sweeter still for love to give its gift,
And you, be liberal in the sweeter way,
You can, I think. At least, as touches me,
You owe her, cousin Romney, no amends.
She is not used to hold my gown so fast,   1180
You need entreat her now to let it go;

572

The lady never was a friend of mine,
Nor capable, – I thought you knew as much, –
Of losing for your sake so poor a prize
As such a worthless friendship. Be content,   1185
Good cousin, therefore, both for her and you!
I'll never spoil your dark, nor dull your noon,
Nor vex you when you're merry, or at rest:
You shall not need to put a shutter up
To keep out this Aurora, – though your north   1190
Can make Auroras which vex nobody,
Scarce known from night, I fancied! let me add
My larks fly higher than some windows. Well;
You've read your Leighs. Indeed 'twould shake a house,
If such as I came in with outstretched hand   1195
Still warm and thrilling from the clasp of one . . .
Of one we know, . . . to acknowledge, palm to palm,
As mistress there, the Lady Waldemar.'

'Now God be with us' . . . with a sudden clash
Of voice he interrupted – 'what name's that?   1200
You spoke a name, Aurora.'
                              'Pardon me;
I would that, Romney, I could name your wife
Nor wound you, yet be worthy.'
                              'Are we mad?'
He echoed – 'wife! mine! Lady Waldemar!
I think you said my wife.' He sprang to his feet,   1205
And threw his noble head back toward the moon
As one who swims against a stormy sea,
Then laughed with such a helpless, hopeless, scorn,
I stood and trembled.
                     'May God judge me so,'
He said at last, – 'I came convicted here,   1210
And humbled sorely if not enough. I came,
Because this woman from her crystal soul
Had shown me something which a man calls light:
Because too, formerly, I sinned by her
As then and ever since I have, by God,   1215
Through arrogance of nature, – though I loved . . .
Whom best, I need not say, since that is writ

Too plainly in the book of my misdeeds:
And thus I came here to abase myself,
And fasten, kneeling, on her regent brows   1220
A garland which I startled thence one day
Of her beautiful June-youth. But here again
I'm baffled, – fail in my abasement as
My aggrandisement: there's no room left for me,
At any woman's foot who misconceives   1225
My nature, purpose, possible actions. What!
Are you the Aurora who made large my dreams
To frame your greatness? you conceive so small?
You stand so less than woman, through being more,
And lose your natural instinct (like a beast),   1230
Through intellectual culture? since indeed
I do not think that any common she
Would dare adopt such monstrous forgeries
For the legible life-signature of such
As I, with all my blots, – with all my blots!   1235
At last then, peerless cousin, we are peers,
At last we're even. Ah, you've left your height,
And here upon my level we take hands,
And here I reach you to forgive you, sweet,
And that's a fall, Aurora. Long ago   1240
You seldom understood me, – but before,
I could not blame you. Then, you only seemed
So high above, you could not see below;
But now I breathe, – but now I pardon! – nay,
We're parting. Dearest, men have burnt my house,   1245
Maligned my motives, – but not one, I swear,
Has wronged my soul as this Aurora has,
Who called the Lady Waldemar my wife.'

'Not married to her! yet you said' . . .
                                        'Again?
Nay, read the lines' (he held a letter out)   1250
'She sent you through me.'
                          By the moonlight there,
I tore the meaning out with passionate haste
Much rather than I read it. Thus it ran.

Ninth Book

Even thus. I pause to write it out at length,
The letter of the Lady Waldemar.

'I prayed your cousin Leigh to take you this,
He says he'll do it. After years of love,
Or what is called so, when a woman frets   5
And fools upon one string of a man's name,
And fingers it for ever till it breaks, –
He may perhaps do for her such a thing,
And she accept it without detriment
Although she should not love him any more.   10
And I, who do not love him, nor love you,
Nor you, Aurora, – choose you shall repent
Your most ungracious letter and confess,
Constrained by his convictions (he's convinced),
You've wronged me foully. Are you made so ill,   15
You woman – to impute such ill to *me*
We both had mothers, – lay in their bosom once.
And after all, I thank you, Aurora Leigh,
For proving to myself that there are things
I would not do, – not for my life, – nor him,   20
Though something I have somewhat overdone, –
For instance, when I went to see the gods
One morning on Olympus, with a step
That shook the thunder from a certain cloud,
Committing myself vilely. Could I think,   25
The Muse I pulled my heart out from my breast
To soften, had herself a sort of heart,
And loved my mortal? He at least loved her,
I heard him say so, – 'twas my recompense,
When, watching at his bedside fourteen days,   30
He broke out ever like a flame at whiles
Between the heats of fever, – "Is it thou?
'Breathe closer, sweetest mouth!" and when at last
The fever gone, the wasted face extinct,
As if it irked him much to know me there,   35

575

He said, " 'Twas kind, 'twas good, 'twas womanly"
(And fifty praises to excuse no love),
"But was the picture safe he had ventured for?"
And then, half wandering, – "I have loved her well,
Although she could not love me." – "Say instead,"   40
I answered, "she does love you." – 'Twas my turn
To rave: I would have married him so changed,
Although the world had jeered me properly
For taking up with Cupid at his worst,
The silver quiver worn off on his hair.   45
"No, no," he murmured, "no, she loves me not;
Aurora Leigh does better: bring her book
And read it softly, Lady Waldemar,
Until I thank your friendship more for that
Than even for harder service." So I read   50
Your book, Aurora, for an hour that day:
I kept its pauses, marked its emphasis;
My voice, empaled upon its hooks of rime,
Not once would writhe, nor quiver, nor revolt;
I read on calmly, – calmly shut it up,   55
Observing, "There's some merit in the book;
And yet the merit in't is thrown away,
As chances still with women if we write
Or write not: we want string to tie our flowers,
So drop them as we walk, which serves to show   60
The way we went. Good morning, Mister Leigh;
You'll find another reader the next time.
A woman who does better than to love,
I hate; she will do nothing very well:
Male poets are preferable, tiring less   65
And teaching more." I triumphed o'er you both,
And left him.
             'When I saw him afterward
I had read your shameful letter, and my heart.
He came with health recovered, strong though pale,
Lord Howe and he, a courteous pair of friends,   70
To say what men dare say to women, when
Their debtors. But I stopped them with a word,
And proved I had never trodden such a road
To carry so much dirt upon my shoe.

Then, putting into it something of disdain,   75
I asked forsooth his pardon, and my own,
For having done no better than to love,
And that not wisely, – though 'twas long ago,
And had been mended radically since.
I told him, as I tell you now, Miss Leigh,   80
And proved, I took some trouble for his sake
(Because I knew he did not love the girl)
To spoil my hands with working in the stream
Of that poor bubbling nature, – till she went,
Consigned to one I trusted, my own maid   85
Who once had lived full five months in my house
(Dressed hair superbly), with a lavish purse
To carry to Australia where she had left
A husband, said she. If the creature lied,
The mission failed, we all do fail and lie   90
More or less – and I'm sorry – which is all
Expected from us when we fail the most
And go to church to own it. What I meant,
Was just the best for him, and me, and her . . .
Best even for Marian! – I am sorry for 't,   95
And very sorry. Yet my creature said
She saw her stop to speak in Oxford Street
To one . . . no matter! I had sooner cut
My hand off (though 'twere kissed the hour before,
And promised a duke's troth-ring for the next)   100
Than crush her silly head with so much wrong.
Poor child! I would have mended it with gold,
Until it gleamed like St Sophia's dome
When all the faithful troop to morning prayer:
But he, he nipped the bud of such a thought   105
With that cold Leigh look which I fancied once,
And broke in, "Henceforth she was called his wife:
His wife required no succour: he was bound
To Florence, to resume this broken bond;
Enough so. Both were happy, he and Howe,   110
To acquit me of the heaviest charge of all – "
– At which I shot my tongue against my fly
And struck him; "Would he carry, – he was just,
A letter from me to Aurora Leigh,

And ratify from his authentic mouth   115
My answer to her accusation?" – "Yes,
If such a letter were prepared in time."
– He's just, your cousin, – aye, abhorrently:
He'd wash his hands in blood, to keep them clean.
And so, cold, courteous, a mere gentleman,   120
He bowed, we parted.
              'Parted. Face no more,
Voice no more, love no more! wiped wholly out
Like some ill scholar's scrawl from heart and slate, –
Aye, spit on and so wiped out utterly
By some coarse scholar! I have been too coarse,   125
Too human. Have we business, in our rank,
With blood i' the veins? I will have henceforth none,
Not even to keep the colour at my lip:
A rose is pink and pretty without blood,
Why not a woman? When we've played in vain   130
The game, to adore, – we have resources still,
And can play on at leisure, being adored:
Here's Smith already swearing at my feet
That I'm the typic She. Away with Smith! –
Smith smacks of Leigh, – and henceforth I'll admit   135
No socialist within three crinolines,
To live and have his being. But for you,
Though insolent your letter and absurd,
And though I hate you frankly, – take my Smith!
For when you have seen this famous marriage tied,   140
A most unspotted Erle to a noble Leigh
(His love astray on one he should not love),
Howbeit you may not want his love, beware,
You'll want some comfort. So I leave you Smith,
Take Smith! – he talks Leigh's subjects, somewhat worse;   145
Adopts a thought of Leigh's, and dwindles it;
Goes leagues beyond, to be no inch behind;
Will mind you of him, as a shoe-string may
Of a man: and women, when they are made like you,
Grow tender to a shoe-string, footprint even,   150
Adore averted shoulders in a glass,
And memories of what, present once, was loathed.
And yet, you loathed not Romney, – though you've played

At "fox and goose" about him with your soul;
Pass over fox, you rub out fox, – ignore   155
A feeling, you eradicate it, – the act's
Identical.
              'I wish you joy, Miss Leigh;
You've made a happy marriage for your friend,
And all the honour, well-assorted love,
Derives from you who love him, whom he loves!   160
You need not wish *me* joy to think of it;
I have so much. Observe, Aurora Leigh,
Your droop of eyelid is the same as his,
And, but for you, I might have won his love,
And, to you, I have shown my naked heart;   165
For which three things I hate, hate, hate you. Hush,
Suppose a fourth! – I cannot choose but think
That, with him, I were virtuouser than you
Without him: so I hate you from this gulf
And hollow of my soul, which opens out   170
To what, except for you, had been my heaven,
And is, instead, a place to curse by! LOVE.'

An active kind of curse. I stood there cursed,
Confounded. I had seized and caught the sense
Of the letter, with its twenty stinging snakes,   175
In a moment's sweep of eyesight, and I stood
Dazed. – 'Ah! not married.'
                              'You mistake,' he said,
'I'm married. Is not Marian Erle my wife?
As God sees things, I have a wife and child;
And I, as I'm a man who honours God,   180
Am here to claim them as my child and wife.'

I felt it hard to breathe, much less to speak.
Nor word of mine was needed. Some one else
Was there for answering. 'Romney,' she began,
'My great good angel, Romney.'
                                Then at first,   185
I knew that Marian Erle was beautiful.
She stood there, still and pallid as a saint,
Dilated, like a saint in ecstasy,

As if the floating moonshine interposed
Betwixt her foot and the earth, and raised her up   190
To float upon it. 'I had left my child,
Who sleeps,' she said, 'and, having drawn this way,
I heard you speaking, . . . friend! – Confirm me now.
You take this Marian, such as wicked men
Have made her, for your honourable wife?'   195

The thrilling, solemn, proud, pathetic voice.
He stretched his arms out toward that thrilling voice,
As if to draw it on to his embrace.
– 'I take her as God made her, and as men
Must fail to unmake her, for my honoured wife.'   200

She never raised her eyes, nor took a step,
But stood there in her place, and spoke again.
– 'You take this Marian's child, which is her shame
In sight of men and women, for your child,
Of whom you will not ever feel ashamed?'   205

The thrilling, tender, proud, pathetic voice.
He stepped on toward it, still with outstretched arms,
As if to quench upon his breast that voice.
– 'May God so father me, as I do him,
And so forsake me, as I let him feel   210
He's orphaned haply. Here I take the child
To share my cup, to slumber on my knee,
To play his loudest gambol at my foot,
To hold my finger in the public ways,
Till none shall need enquire, "Whose child is this?"   215
The gesture saying so tenderly, "My own." '

She stood a moment silent in her place;
Then turning toward me very slow and cold,
– 'And you, – what say you? – will you blame me much,
If, careful for that outcast child of mine,   220
I catch this hand that's stretched to me and him,
Nor dare to leave him friendless in the world
Where men have stoned me? Have I not the right
To take so mere an aftermath from life,
Else found so wholly bare? Or is it wrong   225

To let your cousin, for a generous bent,
Put out his ungloved fingers among briers
To set a tumbling bird's-nest somewhat straight?
You will not tell him, though we're innocent,
We are not harmless, . . . and that both our harms   230
Will stick to his good smooth noble life like burrs,
Never to drop off though he shakes the cloak?
You've been my friend: you will not now be his?
You've known him that he's worthy of a friend,
And you're his cousin, lady, after all,   235
And therefore more than free to take his part,
Explaining, since the nest is surely spoilt
And Marian what you know her, – though a wife,
The world would hardly understand her case
Of being just hurt and honest; while, for him,   240
'Twould ever twit him with his bastard child
And married harlot. Speak, while yet there's time.
You would not stand and let a good man's dog
Turn round and rend him, because his, and reared
Of a generous breed, – and will you let his act,   245
Because it's generous? Speak. I'm bound to you,
And I'll be bound by only you, in this.'

The thrilling, solemn voice, so passionless,
Sustained, yet low, without a rise or fall,
As one who had authority to speak,   250
And not as Marian.
        I looked up to feel
If God stood near me, and beheld His heaven
As blue as Aaron's priestly robe[201] appeared
To Aaron when he took it off to die.
And then I spoke – 'Accept the gift, I say,   255
My sister Marian, and be satisfied.
The hand that gives, has still a soul behind
Which will not let it quail for having given,
Though foolish worldlings talk they know not what
Of what they know not. Romney's strong enough   260
For this: do you be strong to know he's strong:
He stands on Right's side; never flinch for him,
As if he stood on the other. You'll be bound

By me? I am a woman of repute;
No fly-blow gossip ever specked my life;   265
My name is clean and open as this hand,
Whose glove there's not a man dares blab about
As if he had touched it freely. Here's my hand
To clasp your hand, my Marian, owned as pure!
As pure, – as I'm a woman and a Leigh! –   270
And, as I'm both, I'll witness to the world
That Romney Leigh is honoured in his choice
Who chooses Marian for his honoured wife.'

Her broad wild woodland eyes shot out a light,
Her smile was wonderful for rapture. 'Thanks,   275
My great Aurora.' Forward then she sprang,
And dropping her impassioned spaniel head
With all its brown abandonment of curls
On Romney's feet, we heard the kisses drawn
Through sobs upon the foot, upon the ground –   280
'O Romney! O my angel! O unchanged,
Though since we've parted I have passed the grave!
But Death itself could only better *thee*,
Not change thee! – *Thee* I do not thank at all:
I but thank God who made thee what thou art,   285
So wholly godlike.'
                         When he tried in vain
To raise her to his embrace, escaping thence
As any leaping fawn from a huntsman's grasp,
She bounded off and 'lighted beyond reach,
Before him, with a staglike majesty   290
Of soft, serene defiance, – as she knew
He could not touch her, so was tolerant
He had cared to try. She stood there with her great
Drowned eyes, and dripping cheeks, and strange sweet smile
That lived through all, as if one held a light   295
Across a waste of waters, – shook her head
To keep some thoughts down deeper in her soul, –
Then, white and tranquil like a summer-cloud
Which, having rained itself to a tardy peace,
Stands still in heaven as if it ruled the day,   300
Spoke out again – 'Although, my generous friend,

Since last we met and parted you're unchanged,
And, having promised faith to Marian Erle,
Maintain it, as she were not changed at all;
And though that's worthy, though that's full of balm   305
To any conscious spirit of a girl
Who once has loved you as I loved you once, –
Yet still it will not make her . . . if she's dead,
And gone away where none can give or take
In marriage, – able to revive, return   310
And wed you, – will, it Romney? Here's the point,
My friend, we'll see it plainer: you and I
Must never, never, never join hands so.
Nay, let me say it, – for I said it first
To God, and placed it, rounded to an oath,   315
Far, far above the moon there, at His feet,
As surely as I wept just now at yours, –
We never, never, never join hands so.
And now, be patient with me; do not think
I'm speaking from a false humility.   320
The truth is, I am grown so proud with grief,
And He has said so often through His nights
And through His mornings, "Weep a little still,
Thou foolish Marian, because women must,
But do not blush at all except for sin," –   325
That I, who felt myself unworthy once
Of virtuous Romney and his high-born race,
Have come to learn, – a woman poor or rich,
Despised or honoured, is a human soul,
And what her soul is, that, she is herself,   330
Although she should be spit upon of men,
As is the pavement of the churches here,
Still good enough to pray in. And being chaste
And honest, and inclined to do the right,
And love the truth, and live my life out green   335
And smooth beneath his steps, I should not fear
To make him thus a less uneasy time
Than many a happier woman. Very proud
You see me. Pardon, that I set a trap
To hear a confirmation in your voice,   340
Both yours and yours. It is so good to know

'Twas really God who said the same before;
For thus it is in heaven, that first God speaks,
And then His angels. Oh, it does me good,
It wipes me clean and sweet from devil's dirt,   345
That Romney Leigh should think me worthy still
Of being his true and honourable wife!
Henceforth I need not say, on leaving earth,
I had no glory in it. For the rest,
The reason's ready (master, angel, friend,   350
Be patient with me) wherefore you and I
Can never, never, never join hands so.
I know you'll not be angry like a man
(For *you* are none) when I shall tell the truth,
Which is, I do not love you, Romney Leigh,   355
I do not love you. Ah well! catch my hands,
Miss Leigh, and burn into my eyes with yours, –
I swear I do not love him. Did I once?
'Tis said that women have been bruised to death
And yet, if once they loved, that love of theirs   360
Could never be drained out with all their blood:
I've heard such things and pondered. Did I indeed
Love once; or did I only worship? Yes,
Perhaps, O friend, I set you up so high
Above all actual good or hope of good,   365
Or fear of evil, all that could be mine,
I haply set you above love itself,
And out of reach of these poor woman's arms,
Angelic Romney. What was in my thought?
To be your slave, your help, your toy, your tool.   370
To be your love . . . I never thought of that:
To give you love . . . still less. I gave you love?
I think I did not give you anything;
I was but only yours, – upon my knees.
All yours, in soul and body, in head and heart,   375
A creature you had taken from the ground
Still crumbling through your fingers to your feet
To join the dust she came from. Did I love,
Or did I worship? judge, Aurora Leigh!
But, if indeed I loved, 'twas long ago, –   380
So long! before the sun and moon were made,

Before the hells were open, – ah, before
I heard my child cry in the desert night,
And knew he had no father. It may be
I'm not as strong as other women are,   385
Who, torn and crushed, are not undone from love.
It may be I am colder than the dead,
Who, being dead, love always. But for me,
Once killed, this ghost of Marian loves no more,
No more . . . except the child! . . . no more at all.   390
I told your cousin, sir, that I was dead;
And now, she thinks I'll get up from my grave,
And wear my chin-cloth for a wedding-veil,
And glide along the churchyard like a bride
While all the dead keep whispering through the withes,   395
"You would be better in your place with us,
You pitiful corruption!" At the thought,
The damps break out on me like leprosy
Although I'm clean. Aye, clean as Marian Erle!
As Marian Leigh, I know, I were not clean: 400
Nor have I so much life that I should love,
Except the child. Ah God! I could not bear
To see my darling on a good man's knees,
And know, by such a look, or such a sigh,
Or such a silence, that he thought sometimes,   405
"This child was fathered by some cursed wretch" . . .
For, Romney, – angels are less tender-wise
Than God and mothers: even *you* would think
What *we* think never. He is ours, the child;
And we would sooner vex a soul in heaven   410
By coupling with it the dead body's thought,
It left behind it in a last month's grave,
Than, in my child, see other than . . . my child.
We only, never call him fatherless
Who has God and his mother. O my babe,   415
My pretty, pretty blossom, an ill-wind
Once blew upon my breast! can any think
I'd have another, – one called happier,
A fathered child, with father's love and race
That's worn as bold and open as a smile,   420
To vex my darling when he's asked his name

And has no answer? What! a happier child
Than mine, my best, – who laughed so loud tonight
He could not sleep for pastime? Nay, I swear
By life and love, that, if I lived like some,   425
And loved like . . . *some*, aye, loved you, Romney Leigh,
As some love (eyes that have wept so much, see clear),
I've room for no more children in my arms,
My kisses are all melted on one mouth,
I would not push my darling to a stool   430
To dandle babies. Here's a hand shall keep
For ever clean without a marriage-ring,
To tend my boy until he cease to need
One steadying finger of it, and desert
(Not miss) his mother's lap, to sit with men.   435
And when I miss him (not he me) I'll come
And say, "Now give me some of Romney's work,
To help your outcast orphans of the world
And comfort grief with grief." For you, meantime,
Most noble Romney, wed a noble wife,   440
And open on each other your great souls, –
I need not farther bless you. If I dared
But strain and touch her in her upper sphere
And say, "Come down to Romney – pay my debt!"
I should be joyful with the stream of joy   445
Sent through me. But the moon is in my face . . .
I dare not, – though I guess the name he loves;
I'm learned with my studies of old days,
Remembering how he crushed his under-lip
When some one came and spoke, or did not come: 450
Aurora, I could touch her with my hand,
And fly because I dare not.'
       She was gone.
He smiled so sternly that I spoke in haste:
'Forgive her – she sees clearly for herself:
Her instinct's holy.'
     'I forgive!' he said,   455
'I only marvel how she sees so sure,
While others' . . . there he paused, – then hoarse, abrupt, –
'Aurora, you forgive us, her and me?
For her, the thing she sees, poor loyal child,

If once corrected by the thing I know,   460
Had been unspoken, since she loves you well,
Has leave to love you: – while for me, alas,
If once or twice I let my heart escape
This night, . . . remember, where hearts slip and fall
They break beside: we're parting, – parting, – ah,   465
You do not love, that you should surely know
What that word means. Forgive, be tolerant;
It had not been, but that I felt myself
So safe in impuissance and despair,
I could not hurt you though I tossed my arms   470
And sighed my soul out. The most utter wretch
Will choose his postures when he comes to die,
However in the presence of a queen;
And you'll forgive me some unseemly spasms
Which meant no more than dying. Do you think   475
I had ever come here in my perfect mind
Unless I had come here in my settled mind,
Bound Marian's, bound to keep the bond and give
My name, my house, my hand, the things I could,
To Marian! For even I could give as much: 480
Even I, affronting her exalted soul
By a supposition that she wanted these,
Could act the husband's coat and hat set up
To creak i' the wind and drive the world-crows off
From pecking in her garden. Straw can fill   485
A hole to keep out vermin. Now, at last,
I own heaven's angels round her life suffice
To fight the rats of our society,
Without this Romney: I can see it at last;
And here is ended my pretension which   490
The most pretended. Over-proud of course,
Even so! – but not so stupid . . . blind . . . that I,
Whom thus the great Taskmaster of the world
Has set to meditate mistaken work,
My dreary face against a dim blank wall   495
Throughout man's natural lifetime, – could pretend
Or wish . . . O love, I have loved you! O my soul,
I have lost you! – but I swear by all yourself,
And all you might have been to me these years

If that June-morning had not failed my hope, –   500
I'm not so bestial, to regret that day
This night, – this night, which still to you is fair!
Nay, not so blind, Aurora. I attest
Those stars above us, which I cannot see . . . '

'You cannot' . . .
        'That if Heaven itself should stoop,   505
Remix the lots, and give me another chance,
I'd say, "No other!" – I'd record my blank.
Aurora never should be wife of mine.'

'Not see the stars?'
        ''Tis worse still, not to see
To find your hand, although we're parting, dear.   510
A moment let me hold it ere we part:
And understand my last words – these, at last!
I would not have you thinking when I'm gone
That Romney dared to hanker for your love
In thought or vision, if attainable   515
(Which certainly for me it never was)
And wish to use it for a dog today
To help the blind man stumbling. God forbid!
And now I know He held you in His palm,
And kept you open-eyed to all my faults,   520
To save you at last from such a dreary end.
Believe me, dear, that, if I had known like Him
What loss was coming on me, I had done
As well in this as He has. – Farewell, you
Who are still my light, – farewell! How late it is: 525
I know that, now. You've been too patient, sweet.
I will but blow my whistle toward the lane,
And some one comes, – the same who brought me here.
Get in – Good-night.'
        'A moment. Heavenly Christ!
A moment. Speak once, Romney. 'Tis not true.   530
I hold your hands, I look into your face –
You see me?'
        'No more than the blessed stars.
Be blessed too, Aurora. Nay, my sweet,
You tremble. Tender-hearted! Do you mind

Of yore, dear, how you used to cheat old John,   535
And let the mice out slyly from his traps,
Until he marvelled at the soul in mice
Which took the cheese and left the snare? The same
Dear soft heart always! 'Twas for this I grieved
Howe's letter never reached you. Ah, you had heard   540
Of illness, – not the issue, not the extent:
My life long sick with tossings up and down,
The sudden revulsion in the blazing house,
The strain and struggle both of body and soul,
Which left fire running in my veins for blood: 545
Scarce lacked that thunderbolt of the falling beam
Which nicked me on the forehead as I passed
The gallery-door with a burden. Say heaven's bolt,
Not William Erle's, not Marian's father's, – tramp
And poacher, whom I found for what he was,   550
And, eager for her sake to rescue him,
Forth swept from the open highway of the world,
Road-dust and all, – till, like a woodland boar
Most naturally unwilling to be tamed,
He notched me with his tooth. But not a word   555
To Marian! and I do not think, besides,
He turned the tilting of the beam my way, –
And if he laughed, as many swear, poor wretch,
Nor he nor I supposed the hurt so deep.
We'll hope his next laugh may be merrier,   560
In a better cause.'

            'Blind, Romney?'

                    'Ah, my friend,
You'll learn to say it in a cheerful voice.
I, too, at first desponded. To be blind,
Turned out of nature, mulcted as a man,
Refused the daily largesse of the sun   565
To humble creatures! When the fever's heat
Dropped from me, as the flame did from my house,
And left me ruined like it, stripped of all
The hues and shapes of aspectable life,
A mere bare blind stone in the blaze of day,   570
A man, upon the outside of the earth,
As dark as ten feet under, in the grave, –

Why that seemed hard.'
    'No hope?'
       'A tear! you weep,
Divine Aurora? tears upon my hand!
I've seen you weeping for a mouse, a bird, –   575
But, weep for me, Aurora? Yes, there's hope.
Not hope of sight, – I could be learned, dear,
And tell you in what Greek and Latin name
The visual nerve is withered to the root,
Though the outer eyes appear indifferent,   580
Unspotted in their crystals. But there's hope.
The spirit, from behind this dethroned sense,
Sees, waits in patience till the walls break up
From which the bas-relief and fresco have dropt:
There's hope. The man here, once so arrogant   585
And restless, so ambitious, for his part,
Of dealing with statistically packed
Disorders (from a pattern on his nail),
And packing such things quite another way, –
Is now contented. From his personal loss   590
He has come to hope for others when they lose,
And wear a gladder faith in what we gain . . .
Through bitter experience, compensation sweet,
Like that tear, sweetest. I am quiet now,
As tender surely for the suffering world,   595
But quiet, – sitting at the wall to learn,
Content henceforth to do the thing I can:
For, though as powerless, said I, as a stone,
A stone can still give shelter to a worm,
And it is worth while being a stone for that: 600
There's hope, Aurora.'
      'Is there hope for me?
For me? – and is there room beneath the stone
For such a worm? – And if I came and said . . .
What all this weeping scarce will let me say,
And yet what women cannot say at all   605
But weeping bitterly . . . (the pride keeps up,
Until the heart breaks under it) . . . I love, –
I love you, Romney' . . .
      'Silence!' he exclaimed.

'A woman's pity sometimes makes her mad.
A man's distraction must not cheat his soul   610
To take advantage of it. Yet, 'tis hard –
Farewell, Aurora.'
                    'But I love you, sir;
And when a woman says she loves a man,
The man must hear her, though he love her not,
Which . . . hush! . . . he has leave to answer in his turn;   615
She will not surely blame him. As for me,
You call it pity, – think I'm generous?
'Twere somewhat easier, for a woman proud
As I am, and I'm very vilely proud,
To let it pass as such, and press on you   620
Love born of pity, – seeing that excellent loves
Are born so, often, nor the quicklier die, –
And this would set me higher by the head
Than now I stand. No matter: let the truth
Stand high; Aurora must be humble: no,   625
My love's not pity merely. Obviously
I'm not a generous woman, never was,
Or else, of old, I had not looked so near
To weights and measures, grudging you the power
To give, as first I scorned your power to judge   630
For me, Aurora. I would have no gifts
Forsooth, but God's, – and I would use *them* too
According to my pleasure and my choice,
As He and I were equals, you below,
Excluded from that level of interchange   635
Admitting benefaction. You were wrong
In much? you said so. I was wrong in most.
Oh, most! You only thought to rescue men
By half-means, half-way, seeing half their wants,
While thinking nothing of your personal gain.   640
But I who saw the human nature broad
At both sides, comprehending too the soul's,
And all the high necessities of Art,
Betrayed the thing I saw, and wronged my own life
For which I pleaded. Passioned to exalt   645
The artist's instinct in me at the cost
Of putting down the woman's, I forgot

No perfect artist is developed here
From any imperfect woman. Flower from root,
And spiritual from natural, grade by grade   650
In all our life. A handful of the earth
To make God's image! the despised poor earth,
The healthy odorous earth, – I missed with it
The divine Breath that blows the nostrils out
To ineffable inflatus, – aye, the breath   655
Which love is. Art is much, but love is more.
O Art, my Art, thou'rt much, but Love is more!
Art symbolises heaven, but Love is God
And makes heaven. I, Aurora, fell from mine.
I would not be a woman like the rest,   660
A simple woman who believes in love
And owns the right of love because she loves,
And, hearing she's beloved, is satisfied
With what contents God: I must analyse,
Confront, and question; just as if a fly   665
Refused to warm itself in any sun
Till such was *in leone*: I must fret
Forsooth because the month was only May,
Be faithless of the kind of proffered love,
And captious, lest it miss my dignity,   670
And scornful, that my lover sought a wife
To use . . . to use! O Romney, O my love,
I am changed since then, changed wholly, – for indeed
If now you'd stoop so low to take my love
And use it roughly, without stint or spare,   675
As men use common things with more behind
(And, in this, ever would be more behind),
To any mean and ordinary end, –
The joy would set me like a star, in heaven,
So high up, I should shine because of height   680
And not of virtue. Yet in one respect,
Just one, beloved, I am in no wise changed:
I love you, loved you . . . loved you first and last,
And love you on for ever. Now I know
I loved you always, Romney. She who died   685
Knew that, and said so; Lady Waldemar
Knows that; . . . and Marian. I had known the same,

Except that I was prouder than I knew,
And not so honest. Aye, and, as I live,
I should have died so, crushing in my hand   690
This rose of love, the wasp inside and all,
Ignoring ever to my soul and you
Both rose and pain, – except for this great loss,
This great despair, – to stand before your face
And know you do not see me where I stand.   695
You think, perhaps, I am not changed from pride,
And that I chiefly bear to say such words,
Because you cannot shame me with your eyes?
O calm, grand eyes, extinguished in a storm,
Blown out like lights o'er melancholy seas,   700
Though shrieked for by the shipwrecked, – O my Dark,
My Cloud, – to go before me every day
While I go ever toward the wilderness, –
I would that you could see me bare to the soul!
If this be pity, 'tis so for myself,   705
And not for Romney! *he* can stand alone;
A man like *him* is never overcome:
No woman like me, counts him pitiable
While saints applaud him. He mistook the world;
But I mistook my own heart, and that slip   710
Was fatal. Romney, – will you leave me here?
So wrong, so proud, so weak, so unconsoled,
So mere a woman! – and I love you so,
I love you, Romney – '
                        Could I see his face,
I wept so? Did I drop against his breast,   715
Or did his arms constrain me? were my cheeks
Hot, overflooded, with my tears, or his?
And which of our two large explosive hearts
So shook me? That, I know not. There were words
That broke in utterance . . . melted, in the fire, –   720
Embrace, that was convulsion, . . . then a kiss
As long and silent as the ecstatic night,
And deep, deep, shuddering breaths, which meant beyond
Whatever could be told by word or kiss.

But what he said . . . I have written day by day,   725

With somewhat even writing. Did I think
That such a passionate rain would intercept
And dash this last page? What he said, indeed,
I fain would write it down here like the rest,
To keep it in my eyes, as in my ears,   730
The heart's sweet scripture, to be read at night
When weary, or at morning when afraid,
And lean my heaviest oath on when I swear
That, when all's done, all tried, all counted here,
All great arts, and all good philosophies,   735
This love just puts its hand out in a dream
And straight outreaches all things.
                            What he said,
I fain would write. But if an angel spoke
In thunder, should we haply know much more
Than that it thundered? If a cloud came down   740
And wrapt us wholly, could we draw its shape,
As if on the outside and not overcome?
And so he spake. His breath against my face
Confused his words, yet made them more intense
(As when the sudden finger of the wind   745
Will wipe a row of single city-lamps
To a pure white line of flame, more luminous
Because of obliteration), more intense,
The intimate presence carrying in itself
Complete communication, as with souls   750
Who, having put the body off, perceive
Through simply being. Thus, 'twas granted me
To know he loved me to the depth and height
Of such large natures, ever competent,
With grand horizons by the sea or land,   755
To love's grand sunrise. Small spheres hold small fires,
But he loved largely, as a man can love
Who, baffled in his love, dares live his life,
Accept the ends which God loves, for his own,
And life a constant aspect.
                        From the day   760
I brought to England my poor searching face
(An orphan even of my father's grave)
He had loved me, watched me, watched his soul in mine,

Which in me grew and heightened into love.
For he, a boy still, had been told the tale   765
Of how a fairy bride from Italy
With smells of oleanders in her hair,
Was coming through the vines to touch his hand;
Whereat the blood of boyhood on the palm
Made sudden heats. And when at last I came,   770
And lived before him, lived, and rarely smiled,
He smiled and loved me for the thing I was,
As every child will love the year's first flower
(Not certainly the fairest of the year,
But, in which, the complete year seems to blow),   775
The poor sad snowdrop, – growing between drifts,
Mysterious medium 'twixt the plant and frost,
So faint with winter while so quick with spring,
So doubtful if to thaw itself away
With that snow near it. Not that Romney Leigh   780
Had loved me coldly. If I thought so once,
It was as if I had held my hand in fire
And shook for cold. But now I understood
For ever, that the very fire and heat
Of troubling passion in him, burned him clear,   785
And shaped, to dubious order, word and act:
That, just because he loved me over all,
All wealth, all lands, all social privilege,
To which chance made him unexpected heir,
And, just because on all these lesser gifts,   790
Constrained by conscience and the sense of wrong
He had stamped with steady hand God's arrow-mark
Of dedication to the human need,
He thought it should be so too, with his love.
He, passionately loving, would bring down   795
His love, his life, his best (because the best),
His bride of dreams, who walked so still and high
Through flowery poems as through meadow-grass,
The dust of golden lilies on her feet,
That *she* should walk beside him on the rocks   800
In all that clang and hewing out of men,
And help the work of help which was his life,
And prove he kept back nothing, – not his soul.

And when I failed him, – for I failed him, I,
And when it seemed he had missed my love, he thought   805
'Aurora makes room for a working-noon,'
And so, self-girded with torn strips of hope,
Took up his life as if it were for death
(Just capable of one heroic aim),
And threw it in the thickest of the world, –   810
At which men laughed as if he had drowned a dog.
Nor wonder, – since Aurora failed him first!
The morning and the evening made his day.

But oh, the night! oh, bitter-sweet! oh, sweet!
O dark, O moon and stars, O ecstasy   815
Of darkness! O great mystery of love,
In which absorbed, loss, anguish, treason's self
Enlarges rapture, – as a pebble dropt
In some full wine-cup over-brims the wine!
While we two sat together, leaned that night   820
So close, my very garments crept and thrilled
With strange electric life, and both my cheeks
Grew red, then pale, with touches from my hair
In which his breath was, – while the golden moon
Was hung before our faces as the badge   825
Of some sublime inherited despair,
Since ever to be seen by only one, –
A voice said, low and rapid as a sigh,
Yet breaking, I felt conscious, from a smile,
'Thank God, who made me blind, to make me see!   830
Shine on, Aurora, dearest light of souls,
Which rul'st for evermore both day and night!
I am happy.'
                    I flung closer to his breast,
As sword that, after battle, flings to sheath;
And, in that hurtle of united souls,   835
The mystic motions which in common moods
Are shut beyond our sense, broke in on us,
And, as we sat, we felt the old earth spin,
And all the starry turbulence of worlds
Swing round us in their audient circles, till,   840
If that same golden moon were overhead

Or if beneath our feet, we did not know.

And then calm, equal, smooth with weights of joy,
His voice rose, as some chief musician's song
Amid the old Jewish temple's Selah-pause,   845
And bade me mark how we two met at last
Upon this moon-bathed promontory of earth,
To give up much on each side, then take all.
'Beloved,' it sang, 'we must be here to work;
And men who work can only work for men,   850
And, not to work in vain, must comprehend
Humanity and so work humanly,
And raise men's bodies still by raising souls,
As God did, first.'
              'But stand upon the earth,'
I said, 'to raise them (this is human too,   855
There's nothing high which has not first been low,
My humbleness, said One, has made Me great!),
As God did last.'
              'And work all silently
And simply,' he returned, 'as God does all;
Distort our nature never for our work,   860
Nor count our right hands stronger for being hoofs.
The man most man, with tenderest human hands,
Works best for men, – as God in Nazareth.'

He paused upon the word, and then resumed:
'Fewer programmes, we who have no prescience.   865
Fewer systems, we who are held and do not hold.
Less mapping out of masses to be saved,
By nations or by sexes. Fourier's void,
And Comte absurd, – and Cabet,[202] puerile.
Subsist no rules of life outside of life,   870
No perfect manners, without Christian souls:
The Christ Himself had been no Lawgiver
Unless He had given the life, too, with the law.'

I echoed thoughtfully – 'The man, most man,
Works best for men, and, if most man indeed,   875
He gets his manhood plainest from his soul:

While obviously this stringent soul itself
Obeys the old law of development,
The Spirit ever witnessing in ours,
And Love, the soul of soul, within the soul,   880
Evolving it sublimely. First, God's love.'

'And next,' he smiled, 'the love of wedded souls,
Which still presents that mystery's counterpart.
Sweet shadow-rose, upon the water of life,
Of such a mystic substance, Sharon gave   885
A name to! human, vital, fructuous rose,
Whose calyx holds the multitude of leaves,
Loves filial, loves fraternal, neighbour-loves
And civic – all fair petals, all good scents,
All reddened, sweetened from one central Heart!'   890

'Alas,' I cried, 'it was not long ago,
You swore this very social rose smelt ill.'

'Alas,' he answered, 'is it a rose at all?
The filial's thankless, the fraternal's hard,
The rest is lost. I do but stand and think,   895
Across the waters of a troubled life
This Flower of Heaven so vainly overhangs,
What perfect counterpart would be in sight
If tanks were clearer. Let us clean the tubes,
And wait for rains. O poet, O my love,   900
Since *I* was too ambitious in my deed
And thought to distance all men in success
(Till God came on me, marked the place and said,
"Ill-doer, henceforth keep within this line,
Attempting less than others," – and I stand   905
And work among Christ's little ones, content), –
Come thou, my compensation, my dear sight,
My morning-star, my morning, – rise and shine,
And touch my hills with radiance not their own.
Shine out for two, Aurora, and fulfil   910
My falling-short that must be! work for two,
As I, though thus restrained, for two, shall love!
Gaze on, with inscient vision toward the sun,

And, from his visceral heat, pluck out the roots
Of light beyond him. Art's a service, – mark: 915
A silver key is given to thy clasp,
And thou shalt stand unwearied, night and day,
And fix it in the hard, slow-turning wards,
To open, so, that intermediate door
Betwixt the different planes of sensuous form   920
And form insensuous, that inferior men
May learn to feel on still through these to those,
And bless thy ministration. The world waits
For help. Beloved, let us love so well,
Our work shall still be better for our love,   925
And still our love be sweeter for our work,
And both commended, for the sake of each,
By all true workers and true lovers born.
Now press the clarion on thy woman's lip
(Love's holy kiss shall still keep consecrate)   930
And breathe thy fine keen breath along the brass,
And blow all class-walls level as Jericho's [203]
Past Jordan, – crying from the top of souls,
To souls, that, here assembled on earth's flats,
They get them to some purer eminence   935
Than any hitherto beheld for clouds!
What height we know not, – but the way we know,
And how by mounting ever, we attain,
And so climb on. It is the hour for souls,
That bodies, leavened by the will and love,   940
Be lightened to redemption. The world's old,
But the old world waits the time to be renewed,
Toward which, new hearts in individual growth
Must quicken, and increase to multitude
In new dynasties of the race of men;   945
Developed whence, shall grow spontaneously
New churches, new economies, new laws
Admitting freedom, new societies
Excluding falsehood: HE shall make all new.'

My Romney! – Lifting up my hand in his,   950
As wheeled by Seeing spirits toward the east,
He turned instinctively, where, faint and far,

Along the tingling desert of the sky,
Beyond the circle of the conscious hills,
Were laid in jasper-stone as clear as glass   955
The first foundations of that new, near Day
Which should be builded out of heaven to God.
He stood a moment with erected brows
In silence, as a creature might who gazed, –
Stood calm, and fed his blind, majestic eyes   960
Upon the thought of perfect noon: and when
I saw his soul saw, – 'Jasper first,' I said,
'And second, sapphire; third, chalcedony;[204]
The rest in order, – last, an amethyst.'

FROM
The Seraphim and Other Poems
published in 1838

Isobel's Child

> So find we profit,
> By losing of our prayers.
>
> SHAKESPEARE

1

To rest the weary nurse has gone.
   All eight-day watch had watchèd she,
Still rocking beneath sun and moon
   The baby on her knee,
Till Isobel its mother said,   5
'The fever waneth – wend to bed,
   For now the watch comes round to me.'

2

Then wearily the nurse did throw
Her pallet in the darkest place
   Of that sick room, and slept and dreamed: 10
   For, as the gusty wind did blow
   The night-lamp's flare across her face,
She saw, or seemed to see, but dreamed,
   That the poplars tall on the opposite hill,
   The seven tall poplars on the hill,   15
   Did clasp the setting sun until
   His rays dropped from him, pined and still
      As blossoms in frost!
Till he waned and paled, so weirdly crossed,
To the colour of moonlight which doth pass   20
Over the dank ridged churchyard grass.
   The poplars held the sun, and he
The eyes of the nurse that they should not see,
Not for a moment, the babe on her knee,
Though she shuddered to feel that it grew to be   25
   Too chill, and lay too heavily.

3

She only dreamed; for all the while
'Twas Lady Isobel that kept
The little baby, – and it slept
Fast, warm, as if its mother's smile,   30
Laden with love's dewy weight,
And red as rose of Harpocrate
Dropt upon its eyelids, pressed
Lashes to cheek in a sealèd rest.

4

And more and more smiled Isobel   35
To see the baby sleep so well –
   She knew not that she smiled.
Against the lattice, dull and wild
Drive the heavy droning drops,
Drop by drop, the sound being one –   40
As momently time's segments fall
On the ear of God, who hears through all
   Eternity's unbroken monotone.
And more and more smiled Isobel
To see the baby sleep so well –   45
   She knew not that she smiled.
The wind in intermission stops
Down in the beechen forest,
   Then cries aloud
   As one at the sorest,   50
   Self-stung, self-driven,
And rises up to its very tops,
Stiffening erect the branches bowed,
Dilating with a tempest-soul
The trees that with their dark hands break   55
Through their own outline and heavy roll
Shadows as massive as clouds in heaven,
Across the castle lake.
And more and more smiled Isobel
To see the baby sleep so well;   60
She knew not that she smiled;
She knew not that the storm was wild.

Through the uproar drear she could not hear
The castle clock which struck anear —
She heard the low, light breathing of her child.   65

5

O sight for wondering look!
While the external nature broke
Into such abandonment,
While the very mist heart-rent
By the lightning, seemed to eddy   70
Against nature, with a din,
A sense of silence and of steady
Natural calm appeared to come
From things without, and enter in
  The human creature's room.   75

6

So motionless she sat,
The babe asleep upon her knees,
You might have dreamed their souls had gone
Away to things inanimate,
In such to live, in such to moan;   80
And that their bodies had ta'en back,
In mystic change, all silences
That cross the sky in cloudy rack,
Or dwell beneath the reedy ground
In waters safe from their own sound.   85
  Only she wore
The deepening smile I named before,
And *that* a deepening love expressed;
And who at once can love and rest?

7

In sooth the smile that then was keeping   90
Watch upon the baby sleeping,
Floated with its tender light
Downward, from the drooping eyes,
Upward, from the lips apart,
Over cheeks which had grown white   95

With an eight-day weeping.
All smiles come in such a wise,
Where tears shall fall or have of old –
Like northern lights that fill the heart
   Of heaven in sign of cold.   100

8

Motionless she sat.
Her hair had fallen by its weight
On each side of her smile, and lay
Very blackly on the arm
Where the baby nestled warm,   105
Pale as baby carved in stone
Seen by glimpses of the moon
   Up a dark cathedral aisle.
But, through the storm, no moonbeam fell
Upon the child of Isobel –   110
Perhaps you saw it by the ray
   Alone of her still smile.

9

A solemn thing it is to me
To look upon a babe that sleeps;
Wearing in its spirit-deeps   115
The undeveloped mystery
Of our Adam's taint and woe,
Which, when they developed be,
Will not let it slumber so!
Lying new in life beneath   120
The shadow of the coming death,
With that soft, low, quiet breath,
   As if it felt the sun!
Knowing all things by their blooms,
Not their roots, yea, sun and sky,   125
Only by the warmth that comes
Out of each, – earth, only by
The pleasant hues that o'er it run, –
And human love, by drops of sweet
White nourishment still hanging round   130
The little mouth so slumber-bound.

All which broken sentiency
And conclusion incomplete,
Will gather and unite and climb
To an immortality   135
Good or evil, each sublime,
Through life and death to life again.
O little lids, now folded fast,
Must ye learn to drop at last
Our large and burning tears?   140
O warm quick body, must thou lie,
When the time comes round to die,
Still, from all the whirl of years,
Bare of all the joy and pain? –
O small frail being, wilt thou stand   145
    At God's right hand,
Lifting up those sleeping eyes
Dilated by great destinies,
To an endless waking? thrones and seraphim,
Through the long ranks of their solemnities,   150
Sunning thee with calm looks of Heaven's surprise,
    But thine alone on Him? –
Or else, self-willed, to tread the Godless place
(God keep thy will!), feel thine own energies
Cold, strong, objectless, like a dead man's clasp,   155
The sleepless deathless life within thee, grasp, –
While myriad faces, like one changeless face,
With woe *not love's*, shall glass thee everywhere,
And overcome thee with thine own despair?

10

More soft, less solemn images   160
Drifted o'er the lady's heart,
    Silently as snow.
She had seen eight days depart
Hour by hour, on bended knees,
With pale-wrung hands and prayings low   165
And broken, through which came the sound
Of tears that fell against the ground,
Making sad stops: – 'Dear Lord, dear Lord!'
She still had prayed (the heavenly word,

607

Broken by an earthly sigh),　　　　　　　　170
– 'Thou, who didst not erst deny
The mother-joy to Mary mild,
Blessèd in the blessèd child,
Which hearkened in meek babyhood
Her cradle-hymn, albeit used　　　　　　175
To all that music interfused
In breasts of angels high and good!
Oh, take not, Lord, my babe away –
Oh, take not to Thy songful heaven
The pretty baby Thou hast given,　　　　180
Or ere that I have seen him play
Around his father's knees and known
That *he* knew how my love has gone
　　From all the world to him.
Think, God among the cherubim,　　　　185
How I shall shiver every day
In Thy June sunshine, knowing where
The grave-grass keeps it from his fair
Still cheeks! and feel at every tread
His little body which is dead　　　　　190
And hidden in the turfy fold,
Doth make thy whole warm earth a-cold!
O God, I am so young, so young –
I am not used to tears at nights
Instead of slumber – nor to prayer　　　195
With sobbing lips and hands out-wrung!
Thou knowest all my prayings were
"I bless Thee, God, for past delights –
Thank God!" I am not used to bear
Hard thoughts of death; the earth doth cover　200
No face from me of friend or lover.
And must the first who teaches me
The form of shrouds and funerals, be
Mine own first-born belovèd? he
Who taught me first this mother-love?　　205
Dear Lord, who spreadest out above
Thy loving, transpiercèd hands to meet
All lifted hearts with blessing sweet, –
Pierce not my heart, my tender heart,

Thou madest tender! Thou who art   210
So happy in Thy heaven alway!
Take not mine only bliss away!'

11

She so had prayed: and God, who hears
Through seraph-songs the sound of tears,
From that belovèd babe had ta'en   215
The fever and the beating pain.
And more and more smiled Isobel
To see the baby sleep so well
(She knew not that she smiled, I wis),
Until the pleasant gradual thought   220
Which near her heart the smile enwrought,
Now soft and slow, itself, did seem
To float along a happy dream,
    Beyond it into speech like this.

12

'I prayed for thee, my little child,   225
And God has heard my prayer!
And when thy babyhood is gone,
We two together, undefiled
By men's repinings, will kneel down
Upon His earth which will be fair   230
(Not covering thee, sweet!) to us twain,
And give Him thankful praise.'

13

Dully and wildly drives the rain:
Against the lattices drives the rain.

14

'I thank Him now, that I can think   235
    Of those same future days,
Nor from the harmless image shrink
    Of what I there might see –
Strange babies on their mothers' knee,
Whose innocent soft faces might   240

609

From off mine eyelids strike the light,
    With looks not meant for me!'

15

Gustily blows the wind through the rain,
As against the lattices drives the rain.

16

'But now, O baby mine, together   245
We turn this hope of ours again
To many an hour of summer weather,
When we shall sit and intertwine
Our spirits, and instruct each other
In the pure loves of child and mother!   250
Two human loves make one divine.'

17

The thunder tears through the wind and the rain,
As full on the lattices drives the rain.

18

'My little child, what wilt thou choose?
Now let me look at thee and ponder.   255
What gladness, from the gladnesses
Futurity is spreading under
Thy gladsome sight? Beneath the trees
Wilt thou lean all day, and lose
Thy spirit with the river seen   260
Intermittently between
The winding beechen alleys, –
Half in labour, half repose,
Like a shepherd keeping sheep,
Thou, with only thoughts to keep   265
Which never a bound will overpass,
And which are innocent as those
That feed among Arcadian valleys
    Upon the dewy grass?'

19

The large white owl that with age is blind,   270
That hath sat for years in the old tree hollow,
Is carried away in a gust of wind!
His wings could beat him not as fast
As he goeth now the lattice past –
He is borne by the winds; the rains do follow: 275
His white wings to the blast outflowing,
    He hooteth in going,
And still, in the lightnings, coldly glitter
    His round unblinking eyes

20

'Or, baby, wilt thou think it fitter   280
To be eloquent and wise, –
One upon whose lips the air
Turns to solemn verities,
For men to breathe anew, and win
A deeper-seated life within?   285
Wilt be a philosopher,
By whose voice the earth and skies
Shall speak to the unborn?
Or a poet, broadly spreading
The golden immortalities   290
Of thy soul on natures lorn
And poor of such, them all to guard
From their decay, – beneath thy treading,
Earth's flowers recovering hues of Eden, –
And stars, drawn downward by thy looks,   295
To shine ascendant in thy books?'

21

The tame hawk in the castle-yard,
How it screams to the lightning, with its wet
Jagged plumes overhanging the parapet!
And at the lady's door the hound   300
    Scratches with a crying sound.

22

'But, O my babe, thy lids are laid
  Close, fast upon thy cheek, –
And not a dream of power and sheen
Can make a passage up between;   305
Thy heart is of thy mother's made,
  Thy looks are very meek;
And it will be their chosen place
To rest on some belovèd face,
As these on thine – and let the noise   310
Of the whole world go on, nor drown
  The tender silence of thy joys!
Or when that silence shall have grown
Too tender for itself, the same
Yearning for sound, – to look above   315
And utter its one meaning, LOVE,
  That *He* may hear His name!'

23

No wind, no rain, no thunder!
The waters had trickled not slowly,
The thunder was not spent,   320
Nor the wind near finishing.
Who would have said that the storm was diminishing?
No wind, no rain, no thunder!
Their noises dropped asunder
From the earth and the firmament,   325
From the towers and the lattices,
Abrupt and echoless
As ripe fruits on the ground unshaken wholly –
    As life in death!
And sudden and solemn the silence fell,   330
Startling the heart of Isobel
    As the tempest could not.
Against the door went panting the breath
Of the lady's hound whose cry was still,
And she, constrained howe'er she would not,   335
Lifted her eyes, and saw the moon
Looking out of heaven alone

Upon the poplared hill, –
A calm of God, made visible
That men might bless it at their will.   340

24

The moonshine on the baby's face
   Falleth clear and cold.
The mother's looks have fallen back
   To the same place;
Because no moon with silver rack,   345
Nor broad sunrise in jasper skies,
     Has power to hold
     Our loving eyes,
Which still revert, as ever must
Wonder and Hope, to gaze on the dust.   350

25

The moonshine on the baby's face
   Cold and clear remaineth:
The mother's looks do shrink away, –
The mother's looks return to stay,
   As charmèd by what paineth.   355
Is any glamour in the case?
Is it dream or is it sight?
Hath the change upon the wild
Elements, that signs the night,
   Passed upon the child?   360
It is not dream, but sight! –

26

The babe has awakened from sleep,
And unto the gaze of its mother
Bent over it, lifted another!
Not the baby-looks that go   365
Unaimingly to and fro,
But an earnest gazing deep,
Such as soul gives soul at length,
When, by work and wail of years,
It winneth a solemn strength,   370

And mourneth as it wears.
A strong man could not brook
With pulse unhurried by fears
To meet that baby's look
O'erglazed by manhood's tears –   375
The tears of a man full grown,
With a power to wring our own,
In the eyes all undefiled
Of a little three-months' child!
To see that babe-brow wrought   380
By the witnessing of thought,
To judgment's prodigy!
And the small soft mouth unweaned,
By mother's kiss o'erleaned
(Putting the sound of loving   385
Where no sound else was moving,
   Except the speechless cry),
   Quickened to mind's expression,
   Shaped to articulation,
Yea, uttering words – yea, naming woe,   390
In tones that with it strangely went,
Because so baby-innocent,
As the child spake out to the mother so: –

27

'O mother, mother, loose thy prayer!
   Christ's name hath made it strong.   395
It bindeth me, it holdeth me
With its most loving cruelty,
From floating my new soul along
   The happy heavenly air.
It bindeth me, it holdeth me   400
In all this dark, upon this dull
Low earth, by only weepers trod! –
It bindeth me, it holdeth me! –
Mine angel looketh sorrowful
   Upon the face of God.*   405

---

* For I say unto you, That in heaven their angels do always behold the face of my Father which is in heaven.   Matthew 18, 10

28

'Mother, mother, can I dream
Beneath your earthly trees?
I had a vision and a gleam –
I heard a sound more sweet than these
   When rippled by the wind.   410
Did you see the Dove with wings
Bathed in golden glisterings
From a sunless light behind,
Dropping on me from the sky
Soft as mother's kiss, until   415
I seemed to leap, and yet was still?
Saw you how His love-large eye
Looked upon me mystic calms,
Till the power of His divine
Vision was indrawn to mine?   420

29

'Oh, the dream within the dream!
I saw celestial places even.
Oh, the vistas of high palms,
Making finites of delight
Through the heavenly infinite –   425
Lifting up their green still tops
   To the heaven of Heaven!
Oh, the sweet life-tree that drops
Shade like light across the river
Glorified in its for-ever   430
   Flowing from the Throne!
Oh, the shining holinesses
Of the thousand, thousand faces
God-sunned by the throned ONE!
And made intense with such a love,   435
That though I saw them turned above,
Each loving seemed for also me!
And, oh, the Unspeakable, the HE,
The manifest in secrecies,
Yet of mine own heart partaker, –   440
With the overcoming look

Of One who hath been once forsook,
   And blesseth the forsaker.
Mother, mother, let me go
Toward the Face that looketh so.   445
Through the mystic, wingèd Four
Whose are inward, outward eyes
Dark with light of mysteries,
And the restless evermore
"Holy, holy, holy," – through   450
The sevenfold Lamps that burn in view
Of cherubim and seraphim, –
Through the four-and-twenty crowned
Stately elders, white around,
Suffer me to go to Him!   455

30

'Is your wisdom very wise,
Mother, on the narrow earth,
Very happy, very worth
That I should stay to learn?
Are these air-corrupting sighs   460
Fashioned by unlearnèd breath?
Do the students' lamps that burn
All night, illumine death?
Mother, albeit this be so,
Loose thy prayer and let me go   465
Where that bright chief angel stands
Apart from all his brother bands,
Too glad for smiling, having bent
In angelic wilderment
O'er the depths of God, and brought   470
Reeling thence, one only thought
To fill his own eternity.
He the teacher is for me! –
He can teach what I would know –
Mother, mother, let me go!   475

31

'Can your poet make an Eden
   No winter will undo,
And light a starry fire while heeding
   His hearth's is burning too?
Drown in music the earth's din,   480
And keep his own wild soul within
The law of his own harmony? –
Mother, albeit this be so,
Let me to my Heaven go!
A little harp me waits thereby –   485
A harp whose strings are golden all,
And tuned to music spherical,
Hanging on the green life-tree
Where no willows ever be.
Shall I miss that harp of mine?   490
Mother, no! – the Eye divine
Turned upon it, makes it shine;
And when I touch it, poems sweet
Like separate souls shall fly from it,
Each to the immortal fytte.   495
We shall all be poets there,
Gazing on the chiefest Fair.

32

'Love! earth's love! and *can* we love
Fixedly where all things move?
Can the sinning love each other?   500
    Mother, mother,
I tremble in thy close embrace,
I feel thy tears adown my face,
Thy prayers do keep me out of bliss –
    O dreary earthly love!   505
Loose thy prayer and let me go
To the place which loving is
Yet not sad; and when is given
Escape to *thee* from this below,
Thou shalt behold me that I wait   510
For thee beside the happy Gate,

And silence shall be up in heaven
　　To hear our greeting kiss.'

33

The nurse awakes in the morning sun,
And starts to see beside her bed   515
The lady with a grandeur spread
Like pathos o'er her face, – as one
God-satisfied and earth-undone.
　　The babe upon her arm was dead!
And the nurse could utter forth no cry, –   520
She was awed by the calm in the mother's eye.

34

'Wake, nurse!' the lady said;
'*We* are waking – he and I –
I, on earth, and he, in sky!
And thou must help me to o'erlay   525
With garment white, this little clay
Which needs no more our lullaby.

35

'I changed the cruel prayer I made,
And bowed my meekened face, and prayed
That God would do His will! and thus   530
He did it, nurse! He parted *us*.
And His sun shows victorious
The dead calm face, – and *I* am calm,
And Heaven is hearkening a new psalm.

36

'This earthly noise is too anear,   535
Too loud, and will not let me hear
The little harp. My death will soon
Make silence.'

　　　　　　　And a sense of tune,
A satisfièd love meanwhile
Which nothing earthly could despoil,   540
Sang on within her soul.

37

Oh you,
Earth's tender and impassioned few,
Take courage to entrust your love
To Him so named, who guards above
　Its ends and shall fulfil! 545
Breaking the narrow prayers that may
Befit your narrow hearts, away
　In His broad, loving will.

The Deserted Garden

I mind me in the days departed,
How often underneath the sun
With childish bounds I used to run
  To a garden long deserted.

The beds and walks were vanished quite;   5
And wheresoe'er had struck the spade,
The greenest grasses Nature laid,
  To sanctify her right.

I called the place my wilderness,
For no one entered there but I;   10
The sheep looked in, the grass to espy,
  And passed it ne'ertheless.

The trees were interwoven wild,
And spread their boughs enough about
To keep both sheep and shepherd out,   15
  But not a happy child.

Adventurous joy it was for me!
I crept beneath the boughs, and found
A circle smooth of mossy ground
  Beneath a poplar tree.   20

Old garden rose-trees hedged it in,
Bedropt with roses waxen-white
Well satisfied with dew and light
  And careless to be seen.

Long years ago it might befall,   25
When all the garden flowers were trim,
The grave old gardener prided him
  On these the most of all.

Some lady, stately overmuch,
Here moving with a silken noise,   30
Has blushed beside them at the voice
  That likened her to such.

And these, to make a diadem,
She often may have plucked and twined,
Half-smiling as it came to mind   35
  That few would look at   *them*.

Oh, little thought that lady proud,
A child would watch her fair white rose,
When buried lay her whiter brows,
  And silk was changed for shroud! –   40

Nor thought that gardener (full of scorns
For men unlearned and simple phrase),
A child would bring it all its praise
  By creeping through the thorns!

To me upon my low moss seat,   45
Though never a dream the roses sent
Of science or love's compliment,
  I ween they smelt as sweet.

It did not move my grief to see
The trace of human step departed: 50
Because the garden was deserted,
  The blither place for me!

Friends, blame me not! a narrow ken
Hath childhood 'twixt the sun and sward:
We draw the moral afterward—   55
  We feel the gladness then.

And gladdest hours for me did glide
In silence at the rose-tree wall;
A thrush made gladness musical
  Upon the other side.   60

Nor he nor I did e'er incline
To peck or pluck the blossoms white;
How should I know but roses might
  Lead lives as glad as mine?

To make my hermit-home complete,   65
I brought clear water from the spring
Praised in its own low murmuring, –
  And cresses glossy wet.

And so, I thought, my likeness grew
(Without the melancholy tale)   70
To 'gentle hermit of the dale',
  And Angelina too.

For oft I read within my nook
Such minstrel stories; till the breeze
Made sounds poetic in the trees, –   75
  And then I shut the book.

If I shut this wherein I write
I hear no more the wind athwart
Those trees, – nor feel that childish heart
  Delighting in delight.   80

My childhood from my life is parted,
My footstep from the moss which drew
Its fairy circle round: anew
  The garden is deserted.

Another thrush may there rehearse   85
The madrigals which sweetest are;
No more for me! – myself afar
  Do sing a sadder verse.

Ah me, ah me! when erst I lay
In that child's-nest so greenly wrought,   90
I laugh'd unto myself and thought
  'The time will pass away.'

And still I laughed, and did not fear
But that, whene'er was past away
The childish time, some happier play   95
  My womanhood would cheer.

622

I knew the time would pass away,
And yet, beside the rose-tree wall,
Dear God, how seldom, if at all,
  Did I look up to pray! 100

The time is past; – and now that grows
The cypress high among the trees,
And I behold white sepulchres
  As well as the white rose, –

When graver, meeker thoughts are given, 105
And I have learnt to lift my face,
Reminded how earth's greenest place
  The colour draws from heaven, –

It something saith for earthly pain,
But more for Heavenly promise free, 110
That I who was, would shrink to be
  That happy child again.

The Soul's Travelling

Ἤδη νοεροὺς
Πετάσαι ταρσούς.[205]

SYNESIUS

1

I dwell amid the city ever.
The great humanity which beats
Its life along the stony streets,
Like a strong and unsunned river
In a self-made course,   5
I sit and hearken while it rolls.
Very sad and very hoarse,
Certes, is the flow of souls:
Infinitest tendencies
By the finite prest and pent,   10
In the finite, turbulent,
How we tremble in surprise,
When sometimes, with an awful sound,
God's great plummet strikes the ground!

2

The champ of the steeds on the silver bit,   15
As they whirl the rich man's carriage by;
The beggar's whine as he looks at it, –
But it goes too fast for charity;
The trail on the street of the poor man's broom,
That the lady who walks to her palace-home,   20
On her silken skirt may catch no dust;
The tread of the business-men who must
Count their per-cents by the paces they take;
The cry of the babe unheard of its mother
Though it lie on her breast, while she thinks of the other   25
Laid yesterday where it will not wake;
The flower-girl's prayer to buy roses and pinks,
Held out in the smoke, like stars by day;
The gin-door's oath that hollowly chinks
Guilt upon grief and wrong upon hate;   30

The cabman's cry to get out of the way
The dustman's call down the area-grate,
The young maid's jest, and the old wife's scold,
The haggling talk of the boys at a stall,
The fight in the street which is backed for gold,   35
The plea of the lawyers in Westminster Hall;
The drop on the stones of the blind man's staff
As he trades in his own grief's sacredness;
The brothel shriek, and the Newgate laugh,
The hum upon 'Change, and the organ's grinding –   40
The grinder's face being nevertheless
Dry and vacant of even woe,
While the children's hearts are leaping so
At the merry music's winding;
The black-plumed funeral's creeping train,   45
Long and slow (and yet they will go
As fast as Life, though it hurry and strain),
Creeping the populous houses through,
And nodding their plumes at either side, –
At many a house where an infant, new   50
To the sunshiny world, has just struggled and cried, –
At many a house, where sitteth a bride
Trying tomorrow's coronals
With a scarlet blush today:
    Slowly creep the funerals,   55
As none should hear the noise and say,
'The living, the living, must go away
        To multiply the dead.'
    Hark! an upward shout is sent!
In grave strong joy from tower to steeple   60
        The bells ring out –
The trumpets sound, the people shout,
The young queen goes to her Parliament.
She turneth round her large blue eyes,
More bright with childish memories   65
Than royal hopes, upon the people:
On either side she bows her head
    Lowly, with a queenly grace,
And smile most trusting-innocent,
As if she smiled upon her mother;   70

The thousands press before each other
  To bless her to her face;
And booms the deep majestic voice
Through trump and drum, – 'May the queen rejoice
    In the people's liberties!' –   75

3

I dwell amid the city,
And hear the flow of souls in act and speech,
For pomp or trade, for merrymake or folly;
I hear the confluence and sum of each,
  And that is melancholy! –   80
Thy voice is a complaint, O crownèd city,
The blue sky covering thee like God's great pity.

4

O blue sky! it mindeth me
Of places where I used to see
Its vast unbroken circle thrown   85
From the far pale-peakèd hill
Out to the last verge of ocean,
As by God's arm it were done
Then for the first time, with the emotion
Of that first impulse on it still.   90
Oh, we spirits fly at will,
Faster than the wingèd steed
Whereof in old book we read,
With the sunlight foaming back
From his flanks to a misty wrack,   95
And his nostril reddening proud
As he breasteth the steep thundercloud, –
Smoother than Sabrina's [206] chair
Gliding up from wave to air,
While she smileth debonair   100
Yet holy, coldly and yet brightly,
Like her own mooned waters nightly,
    Through her dripping hair.

5

Very fast and smooth we fly,
Spirits, though the flesh be by.   105
All looks feed not from the eye,
Nor all hearings from the ear;
We can hearken and espy
Without either; we can journey
Bold and gay as knight to tourney,   110
And though we wear no visor down
To dark our countenance, the foe
Shall never chafe us as we go.

6

I am gone from peopled town!
It passeth its street-thunder round   115
My body which yet hears no sound:
For now another sound, another
Vision, my soul's senses have –
O'er a hundred valleys deep,
Where the hills' green shadows sleep   120
Scarce known (because the valley-trees
Cross those upland images),
O'er a hundred hills, each other
Watching to the western wave,
I have travelled, – I have found   125
The silent, lone, remembered ground.

7

I have found a grassy niche
Hollowed in a seaside hill,
As if the ocean-grandeur which
Is aspectable from the place   130
Had struck the hill as with a mace
Sudden and cleaving. You might fill
That little nook with the little cloud
Which sometimes lieth by the moon
To beautify a night of June.   135
A cavelike nook, which, opening all

To the wide sea, is disallowed
From its own earth's sweet pastoral;
Cavelike, but roofless overhead,
And made of verdant banks instead   140
Of any rocks, with flowerets spread,
Instead of spar and stalactite,
Cowslips and daisies, gold and white:
Such pretty flowers on such green sward,
You think the sea they look toward   145
Doth serve them for another sky
As warm and blue as that on high.

8

And in this hollow is a seat,
And when you shall have crept to it,
Slipping down the banks too steep   150
To be o'erbrowsèd by the sheep,
Do not think – though at your feet
The cliff's disrupt – you shall behold
The line where earth and ocean meet.
You sit too much above to view   155
The solemn confluence of the two:
You can hear them as they greet;
You can hear that evermore
Distance-softened noise, more old
Than Nereid's singing, – the tide spent   160
Joining soft issues with the shore
In harmony of discontent, –
And when you hearken to the grave
Lamenting of the underwave,
You must believe in earth's communion,   165
Albeit you witness not the union.

9

Except that sound, the place is full
Of silences, which when you cull
By any word, it thrills you so
That presently you let them grow   170
To meditation's fullest length
Across your soul with a soul's strength:

And as they touch your soul, they borrow
Both of its grandeur and its sorrow,
That deathly odour which the clay   175
Leaves on its deathlessness alway.

10

Alway! alway? must this be?
Rapid Soul from city gone,
Dost thou carry inwardly
What doth make the city's moan?   180
Must this deep sigh of thine own
Haunt thee with humanity?
Green visioned banks that are too steep
To be o'erbrowsèd by the sheep,
May all sad thoughts adown you creep   185
Without a shepherd? – Mighty sea,
Can we dwarf thy magnitude,
And fit it to our straitest mood? –
O fair, fair Nature! are we thus
Impotent and querulous   190
Among thy workings glorious,
Wealth and sanctities, – that still
Leave us vacant and defiled,
And wailing like a soft-kissed child,
Kissed soft against his will?   195

11

God, God!
With a child's voice I cry,
Weak, sad, confidingly –
God, God!
Thou knowest, eyelids, raised not always up   200
Unto Thy love (as none of ours are), droop
As ours, o'er many a tear!
Thou knowest, though Thy universe is broad,
Two little tears suffice to cover all:
Thou knowest, Thou, who art so prodigal   205
Of beauty, we are oft but stricken deer
Expiring in the woods – that care for none
Of those delightsome flowers they die upon.

12

O blissful Mouth which breathed the mournful breath
We name our souls, self-spoilt! – by that strong passion   210
Which paled Thee once with sighs, – by that strong death
Which made Thee once unbreathing – from the wrack
Themselves have called around them, call them back,
Back to Thee in continuous aspiration!
    For here, O Lord,   215
For here they travel vainly, – vainly pass
From city-pavement to untrodden sward,
Where the lark finds her deep nest in the grass
Cold with the earth's last dew. Yea, very vain
The greatest speed of all these souls of men,   220
Unless they travel upward to the throne,
Where sittest THOU, the satisfying ONE,
With help for sins and holy perfectings
For all requirements – while the archangel, raising
Unto Thy face his full ecstatic gazing,   225
Forgets the rush and rapture of his wings.

Felicia Hemans [207]

TO L. E. L. [208]

REFERRING TO HER MONODY ON THE POETESS

1

Thou bay-crowned living One that o'er the bay-crowned Dead art bowing,
And o'er the shadeless moveless brow the vital shadow throwing,
And o'er the sighless songless lips the wail and music wedding,
And dropping o'er the tranquil eyes, the tears not of their shedding! –

2

Take music from the silent Dead, whose meaning is completer,   5
Reserve thy tears for living brows, where all such tears are meeter,
And leave the violets in the grass to brighten where thou treadest!
No flowers for her! no need of flowers – albeit 'bring flowers,' thou saidest.

3

Yes, flowers, to crown the 'cup and lute!' since both may come to breaking;
Or flowers, to greet the 'bride!' the heart's own beating works its aching;
Or flowers, to soothe the 'captive's' sight, from earth's free bosom gathered,
Reminding of his earthly hope, then withering as it withered.

4

But bring not near the solemn corse, a type of human seeming,
Lay only dust's stern verity upon the dust undreaming;
And while the calm perpetual stars shall look upon it solely,   15
Her spherèd soul shall look on *them*, with eyes more bright and holy.

5

Nor mourn, O living One, because her part in life was mourning.
Would she have lost the poet's fire for anguish of the burning? –
The minstrel harp, for the strained string? the tripod, for the afflated
Woe? or the vision, for those tears in which it shone dilated?   20

6

Perhaps she shuddered while the world's cold hand her brow was wreathing,
But never wronged that mystic breath which breathed in all her breathing,
Which drew from rocky earth and man, abstractions high and moving,
Beauty, if not the beautiful, and love, if not the loving.

7

Such visionings have paled in sight; the Saviour she descrieth,   25
And little recks *who* wreathed the brow which on His bosom lieth:
The whiteness of His innocence o'er all her garments, flowing,
There, learneth she the sweet 'new song', she will not mourn in knowing.

8

Be happy, crowned and living One! and, as thy dust decayeth,
May thine own England say for thee, what now for Her it sayeth –   30
'Albeit softly in our ears her silver song was ringing,
The footfall of her parting soul is softer than her singing!'

A Seaside Walk

1

We walked beside the sea
After a day which perished silently
Of its own glory – like the princess weird
Who, combating the Genius, scorched and seared,
Uttered with burning breath, 'Ho! victory!'   5
And sank adown a heap of ashes pale.
    So runs the Arab tale.

2

The sky above us showed
A universal and unmoving cloud,
On which the cliffs permitted us to see   10
Only the outline of their majesty,
As master-minds when gazed at by the crowd!
And, shining with a gloom, the water grey
    Swang in its moon-taught way.

3

Nor moon nor stars were out: 15
They did not dare to tread so soon about,
Though trembling, in the footsteps of the sun;
The light was neither night's nor day's, but one
Which, life-like, had a beauty in its doubt,
And Silence's impassioned breathings round   20
    Seemed wandering into sound.

4

O solemn-beating heart
Of nature! I have knowledge that thou art
Bound unto man's by cords he cannot sever –
And, what time they are slackened by him ever,   25
So to attest his own supernal part,
Still runneth thy vibration fast and strong
    The slackened cord along.

5

For though we never spoke
Of the grey water and the shaded rock,   30
Dark wave and stone unconsciously were fused
Into the plaintive speaking that we used
Of absent friends and memories unforsook;
And, had we seen each other's face, we had
    Seen haply, each was sad.   35

FROM
Poems before Congress
published in 1860

A Tale of Villafranca [209]

1

My little son, my Florentine,
  Sit down beside my knee,
And I will tell you why the sign
  Of joy which flushed our Italy,
Has faded since but yesternight;   5
And why your Florence of delight
  Is mourning as you see.

2

A great man (who was crowned one day)
  Imagined a great Deed:
He shaped it out of cloud and clay,   10
  He touched it finely till the seed
Possessed the flower: from heart and brain
He fed it with large thoughts humane,
  To help a people's need.

3

He brought it out into the sun –   15
  They blessed it to his face:
'O great pure Deed, that hast undone
  So many bad and base!
O generous Deed, heroic Deed,
Come forth, be perfected, succeed,   20
  Deliver by God's grace.'

4

Then sovereigns, statesmen, north and south,
  Rose up in wrath and fear,
And cried, protesting by one mouth,
  'What monster have we here?   25
A great Deed at this hour of day?
A great just Deed – and not for pay?
  Absurd, – or insincere.

637

5

'And if sincere, the heavier blow
   In that case we shall bear,   30
For where's our blessed "status quo",
    Our holy treaties, where, –
Our rights to sell a race, or buy,
Protect and pillage, occupy,
    And civilise despair?'   35

6

Some muttered that the great Deed meant
    A great pretext to sin;
And others, the pretext, so lent,
    Was heinous (to begin).
Volcanic terms of 'great'and 'just'?   40
Admit such tongues of flame, the crust
    Of time and law falls in.

7

A great Deed in this world of ours?
    Unheard of the pretence is:
It threatens plainly the great Powers;   45
    Is fatal in all senses.
A just Deed in the world? – call out
The rifles! be not slack about
    The national defences.

8

And many murmured, 'From this source   50
    What red blood must be poured!'
And some rejoined, ' 'Tis even worse;
    What red tape is ignored!'
All cursed the Doer for an evil
Called here, enlarging on the Devil, –   55
    There, monkeying the Lord!

9

Some said, it could not be explained,
    Some, could not be excused;
And others, 'Leave it unrestrained,
    Gehenna's self is loosed.'   60
And all cried, 'Crush it, maim it, gag it!
Set dog-toothed lies to tear it ragged,
    Truncated and traduced!'

10

But HE stood sad before the sun
    (The peoples felt their fate).   65
'The world is many, – I am one;
    My great Deed was too great.
God's fruit of justice ripens slow:
Men's souls are narrow; let them grow.
    My brothers, we must wait.'   70

11

The tale is ended, child of mine,
    Turned graver at my knee.
They say your eyes, my Florentine,
    Are English: it may be:
And yet I've marked as blue a pair   75
Following the doves across the square
    At Venice by the sea.

12

Ah, child! ah, child! I cannot say
    A word more. You conceive
The reason now, why just today   80
    We see our Florence grieve.
Ah, child, look up into the sky!
In this low world, where great Deeds die,
    What matter if we live?

Italy and the World ²¹⁰

1

Florence, Bologna, Parma, Modena.
   When you named them a year ago,
So many graves reserved by God, in a
   Day of Judgment, you seemed to know,
To open and let out the resurrection.   5

2

And meantime (you made your reflection
   If you were English), was nought to be done
But sorting sables, in predilection
   For all those martyrs dead and gone,
Till the new earth and heaven made ready?   10

3

And if your politics were not heady,
   Violent, . . . 'Good,' you added, 'good
In all things! Mourn on sure and steady.
   Churchyard thistles are wholesome food
For our European wandering asses.   15

4

'The date of the resurrection passes
   Human foreknowledge: men unborn
Will gain by it (even in the lower classes),
   But none of these. It is not the morn
Because the cock of France is crowing.   20

5

'Cocks crow at midnight, seldom knowing
   Starlight from dawn-light: 'tis a mad
Poor creature.' Here you paused, and growing
   Scornful, . . . suddenly, let us add,
The trumpet sounded, the graves were open.   25

6

Life and life and life! agrope in
    The dusk of death, warm hands, stretched out
For swords, proved more life still to hope in,
    Beyond and behind. Arise with a shout,
Nation of Italy, slain and buried!   30

7

Hill to hill and turret to turret
    Flashing the tricolor, – newly created
Beautiful Italy, calm, unhurried,
    Rise heroic and renovated,
Rise to the final restitution.   35

8

Rise; prefigure the grand solution
    Of earth's municipal, insular schisms, –
Statesmen draping self-love's conclusion
    In cheap, vernacular patriotisms,
Unable to give up Judaea for Jesus.   40

9

Bring us the higher example; release us
    Into the larger coming time:
And into Christ's broad garment piece us
    Rags of virtue as poor as crime,
National selfishness, civic vaunting.   45

10

No more Jew nor Greek then, – taunting
    Nor taunted; – no more England nor France!
But one confederate brotherhood planting
    One flag only, to mark the advance,
Onward and upward, of all humanity.   50

11

For civilisation perfected
    Is fully developed Christianity.

'Measure the frontier,' shall it be said,
　'Count the ships,' in national vanity?
– Count the nation's heart-beats sooner.　　　　55

12

For, though behind by a cannon or schooner,
　That nation still is predominant,
Whose pulse beats quickest in zeal to oppugn or
　Succour another, in wrong or want,
Passing the frontier in love and abhorrence.　　60

13

Modena, Parma, Bologna, Florence,
　Open us out the wider way!
Dwarf in that chapel of old Saint Lawrence
　Your Michel Angelo's giant Day,
With the grandeur of this Day breaking o'er us!　65

14

Ye who, restrained as an ancient chorus,
　Mute while the coryphaeus spake,
Hush your separate voices before us,
　Sink your separate lives for the sake
Of one sole Italy's living for ever!　　　70

15

Givers of coat and cloak too, – never
　Grudging that purple of yours at the best, –
By your heroic will and endeavour
　Each sublimely dispossessed,
That all may inherit what each surrenders!　　75

16

Earth shall bless you, O noble emenders
　On egotist nations! Ye shall lead
The plough of the world, and sow new splendours
　Into the furrow of things, for seed, –
Ever the richer for what ye have given.　　　80

17

Lead us and teach us, till earth and heaven
   Grow larger around us and higher above.
Our sacrament-bread has a bitter leaven;
   We bait our traps with the name of love,
Till hate itself has a kinder meaning.   85

18

Oh, this world: this cheating and screening
   Of cheats! this conscience for candle-wicks,
Not beacon-fires! this overweening
   Of underhand diplomatical tricks,
Dared for the country while scorned for the counter!   90

19

Oh, this envy of those who mount here,
   And oh, this malice to make them trip!
Rather quenching the fire there, drying the fount here,
   To frozen body and thirsty lip,
Than leave to a neighbour their ministration.   95

20

I cry aloud in my poet-passion,
   Viewing my England o'er Alp and sea.
I loved her more in her ancient fashion:
   She carries her rifles too thick for me,
Who spares them so in the cause of a brother.   100

21

Suspicion, panic? end this pother.
   The sword, kept sheathless at peace-time, rusts.
None fears for himself while he feels for another:
   The brave man either fights or trusts,
And wears no mail in his private chamber.   105

22

Beautiful Italy! golden amber
    Warm with the kisses of lover and traitor!
Thou who hast drawn us on to remember,
    Draw us to hope now: let us be greater
By this new future than that old story.   110

23

Till truer glory replaces all glory,
    As the torch grows blind at the dawn of day;
And the nations, rising up, their sorry
    And foolish sins shall put away,
As children their toys when the teacher enters.   120

24

Till Love's one centre devour these centres
    Of many self-loves; and the patriot's trick
To better his land by egotist ventures,
    Defamed from a virtue, shall make men sick,
As the scalp at the belt of some red hero.   125

25

For certain virtues have dropped to zero,
    Left by the sun on the mountain's dewy side;
Churchman's charities, tender as Nero,
    Indian suttee, heathen suicide,
Service to rights divine, proved hollow: 130

26

And Heptarchy patriotisms must follow.
    – National voices, distinct yet dependent,
Ensphering each other, as swallow does swallow,
    With circles still widening and ever ascendant,
In multiform life to united progression, –   135

27

These shall remain. And when, in the session
    Of nations, the separate language is heard,
Each shall aspire, in sublime indiscretion,
    To help with a thought or exalt with a word
Less her own than her rival's honour.   140

28

Each Christian nation shall take upon her
    The law of the Christian man in vast:
The crown of the getter shall fall to the donor,
    And last shall be first while first shall be last,
And to love best shall still be, to reign unsurpassed.   145

FROM
Last Poems
published in 1862

A Song for the Ragged Schools of London [211]

WRITTEN IN ROME

1

I am listening here in Rome.
   'England's strong,' say many speakers,
'If she winks, the Czar must come,
   Prow and topsail, to the breakers.'

2

'England's rich in coal and oak,'
   Adds a Roman, getting moody,
'If she shakes a travelling cloak,
   Down our Appian roll the scudi.'

3

'England's righteous,' they rejoin,
   'Who shall grudge her exaltations,
When her wealth of golden coin
   Works the welfare of the nations?'

4

I am listening here in Rome.
   Over Alps a voice is sweeping –
'England's cruel! save us some
   Of these victims in her keeping!'

5

As the cry beneath the wheel
   Of an old triumphant Roman
Cleft the people's shouts like steel,
   While the show was spoilt for no man,

6

Comes that voice. Let others shout,
   Other poets praise my land here:
I am sadly sitting out,
   Praying, 'God forgive her grandeur.'

7

Shall we boast of empire, where   25
    Time with ruin sits commissioned?
In God's liberal blue air
    Peter's dome itself looks wizened;

8

And the mountains, in disdain,
    Gather back their lights of opal   30
From the dumb, despondent plain,
    Heaped with jawbones of a people.

9

Lordly English, think it o'er,
    Caesar's doing is all undone!
You have cannons on your shore,   35
    And free parliaments in London,

10

Princes' parks, and merchants' homes,
    Tents for soldiers, ships for seamen, –
Aye, but ruins worse than Rome's
    In your pauper men and women.   40

11

Women leering through the gas
    (Just such bosoms used to nurse you),
Men, turned wolves by famine – pass!
    Those can speak themselves, and curse you.

12

But these others – children small,   45
    Spilt like blots about the city,
Quay, and street, and palace-wall –
    Take them up into your pity!

13

Ragged children with bare feet,
    Whom the angels in white raiment   50
Know the names of, to repeat
    When they come on you for payment.

14

Ragged children, hungry-eyed,
    Huddled up out of the coldness
On your doorsteps, side by side,   55
    Till your footman damns their boldness.

15

In the alleys, in the squares,
    Begging, lying little rebels;
In the noisy thoroughfares,
    Struggling on with piteous trebles.   60

16

Patient children – think what pain
    Makes a young child patient – ponder!
Wronged too commonly to strain
    After right, or wish, or wonder.

17

Wicked children, with peaked chins,   65
    And old foreheads! there are many
With no pleasures except sins,
    Gambling with a stolen penny.

18

Sickly children, that whine low
    To themselves and not their mothers,   70
From mere habit, – never so
    Hoping help or care from others.

19

Healthy children, with those blue
   English eyes, fresh from their Maker,
Fierce and ravenous, staring through   75
   At the brown loaves of the baker.

20

I am listening here in Rome,
   And the Romans are confessing,
'English children pass in bloom
   All the prettiest made for blessing.   80

21

'*Angli angeli!*' (resumed
   From the mediaeval story)
'Such rose angelhoods, emplumed
   In such ringlets of pure glory!'

22

Can we smooth down the bright hair,   85
   O my sisters, calm, unthrilled in
Our heart's pulses? Can we bear
   The sweet looks of our own children,

23

While those others, lean and small,
   Scurf and mildew of the city,   90
Spot our streets, convict us all
   Till we take them into pity?

24

'Is it our fault?' you reply,
   'When, throughout civilisation,
Every nation's empery   95
   Is asserted by starvation?

25

'All these mouths we cannot feed,
    And we cannot clothe these bodies.'
Well, if man's so hard indeed,
    Let them learn at least what God is!   100

26

Little outcasts from life's fold,
    The grave's hope they may be joined in,
By Christ's covenant consoled
    For our social contract's grinding.

27

If no better can be done,   105
    Let us do but this, – endeavour
That the sun behind the sun
    Shine upon them while they shiver!

28

On the dismal London flags,
    Through the cruel social juggle,   110
Put a thought beneath their rags
    To ennoble the heart's struggle.

29

O my sisters, not so much
    Are we asked for – not a blossom
From our children's nosegay, such   115
    As we gave it from our bosom, –

30

Not the milk left in their cup,
    Not the lamp while they are sleeping,
Not the little cloak hung up
    While the coat's in daily keeping, –   120

31

But a place in RAGGED SCHOOLS,
    Where the outcasts may tomorrow
Learn by gentle words and rules
    Just the uses of their sorrow.

32

O my sisters! children small,   125
    Blue-eyed, wailing through the city –
Our own babes cry in them all:
    Let us take them into pity.

The Best Thing in the World

What's the best thing in the world?
June-rose, by May-dew impearled;
Sweet south-wind, that means no rain;
Truth, not cruel to a friend;
Pleasure, not in haste to end;   5
Beauty, not self-decked and curled
Till its pride is over-plain;
Light, that never makes you wink;
Memory, that gives no pain;
Love, when, *so*, you're loved again.   10
What's the best thing in the world?
– Something out of it, I think.

De Profundis [212]

1

The face which, duly as the sun,
Rose up for me with life begun,
To mark all bright hours of the day
With hourly love, is dimmed away, –
And yet my days go on, go on.   5

2

The tongue which, like a stream, could run
Smooth music from the roughest stone,
And every morning with 'Good day'
Make each day good, is hushed away, –
And yet my days go on, go on.   10

3

The heart which, like a staff, was one
For mine to lean and rest upon,
The strongest on the longest day
With steadfast love, is caught away, –
And yet my days go on, go on.   15

4

And cold before my summer's done,
And deaf in Nature's general tune,
And fallen too low for special fear,
And here, with hope no longer here, –
While the tears drop, my days go on.   20

5

The world goes whispering to its own,
'This anguish pierces to the bone';
And tender friends go sighing round,
'What love can ever cure this wound?'
My days go on, my days go on.   25

6

The past rolls forward on the sun
And makes all night. O dreams begun,
Not to be ended! Ended bliss,
And life that will not end in this!
My days go on, my days go on.   30

7

Breath freezes on my lips to moan:
As one alone, once not alone,
I sit and knock at Nature's door,
Heart-bare, heart-hungry, very poor,
Whose desolated days go on.   35

8

I knock and cry, – Undone, undone!
Is there no help, no comfort, – none?
No gleaning in the wide wheat plains
Where others drive their loaded wains?
My vacant days go on, go on.   40

9

This Nature, though the snows be down,
Thinks kindly of the bird of June:
The little red hip on the tree
Is ripe for such. What is for me,
Whose days so winterly go on?   45

10

No bird am I, to sing in June,
And dare not ask an equal boon.
Good nests and berries red are Nature's
To give away to better creatures, –
And yet my days go on, go on.   50

11

I ask less kindness to be done, –
Only to loose these pilgrim-shoon
(Too early worn and grimed), with sweet
Cool deadly touch to these tired feet,
Till days go out which now go on.   55

12

Only to lift the turf unmown
From off the earth where it has grown,
Some cubit-space, and say, 'Behold,
Creep in, poor Heart, beneath that fold,
Forgetting how the days go on.'   60

13

What harm would that do? Green anon
The sward would quicken, overshone
By skies as blue; and crickets might
Have leave to chirp there day and night
While my new rest went on, went on.   65

14

From gracious Nature have I won
Such liberal bounty? may I run
So, lizard-like, within her side,
And there be safe, who now am tried
By days that painfully go on?   70

15

– A Voice reproves me thereupon,
More sweet than Nature's when the drone
Of bees is sweetest, and more deep
Than when the rivers overleap
The shuddering pines, and thunder on.   75

16

God's Voice, not Nature's! Night and noon
He sits upon the great white throne
And listens for the creatures' praise.
What babble we of days and days?
The Dayspring He, whose days go on.   80

17

He reigns above, He reigns alone;
Systems burn out and leave His throne;
Fair mists of seraphs melt and fall
Around Him, changeless amid all, –
Ancient of Days, whose days go on.   85

18

He reigns below, He reigns alone,
And, having life in love forgone
Beneath the crown of sovran thorns,
He reigns the Jealous God. Who mourns
Or rules with Him, while days go on?   90

19

By anguish which made pale the sun,
I hear Him charge His saints that none
Among His creatures anywhere
Blaspheme against Him with despair,
However darkly days go on.   95

20

Take from my head the thorn-wreath brown!
No mortal grief deserves that crown.
O súpreme Love, chief Misery,
The sharp regalia are for THEE
Whose days eternally go on!   100

21

For us, – whatever's undergone,
Thou knowest, willest what is done.
Grief may be joy misunderstood;
Only the Good discerns the good.
I trust Thee while my days go on.   105

22

Whatever's lost, it first was won:
We will not struggle nor impugn.
Perhaps the cup was broken here,
That Heaven's new wine might show more clear.
I praise Thee while my days go on.   110

23

I praise Thee while my days go on;
I love Thee while my days go on:
Through dark and dearth, through fire and frost,
With emptied arms and treasure lost,
I thank Thee while my days go on.   115

24

And having in Thy life-depth thrown
Being and suffering (which are one),
As a child drops his pebble small
Down some deep well, and hears it fall
Smiling – so I. THY DAYS GO ON.   120

A Musical Instrument

1

What was he doing, the great god Pan,
    Down in the reeds by the river?
Spreading ruin and scattering ban,
Splashing and paddling with hoofs of a goat,
And breaking the golden lilies afloat   5
    With the dragon-fly on the river.

2

He tore out a reed, the great god Pan,
    From the deep cool bed of the river:
The limpid water turbidly ran,
And the broken lilies a-dying lay,   10
And the dragon-fly had fled away,
    Ere he brought it out of the river.

3

High on the shore sat the great god Pan,
    While turbidly flowed the river;
And hacked and hewed as a great god can,   15
With his hard bleak steel at the patient reed,
Till there was not a sign of the leaf indeed
    To prove it fresh from the river.

4

He cut it short, did the great god Pan
    (How tall it stood in the river!),   20
Then drew the pith, like the heart of a man,
Steadily from the outside ring,
And notch'd the poor dry empty thing
    In holes, as he sat by the river.

5

'This is the way,' laughed the great god Pan 25
  (Laughed while he sat by the river),
'The only way, since gods began
To make sweet music, they could succeed.'
Then, dropping his mouth to a hole in the reed,
  He blew in power by the river. 30

6

Sweet, sweet, sweet, O Pan!
  Piercing sweet by the river!
Blinding sweet, O great god Pan!
The sun on the hill forgot to die,
And the lilies revived, and the dragon-fly 35
  Came back to dream on the river.

7

Yet half a beast is the great god Pan,
  To laugh as he sits by the river,
Making a poet out of a man:
The true gods sigh for the cost and pain, – 40
For the reed which grows nevermore again
  As a reed with the reeds in the river.

Garibaldi [214]

1

He bent his head upon his breast
  Wherein his lion-heart lay sick: –
  'Perhaps we are not ill-repaid;
Perhaps this is not a true test;
  Perhaps that was not a foul trick;
  Perhaps none wronged, and none betrayed.

2

'Perhaps the people's vote which here
  United, there may disunite,
  And both be lawful as they think;
Perhaps a patriot statesman, dear
  For chartering nations, can with right
  Disfranchise those who hold the ink.

3

'Perhaps men's wisdom is not craft;
  Men's greatness, not a selfish greed;
  Men's justice, not the safer side;
Perhaps even women, when they laughed,
  Wept, thanked us that the land was freed,
  Not wholly (though they kissed us) lied.

4

'Perhaps no more than this we meant,
  When up at Austria's guns we flew,
  And quenched them with a cry apiece,
Italia! – Yet a dream was sent . . .
  The little house my father knew,
  The olives and the palms of Nice.'

5

He paused, and drew his sword out slow,   25
   Then pored upon the blade intent,
   As if to read some written thing;
While many murmured, – 'He will go
   In that despairing sentiment
   And break his sword before the King.'   30

6

He poring still upon the blade,
   His large lid quivered, something fell.
   'Perhaps,' he said, 'I was not born
With such fine brains to treat and trade, –
   And if a woman knew it well,   35
   Her falsehood only meant her scorn.

7

'Yet through Varese's cannon-smoke
   My eye saw clear: men feared this man
   At Como, where this sword could seal
Death's protocol with every stroke: 40
   And now . . . the drop there scarcely can
   Impair the keenness of the steel.

8

'So man and sword may have their use;
   And if the soil beneath my foot
   In valour's act is forfeited,   45
I'll strike the harder, take my dues
   Out nobler, and all loss confute
   From ampler heavens above my head.

9

'My King, King Victor, I am thine!
   So much Nice-dust as what I am   50
   (To make our Italy) must cleave.
Forgive that.' Forward with a sign
   He went.
         You've seen the telegram?
   Palermo's taken, we believe.

A View across the Roman Campagna [215]

1861

1

Over the dumb Campagna-sea,
  Out in the offing through mist and rain,
Saint Peter's Church heaves silently
  Like a mighty ship in pain,
    Facing the tempest with struggle and strain.   5

2

Motionless waifs of ruined towers,
  Soundless breakers of desolate land:
The sullen surf of the mist devours
  That mountain-range upon either hand,
    Eaten away from its outline grand.   10

3

And over the dumb Campagna-sea
  Where the ship of the Church heaves on to wreck,
Alone and silent as God must be,
  The Christ walks. Aye, but Peter's neck
    Is stiff to turn on the foundering deck.   15

4

Peter, Peter! if such be thy name,
  Now leave the ship for another to steer,
And proving thy faith evermore the same,
  Come forth, tread out through the dark and drear,
    Since He who walks on the sea is here.   20

5

Peter, Peter! He does not speak;
  He is not as rash as in old Galilee:
Safer a ship, though it toss and leak,
  Than a reeling foot on a rolling sea!
    And he's got to be round in the girth, thinks he.   25

6

Peter, Peter! He does not stir;
   His nets are heavy with silver fish;
He reckons his gains, and is keen to infer
    – 'The broil on the shore, if the Lord should wish;
    But the sturgeon goes to the Caesar's dish.'   30

7

Peter, Peter! thou fisher of men,
   Fisher of fish wouldst thou live instead?
Haggling for pence with the other Ten,
    Cheating the market at so much a head,
    Griping the Bag of the traitor Dead?   35

8

At the triple crow of the Gallic cock
   Thou weep'st not, thou, though thine eyes be dazed:
What bird comes next in the tempest-shock?
    – Vultures! see, – as when Romulus gazed, –
    To inaugurate Rome for a world amazed!   40

Mother and Poet [216]

1

Dead! One of them shot by the sea in the east,
  And one of them shot in the west by the sea.
Dead! both my boys! When you sit at the feast
  And are wanting a great song for Italy free,
    Let none look at *me*!   5

2

Yet I was a poetess only last year,
  And good at my art, for a woman, men said;
But *this* woman, *this*, who is agonised here,
  – The east sea and west sea rime on in her head
    For ever instead.   10

3

What art can a woman be good at? Oh, vain!
  What art *is* she good at, but hurting her breast
With the milk-teeth of babes, and a smile at the pain?
  Ah, boys, how you hurt! you were strong as you pressed,
    And I proud, by that test.   15

4

What art's for a woman? To hold on her knees
  Both darlings! to feel all their arms round her throat,
Cling, strangle a little! to sew by degrees
  And 'broider the long-clothes and neat little coat;
    To dream and to dote.   20

5

To teach them . . . It stings there! *I* made them indeed
  Speak plain the word *country*. *I* taught them, no doubt,
That a country's a thing men should die for at need.
  I prated of liberty, rights, and about
    The tyrant cast out.   25

6

And when their eyes flashed . . . O my beautiful eyes! . . .
  I exulted; nay, let them go forth at the wheels
Of the guns, and denied not. But then the surprise
  When one sits quite alone! Then one weeps, then one kneels!
    God, how the house feels!   30

7

At first, happy news came, in gay letters moiled
  With my kisses, – of camp-life and glory, and how
They both loved me; and, soon coming home to be spoiled,
  In return would fan off every fly from my brow
    With their green laurel-bough.   35

8

Then was triumph at Turin: Ancona was free!'
  And some one came out of the cheers in the street,
With a face pale as stone, to say something to me.
  My Guido was dead! I fell down at his feet,
    While they cheered in the street.   40

9

I bore it; friends soothed me; my grief looked sublime
  As the ransom of Italy. One boy remained
To be leant on and walked with, recalling the time
  When the first grew immortal, while both of us strained
    To the height he had gained.   45

10

And letters still came, shorter, sadder, more strong,
  Writ now but in one hand, 'I was not to faint, –
One loved me for two – would be with me ere long:
  And *Viva l'Italia!* – *he* died for, our saint,
    Who forbids our complaint.'   50

11

My Nanni would add, 'he was safe, and aware
  Of a presence that turned off the balls, – was imprest
It was Guido himself, who knew what I could bear,
  And how 'twas impossible, quite dispossessed,
    To live on for the rest.'   55

12

On which, without pause, up the telegraph line
  Swept smoothly the next news from Gaeta: – *Shot.*
Tell his mother. Ah, ah, 'his', 'their' mother, – not 'mine',
  No voice says '*My* mother' again to me. What!
    You think Guido forgot?   60

13

Are souls straight so happy that, dizzy with Heaven,
  They drop earth's affections, conceive not of woe?
I think not. Themselves were too lately forgiven
  Through THAT Love and Sorrow which reconciled so
    The Above and Below.   65

14

O Christ of the five wounds, who look'dst through the dark
  To the face of Thy mother! consider, I pray,
How we common mothers stand desolate, mark,
  Whose sons, not being Christs, die with eyes turned away,
    And no last word to say!   70

15

Both boys dead? but that's out of nature. We all
  Have been patriots, yet each house must always keep one.
'Twere imbecile, hewing out roads to a wall;
  And, when Italy's made, for what end is it done
    If we have not a son?   75

16

Ah, ah, ah! when Gaeta's taken, what then?
    When the fair wicked queen sits no more at her sport
Of the fire-balls of death crashing souls out of men?
    When the guns of Cavalli with final retort
        Have cut the game short?   80

17

When Venice and Rome keep their new jubilee,
    When your flag takes all heaven for its white, green, and red,
When *you* have your country from mountain to sea,
    When King Victor has Italy's crown on his head,
        (And *I* have my Dead) –   85

18

What then? Do not mock me. Ah, ring your bells low,
    And burn your lights faintly! *My* country is *there*,
Above the star pricked by the last peak of snow:
    My Italy's THERE, with my brave civic Pair,
        To disfranchise despair!   90

19

Forgive me. Some women bear children in strength,
    And bite back the cry of their pain in self-scorn;
But the birth-pangs of nations will wring us at length
    Into wail such as this – and we sit on forlorn
        When the man-child is born.   95

20

Dead! One of them shot by the sea in the east,
    And one of them shot in the west by the sea.
Both! both my boys! If in keeping the feast
    You want a great song for your Italy free,
        Let none look at *me*!   100

Notes

Poems 1844

Poems 1844 was published in two volumes under the name Elizabeth Barrett Barrett; it was dedicated to her father. She was aged thirty-eight and the collection was the summation of her poetic development thus far, following her first adult collection, *The Seraphim, and Other Poems*, in 1838. A number of the poems had been previously published in periodicals; some were written specifically for the collection.

The Sonnets

The collection begins with twenty-eight sonnets (one of her favourite forms), the majority of which are reflections on her vivid relationship with God and her remarkably clear vision of Christ as a real being. Some of these echo the Metaphysical poets, in the down-to-earthness of the depicted relationship, and in their concerns with philosophical and ethical issues. The imagery is often sacrificial, with reference to Christ's blood, and there is a running theme of suffering balanced by redemption through God's grace. At the same time there is a domesticity of tone which brings these poems very much into the present. The role of the poet, an abiding concern of Barrett's, is also woven into some of these poems. There are also some individual sonnets addressed to living figures.

1 (p. 3) *The Soul's Expression*   Though the sonnet is couched as emanating from the soul, it also has the function of introducing the collection, reminding the reader of the difficulty for the poet of matching her inner intensity with her outward expression: 'This song of soul I struggle to outbear.'

2 (p. 4) *On a Portrait of Wordsworth by B. R. Haydon*   According to Forster, Haydon (Benjamin Robert, 1786–1846) had the portrait, painted in 1842, sent round to Wimpole Street for Elizabeth to see as she was unable to leave her room (Forster, p. 121). William Wordsworth (1770–1850) was Poet Laureate; Helvellyn represented his connection with the Lake District.

3 (p. 4) *My future will not copy fair my past*   Barrett quotes this line in Sonnet 42 of *Sonnets from the Portuguese*.

4 (p. 9) *The Two Sayings, The Look, The Meaning of the Look* These refer to the disciple Peter's denying Christ three times before the crowing of the cock. Barrett emphasises Christ's humanity through the equality of the exchanged look.

5 (p. 15) *To George Sand* George Sand, pseudonym for Aurore Dupin (1804–1876), was a novelist who wrote freely about passion, had many affairs including an important one with the composer Chopin, and was controversial for her lifestyle and the manner of her dress, which was more masculine than feminine. Barrett Browning eventually met her idol in Paris in 1852.

The Ballads

The ballads make up the centrepiece of the 1844 collection and although written in traditional ballad mode using some archaic language they explore contemporary themes. A significant feature is the emphasis on the female either as a central character or in terms of the themes chosen, such as the nature of womanhood. Many of the ballads had been published earlier in periodicals or in *Findens' Tableaux*, an annual publication edited by Mary Russell Mitford, but Barrett made substantial revisions to some of them for *Poems 1844*. Some were written specifically for *Poems 1844*, most notably 'Lady Geraldine's Courtship', which was written in haste to balance the length of Volume One with Volume Two and became one of Barrett's most popular poems.

6 (p. 17) *Romaunt* archaic term for a romantic tale or poem

7 (p. 17) *Palestine* The knight and his page are returning from the Crusades.

8 (p. 19) *Beati, beati, mortui!* Blessed are the dead!

9 (p. 23) *Paynims* archaic term for pagans, in this context the Muslims the Christians were fighting

10 (p. 27) *Ingemisco* sigh

11 (p. 30) *Saint Agnes* patron saint of young girls and engaged couples

12 (p. 35) *weal* well-being, happiness

13 (p. 35) *Aroint thee* Be gone.

14 (p. 37) *shriven* given absolution after confession

15 (p. 40) *vespers* evening prayer

16 (p. 42) *hyaline* smooth as glass (of the sky)

17 (p. 46) *nympholeptic*   having an enthusiastic desire for the unattainable

18 (p. 52) *Camoëns*   Luís de Camões (1524–1580), Portuguese poet

19 (p. 56) *Phemius*   poet in Homer's *Odyssey* who sang to entertain Penelope's suitors in Odysseus's absence

20 (p. 62) *Keats*   John Keats (1795–1821), English poet

21 (p. 69) *Homer*   Greek poet, eighth century BC, author of *The Iliad* and *The Odyssey*. Homer is first in Barrett's pantheon of poets, as follows:

Shakespeare	William Shakespeare (1564–1616), English playwright and poet
Aeschylus	(525–456 BC) Greek dramatist
Euripides	(c.480–405 BC) Greek tragedian
Sophocles	(496–406 BC) Greek tragedian
Hesiod	(eighth century BC) Greek poet
Pindar	(c.522–432 or 438 BC) Greek poet
Sappho	Greek female lyric poet, dates uncertain but c.620–550 BC
Theocritus	(early third century BC) Greek poet
Aristophanes	(455–380 BC) Greek comic playwright
Virgil	(70–19 BC) Roman poet, author of *The Aeneid*
Lucretius	(98 55 BC) Roman poet
Ossian	Scottish warrior and bard, dates unknown but c.third century
Spenser	Edmund Spenser (1552–1599), English poet
Ariosto	Lodovico Ariosto (1474–1533), Italian poet
Dante	Dante Alighieri (1265–1321), author of *The Divine Comedy*
Alfieri	Vittorio Alfieri (1749–1803), Italian dramatist and poet
Boiardo	Matteo Boiardo (1441–1494), Italian poet
Berni	Francesco Berni (1498–1536), Italian poet
Tasso	Torquata Tasso (1544–1595), Italian poet
Racine	Jean Racine (1639–1699), French playwright
Corneille	Pierre Corneille (1606–1684), French playwright
Petrarch	Francesco Petrarca (1304–1374), Italian poet
Lusiad	epic poem (1572) by Luís de Camões
Calderon	Pedro Calderon de la Barca (1600–1681), Spanish dramatist
de Vega	Lope de Vega (1562–1635), Spanish dramatist and poet
Goethe	Johann Wolfgang von Goethe (1749–1832), German writer
Schiller	Friedrich von Schiller (1759–1805), German writer
Plutarch	Lucius Mestrius Plutarchus (c.46–120), Greek biographer

Chaucer	Geoffrey Chaucer (1343–1400), English poet, author of *The Canterbury Tales*
Milton	John Milton (1608–1674), English poet and essayist, author of *Paradise Lost*
Cowley	Abraham Cowley (1618–1677), English Metaphysical poet
Drayton	Michael Drayton (1563–1631) English poet
Browne	Sir Thomas Browne (1605–1682), English writer
Marlowe	Christopher Marlowe (1564–1593), English dramatist and poet
Webster	John Webster (?1580–1625), English dramatist
Fletcher	John Fletcher (1579–1625), English dramatist
Ben	Ben Jonson (1573–1637), English dramatist and poet
Burns	Robert Burns (1756–1796), Scottish poet
Shelley	Percy Bysshe Shelley (1792–1822), English Romantic poet
Byron	George, Lord Byron (1788–1824), English Romantic poet
Coleridge	Samuel Taylor Coleridge (1772–1834), English Romantic poet

22 (p. 74) *Y'varekh* (יברך)   Hebrew priestly blessing: The Lord bless thee, and keep thee (Numbers 6:24)

23 (p. 75) *Aphrodite*   Greek goddess of love, here used to signify the beauty of the harmony

24 (p. 84) *Brocken*   highest mountain in Northern Germany

25 (p. 85) *Jacob and his Bethel stone*   Jacob used a stone on which to rest his head as he slept, then the next morning set it up as a pillar to mark the place he now named Bethel (Genesis 28:18).

26 (p. 91) *Guido*   Guido Reni (1575–1642), Italian painter

27 (p. 96) *muckle*   much

28 (p. 98) *blee*   colour

29 (p. 99) *faulchion*   sword

30 (p. 101) *corse*   corpse

31 (p. 106) *selle*   saddle

32 (p. 114) *Malvern Hills . . . Piers Plowman*   The Malvern Hills in Worcestershire were the setting for the allegorical Middle English poem *Piers Plowman*, attributed to William Langland (*c.*1332–*c.*1400)

33 (p. 115) *Rinaldo*   medieval romance hero

34 (p. 118) *Dryad*   nymph or spirit of the trees

35 (p. 119) *Naiad*   water nymph

36 (p. 119) *Pan or Faunus*   Pan is the Greek god of the wild, Faunus is his Roman equivalent.

37 (p. 121) *lusus*   a freak of nature

38 (p. 122) *Oedipus's grave-place*   Oedipus was the mythical Greek King of Thebes, tragic hero of Sophocles' *Oedipus Rex*; he died in an olive grove at Colonus.

39 (p. 122) *Aladdin*   character in *The Arabian Nights*

40 (p. 126) *mandragore*   plant of the mandrake family, with narcotic powers

Social, historical and personal poems

41 (p. 128) *The Cry of the Children*   This poem was written in response to the 1843 'Report on the Employment of Children and Young Persons in Mines and Manufactories', produced in large part by her friend and correspondent Richard Hengist Horne. It was first published in *Blackwood's Magazine*, 1843, and contributed to the wide-ranging debate about the working and living conditions of workers, especially children, in an increasingly urbanised and industrialised society.

42 (p. 130) *cerement*   wrapping for a dead body

43 (p. 133) *Crowned and Wedded*   Queen Victoria was crowned in 1838 and married to Prince Albert in 1840; both events took place in Westminster Abbey. The poem was first published in *The Athenaeum* in 1840 under the title 'The Crowned and Wedded Queen'.

44 (p. 135) *Napoleon*   Napoleon Bonaparte (1769–1821), Emperor of the French, 1804–1814 and 1815. The poem reflects his various military campaigns, his final exile to St Helena, and the return of his remains to France.

45 (p. 138) *We return Orestes to Electra*   Orestes and Electra were brother and sister, characters in Aeschylus' set of tragedies *The Oresteia*. When Agamemnon, their father, is brutally murdered by their mother Clytemnestra, Orestes returns from exile to avenge his father's death and is reunited with his sister at their father's graveside.

46 (p. 139) *Jupiter . . . Saturnus*   Jupiter/Jove was king of the gods in Roman mythology; his favoured weapon was the lightning bolt. Saturnus, another Roman god, is usually identified as Jupiter's father.

47 (p. 141) *Flush*   the poet's much-loved dog. Mary Russell Mitford gave Flush, a cocker spaniel, to Elizabeth in 1841, after the accidental drowning of her brother Edward in 1840.

48 (p. 149) *My lonely chamber next the sea*   Barrett is referring to her time in Torquay, Devon, where she was sent for her health.

49 (p. 151) *Mitford's bower*   Mary Russell Mitford (1787–1855), Barrett's cherished correspondent, author of the highly successful *Our Village*

50 (p. 151) *Harpocrate*   Harpocrates, Greek god of silence

51 (p. 153) *The Cry of the Human*   a companion poem to 'The Cry of the Children', is, like that poem, a specific response to socio-economic ills, here those caused by the protectionist Corn Laws, first implemented in 1815, which imposed restrictions on the import of grain and pushed the price of bread so high that the poor could not afford to buy it. This, with other factors, led to the period known as the Hungry Forties when many died of starvation. The Corn Laws were repealed in 1846.

52 (p. 154) *'Change*   Corn Exchange, where corn was marketed; includes a larger reference to the capitalist market

53 (p. 157) *Lay*   song; one of several archaic terms used by Barrett for her ballad forms

54 (p. 157) *Romaunt of the Rose*   medieval French poem *Roman de la Rose*, translated by Chaucer as *The Romaunt of the Rose*

55 (p. 162) *obolum da mihi*   give me a penny

56 (p. 181) *L. E. L.'s Last Question*   homage to Letitia Elizabeth Landon (1802–1838), English poet and novelist who signed herself L. E. L.

57 (p. 187) *Catarina to Camoëns*   written from the point of view of Catarina de Atayde whom the poet Camões loved

58 (p. 193) *Una*   pure heroine of Book I of Edmund Spenser's *The Faerie Queene* (1590)

59 (p. 196) *H. S. Boyd*   Hugh Stuart Boyd (1781–1848), Greek scholar, friend and intellectual mentor of Barrett when she lived at Hope End and he in the Malvern Hills. Her diary suggests that her feelings for him were passionate (Forster, pp. 56–9).

60 (p. 196) *Bacchus*   god of wine

61 (p. 196) *Juno*   Roman name for the queen of the gods

62 (p. 196) *Cyclops*   one-eyed giant

63 (p. 196) *Bacchantes*   followers of Bacchus known for their wild and rapturous dancing

64 (p. 197) *Anacreon*　Greek lyric poet known for his drinking songs; dates uncertain but *c.*563–478 BC

65 (p. 197) *Chian*　wine from the Greek island of Chios

66 (p. 197) *Paphia*　of Paphos, on the island of Cyprus. This is a reference to Aphrodite whose mythical birthpace was Paphos.

67 (p. 197) *Hymettus*　mountain range near Athens noted for the honey originating there

68 (p. 198) *Ulysses*　Latin name for Odysseus

69 (p. 199) *Bion*　Greek pastoral poet

70 (p. 199) *Chrysostom*　John Chrysostom (*c.*349–407), Archbishop of Constantinople

71 (p. 199) *Basil*　(329–379), Archbishop of Caesarea when the Church was struggling with the Arian heresy

72 (p. 199) *Heliodorus*　there are several ancients named Heliodorus; this is probably Heliodorus of Athens

73 (p. 199) *Synesius*　(373–414), Greek philosopher and latterly Bishop of Ptolemais

74 (p. 199) *Nazianzen*　Gregory Nazianzen (329–390), Bishop of Sasima under the direction of Archbishop Basil, and later Bishop of Constantinople. He was known for his sermons, and was also a religious poet.

75 (p. 200) *Até*　Greek goddess of mischief and delusion

76 (p. 200) *De Virginitate*　Latin treatise on virginity by Aldhelm (c. 639–709), Abbot of Malmesbury

77 (p. 200) *St Simeon*　Simeon Stylites (*c.*388–459), ascetic saint who lived at the top of a pillar

78 (p. 200) *Cassandra*　daughter of Priam and Hecuba, gifted with the power of prophecy, character in *The Oresteia*

79 (p. 200) *Prometheus*　figure in Greek mythology who stole fire from the gods

80 (p. 200) *Medea*　figure in Greek mythology who avenged the infidelity of her husband Jason by murdering their children

81 (p. 206) *Linnaeus*　Carl Linnaeus (1707–1778), Swedish botanist, the founder of modern botanical classification

82 (p. 207) *The Dead Pan*　The poem is based on the story that, when Christ was on the cross, a cry was heard across the seas, 'Great Pan is

dead!', signifying that Christianity had defeated paganism. Placed symbolically at the end of Volume 2 of *Poems 1844*, it announces Barrett's intention to ally her poetry more clearly to the real. However, as is evident from the following notes, Barrett was still deeply committed to her classical learning.

83 (p. 208) *Oreads* nymphs of the mountain conifers

84 (p. 208) *Plato* (*c*.427–*c*.348 BC), Greek philosopher

85 (p. 209) *Apollo* Greek god of music and poetry

86 (p. 210) *Neptune* Roman god of the sea

87 (p. 210) *Pluto* Roman god of the Underworld, brother to Neptune and Jupiter

88 (p. 210) *Hermes* Greek messenger of the gods

89 (p. 211) *Cybele* mother goddess

90 (p. 211) *Vesta* Roman goddess of hearth, home and family

91 (p. 213) *Dodona's oak* in the shrine of Dodona the rustling of the oak leaves was used as an oracle

92 (p. 213) *Pythia* the Oracle at Delphi

Poems 1850

This collection consolidated *Poems 1844* and is significant in that it postdates Barrett's marriage to Robert Browning, after which Browning became her key literary adviser.

93 (p. 219) *The Runaway Slave at Pilgrim's Point* In 1845 the Boston Anti-Slavery Bazaar asked Barrett to contribute to their annual publication, *The Liberty Bell*. She began the poem then but finished it after her marriage, sending it to America in 1847, though she wondered if it might be 'too ferocious' even for the American abolitionists (Avery and Stott, p. 156). This poem is of particular interest since Elizabeth's father, and thus the whole Barrett family, profited from what were originally slave-holding estates in Jamaica; the extravagant Hope End was built on these profits. She may have felt freed from this influence as well as from her father's personal hold over her when she married Browning and left England, thus being freer artistically to write a poem in the persona of a woman slave.

94 (p. 219) *Pilgrim's Point* Plymouth Rock, the traditional site of the disembarkation of the Pilgrim Fathers from the *Mayflower*

95 (p. 226) *this Union* the Union of the States of America, divided at this point by the issue of slavery

96 (p. 228) *Lydian* language of Anatolia

97 (p. 228) *Hector, son of Priam* unwilling participant in the Trojan War, but a heroic figure

Sonnets from the Portuguese (1846–50)

This sonnet sequence (titled later) was composed during Robert Browning's courtship of Elizabeth Barrett; the earliest version can be found in her manuscript notebook of 1846 (now in the British Library). But she did not show the poems to her husband until 1849, after the birth of Pen, and when Robert was depressed following the death of his mother. He urged their publication, while suggesting that their personal nature be disguised by a title suggesting that they were translations. They were published as part of *Poems* 1850.

98 (p. 283) *Nor breathe my poison on thy Venice-glass* The glass made in Venice was said to be so fine that it would shatter if poison were poured into it.

99 (p. 284) *Aornus* mountain fortress in Northern India besieged and captured (327–6 BC) by Alexander the Great in his Indian campaign

100 (p. 288) *Rialto* market place of Venice

101 (p. 288) *argosies* ships full of rich goods

102 (p. 288) *The nine white Muse-brows* In Greek mythology the nine Muses were the daughters of Zeus and Mnemosyne; they were goddesses of the arts, poetry and music. Pindar depicts them as having purple-black hair, which she is here comparing to her lover's lock of hair.

103 (p. 288) *The bay-crown's shade* the laurel crown awarded to poets (a clear reference to Browning)

104 (p. 292) *dewless asphodel* in Greek mythology a meadow of asphodel is seen as the haunt of the dead

105 (p. 292) *My letters!* the letters written to her by Browning in their courtship

106 (p. 295) *call me by my pet-name!* Ba (for baby), the name used in her family from her birth

107 (p. 297) *the chrism of love* consecrated oil used in certain sacraments, here used to sanctify their love

108 (p. 298) *Mussulmans*   Muslims

109 (p. 298) *Giaours*   term of contempt used by Turks for non-Muslims

110 (p. 298) *Polypheme*   Cyclops blinded by Odysseus

111 (p. 299) *'My future will not copy fair my past'*   quotation from Barrett's poem 'Past and Future' (p. 2)

Aurora Leigh (1856)

Aurora Leigh was called by Barrett Browning a 'sort of novel-poem' (see Introduction); in form it is modelled on the epic, using the classical structure which goes back to Homer and Virgil, and employing blank verse in the manner of her English forebears Milton and Wordsworth. Instead of the usual twelve books it has nine, suggested by Bolton and Bolton Holloway (p. 467) to echo the nine months of a woman's pregnancy, as well as the nine books of prophesy of the Cumaean Sybil. Thus it claims both male and female heritage. Its themes include the role of the woman, and particularly the woman artist, in society; the nature of love and marriage and its consequences for the individual, man or woman; the forces and structures that lead to the oppression of women, particularly their sexual oppression; the nature of poetry and its contribution to the world; class differences and whether they can be bridged; social responsibility in a world of inequality. If this is to make it sound earnest, it is not; Aurora's narrative voice is distinctively ironic and the form is open enough to interweave many different perspectives. The characters depicted are mediated through Aurora's narrative, and through the over-arching vision of Barrett Browning herself, but they speak through their own voices, and as readers we can form different judgements on them in the same way as in a novel. This is thus a highly modern text, both in its concerns and in its dialogic nature.

Aurora Leigh draws deeply on Barrett Browning's considerable learning; fully comprehensive notes are not within the scope of this edition, but a general note is provided for each Book, outlining the key events, noting influences and sources, and explaining context, with occasional specific notes where necessary.

Dedication

John Kenyon (1784–1856) was Barrett Browning's distant cousin and literary promoter and mentor and it was he who encouraged Browning to approach Elizabeth by letter. The Brownings were staying in his London house when Barrett Browning was seeing *Aurora Leigh* into print. He died shortly after its publication.

First Book

Aurora recounts the way her parents met in Florence, their English and Italian origins which combined in her, their child. The name Aurora is significant as meaning dawn; Barrett Browning may also be drawing on Michelangelo's sculpture of Dawn in the Medici Chapel, Florence. After Aurora's mother's death, her father retreats with her to the Italian countryside and teaches her through books while struggling to provide a form of motherhood. His lesson is 'grief and love' (p. 308, l. 186), which is reinforced by the painting of her mother which Aurora dwells on. Then her father dies too, with the message: 'Love, my child, love, love!' (p. 309, l. 212). Orphaned, she is sent to England to be brought up by her father's sister, a stern guardian, who tries to make Aurora conform to moral and social convention, teaching her 'the works of women' (p. 315, l. 456). She meets her cousin Romney Leigh, heir to Leigh Hall. But her real education is through books, and especially the poets. Then poetry becomes hers: 'O life, O poetry' (p. 327, l. 915). As she crochets, conforming to her aunt's ideal of female art, she also composes poetry: 'The inner life informed the outer life' (p. 331, l. 1058). Meanwhile Aurora enjoys walking and talking with Romney, 'not lovers . . . rather . . . thinkers disagreed' (p. 332, ll. 1106–8). In the First Book the culture of England is set against that of Italy; a constrained model of womanhood is set against a freer, more creative one; and Romney's commitment to the actual is set against Aurora's to the ideal.

112 (p. 307) *Psyche*   goddess of the soul

113 (p. 307) *Medusa*   monster with snakes for hair who could turn mortals to stone with her look

114 (p. 307) *Lamia*   character in Keats's poem of the same name, an enchantress who turns into a snake

115 (p. 313) *Athanasius back to Nice*   the Athanasian and the Nicean creeds

116 (p. 319) *Giotto*   Giotto di Bondone (1266–1337), Florentine Renaissance painter

117 (p. 322) *Theophrast*   Theophrastus (371–287 BC), Greek philosopher, successor to Aristotle

118 (p. 322) *Aelian*   Claudius Aelianus (175–235), Roman author and rhetorician

119 (p. 323) *Saul and Nahash*   See 1 Samuel 11.

120 (p. 323) *Alaric*   King of the Visigoths, famous for his sack of Rome in 410

121 (p. 323) *Charlemagne* also known as Charles the Great (*c.*742–814), King of the Franks and Christian Emperor of the West

122 (p. 328) *Ganymede* beautiful youth who, in Greek mythology was abducted by Zeus and taken to Olympus to be his cup-bearer

123 (p. 328) *Heré* Zeus's wife Hera

124 (p. 329) *phorminx* type of lyre played by the ancient Greeks

Second Book

Aurora has reached her twentieth birthday; on the same day, she crowns herself as a poet with a wreath of ivy and rejects Romney's proposal of marriage. Romney and Aurora disagree about what is the best kind of work to dedicate one's life to – his work for people's material betterment, hers, through poetry, for their spiritual good. He has poured scorn on her ambition to be a poet, offering her instead the useful occupation of helping right social ills, asking her to be his wife and helpmate in this task. Aurora refuses on the grounds that 'You have a wife already whom you love, / Your social theory' (p. 345, ll. 409–10), reminding him that 'I too have my vocation, – work to do' (p. 346, l. 455). Their fundamental disagreement is couched in terms of the biblical story of Miriam, sister of Moses (Exodus 15), in which Miriam took up her timbrel, a sort of tambourine (cymbals in the poem) and led the women in singing to celebrate the drowning of Pharaoh's army in the Red Sea, once Moses has led his people through the parted waters. For Romney, such singing is typical women's stuff, wasting time at a serious moment; for Aurora the cymbals and the singing symbolise the power of poetry. Further, Miriam is a prophet, taking that role as a woman. After Romney has departed in distress, their aunt tells Aurora that his proposal would have meant her receiving her rightful inheritance of her father's property, now entailed to Romney. When the aunt dies, she leaves Aurora £300 and all her property, which Romney has tried to supplement with a gift of £30,000 intended for Aurora. Aurora refuses it, and their ways part.

125 (p. 345) *Hagar* handmaid of Sarah, appointed by her to bear a child to Abraham since Sarah was infertile (Genesis 16)

126 (p. 346) *They pick much oakum* the harsh task of unpicking tarred rope into its individual strands for re-use, usually given to prisoners or workhouse inhabitants. Here it represents hard labour for women snared by love.

127 (p. 347) *Fouriers* Charles Fourier (1772–1837), French philosopher

and social reformer who advocated utopian socialism. The plural is to indicate other thinkers like him.

128 (p. 350) *the entail* special arrangement in a will determining a change in the standard line of inheritance

129 (p. 355) *Iphigenia . . . Aulis* *Iphigenia in Aulis* was the last work of Euripides. Agamemnon was commanded to kill his daughter Iphigenia to allow him to sail his ships to Troy.

130 (p. 355) *Griseld* Griselda, folkloric woman noted for her patience even when abused in marriage

131 (p. 356) *sweet Chaldean* The Chaldeans were an ancient people of Babylon; Romney probably refers to their language, Aramaic.

132 (p. 357) *"Siste, viator"* stop, traveller

133 (p. 359) *Babylon or Balbec* both cities of the Middle East on which the sands of the desert encroach

134 (p. 365) *King Solomon* King of Israel whose ring, also known as the Seal of Solomon, was said to be invested with special powers

Third Book

We meet Aurora seven years later, now a seasoned poet but with the shine of youth and hope rubbed off her. She is living independently in London (having used her aunt's £300 to establish herself), is moderately successful, and she finds satisfaction in her work. One day she is visited by Lady Waldemar, who declares that she loves Romney Leigh and she wants to enlist Aurora's help in preventing his marriage to a lowly-born woman. Aurora refuses to comply, but then independently visits Romney's intended, Marian Erle, and hears her sad story. Marian has been brought up in penury, amid drunkenness and violence, but at the same time has learnt the power of books. Her mother sells her to a man from whom she flees, but then collapses and wakes in hospital. There Romney finds her, and offers her work as a seamstress, which allows her an independent life. Thus Aurora hears of Romney's goodness while at the same time understanding Marian. In this book, the emphasis switches from Aurora to Lady Waldemar, the villain of the piece – though she is motivated only by love of Romney – and Marian Erle, the alter-heroine. We also see a rather jaded Aurora; she has lost the first flush of her new dawn, and she hankers after Romney's approval.

135 (p. 370) *phalansteries* buildings designed for utopian communities

136 (p. 371) *Danae*   mother of Perseus, who was conceived when Zeus came down to her in a shower of gold

137 (p. 373) *Descending Sinai . . . Parnassus mount*   Mount Sinai, where the Ten Commandments were given to Moses by God; Mount Parnassus, mythological home of the Muses and poetry. Both are actual mountains carrying symbolic meanings.

138 (p. 373) *Aye, Miriam*   Aurora again identifies herself with the female prophet Miriam.

139 (p. 373) *Collegisse juvat*   extract from Horace, Odes I; the full line reads: 'There are those whose joy it is to gather Olympic dust.'

140 (p. 374) *in Jove's clenched palm*   See Montefiore, pp. 181–5.

141 (p. 376) *Nephelococcygia*   finding shapes in clouds; cloud cuckoo land

142 (p. 378) *Androcles*   Legendary slave Androcles removed a thorn from a lion's paw, and was saved in return by the same lion in the Roman arena.

143 (p. 380) *Blowsalinda*   pretty country girl

144 (p. 380) *Dido*   Dido, Queen of Carthage; in Virgil's *Aeneid*, she and Aeneas fall in love, and she is so distraught when he leaves her to continue his travels that she kills herself. When Aeneas later journeys through the Underworld, he meets Dido's ghost.

145 (p. 382) *Aspasia*   (470–400 BC) an immigrant to Athens, she became the lover of the senior politician Pericles. She is associated with being at the same time sexually free and intelligent and cultured, having founded an intellectual salon in Athens.

146 (p. 383) *Proudhon, Considerant and Louis Blanc*   all socialist reformers

147 (p. 384) *the Ten Hours movement*   the social reform movement which achieved the passing of the Factory Act, 1847, restricting the working day of women and young people to ten hours

Fourth Book

Marian's story continues. She has left her seamstress post to tend to her friend Lucy who is dying, seeing her need as greater than that of the fine ladies she has been sewing for. As Lucy drifts to her death, Romney Leigh appears, and proposes marriage to Marian, in similar terms to those he once offered to Aurora. Marian is to be his helpmate in his struggle against social ills, and in addition their marriage will close the rift ' " 'twixt class and class'" (p. 405, l. 124). This story simply told by Marian leads Aurora to ponder on her own notions of love. Marian wonders if Aurora is displeased at the inequality of the match, but defends herself robustly, suggesting that she'll ' "be a worthier mate, perhaps, than some / Who are wooed in silk among their learned books" ' (p. 408, ll. 230–1). As she finishes with a promise to ' "be a true wife to your cousin Leigh" ' (p. 409, l. 269), Romney enters. Again, he and Aurora are at odds, now over the nature of love, but they both agree that Marian is to be cherished. Romney and Aurora leave together in close conversation. The marriage of Romney and Marian is to take place at St James's Church, and the scene is described ebulliently, the lower orders mixing with the upper. Here Aurora (or perhaps Barrett Browning) betrays her repugnance at this 'hideous interfusion' (p. 416, l. 547). There is a telling imaginative élan in the description of the 'crammed mass' (p. 417, l. 571) which is instinct with a physical disgust. In a long-drawn-out passage describing the waiting guests, it becomes clear that Marian will not appear. Romney announces this, the crowd riots and attacks him, and Aurora falls unconscious as she tries to save him. It emerges that Marian has sent a letter withdrawing from the marriage, which we are shown through Aurora's reading of it. Romney searches for Marian but she has disappeared. Aurora tries, but fails, to disclose her fore-knowledge that Lady Waldemar was plotting against the marriage. The book ends with Romney and Aurora talking as friends, still disagreeing over the commitment each respectively has to socialism and to poetry, both wearier but more compassionate to each other.

148 (p. 410) *an obolus inscribed / With Caesar's image* originally a Greek silver coin stamped with the head of the ruler; here used to continue the theme of women being bought in the exchange of marriage

149 (p. 412) *Athenian wives . . . Eumenides* In the third play of Aeschylus' *The Oresteia*, the Furies appear on stage as an opposing bloody force to the civilised Athenian citizens.

150 (p. 415) *Potiphar's* Potiphar's wife accused their servant Joseph of sexual assault after he had refused her advances (Genesis 39); this is an ironic reference to the chastity of wives.

151 (p. 418) *Madonna of the Bird* Raphael's *Madonna of the Goldfinch* (1506), noted for her gentle expression

152 (p. 422) *Hamlet* first of several references in the following passage to Shakespeare's tragedies *Hamlet* and *King Lear*. The suggestion is that the marriage is play-acting and will end in tragedy.

153 (p. 428) *a spotted Hydra-skin*   the Hydra was a many-headed serpent; for each head cut off it would grow two more. This is an odd analogy to use for the mild Marian.

154 (p. 432) *'Your printer's devils'*   apprentices in a printer's. Romney makes reference to Aurora's success in print while playing on the idea of its bedevilling her.

Fifth Book

This is the central book in the poem, five of nine, the pivotal point in which Aurora looks both backward and forward. Poetry now takes centre stage, and Aurora is free from encumbrances – and other voices – to express her commitment to the poetry of the real, knocking down a few Victorian literary reputations as she goes. She espouses the unfashionable epic, but in the service of representing the current age: 'All men are possible heroes' (p. 440, l. 152). She might say all women too: the metaphors in this midway book are powerfully, triumphantly female. In a knockabout section she rejects the power of drama: it 'Makes lower appeals, submits more menially' (p. 443, l. 269). Aurora also admits to the loneliness of the artist, and especially the woman artist: 'To have our books / Appraised by love, associated with love, / While *we* sit loveless!' And in a touching passage (p. 448, ll.474–6) she voices her sense of loss, at an early age, of the love of her father and mother.

The second half of the book is more novelistic, speeding on the narrative, and airy with light conversation where the first half is stuffed full of matter. But Aurora's sense of isolation is increased in the midst of a dinner party at Lord Howe's, where she hears that Romney is engaged to Lady Waldemar (who is present). She also hears Romney's Christian socialism discussed. In a brutal economic analysis which combines with a cold appraisal of Lady Waldemar's sexual attractions, Romney, it's suggested, is milking her for her money to support his social causes. After a bruising encounter with Lady Waldemar herself, Aurora retreats, writes a worked-over letter of congratulation to her tormentor, and flees in the direction of Italy, having sold her father's books to finance her journey.

155 (p. 439) *Payne Knight*   Richard Payne Knight (1750–1824), scholar interested in theories of the sublime

156 (p. 439) *Helen . . . Hector*   Helen of Troy, the great beauty, and Hector, the great warrior, were also ordinary human beings.

157 (p. 441) *Roland . . . at Roncesvalles*   hero of the French epic poem *La Chanson de Roland* (*c.*1100), who fought at Roncesvalles

158 (p. 444) *Imogen and Juliet*   heroines respectively of Shakespeare's plays *Cymbeline* and *Romeo and Juliet*

159 (p. 444) *Themis' son*   Prometheus

160 (p. 444) *buskin*   thick-soled boot worn by actors in Greek tragedy, which gave them extra height

161 (p. 445) *St Preux*   Saint-Preux is a character in Jean-Jacques Rousseau's novel *The New Eloise* (1761) who falls in love with his pupil Julie.

162 (p. 446) *Pygmalion*   character in Ovid's *Metamorphoses*, a sculptor who falls in love with his own statue

163 (p. 447) *Phoebus Apollo*   Greek god of poetry and music, and also light, hence Phoebus

164 (p. 449) *Ugolino*   in Dante's *Inferno*, Ugolino is forced to eat his own sons

165 (p. 454) *St Lucy*   early Christian martyr who in some versions of her legend has her eyes put out

166 (p. 455) *Pisgah-hill*   Mount Pisgah, where Moses saw the Promised Land spread before him (Deuteronomy 34)

167 (p. 456) *Venus Meretrix*   Venus, Roman goddess of love and beauty; meretrix, a prostitute in ancient Rome

168 (p. 461) *my prophetess at Delphi*   the Oracle at Delphi, who was thought to channel the words of Apollo

169 (p. 468) *Elsevirs*   renowned family of Dutch booksellers, sixteenth to seventeenth century

170 (p. 469) *conferenda hoec cum his*   comparing this with that

171 (p. 469) *Corrupte citat*   wrongly cited

172 (p. 469) *lege potius*   read further

173 (p. 469) *Proclus*   Athenian philosopher

174 (p. 469) *The kissing Judas, Wolf*   Friedrich Wolf (1759–1824), German classical scholar who questioned whether Homer was the sole author of *The Iliad* and *The Odyssey*. This was seen as a sort of heresy in some circles, an opinion endorsed here by calling Wolf a Judas.

175 (p. 469) *Juno's breasts*   Juno, Roman goddess, wife of Jupiter, king of the gods. Stone argues:'Aurora embodies Homer's creativity in the cream from Juno's breasts' (p. 157). This is another of the breast-milk metaphors that run through the poem.

Sixth Book

En route to Italy, Aurora stops in Paris, and expresses her love of France and its ideals, 'musing with myself / On life and art' (p. 476, ll. 204–5). Then she thinks she sees Marian, pursues, but loses her. Drawn to Italy, she can't forget the glimpsed Marian; then she recalls that this Marian clasped a child. She considers contacting Romney, but dismisses it. Then wandering in the early morning she meets her face to face. She insists on going back with Marian to her room, where the child awaits. Aurora initially thinks Marian has stolen the child; then that she has submitted to seduction; then Marian makes clear that the child is a result of force. In a moving passage Marian compares herself to a pebble, shaped, bitten and ground down by the relentless sea, in whose action she includes Aurora and Romney as well as the father of her child. She ends by saying: ' "Marian's dead" ' (p. 493, l. 813). While Aurora struggles with her moral compass, which is initially set against Marian, Marian herself has no moral problem. She loves her child: ' "the mother in me has survived the rest" ' (p. 493, l. 821). As ever, Marian comes out of this far better than anyone else, but the narrative thrust and the tone of Aurora's overarching voice doesn't really allow Marian to set the reader's response. There's an uncomfortable mix of mealy-mouthed admiration and over-effusive affection from Aurora which can't quite hide her unease. Marian requests news of Romney, and is told of his impending marriage to Lady Waldemar. Marian admits that Lady Waldemar was instrumental in making her realise that her marriage to Romney would be problematic, since he: ' "Required a wife more level to himself " ' (p. 498, l.1027). She also arranged the go-between who led Marian to being drugged and used, perhaps in a brothel, but with no protection. The book ends with Marian at her lowest point, and yet her deepest self-understanding: ' "I, Marian Erle, myself, alone, undone," ' (p. 505, l. 1270).

176 (p. 473) *the old Tuileries*   royal palace in Paris

177 (p. 474) *Louis Philippe*   (1773–1850), King of France 1830–1848, when he abdicated during the 1848 Revolution

178 (p. 478) *Dumas*   Alexandre Dumas (1802–1870), French writer

179 (p. 478) *Academicians*   members of the Académie Française, the learned body that is the guardian of the French language

Seventh Book

Marian's tale continues; she has been the main speaker and protagonist in four of the seven books thus far, even though Aurora is the driving narrator. She is taken in as a servant in Paris, then dismissed when her pregnancy is detected; she had not even realised it herself. Aurora, moved by her story, and assuaging her own guilt, asks Marian and her child to come with her to Italy, but in a true statement of equality: ' "I am lonely in the world, / And thou art lonely" ' (p. 509, ll. 120–1). The child will not miss a father, since ' "two mothers shall / Make that up to him" ' (p. 509, ll. 124–5). Marian accepts by offering her child for Aurora's kiss. Aurora is now exercised by what if anything she should tell Romney. And she is haunted by happy memories of him and longing for him, realising that she loves him. She writes not to Romney but to Lord Howe; if Romney is not yet married, he is to release to him the part Lady Waldemar played in Marian's downfall; if he is already married, he is to be told only that Marian is found, and is safe and well. She then writes to Lady Waldemar, in full flood. If they are married, she must tend to Romney tirelessly, at pain of Aurora's revealing her part in Marian's downfall. Then Aurora, Marian and the child travel to Italy. She is both happy to breathe the Italian air, and sad at the thought of her father. She receives a letter from Romney's friend, the painter Vincent Carrington, telling her of his marriage to Kate Ward, a great admirer of Aurora's poetry, and revealing also that Aurora's latest book is a great success. The news of Romney is that he has been ill and that Lady Waldemar has nursed him devotedly. From this Aurora assumes that they are married. Briefly she thinks, of herself, 'Books succeed, / And lives fail' (p. 524, ll. 704–5). But she then has a long disquisition on truth and poetry and their relation to life. Art, as ever, remains important to Aurora: 'Art's the witness of what Is / Behind this show' (p. 528, ll. 834–5). Aurora returns from her aesthetic ruminations to the present world of Italy, where 'Marian's good, / Gentle and loving, – lets me hold the child' (p. 530, ll. 930–1). While she takes pleasure in the beauty of Italy, she is dogged by sadness, and thoughts of Romney.

180 (p. 512) *flagitious*   wicked

181 (p. 514) *Tophet*   place in the valley of Hinnon, near Jerusalem, associated with the sacrifice of children; metaphorically, Hell

182 (p. 519) *I found a house, at Florence*   This passage, with its accurate place names, reflects a view Barrett Browning knew well from her life in Florence.

183 (p. 523) *the Pitti*   the Pitti Palace in Florence. The Palatine Galleries, rich in works of art, were by this stage open to the public.

184 (p. 524) *nepenthe*   in the *Odyssey*, magical potion which takes away sorrow

185 (p. 525) *Phaedons*   reference to Plato's *Phaedo*, his meditation on the soul

186 (p. 526) *Antinous*   beautiful Greek youth, loved by the Emperor Hadrian

187 (p. 529) *digamma*   archaic letter of the Greek alphabet

188 (p. 529) *Medaean boil-pot of the sun*   Medea, granddaughter of the sun god Helios; in Euripides' *Medea*, the murderer of her own children

189 (p. 539) *benigna sis*   you are good to us (part of a prayer to the Virgin Mary)

Eighth Book

As Aurora struggles for some personal equilibrium in the late summer evening, Romney suddenly arrives. It appears that letters have gone astray; Aurora mistakes what their import might have been, assuming they spoke of Romney's marriage. As ever, Aurora and Romney are at cross purposes, neither saying what is the case, each imagining what is not. Romney praises Aurora's book of poetry, and in a deliberate echo calls her ' "My Miriam, whose sweet mouth, when nearly drowned / I still heard singing on the shore!" ' (p. 550, ll. 334–5), reversing his position in Book 2. If this were not enough for Aurora, he calls her ' "My Italy of women" '. He also quotes her words back to her, the words from Book 2, commending the cause of poetry over his concern for social reform. Indeed throughout this book each quotes to the other either direct phrases or reversals of phrases which they exchanged in Book 2. Now Romney capitulates completely in relation to that earlier argument, and condemns all his social efforts as failures. But Aurora answers with her own sense of failure, reminding Romney that God will never fail them, and reiterating the importance of keeping on working. Romney remains in bitter despair about the emptiness of all he has attempted: ' "My vain phalastery dissolved itself" ' (p, 565, l. 888). At the same time, his rural neighbours opposed his efforts, breaking windows and ostracising him. Only now does he reveal to Aurora the final blow, that those who opposed him burnt down Leigh Hall, helped by the inmates themselves: ' " 'Tis somewhat easier, though, to burn a house / Than build a system" ' (p. 566, ll. 946–7). Although Aurora is full of compassion, she feels constrained as she still labours under the belief that Romney is married to Lady Waldemar. At the end of the book he realises this misunderstanding, and gives Aurora a letter from that lady, which he says will explain all.

190 (p. 541) *Boccaccio* Giovanni Boccaccio (1313–1375), Italian poet. 'The Falcons' is a reference to one of the stories in his *Decameron*.

191 (p. 543) *the Austrian boar* Austria was seeking to subjugate Tuscany to its power; the cause of Italian unification and independence was close to Barrett Browning's heart.

192 (p. 552) *that Phalarian bull* Phalaris was a Sicilan tyrant who had a bronze bull fashioned in which he tortured and killed his enemies by roasting them alive, including the sculptor who made the bull.

193 (p. 554) *writ in Sanscrit* classical language of India, here used to suggest that the language of Aurora's heart is indecipherable

194 (p. 559) *nostrum* easy solution

195 (p. 560) *cashiered* dismissed from service (usually from the armed forces)

196 (p. 565) *Arcadian peace* perfect rural peace; in antiquity a province of Greece idealised as embodying pastoral perfection

197 (p. 568) *Druid gods* pagan priests of the Iron Age

198 (p. 571) *Buonarroti* Michelangelo di Buonarroti (1475–1564), Italian artist

199 (p. 571) *One fills their cup . . . vinegar and gall* reference to Christ's ordeal on the Cross

200 (p. 572) *Moses' bulrush-boat* Miriam, Moses' sister, hid Moses in a wicker basket among the bulrushes when it was decreed that all Hebrew baby boys should be killed.

Ninth Book

Aurora reads Lady Waldemar's letter, in which she upbraids her for the tone of Aurora's letter to her; she admits that Romney does not love her, but refuses responsibility for Marian's fate. She tells Aurora that Romney has decided that Marian is his wife in true spirit and that he must seek her out. However, she expresses her belief that Romney and Aurora love each other. She ends by cursing Aurora on the Bible of Love. As Aurora realises, out loud, that Romney is not married, he in turn says that he is, to Marian. Marian appears and asks confirmation first from Romney that he accepts her and her child as they are, and from Aurora that she gives her consent to this. She then reverses both their acceptances with her own refusal, on the grounds that she does not love Romney. Perhaps once she worshipped him: ' "I haply set you above love itself, / And out of reach of these poor woman's arms, / Angelic Romney" ' (p. 584, ll. 367–9). She reiterates her earlier statement, that her experiences have killed her, except for the love of her child. She will now dedicate herself to him; he needs no father when he has ' "God and his mother" ' (p. 585, l. 415). When her child has grown, then she'll be happy to work for Romney's causes, but not as his wife. Instructing Aurora and Romney to ' "open on each other your great souls" ' (p. 586, l. 441), she returns to her child. We have come full circle to Aurora and Romney. One last revelation is to come; Aurora has not picked up the many hints in the Eighth Book, but Romney now tells her that he is blind. A beam falling on him in the fire at Leigh Hall, aided perhaps by the spite of Marian's father, has taken his eyesight (in an obvious echo of *Jane Eyre*). Now at last, it seems, she can declare her love, not only to him but to herself. If poor Romney has to lose his sight to achieve that, so did Rochester. But Aurora's declaration is truly humble, and she sees her failings and her pride. If Romney has to give up his sight to gain the dawn light of Aurora, she has to give up her art: ' "Art is much, but love is more!" ' Thus the earlier radical message of the poem is overturned and like all good nineteenth-century novels, *Aurora Leigh* ends with the coming together of a man and a woman. At least, though, it does not end on marriage (though that is assumed) but on an ecstatic note, a long kiss, 'deep, deep, shuddering breaths' (p. 593, l. 723), and Aurora 'thrilled / With strange electric life' (p. 596, ll. 821–2). God's in there as well, with references to the New Jerusalem, and 'work for two' (p. 598, l. 911), and even the prospect still of blowing ' "all class-walls level as Jericho's" ' (p. 599, l. 932). But finally, as they look out, one unseeingly, towards the east and the new dawn, the poem ends on the age-old prospect of love and hope between two people who have struggled with life but found their way forward.

201 (p. 581) *Aaron's priestly robe* Aaron the brother of Moses and Miriam, the first High Priest of the Israelites

202 (p. 597) *Comte, Cabet* Auguste Comte (1798–1857), Etienne Cabet (1788–1856), both French philosophers who tried to link philosophy to the contemporary social and industrial context. Cabet was a utopian socialist.

203 (p. 599) *blow all class-walls level as Jericho's* the Israelites brought the walls of Jericho down by prayer and faith

204 (p. 600) *Jasper . . . sapphire . . . chalcedony . . . amethyst* In Revelation 21,

---

the new Jerusalem is depicted as a bride adorned for her husband, and in verses 18–20 these and other specific jewels are mentioned as part of its foundations.

From *The Seraphim and Other Poems*

205 (p. 624) Ἤδη νοεροὺς / Πετάσαι ταρσούς Now spread your intellectual wings

206 (p. 626) *Sabrina* goddess of the River Severn

207 (p. 631) *Felicia Hemans* (1793–1835), English poet

208 (p. 631) *L. E. L.* Letitia Elizabeth Landon, 1802–38

From *Poems before Congress* (1860)

209 (p. 637) *Villafranca* The Conference of Villafranca, which led to the Treaty of Villafranca, 1859, gravely disappointed Italian nationalist hopes for unification. Napoleon III is the great man who imagined a great deed (unification) but failed to deliver it.

210 (p. 640) *Italy and the World* again, a hymn to Italian unification

From *Last Poems* (1862)

211 (p. 649) *A Song for the Ragged Schools of London* Ragged Schools were charitable schools run to ensure an education for the poor and destitute. The poem was originally published in 1854 to help with her sister Arabella's charitable work. The poem is of a piece with Barrett Browning's 'Condition of England' poems.

212 (p. 655) *De Profundis* from the depths

213 (p. 660) *A Musical Instrument* one of Barrett Browning's best-known poems, perhaps because it has been frequently anthologised. It takes up the same theme as 'The Dead Pan'.

214 (p. 662) *Garibaldi* Giuseppe Garibaldi (1807–1882), key figure and general in the Italian Risorgimento. This poem celebrates his leadership of the Red Shirts.

215 (p. 664) *Campagna* the countryside surrounding Rome

216 (p. 666) *Mother and Poet* again refers to one of the stages in the battle for Italian unification

Index of Poem Titles

Index of First Lines

Fast this Life of mine was dying 270
First time he kissed me, he but only kissed 297
Five months ago the stream did flow 263
Florence, Bologna, Parma, Modena 640
Free Heart, that singest today 246

Go from me. Yet I feel that I shall stand 281
GOD be with thee, my belovèd – GOD be with thee! 43
God, who, with thunders and great voices kept 235
God would not let the spheric Lights accost 236
Gods of Hellas, gods of Hellas 207
Grief sat upon a rock and sighed one day 255

He bent his head upon his breast 662
He listened at the porch that day 261
Her azure eyes, dark lashes hold in fee 232
How do I love thee? Let me count the ways 300
How he sleepeth, having drunken 126

I am listening here in Rome 649
I am no trumpet, but a reed 264
I classed, appraising once 173
I count the dismal time by months and years 16
I dwell amid the city ever 624
I have a smiling face, she said 244
I have been in the meadows all the day 5
I lift my heavy heart up solemnly 281
I lived with visions for my company 291
I mind me in the days departed 620
I never gave a lock of hair away 287
I see thine image through my tears tonight 293
I stand by the river where both of us stood 172
I stand on the mark beside the shore 219
I tell you, hopeless grief is passionless 6
I thank all who have loved me in their hearts 299
I think of thee! – my thoughts do twine and bud 293
I think that look of Christ might seem to say 10
I think we are too ready with complaint 13
I thought once how Theocritus had sung 279
I will paint her as I see her 192

One eve it happened when I sat alone 541
'Onora, Onora,' – her mother is calling 28
Over the dumb Campagna-sea 664

Pardon, oh, pardon, that my soul should make 297
Put the broidery-frame away 164

Said a people to a poet – 'Go out from among us straight! 112
Say over again, and yet once over again 289
She has laughed as softly as if she sighed 257
Sleep on, baby, on the floor 194
Speak low to me, my Saviour, low and sweet 7

Thank God, bless God, all ye who suffer not 5
The English have a scornful insular way 471
The face of all the world is changed, I think 282
The face which, duly as the sun 655
The first time that the sun rose on thine oath 294
The poet hath the child's sight in his breast 233
The Saviour looked on Peter. Aye, no word 9
The seraph sings before the manifest 3
The shadow of her face upon the wall 232
The ship went on with solemn face 241
The simple goatherd, between Alp and sky 233
The soul's Rialto hath its merchandise 288
The wind sounds only in opposing straits 231
The woman singeth at her spinning-wheel 11
'The woman's motive? shall we daub ourselves 506
'There is no God' the foolish saith 153
There is no one beside thee and no one above thee 276
They met still sooner. 'Twas a year from thence 402
They say Ideal beauty cannot enter 234
They say that God lives very high 254
Thou bay-crowned living One that o'er the bay-crowned
    Dead art bowing 631
Thou comest! all is said without a word 294
Thou hast thy calling to some palace-floor 280
Thou large-brained woman and large-hearted man 15
Three gifts the Dying left me, – Aeschylus 237
Times followed one another. Came a morn 334